*Dale and Appelbe's*

# Pharmacy
# Law and
# Ethics

**Gordon E Appelbe**, LL B, PhD, MSc, BSc(Pharm), FRPharmS, Hon-MPS(Aus), FCPP, is an independent pharmaceutical/legal consultant. He qualified as a pharmacist in 1956 and then worked for nine years in community pharmacy. He joined the staff of the Pharmaceutical Society in 1965, first as an inspector under the Pharmacy Acts and then, in 1971, as secretary to the Statutory Committee. He was appointed deputy head of the Law Department in 1974 and was head of the Law Department and Chief Inspector from 1978 to 1991.

**Joy Wingfield**, LL M, MPhil, BPharm, FRPharmS, Dip Ag Vet Pharm, FCPP, is Boots Special Professor of Pharmacy Law and Ethics at the University of Nottingham and a pharmacy practice consultant for Boots The Chemists Ltd. She qualified as a pharmacist in 1971 and then worked for five years in community pharmacy. She joined the staff of the Pharmaceutical Society in 1976 as an inspector under the Pharmacy Acts. From 1986 to 1991 she was the senior administrator, and later head of Ethics Division in the Law Department, responsible for professional and registration matters. This was followed by nine years as the assistant pharmacy superintendent for Boots. She now occupies a part-time chair as Boots special professor in pharmacy law and ethics at Nottingham University, and retains a part-time practice consultancy for Boots The Chemists.

*Dale and Appelbe's*

# Pharmacy Law and Ethics

## SEVENTH EDITION

### Gordon E Appelbe
LL B, PhD, MSc, BSc(Pharm), FRPharmS, Hon MPS(Aus), FCPP

### Joy Wingfield
LL M, MPhil, BPharm, FRPharmS, Dip Ag Vet Pharm, FCPP

Pharmaceutical Press

**Published by the Pharmaceutical Press**
1 Lambeth High Street, London SE1 7JN, UK

© 2001 jointly by Gordon E Appelbe, Joy Wingfield and the
Pharmaceutical Press

First published 1976
Second edition 1979
Third edition 1983
Fourth edition 1989
Fifth edition 1993
Sixth edition 1997
Reprinted 1998, 1999
Seventh edition 2001

Text design by Barker/Hilsdon, Lyme Regis, Dorset
Typeset by Photoprint, Torquay, Devon
Printed in Great Britain by TJ International, Padstow, Cornwall

ISBN 0 85369 475 3

A catalogue record for this book is available from the British
Library

# Contents

**15    Medicines Act 1968:**
**Pharmacopoeias and Other Publications    152**

**16    Misuse of Drugs Act 1971    157**

# Preface to the
# Seventh Edition

This book seeks to provide in one volume an outline of the law that affects the practice of pharmacy in Great Britain, together with an account of the way in which British pharmacy has developed and maintained its standards of professional conduct. The authors hope that the book will prove useful not only to pharmacy undergraduates, pre-registration students, and pharmacists in all branches of the profession, but also to others in Britain and overseas who may need some knowledge of contemporary British law relating to medicines and poisons, and of the development of professional ethics in British pharmacy.

The whole text has again been extensively revised for this edition, new material being added to most chapters. Once again, major changes to the National Health Service have necessitated a substantial rewrite of Chapter 23 to reflect the sweeping changes to structure, organisation, duties of quality and collaboration required by the Health Act 1999. Even so, the Government's new NHS plan and its blueprint for pharmacy are yet to be implemented.

The major legislation affecting pharmacy – the Medicines Act (Chapters 1–15) and Misuse of Drugs Act (Chapter 16) – together with the regulations made thereunder, are dealt with in detail. With the loss of Crown immunity, it is important to stress that hospital pharmacists are aware that all this legislation now applies to NHS hospitals as well as to community pharmacies and hospitals in the private sector. The 'miscellaneous' chapter (Chapter 25) has been completely revised and enlarged to incorporate many of the changes which have occurred since the last edition with respect to consumer and environmental legislation. This includes data protection, competition law, and employment disability legislation. Chapter 28 on European legislation has been updated.

The law is that of Great Britain except where otherwise stated in the text. The aim has been to state the law as concisely as accuracy permits, but it should be borne in mind that only the courts can give a legally binding decision on any question of interpretation. The responsibility for the text and any views expressed therein lies with the authors.

Standards of professional conduct in pharmacy have developed considerably over the past 60 years. The Royal Pharmaceutical Society has been undertaking a complete review of its Code of Ethics and this has only been partially completed. A working party of the Society has also been looking at its disciplinary procedures and other aspects of the Society's work in the light of the new Health Act 1999. Much of this work has still to be completed. The chapters on professional conduct, and on the procedures and decisions of the Statutory Committee have been rewritten with these issues in mind. A new series of disciplinary cases has been incorporated in Chapter 21. The proposed Code of Ethics and Professional Standards is discussed and reproduced.

The other health care professions are also undergoing change which will effect them variably over the next one to two years including a new Nursing Council to replace the UKCC and a new Council to replace the present Council for the professions Supplementary to Medicine (Chapter 22)

We gratefully acknowledge the help and advice we have received from numerous sources. Thanks are due to Susan Sharpe and Helen Darracott and other members of the Law Department of the Royal Pharmaceutical Society, for their assistance on various aspects of this book. Valuable help was received from Dr John Farwell, hospital pharmaceutical consultant, on matters concerning the NHS hospital service, from Edward Mallinson concerning the NHS in Scotland, and from Harold Gay of Boots The Chemists Ltd, Nottingham, with regard to environmental and consumer legislation. Thanks also go, once again, to our publishers, in particular to Charles Fry, John Wilson and Paul Weller, for their guidance and cheerfulness.

Gordon E Appelbe
Joy Wingfield

April 2001

# Foreword

Preparing a new edition of any book concerning health care law and ethics has become a nightmare. Novel developments in science and technology and the pace of change within the NHS mean that no sooner is a draft chapter complete than it is out of date. Gordon Appelbe and Joy Wingfield have been fortunate to remain sane as they struggle to complete their work. The major changes in relation to regulation of the professions, the Health Act and the amendments to the Code of Ethics are just some of the challenges confronting the authors on this occasion. The changing face of pharmacy will have posed even greater difficulties. Alterations in the way the NHS will provide pharmacy services must be factored into the book. The prospect of the cyber-pharmacist has to be addressed. Routine developments such as amendments of secondary legislation and case-law may come as a blessed relief. *Dale and Appelbe* is an important work. Pharmacy is still a discipline neglected by scholars outside its boundaries.

We have seen a flowering of interest in, and controversy surrounding, ethical and legal aspects of health care generally. Health professionals, with the doctors in the front line, have been confronted with critical analysis of their practice from diverse commentators outside their own professions. Lawyers, moral philosophers and social scientists queue up to offer their perspective on what does, and does not, constitute ethical and responsible professional practice. The rising tide of litigation provokes fears of a malpractice crisis. Rarely a day passes without the media focusing on the failings of health care providers. Such a battery of criticism has triggered chagrin. Doctors feel understandable resentment at the constant dissection of their ethics and their practice by scholars from other disciplines – scholars who do not ever have to face the reality of everyday practice. Nurses feel increasingly vulnerable to similar pressures. Dentists and veterinary surgeons begin to lose sleep about the threat of the law, and challenges to internally determined ethics. Pharmacists, while not immune from such developments, appear to have attracted much less external *academic* criticism of their ethics and practice. With one or two notable exceptions, pharmacists, consciously or unconsciously, have retained their relatively low profile.

A number of reasons may explain the so-far happy lot of the pharmacist. Let me address first what I consider to be a bad reason. Philosophers, social scientists and academic lawyers continue to demonstrate a worrying tendency to concentrate almost exclusively on ethical dilemmas of high drama and low incidence. The fate of the unfortunate patient in PVS, the ethics of transplanting organs from genetically altered pigs to human recipients, the tragedy of conjoined twins – these are the everyday menu of discourse in academic journals and university common rooms. These same heartrending questions are often transformed into media events. The daily round of the pharmacist in hospital or the community simply lacks that drama. Yet important though the ethics of caring for patients in PVS, or of transplantation, or the conjoined twins, are, they are not in fact the everyday stuff of life. They actually affect only a very few members of our society. The pharmacist's work reaches out to the entire community. The impact of his or her practice affects us all, but when pharmacists do their job properly, we barely even notice its importance.

No drug is one hundred per cent safe. All medication must be handled with care and respect. For most ills, great or small, some medication will be indicated. The pharmacist is the gatekeeper of that process. Whether dispensing a prescription medicine, or selling a medicinal product, pharmacists are the experts. We, the lay public, rely on the pharmacists, to ensure our welfare. We expect them to exercise not just technical skills, but to take steps to educate us in the safe use of our medicines. Nonetheless, we do not accord them the professional status their training and discipline truly merits. The man or woman in the white coat is taken for granted by the customer rushing in and out of the pharmacy. And a form of intellectual snobbery, too, downgrades the provision of medicine, accepting the claims of medical practitioners that they are *the* crucial health profession.

The pharmacy profession has actively sought to enhance the image and status of the profession. The public are encouraged to seek advice from their pharmacists. The community pharmacist is so much more than a 'pedlar of pills'. He or she is an accessible, and usually local, source of care for minor ills and a professional able to help the layperson distinguish minor from major ills. In the last ten years, more and more licensed medicines have moved from Prescription Only to Pharmacy status. On their own authority, pharmacists can now grant access to more and more powerful medicines. The hospital pharmacist is encouraged to play a larger role as the hospital expert on medicines, a source of advice to his or her other professional colleagues. The modern pharmacist is truly a butterfly emerging from its constraining chrysalis.

Pharmacists are well aware that enlarged powers and enhanced status will bring their own disadvantages as well as advantages. Adopting a more fully advisory function and taking exclusive responsibility for providing a greater range of drugs necessarily increases the possibility of error. When medicines are sold, rather than dispensed on the NHS, the pharmacist guarantees the quality and safety of the medicines. In an increasingly litigious society, pharmacists must brace themselves for more lawsuits. Pharmacists in the community operate in the marketplace. They must run successful businesses as well as deliver professional services. They have to reconcile the demands of professional ethics with the desire to maximise profit. The climate of the times does not help. Once a medicine is available in pharmacies, it can be generally advertised, and advertising medicines is now itself big business. In a consumerist society, a customer who has decided that he wants the 'Wonderdrug' advertised last night on the television may resent what he perceives as interference when the pharmacist seeks to assess whether 'Wonderdrug' is safe and appropriate for him. Medicines themselves are also big business with the supermarkets in vigorous competition with pharmacies for what they hope will be a lucrative market. We await the final outcome of the bid to end retail price maintenance on medicines. The pressure to maintain responsible and ethical practice will be demanding in the face of such conflicting pressures. The slightest evidence of failure to meet those demands will bring pharmacists into the limelight.

In 2001, one highly publicised development may cast an uncomfortable spotlight on community pharmacists. Deregulation of post-coital contraception allowing pharmacists to sell the erroneously named 'morning after' pill to women over 16 will continue to attract controversy. The ability of pharmacists to undertake professional consultations and sell a product which a vociferous minority considers to be hazardous and immoral will be sorely tested. The test in principle should be embraced. Pharmacists could prove their mettle. Alas, the test may not be conducted in strictly fair conditions. Any suggestion of sale to under-age girls, or claims that a woman took the drug while pregnant and it harmed her child, will receive instant publicity. Pharmacists will have to get used to some rough treatment. Let us hope that the interest of the media will provoke a more reflective interest on the part of other better informed commentators.

Pharmacists are nonetheless fortunate in two respects. First, one reason for the relative lack of furore over pharmacy practice so far and the comparative rarity of litigation against pharmacists suggests a job done well. Second, pharmacists have for 25 years now benefited from a text which clearly and in great detail spells out their professional and legal obligations. *Dale and Appelbe's Pharmacy Law and Ethics* offers to every pharmacist a guide to ensure that he or she has no excuse for falling short of what their profession and the law requires. Written by authors who are themselves pharmacists, but with great legal and ethical expertise, this edition should be read and absorbed by every pharmacist. My first exposure to teaching health professionals was to deliver a term's lectures on law for pharmacists in the mid-1970s, when virtually no medical school in England taught medical law or ethics. Pharmacy recognised the need for pharmacists to understand the legal framework of their practice. Joe Dale and Gordon Appelbe sought to meet that need and, after Joe Dale's death, Joy Wingfield joined Gordon Appelbe in continuing that work. That far-sighted policy of anticipating the importance of professional appreciation of law and ethics has helped pharmacy avoid some of the pitfalls of their fellow professions.

*Dale and Appelbe* acknowledges the centrality of law in professional practice. It is an essential reference for the pharmacist and a key source to those of us outside pharmacy who do believe that pharmacy law and ethics is just as important as medical law and ethics.

Margaret Brazier
Professor of Law
Institute of Medicine, Law and Bioethics
University of Manchester

# Introduction

# Development of the Law in

# Relation to Pharmacy, Medicines

# and Poisons

Between 1968 and 1978 the statutes relating to medicines, poisons and drugs were almost entirely repealed and replaced by new legislation. The Medicines Act 1968 now controls the manufacture and distribution of medicines; the Poisons Act 1972 regulates the sale of non-medicinal poisons, whilst the Misuse of Drugs Act 1971 deals with the abuse of drugs. In 1973 the National Health Service Reorganisation Act brought about a major revision in the pharmaceutical services of the National Health Service. A new National Health Service Act in 1977 together with many amending Health Service Acts now regulate the pharmaceutical services. All these Acts are described in detail in later chapters together with the orders and regulations which have been made under them. This introduction gives a brief account of how the law developed to this point, including references to most of the early statutes, all of which have now been repealed either wholly or in part.

Before the middle of the nineteenth century there were no legal restrictions in England on the sale of poisons or drugs, and anyone could describe themselves as a pharmaceutical chemist. Statutory control over sales was first applied to arsenic because, as the preamble to the Arsenic Act 1851 stated, *the unrestricted sale of arsenic facilitates the commission of crime*. The first statute relating to pharmacy followed the next year. The Pharmacy Act 1852 confirmed the charter of incorporation of the Pharmaceutical Society of Great

Britain, hereinafter called *the Society*, which had been granted in 1843 (see p.212). The 1852 Act established the framework of the Society and gave it power to hold examinations and to issue certificates. It also restricted the use of the title *pharmaceutical chemist* to members of the Society, although it did not restrict the use of the titles *chemist* or *druggist*. The Society received its *Royal* prefix in 1988.

The Pharmacy Act 1868 brought new developments. It introduced a Poisons List (with 15 entries) and empowered the Society to add other substances to it, subject to the approval of the Privy Council. A *poison* was defined as any substance included in the Poisons List. Articles and preparations containing poisons could be sold by retail only by *pharmaceutical chemists* or by a new legal class of *chemists and druggists*. Both titles were protected by the Act. The class of *chemists and druggists* comprised (i) all those who before the passing of the Act had been engaged *in the keeping of open shop for the compounding of the prescriptions of duly qualified medical practitioners*, and (ii) all those persons who had been registered as *assistants* under the provisions of the Pharmacy Act 1852.

The registrar of the Society was thereafter required to keep registers of pharmaceutical chemists, of chemists and druggists, and of apprentices or students. The qualification of *chemist and druggist* (the *Minor* examination) became the statutory minimum for persons carrying on a business comprising the sale of poisons. Chemists and druggists were eligible to be elected members or associates of the Pharmaceutical Society, but did not have all the privileges of a member who had qualified as a pharmaceutical chemist (by passing the *Major* examination). That state of affairs continued – slightly modified by a statute of 1898 – until the Pharmacy Act 1953 combined the two qualifications in one Register of Pharmaceutical Chemists. The profession of pharmacy is now regulated by the Pharmacy Act 1954, which absorbed the 1953 Act. The 1954 Act is described in detail in Chapter 19.

The 1868 Act not only introduced the first list of poisons but also regulated the manner in which they could be sold, specifying more stringent restrictions on sale for the more dangerous poisons. Fixed penalties, recoverable in the civil courts, were prescribed for breaches of the Act. The list of poisons was extended by the Poisons and Pharmacy Act 1908 which also provided that poisons for agricultural and horticultural purposes could be sold by licensed dealers as well as by pharmacists. This Act also prescribed conditions under which corporate bodies could carry on the business of a chemist and druggist. This had become necessary because it had been held in the High Court in 1880 that an incorporated company was not covered by the word *person* as used in the 1868 Act, and was therefore not liable for penalties under the Act (*Pharmaceutical Society* v. *London and Provincial Supply Association Ltd*, see p.360).

Under the Pharmacy and Poisons Act 1933 a Poisons Board was established to advise the Secretary of State on what should be included in the Poisons List. Poisons in Part I of the list could be sold by retail only at pharmacies; poisons in Part II could be sold also by traders on a local authority list. Poisons were further classified by means of the Schedules to the Poisons Rules made under the Act. Schedule 4, for example, comprised a class of poisons which could be supplied to the public only on the authority of a prescription written by a practitioner. A Register of Premises was set up under the Act, and all registered pharmacists were required to be members of the Pharmaceutical Society.

One of the main features of the 1933 Act was the establishment of a disciplinary body (the Statutory Committee) which had authority not only over pharmacists who committed misconduct, but also over pharmacists and corporate bodies convicted of offences under the Pharmacy Act. The Society was placed under a duty to enforce the Act, and was authorised to appoint inspectors for the purpose. Proceedings under the Act were to be taken in courts of summary jurisdiction and not, as previously, in the civil courts. The Pharmacy and Poisons Act 1933 was repealed by the Medicines Act 1968. The Poisons Act 1972 deals only with non-medicinal poisons (Chapter 17). Chapter 21 deals with the powers of the Statutory Committee and includes reports of important Statutory Committee decisions.

Pharmacy and poisons were firmly linked together by statute, but the sale and manufacture of medicines was not regulated in any way except for medicines containing poisons. Some control over quality was provided by a series of Food and Drugs Acts, culminating in the Food and Drugs Act 1955. Under those Acts it was an offence to sell adulterated drugs, or to sell, to the prejudice of the purchaser, any drug not of the nature, substance or quality demanded. The effectiveness of those provisions was limited by the fact that most drugs were of vegetable origin and, for many of them, there were no precise standards. Furthermore, a manufacturer of a proprietary medicine did not have to disclose its composition, provided that s/he paid the appropriate duty by way of fixing the appropriate excise stamps to each bottle or packet as required by the Medicine Stamp Acts. That state of affairs was changed by the Pharmacy and Medicines Act 1941, which abolished medicines stamp duty and required, instead, a disclosure of composition of each container. It also restricted the sale of medicines to shops (as distinct from market stalls, etc.) and made it unlawful to advertise any article for the treatment of eight named diseases, including diabetes, epilepsy and tuberculosis. This was the first statute in which pharmacy and medicines were directly linked. The 1941 Act, however, did not apply to animal medicines.

The Therapeutic Substances Act 1925 controlled by licence the manufacture (but not the sale or supply) of a limited number of products the purity or potency of which could not be tested by chemical means e.g. vaccines, sera, toxins, antitoxins and certain other substances. The list was greatly extended when antibiotics came into use. It had not been held necessary to restrict the retail sale or supply of vaccines, sera and antitoxins, but penicillin and most other antibiotics were found to be substances which were *capable of causing danger to the health of the community if used without proper safeguards.* Consequently, the Penicillin Act 1947 and the Therapeutic Substances (Prevention of Misuse) Act 1953 permitted the supply of antibiotics to the public only by practitioners, or from pharmacies on the authority of practitioners' prescriptions. The Therapeutic Substances Act 1956 replaced the earlier Acts, so bringing under the control of one statute both the manufacture and the supply of therapeutic substances. It could be regarded as the precursor to the Medicines Act 1968, which has now replaced it.

Legislation relating to medicines developed in a piecemeal manner, each problem being dealt with as it arose, and the law was scattered throughout a number of statutes. However, rapid developments in pharmaceutical research after the 1939/45 war made available an increasing number of potent substances for use in medicine, and a working party was set up by the Government in 1959 to examine the need for new controls. The thalidomide tragedy in 1961 almost certainly precipitated proposals for new legislation which was published in 1967 in a White Paper entitled *Forthcoming Legislation on the Safety, Quality and Description of Drugs and Medicines* (Cmnd. 3395). The Medicines Act 1968, which is designed to replace all earlier legislation relating to medicines, was based on the proposals in the White Paper. It is considered in detail in Chapters 1 to 15.

European Community legislation has had, and still has, a large impact on United Kingdom law. The Treaty of Rome and the issue of Regulations, Directives, Decisions and Recommendations by the Council of Ministers in Brussels has led to amendments of pharmacy law in Great Britain particularly with regard to the mutual recognition of pharmaceutical qualifications and the manufacture and distribution of medicines. This is discussed in Chapter 28.

International agreement about the control of narcotics began with the International Opium Convention signed at the Hague in 1912, although the Convention was not implemented until after the 1914/18 war. A series of Dangerous Drugs Acts, beginning with the Dangerous Drugs Act 1920, brought the various international agreements into force in Great Britain. The Single Convention on Narcotic Drugs 1961 replaced all the earlier international agreements and was reflected in the Dangerous Drugs Act 1965.

The misuse of amphetamines and other psychotropic drugs widened the problems of abuse, and an International Convention on Psychotropic Substances was signed in 1971. In Great Britain, however, the Drugs (Prevention of Misuse) Act 1964 had provided a measure of control by making the unlawful possession of amphetamines, and certain other drugs, an offence. As problems of drug abuse continued to increase, the law was extended and recast in the Misuse of Drugs Act 1971, which repealed the various Dangerous Drugs Acts and the 1964 Act. The provision of the 1971 Act and the regulations made under it are described in detail in Chapter 16.

The National Health Service Act 1946 and the National Health Service (Scotland) Act 1947 provided for a comprehensive health service, including the provision of pharmaceutical services. There have since been a number of amending Acts. The current structure of the National Health Service is outlined in Chapter 23 and a full description is given of the arrangements for providing a pharmaceutical service.

Miscellaneous legislation impinging on pharmacy is dealt with in Chapters 18, 24 and 25, and a discussion on allied health professions is provided in Chapter 22.

# List of Statutes

# and Statutory Instruments

*Statutes marked with a cross have been repealed*

Access to Health Records Act 1990

Agriculture Act 1947

Agriculture Act 1970

Alcoholic Liquor Duties Act 1979

Animal (Cruel Poisons) Act 1962
   SI 1963 No.1278          Animal (Cruel Poisons) Regulations 1963

Animal Health and Welfare Act 1984

Animals (Scientific Procedures) Act 1986

Apothecaries Act 1815

Arsenic Act 1851

Business Names Act 1985

Competition Act 1998

Companies Act 1985

Consumer Protection Act 1987
   SI 1988 No.2078          Consumer Protection (Code of Practice for Traders on
                            Price Indications) (Approved) Order 1988

Medicines

| | |
|---|---|
| SI 1974 No.832 | —(Renewal Applications for Licences and Certificates) Regulations 1974 |
| | amended 1977/180; 1982/1789; 1992/755 |
| SI 1974 No.1150 | —(Exemption from Licences) (Ingredients) Order 1974 |
| SI 1975 No.298 | —(Advertising of Medicinal Products) Regulations 1975 |
| SI 1975 No.533 | —(Dental Filling Substances) Order 1975 |
| SI 1975 No.761 | —(Termination of Transitional Exemptions) (No.3) Order 1975 |
| SI 1975 No.762 | —(Exemptions from Licences) (Wholesale Dealing in Confectionery) Order 1975 |
| SI 1975 No.1169 | —(Medicines Act 1968 Amendment) Regulations 1975 |
| SI 1975 No.1349 | —(Feeding Stuffs Additives) Order 1975 |
| SI 1975 No.2000 | —(Child Safety) Regulations 1975 |
| | amended 1976/1643; 1987/877; 1994/1402 |
| SI 1976 No.31 | —(Feeding Stuff Limits of Variation) Order 1976 |
| SI 1976 No.968 | —(Specified Articles and Substances) Order 1976 |
| | amended 1994/3119 |
| SI 1976 No.1726 | —(Labelling) Regulations 1976 |
| | amended 1977/996; 1977/2168; 1978/41; 1978/1140; 1981/1791; 1983/1729; 1985/1558; 1985/2008; 1989/1183; 1992/3273; 1994/104; 1994/3114 |
| SI 1977 No.161 | —(Exemption from Licences) (Medicinal Tests on Animals) Order 1977 |
| SI 1977 No.670 | —(Bal Jivan Chamcho Prohibition) (No.2) Order 1977 |
| | amended 1997/856 |
| SI 1977 No.1038 | —(Manufacturer's Undertakings for Imported Products) Regulations 1977 |
| | amended 1992/2845; 1994/3144 |
| SI 1977 No.1050 | —(Medicines Act 1968) Amendment Regulations 1977 |
| SI 1977 No.1055 | —(Leaflets) Regulations 1977 |
| | amended 1992/3274; 1994/104 |
| SI 1977 No.1399 | —(Certificate of Analysis) Regulations 1977 |
| SI 1977 No.1488 | —(Breathing Gases) Order 1977 |
| SI 1977 No.2126 | —(Pharmacy and General Sale) (Appointed Day) Order 1977 |
| SI 1977 No.2130 | —(Retail Sale or Supply of Herbal Remedies) Order 1977 |
| SI 1977 No.2131 | —(Prohibition of Non-Medicinal Antimicrobial Substances) Order 1977 |
| | amended 1992/2684 |
| SI 1978 No.40 | —(Fluted Bottles) Regulations 1978 |
| SI 1978 No.41 | —(Labelling and Advertising to the Public) Regulations 1978 |
| SI 1978 No.1004 | —(Radioactive Substances) Order 1978 |
| SI 1978 No.1006 | —(Administration of Radioactive Substances) Regulations 1978 |
| | amended 1995/2147 |

# Table of Abbreviations

AC—Appeal Court
All ER—All England Law Reports
AMTRA—Animal Medicines Training Regulatory Authority
App Cases—Law Reports Appeal Cases
BNF—British National Formulary
BP—British Pharmacopoeia
BPC—British Pharmaceutical Codex
B.Vet.C—British Veterinary Codex
Ch—Law Reports Chancery Division
cm—centimetre
Cmmd—Command paper
CVMP—Committee for Veterinary Medicinal Products
EC—European Economic Community
EEC—European Economic Community
EMEA—European Agency for the Evaluation of Medicinal Products
EU—European Union
fl.oz—fluid ounce
GDS—general dental services
GMC—General Medical Council
GMP—Good Manufacturing Practice
GMS—general medical services
GP—General Practitioner
g—gram
HA—Health Authority
HSC—Health Service Circular
INN—international non-proprietary name
iu—international unit
KB—Law Reports King's Bench Division
kg—kilogram
LPC—Local Pharmaceutical Committee
LT—Law Times reports

MCA—Medicines Control Agency
MDA—Medical Devices Agency
μg—micrograms
md—maximum dose
mdd—maximum daily dose
mg—milligram
ml—millilitre
MRL—maximum residue limit
ms—maximum strength
NHS—National Health Service
NMC—Nursing and Midwifery Council
PALS—Patient Advocacy and Liaison Service
PDS—personal dental services
PGD—Patient Group Direction
*Pharm J*—Pharmaceutical Journal
PMS—personal medical services
POM—Prescription Only Medicine
QB—Law Reports Queen's Bench Division
reg.—Regulation
RPM—Resale Price Maintenance
s.—section
Sch.—Schedule
SI—Statutory Instrument
SI(S)—Statutory Instrument (Scotland)
SSP—Statutory Sick Pay
UKCC—United Kingdom Central Council for Nurses, Midwives and Health Visitors
VMD—Veterinary Medicines Directorate
v/v—volume in volume
v/w—volume in weight
w/v—weight in volume
w/w—weight in weight

# CHAPTER ONE

# Medicines Act 1968

## Scope and Administration

European Community Council Directives and Regulations together with the Medicines Act 1968 (from now on referred to as *the Act*) regulate the manufacture, distribution and importation of (a) medicines for human use; (b) medicines for administration to animals; and (c) medicated animal feeding stuffs. At present their application to products for export is limited (see Chapter 2). The Health and Agriculture Ministers of the United Kingdom are responsible for the administration of the Act and they have the benefit of advice from a Medicines Commission.

Medicinal products placed on the market in the United Kingdom require a marketing authorisation, formerly called a product licence. Similarly the manufacture, wholesaling, importation and distribution of medicines are controlled through a licensing system operated by the Ministers and enforced by the Medicines Control Agency (see Chapter 2). Since the removal of Crown Immunity in April 1991 manufacturing units in National Health Service hospitals are also within the licensing system and are subject to the oversight of the Medicines Control Agency of the Department of Health and its Inspectorate. The animal medicines legislation is monitored by the Veterinary Medicines Directorate of the Ministry of Agriculture, Fisheries and Food.

The Act also deals with the registration of retail pharmacies and provides that medicines may be supplied to the public only from pharmacies, except those medicines which can with reasonable safety be sold without the supervision of a pharmacist. The Minister can make regulations relating to the labelling of medicines, the containers in which they are supplied, and the manner in which their sale is promoted, whether by advertisement or oral representation.

In Great Britain the Royal Pharmaceutical Society of Great Britain (*the Society*) has duties of enforcement in connection with pharmacies and the retail distribution of medicines. Other enforcement duties may be given to the Society and to local authorities, as the appropriate Minister may decide (see p.6).

Preparation of the *British Pharmacopoeia* and other books of standards also falls within the scope of the Act.

The Animal Health and Welfare Act 1984 (ss.13, 14 and 15) increased the powers under the Medicines Act to:

1   regulate the manufacture and sampling of animal feeding stuffs; and
2   provide for registration of suppliers of veterinary drugs and medicated feeding stuffs and for the maintenance of those registers in Great Britain by the Society (see Chapter 12).

## Medicinal Product

The term used is not *medicine* but *medicinal product*, which is defined in Council Directive 65/65/EEC as:

1   Any substance or combination of substances presented for treating or preventing disease in human beings or animals.
2   Any substance or combination of substances which may be administered to human beings or animals with a view to making a medical diagnosis or to restoring, correcting, or modifying physiological functions in human beings or animals is likewise considered a medicinal product.

This is a broader definition than that in the Medicines Act and can be defined as being a medicinal product (a) by presentation and (b) by function.

The term *a medicinal product to which Chapters II to V of the 1965 Directive apply* includes all medicinal products for human use *except* those prepared on the basis of a *magistral* or *official formula*, medicinal products intended for research, or intermediate products intended for further processing by an authorised manufacturer (Council Directive 65/65/EEC, as amended).

*Magistral* means any medicinal product prepared in a pharmacy in accordance with a prescription for an individual patient.

*Official formula* means any medicinal product which is prepared in accordance with the prescriptions of a pharmacopoeia and is intended to be supplied directly to the patients served by the pharmacy in question.

*Ingredient* may be the sole active ingredient present in a medicinal product.

*Hospital* includes a clinic, nursing home or similar institution.

*Animal* includes any bird, fish or reptile (s.132).

*Medicinal purpose* means one or more of the following: (a) treating or preventing disease; (b) diagnosing disease or ascertaining the existence, degree or extent of a physiological condition; (c) contraception; (d) inducing anaesthesia; (e) otherwise preventing or interfering with the normal operation of a physiological function [s.130(2)].

*Administer* means administer to a human being or an animal, whether orally, by injection or by introduction into the body in any other way, or by external application, a substance or article either in its existing state or after it has been dissolved or dispersed in, or diluted or mixed with, some other substance used as a vehicle [s.130(9)].

By ministerial order (s.104) the Act, or specified parts of the Act, can be applied to any article or substance which is not a medicinal product but is made wholly or partly for a medicinal purpose. In the past Orders have been made in respect of surgical ligatures and sutures, dental filling substances, contact lenses and associated substances, and intra-uterine contraceptive devices. However since 1994 these substances have been considered to be medical devices rather than medicines and are now controlled under the Medical Devices Regulations 1994 (SI 1994 No.3017, as amended) made under the Consumer Protection Act 1987 (see p.32).

An order may also be made (s.105) in respect of any substance which (a) is used as an ingredient in the manufacture of a medicinal product; or (b) is capable of causing danger to the health of the community or to the health of animals if used without proper safeguards. The order may specify which parts of the Act are to apply. Some substances used as ingredients in the manufacture of medicinal products, and certain other substances, have been controlled by orders of this kind (SIs 1971 No.1200, 1973 No.367 and 1985 No.1403) (see Appendix 1).

Orders can also be made under the European Communities Act 1972, e.g. the Medicines for Human Use (Marketing Authorisations, etc) Regulations 1994 (SI 1994 No.3144).

Certain things are specifically declared *not* to be medicinal products (s.130). These include:

1   Substances or articles manufactured for administration to human beings or animals in the course of the manufacturer's business, or in a laboratory on behalf of the manufacturer, solely by way of a test for ascertaining what effects they have, and in circumstances where the manufacturer has no knowledge that the effects are likely to be beneficial.

2   Substances and articles as may be specified in a ministerial order. Chemical substances used to sterilise animals which are neither domestic nor held in captivity are not medicinal products (SI 1986 No.2177).

*Breathing gases* for human use in conditions in which respiration is adversely affected by abnormal atmospheric pressure or otherwise are not medicinal products when they are not administered for the treatment or diagnosis of disease. This exemption applies to oxygen, air or any mixture of both, or of either or both with any inert gas or gases or with nitrogen (SI 1977 No.1488).

An animal feeding stuff into which a medicinal product has been incorporated is also classed as a medicinal product. Special provisions relate to such feeding stuffs (s.130).

## Administration

The Medicines Act extends to Scotland and Northern Ireland, and the terms the *Health Ministers* and the *Agricultural Ministers* include the relevant Ministers of those countries (s.1), as well as those for England and Wales. All these Ministers, taken together, comprise the *Ministers* who act jointly in certain matters, e.g. the appointment of the Medicines Commission (s.2). The Ministers also comprise the *licensing authority* (s.6), but these licensing functions are carried out by either the Medicines Control Agency or the European Agency for the Evaluation of Medicinal Products.

*Medicines Control Agency* (MCA) is the licensing authority for the decentralised system, i.e. mutual recognition and national procedures, for market authorisations under the terms of the Council Directives (see Chapter 2). It is also the licensing authority for all other licences required under the Act, e.g. manufacturers, wholesale dealers, etc. and is also the enforcement authority for these matters in the United Kingdom.

*European Agency for the Evaluation of Medicinal Products* (EMEA), established under EC Council Regulation 2309/93/EEC, is the licensing authority for the centralised procedures for market authorisations under the terms of the EC Council Directives (see Chapter 2).

*Veterinary Medicines Directorate* (VMD) is the organisation for animal medicines equivalent to the Medicines Control Agency.

Before exercising any power to make orders or regulations the Ministers must, except in certain cases of emergency, consult in advance organisations which appear to them (the Ministers) to represent interests likely to be affected (s.129). In relation to matters not connected with veterinary drugs or animal medicines *appropriate Ministers* means the *Health Ministers*.

The *Medicines Commission* (s.2) is a body appointed by the Ministers to advise them on the administration of the Act and on any matters relating to medicinal products. It is a body corporate which must have at least eight members (there are in fact 19). It must include at least one member who, in relation to each of the following activities, has had wide and recent experience and has shown capacity in: (a) the practice of medicine; (b) the practice of veterinary medicine; (c) the practice of pharmacy; (d) chemistry other than pharmaceutical chemistry; (e) the pharmaceutical industry [s.2(3)]. The chairman is appointed by the Ministers from amongst the members of the Commission [s.2(4)].

The Commission is required to make recommendations to the Ministers about the numbers of committees required under section 4 (*appropriate committees*) and about their functions and membership [s.3(2)]. These committees may be set up by the Ministers for any purpose in connection with the execution of the Act, but specific reference is made to the establishment of committees: (a) to give advice with respect to safety, quality or efficacy; (b) to promote the collection and investigation of information relating to adverse reactions; and (c) to prepare further editions of the *British Pharmacopoeia* and other compendia. The Commission itself is required to undertake any of these functions which have not been assigned to any committee.

Three section 4 committees are still functioning: the Committee on the Safety of Medicines (SI 1970 No.1257); the Veterinary Products Committee (SI 1970 No.1304); and the British Pharmacopoeia Commission (SIs 1970 No.1256 and 1982 No.1335).

The most recently established committee is the Advisory Board on the Registration of Homoeopathic Products which gives advice with respect to the safety and quality of any homoeopathic product in respect of which a certificate of registration could be granted (SI 1995 No.309) (see Chapter 2).

Administrative provisions relating to the Medicines Commission and the section 4 committees are in Schedule 1 to the Act and in regulations made thereunder (SI 1970 No.746). The Medicines Commission can appoint its own ad hoc committees, and section 4 committees can set up their own sub-committees.

The Ministers can extend the functions of the Medicines Commission and can vary or terminate any of the Commission's functions, subject to the approval of a resolution of both Houses of Parliament. Annual reports about the work of the Medicines Commission and its committees and of the committees set up under section 4 of the Act must be submitted to the Ministers (s.5).

## Enforcement

The primary duty of enforcing the Act rests with the *appropriate Minister* in England and Wales [s.108(1)], the Secretary of State in Scotland [s.109(1)] and the Minister of Health and Social Services in Northern Ireland [s.110(1)]. There are provisions for these Ministers to delegate many of their functions to other authorities, but licensing requirements and those provisions which affect hospitals or the premises of practitioners are solely the responsibility of the Ministers. In England, Wales and Scotland arrangements can be made or directions given whereby local food and drug authorities and/or the Royal Pharmaceutical Society can have certain duties or exercise certain powers, concurrently with the Ministers [s.108(2)]. In Scotland, these enforcement authorities cannot themselves institute proceedings (s.109).

**Role of the Royal Pharmaceutical Society**

The Society is responsible under this Act for the maintenance of the Register of Pharmacy Premises (see Chapter 4) and for disciplinary control over bodies corporate and representatives of pharmacists carrying on retail pharmacy businesses (see Chapter 21).

The Royal Pharmaceutical Society, concurrently with the Minister, is also required to enforce in Great Britain [ss.108(6) and 109(2)] the provisions relating to:

1  Sale and supply of medicinal products not on a General Sale List (s.52).
2  Sale, supply or administration of medicinal products on prescription only (s.58).
3  Regulations restricting sale, supply or administration of certain medicinal products except with the authority of specially certified practitioners (s.60).
4  Regulations restricting sale or supply of medicinal products to persons in a specified class (s.61).
5  Annual return of premises to the registrar (s.77).
6  Restrictions on use of titles, descriptions and emblems (s.78).
7  Regulations imposing further restrictions on titles [s.79(2)].

The appropriate Minister *must* arrange for the Society, and/or Food and Drug Authorities (as designated in s.198 of the Local Government Act 1972) to have a power, or a duty, to enforce in connection with retail sale, supply, etc. of medicinal products provisions relating to:

8  Prohibition of sale, supply or importation of medicinal products specified by order (s.62) (see Chapter 13).
9  Sale and supply and offer of sale or supply of adulterated medicinal products (s.63).
10 Sale of medicinal products not of the nature or quality demanded (s.64).
11 Compliance with standards specified in monographs in certain publications (s.65).
12 Regulations relating to labelling and marking of containers and packages [s.85(3),(4) and (5)].
13 Regulations relating to requirements for containers [s.87(2)].
14 Regulations relating to distinctive colours, shapes and marking of medicinal products [s.88(3)].
15 Regulations relating to display of information on automatic machines [s.89(2)].
16 Regulations relating to leaflets to be supplied with medicinal products [s.86(2) and (3)].
17 False or misleading representations or advertisements (s.93).

18   Advertisements requiring consent of product licence holder (s.94).
19   Regulations relating to issue of advertisements (s.95).

Such arrangements for enforcement have been made with the Society relating to 9 to 13. Enforcement by the Society in respect of 17, 18 and 19 is limited to premises, ships, aircraft, vehicles, or places where retail sales take place, and to the display of advertisements in close proximity to automatic machines.

The Society and the Food and Drug Authorities *may* be given a power or duty to enforce provisions relating to:

20   Sale of medicinal products on General Sale List (s.53).
21   Sale of medicinal products from automatic machines (s.54).
22   Regulations relating to premises where medicinal products are prepared or dispensed and to dealings in medicinal products including the super-vision, storage, safekeeping, record-keeping, disposal, supply as samples or precautions to be taken before sale, and to the construction, etc. of automatic machines (s.66).

The Society has been given the power and is under a duty to enforce sections 53, 54 and 66 in respect of registered pharmacies and of premises where certain exempted veterinary drugs are sold (see Chapter 12). Food and Drug Authorities have a power and are under a duty to enforce these sections in respect of all other premises (SI 1980 No.1923).

An enforcement authority must give 28 days' notice to the Minister before instituting proceedings under any of the sections in 8 to 22 above.

County Councils have a duty to enforce the provisions of the Act relating to the proper labelling and description of medicated animal feeding stuffs (ss.90 and 108). These authorities also have a duty to enforce any order made under section 62(1) prohibiting the sale, supply or importation of any specified animal feeding stuffs. The Council of any county district which is not a Food and Drug Authority and the overseers of the Inner Temple and the Middle Temple may be required to enforce the regulations made under section 66 (see 22 above).

## Inspection and Sampling

A right of entry and a right to inspect, take samples and seize goods and documents is given (ss.111 and 112) to *any person duly authorised in writing by an enforcement authority* in order to ascertain whether there has been a contravention of the Act. The right to inspect extends to any substance or article appearing to be a medicinal product; to any plant or equipment used to manufacture or assemble medicinal products; and to any labels, leaflets, containers or packages. An authorised person, having produced his credentials if required to do so, is empowered:

1    to enter any premises, stall or place other than any vehicle or home-going ship, to ascertain whether there has been a contravention of the Act, or generally for the purposes of performing the functions of the enforcement authority; and to enter any ship, aircraft or hover-vehicle to ascertain whether there is in it any article or substance imported in contravention of the Act;

2    to take a sample (by purchase or otherwise) of any medicinal product sold or supplied or any substance to be used in the manufacture of a medicinal product;

3    to require the production of any books or documents relating to the business;

4    to take copies of any entry in any such book or document;

5    to seize and detain any substance or articles or any document which he has reasonable cause to believe may be required for proceedings under the Act (the person from whom the seizure is made must be informed).

A person duly authorised in writing by the licensing authority, i.e. an inspector of the Medicines Control Agency of the Department of Health, may exercise these rights in respect of the business of any applicant for a licence or certificate under Part II of the Act in order to verify any statement made in the application.

Twenty-four hours' notice must be given to the occupier if it is intended to enter any premises used only as a private dwelling house. In cases of urgency, or where refusal is apprehended, or where the giving of notice will defeat the object of entry, or where the premises are unoccupied, a justice of the peace may issue a warrant authorising entry, by force if necessary. Any person entering any property in the exercise of a right of entry may take with him/her such other persons and such equipment as may be necessary. On vacating any unoccupied property entered in pursuance of a warrant, s/he must leave it as effectively secured as s/he found it.

It is an offence wilfully to obstruct a duly authorised person, or wilfully to fail to comply with any proper request made by him/her or, without reasonable cause, to fail to give him/her any assistance or information s/he may reasonably require within his/her functions under the Act. It is also an offence to give such a person false information (s.112).

A person who has exercised a right of entry and discloses to any other person, except in the performance of his/her duty, information about any manufacturing process or trade secret obtained by him/her in the premises, commits an offence. It is similarly an offence for any person to disclose any information obtained by him/her in pursuance of the Acts (s.118).

A detailed procedure is set out in Schedule 3 for dealing with samples taken by a *sampling officer* (i.e. a person authorised by the relevant enforcement authority) either for any purpose in connection with that authority's functions under the Act, or to ascertain whether there has been a contravention of the Act.

A sample must be divided forthwith into three parts, two being retained by the sampling officer and the third given to the vendor or dealer in the manner prescribed in the Schedule, according to the circumstances. One of the parts retained by the sampling officer may be submitted for analysis to a public analyst, or to a laboratory with which an arrangement has been made by the enforcement authority with the approval of the Minister.

A certificate, in the prescribed form, specifying the result of the analysis must be issued by the person having control of the laboratory, or by the public analyst carrying out the analysis. The certificate must be signed by the person issuing it and, in any proceedings, a document purporting to be such a certificate shall be sufficient evidence of the facts stated in the document, unless the other party requires that the person who issued the certificates shall be called as a witness. The second part of the sample retained by the sampling officer must be produced as evidence and, if required by either party or at the direction of the court, must be submitted to the Government Chemist for analysis. The prescribed forms of certificates of analysis are in SI 1977 No.1399 (see Appendix 7).

A sampling officer must pay the value of a sample if it is demanded by the person from whom it is taken; there is provision for arbitration about the value in case of a dispute. The taking of a sample by a sampling officer has effect as though it were a sale of a medicinal product and the provisions of section 64 of the Act relating to the protection of purchasers apply (see Chapter 13).

Where a substance or article has been seized by a person exercising a right of seizure (referred to as an *authorised officer*) (s.113) s/he must either treat it as a sample, or set aside part of it as a sample, if requested to do so within 21 days by the person entitled to be informed of the seizure. This does not apply if the nature of the substance is such that it is not reasonably practicable to do either of these things. A substance or article treated as a sample under these provisions is subject to the procedure of division, analysis, etc., set out in Schedule 3 as described above.

Any person, other than a person authorised by an enforcement authority, who has purchased a medicinal product may submit a sample of it for analysis to the public analyst for the area where it was purchased, subject to the analyst's right to demand payment of the prescribed fee in advance. The public analyst must analyse the sample as soon as is practicable and issue a certificate in the form prescribed (s.115) (see Appendix 7).

There are special enforcement and sampling provisions relating to animal feeding stuffs (s.117). The Agriculture Minister may by regulation modify, for animal feeding stuffs, the ordinary sampling procedure. These regulations may prescribe a method of analysis to be used in analysing samples of feeding stuffs, and provide that the results of analysis by other methods shall not be admissible in evidence. The Agriculture Minister may by order specify the discrepancy which will be tolerated between the amount of medicinal product present in an animal feeding stuff and the amount declared on the label.

Deficiencies or excesses within the prescribed limits are not regarded as contraventions of the Act.

## Legal Proceedings

Where a contravention is due to the default of another person, that person may be charged and convicted, whether or not proceedings are taken against the person committing the contravention. A person charged with an offence who proves to the satisfaction of the court (a) that s/he exercised all due diligence to prevent the contravention, and (b) that it was due to the act or default of another person, shall, subject to certain procedural requirements, be acquitted of the offence (s.121).

When an offence is committed by a body corporate, any director, manager, company secretary or other similar officer may be proceeded against, as well as the body corporate, if it is proved that the offence was committed with his/her consent and connivance, or was attributable to his/her neglect. *It is specifically provided that the superintendent pharmacist of a pharmacy company (whether or not a member of the board), and any pharmacist in personal control of a pharmacy and acting under his/her direction, shall be regarded as officers for this purpose* (s.124).

Medicinal products and animal feeding stuffs proved to have been found on a vehicle from which those goods are sold are presumed to have been offered for sale, unless the contrary is proved (s.126). This presumption applies when the offences concern the offering for sale of: (a) a medicated animal feeding stuff without the authority of a product licence, animal test certificate, or a veterinary direction (s.40); or (b) a medicinal product contrary to the restriction on retail sales (ss.52 and 53); or (c) an adulterated medicinal product [s.63(b)]. There is also a presumption in respect of the possession of medicinal products or medicated animal feeding stuffs (or leaflets referring to them) on premises at which the person charged carries on a business including the supply of those goods.

When the offence concerns adulteration [s.63(b)], false or misleading labels or leaflets (ss.85 and 86), requirements as to containers (s.87) or requirements as to marking of medicinal products (s.88), a person is presumed, unless the contrary is proved, to have had medicinal products in his/her possession for the purpose of sale or supply. Warranty can be pleaded as a defence to a charge of contravening any of these sections, or of sections 64 and 65. These relate to sales made to the prejudice of the purchaser (s.64) or failure to comply with standards specified in official monographs (s.65).

Subject to certain formalities a defendant can rely on warranty if s/he proves:

1    that s/he purchased the substance or article as one which could lawfully be sold, supplied or offered for sale and with a written warranty to that effect;

2    that at the time of the alleged offence s/he had no reason to believe that it was otherwise; and

3    that the substance or article was then in the same state as when s/he purchased it (s.122).

A defendant who is the servant of the person who purchased under warranty can rely on the same defence as his/her employer, and a name or description entered in an invoice is deemed to be written warranty that the article described can be sold under that description.

It is an offence for a person to give a false warranty unless s/he can prove that at the time s/he gave it s/he had reason to believe that the statement of description was accurate. It is also an offence wilfully to apply to any article or substance (a) a warranty; or (b) a certificate of analysis issued under the Act (see p.9), if that warranty or certificate relates to a different substance or article.

Any document purporting to be an authorised copy of the *British Pharmacopoeia*, or a compendium or a list of names as described in Part VII of the Act or of an amendment thereto, shall be received in evidence as being a true copy of the subject matter contained therein and shall be evidence of the date on which it came into operation (s.102).

The validity of licences and licensing decisions is considered under licensing (Chapter 2), and certificates issued by the registrar relating to the premises are dealt with under pharmacies (see Chapter 4).

## Summary

*   The legal sources for the marketing authorisations of medicinal products and the licensing of manufacturers, wholesalers, and other distributors of medicines are the European Directives and the United Kingdom Medicines Act 1968.
*   The advisory structure for the Ministers is a Medicines Commission and several statutory committees including the Committee on the Safety of Medicines.
*   The two licensing authorities The Medicines Control Agency (MCA) and the European Evaluation Agency for Medicinal Products (EMEA) deal with the decentralised and centralised licensing procedures for medicinal products.
*   The definition of a medicinal product is set out in Council Directive 65/65/EEC.
*   Certain substances, e.g. surgical ligatures and sutures, dental fillings, contact lenses and intra-uterine devices, are no longer controlled under the Medicines Act but under the Medical Devices Regulations made under the Consumer Protection Act.
*   The enforcement of the Act and regulations fall upon the Medicines Control Agency and the Royal Pharmaceutical Society of Great Britain.

- The powers of the inspectors are laid down and stringent conditions relate to the taking of sampling within a sampling procedure.
- Those liable to commit offences under the Act are listed together with any defences that can be raised.

## Further Reading

AMELIA Guidance notes. Veterinary Medicines Directorate.
MAIL publications. Medicines Control Agency.
MAVIS advisory leaflets. Veterinary Medicines Directorate.
*Rules Governing Medicinal Products for Human Use in the European Community* vol. I. The Stationery Office.
*Rules Governing Medicinal Products for Animal Use in the European Community* vol. Va. The Stationery Office.

CHAPTER TWO

# Medicines Act 1968

## The Licensing System

Licensing requirements are set out in EC Council Directives and in the Medicines Act, which provide for marketing authorisations, manufacturers' licences, wholesale dealers' licences, clinical trial certificates and animal test certificates. The licensing system applies to medicinal products and to substances incorporated in animal feeding stuffs for a medicinal purpose. (Retailers of licensed products, unless responsible for the composition of the products they sell, do not require any licences, but medicinal products which are not on a General Sale List may be sold or supplied by retail, subject to certain exemptions, only from registered pharmacies (see Chapter 5).)

Without the appropriate marketing authorisation, licence or certificate it is not lawful for any person, in the course of a business carried on by him/her, to manufacture, sell, supply, export, or import into the United Kingdom any of these products unless some exemption is provided in the Act or regulations.

In this chapter the provisions of the Directives and the Act and its statutory instruments are collated and summarised under appropriate headings. The statutory instruments mentioned are those in force on 1 January 2001. Explanatory leaflets are available from the Medicines Control Agency of the Department of Health in the case of human medicines and the Veterinary Medicines Directorate of the Ministry of Agriculture, Fisheries and Food for medicines for animal use.

**Issue of Licences**

Market authorisations and licences are issued by the licensing authorities, i.e. the Medicines Control Agency (MCA) or the European Agency for the Evaluation of Medicinal Products (EMEA), who may grant, refuse, review, suspend, revoke or vary them (ss.20 and 28 and SI 1994 No.3144). They expire at the end of five years or such shorter period as is specified in the marketing authorisation/licence. If a marketing authorisation/licence, subsequent to its issue, contravenes any European Community obligation, a notice terminating it may be served on the holder (s.24 and SI 1994 No.3144). The authority must send copies of licences to the appropriate section 4 Committees (see p.5). When an application for a marketing authorisation/ licence is refused, the licensing authority must state the reasons for refusal in a notice served on the applicant. Refusal may not be based on any ground relating to the price of a product, and the licensing authority must consult the appropriate committee, that is the Committee on the Safety of Medicines or the Veterinary Products Committee, before refusing an application on grounds of safety, quality or efficacy (s.20).

**Marketing Authorisations for Human Medicines**

Prior to 1994 product licences were granted for medicines by the Medicines Control Agency and these were designated by the initials 'PL'. In 1990 the European Community issued proposals for a two-tiered system for obtaining marketing authorisations and this system was implemented in 1994, thus replacing product licences with marketing authorisations. The system comprises a centralised system and a national (member state) system. The centralised licensing system is administered by the European Agency for the Evaluation of Medicinal Products and is used for new active substances and certain high-technology and biotechnology products. The centralised procedure is set out in Regulation 2309/93/EEC, which has direct effect on member states without any separate implementation by a member state.

The decentralised system, also known as the mutual recognition procedure, is for the other products and involves the Medicines Control Agency and its marketing authorisations may be recognised by the other member states. Council Directive 65/65/EEC, as amended, together with the other European pharmaceutical Directives, implemented by United Kingdom regulations (SI 1994 No.3144), establish the procedures for the decentralised system. The regulations implement the Directives concerned by cross-reference to the Directives themselves, rather than setting out the details in full.

No medicinal product may be placed on the market of a member state and no such product can be distributed by way of wholesale dealing unless a marketing authorisation has been issued by the Medicines Control Agency or the European Agency for the Evaluation of Medicinal Products. Medicinal products include immunological products, medicinal products based on human blood or blood constituents and medicinal products based on radio-isotopes (radiopharmaceuticals). However, these provisions do not apply to whole human blood, plasma or blood cells of human origin, nor a radio-pharmaceutical in which the radionuclide is in a sealed source. Homoeopathic medicinal products are dealt with separately (see p.17).

*Proprietary medicinal product* means any ready-prepared medicinal product placed on the market in the United Kingdom under a special name and in a special pack (Council Directive 65/65/EEC, Art.1).

*Radiopharmaceutical* means a medicinal product which, when ready for use, contains one or more radionuclides included for a medicinal purpose (SI 1992 No.604).

*Blood product* means any industrially prepared medicinal product for human use derived from human blood or blood plasma and includes albumin, coagulating factors and immunoglobulins of human origin but does not include whole blood, human plasma or blood cells of human origin (SI 1992 No.755).

The holder of a marketing authorisation for a medicinal product may: (a) sell, supply or export the product; (b) procure its sale, supply or exportation; (c) procure its manufacture or assembly, in accordance with the marketing authorisation.

In dealing with an application for a marketing authorisation, the licensing authority must give particular consideration to the safety, quality and efficacy of the products (s.19). Considerations of safety are taken to include the extent to which the product:

1    if used without proper safeguards, is capable of causing danger to the health of the community, or of causing danger to the health of animals generally or of one or more species of animals; or
2    if administered to an animal, may be harmful to the animal or may induce disease in other animals or may leave a residue in the carcass or product of the animal which may be harmful to human beings; or
3    may interfere with the treatment, prevention or diagnosis of disease; or
4    may be harmful to the person administering it or (in the case of an instrument, apparatus or appliance) the person operating it (s.132).

When considering the *efficacy* of a product, the licensing authority must not take into account any question of the superior efficacy of another product (s.19), or refuse to grant a licence on any grounds relating to price (s.20).

For imported products the licensing authority must have particular regard to the methods, standards and conditions of manufacture. The applicant may be required to produce one or more of the following:

1    an undertaking by the manufacturer that s/he will permit inspection by the licensing authority;
2    an undertaking by, or on behalf of, the manufacturer that s/he will comply with prescribed conditions (SI 1977 No.1038, as amended by SI 1992 No.2845) (see also Appendix 4);

3     a declaration by or on behalf of the manufacturer that the product has
      been manufactured in accordance with the law of the country where it
      was manufactured (s.19).

An application for a marketing authorisation for a medicinal product for
human use in either of the procedures must be accompanied by the particulars
set out in Council Directive 65/65/EEC (Arts.4 and 4a), Council Directive
75/319/EEC (Art.2) and Council Directive 75/318/EEC (the Annex). Article
4a sets out the details of the Summary of Product Characteristics (SPC) (see
Appendix 3).

*Summary of Product Characteristics* means the information required to
accompany any application for a marketing authorisation under Council
Directive 65/65/EEC (Art.4a). (for details see p.396).

Apart from the Summary of Product Characteristics, the particulars
required to be given in a full application include: the kind of activity to be
undertaken (e.g. selling, procuring manufacture, etc.); the pharmaceutical
form of the product; its composition, physical characteristics and medicinal
use; method of manufacture and assembly; quality control procedures; containers and labelling; reports of experimental and biological studies and of
clinical trials and studies; any adverse reactions; and, where the product is
made abroad, documentary evidence of authorisation relating to manufacture,
assembly, etc. Special additional conditions apply for applications concerning
immunological products, radiopharmaceuticals, and medicinal products
derived from human blood or human plasma (see Appendix 3).

Abridged applications are permitted where the relevant data have been
submitted in an earlier application, or data about the kind of product in
question are well documented. (Renewal applications for licenses and certificates are dealt with in SI 1994 No.3144.)

Standard conditions and obligations for marketing authorisations are prescribed in the relevant EC Directives (see Appendix 5). These provisions are
incorporated in the marketing authorisation unless the applicant desires that
any of them shall be excluded or modified in respect of his/her product and
his/her request is granted.

## Borderline Products

Where the licensing authority are of the opinion that a product is a relevant
medicinal product they may by notice in writing serve on any person who has
placed the product on the market informing him/her that the product is a
relevant medicinal product and needs to be licensed together with the reasons
why they are so minded. Statutory provisions provide for initial representations to be made to the licensing authority and, if necessary, for further
representations to be made to an independent review body. Once a final
determination has been made the licensing authority may serve notice requiring

the person not to put the product on the market or to stop marketing it from a date specified. Detail procedures are set out in the legislation (SI 2000 No.292).

## Registration Certificates for Homoeopathic Medicines for Human Use

*Homoeopathic Medicinal Products* means any medicinal product (which may contain a number of principles) prepared from products, substances or compositions called homoeopathic stocks in accordance with a homoeopathic manufacturing procedure described by the *European Pharmacopoeia* or, in the absence thereof, by any pharmacopoeia used officially in a member state (Council Directive 92/73/EEC).

*Certificate of Registration* means a certificate granted under the Medicines (Homoeopathic Medicinal Products for Human Use) Regulations 1994 (SI 1994 No.105, as amended).

In the case of a homoeopathic medicinal product a marketing authorisation is not required provided that a certificate of registration has been granted (SI 1994 No.276). Only homoeopathic medicines which satisfy all of the following conditions may be subject to this simplified registration procedure:

1    they are administered orally or externally;
2    no specific therapeutic indication appears on the label of the product or in any information relating thereto;
3    there is a sufficient degree of dilution to guarantee the safety of the product, in particular, the product may not contain either more than one part per 10 000 of the mother tincture or more than 1/100th of the smallest dose used in allopathy with regard to active principles whose presence in an allopathic product would result in it requiring a doctor's prescription.

Applications for a certificate of registration for a homoeopathic medicinal product must be made in the manner prescribed in the regulations (SI 1994 No.105, as amended). The application must be in writing, in English and include the particulars required by Council Directive 92/73/EEC (see Appendix 3). Fees and Standard variations are covered by SI 1998 No.574.

## Product Licences (Parallel Importing)

The importation from a member state of the European Community of a medicinal product which is a version of one already the subject of a United Kingdom marketing authorisation is known as 'parallel importing'.

A modified form of licence application may be considered for such a product, subject to the following conditions:

1    the product to be imported must be a *proprietary medicinal product* (as defined in Art.1 of Council Directive 65/65/EEC) which is not a vaccine,

toxin, serum or based on human blood, a blood constituent, or a radioactive isotope, or homoeopathic product, as specified in Council Directive 75/319/EEC;

2    it must be covered by a currently valid market authorisation granted by the regulatory body of a European Community member state;

3    it must have no different therapeutic effect from the product covered by the United Kingdom licence; and

4    it must be made by, or under licence to, the United Kingdom manufacturer, or by a member of the same group of companies.

A licence granted in these circumstances is known as a Product Licence (Parallel Import) (PL(PI)).

These requirements apply to the parallel importing of medicines for human use and are taken from an administrative document issued by the Department of Health and Social Security (MAL2/PI). Comparable requirements for veterinary medicines appear in the Medicines (Veterinary Drugs) (Exemption from Licences) (Importation) Order 1986 (SI 1986 No.228).

## Marketing Authorisations for Animal Medicines

*Ready made veterinary drug* means a ready-prepared veterinary drug placed on the market in the United Kingdom in a pharmaceutical form in which it may be used without further processing, *not* being a drug placed on the market under a special name and in a special pack (SI 1992 No.604).

Again, as with human medicines, there are two types of system; centralised and decentralised with full data being required. The Marketing Authorisations for Veterinary Medicinal Products Regulations 1994 (SI 1994 No.3142) implement the Council Directive 81/851/EEC, as amended, for the decentralised system and the centralised procedure is set out in Regulation 2309/93/EEC, which has direct effect. Council Directive 92/74/EEC sets out a simplified procedure for veterinary homoeopathic products similar to that for human medicines.

An application for a marketing authorisation for a medicinal product for animal use in either of the procedures must be accompanied by the particulars set out in Council Directive 81/851/EEC, Council Directive 81/852/EEC (Art.2) and Council Directive 90/676/EEC, and are similar to those for human medicines. The Committee for Veterinary Medicinal Products (CVMP), established under Council Directive 81/851/EEC, gives advice to the Commission and to the national authorities.

Council Regulation 2377/90/EEC lays down the procedures for the evaluation of the safety of residues and the establishment of maximum residue limits (MRLs) in foodstuffs. Provisions for the renewal of applications are set out in SI 1994 No.3142.

Standard conditions for marketing authorisations are prescribed in the relevant EC Directives. These provisions are incorporated in the marketing authorisation unless the applicant desires that any of them shall be excluded or modified in respect of his/her product and his/her request is granted.

## Registration Certificates for Homoeopathic Medicines for Animal Use

No person may market a veterinary homoeopathic medicine for animals unless the product is registered in accordance with the provisions of EC Council Directives 81/851/EEC and 92/74/EEC and the Registration of Homoeopathic Veterinary Medicinal Products Regulations 1997 (SI 1997 No.322).

## Manufacturer's Licence

A manufacturer's licence is required by a person who, in the course of a business carried on by him/her, manufactures or assembles a medicinal product (s.8). The medicinal product to be manufactured or assembled must be the subject of a marketing authorisation unless some exemption is provided in the Act or regulations. The manufacturer must hold a marketing authorisation or be acting to the order of the marketing authorisation holder (s.23).

*Manufacture* includes any process carried out in the course of making the product, but does not include dissolving or dispensing the product in, or diluting or mixing it with, some other substances used as a vehicle for administration.

*Assemble* means the enclosing of the products (with or without other medicinal products of the same description) in a container which is labelled before the product is sold or supplied or, where the product (with or without medicinal products of the same description) is already enclosed in a container in which it is to be sold or supplied, labelling the container before the product is sold or supplied in it (s.132). *Assembly* has a corresponding meaning.

A licence is not required for the manufacture of chemicals and other substances used in the manufacture of ingredients of medicinal products. Nor is a licence required for the manufacture of ingredients supplied in bulk to other manufacturers (see definition of *medicinal products*, p.2). A manufacturer's licence covering assembly must be held for breaking bulk supplies of a medicinal product if it involves the enclosure of the product in different containers or labelling the containers.

In dealing with applications for manufacturer's licences, the licensing authority must, in particular, take into consideration:

1    the operations proposed to be carried out in pursuance of the licence;
2    the premises in which those operations are to be carried out;
3    the equipment which is or will be available on those premises for carrying out those operations;

4    the qualifications of the persons under whose supervision those operations will be carried out; and

5    the arrangements made or to be made for ensuring the safe-keeping of, and the maintenance of adequate records in respect of, medicinal products manufactured or assembled in pursuance of the licence [s.19(5)].

N.B. Council Directive 91/356/EEC lays down the principles and guidelines of *Good Manufacturing Practice* (GMP) which is applicable to all activities which require a licence under Council Directive 75/319/EEC (Art.16).

Applications must be made in the manner prescribed in the regulations (SI 1971 No.974 and SI 1977 No.1052, as amended) indicating whether the licence is to relate to manufacturing or assembly or to both, and giving the particulars mentioned in 1 to 5 above. The applicant must describe the products to be manufactured or assembled and give details of any manufacturing operations to be carried out. The qualifications of the production manager and of the person in charge of quality control must be given, and the name and function of the person to whom they are responsible. Where relevant the qualifications of the person in charge of animals, and of the person responsible for the culture of any living tissue, must also be given.

At least one 'qualified person' is required to be nominated whose responsibilities are set out in the regulations (see Appendix 5). A *qualified person* means a person who as respects qualification and experience satisfies the provisions of Articles 23 and 24 of Council Directive 75/319/EEC.

The standard provisions for a manufacturer's licence (see Appendix 5) are incorporated in every licence unless the applicant has successfully applied for any to be excluded or modified (s.47). Renewal applications are dealt with in SI 1974 No.832, as amended.

## Wholesale Dealer's Licence

Council Directive 92/25/EEC requires a wholesale dealer's licence to be held by any person who, in the course of a business carried on by him/her:

1    sells, or offers for sale, any medicinal products by way of wholesale dealing; or

2    distributes, otherwise than by way of sale, any medicinal product, ready made veterinary drug or industrially produced medicinal product other than a veterinary drug which has been imported, but was not consigned from a member state of the European Union (s.8 and SIs 1977 No.1050, 1983 No.1724 and 1992 No.604).

No person may distribute by way of wholesale any medicinal product which is subject to Directive 65/65/EEC (proprietary and generic medicinal products) except in accordance with a wholesale dealer's licence and from premises specified in that licence. The latter provision does not apply to whole human blood, plasma or blood cells of human origin, a radiopharmaceutical in which the radionuclide is in a sealed source, or a homoeopathic product. Neither does it apply to veterinary drugs which are immunological products, radio-pharmaceuticals, homoeopathic, additives for animal feeding stuffs, or a product specially prepared for a veterinary surgeon for an animal or herd under his/her care.

A wholesale dealer's licence is also required for exportation of any medicinal product which is subject to Directive 65/65/EEC (proprietary and generic medicinal products) if it is to be exported to a member state of the European Union (SI 1993 No.834).

No licence under 2 is required by a person who provides facilities solely for the transport of the medicinal product, or who, in the course of his/her business as an import agent, imports a medicinal product solely to the order of another person who intends to distribute it (SI 1990 No.566). Neither is a licence required by the holder of a marketing authorisation or by a person who has assembled the product to the order of the marketing authorisation holder and where the product has not left the premises of the manufacturer or assembler until the sale of the product (SI 1990 No.566).

Distribution of a medicinal product by way of wholesale dealing means:

1   selling or supplying it; or
2   procuring, holding or exporting it for the purposes of sale or supply to a person who receives it for the purposes of:

   (a)   selling or supplying it; or
   (b)   administering it, or causing it to be administered, to one or more human beings in the course of a business carried on by that person.

The term *business* includes a professional practice and any activity carried on by a body of persons, whether corporate or unincorporated (s.132). Consequently, all sales that are made to practitioners (whether medical or dental) for use in their practices constitute sales by way of wholesale dealing. The provision of services under the National Health Service is treated as the carrying on of a business by the appropriate Minister, Secretary of State or Ministry [s.131(5)].

Sales made by the manufacturer of a product are excluded from the definition of wholesale dealing so that s/he does not require a licence in order to sell his/her own products (s.131). A further concession is provided (SI 1972 No.640) in respect of wholesale sales made by a marketing authorisation holder who is not also the manufacturer, or by a person assembling to his/her order. Provided that such products do not leave the premises of the licensed manufacturer or licensed assembler until the actual sale, no wholesale dealer's licence is required.

The activities of a group of retailers or practitioners who buy medicinal products in bulk and divide the stock amongst themselves for resale does not normally require a licence. If the group has a separate legal identity of its own, or if purchases are made by it collectively for resale to members of the group, a wholesale dealer's licence may be necessary (see also Exemptions for Pharmacists below).

In dealing with an application for a wholesale dealer's licence, the licensing authority must, in particular, take into consideration:

1    the premises on which medicinal products of the description to which the application relates will be stored;
2    the equipment which is or will be available for storing medicinal products on those premises;
3    the equipment and facilities which are or will be available for distributing medicinal products from those premises; and
4    the arrangements made or to be made for securing the safe-keeping of, and the manufacture of adequate records in respect of, medicinal products stored on or distributed from those premises [s.19(6)].

Applications must be made in the manner prescribed in the regulations (SIs 1971 No.974 and 1977 No.1052) and state the classes of medicinal products which are the subject of the application and the uses for which they are intended, together with the particulars mentioned above. The applicant must also give the name and address and qualifications of the responsible person, details of an emergency plan for the recall of products, and details for keeping records either by way of invoices, on computer or in any other form relating to all products received or despatched (SI 1993 No.832).

The standard provisions for wholesale dealer's licences (see Appendix 5) are incorporated in every licence unless the applicant has successfully applied for any to be excluded or modified (s.47 and SI 1971 No.972, as amended).

### Fees

Holders of marketing authorisations, manufacturers' licences and wholesale dealer's licences have to pay a fee in connection with the holding of authorisations/licences in respect of each licence period. Such fees are prescribed in regulations made under the Medicines Act 1971, for human medicines (SI 1995 No.1116, as amended), for animal medicines (SI 1997 No.1469) and for homoeopathic medicines (SI 1996 No.482, as amended).

### Clinical Trial and Animal Test Certificates

*Clinical trials* means an investigation or series of investigations consisting of the administration of one or more medicinal products, where there is evidence that they may be beneficial to a patient or patients, by one or more doctors or dentists for the purpose of ascertaining what effects, beneficial or harmful, the products have (s.31). (For circumstances in which the administration of a substance does not constitute a clinical trial or bring the substance within the definition of a medicinal product, see Chapter 1.) For the manufacture or assembly of a medicinal product to be used only for the purpose of a clinical trial, a manufacturer's licence or a marketing authorisation is not required (s.35). There is a comparable definition for *medicinal test on animals* (s.32).

The provisions relating to clinical trials and medicinal tests on animals are in sections 31 to 39 of the Act. No person may, in the course of a business carried on by him/her, (a) sell or supply, or (b) procure the sale or supply of, or (c) procure the manufacture of or assemble for the purpose of sale or supply a medicinal product for the purpose of a clinical trial or a medicinal test on animals unless s/he is, or acts to the order of, the holder of a marketing authorisation which authorises the clinical trial, or unless a clinical trial certificate or animal test certificate, as appropriate, has been issued and is in force, and the trial or test is to be carried out in accordance with it.

### Exemptions for Clinical Trials

A marketing authorisation or clinical trial certificate is not required for the sale, supply, manufacture or assembly of a medicinal product for the purpose of a clinical trial provided the conditions imposed by the exempting orders are met (SIs 1995 No.2808 and 1995 No.2809). Notification of the supplier's intention must be sent to the licensing authority. The notice must be accompanied by particulars of the trial and summaries of pharmaceutical data and of reports made and tests performed as specified in Schedule 1 to the Order (SI 1995 No.2808). There is provision for termination of the exemption in certain circumstances, usually on the grounds of safety.

A certificate is not required if the product to be the subject of the clinical trial is covered by a marketing authorisation and the conditions set out in SI 1974 No.498 are met. Similar conditions applicable to licensed products to be used in medicinal tests on animals are in SI 1977 No.161. The principal requirements are that the product is to be used strictly in accordance with the marketing authorisation and that the licensing authority is notified of any adverse reactions or effects.

A doctor or dentist wanting to have a product manufactured or imported for use in a clinical trial does not need a certificate if certain conditions are met. The products must have been manufactured or imported specially for the trial and only for administration to the practitioner's own patients. The trial must not have been arranged by, or at the request of, a third party [s.31(5) and (6) and SI 1972 No.1200]. A similar exemption applies where a product is specially manufactured for a veterinarian to use in a medicinal test on animals [s.33(2) and (3)].

When practitioners' prescriptions are dispensed in a registered pharmacy, hospital or health centre under the supervision of a pharmacist there is no need for any certificate [ss.31(7) and 33(4)].

Exemptions for Tests on Animal Licences or Animal Test Certificates are not required for the sale, supply or administration of veterinary drugs (not including immunological drugs) for the purposes of medicinal tests on animals subject to the conditions set out in SI 1986 No.1180.

## Exemptions for Imports

No marketing authorisation is required for the importation of a medicinal product:

1    by any person for administration to him/herself or to any person or persons who are members of his/her household; or
2    where it is specially imported by or to the order of a doctor or dentist (ss.9 and 13) for the purposes described in the section Exemptions for Practitioners (see below); or
3    intended for re-export (see below).

No exemption exists for the veterinary surgeon who may not import unlicensed veterinary medicines.

Marketing authorisations are not required for imported medicinal products which are to be exported in the form in which they were imported (see Exemptions for Exports below).

## Exemptions for Exports

The application of the licensing system to exports is postponed until a *special appointed day* at some time in the future (s.48). The result is that although a manufacturer's licence must be held in order to manufacture medicinal products for export, no marketing authorisations are required, except for certain products, the purity and potency of which cannot be adequately tested by chemical means. Those which are for human use are listed in SI 1971 No.1198, namely, antigens, antitoxins, antisera, sera, toxins or vaccines. Those which are veterinary products are listed in SI 1971 No.1309, namely, antigens, antisera, antitoxins, corticotrophin, heparin, hyaluronidase, insulin, plasma, preparations of pituitary (posterior lobe), sera, toxins, vaccines and other medicinal products or substances derived from animals.

Marketing authorisations are not required for imported medicinal products which are to be exported in the form in which they were imported and are either:

1    not assembled in a way different from the way in which they were assembled on being imported; or
2    assembled in a way different from the way they were assembled on being imported but, the assembler, being the holder of a manufacturer's licence and having supplied the licensing authority with required information, has been notified that s/he may import the product (s.13 and SIs 1971 No.1326 and 1977 No.640).

This exemption for re-exported products does not apply to the veterinary products listed in SI 1971 No.1309 which are set out in the paragraph above.

## Exemptions for Practitioners

A doctor, dentist or veterinarian does not require a licence of any kind in respect of medicinal products specially prepared by him/her for administration to a particular patient (Sch.1 to SI 1994 No.3144). The exemption extends to the preparation of a medicinal product at the request of another practitioner for administration to one of his/her patients or to an animal or herd under his/her care.

There is no exemption from licensing for veterinary surgeons or veterinary practitioners in respect of any vaccine for administration to poultry, but there is exemption in respect of a vaccine for administration to an animal (other than poultry) provided it is an autogenous vaccine. Any plasma or serum specially prepared for administration to one or more animals in the herd from which it is derived is also exempt from licensing [s.9(3)].

A practitioner may hold a stock of medicinal products for the purposes described above without the need to hold marketing authorisations. The total stock of such products which may be held by him/her must not exceed 5 litres of fluids and 2.5 kg of solids (SI 1994 No.3144), and they must have been procured from a person holding an appropriate manufacturer's licence (SIs 1971 No.1450 and 1972 No.1200). (See also 'Special' Dispensing, Manufacturing and Assembly Exemptions below.)

A doctor or dentist does not require any licence for any medicinal product specially imported by him/her or to his/her order for administration to a particular patient of his/hers or at the request of another doctor or dentist for administration to one of his/her patients (ss.9 and 13). There is a similar exemption from licensing for medicinal products imported by a hospital, wholesaler or retail pharmacy business provided the sale or supply is to a doctor or dentist for administration to a particular patient of his/hers. This exemption from licensing is subject to the requirements of SI 1994 No.3144, namely, notification to the licensing authority, maintenance of written records including adverse drug reactions (for five years), and certain other conditions.

## Exemptions for Nurses and Midwives

A registered nurse or a registered midwife is not required to have a manufacturer's licence in order to assemble medicinal products in the course of his/her profession (s.11).

## Exemptions for Pharmacists

The exemptions from licensing for pharmacists are contained in section 10 of the Act, to which a number of subsections were added by SI 1971 No.1445.

Subject to the work being done by or under the supervision of a pharmacist, no licence of any kind is required for any of the following activities being carried out in a registered pharmacy:

1    Preparing or dispensing a medicinal product in accordance with a prescription given by a practitioner, or preparing a stock of medicinal products for this purpose. The stock of medicinal products may be procured from a manufacturer holding the appropriate special licence (see 'Special' Dispensing, Manufacturing and Assembly Exemptions below). This exemption also applies to hospitals and health centres [s.10(1) and (4) and SI 1972 No.1200]. In respect of vaccines, sera and plasma for administration to animals, the exemption from licensing for pharmacists is subject to the same limitation which applies to veterinarians (see Exemptions for Practitioners above).

2    Preparing or dispensing a medicinal product in accordance with a specification furnished by the person to whom the product is to be sold for administration to that person, or to a person under his/her care, or an animal or herd under his/her control, or preparing a stock of medicinal products for these purposes [s.10(3)]. This exemption does not cover any vaccine, plasma or serum for animal use.

3    Preparing or dispensing a medicinal product for administration to a person when the pharmacist is requested by or on behalf of that person to do so in accordance with the pharmacist's own judgment as to the treatment required, and that person is present in the pharmacy at the time of the request (*counter prescribing*); a stock of medicinal products prepared in a registered pharmacy in accordance with 1 and 2 above and under this paragraph may be sold or supplied from any other registered pharmacy forming part of the same retail pharmacy business.

4    Preparing a medicinal product or a stock of medicinal products, not to the order of another person, but with a view to retail sale or supply, provided that the sale or supply is made from the registered pharmacy where it was prepared and the product is not the subject of an advertisement [s.10(5)]. In this connection, *advertisement* does not include words appearing on the product or its container or package or the display of the product itself, but does include a show-card [s.10(8)].

5    Assembling a medicinal product [s.10(1)]. This exemption also applies to hospitals and health centres. When medicinal products are assembled in a registered pharmacy for retail sale or supply, they may not be the subject of any advertisement and may only be sold or supplied at the registered pharmacy where they are assembled or at some other

registered pharmacy forming part of the same retail pharmacy business (SI 1971 No.1445).

6    Wholesale dealing, where such dealing constitutes no more than an inconsiderable part of the business carried on at that pharmacy. This covers occasional sales to practitioners or to other pharmacists (SI 1971 No.1445) (see p.98).

A retail pharmacist who is responsible for the composition of a medicinal product which s/he intends to sell or supply in the course of his/her business must hold a marketing authorisation if his/her activities fall outside the exemptions set out above. S/he must also have a manufacturer's licence or arrange for the product to be made by a manufacturer who has an appropriate licence.

## Exemptions for Chiropodists, etc.

A person who is either a member of a registering body or customarily administers medicinal products to human beings in the course of a business in the field of osteopathy, chiropody, naturopathy or other similar field does not require a manufacturer's licence to assemble medicinal products for human use which are on general sale. The product must be for administration to a particular person who has requested the naturopath, etc. to use his/her own judgment as to the treatment required. Exemption is obtained by notification to the licensing authority (SI 1979 No.1114).

## Exemptions for Herbal Remedies

A *herbal remedy* is a medicinal product consisting of a substance produced by subjecting a plant or plants to drying, crushing or any other process, or of a mixture whose sole ingredients are two or more substances so produced, or of a mixture whose sole ingredients are one or more substances so produced and water or some other inert substances (s.132).

No marketing authorisation/licence is required for the sale, supply, manufacture or assembly of any such herbal remedy in the course of a business in which the person carrying on the business sells or supplies the remedy for administration to a particular person after being requested by or on behalf of that person, and in that person's presence, to use his/her own judgment as to the treatment required. The person carrying on the business must be the occupier of the premises where the manufacture or assembly takes place and must be able to close them so as to exclude the public [s.12(1)].

No marketing authorisation/licence is required for the sale, supply, manufacture or assembly of those herbal remedies where the process to which the plant or plants are subjected consists only of drying, crushing or comminuting and the remedy is sold or supplied under a designation which only specifies the plant or plants and the process and does not apply any other name to the remedy; and without any written recommendation (whether by means of a labelled container or package or a leaflet or in any other way) as to the use of the remedy [s.12(2)]. This exemption does not extend to imported products.

Presumably, unless a herbal product is sold or supplied for a medicinal purpose, it is not even a medicinal product; no doubt there will be circumstances in which herbs of this kind will be sold for other than medicinal purposes.

## Exemptions for Wholesale Dealing in Confectionery

No wholesale dealer's licence is required for the sale, or offer for sale by way of wholesale dealing, of a medicinal product, other than a veterinary drug, which is for sale as confectionery if the marketing authorisation in respect of the medicinal product provides that the exemption shall apply, and if the medicinal product is not sold or offered for sale accompanied by or having in relation to it any particulars in writing specifying that product's curative or remedial function in relation to a disease specified, other than in relation to the relief of symptoms of coughs, colds or nasal congestion (SI 1975 No.762).

## Exemptions for Foods and Cosmetics

It is provided by orders (SIs 1971 No.1410 and 1973 No.2079) that licensing provisions do not apply to anything done in relation to a medicinal product which is wholly or mainly for use by being administered to one or more human beings and which is for sale, or is to be for sale, either for oral administration as a food or for external use as a cosmetic.

The definition of *food* includes beverages, confectionery, ingredients in the preparation of foods and advertised dietary supplements which contain added vitamins.

*Vitamins* are any of the following: vitamins A, B1, B2, B6, C, D and E, biotin, nicotinamide, nicotinic acid, pantothenic acid and its salts, bioflavonoids, inositol, choline, p-aminobenzoic acid, cyanocobalamin or folic acid.

*Vitamin preparation* means any medicinal product, the active ingredients of which consist only of vitamins, or vitamins and mineral salts, that is, salts of any one or more of the following: iron, iodine, calcium, phosphorus, fluorine, copper, potassium, manganese, magnesium or zinc.

A *cosmetic* is defined as 'any substance or preparation intended to be applied to the various surfaces of the human body including epidermis, pilary system and hair, nails, lips and external genital organs, or the teeth and buccal mucosa, wholly or mainly for the purpose of perfuming them, cleansing them, protecting them, caring for them or keeping them in condition, modifying their appearance (whether for aesthetic purposes or otherwise) or combating body odours or normal body perspiration'.

This general exemption from licensing requirements does not apply if the food or cosmetic is sold with some particulars, in writing, specifying the product's curative or remedial function in relation to a specified disease, or the use of the product for such curative or remedial purposes. A marketing authorisation is required for any product promoted to practitioners. In addition, *no exemption* applies to the following:

1   Cosmetics for external use containing any antibiotic; or hexachlorophane (but not if less than 0.1 per cent and labelled with a statutory caution); or any hormone in excess of 0.004 per cent w/w; or resorcinol in excess of 1 per cent w/w.
2   Any *vitamin preparation* for oral administration as a food in relation to which there are no written particulars or directions as to dosage.
3   Any *vitamin preparation* for oral administration as a food in relation to which there are written particulars or directions specifying a recommended daily dosage for adults involving a daily intake in excess of: vitamin A, 2500 iu; or antirachitic activity, 250 iu; or folic acid, 25 µg; or cyanocobalamin, 5 µg.
4   Any medicinal product for oral administration as a food, not being a *vitamin preparation*, to which one or more of the ingredients, vitamin A or D, folic acid or cyanocobalamin has been added; and in relation to which product there are written particulars or directions as to recommended use of that substance which involves a daily intake in excess of the quantities and ingredients specified in 3.
5   Any medicinal product not covered by 2, 3 or 4 above, which is to be sold with, accompanied by, or having in relation to it any particulars in writing specifying the dosage relevant to that product's medicinal properties.

Exemption from marketing authorisations or licensing does not exempt a medicinal product from any labelling requirements which may be made under the Act (see Containers, Packages and Identification, Chapter 14).

Whether or not a substance or article is a medicinal product depends upon the purpose for which it is sold or supplied (see Chapter 1). Some substances have both medicinal and non-medicinal uses. Although the exemptions for foods and cosmetics cover a wide field, borderline cases will inevitably occur where there is doubt as to the status of a product. A legally binding decision can only be given in the courts, but inquiries can be made of the Medicines Control Agency about the status of any product which is being promoted in a particular way. It is quite possible that a slight alteration in wording of a label may alter the standing of a product under the Act.

Certain examples have been mentioned in the Department's leaflet, MAL8. On the one hand, anti-smoking preparations which create an unpleasant taste in the mouth when the person taking them smokes tobacco, and tablets and cachets sucked in order to freshen the breath, are not considered to be medicinal products. On the other hand, hair restorers, whether to be taken orally or applied externally, and insect repellents for external application to cats and dogs, are regarded as medicinal products.

### Exemptions for Ingredients

Ingredients used in pharmacies, in hospitals or in businesses where herbal remedies are sold and those used by practitioners, are medicinal products (s.130), but they are exempted from licensing requirements (SI 1974 No.1150) provided particulars of the activity have been notified to the licensing authority by the manufacturer or supplier. The exemption may, in the interest of safety, be withdrawn by the licensing authority. Certain substances which are not themselves medicinal products but may be used as ingredients are subject to licensing. They are listed in SIs 1971 No.1200 and 1985 No.1403 (see Appendix 1).

### 'Special' Dispensing, Manufacturing and Assembly Exemptions

In order *to fulfil special needs* Council Directive 65/65/EEC (Art.2.4) and SI 1994 No.3144 (Sch.1) enable a *special* dispensing or manufacturing service to be provided in response to a bona fide unsolicited order, formulated in accordance with the specification of a doctor or dentist and for use by his/her individual patients on his/her direct personal responsibility without the need for the manufacturer to hold a marketing authorisation for the medicinal product concerned. The conditions which apply are:

1    The medicinal product must be supplied to a doctor or dentist, or for use in a pharmacy, hospital or health centre under the supervision of a pharmacist.
2    The medicinal product must not be the subject of any advertisement or representation. However, the service provided may be advertised.
3    Manufacture or assembly must be carried out under the supervision of such staff and such precautions must be taken as are adequate to ensure that the product is of the character required by, and meets the specifications of, the doctor or dentist who requires it.
4    Written records as to the manufacture/assembly must be maintained and available to the licensing authority.
5    The medicinal product is manufactured/assembled by the holder of a manufacturer's licence.
6    The medicinal product is distributed by way of wholesale dealing by the holder of a wholesale dealer's licence.

Medicinal products to which these special licensing provisions apply and the circumstances in which they may be supplied are:

1    Products supplied to a doctor or dentist for administration to a particular patient (but there is a limit on the amount of stock which may be held by a doctor or dentist) (see p.25).

2    Products, or stocks of products, supplied to retail pharmacists, hospitals or health centres for dispensing, or with a view to dispensing, practitioners' prescriptions.

3    Products, or stocks of products, supplied to retail pharmacists for administration to particular persons in accordance with the pharmacist's own judgment, or in accordance with the specification of a customer for administration to him/herself or a person under his/her care.

4    Herbal remedies supplied to a retailer for administration to a particular person in accordance with the retailer's own judgment.

5    Products (not being Prescription Only or Pharmacy Only products) supplied to a person for administration to him/herself or a member of his/her household.

6    Products (not being Prescription Only products) for sale or supply to a person exclusively for use by him/her in the course of his/her business for administration to human beings, but not by way of sale, e.g. a special formula for use in a first-aid room. These products must be prepared under the supervision of a pharmacist.

7    Products supplied to licensed wholesale dealers for supply in the circumstances specified in 1 to 6 above.

## Hospitals

On 1 April 1991, by virtue of the National Health Service and Community Care Act 1990, all National Health Service hospitals lost their Crown immunity and became liable to the licensing provisions of the Medicines Act. The type of activities relating to manufacture, assembly, and wholesaling varies considerably from one hospital to another and whether any particular licence is required depends on the individual activity. Certain exemptions exist where an activity takes place under the supervision of a pharmacist either in a registered pharmacy (see p.26) or in a hospital (s.10). The Medicines Control Agency has issued a document entitled *Guidance to the NHS on the Licensing Requirements of the Medicines Act 1968* (September 1992). Hospital pharmacists requiring further details should contact the Medicines Control Agency.

## Export Certificates

The licensing authority may, on the application of an exporter of medicinal products, issue to him/her a certificate containing such statements relating to the products as the authority considers appropriate, having regard to any requirements (whether having the force of law or not) which have effect in the country to which the products are to be exported and to the provisions of the

Medicines Act, and to any licence granted or other things done by virtue of the Act (s.50).

## Medical Devices

Such devices include intra-uterine devices and diaphragms, dental fillings, contact lens care products, non-medicated dressings, sutures and ligatures, etc. These are no longer controlled under the Medicines Act but under consumer protection legislation (The Medical Devices Regulations 1994, SI 1994 No.3017).

A *device* means a medical device, that is to say an instrument, apparatus, appliance, material or other article, whether used alone or in combination, together with any software necessary for its proper application which:

1    is intended by the manufacturer to be used for human beings for the purpose of:

  (a)   diagnosis, prevention, monitoring, treatment or alleviation of disease;

  (b)   diagnosis, monitoring, treatment or alleviation of or compensation for an injury or handicap;

  (c)   investigation, replacement or modification of the anatomy or of any physiological process; or

  (d)   control of contraception; and

2    does not achieve its principal intended action in or on the human body by pharmacological, immunological or metabolic means, even if it is assisted in its function by such means,

even if it is intended to administer a medicinal product as defined in Council Directive 65/65/EEC or incorporates as an integral part of a substance which, if used separately, would be a medicinal product and which is liable to act upon the body with action ancillary to that of the device.

Such devices must comply with the regulations with regard to the essential requirements set out in Council Directive 93/42/EEC and with specific labelling. There is a Medical Devices Agency which administers and enforces the legislation. Manufacturers have to be registered and fees are payable (SI 1995 No.449, as amended).

## Summary

•    All dealings in medicinal products are subject to a licensing system unless specifically exempted. Marketing authorisations or licences are needed to *place a medicine on the market*, to manufacture, wholesale or distribute medicinal products. Certification is needed for human and animal clinical trials.

- The national (decentralised) marketing authorisations are administered by the Medicines Control Agency and the centralised system by the EMEA.
- A simplified system of licensing (*certification*) applies to homoeopathic products.
- Stringent requirements, set out in a Guide to Good Manufacturing Practice, apply to manufacturing licences and introduce the concept of a *qualified person*. Similar conditions apply to wholesale dealer's licences which have a *responsible person*.
- Clinical trials are subject to certification by the licensing authority unless specifically exempted.
- Certain exemptions from licensing exist for doctors, nurses, pharmacists, other health professionals, and hospitals.
- No licences are required for certain activities carried out in a pharmacy under the supervision of a pharmacist.
- Certain products are exempt from licensing, e.g. herbal remedies, confectionery, food, cosmetics and vitamins.
- Provisions are made for *special* dispensing or manufacturing services.
- Medical devices, e.g. dental fillings, contact lenses, intra-uterine devices, etc. are now controlled under consumer protection legislation.

## Further Reading

AMELIA publications. Veterinary Medicines Directorate.

*Code of Practice for Qualified Persons.* European Industrial Pharmacists Group, The Royal Pharmaceutical Society of Great Britain.

MAIL publications. Medicines Control Agency.

MAL Advisory leaflets. Medicines Control Agency.

MAVIS advisory leaflets. Veterinary Medicines Directorate.

*Rules and Guidance for Pharmaceutical Manufacturers (GMP)* (1997). The Stationery Office.

*Rules Governing Medicinal Products for Human Use in the European Community* vol. I. The Stationery Office.

*Rules Governing Medicinal Products for Animal Use in the European Community* vol. Va. The Stationery Office.

CHAPTER THREE

# Medicines Act 1968

# Sales Promotion of Medicinal Products

### Advertisements and Representations

The Medicines (Advertising) Regulations 1994 (SI 1994 No.1932, as amended) and the Medicines (Monitoring of Advertising) Regulations 1994 (SI 1994 No.1933, as amended) implement Council Directive 92/28/EEC and both sets of regulations supplement the existing controls under the Medicines Act (Part VI) and ensure that a relevant medicinal product is only promoted in accordance with its marketing authorisation.

A distinction is drawn between *advertisements* and *representations* in the Act (see below). In the regulations governing the advertising of relevant medicinal products (SI 1994 No.1932) the definition of *advertisement* includes a *representation* (see p.36) but does not include reference material, factual, informative statements or announcements, a trade catalogue or a price list provided there is no product claim (c.f. s.92 of the Act).

In the regulations the word *representation* has the same meaning as in the Act, except it does not include the making of a factual, informative statement or announcement which includes no product claim.

*Advertisement* includes every form of advertising, whether in a publication, or by the display of any notice, or by means of any catalogue, price list, letter (whether circular or addressed to a particular person) or other document, or by words inscribed on any article, or by the exhibition of a photograph or a cinematograph film, or by way of sound recording, sound broadcasting or television, or in any other way (s.92).

*Representation* means any statement or undertaking (whether constituting a condition or a warranty or not) which consists of spoken words other than words broadcast by way of sound recording, sound broadcasting or television, or forming part of a sound recording or embodied in a cinematograph film soundtrack [s.92(5)].

Words spoken, other than by way of sound or television broadcasting, or as part of a sound recording or film soundtrack, do not fall within the definition of advertisement. Similarly, unless provided for in regulations made under section 95, neither the sale or supply of a medicinal product in a labelled container, nor the inclusion of a leaflet relating to a specific medicinal product, constitute the issue of an advertisement (s.92).

*Sound recording* has the meaning assigned to it by section 12 of the Copyright Act 1956, that is 'the aggregate of the sounds embodied in, and capable of being reproduced by means of, a record of any description, other than a soundtrack associated with a cinematograph film'.

To secure that adequate information is given about medicinal products, to promote safety in relation to them, and to prevent the giving of misleading information about them, the appropriate Minister may impose by regulation any requirements which may be necessary or expedient. They may concern the form of any advertisement and the particulars contained therein and, in the case of television or cinematograph film advertisements, their duration and manner of exhibition may be controlled. Advertisements of particular kinds, as specified in the regulations, may be prohibited, either totally or subject to some exceptions [s.95(3)].

## Control of Advertisements and Representations

No commercially interested party, and no person acting on his/her behalf, may issue an advertisement relating to a medicinal product without the consent of the holder of the marketing authorisation (s.94). The licensing authority may obtain up to 12 copies of any advertisement (including any data sheet) relating to medicinal products by serving a notice on the person who issued it or caused it to be issued (s.97).

The appropriate Ministers may, by regulation, prohibit the issue of advertisements (s.95):

1    relating to medicinal products of a specific description or class;
2    likely to lead to the use of any medicinal product, or any other substance or article, for the purpose of treating or preventing a specified disease, or diagnosing a specified disease, or ascertaining the existence, degree or extent of a specified physiological condition, or permanently or temporarily preventing or otherwise interfering with the normal operation of a specified physiological function, or artificially inducing a specified condition of mind or body;

3  likely to lead to the use of a particular class of medicinal products, or other substances or articles, for the purposes set out in (b) below;

4  relating to medicinal products and containing a specified word or phrase which, in the opinion of the Minister, is likely to mislead the public as to the nature or effects of the products, or as to any condition of mind or body in connection with which the products might be used.

The regulations may also extend the prohibitions mentioned in 2, 3 and 4 above to cover any representations made:

(a)  in connection with the sale or supply or offer for sale or supply of a medicinal product or other substance or article to which the regulations apply; or

(b)  for the purpose of inducing any person to buy the medicinal product, substance or article from a retailer; or,

(c)  to a practitioner, or a patient or client, for the purpose of inducing the practitioner to prescribe medicinal products of a specified description.

Regulations relating to advertisements for medicinal products for human use addressed to doctors or dentists and the public are in SI 1994 No.1932. Other regulations (SI 1979 No.1760) specify particulars which must be included in advertisements in the form of information sheets and sent to pharmacists and opticians about substances and fluids for use with contact lenses or blanks.

## Advertising in General

### Definitions

Certain terms used in advertising are further defined in SI 1994 No.1932 in relation to *relevant* medicinal products as follows:

*Advertisement* has the meaning as in section 92 of the Act (see p.34), except that in relation to a relevant medicinal product (see p.131): (a) provided that it makes no product claim, reference material, a factual informative statement or announcement, a trade catalogue or price list shall not be taken to be an advertisement, and (b) an advertisement includes a representation, and for the purposes of this representation has the meaning as in section 92 of the Act (see p.35) except that it does not include the making of a factual informative statement or announcement which includes no product claim.

*Essential information compatible with the summary of product characteristics* means essential information compatible (a) with the summary of product characteristics, if there is one, or (b) if there is no summary of product characteristics, with the data sheet.

*Promotional aid* means a non-monetary gift made for a promotional purpose by a commercially interested party.

*Reference material* includes entries which are in the form of, and limited to, a brief description of a medicinal product, its uses and any relevant contra-indications and warnings appearing without charge in a publication consisting wholly or mainly of such entries where the publication is sent or delivered to persons qualified to prescribe or supply relevant medicinal products by a person who is not a commercially interested party.

## General Principles

1    No person may issue an advertisement for a relevant medicinal product unless that product has a marketing authorisation. This general regulation does not apply to registered homoeopathic medicinal products (SI 1994 No.1932).

2    No person shall issue an advertisement relating to a relevant medicinal product unless that advertisement:

(a)    complies with the particulars listed in the summary of product characteristics, and

(b)    encourages the rational use of that product by presenting it objectively and without exaggerating its properties (SI 1999 No.267).

3    No person shall issue a misleading advertisement relating to a relevant medicinal product (SI 1999 No.267).

## Duties of Holders of Marketing Authorisations

Any person who holds a marketing authorisation must (reg.4):

1    establish a scientific service to compile and collate all information, whether received from medical sales representatives employed by him/her or from any other source relating to that product;

2    ensure that, in relation to any such product which sales representatives promote, those medical sales representatives are given adequate training and have sufficient scientific knowledge to enable them to provide information which is as precise and as complete as possible about that product;

3    keep available for Health Ministers, or communicate to them within such period as may be specified in a notice served by them on him/her, a sample of any advertisement for which s/he is responsible relating to that product, together with a statement indicating the persons to whom the advertisement is addressed, the method of dissemination and the date of its first dissemination (SI 1999 No.267), and

4    supply, within the period specified in a notice served by the Health Ministers on him/her, any information and assistance requested by them in order to carry out their functions under the regulations or the Monitoring of Advertising Regulations (SI 1999 No.267).

### Advertising to Persons Qualified to Prescribe or Supply

*Persons qualified to prescribe or supply* includes persons, and employees of such persons, who in the course of their profession or in the course of a business may lawfully prescribe, sell by retail or supply in circumstances corresponding to retail sale relevant medicinal products.

The regulations (SI 1994 No.1932, as amended by SI 1999 No.267) implement Council Directive 92/28/EEC in connection with the control of advertising to persons who are qualified to prescribe or supply. The regulations do not relate to advertisements aimed at veterinary surgeons or veterinary practitioners.

No person may issue an advertisement relating to a relevant medicinal product and aimed at persons qualified to prescribe or supply unless the advertisement (reg.14 and Sch.2):

1     contains essential information compatible with the summary of product characteristics (SPC); and
2     contains the following particulars:

   (a)   the licence number of the product;
   (b)   the name and address of the marketing authorisation holder which relates to the product or the business name and address of his/her business that is responsible for its sale or supply;
   (c)   the classification of the product, i.e. Prescription Only, Pharmacy Only, or General Sale List;
   (d)   the name of the product and a list of active ingredients using the common name placed immediately adjacent to the most prominent display of the name;
   (e)   the indications as within the terms of the licence;
   (f)   a succinct statement of the entries in the SPC or where there is no SPC the data sheet, relating to side effects, precautions and relevant contra-indications;
   (g)   a succinct statement of the entries in the SPC, or where there is no SPC the data sheet, relating to the dosage and method of use relevant to the indications shown. The method of administration should also be shown where this is not obvious;
   (h)   a warning issued by the licensing authority under Part II of the Act which is required to be included;
   (i)   the cost, excluding VAT, of either a specified package of the product, or a specified quantity or recommended daily dose, calculated by reference to any specified package of the product, except that the cost may be omitted in the case of an advertisement inserted in a publication which is printed in the United Kingdom but with a circulation outside the United Kingdom of more than 15 per cent of its total circulation;

(j)  the particulars in paragraphs (f), (g) and (h) above shall be printed in a clear and legible manner and be placed in such a position in the advertisement that their relationship to the claims and indications for the product can readily be appreciated by the reader.

## Abbreviated Advertisements

*Abbreviated advertisement* means an advertisement, other than a loose insert, which does not exceed in size an area of 420 cm$^2$, in a publication sent or delivered wholly or mainly to persons qualified to prescribe or supply relevant medicinal products.

No person may issue such an advertisement unless it:

1  contains essential information compatible with the summary of product characteristics; and,
2  the following particulars:

(a)  the name of the medicinal product and a list of the active ingredients using the common name placed immediately adjacent to the most prominent display of the name;
(b)  the name and address of the marketing authorisation holder or the business name and address of the part of the business responsible for the sale or supply;
(c)  the classification of the products, i.e. Prescription Only, Pharmacy Only, or General Sale List;
(d)  a form of words which clearly indicates that further information is available on request to the licence holder or in the summary of product characteristics or, if there is no SPC, the data sheet, relating to the product.

and any warning issued in relation to the product by the licensing authority.

## Audio-visual Advertisements

No person may issue in a programme service or video recording any advertisement unless the advertisement:

1  contains essential information compatible with the summary of product characteristics;
2  contains the following particulars:

(a)  the licence number of the product,
(b)  the name and address of the marketing authorisation holder which relates to the product or the business name and address of his/her business that is responsible for its sale or supply;
(c)  the classification of the product, i.e. Prescription Only, Pharmacy Only, or General Sale List;

(d)   the name of the product and a list of active ingredients using the common name placed immediately adjacent to the most prominent mention or display of the name;

(e)   the indications as within the terms of the licence;

(f)   a succinct statement of the entries in the SPC or, where there is no SPC, the data sheet relating to side effects, precautions and relevant contra-indications;

(g)   a succinct statement of the entries in the SPC or, where there is no SPC, the data sheet relating to the dosage and method of use relevant to the indications shown. The method of administration should also be shown where this is not obvious.

(h)   a warning issued by the licensing authority under Part II of the Act which is required to be included.

## Promotional Aids

The requirements set out above in relation to advertisements, abbreviated advertisements and audio-visual advertisements do not apply to promotional aids if:

1   the advertisement consists solely of the name of the product; and,

2   the advertisement is intended solely as a reminder.

## Written Material Accompanying Promotions

No person may send or deliver to prescribers or suppliers of medicinal products as part of a promotion any written material unless it:

1   contains essential information compatible with the summary of product characteristics;

2   contains the classification of the product, i.e. Prescription Only, Pharmacy Only, or General Sale List;

3   states the date on which it was drawn up or last revised.

Any such written material shall be accurate, up-to-date, verifiable and complete and not state any quotation, table or other illustrative matter taken from a medical journal or other scientific work unless it is accurately reproduced and the precise source is indicated.

## Free Samples

A person may supply a sample only:

1   to a person qualified to prescribe medicinal products;

2   if the sample is not a narcotic or a psychotropic substance; and subject to the following:

(a)  the sample is supplied on an exceptional basis only;

(b)  a limited number only of samples of each product may be supplied in one year to one recipient;

(c)  samples supplied may only be in response to a written request, signed and dated from the recipient;

(d)  suppliers of samples must maintain an adequate system of control and accountability;

(e)  every sample shall be no bigger than the smallest presentation available for sale in the United Kingdom;

(f)  every sample must be marked 'free medical sample – not for resale' or bear a similar description;

(g)  every sample must be accompanied by a copy of the SPC or, where there is no SPC, a copy of the data sheet.

## Medical Sales Representatives

All sales representatives promoting medicinal products to prescribers or suppliers of medicines must give to all persons they visit a copy of the SPC or, in the absence of a SPC, a copy of the data sheet. Such representatives must report all information which they receive from prescribers, including any adverse drug reactions, to the scientific service established under the regulations.

## Inducements and Hospitality

When products are being promoted to health professionals no person may supply, offer or promise any gift, pecuniary advantage or benefit in kind unless it is inexpensive and relevant to the practice of medicine or pharmacy.

Hospitality may be offered at events for purely professional or scientific purposes and/or for medicine promotion only to health professionals and, provided that such hospitality is reasonable in level, is subordinate to the main scientific objective or main purpose of the meeting.

It is an offence for a health professional to solicit or accept any gift, pecuniary advantage, benefit in kind, hospitality or sponsorship prohibited by the regulations.

## Advertisements Directed to the Public

The regulations dealing with advertisements which are directed to the public, relating to medicinal products for human use (SI 1994 No.1932, as amended) impose a range of prohibitions, restrictions and requirements which are set out below.

No advertisement may be issued which is likely to lead to the use of a relevant medicinal product:

1     which is a Controlled Drug which is listed in Schedules I, II or IV of the Narcotic Drugs Convention or Schedules I–IV of the Psychotropic Substances Convention (reg.8);

2     which is for human use and is a Prescription Only Medicine (reg.7);

3     or any other medicinal product, substance or article for the purpose of inducing an abortion in women (reg.6);

4     for the purpose of treatment, prevention or diagnosis of any disease specified in Table 3.1 (reg.6, as amended):

**Table 3.1**  Diseases for which advertisements for relevant medicinal products may not be issued

| | |
|---|---|
| Bone diseases | Diseases of the liver, biliary system and pancreas |
| Cardiovascular diseases | |
| Diabetes and other metabolic diseases | Malignant diseases |
| Endocrine diseases | Serious neurological and muscular diseases |
| Serious disorders of the eye and ear | |
| Serious gastrointestinal diseases | Psychiatric diseases |
| Genetic disorders | Serious renal diseases |
| Serious infectious diseases including HIV-related diseases and tuberculosis | Serious respiratory diseases |
| | Sexually transmitted diseases |
| Chronic insomnia | Serious skin disorders |
| Joint, rheumatic and collagen diseases | |

N.B. the prohibition under 4 above does not apply to advertisements which lead to the use of a medicinal product for the purpose of:

(a)    the prevention of neural tube defects (reg.6), or

(b)    the treatment of the symptoms of rheumatic or non-serious arthritic conditions (SI 1996 No.1552).

## Prohibition of Certain Material in Advertisements

No person shall issue an advertisement relating to a relevant medicinal product which contains any material which (reg.9):

1     gives the impression that a medical consultation or surgical operation is unnecessary, in particular by offering a telephone number;

2     suggests that the effects of taking the medicinal product are guaranteed, are unaccompanied by side effects or are better than, or equivalent to, those of another identifiable treatment or medicinal product;

3     suggests that health can be enhanced by taking the medicinal product;

4     suggests that health could be affected by not taking the product;

5     is directed exclusively or principally at children;

6     refers to a recommendation by scientists, health professionals, or persons who are neither of the foregoing but who, because of their celebrity, could encourage the consumption of medicinal products;

7    suggests that the medicinal product is a foodstuff, cosmetic, or other consumer product;
8    suggests that the safety and efficacy of the medicinal product is due to the fact that it is natural;
9    might, by a description or detailed representation of a case history, lead to erroneous self-diagnosis;
10   refers, in improper, alarming or misleading terms, pictorial representations of changes in the human body caused by disease or injury, or of the action of a medicinal product on the human body or parts thereof; or
11   mentions that the medicinal product has been granted a marketing authorisation.

## Form and Contents of Advertisements

No person shall issue an advertisement relating to a relevant medicinal product unless that advertisement (reg.10):

1    is set out in such a way that it is clear that the message is an advertisement and so that the product is clearly identified as a medicinal product, and
2    excluding advertisements for homoeopathic medicinal products, includes the following:
     (a)   the name of the medicinal product;
     (b)   if it contains only one active ingredient, the common name of the medicinal product;
     (c)   the information necessary for correct use of the product; and
     (d)   an express and legible invitation to read carefully the instructions on the leaflet contained within the package or on the label, as the case may be.

These provisions do not apply if the advertisement relates to a relevant medicinal product which is on a promotional aid if the advertisement consists solely of the name of the product (or in the case of a homoeopathic medicinal product the scientific name of the stock) and the advertisement is solely intended as a reminder (reg.10).

## Vaccination Campaigns

The regulations as set out above do not apply to any advertisement which is part of a vaccination campaign relating to a relevant medicinal product provided that such a campaign has been approved by the Health Ministers (reg.11).

## Sales or Supplies for Promotional Purposes

No person who:

1    is the holder of a marketing authorisation, or

2     carries on a business which consists wholly or partly of the manufacturing, or of selling and supplying of relevant medicinal products

shall, for a promotional purpose (whether a promotional purpose of his/her own or of a third party), sell or supply relevant medicinal products to any member of the public (SI 1999 No. 267).

## Advertisements for Registered Homoeopathic Products

An advertisement relating to homoeopathic medicinal products may not mention any specific therapeutic indications and may only contain the following details:

1     the scientific name of the stock(s) followed by the degree of dilution, making use of the pharmacopoeia symbols used in relation to the homoeopathic procedure described for that stock(s);
2     the name and address of the holder of the certificate of registration and, where different, the name and address of the manufacturer;
3     the method of administration and, if necessary, the route;
4     the expiry date of the product stating the month and year;
5     the pharmaceutical form;
6     the contents of the sales presentation;
7     any special storage precautions;
8     any special warnings;
9     the manufacturer's batch number;
10    the registration number allotted by the licensing authority preceded by the letters *HR* in capital letters (reg.22);
11    the words *homoeopathic product without approved therapeutic indications*;
12    a warning advising the user to consult a doctor if the symptoms persist during the use of the product.

## Monitoring of Advertising

Monitoring of advertising is governed by the Medicines (Monitoring of Advertising) Regulations 1994 (SI 1994 No.1933, as amended by SI 1999 No.267). However, the existing voluntary control under the Medicines Act is encouraged and the existing Codes of Advertising Practice administered by the Association of the British Pharmaceutical Industry (for Prescription Only Medicines) and by the Proprietary Association of Great Britain (for over-the-counter medicines) will continue.

Complaints, in the first instance, will be referred to the appropriate self-regulatory body, but the Minister has the power of civil injunction. A person holding a marketing authorisation will be required to issue corrective statements if their advertising is found to be in breach of the regulations.

In the amending regulations (SI 1999 No.267) a Schedule has been introduced relating to the scrutiny of certain published or proposed advertisements. The Schedule gives the Health Ministers powers for determining whether or not certain advertisements, proposed or published, breach the Advertising Regulations. There is an opportunity for representations to be made to an Independent Review Panel before the Health Ministers determine the case and breaches of notices issued by the Health Ministers create an offence. Details of the operation of the Review Panel are available from the Medicines Control Agency.

## Prohibition of Representations

No representation may be made by a commercially interested party which is likely to lead to the use of a medicinal product or, where relevant, any other substance or article for any of the diseases for which advertisements are prohibited (see p.42) if the representation:

1    is made in connection with the sale or supply, or offer for sale or supply, of that product, substance or article;
2    is made to any person for the purpose of inducing him/her to purchase from a retailer that product, substance or article;
3    is made, in connection with medicinal products, to the patient of a doctor or dentist for the purpose of inducing him/her to request the doctor or dentist to prescribe medicinal products of that description.

The prohibition on representations does not apply to any representation:

(a)    made by a pharmacist who sells or supplies a medicinal product when dispensing a prescription given by a doctor or dentist, or when using his/her own judgment as to the treatment required by a person, i.e. counter prescribing, or
(b)    made by a State Registered chiropodist (see p.84) in relation to a medicinal product which s/he supplied to his/her patient for the purpose of treatment by being administered to the surface of the foot; or
(c)    made by a registered nurse or certified midwife to a patient in relation to a medicinal product.

## Exceptions for Labels and Leaflets

None of the prohibitions, restrictions and requirements imposed by the regulations applies to any labelled container or package of a medicinal product or any other substance or article or any leaflet supplied with such product where that product is prepared or dispensed with a view to administration to a person in accordance with the prescription of a doctor or dentist (SI 1978 No.41).

The prohibitions on advertising imposed under the current regulations do not apply to labelled containers or packages of medicinal products or to leaflets supplied, or intended to be supplied, with medicinal products which:

1    are herbal remedies which are not restricted under the Herbal Remedies Order (SI 1977 No.2130) (see p.108); or
2    are homoeopathic preparations with licences of right; or
3    are 'counter prescribed' by a pharmacist in a registered pharmacy (see p.26).

These exceptions are subject to the condition that certain words or phrases are not included in labels or leaflets except in so far as it is necessary to explain the contra-indications or precautions or the action to be taken in the event of overdosage of the medicinal products. The words and phrases are:

- Amenorrhoea
- Angina
- Atherosclerosis
- Erysipelas
- Gallstones
- Multiple sclerosis
- Osteoarthritis
- Phlebitis
- Thrombosis
- Ulcer (except when used in the phrase 'aphthous ulcer' or 'mouth ulcer').

There is a further condition for herbal, biochemic and anthroposophic remedies, namely that every container and package of these medicinal products must be labelled with appropriate particulars and warning thus:

(a)    *A herbal remedy for (name of disease)*, or as appropriate, *A biochemic remedy for*, or *An anthroposophic remedy for.*
(b)    *Warning. If you think you have (name of disease, as above) consult a registered medical practitioner before taking this product. If you are already receiving treatment, tell your doctor that you are also taking this product.*

The name of the product may be used in the warning instead of the words *this product* and the warning must be within a rectangle within which there shall be no other matter of any kind.

## Summary

- The regulations prohibit advertisements for medicinal products for the treatment, prevention or diagnosis of certain diseases to the public. These include cardiovascular diseases, diabetes, malignant diseases, psychiatric diseases, etc.

- The regulations prohibit the advertising to the public of Controlled Drugs and Prescription Only Medicines.
- Requirements as to the information on medicinal products which has to be given to persons qualified to prescribe or supply medicines includes essential information compatible with the summary of product characteristics. This may be given by way of written information accompanying promotions, or by promotion by medical representatives.
- A limited number only of free samples may be supplied to a person qualified to prescribe relevant medicinal products. The samples may only be supplied in response to a written request and suppliers must maintain an adequate system of control.
- No person who is the holder of a marketing authorisation or who carries on a business which consists of the manufacturing, or of selling or supplying medicinal products shall, for promotional purposes, sell or supply medicinal products to any member of the public.
- Hospitality given to persons qualified to prescribe or supply medicines must be reasonable in level and subordinate to the main objective of meetings held for scientific or professional purposes. No person may supply or promise any gift, pecuniary advantage or benefit in kind unless it is inexpensive and relevant to the practice of medicine or pharmacy.
- Monitoring of advertising is to be undertaken by self-regulatory bodies but there are also legal provisions involving the Health Ministers.

## Further Reading

*ABPI Compendium of Summaries of Product Characteristics 1999–2000.* Association of the British Pharmaceutical Industry.
*Advertising and Promotion of Medicines in the UK.* HMSO.
MAIL 85 and MAIL 91 leaflets. Medicines Control Agency.

# CHAPTER FOUR

# Medicines Act 1968

## Retail Pharmacy Businesses

A *retail pharmacy business* means a business (not being a professional practice carried on by a practitioner) which consists of or includes the retail sale of medicinal products other than medicinal products on a General Sale List (whether medicinal products on such a list are sold in the course of that business or not) (s.132). Such a business may, subject to certain conditions, lawfully be conducted by (s.69):

1   a pharmacist, or a partnership where each partner is a pharmacist, or, in Scotland, a partnership where one or more partners is a pharmacist; or

2   a body corporate where the business so far as concerns the keeping, preparing and dispensing of medicinal products other than medicinal products on a General Sale List, is under the management of a super-intendent who is a pharmacist, and who does not act in a similar capacity for any other body corporate. A statement in writing signed by him/her, and signed on behalf of the body corporate, specifying his/her name and stating whether or not s/he is a member of the board, must have been sent to the registrar [s.71(2)]; or

3   a representative of a deceased, bankrupt or mentally ill pharmacist, whose name, together with the names and address of the representative, has been notified to the registrar [s.72(2)].

The *certain conditions* are that at all premises where the business is carried on and medicinal products, other than medicinal products on a General Sale List, are sold by retail, and:

(a)  the business, so far as concerns the retail sale at those premises of medicinal products (whether they are on a General Sale List or not), or the supply at those premises of such products in circumstances corresponding to retail sale, is under the personal control of a pharmacist; and

(b)  the pharmacist's name and certificate of registration under the Pharmacy Act 1954 are conspicuously exhibited (ss.70–72).

The effect is that, in a pharmacy business, personal control must be exercised by a pharmacist over the sale or supply of all medicinal products including those in a General Sale List. [The meaning of *personal control* has been considered by the High Court and the Statutory Committee (see Chapters 21 and 26).]

Where the business is owned by a partnership, one or more of the partners (or, in Scotland, one or more of the pharmacist partners) may be in personal control. In either case, and in the case of a proprietor pharmacist, some other pharmacist may be in personal control (s.70).

A retail pharmacy business owned by a body corporate may be under the personal control of the superintendent, or of a manager or assistant who is a pharmacist subject to the superintendent's directions (s.71). In relation to a body corporate *the board* means the body of persons controlling the body corporate by whatever name called (s.69).

The owner of a pharmacy business who complies with appropriate conditions described above is a *person lawfully conducting a retail pharmacy business*. Registration of the premises, which is dealt with below, is not one of these conditions. Nevertheless, such registration is essential, as the retail activities controlled under the Medicines Act 1968 and the Poisons Act 1972 must take place at *registered pharmacies*.

## Representatives of Pharmacists

There are some situations in which the retail pharmacy business of a pharmacist may lawfully be conducted by his/her representatives subject to the conditions already set out and the further conditions described here. The meaning of *representatives* differs according to the circumstances as follows (s.72):

1    In relation to a pharmacist who has died, 'representative' means his/her executor or administrator and, for a period of three months from the date of his/her death, if s/he has died leaving no executor who is entitled and willing to carry on the business, includes any person beneficially interested in his/her estate. The representative of a deceased pharmacist may carry on the business for a period of up to five years from the date of his/her death. Should s/he cease to be a representative before the expiry of five years, on completing the distribution of the deceased

pharmacist's estate, his/her authority lawfully to carry on the pharmacy business would also come to an end.

2 Where a pharmacist is adjudged bankrupt or, in Scotland, sequestration of his/her estate is awarded, the trustee in bankruptcy or in the sequestration is the pharmacist's representative. S/he may carry on the pharmacist's business for a period of three years from the date on which s/he is adjudged bankrupt or the date of the award of sequestration, as the case may be.

3 Where a pharmacist enters into a composition or scheme or deed of arrangement with his/her creditors, or in Scotland makes a trust deed for behoof of his/her creditors, or a composition contract, then the trustee appointed under any such arrangement is the pharmacist's representative. S/he may carry on the business for a period of three years from the date on which s/he became entitled to do so.

4 Where a receiver is appointed for a pharmacist under Part VIII of the Mental Health Act 1959 or, in Scotland, a curator bonis or judicial factor is appointed for him/her on the grounds that s/he suffers from some mental disorder, or in Northern Ireland a committee, receiver or guardian is appointed in his/her case under the Lunacy Regulation (Ireland) Act 1871, then that person is the pharmacist's representative. S/he may carry on the business for three years from the date of his/her appointment.

A person lawfully conducting a retail pharmacy business as the representative of a pharmacist may take or use in connection with that business any title, emblem or description which the pharmacist him/herself could have used [s.78(8)] (see p.53).

The Health Ministers may, by order, add to, revoke or vary any of these conditions relating to the carrying on of retail pharmacy business, or provide for alternative or modified conditions. Such an order must receive the approval of each House of Parliament (s.73).

## Registration of Pharmacy Premises

The *registrar* is the Registrar of the Royal Pharmaceutical Society of Great Britain or, where appropriate, the Pharmaceutical Society of Northern Ireland (s.69). It is the registrar's duty to keep the register of pharmacy premises and, subject to the provisions described later, to enter in the register, on payment of the prescribed fee, any premises in respect of which application is made [s.75(1)]. A document purporting to be a certificate signed by the registrar and stating that, on a specified date, specified premises were, or were not, entered in the register shall be admissible in any proceedings as evidence (and, in Scotland, shall be sufficient evidence) that those premises were, or were not, entered in the register on that date [s.76(7)].

*Registered pharmacy* means premises entered for the time being in the register [s.74(1)]. Where a business which concerns the retail sale or supply of medicinal products is carried on in one or more separate or distinct parts of a building, each part is taken to be separate premises [s.69(2)]. A departmental store, for example, might have a department which is a registered pharmacy and a separate department (which is not a pharmacy) where General Sale List medicines are sold.

Registration of pharmacy premises must be effected in a prescribed manner [s.75(2) and SI 1973 No.1822]. An application must be in writing and be given or sent to the registrar with the prescribed fee. It must be made and signed by or on behalf of the person carrying on, or who intends to carry on, a retail pharmacy business at the premises to which the application relates. A separate application must be made in respect of each premises and each application must contain, or be accompanied by, the following particulars:

1   The name of the person carrying on, or intending to carry on, a retail pharmacy business and his/her private residential address. In the case of a partnership the names and such addresses of all the partners must be given. In the case of a body corporate, the registered name and address of the registered office of the body must be given. Where a business is being carried on by a representative of a pharmacist and the business is under the personal control of a pharmacist, the name of the pharmacist in personal control and the number of his/her certificate of registration must be given.

2   The business name where a person or a partnership or body corporate is carrying on or intends to carry on such a business under a business name which is different from the name of the person or of the partners or of the corporate body.

3   The name of the pharmacist or, if more than one, the names of all the pharmacists under whose personal control the business is, or is to be, carried on at all the premises to which the application relates, and in the case of a body corporate the name of the superintendent under whose management the business is, or is to be, carried on, and the number of the certificate of each such pharmacist and, as the case may be, superintendent.

4   The full postal address of the premises to which the application relates.

5   Where the application for registration relates to premises in respect of which there has been a change of ownership of the business, the name and address of the immediate former owner of that business and the date of such change of ownership.

6   The date or intended date of the commencement of the business.

7   A brief description of the premises including the internal layout of the premises as regards the areas where medicinal products are or are intended to be sold or supplied, prepared, dispensed or stored together with:

(a)    a statement showing whether or not there are arrangements so as to enable supervision to be exercised by a pharmacist of any dispensing and sale of medicinal products at one and the same time; and

(b)    a sketch plan, drawn to scale, showing the areas and the layouts to which this paragraph relates.

The registrar must notify the appropriate Ministers (in England and Wales, the Minister of Health; in Northern Ireland, the Minister of Health and Social Services; in Scotland, the Secretary of State) whenever an application is made. S/he may not enter the premises in the register until two months from that date, unless the Minister otherwise consents [s.75(3)]. Premises are not to be entered in the register unless the registrar is reasonably satisfied that the applicant is a person lawfully conducting a retail pharmacy business or will be so at the time of commencement of business [s.75(7)].

If it appears to the Minister that in a material respect the premises do not comply with the requirements of section 66 regulations (see p.55), s/he must within the two-month period serve on the applicant a notice stating his/her reasons for proposing to certify that the premises are unsuitable for registration. A copy of the notice must be served on the registrar, who may not then enter the premises in the register unless the Minister, after hearing the applicant, directs otherwise [s.75(4)]. An applicant may, within 28 days of receiving a notice from the Minister, submit written representations or seek to be heard by a person appointed by the Minister. Following this procedure the Minister must either:

1    send to the registrar a certificate that the premises are unsuitable for registration and notify the applicant that s/he has done so, stating his/her reasons if so requested; or

2    notify the applicant and the registrar that s/he has determined not to issue a certificate and the registrar must forthwith enter the premises in the register [s.75(5) and (6)].

## Change of Ownership

Where a change occurs in the ownership of a registered pharmacy, the registration becomes void at the end of the period of 28 days from the date on which the change occurs. If it occurs on the death of the person carrying on the business, that is on the death of a pharmacist owner or, in the case of a partnership, one of the partners, the period is three months from the date of the death [s.76(3)].

When the registration of pharmacy premises becomes void following a change of ownership, an application for restoration to the register may be made by the new owner. The registrar must restore the premises to the register if s/he is reasonably satisfied that the new owner is a person lawfully conducting a retail pharmacy business or will be so at the time s/he commences business at the premises. A fee equal to a retention fee must be paid by the new owner, but only if the retention fee for the year has not already been paid [s.76(5)]. No description of the premises or sketch plan need be submitted.

## Premises Retention Fees

A *retention fee* is payable annually in respect of any premises entered in the register for each year subsequent to the year in which they were registered [s.76(1)]. In this context, *year* means a period of 12 months beginning on such date as the Council (i.e. the Council of the Royal Pharmaceutical Society) may from time to time determine [s.74(3)]. The Council has decided that the registration year shall commence on the first day of January.

In January each year, every person who carries on a retail pharmacy business must send to the registrar a list of all premises at which his/her business, so far as it consists of the retail sale of medicinal products, is carried on. S/he must also state the name of the pharmacist in charge of each pharmacy. This means, in effect, that the owner of a pharmacy or pharmacies must inform the registrar each January of all the addresses of businesses where s/he sells medicinal products of any kind, and pay retention fees in respect of those which are registered pharmacies (s.77).

The Council may direct the registrar to remove any premises from the register if the person carrying on the retail pharmacy business fails to pay a retention fee within two months from the date on which a demand for it has been made to him/her in the prescribed manner. If, before the end of the year, or whatever period is permitted by the Council in any particular case, the retention fee is paid, together with any prescribed sum by way of penalty, the registrar must restore the premises to the register. If the Council so directs, the restoration shall be deemed to have had effect as from the date on which the premises were removed from the register [s.76(2)]. (For Northern Ireland, any reference to the Council in this section should be construed as a reference to the Minister of Health and Social Services for Northern Ireland.)

The Health Ministers are responsible for making any regulations relating to the registration of pharmacies [s.76(6)]. Any fees received by the registrar may be used for the purposes of the Royal Pharmaceutical Society [s.76(8)].

## Titles, Descriptions and Emblems

No person may, in connection with any business, use any title, description or emblem likely to suggest that s/he possesses any qualification with respect to the sale, manufacture or assembly of medicinal products which s/he does not in fact possess; or that any person employed in the business possesses any such qualification which that person does not in fact possess [s.78(6)].

Furthermore, the use of certain titles and descriptions is specifically restricted as follows:

1      The description *pharmacy* may only be used in respect of a registered pharmacy or the pharmaceutical department of a hospital or a health centre. It may not be used in connection with any business, other than a pharmacy, which consists of or includes the retail sale of any goods, or the supply of any goods in circumstances corresponding to retail sale [s.78(4)].

Its use in connection with a business carried on at any premises shall be taken as likely to suggest that the person carrying on the business (where that person is not a body corporate) is a pharmacist, and that any other person under whose personal control the business (so far as concerns the retail sale of medicinal products or the supply of such products in circumstances corresponding to retail sale) is carried on at those premises, is also a pharmacist.

2      The titles *Pharmaceutical Chemist, Pharmaceutist, Pharmacist, Member of the Pharmaceutical Society* or *Fellow of the Pharmaceutical Society* may only be taken or used by pharmacists [s.78(5)].

These titles may not be used at any premises connected with a business which includes the retail sale or supply of any goods unless those premises are a registered pharmacy or a hospital or health centre [s.78(5)].

3      The titles *Chemist and Druggist, Druggist, Dispensing Chemist* or *Dispensing Druggist* may only be taken or used by a person lawfully conducting a retail pharmacy business [s.78(2)].

The taking or using of the title *Chemist* is also restricted to a person lawfully conducting a retail pharmacy business, but only in connection with the sale of any goods by retail or the supply of any goods in circumstances corresponding to retail sale [s.78(2)].

Where the person lawfully conducting the retail pharmacy business is a body corporate, these titles may only be used if the pharmacist who is superintendent is also a member of the board of the body corporate [s.78(3)].

None of these titles may be used at any premises connected with a business which includes the retail sale or supply of any goods unless those premises are a registered pharmacy [s.78(3)].

The Health Ministers may by order, and after consultation with the Council of the Pharmaceutical Society, impose further restrictions or requirements with respect to the use of titles, descriptions and emblems. The Ministers may also provide that existing restrictions shall cease to have effect or be subject to specified exceptions. Regulations for these purposes must be approved by resolution of each House of Parliament (s.79).

## Accommodation, Storage, Records, Equipment, etc.

The appropriate Ministers have wide powers under the Act (s.66) to make regulations with respect to any of the following matters, although at the time this book closed for press such regulations had been made only in relation to 9 and 10 below (see p.72):

(see p.72)

1   the manner in which, or persons under whose supervision, medicinal products may be prepared or may be dispensed;
2   the amount of space to be provided in any premises for preparing or dispensing medicinal products, the separation of any such space from the remainder of the premises, and the facilities to be provided in any premises for such persons;
3   the amount of space to be provided in any premises for the sale or supply of medicinal products;
4   the accommodation (including the amount of space) to be provided in any premises for members of the public to whom medicinal products are sold or supplied or for whom medicinal products are being prepared or assembled;
5   the amount of space to be provided in any premises for the storage of medicinal products;
6   the safekeeping of medicinal products;
7   the disposal of medicinal products which have become unusable or otherwise unwanted;
8   precautions to be observed before medicinal products are sold or supplied;
9   the keeping of records relating to the sale or supply of medicinal products;
10   the supply of medicinal products distributed as samples;
11   sanitation, cleanliness, temperature, humidity or other factors relating to the risks of deterioration or contamination in connection with the manufacture, storage, transportation, sale or supply of medicinal products;
12   the construction, location and the use of automatic machines for the sale of medicinal products.

The Ministers can also prescribe requirements in respect of:

(a)   the construction, layout, drainage, equipment, maintenance, ventilation, lighting and water supply of premises at or from which medicinal products are manufactured, stored, transported, sold or supplied;
(b)   the disposal of refuse at or from any such premises; and
(c)   any apparatus, equipment, furnishings or utensils used at any such premises.

**Disqualification of Retail Pharmacy Owner**

It is an offence to contravene any of the regulations made under section 66 (s.67). Any person who is convicted of such an offence may, by order of the court, be disqualified from using the premises concerned for the purposes of a retail pharmacy business for a period not exceeding two years (s.68).

**Summary**

- Retail businesses which sell medicines not on a General Sale List must be registered as pharmacies. They may be owned by a pharmacist, a partnership, a body corporate or a representative of a deceased pharmacist.
- Detailed requirements relating to the premises, together with a fee, must be forwarded to the Royal Pharmaceutical Society in order for registration to take place.
- Certain titles may only be used by pharmacists, e.g. *pharmacist, pharmaceutical chemist, member of the Pharmaceutical Society.*
- A body corporate may use the title *dispensing chemist, chemist and druggist* or *chemist* only if the superintendent is a member of the board, otherwise the body corporate may only use the title *pharmacy* in connection with its pharmacy premises.
- Ministers, by way of regulations, may impose a large range of conditions relating to premises from which medicines are sold.

# CHAPTER FIVE

# Medicines Act 1968

## Pharmacy Medicines

Part III of the Act is concerned with the regulation of dealings with medicinal products. The basic principle, set out in section 52, is that medicinal products may be sold or supplied by retail only from registered pharmacies, unless they are products included in a General Sale List (see Chapter 6) or subject to some other exemption under the Act.

Section 52 provides that medicinal products, which are not included in a General Sale List, shall not be sold, offered or exposed for sale by retail, or supplied in circumstances corresponding to retail sale by any person in the course of a business carried on by him/her unless:

1  that person is, in respect of that business, a person lawfully conducting a retail pharmacy business;
2  the product is sold, offered or exposed for sale, or supplied on premises which are a registered pharmacy; and
3  that person, or, if the transaction is carried out on his/her behalf by another person, then that other person is, or acts under the supervision of, a pharmacist.

N.B. A retail pharmacy business must be under the personal control of a pharmacist so far as it concerns the sale of medicinal products including products on a General Sale List (ss.70–72). The meaning of *supervision* and *personal control* have been considered by the High Court and the Statutory Committee (see Chapters 21 and 26).

Selling by retail or retail sale includes all those sales which do not fall within the definition of selling by way of wholesale dealing [s.131(3)]. Supplying in circumstances corresponding to retail sale has a comparable meaning [s.131(4)]. Retail sale or supply, therefore, comprises all those sales or supplies of medicinal products made in the course of a business to a person who buys (or receives) them for the purpose other than that of (a) selling or supplying them; or (b) administering them or causing them to be administered to one or more human beings in the course of a business carried on by him/her.

The requirements of section 52 apply to sales and supplies made in 'the course of a business'. The provision of services under the National Health Service is treated as the carrying on of a business [s.131(5)]. However, the dispensing of a medicinal product on a National Health Service prescription is not a sale but a 'supply in circumstances corresponding to retail sale' (*Appleby* v. *Sleep* [1968] 2 All ER 265) (see p.370).

## Pharmacy Medicine Defined

Certain medicinal products may only be sold or supplied from pharmacies in accordance with a prescription given by an appropriate practitioner. These products, called *Prescription Only Medicines* (POMs) are specified in a 'prescription only' order (SI 1997 No.1830, as amended) (see p.71). Any medicinal product which is not a *Prescription Only Medicine* or a medicinal product on a General Sale List is a *Pharmacy Medicine* (P) (SI 1980 No.1924, as amended). There is no definitive list of Pharmacy Medicines, as the total in the class cannot be determined. It comprises all those medicines which are not in a 'Prescription Only' or 'General Sale List', and includes all medicines made in a pharmacy for retail sale under the exemptions from licensing granted to retail pharmacists (see p.26).

Some General Sale List medicines, when presented in packs exceeding specified quantities, may only be sold or supplied from pharmacies. They are designated *Pharmacy Medicines* (SI 1980 No.1923, as amended) although there is no legal requirement for supervision by a pharmacist (see Retail Pack Sizes of Certain Products, Chapter 6).

Some Prescription Only Medicines when presented in packs **not** exceeding specified quantities, may only be sold or supplied from pharmacies (see Retail Pack Sizes of Certain Products, Chapter 6).

## Exemptions in Cases Involving Another's Default

The restrictions imposed by section 52 of the Act shall not apply to the sale, offer or exposure for sale or supply of a medicinal product by a person who, having exercised all due diligence, believes on reasonable grounds that the product is a medicinal product on a General Sale List or subject to a temporary exemption but which due to the act or default of another person is not such a medicinal product, if and so long as the conditions applying to the sale of medicinal products on a General Sale List are fulfilled (SI 1980 No.1924) (see Chapter 6).

## Temporary Exemptions

Where the product licence, or a variation of a product licence, provides for the sale or supply of a medicinal product without the supervision of a pharmacist, it may be sold under General Sale conditions despite the fact that it is not included in the current General Sale List. This temporary exemption is for two years from the date of the grant of the licence, or for one year from the date of a variation in a licence (SI 1980 No.1924). It appears that the General Sale List should be updated each year.

The conditions under which General Sale List medicines may be sold are described in Chapter 6.

## Collection and Delivery Arrangements – Exemption

A *collection and delivery arrangement* means any arrangement whereby a person is enabled to take or send a prescription given by a doctor or dentist to premises other than a registered pharmacy and to collect or have collected on his/her behalf from such premises a medicinal product prepared or dispensed in accordance with such prescription at a registered pharmacy by or under the supervision of a pharmacist if such premises at which the medicinal product is supplied are capable of being closed so as to exclude the public (SI 1978 No.1421).

When an arrangement of this kind is used by a person lawfully conducting a retail pharmacy business the supply of dispensed medicines for human use at the non-pharmacy premises without the supervision of a pharmacist is rendered lawful by an exemption provided in SI 1978 No.1421.

## Summary

- Pharmacy Medicines comprise all medicinal products which are not on the General Sale List, are not on the Prescription Only List or are exempt in some form or other from the latter.
- The legislation requires that retail sales or supplies of Pharmacy Medicines have to be made by a person conducting a retail pharmacy business, at a registered pharmacy, and by, or under the supervision of, a pharmacist.
- The conditions under which Pharmacy Medicines must be sold do not apply where there is a collection and delivery arrangement in place.

## Further Reading

*Medicines, Ethics and Practice*, published annually. The Royal Pharmaceutical Society of Great Britain.

CHAPTER SIX

# Medicines Act 1968

## General Sale Medicines

General Sale Medicines are those which in the opinion of the appropriate Minister can with reasonable safety be sold or supplied otherwise than by or under the supervision of a pharmacist (s.51). Medicines for human use are listed in SI 1984 No.769, as amended. Veterinary drugs are listed in SI 1984 No.768.

### Conditions Applying to Retail Sale or Supply

Medicinal products on a General Sale List may only be sold by retail, offered or exposed for sale by retail, or supplied in circumstances corresponding to retail sale either at registered pharmacies, or in circumstances where the following conditions are fulfilled:

1   the place at which the medicinal product (unless it is a veterinary drug) is sold, offered, exposed or supplied, must be premises at which the person carrying on the business in question is the occupier and which s/he is able to close so as to exclude the public;

N.B. As veterinary drugs are specifically exempted [s.53(2)] they may be sold from stalls and vans. Similarly, the restriction as to premises does not apply to foods and cosmetics that are medicinal products (SI 1980 No.1924).

2    the medicinal product must have been made up for sale in a container elsewhere than at the place at which it is sold, offered, exposed for sale or supplied, and the container must not have been opened since the product was made up for sale in it;

3    the business, so far as concerns the sale or supply of medicinal products, must be carried on in accordance with such conditions as may be prescribed (s.53).

## General Sale List Medicines for Human Use

The classes of medicinal products on general sale for administration to human beings are set out in Schedules 1 and 2 to SI 1984 No.769, as amended. Those in Schedule 2 are licence of right products.

The list is made up as follows:

1    Appended to each of the Schedules are two lists of products, namely Table A (those for internal and external use) and Table B (those for external use only). Where a product contains a substance listed in one of the tables it must satisfy any stated specification as to maximum strength (ms); use; pharmaceutical form; or route of administration. Similarly, products for internal use (Table A) must satisfy any specification as to maximum dose (md) or maximum daily dose (mdd). Containers and packages must be labelled with the required information given in the specification.

2    Aqueous and alcoholic extracts, spirits, syrups and liquid suspensions derived from the substances in 1 above.

3    Excipients (that is substances which do not contribute directly to the pharmacological action of the medicinal product otherwise than by regulation of the release of the active ingredient).

4    Licence of right products containing one or more of the following:

   (a)    haemoglobin or the following parts of animals, namely bone, brain, genitals, horn, prostate and spleen but not extracts from such parts;

   (b)    glycerine extracts of bone marrow;

   (c)    bovine blood derivatives;

   (d)    substances of vegetable origin and extracts of such substances used in the United Kingdom as food.

5    Medicinal products for human use which are for sale or supply, either for oral administration as food, or external use as a cosmetic, other than products which are eye drops, eye ointments or Prescription Only Medicines or contain either:

   (a)    Vitamin A, Vitamin A acetate, and Vitamin A palmitate with a maximum daily dose equivalent to more than 7500 iu of Vitamin A or 2250 μg of retinol; or

(b)  Vitamin D with a maximum daily dose of more than 400 iu of antirachitic activity.

## General Sale List Medicines for Animal Use

The medicinal products permitted for general sale as veterinary medicines are set out in Schedule 1 to SI 1984 No.768 as follows:

1   Those listed in Table A (substances for internal and external use) or Table B (substances for external use only). Where a product contains an ingredient which is listed in Table A or B it must comply with specifications in the table as to maximum strength (ms), maximum dose (md), maximum daily dose (mdd), use, pharmaceutical form or route of administration and be labelled accordingly.
2   Excipients.
3   Substances of animal origin (including extracts of such substances) used in the United Kingdom as a human or animal food.
4   Substances of vegetable origin (including extracts and residues of such substances) used in the United Kingdom as a human or animal food.
5   Grit in veterinary drugs for birds.

## Automatic Machines

Medicinal products which are on a General Sale List (other than veterinary drugs) may be sold from automatic machines. Such machines must be located in premises which the occupier is able to close so as to exclude the public (s.66 and SI 1980 No.1923).

## Retail Pack Sizes of Certain Products

Limits are imposed on the pack sizes of certain General Sale List products when they are sold or supplied by retail from businesses other than pharmacies. If sold outside the limits laid down the medicinal products concerned are classed as *Pharmacy Medicine* or *Prescription Only Medicines*

The limits for General Sale are:

### 1 Aloxiprin

Medicines for human use containing aloxiprin may only be presented for sale in separate and individual containers or packages containing not more than: (a) 30 tablets (effervescent tablets); (b) 16 capsules or tablets (non-effervescent); and (c) 10 sachets (powders or granules) (s.53) (SI 1980 No.1923, as amended).

## 2 Aspirin and Paracetamol

Medicines for human use containing aspirin or paracetamol may only be presented for sale in separate and individual containers or packages containing not more than: (a) 16 capsules or tablets (non-effervescent) (SI 1999 No.644); (b) 10 sachets (powder or granules); (c) 30 tablets containing not more than 325 mg (effervescent tablets); (d) 20 tablets where the amount of aspirin exceeds 325 mg but does not exceed 500 mg (effervescent tablets) (SI 1994 No.2411).

*Effervescent*, in relation to a tablet, means containing not less than 75 per cent by weight of the tablet, of ingredients included wholly or mainly for the purpose of releasing carbon dioxide when the tablet is dissolved or dispersed in water.

In the case of liquid preparations of paracetamol:

(a)    which are intended for persons over 12 years not more than 160 ml;
(b)    which are intended for persons less than 12 years individual doses of not more than 5 ml and no greater quantity than 20 doses (SI 1997 No.2045).

## 3 Bisacodyl

Tablets for human use containing bisacodyl may only be presented for sale in a separate and individual container or package containing not more than 10 tablets (s.53) (SI 1990 No.1124).

## 4 Ibuprofen

Medicines for human use containing ibuprofen may only be presented for sale in separate and individual containers or packages containing: (a) in the case of tablets or capsules, not more than 16 tablets (SI 1999 No.644); (b) in the case of powder or granules, not more than 12 sachets; and (c) in the case of a topical product, not more than 2.5 g of ibuprofen (SI 1995 No.3215).

## 5 Clotrimazole

A medicinal product for topical use containing clotrimazole may only be presented for sale in separate and individual containers or packages containing not more than 500 mg of clotrimazole (SI 1995 No.3215).

## 6 Sodium Picosulphate

Medicines for human use containing sodium picosulphate may only be presented for sale in separate and individual containers or packages containing not more than 60 ml (SI 1997 No.2045).

### 7 Loperamide Hydrochloride

Medicines for human use containing loperamide hydrochloride may only be presented for sale in separate and individual containers or packages containing not more than six tablets or capsules (SI 1997 No.2045).

### 8 Mepyramine Maleate

Medicines for human use containing mepyramine maleate may only be presented for sale in separate and individual containers or packages containing not more than 20 g with a maximum strength of 2 per cent for the symptomatic relief of insect stings and bites, and nettle stings, in adults and in children aged 2 and over (SI 2000 No.1070).

### 9 Ranitidine Hydrochloride

Medicines for human use containing ranitidine hydrochloride may only be presented for sale in separate and individual containers or packages containing not more than 12 tablets ms 75 mg (SI 1999 No.2510).

### 10 Veterinary Medicines

For veterinary drugs the quantities permitted in individual containers or packages are listed in Table 6.1:

**Table 6.1** Quantities permitted in individual containers or packages for veterinary drugs

| | |
|---|---|
| Aminonitrothiazole | 100 ml of solution or 50 capsules |
| Aspirin | 25 tablets or 25 sachets of powder |
| Bromhexine hydrochloride | 20 g |
| Paracetamol | 25 tablets |
| Phenylephrine hydrochloride | 15 ml |
| Potassium chlorate | 30 ml |

Packs containing more than these quantities may only be sold or supplied from pharmacies and must be labelled P (SI 1981 No.1791).

## Products Not To Be On General Sale

The General Sale List Orders relating to medicinal products for human use (SI 1984 No.769) and for veterinary drugs (SI 1984 No.768) specify certain classes of products which are not to be on general sale. They are:

1    Medicinal products for human use or veterinary drugs promoted, recommended, or marketed:

(a)    for use as eye drops or eye ointments;

(b)    for administration by parenteral injection; or

(c)    for use as anthelmintics, except veterinary drugs consisting or containing dichlorophen, diethylcarbamazine citrate, piperazine adipate, piperazine calcium adipate, piperazine citrate, piperazine dihydrochloride, piperazine hydrate or piperazine phosphate.

2    Veterinary drugs promoted, recommended or marketed for the internal treatment of ringworms.

3    Medicines for human use promoted, recommended or marketed:

(a)    for use as enemas (SI 1985 No.1540);

(b)    for use wholly or mainly for irrigation of wounds or of the bladder, vagina, or rectum (SI 1985 No.1540);

(c)    for administration wholly or mainly to children being a preparation of aloxiprin or aspirin (SI 1987 No.910).


## Summary

- Medicines which in the opinion of the Minister can with reasonable safety be sold other than by or under the supervision of a pharmacist are listed as General Sale List medicines for both human and animal use. They may only be sold from closable premises and in their original packs.
- Certain medicines may be sold other than by or under the supervision of a pharmacist subject to certain pack sizes. These include aspirin, aloxiprin, bisacodyl, ibuprofen, topical clotrimazole and ranitidine hydrochloride.
- Certain medicines cannot be on general sale. These include eye drops and ointments, most anthelmintics, parenterals, those medicines promoted as enemas or for use as irrigations, and aspirin for children.


## Further Reading

*Medicines, Ethics and Practice*, published annually. The Royal Pharmaceutical Society of Great Britain.

# CHAPTER SEVEN

# Medicines Act 1968

## Prescription Only Medicines

A *Prescription Only Medicine* (POM) means a medicinal product which may only be sold or supplied by retail in accordance with a prescription given by *an appropriate practitioner* (s.58).

For the purposes of SI 1997 No.1830 – which lists Prescription Only Medicines for human use – doctors, dentists, veterinary surgeons and veterinary practitioners are designated as *appropriate practitioners*. For the purposes of SI 1991 No.1392 – which lists Prescription Only Medicines which are for animal use – veterinary surgeons and veterinary practitioners only are described as *appropriate practitioners*.

The Medicinal Products: Prescription by Nurses etc. Act 1992, amended the Medicines Act 1968 and provides that registered nurses, midwives and health visitors who are of such a description and who comply with certain conditions are considered to be *appropriate practitioners*. An appropriate nurse practitioner is defined and the medicines in relation to which they are such a practitioner is stated in the regulations (SI 1997 No.1830).

*Appropriate nurse practitioner* means:

1    a person who:

    (a)    is registered in the register maintained by the United Kingdom Central Council for Nursing, Midwifery and Health Visiting (the professional register); and

(b) has a district nursing qualification additionally recorded in the professional register; or

2 a person registered in the professional register as a health visitor.

Such nurse practitioners may prescribe: Co-danthramer capsules and oral suspensions; Co-danthrusate capsules and oral suspensions; Mebendazole tablets and oral suspension; Miconazole oral gel; Nystatin pastilles and oral suspension; and Streptokinase and Streptodornase topical powder (SI 1997 No.1830, as amended).

On 25 October 2000 the Department of Health issued a consultation document entitled *Proposals to Extend Nurse Prescribing*. It includes the kind of principles which should guide nurse prescribing, the medical conditions and nursing formulary for such prescribing and plans for preparation and training for nurse prescribers. The document set out a range of options to extend nurse prescribing and sought comments by 10 January 2001.

**Prescription Only Medicines for Human Use**

The criteria to be applied in specifying which medicinal products are to be Prescription Only are laid down in regulations (SI 1992 No.3271) implementing Council Directive 92/26/EEC (the Classification of Human Medicines Directive) and Council Directive 81/851/EEC, as amended by Council Directive 90/676/EEC (the Veterinary Medicines Directives).

Prescription Only Medicines which are not for animal use are listed in SI 1997 No.1830, as amended. Unless exempt they are:

1 Medicinal products consisting of or containing a substance listed in Column I of Schedule 1 to the Order.
2 Medicinal products that are Controlled Drugs.
3 Medicinal products that are for parenteral administration whether or not they include any substance included in the Prescription Only List.
  *Parenteral administration* means administration by breach of the skin or mucous membrane.
4 Cyanogenetic substances other than preparations for external use.
5 Medicinal products that on administration emit radiation, or contain or generate any substance which emits radiation, in order that radiation may be used.
6 Medicinal products for human use which are classified as prescription only in their marketing authorisation granted under Council Regulation 2309/93/EEC.

**Exemptions from Prescription Only**

*1 Medicinal Products Exempt Due to Conditions*

A medicinal product is exempt if it is listed in Column 1 of Schedule 1 and there is:

(a)   an entry in Columns 2, 3, 4, or 5 of that Schedule which contains a condition and that condition is satisfied; or

(b)   there is more than one such condition which applies where that substance is used in that product and each of those conditions are satisfied.

The conditions are that the medicinal product is:

   (i) a particular strength;
   (ii) a particular pharmaceutical form;
   (iii) the route of administration specified in the schedule; and
   (iv) in or from containers or packages labelled to show doses not exceeding the maximum dose (md), or the maximum daily doses (mdd), or both as specified in the Schedule.

All these exempted medicinal products will be a *Pharmacy Medicine*.
   *Maximum strength* or *ms* means either:

(a)   the maximum quantity of a substance by weight or volume contained in a dosage unit of a medicinal product;

(b)   the maximum percentage of a Prescription Only Medicines substance contained in a medicinal product calculated in terms of weight in weight (w/w), weight in volume (w/v), volume in weight (v/w) or volume in volume (v/v) and if the maximum percentage calculated in those ways differ, the higher or highest percentage.

*Maximum dose* or *md* means the maximum quantity of a substance contained in the amount of a medicinal product for internal use which it is recommended should be taken or administered at any one time.

   *Maximum daily dose* or *mdd* means the maximum quantity of a substance contained in the amount of a medicinal product which it is recommended should be taken or administered in any period of 24 hours.

## 2 Retail Pack Sizes of Certain Products

Some Prescription Only Medicines when presented in packs **not** exceeding specified quantities, may only be sold or supplied from pharmacies. These are:

(a)   *Aspirin* where if the pack size for non-effervescent tablets or capsules does not exceed 32 and the ms 500 mg then the product is a *Pharmacy Medicine*. The total quantity sold to a person at any one time must not exceed 100.

(b)   *Aspirin* where if the pack size for non-effervescent tablets or capsules does not exceed 100 and the ms 75 mg then the product is a *Pharmacy Medicine*.

(c)   *Paracetamol* where if the pack size for non-effervescent tablets or capsules does not exceed 32 and the ms 120 mg (for children under 12) or ms 500 mg (for adults or children over 12) then the product is a

*Pharmacy Medicine.* The total quantity sold to a person at any one time must not exceed 100 (SI 1997 No.2044).

Aspirin and paracetamol in preparations other than non-effervescent tablets and capsules are also Pharmacy Medicines.

### 3 Exempted Controlled Drugs

Maximum strengths are specified in Part II of Schedule 1 to the Prescription Only order for certain Controlled Drugs. A medicinal product containing only one of those substances not in excess of the maximum strength is a *Pharmacy Medicine*, provided it is not a veterinary medicinal product and does not contain any other substances at a strength which would render the product a Prescription Only Medicine, and it is sold, supplied or administered:

(a)  in the pharmaceutical form specified in the order; and
(b)  in or from containers or packages labelled to show a dose not exceeding a maximum dose as specified in the order.

That exemption applies to the six Controlled Drugs set out in Table 7.1 below. Subject to the limitations as to maximum strength, maximum dosage and pharmaceutical form shown they are Pharmacy Medicines.

**Table 7.1**   Exempt Controlled Drugs

| Substance | Maximum Strength | Maximum Dose |
|---|---|---|
| Codeine; its salts | Equivalent of 1.5 % of Codeine monohydrate base | Equivalent of 20 mg of Codeine monohydrate base |
| Dihydrocodeine; its salts | Equivalent of 1.5 % of Dihydrocodeine base | Equivalent of 10 mg of Dihydrocodeine base |
| Ethylmorphine; its salts | Equivalent of 0.2 % of Ethylmorphine base | Equivalent of 7.5 mg of Ethylmorphine base |
| Morphine; its salts | (1) Liquid: Equivalent of 0.02 % of anhydrous Morphine (2) Solid; Equivalent of 0.04 % and 300 $\mu$g of anhydrous Morphine base | Equivalent of 3 mg of anhydrous Morphine base Equivalent of 3 mg of anhydrous Morphine base |
| Medicinal Opium | (1) Liquid: Equivalent of 0.02 % of anhydrous Morphine base (2) Solid: Equivalent of 0.04 % of anhydrous Morphine base | Equivalent of 3 mg of anhydrous Morphine base Equivalent of 3 mg of anhydrous Morphine base |
| Pholcodine; its salts | Equivalent of 1.5 % of Pholcodine monohydrate base | Equivalent of 20 mg of Pholcodine monohydrate base |

### Prescription Only Medicines for Animal Use

Prescription Only medicinal products for animal use are listed in SI 1991 No.1392. They are:

1    Those veterinary medicinal products containing one or more substances listed in Part I of Schedule 1 to the Order. Maximum strengths are shown in the Schedule for certain substances. A veterinary medicinal product containing such a substance at or below the maximum strength and complying with any other specification in the Schedule as to use, pharmaceutical form or route of administration is not a Prescription Only Medicine.
2    Veterinary Medicinal Products that are Controlled Drugs.
3    Veterinary Medicinal Products for parenteral administration. But any parenteral preparation which contains a substance in Schedule 2 to the Order is not a Prescription Only Medicine provided that substance does not exceed any specified maximum strength and the preparation is sold or supplied for the purpose stated in the Schedule. These are:

   • Lignocaine
   • Lignocaine hydrochloride
   • Procaine hydrochloride

4    Medicinal products which are veterinary medicinal products by reason of their having been sold or supplied for the administration to animals and which prior to such sale or supply were Prescription Only Medicines as defined in the Prescription Only Medicines (Human Use) Order (SI 1997 No.1830).

### New Medicinal Products

Where a marketing authorisation has been issued in respect of a new medicinal product restricting it to Prescription Only use, that restriction will normally apply for five years from the date of the granting of the licence. Normally, it is intended that the Prescription Only Order will be updated to include the product before the expiry of the five-year period.

### Administration of Prescription Only Medicines

The Act provides that no person shall administer a Prescription Only Medicine, otherwise than to him/herself, unless s/he is a practitioner or is acting in accordance with the direction of a practitioner [s.58(2)(b)]. However, certain injectable products may be administered by way of parenteral injection to human beings for the purpose of saving life in an emergency. They are set out in Table 7.2:

**Table 7.2**  Injectable products which may be administered by way of parenteral injection to human beings for the purpose of saving life in an emergency

| | |
|---|---|
| Adrenaline injection (1 in 1000) | Hydrocortisone injection |
| Atropine sulphate injection | Mepyramine injection |
| Chlorpheniramine injection | Promethazine hydrochloride injection |
| Cobalt edetate injection | Snake venom antiserum |
| Dextrose injection strong BPC | Sodium nitrite injection |
| Diphenhydramine injection | Sodium thiosulphate injection |
| Glucagon injection | Sterile pralidoxime |

## Radioactive Medicinal Products

*Radioactive substance* means any substance that contains one or more radionuclides of which the activity or concentration cannot be disregarded as far as radiation protection is concerned (SI 1978 No.1006).

Only a doctor or dentist holding an appropriate certificate issued by the Health Minister or a person acting under the directions of such a doctor or dentist may lawfully administer a *radioactive medicinal product*, that is a medicinal product which is, which contains or which generates a radioactive substance and which is, contains or generates that substance in order, when administered, to utilise the radiation emitted therefrom. Certain other conditions are laid down in the regulations (SI 1978 No.1006, amended by SI 1995 No.2147).

## Prescriptions

A Prescription Only Medicine may only be sold or supplied in accordance with a prescription given by a practitioner [s.58(a)]. To meet that requirement, certain conditions must be satisfied (SI 1997 No.1830).

The prescription:

(a)  shall be signed in ink with his/her own name by the practitioner giving it;

(b)  shall, without prejudice to subparagraph (a), be written in ink or otherwise so as to be indelible, unless it is a health prescription which is not for a Controlled Drug specified in Schedule 1, 2 or 3 to the Misuse of Drugs Regulations, in which case it may be written by means of carbon paper or similar material;

(c)  shall contain the following particulars:

    (i)  the address of the practitioner giving it;

    (ii)  the appropriate date (see below);

    (iii)  such particulars as indicate whether the practitioner giving it is a doctor, a dentist, an appropriate nurse practitioner, a veterinary surgeon or a veterinary practitioner;

(iv) where the practitioner giving it is a doctor, dentist, or an appropriate nurse practitioner, the name, address and the age, if under 12, of the person for whose treatment it is given; and

(v) where the practitioner giving it is a veterinary surgeon or a veterinary practitioner, the name and address of the person to whom the Prescription Only Medicine is to be delivered and a declaration that it is for an animal or herd under his/her care.

(d)   shall not be dispensed after the end of the period of six months from the appropriate date, unless it is a repeatable prescription in which case it shall not be dispensed for the first time after the end of that period nor otherwise than in accordance with the direction contained in the repeatable prescription;

(e)   in the case of a repeatable prescription that does not specify the number of times it may be dispensed, shall not be dispensed on more than two occasions unless it is a prescription for oral contraceptives in which case it may be dispensed six times before the end of the period of six months from the appropriate date.

Where a prescription given by an appropriate practitioner does not fulfill a required condition, the sale or supply is not rendered unlawful if the person making the sale or supply, having exercised all due diligence, believes on reasonable grounds that that condition is fulfilled in relation to that sale or supply.

Similarly, the sale or supply is not rendered unlawful if made against a forged prescription provided the pharmacist has exercised all due diligence and believes on reasonable grounds that the prescription is genuine.

*Repeatable prescription* means a prescription which contains a direction that it may be dispensed more than once.

*Health prescription* means a prescription issued by a doctor or dentist under or by virtue of:

1    in England and Wales, the National Health Service Act 1977;
2    in Scotland, the National Health Service (Scotland) Act 1978; and
3    in Northern Ireland, the Health and Personal Social Services (Northern Ireland) Order 1972.

The *appropriate date* is the date on which the prescription was signed by the practitioner, or, in the case of a health prescription only, the date indicated by him/her as being the date before which it shall not be dispensed. Where a health prescription bears both dates, the later of those dates is the appropriate one.

## Pharmacy Records

Every person lawfully conducting a retail pharmacy business is required to keep a record in respect of every sale or supply of a Prescription Only Medicine, unless:

1   it is a sale or supply in pursuance of a health prescription or a prescription for oral contraceptives; or
2   a separate record of the sale or supply is made in accordance with regulation 19 of the Misuse of Drugs Regulations (see Chapter 16, p.178) or regulation 19 of the Misuse of Drugs (Northern Ireland) Regulations 1974; or
3   the sale or supply is to a person employed or engaged in connection with a scheme for testing the quality and checking the amount of drugs and appliances supplied under the National Health Service legislation of England and Wales, or Scotland, or Northern Ireland; or
4   in Scotland, the sale or supply is to a doctor of drugs or appliances which, under the National Health Service, the doctor is entitled or required to supply; or
5   in Northern Ireland, the sale or supply is in response to an order for a doctor of medicinal products which are drugs required by him/her under the National Health Service for immediate administration or in other similar cases (SI 1980 No.1923).

For records of wholesale transactions in Prescription Only Medicines see Chapter 9.

An entry must be a written or computerised record kept for the purpose in respect of each sale or supply (SI 1997 No.1831). The entry must be made on the day the sale or supply takes place, or, if that is not reasonably practicable, on the following day.

For an emergency supply made on a doctor's undertaking to furnish a prescription within 72 hours the recording of (a) the date of the prescription and (b) the date on which the prescription is received, may be made on the day that the prescription is received (SI 1980 No.1923).

## Particulars of Prescriptions to be Recorded

The particulars to be recorded in the case of a sale or supply of a Prescription Only Medicine in pursuance of a prescription are:

1   the date on which the medicine was sold or supplied;
2   the name, quantity and, except where it is apparent from the name, the pharmaceutical form and strength of the medicine;
3   the date on the prescription and the name and address of the practitioner giving it;
4   the name and address of the person for whom or for whose animal, as the case may be, the medicine was prescribed.

For second and subsequent supplies made on a repeat prescription it is sufficient to record the date of supply and a reference to the entry in the register relating to the first supply.

Additional particulars must be recorded in the case of emergency supplies to patients (see below).

**Preservation of Pharmacy Records**

The Prescription Only Record must be preserved by the owner of the retail pharmacy business for a period of two years from the date of the last entry in the record. A prescription must be retained for two years from the date on which the Prescription Only Medicine was sold or supplied, or, for a repeat prescription, the date on which the medicine was supplied for the last time (see also Chapter 16).

**Labelling of Dispensed Medicines**

See page 136.

**Exemptions for Persons Conducting Retail Pharmacy Businesses**

In the Act, and in the orders made under the Act, there are specific exemptions for persons lawfully conducting retail pharmacy businesses from the conditions or restrictions on the retail sale and supply of Prescription Only Medicines (SI 1997 No.1830) and from the supply and administration of Prescription Only Medicines (SI 2000 No.1917). Exemptions from control for other persons are to be found in Chapter 8.

In an emergency a person lawfully conducting a retail pharmacy business can sell or supply a Prescription Only Medicine if and so long as certain conditions are satisfied. There are two kinds of emergency supply (those made at the request of a doctor, and those made at the request of a patient) and different conditions apply to them.

*Exemption for Emergency Supply Made at the Request of a Doctor*

The conditions that apply are:

1   that the pharmacist by or under whose supervision the Prescription Only Medicine is to be sold or supplied is satisfied that the sale or supply has been requested by a doctor who by reason of an emergency is unable to furnish a prescription immediately;
2   that that doctor has undertaken to furnish the person lawfully conducting the retail pharmacy business with a prescription within 72 hours;
3   that the Prescription Only Medicine is sold or supplied in accordance with the directions of the doctor requesting it;
4   that the Prescription Only Medicine is not a Controlled Drug specified in Schedule 1, 2, or 3 to the Misuse of Drugs Regulations (see Appendix 11);

5    that an entry is made in the Prescription Only Register (see above) stating:

(a)    the date on which the medicine was sold or supplied;

(b)    the name, quantity and, except where it is apparent from the name, the pharmaceutical form and strength of the medicine;

(c)    the name and address of the person for whom the Prescription Only Medicine was supplied;

(d)    the date on which the prescription was received and the name and address of the practitioner giving it;

(e)    the date on the prescription (SI 1997 No.1830).

### Exemption for Emergency Supply Made at the Request of a Patient

The conditions that apply are:

1    that the pharmacist by or under whose supervision the Prescription Only Medicine is to be sold or supplied has interviewed the person requesting the medicine and has satisfied him/herself:

(a)    that there is an immediate need for the Prescription Only Medicine requested to be sold or supplied and that it is impracticable in the circumstances to obtain a prescription without undue delay;

(b)    that treatment with the Prescription Only Medicine requested has on a previous occasion been prescribed by a doctor for the person requesting it; and

(c)    as to the dose which in the circumstances it would be appropriate for that person to take.

2    that no greater quantity of the Prescription Only Medicine in question than will provide five days' treatment is sold or supplied except that there may be sold or supplied, where the medicine in question is:

(a)    an aerosol dispenser for the relief of asthma, an ointment or cream which has been made up for sale in a container elsewhere than at the place of sale or supply, the smallest pack that the pharmacist has available for sale or supply;

(b)    an oral contraceptive sufficient for a full cycle;

(c)    an antibiotic for oral administration in liquid form, the smallest quantity that will provide a full course of treatment.

3    that the pharmacist by or under whose supervision the medicine is sold or supplied ensures that an entry in the Prescription Only Register is made (see above) stating:

(a)    the date on which the Prescription Only Medicine was sold or supplied;

(b)  the name, quantity and, except where it is apparent from the name, the pharmaceutical form and strength of the medicine;

(c)  the name and address of the person requiring the medicine; and

(d)  the nature of the emergency.

4    that the container or package of the medicine is labelled with:

(a)  the date on which the Prescription Only Medicine was sold or supplied;

(b)  the name, quantity and, except where it is apparent from the name, the pharmaceutical form and strength of the Prescription Only Medicine;

(c)  the name of the person requiring the Prescription Only Medicine;

(d)  the name and address of the registered pharmacy from which the Prescription Only Medicine was sold or supplied; and

(e)  the words 'Emergency Supply'.

5    that the Prescription Only Medicine:

(a)  is not a Controlled Drug specified in Schedule 1, 2 or 3 to the Misuse of Drugs Regulations (see Appendix 11); or

(b)  does not contain one or more of the following substances (see Table 7.3):

**Table 7.3**  Substances one or more of which may **not** be contained in a Prescription Only Medicine supplied at the request of a patient (SI 1997 No.1830, as amended)

| | |
|---|---|
| Ammonium bromide | Methohexitone sodium |
| Calcium bromide | Pemoline |
| Calcium bromidolactobionate | Piracetam |
| Embutramide | Potassium bromide |
| Fencamfamin hydrochloride | Prolintane hydrochloride |
| Fluanisone | Sodium bromide |
| Hexobarbitone | Strychnine hydrochloride |
| Hexobarbitone sodium | Tacrine hydrochloride |
| Hydrobromic acid | Thiopentone sodium |
| Meclofenoxate hydrochloride | |

An emergency sale or supply is permitted of a Prescription Only Medicine which consists of or contains Phenobarbitone or Phenobarbitone sodium provided that it is for use in the treatment of epilepsy and does not contain any of the other substances listed above or any substances in Schedule 1, 2 or 3 to the Misuse of Drugs Regulations.

## Exemption for Supply or Administration of Prescription Only Medicines under a Patient Group Direction (PGD)

*Patient Group Direction* means:

1    a written direction relating to the supply and administration of a description or class of Prescription Only Medicines; or
2    a written direction relating to the administration of a description or class of Prescription Only Medicines, and which in either case:

(a)    is signed by a doctor or dentist, and by a pharmacist, and
(b)    relates to supply and administration, or to administration only, to persons generally (subject to any exclusions which may be set out in the Direction).

The restrictions on retail sale, supply or administration of Prescription Only Medicines do not apply to the supply or administration of any such medicine by a person lawfully conducting a retail pharmacy business where the medicine is supplied or is administered, by such a person subject to an arrangement made with the Common Services Agency, a Health Authority, a Special Health Authority, a National Health Service Trust, or a Primary Care Trust; where the medicine is supplied for the purpose of being administered or, is administered, to a particular person in accordance with a Patient Group Direction (PGD); and where the following conditions are satisfied:

1    The PGD relates to the supply, or the administration, of a description or class of Prescription Only Medicine by a person lawfully conducting a retail pharmacy business who supplies or administers such a medicine.
2    The PGD has effect at the time at which the medicine is supplied or is administered.
3    The PGD contains the particulars specified in the regulations (see Appendix 8). If the PGD is for administration only any restrictions on quantity may be omitted.
4    The PGD is signed on behalf of the authority with whom the arrangement is made by a doctor (or dentist) **and** a pharmacist.
5    At the time at which the medicine is supplied or administered the medicine has a marketing authorisation or a homoeopathic certificate of registration (SI 2000 No.1917).
6    Where the medicine is administered by the person lawfully conducting a retail pharmacy business, the individual who administers the medicine belongs to one of the classes specified in the Order (see Appendix 8) and is designated in writing on behalf of the body with which an arrangement has been made (added by SI 2000 No.2899).

N.B. As far as pharmacies are concerned there is no provision to use Patient Group Directions to permit the supply or administration of Pharmacy Medicines and General Sale List medicines.

*Exemptions from Prescription Only for Certain Persons, etc.*

See Chapter 8.

## Summary

- Practitioners for the purpose of prescribing Prescription Only Medicines are doctors, dentists and veterinary surgeons. Certain nurses are also appropriate nurse practitioners and may prescribe medicines from a limited list.
- Certain medicines are Prescription Only by description or class including Controlled Drugs (some are exempt due to maximum strength or maximum dose), parenterals, and cyanogenetic substances.
- Certain Prescription Only Medicines are exempt, dependent on strength, daily dosage, specified condition for use, etc., e.g. cimetidine.
- Certain Prescription Only Medicines may be administered in an emergency, e.g. adrenaline injection.
- Detailed prescription requirements are laid down including name and address of patient, signature and address of doctor, date, age of patient if under 12, etc.
- Detailed record requirements are imposed for Prescription Only Medicines except those on a health prescription or oral contraceptives.
- Prescription Only Medicines, except Controlled Drugs, may be supplied at the request of a doctor who by reason of any emergency is unable to furnish a prescription immediately.
- Prescription Only Medicines, except Controlled Drugs, may be supplied at the request of a patient if the pharmacist has interviewed the patient, is satisfied that there is an immediate need, it is impracticable to obtain a prescription without undue delay and the medicine has been prescribed before by a doctor. Detailed quantity, labelling and record conditions apply.
- Under certain conditions Prescription Only Medicines may be supplied under Patient Group Directions.

## Further Reading

*Medicines, Ethics and Practice*, published annually. The Royal Pharmaceutical Society of Great Britain.
(Lists of Prescription Only Medicines are included.)

CHAPTER EIGHT

# Medicines Act 1968

# Retail Sale and Supply –

# Exemptions from Controls for

# Other Persons

In the Act, and in orders made under the Act, there are specified exemptions for certain classes of persons from the conditions or restrictions on retail sale and/or supply which apply to medicines on a General Sale List (s.53), Pharmacy Medicines (s.52), and Prescription Only Medicines (s.58). Exemption from the restriction on the administration of Prescription Only Medicines for parenteral use is also conferred on certain persons (SI 1997 No.1830, as amended).

The classes of persons and the bodies exempted, the medicinal products to which the exemptions apply, and the conditions (if any) which attach to the retail sale, supply or administration by these exempted persons are described in this chapter.

The sale of a Prescription Only Medicine or a Pharmacy Medicine to any of these persons in accordance with the exemptions granted to them is a sale by way of wholesale dealing (SI 1980 No.1923, amended by SI 2000 No.1918). The persons who may engage in wholesale dealing, the extent to which it may be carried on at retail pharmacy businesses and the records to be kept in respect of wholesale transactions are described in Chapter 9.

## Hospitals and Health Centres

The restrictions on retail sale or supply of Prescription Only Medicines do not apply to the sale or supply of any such medicine in the course of the business of a hospital where the medicine is sold or supplied for the purpose of being administered (whether in the hospital or elsewhere) to a particular person in accordance with the written directions of a doctor or dentist relating to that person. The written directions need not satisfy the requirements for a prescription given in the Prescription Only order (SI 2000 No.1917) (see pp.71–72).

The restrictions on the sale, offer for sale, or supply of any other medicinal products (not being Prescription Only Medicines) do not apply when the sale, offer for sale, or supply is in the course of the business of a hospital or health centre for the purpose of being administered (whether in the hospital or health centre or elsewhere) in accordance with the directions of a doctor or dentist (s.55).

## National Health Service Bodies

1   The restrictions on retail sale or supply of Prescription Only Medicines do not apply to the supply of any such medicine, by:
  (a)   the Common Services Agency;
  (b)   a Health Authority or Special Health Authority;
  (c)   a National Health Service Trust;
  (d)   a Primary Care Trust; or
  (e)   a person, other than an excepted person, subject to an arrangement made with one of the bodies in (a)–(d) above for the supply of Prescription Only Medicines where the medicine is supplied for the purpose of being administered to a particular person in accordance with the written directions of a doctor or dentist relating to that person. The written directions need not satisfy the requirements for a prescription given in the Prescription Only order (SI 2000 No.1917) (see pp.71–72).

*Excepted person* means: a doctor, a dentist, or a person lawfully conducting a retail pharmacy business.

1   The restrictions on retail sale or supply of Prescription Only Medicines do not apply to the supply, or as the case may be, the administration of any such medicine by:
  (a)   the Common Services Agency;
  (b)   a Health Authority or Special Health Authority;
  (c)   a National Health Service Trust;
  (d)   a Primary Care Trust; or
  (e)   a person, other than an excepted person, subject to an arrangement made with one of the persons in (a)–(d) above for the supply,

or, the administration of Prescription Only Medicines where the medicine is supplied for the purpose of being administered, or as the case may be, is administered, to a particular person in accordance with a Patient Group Direction (PGD) and where the following conditions are satisfied:

(i) The PGD relates to the supply, or the administration, of a description or class of Prescription Only Medicine by the person who supplies or administers a Prescription Only Medicine.

(ii) The PGD has effect at the time at which the medicine is supplied or is administered.

(iii) The PGD contains the particulars specified in the regulations (see Appendix 8). If the PGD is for administration only any restrictions on quantity may be omitted.

(iv) The PGD is signed on behalf of the person specified in (a)–(d) above (*the authorising person*) by a doctor (or dentist) **and** a pharmacist.

(v) The individual who supplies or administers the medicine belongs to a class of health professionals (see Appendix 8) and is designated in writing on behalf of the authorising body for the purpose of supply or administration under the PGD.

(vi) At the time at which the medicine is supplied or administered the medicine has a marketing authorisation or a homoeopathic certificate of registration (SI 2000 No.1917).

For definition of *Patient Group Direction* see p. 77.

N.B. The particulars required in the PGD (iii) and the list of designated health professionals (v) are set out in Appendix 8.

Similar provisions apply to permit the supply or administration of Pharmacy medicines and General Sale List medicines by means of PGDs (SI 2000 No.1919).

## Doctors, Dentists and Veterinarians

The restrictions on retail sale or supply do not apply to the sale, offer for sale or supply of any medicinal products:

1   by a doctor or dentist to a patient of his/hers, or to a person under whose care such a patient is; or

2   by a veterinary surgeon or veterinary practitioner for administration by him/her or under his/her direction to an animal or herd under his/her care (ss.55 and 58).

For interpretation of *patient of his/hers* see Chapter 26.

**Unorthodox Practitioners**

Persons who at 11 February 1982 were customarily administering medicinal products to human beings by parenteral administration in the course of a business in the field of osteopathy, naturopathy, acupuncture or other similar field (except chiropody) may *administer* Prescription Only Medicines which are only so classified because they are for parenteral use and provided they do not contain an ingredient which would otherwise make them Prescription Only. The person administering the medicine must, at the request of the person to whom it is to be administered, use his/her own judgment as to the treatment required (SI 1997 No.1830).

**Midwives**

*Sale or Supply*

The restrictions on retail sale or supply do not apply to the supply or sale (but not offer for sale) of certain medicinal products by a registered midwife in the course of his/her professional practice.

The medicinal products to which this exemption applies (SI 1997 No.1830) are:

1    all medicinal products that are not Prescription Only Medicines;
2    Prescription Only Medicines containing any of the following substances but no other Prescription Only Medicine:

- Chloral hydrate
- Ergometrine maleate (only when contained in a medicinal product which is not for parenteral administration)
- Pentazocine hydrochloride
- Phytomenadione (SI 1998 No.2081)
- Triclofos sodium

*Administration*

Registered midwives may also administer parenterally in the course of their professional practice Prescription Only Medicines containing any of the following substances (SI 1997 No.1830):

- Ergometrine maleate
- Lignocaine
- Lignocaine hydrochloride
- Naloxone hydrochloride
- Oxytocin, natural and synthetic
- Pentazocine lactate
- Pethidine hydrochloride

- Phytomenadione
- Promazine hydrochloride

Additionally lignocaine, lignocaine hydrochoride and promazine hydrochloride may only be administered by a midwife while attending a woman in childbirth.

Midwives may also supply or administer Prescription Only Medicines, Pharmacy Medicines, and General Sale List medicines under PGDs (see p.80).

## Registered Nurses

The restrictions on retail supply or sale do not apply to the supply or sale (but not offer for sale) by a registered nurse in the course of his/her professional practice of any medicinal product specified in an order made by the Health Ministers (s.55). No such order has yet been made. *Registered nurse* does not include enrolled nurses (see Nurses, Midwives and Health Visitors, Chapter 22).

*Nurse practitioners* may prescribe, but not sell or supply, a limited list of Prescription Only Medicines (see p.66).

Registered nurses may also supply or administer Prescription Only Medicines, Pharmacy Medicines, and General Sale List medicines under PGDs (see p.80).

## Ophthalmic Opticians

The restrictions on retail supply or sale do not apply to the sale or supply of certain medicinal products (those in 3 and 4 below) by registered ophthalmic opticians provided they are only in the course of their professional practice and only in an emergency.

The medicinal products to which this exemption applies are:

1    all medicinal products on a General Sale List;
2    all Pharmacy Medicines;
3    Prescription Only Medicines that are either:

   (a)    eye drops containing not more than 0.5 per cent chloramphenicol; or
   (b)    eye ointments containing not more than 1.0 per cent chloramphenicol;

4    Medicines which are Prescription Only by reason only that they contain any of the following substances:

   - Atropine sulphate
   - Bethanecol chloride
   - Carbachol
   - Cyclopentolate hydrochloride

- Homatropine hydrobromide
- Naphazoline hydrochloride
- Naphazoline nitrate
- Physostigmine salicylate
- Physostigmine sulphate
- Pilocarpine hydrochloride
- Pilocarpine nitrate
- Tropicamide

Supplies of these Prescription Only Medicines may be obtained by opticians for use in their practice from a retail pharmacy business subject to the presentation of an order signed by a registered ophthalmic optician (SI 1997 No.1830).

Ophthalmic opticians may also *purchase* for use in their practice (but not for sale or supply) medicines which are Prescription Only by reason only that they contain any one or more of the following substances (SI 1980 No.1923):

- Amethocaine hydrochloride
- Framycetin sulphate
- Lignocaine hydrochloride
- Oxybuprocaine hydrochloride
- Proxymetacaine hydrochloride
- Thymoxamine hydrochloride

Registered ophthalmic opticians may also supply or administer, Prescription Only Medicines, Pharmacy Medicines, and General Sale List medicines under PGDs (see p.80).

### Chiropodists

#### Sale or Supply

The restrictions on retail sale or supply do not apply to the sale or supply of certain medicinal products by state registered chiropodists provided:

1    the sale or supply is made in the course of their professional practice; and
2    the product has been made up for sale or supply in a container elsewhere than at the place at which it is sold or supplied.

The medicinal products to which this exemption applies are:

1    medicinal products for external human use that are on a General Sale List; and
2    any of the following *Pharmacy Medicines* for external use only: ointment of heparinoid and hyaluronidase, potassium permanganate crystals or solution, and products containing, as their only active ingredients, any of the following substances, at a strength, in the case of each

substance, not exceeding that specified in relation to that substance (SI 1982 No.27):

- 9.0 per cent Borotannic complex
- 10.0 per cent Buclosamide
- 3.0 per cent Chlorquinaldol
- 1.0 per cent Clotrimazole
- 10.0 per cent Crotamiton
- 5.0 per cent Diamthazole hydrochloride
- 1.0 per cent Econazole nitrate
- 1.0 per cent Fenticlor
- 10.0 per cent Glutaraldehyde
- 0.4 per cent Hydrargaphen
- 2.0 per cent Mepyramine maleate
- 2.0 per cent Miconazole nitrate
- 2.0 per cent Phenoxypropan-2-ol
- 20.0 per cent Podophyllum resin
- 10.0 per cent Polynoxylin
- 70.0 per cent Pyrogallol
- 70.0 per cent Salicylic acid
- 0.1 per cent Thiomersal

and

- Ibuprofen; other than preparations of Ibuprofen which are Prescription Only Medicines and in an amount sufficient for three days' treatment where the md is 400 mg, the mdd 1200 mg and the maximum pack is 3600 mg (SI 1998 No.107).

State registered chiropodists who hold a certificate of competence, in the use of the following Prescription Only Medicines, issued by or with the approval of the Chiropodists Board may sell or supply any one of the following substances in the course of their professional practice:

| | |
|---|---|
| Co-dydramol 10/500 tablets: | the quantity sold or supplied to a person at any one time not to exceed an amount sufficient for three days' treatment to a maximum of 24 tablets. |
| Amorolfine HCl cream: | the maximum strength of Amorolfine not to exceed 0.25 per cent w/w. |
| Amorolfine HCl lacquer | the maximum strength of Amorolfine not to exceed 5 per cent w/v. |
| Topical Hydrocortisone | the maximum strength of Hydrocortisone in the medicinal product not to exceed 1 per cent w/w. |

The medicinal product must have been be made up for sale or supply in a container elsewhere than at a place at which it is sold (SI 1998 No.107).

## Administration

State registered chiropodists who hold a certificate of competence in the use of analgesics issued by or with the approval of the Chiropodists Board may administer parenterally in the course of their professional practice Prescription Only Medicines containing any one of the following substances (SI 1998 No.108):

- Bupivacaine hydrochloride
  Bupivacaine hydrochloride with adrenaline where the maximum strength of the adrenaline does not exceed 1 mg in 200 ml of bupivacaine hydrochloride
- Lignocaine hydrochloride
  Lignocaine hydrochloride with adrenaline where the maximum strength of the adrenaline does not exceed 1 mg in 200 ml of lignocaine hydrochloride
- Mepivacaine hydrochoride (SI 1998 No.2081)
- Prilocaine hydrochloride

State registered chiropodists may also supply or administer Prescription Only Medicines, Pharmacy Medicines, and General Sale List medicines under PGDs (see p.80).

## Ambulance Paramedics

Persons who hold a certificate of proficiency in ambulance paramedic skills issued by, or with the approval of, the Secretary of State may parenterally administer (but not sell or supply) the following Prescription Only Medicines:

1 Diazepam 5 mg per ml emulsion for injection
2 Succinylated gelatin (modified fluid gelatin) 4 per cent intravenous infusion
3 Medicines containing Ergometrine maleate 500 μg per ml with Oxytocin 5 iu per ml but no other active ingredient
4 Prescription Only Medicines containing one or more of the following substances, but no other active ingredient:

- Adrenaline acid tartrate
- Anhydrous glucose
- Benzylpenicillin
- Bretylium tosylate
- Compound sodium lactate intravenous infusion (Hartmann's Solution)
- Ergometrine maleate
- Frusemide
- Glucose
- Heparin sodium

- Lignocaine hydrochloride
- Metoclopramide
- Morphine sulphate
- Nalbuphine hydrochloride
- Naloxone hydrochloride
- Polygeline
- Sodium bicarbonate
- Sodium chloride
- Streptokinase

The administration may only be for the immediate, necessary treatment of sick or injured persons. In the case of a Prescription Only Medicine containing heparin sodium it may only be used for cannula flushing (SI 1997 No.1830).

Individuals who hold a certificate of proficiency in ambulance paramedic skills issued by the Secretary of State or individuals who are state registered paramedics may also supply or administer Prescription Only Medicines, Pharmacy Medicines, and General Sale List medicines under PGDs (see below).

## Health Professionals who Supply or Administer Prescription Only Medicines under a Patient Group Direction in Order to Assist Doctors or Dentists in Providing National Health Services

For the definition of a *Patient Group Direction* see page 77.

*Primary Medical (Dental) Services* means: the provision of general medical (dental) services under the National Health Service Act 1977, or the performance of personal medical (dental) services in connection with a pilot scheme under the National Health Service (Primary Care) Act 1997.

The restrictions on retail sale or supply of Prescription Only Medicines do not apply to the supply, or as the case may be, the administration of any such medicine by any of the following individuals: pharmacists, registered nurses and midwives, registered health visitors, registered ophthalmic opticians, state registered chiropodists, state registered ambulance paramedics, and registered orthoptists, physiotherapists and radiographers where the individual supplies or administers a medicine in order to assist a doctor or dentist in the provision of National Health Service primary medical (or dental) service. The medicine is supplied in accordance with a PGD and the following conditions apply:

1    The PGD relates to the supply, or the administration of a description or class of Prescription Only Medicine in order to assist the doctor or dentist in question in the provision of National Health Service primary medical (dental) services.

2    The PGD has effect at the time at which the medicine is supplied or is administered.

3    The PGD contains the particulars specified in the regulations (see Appendix 8). If the PGD is for administration only any restrictions on quantity may be omitted.

4    The PGD is signed by the doctor or dentist in question and, on behalf of the health authority, by a doctor **and** a pharmacist.

5    The health professional (see Appendix 8) who supplies or administers the medicine is designated in writing by the doctor or dentist in question.

6    At the time at which the medicine is supplied or administered the medicine has a marketing authorisation or a homoeopathic certificate of registration (SI 2000 No.1917).

### Persons Authorised to be Sold Cyanide Salts under the Poisons Act 1972

Pharmacists may sell amyl nitrite to such persons who would include a person or institution concerned with scientific education or research, a person who requires the article for the purpose of his/her trade or business, and a person who requires the article for the purpose of enabling him/her to comply with any requirements made by or in pursuance of any enactment with respect to the medical treatment of persons employed by that person in any trade or business carried on by him/her (see also p.90). The sale or supply must only be so far as it is necessary to enable an antidote to be available to persons at risk of cyanide poisoning (SI 1997 No.1830).

### Manufacturers of Products for Treatment of the Hair and Scalp

The holder of a manufacturer's licence for a medicinal product which is for external use in the treatment of hair and scalp conditions may sell or supply the product free from the statutory restrictions or conditions applicable to retail sales provided that:

1    the licence in question contains a provision that the licence holder shall only manufacture the medicinal product for a particular person after being requested by or on behalf of that person and in that person's presence to use his/her own judgment as to the treatment required; and

2    the sale or supply is made only upon receipt of such a request.

The medicinal products to which this exemption applies are:

1    medicinal products on a General Sale List which are for human external use; and

2    Pharmacy Medicines which are for external use in the treatment of hair and scalp conditions and which contain any of the following substances:

- not more than 5 per cent of boric acid
- isopropyl myristate or lauryl sulphate
- not more than 0.004 per cent oestrogens
- not more than 1 per cent of resorcin
- not more than 3 per cent of salicylic acid
- not more than 0.2 per cent of sodium pyrithione or
- zinc pyrithione (SI 1980 No.1924)

## Public Analysts, Sampling Officers, etc.

The restrictions on retail sale or supply do not apply to persons who sell or supply any medicinal product to any of the following:

1   a public analyst appointed under section 27 of the Food Safety Act 1990 or Article 36 of the Food (Northern Ireland) Order 1989;

2   an authorised officer within the meaning of section 5(6) of the Food Safety Act 1990;

3   a sampling officer within the meaning of Article 38(1) of the Food (Northern Ireland) Order 1989;

4   a person duly authorised by an enforcement authority under sections 111 and 112 of the Act;

5   a sampling officer within the meaning of Schedule 3 to the Act (see p.7).

The sale or supply is subject to the presentation of an order signed by or on behalf of the analyst, authorised officer, sampling officer or enforcement officer, as the case may be. It must state the status of the person signing it and the amount of the Prescription Only Medicine required and shall be only in connection with the exercise by those persons of their statutory functions (SI 1997 No.1830).

## National Health Service Drug Testing

The restrictions on retail sale or supply do not apply to persons who sell or supply any medicinal product to any person employed or engaged in connection with the scheme for testing the quality and amount of the drugs, preparations and appliances supplied under the National Health Service Act 1977, the National Health Service (Scotland) Act 1978 and the Health and Personal Social Services (Northern Ireland) Order 1972 or any subordinate legislation made under those Acts or that Order (SIs 1980 No.1924 and 1983 No.1830).

The sale or supply must be for the purpose of the relevant scheme and is subject to the presentation of an order signed on behalf of the person so employed or engaged stating:

1    the status of the person signing it;
2    the amount of the medicinal product required.

## Owners and Masters of Ships

The restrictions on supply (but not sale) of any medicinal product do not apply when the supply is made by the owner or the master of a ship which does not carry a doctor on board as part of her complement. An owner or master may also administer Prescription Only Medicines that are for parenteral administration. The supply or administration shall be only so far as is necessary for the treatment of persons on the ship (SI 1997 No.1830).

## Offshore Installations

Persons employed as qualified first-aid personnel on offshore installations may:

1    supply any medicinal product; and
2    administer all parenteral Prescription Only Medicines

only so far as is necessary for the treatment of persons on the installation (SI 1997 No.1830).

## British Standards Institution

The restrictions on the retail sale or supply do not apply to persons who sell or supply any Prescription Only Medicine, any Pharmacy Medicine or any medicinal product on a General Sale List to the British Standards Institution. The British Standard Institution **itself** cannot sell, supply or administer medicinal products.

The sale or supply shall only be for the purpose of testing containers of medicinal products or determining the standards for such containers and is subject to the presentation of an order signed on behalf of the British Standards Institution stating the status of the person signing it and the amount of the medicinal product required (SIs 1980 No.1924 and 1997 No.1830).

## Statutory Requirements as to Medical Treatment

The restrictions on retail supply (but not sale) of medicinal products do not apply to supplies made by persons requiring medicinal products for the purpose of enabling them, in the course of any business carried on by them, to comply with any requirements made by or in pursuance of any enactment with respect to the medical treatment of employees. The exemption extends to the Prescription Only Medicines and the Pharmacy Medicines specified in the relevant enactment and to medicinal products on a General Sale List.

The supply shall be:

1    for the purpose of enabling them to comply with any requirements made by or in pursuance of any such enactment; and
2    subject to such conditions and in such circumstances as may be specified in the relevant enactments (SIs 1980 No.1924 and 1997 No.1830).

## Licences and Group Authorities

The restrictions on the supply of Prescription Only Medicines do not apply to persons authorised by licences granted under regulation 5 of the Misuse of Drugs Regulations 1973 to supply the Controlled Drugs specified in the licence.

The supply shall be subject to such conditions and in such circumstances and to such an extent as may be specified in the licence.

Similarly, the restrictions on the administration of Prescription Only Medicines do not apply to persons who are authorised as members of a group by group authority granted under regulations 8(3) or 9(3) of the Misuse of Drugs Regulations 1985. The exemption is limited to the administration of Controlled Drugs that are specified in the group authority and is subject to such conditions and in such circumstances and to such an extent as may be specified in the group authority (SI 1997 No.1830).

## Royal National Lifeboat Institution

The restrictions on the retail supply of any medicinal product do not apply to supply by the Royal National Lifeboat Institution or certificated first-aiders of the Institution. The supply of any Prescription Only Medicine shall be only so far as it is necessary for the treatment of sick or injured persons in the exercise of the functions of the Institution (SI 1997 No.1830).

## British Red Cross Society, etc.

The restrictions on the retail supply of Pharmacy Medicines and all medicinal products on a General Sale List (but *not* Prescription Only Medicines) do not apply to supply by the bodies specified below and their certificated first-aid and certificated nursing members. In all cases the supply shall be only so far as it is necessary for the treatment of sick or injured persons. The bodies concerned are:

*    British Red Cross Society
*    St John Ambulance Association and Brigade

- St Andrew's Ambulance Association
- Order of Malta Ambulance Corps (SI 1980 No.1924)

### Dental Schemes

Pharmacy Medicines that are for use in the prevention of dental caries and consist of or contain sodium fluoride (see below) may be supplied, in the course of 'pre-school dental schemes', by health authorities and, in the course of 'school dental schemes', by persons carrying on the business of a school providing full-time education.

A *pre-school dental scheme* means a scheme supervised by a doctor or dentist in which medicinal products are supplied to parents or guardians of children under five for use by such children for the purpose of preventing dental caries. The supplies must be made by a registered nurse or an enrolled nurse.

A *school dental scheme* means a scheme supervised by a doctor or dentist in which medicinal products are supplied at a school to pupils of that school for the purpose of preventing dental caries. A supply may also be made to a child under 16 years of age with the consent of the parent or guardian of that child (SI 1980 No.1924).

N.B. The following are the Pharmacy Medicines affected:

1    Preparations of sodium fluoride for use in the prevention of dental caries in the form of:

   (a)    tablets or drops (maximum daily dose 2.2 mg);
   (b)    mouth rinses containing not more than 0.2 per cent (other than those for daily use);
   (c)    mouth rinses for daily use (containing not more than 0.05 per cent);
   (d)    dentifrices containing not more than 0.33 per cent.

Other medicinal products containing sodium fluoride are Prescription Only Medicines and may not be sold, supplied or administered.

### Occupational Health Schemes

Pharmacy Medicines and Prescription Only Medicines may be supplied by a person operating an *occupational health scheme*, that is, a scheme in which persons, in the course of a business carried on by them, provide facilities for their employees for the treatment or prevention of disease.

The supply must be made in the course of the scheme. The medicinal products may be supplied to the person operating the scheme in response to an order in writing signed by a doctor, a registered nurse or an enrolled nurse.

The individual supplying or administering the medicines in the course of the scheme, if not a doctor, must be:

1    a registered nurse or an enrolled nurse; and
2    where the medicinal product in question is a Prescription Only Medicine, acting in accordance with the written instructions of a doctor as to the circumstances in which Prescription Only Medicines of the description in question are to be used in the course of the occupational health scheme (SIs 1980 No.1924 and 1997 No.1830).

## Aircraft Commanders

The commander of an aircraft or the operator, that is, the person for the time being having the management of the aircraft, may supply certain medicinal products but only so far as is necessary for the immediate treatment of sick or injured persons on the aircraft. S/he may supply any medicinal products on a General Sale List, any Pharmacy Medicine and Prescription Only Medicines which are *not* for parenteral administration and which have been sold or supplied to him/her in response to an order in writing signed by a doctor. The supply of those Prescription Only Medicines by the commander or operator shall be in accordance with the written instructions of a doctor as to the circumstances in which Prescription Only Medicines of the description in question are to be used on the aircraft (SIs 1980 No.1924 and 1997 No.1830).

In addition the commander or operator of an aircraft may administer Prescription Only Medicines for parenteral use which have been sold or supplied to him/her in response to an order in writing signed by a doctor. The administration shall be only so far as is necessary for the immediate treatment of sick or injured person on the aircraft and shall be in accordance with the written instructions of a doctor as to the circumstances in which Prescription Only Medicines of the description in question are to be used on the aircraft (SI 1997 No.1830).

## Universities, etc.

The restrictions on retail sale or supply do not apply to persons selling or supplying any medicinal product to a university, an institution concerned with higher education or an institution concerned with research but only for the purposes of the education or research with which the institution is concerned. The sale or supply is subject to the presentation of an order signed by the principal of the institution with education or research or the appropriate head of department in charge of a specified course of research (SIs 1980 No.1924 and 1997 No.1830).

The order must state:

1    the name of the institution for which the medicinal product is required;
2    the purpose for which it is required; and
3    the total quantity required.

## Sales by Licence Holders

The restrictions on sale or supply do not apply to holders of marketing authorisations and holders of manufacturing licences who sell or supply medicinal products referred to in the licences to pharmacists so as to enable them to prepare an entry relating to the medicinal product in question in a tablet or capsule identification guide or similar publication. No greater quantity than is reasonably necessary for that purpose may be supplied (SI 1997 No.1830).

## Veterinary Drugs

The exemptions which apply to the retail sale or supply of certain veterinary drugs are dealt with in Chapter 12.

## Summary

- Doctors and dentists may sell or supply all medicines to their own patients.
- Veterinary practitioners and veterinary surgeons may sell or supply all medicines for administration by them, or under their direction to an animal or herd under their care.
- For the purposes of their professional practice midwives have a list of medicines which can be sold or supplied by them and another list of medicines which they may administer.
- In the course of their professional practice, and only in an emergency, ophthalmic opticians have a list of medicines which they may sell or supply to their patients. They may also purchase for use in their practice, but not for sale or supply, a limited list of Prescription Only Medicines.
- In the course of their professional practice chiropodists may sell or supply to their patients any General Sale List medicine for external use and a limited list of Pharmacy Medicines. Chiropodists holding a certificate of competence in the use of analgesics may administer, in their practice, a named list of local parenteral analgesics.
- Persons who hold a certificate of proficiency in ambulance paramedic skills may parenterally administer certain medicines for the immediate, necessary treatment of the sick or injured.

- Other categories of activities also have limited lists of medicines which they may sell or supply. These include: dental and occupational health schemes; owners and masters of ships; offshore installations; the Royal National Lifeboat Institution; public analysts; aircraft commanders; universities; and the British Red Cross.
- National Health Service Bodies and certain health professionals can supply medicines under Patient Group Directions. These include registered nurses and midwives, registered health visitors, registered ophthalmic opticians, state registered chiropodists, state registered ambulance paramedics, and registered orthoptists, physiotherapists and radiographers.

CHAPTER NINE

# Medicines Act 1968

# Wholesale Dealing

Regulations (SI 1980 No.1923, as amended) made under the Act (s.61) control the sale of medicinal products by way of wholesale dealing, that is, the sale of medicinal products to a person for the purpose of (a) selling or supplying them; or (b) administering them to human beings in the course of a business (see p.20). Sales of medicinal products by way of wholesale dealing can be made as set out below by:

1    the holder of a marketing authorisation; or
2    a person carrying on a business which consists (wholly or partly) of manufacturing medicinal products or of selling them by way of wholesale dealing. The sales must be made in the course of the business. (Retail pharmacy owners, who are not licensed as wholesalers, may sell by way of wholesale dealing provided the sales constitute no more than an inconsiderable part of the business (see p.27).)

### A Person Making Sales by Way of Wholesale Dealing

A person making sales by way of wholesale dealing must possess a wholesale dealer's licence (see p.20). Such sales must be from a specified place and the licence holder must (SI 1993 No.833):

1    Keep records, which may be in the form of invoices or on computer or in any other form, giving the following information in respect of such products which have been received or despatched:

   (a)   the date of receipt and of despatch;
   (b)   the name of the products;
   (c)   the quantity of the products received or despatched;
   (d)   the name and address of the person from whom, or to whom, the products are sold or supplied as appropriate.

2    Have at all times at his/her disposal the services of a person – *a responsible person* – who possesses in the opinion of the licensing authority:

   (a)   knowledge of the activities to be carried out and of the procedures to be performed under the licence; and
   (b)   experience in those activities and procedures which is adequate for those purposes.

   The functions of the responsible person shall be to ensure that the conditions under which the licence has been granted have been, and are being, complied with and that the quality of the products is maintained in accordance with the requirements of the appropriate marketing authorisation.

3    Obtain supplies of medicinal products only from:

   (a)   any person who is the holder of a manufacturer's licence or a wholesale dealer's licence which relates to those products; or
   (b)   any person who holds an authorisation granted by the competent authority of a member state other than the United Kingdom authorising the manufacture of such products or the distribution by way of wholesale dealing of such products.

4    Institute an emergency plan which ensures effective implementation of any recall from the market.

## Pharmacy Medicines by Wholesale Dealing

Pharmacy Medicines may be sold by way of wholesale dealing to (SI 1980 No.1923):

1    practitioners;
2    any person lawfully conducting a retail pharmacy business;
3    authorities or persons carrying on the business of a hospital or health centre;
4    holders of wholesale dealer's licences, or persons to whom the requirements to hold a wholesale dealer's licence do not apply by virtue of an exemption conferred by or under the Act;

5    Ministers of the Crown and Government Departments and officers thereof;

6    a National Health Service Trust established under the National Health Service and Community Care Act 1990 or the National Health Service (Scotland) Act 1978;

7    the Common Services Agency in Scotland;

8    any person who requires Pharmacy Medicines for the purpose of administering them to human beings in the course of a business where the medicines are for the purpose of being so administered;

9    any person who may sell or supply in circumstances corresponding to retail sale Pharmacy Medicines as specified in an exemption order (SI 1980 No.1924, as amended) (see Chapter 8) or certain herbal remedies (s.56 and SI 1977 No.2130) (see Chapter 11), or veterinary drugs (see Chapter 12).

## Prescription Only Medicines by Wholesale Dealing

Prescription Only Medicines may be sold by way of wholesale dealing to the same persons and authorities as in 1, 2, 3, 4, 5, 6 and 7 as for Pharmacy Medicines above, plus:

10    any person who is the subject of an exemption in Schedule 3 to the Prescription Only Order (SI 1997 No.1830) but only in respect of the medicinal products covered by the exemption (see Chapter 8);

11    registered ophthalmic opticians: there are certain Prescription Only Medicines which opticians are entitled to supply to their patients or use in their practice (see p.83);

12    any person selling or supplying by retail, or administering, unit preparations of Prescription Only Medicines (other than Controlled Drugs) diluted to one part in a million (6x) having been requested by or on behalf of the particular person and in that person's presence to use their own judgment as to the treatment required (see also Homoeopathic Medicines, Chapter 10).

## Wholesale Sales from a Pharmacy

A pharmacist may supply medicines by way of wholesale dealing provided that the sales constitute no more than an inconsiderable part of the business carried on at that pharmacy [s.10(7)] (see also p.27). This figure is generally accepted as not more than 5 per cent of the turnover in medicinal products; above that figure a wholesale dealer's licence would be required.

If the pharmacist does not possess a wholesale dealer's licence, then the only records required to be kept are a copy of the order or invoice relating to the supply, or alternatively an entry made in the Prescription Only Register by the owner of the retail pharmacy business (SI 1980 No.1923). Orders or invoices (and all orders required as a condition in connection with any exempted sale of a Prescription Only Medicine (see Chapter 8)) must be kept for two years from the date of the sale or supply.

If the pharmacist does possess a wholesale dealer's licence, then all the provisions of such a possession apply (see above).

### Summary

- Normally, a person who sells medicines by way of wholesale dealing requires a wholesale dealer's licence which requires special premises, records to be kept and the appointment of a responsible person whose functions are to ensure that the conditions of the licence are being complied with and that the quality of the products is maintained in accordance with the requirements of the appropriate marketing authorisation.
- A pharmacist may supply medicines by way of wholesale dealing, e.g. to a doctor, provided the sales constitute no more than an inconsiderable part of the business carried on at that pharmacy [s.10(7)] (see also p.27). This value is generally accepted as not more than 5 per cent of the turnover in medicinal products.

CHAPTER TEN

# Medicines Act 1968
# Sale and Supply of
# Homoeopathic Medicines

Most homoeopathic medicines for human use are subject to licensing procedures but, provided certain conditions are met, a simplified system of certification is permitted under regulations made under EC Council Directive 92/73/EEC (see p.17). A similar scheme is in force regarding registration of veterinary homoeopathic medicines under EC Council Directive 81/851/EEC (see p.19).

## Medicinal Products at High Dilutions (Homoeopathic Medicines)

Medicinal products at high dilutions are prepared from 'unit preparations'. *Unit preparation* means 'a preparation, including a mother tincture, prepared by a process of solution, extraction or trituration with a view to being diluted tenfold or one hundredfold, either once or repeatedly, in an inert diluent, and then used either in this diluted form or, where applicable, by impregnating tablets, granules, powders or other inert substances' (SI 1997 No.1830).

## Homoeopathic Medicines for Human Use – Licensing

See page 17.

## Homoeopathic Medicines for which General Sale is Permitted

If the seller complies with the conditions which apply to the sale or supply of products in the General Sale List (s.53) (see p.60), then s/he may sell by retail, offer or expose for sale or supply certain medicinal products which consist of one or more unit preparations diluted to the extent specified and for the use specified but not any Controlled Drug or product for parenteral administration (SI 1980 No.1924).

### Products for Internal or External Use

1   Any substance where the unit preparation has been diluted to at least one part in a million million (6c).
2   Any substance in Part II of Schedule 2 to the Pharmacy and General Sale Exemption Order (SI 1980 No.1924), where the unit preparation has been diluted to at least one part in a million (6x). These substances are listed in Table 10.1:

**Table 10.1**   Substances in Part II of Schedule 2 to SI 1980 No.1924 where the unit preparation has been diluted to at least one part in a million (6x)

| | |
|---|---|
| Adonis vernalis | Boletus laricis |
| Agaricus bulbosus | Bovista |
| Agaricus muscarius | Cade oil |
| Agnus castus | Calcium fluoride |
| Ailanthus glandulosa | Cantharis |
| Alum | Carduus marianus |
| Amethyst | Cedar wood oil |
| Ammonium iodide | Cerium oxalicum |
| Amygdalae amarae | Chalcocite |
| Apatite | Chalcopyrite |
| Apocynum androsaemifolium | Chelidonium majus |
| Apocynum cannabinum | Chenopodium oil |
| Argentite | Colocynthis |
| Argentum chloride | Convallaria majalis |
| Argentum iodide | Copper silicate, Nat. |
| Arnica | Crotalus horridus |
| Artemisia cina | Cucumis melo |
| Aspidium anthelmintica | Cucurbita |
| Aspidium filix-mas | Datura stramonium |
| Aurum sulphide | Derris |
| Balsamum copaivae | Diamond |
| Balsamum peruvianum | Ephedra vulgaris |
| Barium citrate | Ferric acetate |
| Barium sulphate | Ferrous iodide |
| Bismuth metal | Ferrous oxalate |
| Bismuth subgallate | Ferrous sulphide |
| Bismuth subnitrate | Formic acid |

*Table 10.1 contd*

| | |
|---|---|
| Gall | Potassium silicate |
| Gelsemium sempervirens | Pyrethrum |
| Gneiss | Pyrolusite |
| Granatum (Pomegranate bark) | Ranunculus acris |
| Hamamelis virginiana | Ranunculus bulbosus |
| Hepar sulfuris | Ranunculus flammula |
| Hyoscyamus niger | Ranunculus repens |
| Iris florentine | Ranunculus sceleratus |
| Jaborandi | Rhodium oxynitrate |
| Juniperus sabina | Rhododendron chrysanthemum |
| Kaolinite | Rhus toxicodendron |
| Lachmanthus tinctoria | Salicylic acid |
| Lapis albus | Scrophularia aquatica |
| Lycopodium | Sodium aluminium chloride |
| Magnesium | Sodium auro-chloride |
| Magnesium acetate | Sodium hypochlorite |
| Magnesium chloride | Sodium nitrate |
| Magnetite | Squill |
| Manganese acetate | Stannum metal |
| Nicotiana tabacum | Staphisagria |
| Nicotiana tabacum oil | Sulphur iodide |
| Oleander | Tamus communis |
| Opuntia vulgaris | Tannic acid |
| Oxalic acid | Terebinthinae oleum |
| Petroleum | Theridion |
| Phellandrum acquaticum | Topaz |
| Pix liquida | Uric acid |
| Platinum | Zinc hypophosphite |
| Platinum chloride | Zinc isovalerate |
| Potassium hydroxide | |

3    Any substance in Table A of Schedule 2 to the General Sale List Order (ingredients of licences of right) (SI 1984 No.769), where the unit preparation has been diluted to at least one part in ten (1x).

4    Any substance in Part III of Schedule 2 to the Pharmacy and General Sale Exemption Order (SI 1980 No.1924), where the unit preparation has been diluted to at least one part in ten (1x). The substances are listed in Table 10.2:

**Table 10.2**  Substances in Part III of Schedule 2 to SI 1980 No.1924, where the unit preparation has been diluted to at least one part in ten (1x)

| | |
|---|---|
| Abies excelsa | Alstonia scholaris |
| Abies nigra | Aluminium |
| Abies nobilis | Amber (Succinum) |
| Acalypha indica | Ambra grisea |
| Agate | Ammonium phosphate |
| Alisma plantago aquaticum | Angostura vera |

*Table 10.2 contd*

Anthoxanthum
Apis mellifera
Aqua marina
Aqua mellis
Aralia racemosa
Aranea diadema
Arum maculatum
Arum triphyllum
Asarum
Asperula odorata
Astacus fluviatilis
Auric chloride
Badiaga
Beech (Fagus sylvestris)
Bellis perennis
Berberis aquifolium
Borago officinalis
Butyric acid
Calcium metal
Calcium chloride
Calcium oxide
Calcium sulphate
Castoreum
Ceanothus americanus
Cedron
Cerato (Ceratostigma willmottiana)
Cherry plum (Prunus cerasifera)
Chestnut, Red and Sweet
Cholesterinum
Chrysolite
Cistus canadensis
Clematis erecta
Conchae vera
Conchiolinum
Corallium rubrum
Crab Apple
Crocus sativus
Erbium
Erigeron canadense
Fuligo
Genista tinctoria
Geum urbanum
Glycogen
Gnaphalium leontropodium
Gold
Gorse (Ulex europocus)
Graphites
Gratiola officinalis
Gymnocladus (American Coffee Tree)

Haematoxylon campechianum
Hecla Lava (Ash from Mount Hecla)
Hedeoma pulegioidies
Hedera helix
Heliotrope
Heracleum spondylium
Herniaria
Hornbeam (Carpinus betulus)
Iberis amara
Impatiens
Iris germanica
Iris pseudacorus
Jacaranda procera
Jatropha curcas
Juncus communis
Justicia adhatoda
Lamium album
Laurocerasus
Laurus nobilis oil
Ledum palustre
Lilium tigrinum
Lonicera caprifolium
Lysimachia vulgaris
Magnesium phosphate
Magnesite
Magnolia
Marum verum
Melilotus officinalis
Menispermum canadense
Mephitis putorius
Mercurialis perennis
Mimulus (Mimullis guttatus)
Moschus
Myrica gale
Myrtus communis
Ocimum basilicum
Olive
Oxalis acetosella
Pangamic acid
Paullinia cupana
Penthorum sedoides
Pollen (mixed)
Polygonatum multiflorum
Polygonum aviculare
Polypodium vulgare
Primula vulgaris
Prunella vulgaris
Ptelea trifoliata

*Table 10.2 contd*

Ratanhia
Robinia pseudoacacia
Rubia tinctorum
Rumex acetosella
Sal marina
Sarcolactic acid
Sarracenia purpurea
Scleranthus (Scleranthus annus)
Silica
Silphium laciniatum

Sodium benzoate
Spongia marina
Star of Bethlehem (Ornithogalum umbellatum)
Ulmus campestris
Vine
Walnut (Juglerus regia)
Water violet (Hottonia palustris)
Wild oat
Wild rose

### Products for External Use Only

1   Any substance in Table B of Schedule 2 to the General Sale List Order (ingredients of licences of right) (SI 1984 No.769) where the unit preparation has been diluted to at least one part in ten (1x).

2   Any substance in Part IV of Schedule 2 to the Pharmacy and General Sale Exemption Order (SI 1980 No.1924), where the unit preparation has been diluted to at least one in part in ten (1x). The substances are listed in Table 10.3:

**Table 10.3** Products for external use only listed in Part IV of Schedule 2 to SI 1980 No.1924 where the unit preparation has been diluted to at least one part in ten (1x)

Adonis vernalis
Agaricus bulbosus
Agaricus muscarius
Agnus castus
Ailanthus glandulosa
Alum
Amethyst
Ammonium iodide
Amygdalae amarae
Apatite
Apocynum androsaemifolium
Apocynum cannabinum
Argentite
Argentum chloride
Argentum iodide
Artemisia cina
Aspidium anthelmintica
Aspidium filix-mas
Aurum sulphide
Balsamum copaivae
Balsamum peruvianum
Barium citrate
Barium sulphate

Bismuth metal
Bismuth subgallate
Bismuth subnitrite
Boletus laricus
Bovista
Cade oil
Calcium fluoride
Carduus marianus
Cedar wood oil
Cerium oxalicum
Chalcocite
Chalcopyrite
Chelidonium majus
Chenopodium oil
Colocynthis
Convallaria majalis
Copper silicate, Nat.
Crotalus horridus
Cucumis melo
Cucurbita
Datura stramonium
Derris
Diamond

*Table 10.3 contd*

Ephedra vulgaris
Ferric acetate
Ferrous iodide
Ferrous oxalate
Ferrous sulphide
Formic acid
Gall
Gelsemium sempervirens
Gneiss
Hamamelis virginiana
Hepar sulfuris
Hyoscyamus niger
Iris florentine
Jaborandi
Juniperus sabina
Kaolinite
Lachmanthus tinctoria
Lapis albus
Lycopodium
Magnesium
Magnesium acetate
Magnesium chloride
Magnetite
Manganese acetate
Nicotiana tabacum
Nicotiana tabacum oil
Oleander
Opuntia vulgaris
Oxalic acid
Petroleum
Phellandrium aquaticum

Pix liquida
Platinum
Platinum chloride
Potassium hydroxide
Potassium silicate
Pyrethrum
Pyrolusite
Ranunculus acris
Ranunculus bulbosus
Ranunculus flammula
Ranunculus repens
Ranunculus sceleratus
Rhodium oxynitrate
Rhododendron chrysanthemum
Rhus toxicodendron
Salicylic acid
Scrophularia aquatica
Sodium aluminium chloride
Sodium auro-chloride
Sodium hypochlorite
Sodium nitrate
Squill
Stannum metal
Sulphur iodide
Tannic acid
Terebinthinae oleum
Topaz
Uric acid
Zinc hypophosphite
Zinc isovalerate

## Homoeopathic Medicines for Treatment According to the Judgment of the Seller

If the person selling the product is requested by or on behalf of a particular person and in that person's presence to use their own judgment as to the treatment required then they may sell by retail, offer or expose for sale or supply certain medicinal products (other than excluded products) which are registered or consist solely of one or more unit preparations diluted to the extent specified and for the use specified. The substances to which this exemption applies and which are subject to section 53 of the Act (see p.60) are listed below:

### Products for Internal or External use

1   Any substance, where the unit preparation has been diluted to at least one part in a million (6x).

2     Any substance listed in Part I of Schedule 2 to the Pharmacy and General Sale Exemption Order (SI 1980 No.1924) where the unit preparation has been diluted to at least one part in a thousand (3x). The substances are listed in Table 10.4:

**Table 10.4**   Substances listed in Part I of Schedule 2 to SI 1980 No.1924, where the unit preparation has been diluted to at least one part in a thousand (3x)

| | |
|---|---|
| Agaricus muscarius | Chenopodium oil |
| Ailanthus glandulosa | Cina |
| Apocynum cannabinum | Colocynthis |
| Aurum iodatum | Convallaria majalis |
| Belladonna | Gelsemium sempervirens |
| Bismuth subgallate | Hyoscyamus niger |
| Bryonia alba dioica | Lycopodium |
| Calcium fluoride | Manganese acetate |
| Cantharis | Ranunculus bulbosus |
| Cerium oxalicum | Terebinthinae oleum |
| Chelidonium majus | |

3     Any substance in Table A of Schedule 2 to the General Sale List Order (SI 1984 No.769) (ingredients of licence of right products), where the unit preparation has been diluted to at least one part in ten (1x).
4     Any substance in Part III of Schedule 2 to the Pharmacy and General Sale Exemptions Order (SI 1980 No.1924), where the unit preparation has been diluted to at least one part in ten (1x). The substances are listed above, in Tables 10.1, 10.2 and 10.3.
5     any **registered** homoeopathic medicinal product for human use other than an excluded product (SI 1998 No.2368).

*Excluded products* include Controlled Drugs, Prescription Only Medicines and any in a class specified in Schedule 3 of the main order (SI 1984 No.769), i.e. medicines for use as anthelmintics, for parenteral administration, or for use as eye drops or eye ointments.

### Products for External Use Only

The substances and unit dilutions for external use are the same as those for homoeopathic medicines for which General Sale is permitted.

### Homoeopathic Medicines for Animal Use – Licensing

See page 19.

## Summary

- Most homoeopathic medicines are on the General Sale List and may be sold from any retail shop which is closable to the public.
- Certain listed homoeopathic medicines may be sold if the seller is requested by a customer to use the seller's own judgment as to the treatment required. There are certain excluded categories.

## Further Reading

MAL leaflet No.21 (to be revised). Medicines Control Agency.

# CHAPTER ELEVEN

# Medicines Act 1968

## Herbal Remedies

A *herbal remedy* is a medicinal product consisting of a substance produced by subjecting a plant or plants to drying, crushing or any other process, or of a mixture whose sole ingredients are two or more substances so produced, or of a mixture whose sole ingredients are one or more substances so produced and water or some other inert substance (s.132).

### Exemption from Licensing

Subject to the limitations described in this chapter, herbal remedies are exempted from licensing requirements by section 12 of the Act which describes remedies of two kinds thus:

1   Any herbal remedy which is manufactured or assembled on premises of which the person carrying on the business is the occupier and which s/he is able to close so as to exclude the public, and the person carrying on the business sells or supplies the remedy for administration to a particular person after being requested by or on behalf of that person and in that person's presence to use his/her own judgment as to the treatment required.

    (For convenience these can be described as 'herbal practitioner's remedies', although that term is not used in the statute.)

2    Any herbal remedy where the process to which the plant or plants are subjected in producing the remedy consists only of drying, crushing or comminuting, and the remedy is, or is to be, sold or supplied:

(a)    under a designation which only specifies the plant or plants and the process and does not apply any other name to the remedy; and

(b)    without any written recommendation (whether by means of a labelled container or package or a leaflet or in any other way) as to the use of the remedy (see also p.46).

## Exemptions from Controls on Retail Sale

There is an exemption for herbal remedies in section 56 of the Act from the restrictions on retail sale and supply of medicinal products in sections 52 and 53 (see Chapters 5 and 6). The exemption, which extends to both classes 1 and 2 described above, applies to anything done at premises of which the person carrying on the business in question is the occupier and which s/he is able to close so as to exclude the public (s.56).

This general exemption is modified by the Herbal Remedies Order (SI 1977 No.2130) so that there is no exemption (except as below) from the restriction on retail sale or supply for herbal remedies:

1    that are not on the General Sale List;
2    that are not exempted from licensing as in 2 above;
3    that are exempted from licensing as in 2 above but contain one or more of the substances listed in Part I or Part II of the Schedule to the order (see Exemption of 'Herbal Practitioners', below).

The effect of this is that any shopkeeper can sell:

(a)    any herbal remedy on the General Sale List; or
(b)    any herbal remedy which is exempted from licensing as in 1 above, except those in Part I and Part II of the Schedule.

## Further Exemption for Shopkeepers

The order further modifies the controls on retail sale so that any person can, subject to certain conditions, sell or supply by retail any herbal remedy included under 1, 2 or 3 above where the process to which the plant or plants are subjected consists of drying, crushing or comminuting with or without any subsequent process of tabletting, pill-making, compressing or diluting with water but not any other process.

The conditions are that:

4    the herbal remedy does not contain a substance listed in Part I or Part II of the Schedule (see below);

5    the seller (or supplier) of the herbal remedy either:

(a)   has notified the enforcement authority in the United Kingdom in writing that s/he is selling or supplying or intending to sell or supply herbal remedies included in 1, 2 or 3 in the section above on Exemptions from Controls on Retail Sale, which are prepared by the limited processes described in the opening paragraph of this chapter; or

(b)   has a manufacturer's licence granted under Part II of the Act in respect of that remedy.

## Exemption of 'Herbal Practitioners'

In addition to the exemptions already described, the order (SI 1977 No.2130) provides further exemptions for herbal remedies, prepared by any process, from the controls on retail sale or supply provided:

1    the herbal remedy concerned does not contain:

(a)   any substance included in Part I of the Schedule to the order; or

(b)   any substance in Part III of the order, except for internal remedies, when sold or supplied in or from containers or packages labelled to show a dosage not exceeding that specified, or for external remedies, when sold or supplied with the strength of the substance not exceeding the percentage specified.

2    the person selling or supplying the herbal remedy (a *herbal practitioner*):

(a)   has been requested by or on behalf of a particular person and in that person's presence to use his/her own judgment as to the treatment required; and

(b)   has notified the enforcement authority in writing that s/he is selling or supplying or intends to sell or supply from the premises specified in the notice herbal remedies as in 1, 2 or 3 in the section above on Exemptions from Controls on Retail Sale.

A person (*herbal practitioner*) selling or supplying herbal remedies, to which the exemption described in this section applies, may be required to furnish to the enforcement authority a list of the substances contained in those herbal remedies. The exemption will not apply if the *herbal practitioner* fails to furnish the list within the time specified in the notice served upon him/her by the enforcement authority.

## Enforcement Authority

The term *enforcement authority* includes the Secretaries of State and the Royal Pharmaceutical Society of Great Britain.

**Schedule to the Herbal Remedies Order**

The Schedule to the Medicines (Retail Sale or Supply of Herbal Remedies) Order 1977 (SI 1977 No.2130) is in three parts, reflecting the different degrees of control over the retail sale or supply of the substances in each part.

*Part I*

The substances in this part (see Table 11.1) may only be sold by retail at registered pharmacies and by or under the supervision of a pharmacist.

**Table 11.1**  Substances in Part I of the Schedule to SI 1977 No.2130

| Common Name | Botanical Name |
| --- | --- |
| Areca | *Areca catechu* |
| Canadian Hemp | *Apocynum cannabinum* |
| Catha | *Catha edulis* |
| Chenopodium | *Chenopodium ambrosioides* var. *anthelminticum* |
| Crotalaria fulva | *Crotalaria berberoana* |
| Crotalaria spect. | *Crotalaria spectabilis* |
| Cucurbita | *Cucurbita maxima* |
| Duboisia | *Duboisia leichardtii* |
|  | *Duboisia myoporoides* |
| Elaterium | *Ecballium elaterium* |
| Embelia | *Embelia ribes* |
|  | *Embelia robusta* |
| Erysimum | *Erysimum canescens* |
| Holarrhena | *Holarrhena antidysenterica* |
| Kamala | *Mallotus philippinensis* |
| Kousso | *Brayera anthelmintica* |
| Male fern | *Dryopteris filix mas* |
| Mistletoe berry | *Viscum album* |
| Poison ivy | *Rhus radicans* |
| Pomegranate bark | *Punica granatum* |
| Santonica | *Artemisia cina* |
| Savin | *Juniperus sabina* |
| Scopolia | *Scopolia carniolica* |
|  | *Scopolia japonica* |
| Stavesacre seeds | *Delphinium staphisagria* |
| Strophanthus | *Strophanthus courmonti* |
|  | *Strophanthus emini* |
|  | *Strophanthus gratus* |
|  | *Strophanthus hispidus* |
|  | *Strophanthus kombe* |
|  | *Strophanthus nicholsoni* |
|  | *Strophanthus sarmentosus* |
| Slippery elm bark | *Ulmus fulva* |
| (whole or unpowdered) | *Ulmus rubra* |
| Yohimbe bark | *Pausinystalia yohimbe* |

## Part II

The list of substances in this part is the same as that in Part III. They may only be sold by retail from registered pharmacies and by or under the supervision of a pharmacist except when the conditions under Part III are met (see below).

## Part III

Persons who comply with the requirements set out on page 110 (commonly known as *herbal practitioners*) can sell or supply by retail herbal remedies containing any of the substances listed in Table 11.2 subject to the maximum dosages and strengths indicated.

**Table 11.2**    Substances in Part III of the Schedule to SI 1977 No.2130

| | Column 1 | Column 2 | Column 3 |
|---|---|---|---|
| Common Name | *Substance*<br><br>*Botanical Name* | *Maximum dose and maximum daily dose* | *Percentage* |
| Aconite | *Aconitum balrourii*<br>*Aconitum chasmanthum*<br>*Aconitum deinorrhizum*<br>*Aconitum lycoctonum*<br>*Aconitum napellus*<br>*Aconitum spicatum*<br>*Aconitum stoerkianum*<br>*Aconitum uncinatum* var.<br>    *japonicum* | | 1.3% |
| Adoni vernalis | *Adonis vernalis* | 100 mg (md)<br>300 mg (mdd) | |
| Belladonna herb | *Atropa acuminata*<br>*Atropa belladonna* | 150 mg (mdd)<br>50 mg (md) | |
| Belladonna root | *Atropa acuminata*<br>*Atropa belladonna* | 90 mg (mdd)<br>30 mg (md) | |
| Celandine | *Chelidonium majus* | 2 g   (md)<br>6 g   (mdd) | |
| Cinchona bark | *Cinchona calisaya*<br>*Cinchona ledgerana*<br>*Cinchona micrantha*<br>*Cinchona officinalis*<br>*Cinchona succirubra* | 250 mg (md)<br>750 mg (mdd) | |
| Colchicum corm | *Colchicum autimnale* | 100 mg (md)<br>300 mg (mdd) | |
| Conium leaf | *Conium maculatum* | | 7% |
| Conium fruits | *Conium maculatum* | | 7% |
| Convallaria | *Convallaria majalis* | 150 mg (md)<br>450 mg (mdd) | |

*Table 11.2 contd.*

| Common Name | Column 1 | Column 2 | Column 3 |
|---|---|---|---|
| | Substance | Maximum dose and maximum | |
| Common Name | Botanical Name | daily dose | Percentage |
| Ephedra | Ephedra distachya | | |
| | Ephedra equisetina | | |
| | Ephedra gerardiana | 1800 mg (mdd) | |
| | Ephedra sinica | | |
| Gelsemium | Gelsemium sempervirens | 25 mg (md) | |
| | | 75 mg (mdd) | |
| Hyoscyamus | Hyoscyamus albus | 300 mg (mdd) | |
| | Hyoscyamus muticus | | |
| | Hyoscyamus niger | 100 mg (md) | |
| Jaborandi | Pilocarpus jaborandi | | 5% |
| | Pilocarpus microphyllus | | |
| Lobelia | Lobelia inflata | 200 mg (md) | |
| | | 600 mg (mdd) | |
| Poison Oak | Rhus toxicodendron | | 10% |
| Quebracho | Aspidosperma | 50 mg (md) | |
| | quebrachoblanco | 150 mg (mdd) | |
| Ragwort | Senecio jacobaea | | 10% |
| Stramonium | Datura innoxia | 150 mg (mdd) | |
| | Datura stramonium | 50 mg (md) | |

## Banned Herbal Remedies

### Aristolochia

The various forms of *Aristolochia* were made Prescription Only Medicines on 13 January 1997. Since then the sale, supply and importation of medicinal products consisting or containing a plant belonging to the species of the genus *Aristolochia* or belonging to any of the species *Akebia quinata, Akebia trifoliata, Clematis armandi, Clematis montana, Cocculus laurifolius, Cocculus orbiculatus, Cocculus trilobus* and *Stephania tetrandra*, consisting of or containing an extract from such a plant are prohibited. The ban was extended on 16th June 2000 (SI 2000 No.1368).

### Mu Tong and Fangji

The sale, supply and importation of medicinal products is prohibited where, at the time of the sale, supply or importation, the label on the container or package, or any document accompanying the product indicates in any language that the product consists of or contains Mu Tong or Fangji or that the product consists of or contains *Akebia quinata, Akebia trifoliata, Clematis armandi, Clematis montana, Cocculus laurifolius, Cocculus orbiculatus, Cocculus trilobus* and *Stephania tetrandra,* or an extract from such a plant.

The prohibitions relating to *Aristolochia,* Mu Tong and Fangji do not apply to the importation from the states of the European Union or European Economic Area states, to the importation made by or on behalf of food and medicines enforcement agencies, or to products which possess a marketing authorisation or a homoeopathic certificate of registration (SI 2000 No.1368).

## Summary

- Ordinary shopkeepers can sell herbal remedies on the General Sale List and herbal remedies which are merely dried, crushed or comminuted without any written recommendation, but not those in the Schedule to the order.
- Shopkeepers who have a manufacturer's licence, or choose to notify the enforcement authority, can sell dried, crushed and comminuted herbs which have also been subjected to certain other limited processes, but not those in the Schedule to the order.
- Herbal practitioners can sell herbal remedies of the kind described above which shopkeepers can sell and also those remedies containing substances in and subject to the requirements of Part III of the Schedule to the order.
- Herbal remedies containing substances in Part I or Part II of the Schedule to the order may only be sold from pharmacies.
- Certain herbals have been banned, e.g. *Aristolochia,* and Mu Tong and Fangji.

## Further Reading

Newall A. N., Anderson L. A., Phillipson J. D. (1996). *Herbal Medicines.* London: Pharmaceutical Press.

# CHAPTER TWELVE

# Medicines Act 1968

# Veterinary Medicinal Products –

# Exemptions from Controls

A *veterinary medicinal product* means a medicinal product which is manufactured, sold, supplied, imported or exported for the purpose of being administered to animals (including birds, fish and reptiles), but not for the purpose of being administered to human beings (s.132).

## Classes of Veterinary Medicinal Products

All medicinal products, whether for administration to human beings or veterinary medicinal products, fall into one of three categories, namely:

1 those on a General Sale List;
2 those on a Prescription Only List; or
3 those not included in either the Prescription Only List or the General Sale List. When for administration to human beings these are Pharmacy Medicines for sale only in pharmacies.

The requirements of the Medicines Act and the restrictions it imposes on the retail sale or supply of these categories of medicinal products have been fully explained in Chapter 5 (Pharmacy Medicines), Chapter 6 (General Sale Medicines) and Chapter 7 (Prescription Only Medicines).

Orders made under the Act provide some exemptions for certain classes of persons from the restrictions on retail sale or supply of veterinary medicinal products. Sales made by these persons are exempted retail sales. Sales made to them are sales by way of wholesale dealing (see Chapter 9).

The extent of the various exemptions and the conditions, if any, attached to them are dealt with in this chapter. The relevant Statutory Instruments are those dealing with Prescription Only Medicines (SI 1991 No.1392, as amended); Pharmacy and General Sale exemptions (SI 1980 No.1924); Veterinary medicinal products exemptions for merchants (SI 1998 No.1044) and the miscellaneous provisions (SI 1980 No.1923, as amended).

## Record Keeping for Veterinary Products

Any person who sells veterinary medicinal products by retail intended for administration to animals whose flesh or products are intended for human consumption and in respect of which a withdrawal period must be observed must keep a record.

Similarly any person who sells any other veterinary medicinal products by retail intended for administration to such animals, unless the products are on a General Sale List must keep records.

For each incoming and outgoing transaction a record must be kept of the:

1    date of transaction;
2    name of the product sold;
3    manufacturer's batch number;
4    quantity sold or received;
5    name and address of supplier or recipient; and
6    name and address of the prescribing veterinarian (where relevant) and a copy of the prescription.

All records must be durable but may be kept by electronic means. They must be kept for three years and be made available on request to any person having a duty of enforcement. The Royal Pharmaceutical Society has the duty to enforce concurrently with the Ministers in England and Scotland and the National Assembly for Wales (SI 2000 No.7).

## Veterinary Surgeons and Practitioners

The restrictions on retail sale or supply do not apply to the sale, offer for sale or supply of any medicinal product by a veterinary surgeon or practitioner for administration by him/her or under his/her direction to an animal or herd under his/her care (ss.55 and 58). Furthermore, the restrictions on retail sale or supply do not apply to any person who sells any medicinal product to a veterinary surgeon or practitioner (SIs 1980 No.1924 and 1991 No.1392).

## Poultry Vaccine Suppliers

Persons providing a poultry vaccination service may sell a poultry vaccine whose name and authorisation number appears on a list kept by the Minister of Agriculture, Fisheries and Food in accordance with Article 3 of the Exemption Order (SI 1998 No.1044) and which, if or when for parenteral administration, is a Prescription Only Medicine. However, such sales or supplies may only be made to a person who has charge of animals for the purpose of and in the course of carrying on a business, whether as his/her sole business activity or as a substantial part of his/her business activities (SI 1991 No.1392).

Similarly, the restrictions on retail sale or supply do not apply to a person who sells or supplies any of those vaccines to a person providing a poultry vaccination service, subject to the presentation of an order signed by the purchaser stating the amount of the vaccines required (SIs 1980 No.1924 and 1991 No.1392).

## Exempted Veterinary Medicinal Products – Sale or Supply

The Medicines (Exemptions for Merchants in Veterinary Drugs) Order 1998 (SI 1998 No.1044) permits certain licensed medicinal products (known as PML medicinal products) which are not on a General Sale List to be sold or supplied by retail by:

1    the holders of marketing authorisations;
2    a specially authorised person, that is, a person specially authorised either, by a direction of the licensing authority, to assemble the veterinary drug otherwise than in accordance with the manufacturer's licence or, by the marketing authorisation, to sell the drug under the alternative name specified in the licence/authorisation;
3    by certain categories of dealers.

N.B. Veterinarians and pharmacists are permitted to sell PML products.

The order applies to any veterinary drug whose name and authorisation number appears on a list kept by the Minister of Agriculture, Fisheries and Food. The explanatory note to the Statutory Instrument states that this list will be open for inspection at the office of the Veterinary Medicines Directorate, Woodham Lane, Addlestone, Surrey KT15 3NB and copies will be made publicly available and published in a regular bulletin.

Two classes of dealers are described in the order:

1    *Agricultural Merchants* who may sell any veterinary medicinal products listed by the Minister subject to certain conditions (see below).

An *Agricultural merchant* means a person who carries on a business involving in whole or in part the sale of agricultural requisites, being things used for soil cultivation or keeping of animals for production of food or game, equipment for collecting produce from animals kept for production of food, things for the maintenance of that equipment, and protective clothing.

2     *Saddlers* who may sell any veterinary medicinal product listed by the Minister which is a horse wormer, dog wormer or cat wormer.

A *saddler* means a person carrying on a business involving in whole or in part the sale of saddlery requisites, being products and equipment and things for the maintenance of that equipment, for keeping of horses or ponies, and including human clothing for that purpose.

## Restrictions on Sale or Supply of Veterinary Medicinal Products and Horse Wormers Listed by the Minister

The sale of listed veterinary medicinal products and wormers by merchants and saddlers is subject to the certain conditions.

### Registration Requirements

Registration requirements are set out in SI 1998 No.1044, made under the Medicines Act 1968, as amended by the Animal Health and Welfare Act 1984. The *register* is maintained by the Royal Pharmaceutical Society of Great Britain, which is also responsible for inspection and enforcement. In Northern Ireland, the register is kept by the Department of Health and Social Services for Northern Ireland.

An agricultural merchant or saddler is subject to conditions in respect of inclusion and retention on the register, namely s/he must:

1     Register his/her name and details of all premises where s/he sells or stores veterinary medicinal products.
2     Give details for each premises of the name and qualifications of a person nominated to be a suitably qualified person for the premises.
3     Pay the appropriate fee for each set of premises.
4     Pay a retention fee annually in respect of each premises and notify any change in particulars as soon as possible. Failure to pay the retention fees leads to removal from the register and the payment of higher fees to have the premises restored to the register.
5     Be a fit and proper person to sell such veterinary drugs.

In addition:

6     All premises used for sale or storage must be suitable for the purpose, and premises to be used for sale, which may include a stall of a permanent nature at a market or agricultural showground, must be capable of being closed so as to exclude the public. Any alteration to

premises which affect their suitability must be notified to the registration authority.

7   Any proposed permanent change to the suitably qualified person nominated must be notified to the registration authority.

## Conditions of Sale

The conditions which must be complied with by an agricultural merchant or a saddler are that:

1   The premises at which sales of veterinary drugs are made must be occupied by him/her and under his/her control at all times when the premises are open for business, and s/he must store those products in a part of the premises partitioned off or otherwise separated from the rest of the premises and to which the public have no access.

2   The suitably qualified person nominated and notified or, in his/her temporary absence, an alternative suitably qualified person, shall authorise each sale of veterinary drugs.

3   Only exempted veterinary drugs listed by the Minister may be sold.

4   Each veterinary drug sold must be in the container in which it was made up for sale by the manufacturer or assembler, which has not been opened since then, and must bear the manufacturer's label, which has not been altered, and not be sold after the date of expiry indicated on its label.

5   The sale is not by self-service methods.

6   If the product is a cat wormer, a dog wormer, or a horse wormer, the sale to is to a person whom s/he knows or has reasonable cause to believe has in his/her charge a cat if it is a cat wormer, a dog if it is a dog wormer or a horse or pony if it is a horse wormer and will use the product for the treatment of the animal concerned.

7   S/he must keep records (see below).

Additional conditions to be complied with by an agricultural merchant are:

8   If the product is **not** a cat wormer, dog wormer, or horse wormer, the sale to is to a person whom s/he knows or has reasonable cause to believe has animals under his/her control for the purpose of, and in the course of, carrying on a business either as his/her sole business activity or as a part of his/her business activities. N.B. This does not extend to a business wholly or mainly concerned with sales to the owners of pet animals. The keeping of animals as pets or the keeping of poultry, etc. for the sole use of the owner or his/her family or to give away is not 'carrying on a business'.

9   If the product is an organophosphate sheep dip or if the product is a sheep dip, not intended for export, the sale is made to a person whom the seller knows, or has reasonable cause to believe, is the holder, or the employer of or a person acting on behalf of the holder, of a Certificate of

Competence, and the agricultural merchant keeps a record of the certificate number for three years from the date of the sale.

*Certificate of Competence* means a Certificate of Competence in the Safe Use of Sheep Dips issued by the National Proficiency Tests Council or by that Council and the Department of Agriculture in Northern Ireland showing that parts 1 and 2 of the assessment have been satisfactorily completed.

### Records

For each incoming and outgoing transaction an agricultural merchant or a saddler must keep the following records:

1    the date of the transaction;
2    the identity of the products;
3    the manufacturer's batch number;
4    the quantity received or supplied; and
5    the name and address of the supplier or recipient.

At least once a year a detailed audit of all transactions has to be carried out and recorded, with incoming and out goings reconciled with those held in stock and any discrepancies recorded.

All records shall be durable, but may be kept by electronic means, and shall be kept for a period of three years from the date of the transaction or audit and made available to the registration authority or any person authorised by the enforcement authority (SI 1998 No.1044).

### Code of Good Practice

There is a code of good practice for the sale and supply of animal medicines prepared by the Animal Medicines Training Regulatory Authority (AMTRA) which sets out the standards which agricultural merchants and saddlers dealing with animal medicines are expected to meet. The code has no legal status but supplements the principal legal requirements with other provisions relating to personnel, sale and storage arrangements and standards of premises.

### Labelling Requirements for Veterinary Medicinal Products

See Chapter 14.

## Prescriptions

A prescription for a Prescription Only Medicine must comply with the requirements given on pages 71–72. In addition, it must carry a declaration by the veterinarian giving it that the medicine is prescribed for an animal or herd under his/her care (SI 1991 No.1392).

## Summary

* Veterinary surgeons and practitioners may sell or supply any medicinal product for administration by them, or under their direction, to an animal or herd under their care.
* There is a class of veterinary medicines known as Medicines Listed by the Minister which may be sold by pharmacists or veterinarians and by registered agricultural merchants and registered saddlers.
* When sold by an agricultural merchant or saddler, specific conditions apply to the sale and detailed records have to be kept.
* There is a code of practice for agricultural merchants and for saddlers.

## Further Reading

MAVIS advisory leaflets. Veterinary Medicines Directorate.

CHAPTER THIRTEEN

# Medicines Act 1968

# Prohibitions for Protection of

# the Purchaser

A prohibition, either total or limited in some way, on the sale, supply or importation of specified classes of medicinal products or of particular medicinal products may be imposed by order of the appropriate Ministers if it appears to them necessary to do so in the interest of safety. Before making such an order the Ministers are required to consult the appropriate committee (or the Medicines Commission) and to consider representations made by other organisations who have been consulted. These requirements may be waived if, in the opinion of the Ministers, it is essential to make the order with immediate effect to avoid serious danger to health, whether of human beings or of animals. An order made without consultation is effective for three months only but may be renewed (s.62).

Any person who, otherwise than for performing or exercising a statutory duty or power, is in possession of such a medicinal product, knowing or having reasonable cause to suspect that it was sold, supplied or imported in contravention of the order, is guilty of an offence (s.67) (see also p.6).

### Section 62 Orders

*Bal Chivan Chamcho*

The sale, supply, or importation of this medicinal product is prohibited. It is a baby tonic in the form of a dark brown aromatic solid substance affixed to a spoon-shaped metal appliance (SI 1977 No.670, as amended). The prohibition does not apply to importation from a member state of the European Union or if it originated in a state within the European Economic Area. Neither does the prohibition apply to the sale or supply to a public analyst, a sampling officer, or a person duly authorised by an enforcement authority under the Act.

### Non-medicinal Antimicrobial Substances

There are a number of antimicrobial substances which have medicinal and non-medicinal uses (e.g. sulphanilamide, streptomycin and certain other antibiotics). For medicinal purposes they are classed as Prescription Only medicinal products. When used for non-medicinal purposes they are also within the control of the Medicines Act by virtue of an order made under section 105 (see p.3). Further orders under section 62 (SIs 1977 No.2131 and 1992 No.2684) prohibit the sale or supply of these substances when used for non-medicinal purposes except for certain purposes. The list of substances and the exceptions to the prohibition on sale are set out in Appendices 1 and 2.

### Stilbenes and Thyrostatic Substances

Regulations (SI 1982 No.626) made under the European Communities Act 1972 prohibit the administration to farm animals of any of these substances or of medicinal products or animal feeding stuffs containing them. Administration is not prohibited if prior steps are taken to ensure that the animals and their products are unavailable for animal or human consumption.

### Chloroform

The sale or supply of medicinal products for human use which consist of or contain chloroform is prohibited (SI 1979 No.382) subject to the following exceptions. A sale or supply made:

1   by a doctor or dentist to a patient of his/hers, where the medicinal product has been specially prepared by that doctor or dentist for administration to that particular patient; or
2   by a doctor or dentist who has specially prepared the medicinal product at the request of another doctor or dentist for administration to a particular patient of that other doctor or dentist; or
3   from a pharmacy or hospital where the medicinal product has been specially prepared in accordance with a prescription given by a doctor or dentist for a particular patient; or
4   to a hospital, a doctor or a dentist for use as an anaesthetic; or
5   to a person who buys it for the purpose of reselling it to a hospital, a doctor or a dentist for use as an anaesthetic; or

6   where the medicinal product contains chloroform in a proportion of not more than 0.5 per cent (w/w) or (v/v); or

7   where the medicinal product is solely for use in dental surgery; or

8   where the medicinal product is solely for use by being applied to the external surface of the body which for the purpose of this order does not include any part of the mouth, teeth or mucous membranes; or

9   where the medicinal product is for export; or

10   where the medicinal product is sold for use as an ingredient in the preparation of a substance or article in a pharmacy, a hospital or by a doctor or dentist.

For the purposes of sale or supply (but not of importation) of medicines for human use the exemption limits for chloroform given in the Prescription Only and General Sale List orders are overridden by this order. The practical effect is that only products falling within 6 and 8 above may be sold by retail to the general public. But for the purposes of record keeping the exemption levels in the Prescription Only order still apply, so that records are required to be kept only of sales or supplies of products for internal use which contain more than 5 per cent of chloroform w/w or v/v as appropriate.

## Adulteration of Medicinal Products

It is an offence:

1   to add any substance to, or abstract any substance from, a medicinal product so as to affect injuriously the composition of the product, with intent that the product shall be sold or supplied in that state; or

2   to sell or supply, or offer or expose for sale or supply, or have in possession for the purpose of sale or supply, any medicinal product whose composition has been injuriously affected by the addition or abstraction of any substance (s.63).

It is also an offence to sell (or supply on a practitioner's prescription) to the prejudice of the purchaser (or patient) any medicinal product which is not of the nature or quality demanded by the purchaser (or specified in the prescription) (s.64).

There is no offence if the medicinal product contains some extraneous matter, the presence of which is proved to be an inevitable consequence of the process of manufacture, nor is it an offence where:

1   a substance has been added to, or abstracted from, the medicinal product which did not injuriously affect the composition of the product and was not carried out fraudulently; and

2    the product was sold having attached to it, or to a container or package in which it was sold, a conspicuous notice of adequate size and legibly printed specifying the substance added or abstracted.

## False or Misleading Advertisements or Representations

An advertisement or representation (whether it contains an accurate statement of the composition of medicinal products of the description or not) is taken to be false or misleading if (but only if) it falsely describes the medicinal products to which it relates, or is likely to mislead as to the nature or quality of medicinal products of that description or as to their uses or effects (s.93).

A document, advertisement or representation is taken to be likely to mislead as to the uses or effects of medicinal products of a particular description if it is likely to mislead as to any of the following matters:

1    any purposes for which medicinal products of that description can with reasonably safety be used;
2    any purposes for which such products cannot be so used;
3    any effects which such products when used (or when used in any particular way referred to in the document, advertisement or representation) produce or are intended to produce [s.130(10)].

Medicinal products are 'of the same description' if (but only if) they are manufactured to the same specifications, and they are or are to be, sold, supplied, imported or exported in the same pharmaceutical form [s.130(8)].

The purposes for which medicinal products of any description may be recommended for use are limited to those specified in the licence relating to them. Any recommendation that they may be used for purposes other than those specified is an *unauthorised recommendation* [s.93(1) and (10)].

Any commercially interested party, or other person acting at that party's request or with their consent, who issues or causes to be issued a false or misleading advertisement or one containing an unauthorised recommendation relating to medicinal products of any description is guilty of an offence (s.93). It is also an offence [s.93(3)] to make, in the course of a relevant business, a false or misleading representation or one which amounts to an unauthorised recommendation:

1    in connection with the sale or offer for sale of a medicinal product; or
2    to a practitioner, or to a patient or a client, for the purpose of inducing the practitioner to prescribe medicinal products of a particular description; or
3    to a person for the purpose of inducing him/her to purchase medicinal products of a particular description from a retailer.

A *relevant business* is one which consists of or includes the sale or supply of medicinal products [s.92(4)].

**Summary**

- The sale or supply of some medicinal products is either prohibited (e.g. Bal Chivan Chamcho) or prohibited subject to exceptions (e.g. stilbenes and thyrostatic substances, non-medicinal antimicrobials and chloroform).
- It is an offence to adulterate, by way of addition or abstraction, a medicinal product, or to sell, supply or possess an adulterated product.
- It is an offence to sell or supply to the prejudice of the purchaser (or patient) any medicinal product which is not of the nature or quality demanded by the purchaser (or specified on a prescription).
- An advertisement is false or misleading if it falsely describes the medicinal product to which it relates or is likely to mislead as to the nature and quality of the product or to its use.

# CHAPTER FOURTEEN

# Medicines Act 1968

## Containers, Packages and Identification

### Regulations and Penalties

Regulations may be made as the appropriate Ministers consider expedient or necessary for promoting the safety of medicinal products and for securing (i) that such products are correctly described and readily identifiable, and (ii) that any appropriate warning or information or instruction is given, and that false or other misleading information is not given. These regulations may apply to:

1    the labelling of containers [s.85(1)];
2    the labelling of packages [s.85(1)];
3    the display of distinctive marks on containers and packages [s.85(1)];
4    leaflets [s.86(1)];
5    colour or shape [s.88(1)];
6    distinctive marks to be displayed on such products [s.88(1)];
7    information to be displayed on automatic machines (s.89).

For the same purposes and also for preserving the quality of the products, regulations may prohibit the sale of medicinal products in containers which do not comply with specified requirements, in particular as to the strength, shape or pattern of the containers or of the materials of which they are made (s.87).

It is an offence for any person in the course of a business carried on by him/her to sell or supply, or have in their possession for the purpose of sale or supply, any medicinal product or any leaflet relating to medicinal products in such circumstances as to contravene any requirements which may be imposed by these regulations [ss.85(3) and 86(2)].

The sale of a medicinal product without its being enclosed in a container is regarded as a contravention of the regulations concerning the labelling of containers [s.85(4)].

It is an offence for any person in the course of a business carried on by him/her to supply a product to which Chapters II to V of Council Directive 65/65/EEC applies, unless:

1    a leaflet is enclosed in, or supplied with, the container or package; or
2    the container or package itself contains the particulars which a leaflet relating to the product is required by the regulations to contain and does so in the manner required (SI 1994 No.276).

It is also an offence for a person in the course of a business carried on by him/her to sell or supply or have in their possession for the purpose of sale or supply a medicinal product in a container or package which is labelled or marked in such a way, or supplied with a leaflet so that the container, package or leaflet falsely describes the product, or is likely to mislead as to the nature or quality of the product or as to its uses or the effects of medicinal products of that description [ss.85(5) and 86(3)].

Any person contravening the labelling regulations (see below) is liable on summary conviction to a fine of up to £5000 and, on conviction or indictment, to a fine or to imprisonment for a term not exceeding two years or to both.

## Definitions

The terms defined here are those used in the Act and regulations in connection with labelling which are not explained elsewhere in the text.

*Appropriate non-proprietary name* means, briefly:

1    any name, or abbreviation or suitable inversion of such name, at the head of a monograph in a 'specified publication' (see below);
2    where the product is not described in a monograph, the British approved name;
3    where there is no monograph name or British approved name, the international non-proprietary name (INN); or
4    where there is no monograph name, British approved name or INN, the accepted scientific name or other name descriptive of the true nature of the product (SI 1976 No.1726).

*Appropriate quantitative particulars* means the quantity of each active ingredient (or that part of the active molecule responsible for the therapeutic or pharmacological activity) identified by its appropriate INN and expressed in terms of weight, volume, capacity or for certain products, in units of activity or as a percentage.

The quantity to be shown is:

1    the quantity in each dosage unit (for pastilles and lozenges only, it can be shown as a percentage); or
2    if there is no dosage unit, the quantity of each active ingredient in the container; or
3    if the product contains any active ingredient which cannot be definitively characterised, the quantity of the ingredient present in the highest proportion other than diluents, excipients, etc.

The quantity of antimicrobial preservative added to a biological medicinal product must be stated. That applies to antigens, toxins, antitoxins, sera, antisera and vaccines.

The quantity can be expressed in terms of the dilution of the unit preparation for a *homoeopathic product* (that is, a product prepared in accordance with the methods of homoeopathic medicine or similar system which is sold or supplied as a homoeopathic product and is so described by the person who sells or supplies it) (SI 1976 No.1726).

*Strength* in relation to a relevant medicinal product means the content of active ingredient in that product expressed quantitatively per dosage unit, per unit volume or by weight, according to the dosage form.

*Dosage unit* means:

1    where the medicinal product is in the form of a tablet or capsule or is an article in some other similar pharmaceutical form, that tablet, capsule or other similar article; or
2    where the medicinal product is not in the form of aforesaid that quantity of the medicinal product which is used as the unit by reference to which the dose of the medicinal product is measured (SI 1976 No.1726).

*Quantity* means, where the quantity is not the exact quantity, the quantity which is as near the exact quantity as is reasonably practicable or which differs from the exact quantity only to such extent as is reasonably necessary in the circumstances having regard to the nature of the medicinal product in question (SI 1976 No.1726).

A *container*, in relation to a medicinal product, means the bottle, jar, box, packet or other receptacle which contains, or is to contain it, not being a capsule, cachet or other article in which the product is or is to be administered; and where any such receptacle is or is to be contained in another such receptacle, includes the inner receptacle but not the outer (s.132).

It should be noted that a capsule, cachet or other article in which a medicinal product is to be administered is not normally a container, but if the capsule, etc., is not to be administered, then it is a container.

A *package*, in relation to any medicinal products, means any box, packet or other article in which one or more containers of the products are to be enclosed, and where any such box, package or other article is or is to be itself enclosed in one or more other boxes, packets or other articles, includes each of the boxes, packets or other articles in question (s.132).

In effect, the inner receptacle which actually contains the medicinal products is a container, every outer receptacle is a package.

*Labelling*, in relation to a container or package of medicinal products, means affixing to or otherwise displaying on it a notice describing or otherwise relating to the contents (s.132).

*Expiry date* means the date after which, or the month and year after the end of which, the medicinal product should not be used or the date before which or the month and year before the beginning of which, the medicinal product should be used (SI 1977 No.996).

*External use* means:

1    in relation to medicinal products for use by being administered to human beings, application to the skin, hair, teeth, mucosa of the mouth, throat, nose, ear, eye, vagina or anal canal;
2    in relation to veterinary drugs, application to the skin, hair, fur, feathers, scales, hoof, horn, ear, eye, mouth, or mucosa of the throat or prepuce;

in either case when a local action only is necessary and extensive systemic absorption is unlikely to occur; and references to *medicinal products for external use* shall be read accordingly, except that in relation to 1 above the references shall not include throat sprays, throat pastilles, throat lozenges, throat tablets, nasal sprays, nasal inhalations or teething preparations (SI 1997 No.1830).

*Proprietary medicinal product* means a ready-prepared medicinal product placed on the market in the United Kingdom under a special name and in a special pack (SI 1992 No.604).

*Ready-made veterinary drug* means a ready-prepared veterinary drug placed on the market in the United Kingdom in a pharmaceutical form in which it may be used without further processing, not being a drug placed on the market under a special name and in a special pack.

*Specified publication* means the *European Pharmacopoeia*, the *British Pharmacopoeia*, the *British Pharmaceutical Codex*, the *British Veterinary Codex* (or other official compendia which may in the future be produced under the Medicines Act) and the list of British approved names (Medicines Act, s.100).

## Labelling Regulations

The regulations apply at all stages of distribution, except where otherwise stated. Medicinal products which are Controlled Drugs must also be labelled in accordance with the Misuse of Drugs Regulations 1985 (see p.178).

Regulations implementing Council Directive 92/27/EEC have been issued dealing with *relevant medicinal products* (SI 1992 No.3273) (see the definition, below). Regulations dealing with homoeopathic medicinal products (SI 1994 No.104) have also been issued.

## Labelling of Relevant Medicinal Products

*Relevant medicinal product* means a product to which Chapters II to V of Council Directive 65/65/EEC applies in respect of which a marketing authorisation is granted or renewed on or after 1 January 1994. Thus, all medicinal products for human use are included except those prepared on the basis of magistral (see p.2) or official formula, those intended for research or development trials, or intermediate products intended for further processing.

## General Labelling Provisions for Relevant Medicinal Products for Human Use

All labelling of containers and packages must be:

1    legible;
2    comprehensible;
3    indelible;
4    either in the English language only or in English and in one or more other languages provided that the same particulars appear in all the languages used.

Where the holder of a marketing authorisation for a relevant medicinal product proposes to alter the labelling relating to it in any respect s/he must notify the licensing authority and, unless the licensing authority has notified him/her that it does not approve the alterations s/he may, after a period of 90 days from the date of notification by him/her, supply the product with the altered labelling (SI 1992 No.3273).

## Standard Labelling Requirements for Relevant Medicinal Products for Human Use

The standard requirements for the labelling of containers and packages of relevant medicinal products are set out in Council Directive 92/27/EEC and SI 1992 No.3273. There are modifications for small containers and blister packs (see p.133).

The standard requirements are:

1    The name of the medicinal product, followed by the common name where the medicinal product contains only one active ingredient and if its name is an invented name; where a medicinal product is available

in several pharmaceutical forms and/or several strengths, the pharmaceutical form and/or strength (baby, child or adult as appropriate) must be included in the name of the medicinal product.

*Common name* means the international non-proprietary name or, if one does not exist, the usual common name.

*Strength* in this context means: the suitability of the product for a baby, child or adult.

2   A statement of the active ingredients expressed qualitatively and quantitatively per dosage unit or according to the form of administration for a given volume or weight, using their common names.

3   The pharmaceutical form of the product and the contents by weight, by volume or by number of doses of the product.

4   A list of those excipients known to have a recognised action or effect and included in the guidelines published in pursuant to Article 12. However, if the product is injectable or a topical or eye preparation, all excipients must be stated.

5   The method and, if necessary, the route of administration.

6   A special warning that the medicinal product must be stored out of the reach of children.

7   Any special warning if this is necessary for the medicinal product concerned.

8   The expiry date in clear terms (month/year).

9   Special storage precautions, if any.

10   Special precautions for disposal of unused medicinal products, if appropriate, or waste materials derived from such products.

11   The name and address of the holder of the marketing authorisation.

12   The marketing authorisation number.

13   The manufacturer's batch number.

14   In the case of self-medication, instructions on the use of the medicinal product.

The outer packaging may be labelled to show symbols or pictograms designed to clarify certain information mentioned in 1 to 14 above and other information compatible with the summary of product characteristics which is useful for health education, to the exclusion of any element of a promotional nature.

In addition, member states of the European Union may require certain additional labelling, e.g. the price of the product, the reimbursement conditions, and the classification, e.g. POM.

*Summary of product characteristics* means the information required to accompany any application for a marketing authorisation which expression shall include, where there is no such information:

1   the data sheet, if there is one; or

2   if there is no data sheet, the information which would be required to accompany an application for a marketing authorisation product under Council Directive 65/65/EEC.

## Small Containers for Relevant Medicinal Products for Human Use

Where the container of a relevant medicinal product is *not* a blister pack but is too small to include all the standard particulars for relevant medicinal products it must be labelled with:

1    the name of the medicinal product as laid down in standard labelling (see p.131);
2    the contents of the product by weight, by volume or by unit
3    the method, and if necessary the route, of administration;
4    the expiry date;
5    the batch number.

## Blister Packs for Relevant Medicinal Products for Human Use

Where the container of a relevant medicinal product is a blister pack and is enclosed within a package which complies with the standard labelling (see above), the container must be labelled with:

1    the name of the medicinal product as laid down in standard labelling (see p.131);
2    the expiry date;
3    the name of the holder of the marketing authorisation;
4    the batch number.

## Standard Labelling Requirements for Containers and Packages for Radiopharmaceuticals for Human Use

Containers and packages for radiopharmaceuticals must be labelled with the standard particulars for relevant medicinal products (see p.131) together with the following additional particulars:

1    the container and package must be labelled in accordance with the current edition of the Regulations for the Safe Transport of Radioactive Materials;
2    the labelling on the shielding must explain in full the codings used on the vial and shall indicate where necessary, for a given time and date, the amount of radioactivity per dose or per vial and the number of capsules, or for liquids the number of millilitres in the container;
3    the vial shall be labelled to show:

     (a)    the name or code of the medicinal product, including the name or chemical symbol of the radionuclide;

(b)   the international symbol for radioactivity;
(c)   the name of the manufacturer;
(d)   the amount of radioactivity as specified in 2 above.

## Labelling of Relevant General Sale List Medicinal Products

All relevant medicinal products for human use on a General Sale List when sold or supplied by retail must be labelled as follows (SI 1994 No.3144, Sch.5). If the product contains:

1   aloxiprin, aspirin or paracetamol, with the words *If symptoms persist, consult your doctor* and, except where the product is for external use only, the recommended dosage;
2   aloxiprin, with the words *Contains an aspirin derivative*;
3   aspirin, except where the product is for external use only or where the name of the product includes the word *aspirin* and appears on the container or package, the words *Contains aspirin*;
4   paracetamol, except where the name of the product includes the word *paracetamol* and appears on the container or package, the words *Contains paracetamol*;
5   paracetamol, the words *Do not exceed the stated dose* (these words must appear adjacent to either the directions for use or the recommended dosage);
6   paracetamol, unless it is wholly or mainly intended for children who are 12 years old or younger (i.e. a product for children 12 and over), the words *Do not take with any other paracetamol containing products* and

(a)   if a package leaflet accompanying the product displays the words *Immediate medical advice should be sought in the event of overdose, even if you feel well, because of the risk of delayed, serious liver damage* the words *Immediate medical advice should be sought in the case of overdose, even if you feel well* must be added to the label; or
(b)   if no package leaflet accompanies the product or the package leaflet does not display the words *Immediate medical advice should be sought in the event of overdose, even if you feel well, because of the risk of delayed, serious liver damage* then those words must be added to the label (SI 1998 No.3105).

7   paracetamol, and is wholly or mainly intended for children who are 12 years old or younger, the words *Do not give with any other paracetamol containing products* and

(a)   if a package leaflet accompanying the product displays the words *Immediate medical advice should be sought in the event of overdose, even if the child seems well, because of the risk of delayed, serious liver damage* the words *Immediate medical advice should be sought in the case of overdose, even if the child seems well* must be added to the label; or

(b) if no package leaflet accompanies the product or the package leaflet does not display the words *Immediate medical advice should be sought in the event of overdose, even if the child seems well, because of the risk of delayed, serious liver damage* then those words must be added to the label (SI 1998 No.3105).

Where more than one of the phrases in 2, 3 and 4 above apply they may be combined, for example, *Contains aspirin, an aspirin derivative and paracetamol.* Those phrases must be within a rectangle in which there is no other matter and must be in a prominent position.

On those General Sale List medicines which are subject to pack size provisions (see p.62) the larger pack sizes must be labelled with a 'P' within a rectangle in which there is no other matter.

## Labelling of Relevant Medicinal Products for Pharmacy Sale Only

All medicinal products for pharmacy sale only when sold or supplied by retail must be labelled as follows (SI 1994 No.3144, Sch.5):

1   With the capital letter 'P' in a rectangle containing no other matter. This also applies:

   (a)   to sales of Pharmacy Medicines by way of wholesale dealing, and
   (b)   to General Sale List Medicines in pack sizes restricted to pharmacy sale (SI 1994 No.3144).

2   If containing aspirin, aloxiprin or paracetamol, in the manner described above for medicinal products on a General Sale List.

3   If for human use and exempt from Prescription Only control by reason of the proportion or level in such a product of the Prescription Only substance, with the words *Warning. Do not exceed the stated dose.* (This does not apply to products for external use or products containing any of the substances set out in 5 below.)

4   If for the treatment of asthma or other conditions associated with bronchial spasm or contains ephedrine or any of its salts, with the words *Warning. Asthmatics should consult their doctor before using this product.* (This does not apply to products for external use.)

5   If the product contains an antihistamine or any of its salts or molecular compounds, with the words *Warning. May cause drowsiness. If affected do not drive or operate machinery. Avoid alcoholic drink.* (This does not

apply to products for external use or where the marketing authorisation contains no warning to the sedating effect of the product in use.)

6    If the product is an embrocation, liniment, lotion, liquid antiseptic or other liquid preparation or gel and is for external application, with the words *For external use only.*

7    If the product contains hexachlorophane, either with the words *Not to be used for babies* or a warning that the product is not to be administered except on medical advice to a child under two years.

The relevant warning phrase or phrases described under Labelling of Relevant General Sale List Medicinal Products and Labelling of Relevant Medicinal Products for Pharmacy Sale Only above must be in a rectangle within which there is no other matter. That does not apply to the phrases *Do not exceed the stated dose* or *If symptoms persist consult your doctor* on the labels or products for human use required to be labelled because of their aspirin, aloxiprin, or paracetamol content.

## Labelling of Relevant Prescription Only Medicinal Products

The container and package of every medicinal product included in a Prescription Only list must be labelled to show:

1    The letters 'POM' in capital letters within a rectangle within which there shall be no other matter of any kind. That requirement applies to wholesale transactions (which include sales to doctors or dentists) but does not apply to dispensed medicines.

2    If the product is an embrocation, liniment, lotion, liquid antiseptic or other liquid preparation or gel and is for external application, with the words *For external use only.*

3    If the product contains hexachlorophane, either with the words *Not to be used for babies* or a warning that the product is not to be administered except on medical advice to a child under two years.

## Labelling of Relevant Dispensed Medicinal Products

The standard labelling requirements do not apply to dispensed medicines.

A *dispensed relevant medicinal product* means a relevant medicinal product prepared or dispensed in accordance with a prescription given by a practitioner.

The container of a dispensed relevant medicinal product must be labelled to show the following particulars:

1   the name of the person to whom the medicine is to be administered;
2   the name and address of the person who sells or supplies the relevant medicinal product;
3   the date of dispensing; and
4   where the product has been prescribed by a practitioner such of the following particulars as s/he may request:

    (a)   the name of the product or its common name;
    (b)   directions for use of the product;
    (c)   precautions relating to the use of the product; or

where a pharmacist, in the exercise of his/her professional skill and judgment, is of the opinion that any of such particulars are inappropriate and has taken all reasonable steps to consult with the practitioner and has been unable to do so, particulars of a same kind as those requested by the practitioner which the pharmacist considers appropriate;

5   the words *Keep out of the reach of children* or words of direction bearing a similar meaning;
6   the phrase *For external use only* if the product is not on a General Sale List and is an embrocation, liniment, lotion, liquid antiseptic or other liquid preparation or gel and is for external use only.

A container need not be labelled if it is enclosed in a package which is labelled with the required particulars.

## Labelling of Medicinal Products Exempt from Product Marketing Authorisations

The following classes of medicinal products, exempt from marketing authorisations (product licences) by various orders made under the Medicines Act, are subject to modified labelling requirements.

### Foods and Cosmetics

Certain medicinal products which are foods are exempt from marketing authorisations (product licences) by the Foods and Cosmetics Order (SI 1971 No.1410) and the labelling particulars (see above) which apply to these products are:

1   name of product (container and package);
2   description of pharmaceutical form (package only);
3   appropriate quantitative particulars (container only);
4   quantity (container and package);
5   any special handling and storage requirements (container and package);
6   expiry date (container only).

The labels of the container and of the package must also bear the name and address of the manufacturer or the person responsible for its composition or the person who first sells or supplies it as a medicinal product.

These labelling requirements do not apply to any product which is subject to the Labelling of Food Regulations. There are no labelling requirements for cosmetics.

### Special and Transitional Cases

'Special' dispensing and manufacturing services provided by manufacturers for practitioners, pharmacists and others are the subject of two orders (SIs 1971 No.1450 and 1972 No.1200) under the Medicines Act which provide exemptions from marketing authorisations (see Chapter 2). These orders also extend to certain other special cases. The label of the container of medicinal products affected, and the packages immediately enclosing them, must show the following labelling particulars:

1  name of the product;
2  pharmaceutical form (package only);
3  appropriate quantitative particulars;
4  quantity;
5  any special handling and storage requirements;
6  batch reference;
7  manufacturer's licence number, or name and address.

The package must also bear the name and address of the manufacturer, or of the person responsible for the composition of the product, or of the person who first sells or supplies it as a medicinal product.

### Other Exempt Medicinal Products

Apart from the orders mentioned under Foods and Cosmetics and Special and Transitional Cases above, the Medicines Act provides other exemptions from marketing authorisation (product licence) requirements for certain medicinal products.

The following requirements apply, for example, to medicinal products which are prepared in a registered pharmacy for retail sale from that pharmacy and which are not advertised. (Such products are familiarly known as 'chemist's nostrums'.)

The label of the container of such a medicinal product and the package immediately enclosing it must show the following labelling particulars:

1  name of the product;
2  pharmaceutical form (package only);
3  appropriate quantitative particulars;
4  quantity;
5  directions for use;

6     any special handling and storage requirements;
7     expiry date (if relevant).

The label of the container and the package must also show the name and address of the seller.

## Ingredient Medicinal Products

The label of the container and of the package of ingredients which are to be used in the preparation of medicinal products must show the following labelling particulars:

1     name of the product (i.e. ingredient);
2     pharmaceutical form;
3     appropriate quantitative particulars;
4     quantity;
5     any special handling and storage requirements;
6     expiry date (if relevant);
7     marketing authorisation number (or the name and address of the holder of the marketing authorisation);
8     batch reference;
9     manufacturer's licence number, or name and address;
10    particulars required by the marketing authorisation.

## Contract Manufacture or Assembly

Where a medicinal product is supplied solely for the purpose of assembly and the supply is between persons concerned in the manufacture or assembly of the product, the package immediately enclosing the container must be labelled to show:

1     name of the product;
2     name and address of the person supplying the product;
3     marketing authorisation number (if any);
4     batch reference.

The person taken to be concerned in the manufacture or assembly of a medicinal product is (a) the marketing authorisation holder or, if there is no authorisation, the person responsible for the composition of the product, or (b) the person who manufactures or assembles the product to the order of the authorisation holder, etc. or to the order of the Crown.

Those are the only requirements which apply to stocks held in the manufacturing process.

## Delivery and Storage

The labelling particulars required for delivery and storage must appear on the outer package, that is to say, the package enclosing the package immediately enclosing the container. The required labelling particulars are:

1   any special handling and storage particulars;
2   the expiry date of the product;
3   the manufacturer's batch number.

## Clinical Trials

Where a medicinal product is for administration in a clinical trial, the labelling on the container and package must sufficiently identify the clinical trial, the product (if more than one product is supplied in the course of the trial) and such designation as will identify the person to whom the product is to be administered. It must also show the name and address of the premises where the clinical trial is to be carried out (or the name and address of the product licence holder) and particulars required to be stated on the labels by the product licence or clinical trial certificate.

## Standard Labelling Requirements for Containers and Packages of Homoeopathic Products for Human Use

All containers and packages for homoeopathic products must be labelled clearly and make reference to their homoeopathic nature by clear use of the words *homoeopathic medicinal product*. In addition they must carry the following particulars and no others (SI 1994 No.104):

1   the scientific name of the stock or stocks followed by the degree of dilution, making use of the symbols of the pharmacopoeia used in relation to the homoeopathic manufacturing procedure described therein for that stock or stocks;
2   the name and address of the holder of the certificate of registration and, where different, the name and address of the manufacturer;
3   the method of administration and, if necessary, route;
4   the expiry date of the product in clear terms, stating the month and year;
5   the pharmaceutical form;
6   the contents of the sales representation;

7    any special storage precautions;
8    any special warning necessary for the product concerned;
9    the manufacturer's batch number;
10   the registration number allocated by the licensing authority preceded by
     the letters 'HR' in capital letters;
11   the words *homoeopathic medicinal product without approved thera-
     peutic indications*;
12   a warning advising the user to consult a doctor if the symptoms persist
     during the use of the product.

## Surgical Materials

Certain surgical materials (for example, ligatures and sutures) are medicinal
products by virtue of the Medicines (Surgical Materials) Order 1971 (SI 1971
No.1267). The label of the container of such a product and the package
immediately enclosing it, must show the following labelling particulars:

1    name of the product;
2    description of the pharmaceutical form;
5    directions for use;
6    contra-indications, warnings and precautions (if any);
9    any special handling and storage requirements;
10   expiry date where relevant;
11   name and address of the holder of the marketing authorisation;
12   marketing authorisation number;
13   batch reference;
14   manufacturer's licence number, or name and address;
15   particulars required by the marketing authorisation (product licence).

The label must also show the nature and origin of the article or substance and
the quantity of the product in the container expressed in terms of weight or
volume or length.

## Labelling of Animal Medicines

Animal medicines which possessed product licences prior to 1 January 1995
are subject to the same general and standard labelling requirements as
medicinal products for human use (see p.131).

As from January 1995 all medicinal products for animal use obtaining new
marketing authorisations or having their licences renewed have to comply
with the provisions of the Marketing Authorisations for Veterinary Medicinal
Products Regulations 1994 (SI 1994 No.3142, reg.6). These regulations
implement Council Directive 81/851/EEC, as amended.

It is an offence not to label animal medicines under the new regulations but
a defence is provided where such products were placed on the market after

1 January 1995 but on or before 31 December 1996 and conformed to the old regulations.

The new regulations require the following information to appear in legible characters on the containers and outer packages:

1    the name of the veterinary medicinal product;
2    a statement of the active ingredients expressed qualitatively and quantitatively per dosage unit or according to the form of administration for a given volume or weight, using the international non-proprietary name or where none exists the usual non-proprietary name;
3    manufacturer's batch number;
4    marketing authorisation number;
5    name and address or registered business address of the person responsible for marketing and of the manufacturer if different;
6    the species of animal for which the product is intended together with the method and route of administration;
7    the withdrawal period, even if nil, in the case of products administered to food-producing animals;
8    the expiry date in plain language;
9    special storage precautions, if any;
10   special precautions for disposal of unused product or waste material;
11   any special precautions relating to use or other particulars essential for safety or health protection;
12   the words *For animal treatment only*;
13   the words *Store out of the reach of children*;
14   the indications 'POM', 'P', 'PML', or 'GSL' in a box in which there is no other written material.

## Labelling Small Containers for Animal Medicinal Products

For containers such as ampoules the information required is:

1    the name of the veterinary medicinal product;
2    quantity of the active ingredients;
3    manufacturer's batch number;
4    route of administration;
5    the expiry date in plain language;
6    the words *For animal treatment only*.

## Sales by Agricultural Merchants and Saddlers

Exempted veterinary drugs must be labelled in accordance with the principal labelling regulations (see p.131), as amended and with the additional labelling requirements in SI 1977 No.2168.

The containers and the immediately enclosed package of an exempted veterinary drug, when sold or supplied by retail, must be labelled:

1    'PML' (Schs.1 and 2) or 'POM' (Sch.3), as appropriate. The letters must be in capitals within which there shall be no other matter of any kind.
      N.B. For wholesale transactions the letters need only appear on the immediately enclosing package.
2    If containing hexachlorophane and for oral administration for the prevention or treatment of liver fluke disease in cattle, with a warning that it is not for use in lactating cattle, and also, if for liver fluke disease in sheep or cattle, with a warning that protective clothing must be worn when the product is being administered.
3    If containing aloxiprin, with the words *Unsuitable for cats* and *Contains an aspirin derivative.*
4    If containing aspirin, with the words *Unsuitable for cats* and *Contains aspirin.* (*Contains aspirin* may be omitted where the word *aspirin* is included in the name of the product.)
5    If containing salicylamide, with the words *Unsuitable for cats.*

In 3, 4 and 5 the special *Unsuitable for cats* words must be within a rectangle within which there shall be no other matter.


## Labelling of Medicinal Tests on Animals

The labelling requirements of containers and packages of a medicinal product or medicated feeding stuff for medicinal tests on animals are set out in separate regulations (SI 1988 No.1009) and are briefly as follows. (The general provisions as to the English language, indelibility and legibility apply.)

1     Designations to identify the animal test.
2     Where there is more than one medicinal product or medicated feeding stuff in the course of a test such designation to identify each medicinal product or excepted medicated feeding stuff.
3     Quantity.
4     Purpose for which to be used, the species, and the directions for use including dosage and any warning statements.
5     Requirements (if any) for incorporation in animal feeding stuffs.
6     Any special handling and storage requirements.
7     Expiry date.
8     Any other particulars required by the licence or certificate.
9     In the case of small-sized labels the statement that a leaflet of instructions is supplied with each product.
10    The words *For animal test use only.*

Where any container is of a size which makes it impracticable to be labelled to show all the particulars above it must be labelled with items 1, 2, 7 and 8, and a leaflet containing all the particulars must be supplied with the product and delivered to the purchaser.

## Leaflets

### Medicinal Products Which are Relevant Medicinal Products for Human Use

All leaflets included in the package or container of any relevant medicinal product (see p.131) must comply with section 7(1) of SI 1994 No.3144 and contain the particulars as set out in Council Directive 92/27/EEC.

All particulars must be drawn up in accordance:

1  with the summary of product characteristics (see p.132), if there is one;
2  if there is no summary of product characteristics, with the data sheet, if there is one;
3  if there is no summary of product characteristics and no data sheet, with the information which would be required to accompany an application for a product licence under Council Directive 65/65/EEC.

The particulars must be written in clear and understandable terms for the patient, and be clearly legible in the language of the member state where the product was placed on the market. Other languages may be used provided that the same particulars appear in all the languages used.

The particulars which must be included are:

1  For identification of the medicinal product:

   (a)  the name of the product, followed by the common name if the product contains only one active ingredient and if its name is an invented name; where a medicinal product is available in several pharmaceutical forms and/or several strengths, the pharmaceutical form and/or strength (for example, baby, child, adult) must be included in the name of the product;

   (b)  a full statement of the active ingredients and excipients expressed qualitatively and a statement of the active ingredients expressed quantitatively, using their common names, in the case of each presentation of the medicinal product;

   (c)  the pharmaceutical form and the contents by weight, by volume or by number of doses of the product, in the case of each presentation of the product;

   (d)  the pharmaco-therapeutic group, or type of activity in terms easily comprehensible for the patient;

   (e)  the name and address of the holder of the marketing authorisation and of the manufacturer.

2  The therapeutic indications.

3    A list of information which is necessary before taking the medicinal product, as follows:

(a)    contra-indications;

(b)    appropriate precautions for use;

(c)    forms of interaction with other medicinal products and other forms of interaction (e.g. with alcohol, tobacco and foodstuffs) which may affect the action of the medicinal product;

(d)    special warnings, which:

> (i)  take into account the particular condition of certain categories of users (e.g. children, pregnant or breastfeeding women, the elderly, and persons with specific pathological conditions);
>
> (ii)  mention, if appropriate, potential effects on the ability to drive vehicles or operate machinery;
>
> (iii)  give details of those excipients, knowledge of which is important for the safe and effective use of the medicinal product.

4    The necessary and usual instructions for proper use, in particular:

(a)    dosage;

(b)    method and, if necessary, route of administration;

(c)    the frequency of administration, specifying if necessary, the time at which the medicinal product may or must be administered;
and, where the nature of the product makes it appropriate:

(d)    the duration of treatment, where it should be limited;

(e)    the action to be taken in the case of an overdose (e.g. symptoms and emergency procedures);

(f)    the course of action to be taken where one or more doses have not been taken;

(g)    indication, if necessary, of the risk of withdrawal effects.

5    A description of the undesirable effects which can occur with normal use of the medicinal product and, if necessary, the action to be taken in such a case, together with an express invitation to the patient to communicate any undesirable effect which is not mentioned in the leaflet to his/her doctor or pharmacist.

6    A reference to the expiry date indicated on the label with:

(a)    a warning against using the product after this date;

(b)    where appropriate, special storage precautions;

(c)    if necessary, a warning against certain visible signs of deterioration.

7    The date upon which the leaflet was last revised.

The licensing authority may decide that certain therapeutic indications need not be included in a leaflet where the dissemination of such information might have serious disadvantages for the patient.

A leaflet for a relevant medicinal product may include:

1    a symbol or pictogram designed to clarify the particulars set out in 1 to 7 above;
2    other information compatible with the summary of product characteristics which is useful for health education, to the exclusion of any element of a promotional nature.

### Paracetamol

Where a package leaflet is included in the packaging of a relevant medicinal product containing paracetamol, unless the product is wholly or mainly intended for children who are 12 years old or younger, the leaflet shall display the words *Immediate medical advice should be sought in the event of overdose, even if you feel well, because of the risk of delayed, serious liver damage*, i.e. where the product is intended for children 12 and over.

Where a package leaflet is included in the packaging of a relevant medicinal product containing paracetamol, and the product is wholly or mainly is intended for children who are 12 years old **or younger**, the leaflet shall display the words *Immediate medical advice should be sought in the event of overdose, even if the child seems well, because of the risk of delayed, serious liver damage* (SI 1998 No.3105).

### Radiopharmaceuticals and Radiopharmaceutical-Associated Products

A leaflet enclosed with a radiopharmaceutical or radiopharmaceutical-associated products must in addition to containing particulars required in the regulations (SI 1994 No.3144) contain:

1    details of any precautions to be taken by the user and the patient during the preparation and administration of the product;
2    details of any special precautions to be taken in respect of the disposal of the container and its unused contents.

### Homoeopathic Medicinal Products

Any leaflet enclosed in or supplied with the packaging of a homoeopathic product which is placed on the market in accordance with a certificate of registration must bear the words *homoeopathic medicinal product*. In addition the leaflet must carry the following particulars and no others (SI 1994 No.104):

1    the scientific name of the stock or stocks followed by the degree of dilution, making use of the symbols of the pharmacopoeia used in

relation to the homoeopathic manufacturing procedure described therein for that stock or stocks;

2   the name and address of the holder of the certificate of registration and, where different, the name and address of the manufacturer;

3   the method of administration and, if necessary, route;

4   the expiry date of the product in clear terms, stating the month and year;

5   the pharmaceutical form;

6   the contents of the sales representation;

7   any special storage precautions;

8   any special warning necessary for the product concerned;

9   the manufacturer's batch number;

10  the registration number allocated by the licensing authority preceded by the letters 'HR' in capital letters;

11  the words *homoeopathic medicinal product without approved therapeutic indications*;

12  a warning advising the user to consult a doctor if the symptoms persist during the use of the product.

### Animal Medicines

Leaflets supplied with proprietary veterinary drugs or ready-made veterinary drugs must contain the particulars set out in the regulations (SI 1983 No.1727, as amended). The requirements are similar to those for human relevant medicinal products (see above) and include 1 to 3, and 5 to 7 inclusive, with the substitution of the words 'proprietary veterinary drug' or 'ready-made veterinary drug' for the words 'proprietary medicinal product'. Numbers 4, 8, and 9 are substituted by the following:

4   The species of animal for which the proprietary veterinary drug or ready-made veterinary drug is intended, the dosage for each species, the method and route of administration and, if necessary, advice on correct administration.

8   The name and address of the holder of the product licence which relates to the proprietary veterinary drug or ready-made veterinary drug, and, if different therefrom, the name and address of the person responsible for the composition of the drug.

9   The withdrawal period specified in the product licence before an animal which has been treated with the proprietary veterinary drug or ready-made veterinary drug is slaughtered for the production of food and before products derived from such an animal are used as food.

### Relevant Animal Medicines

See Labelling, pages 141–142.

## Child Safety Regulations

Special requirements apply to the retail sale or supply of medicinal products in unit-dose forms which contain aspirin (except effervescent tablets containing less than 25 per cent w/w) or paracetamol and are exclusively for administration to human beings (SI 1975 No.2000, as amended). These medicinal products must be packed in child-resistant containers, that is:

1    opaque or dark-tinted reclosable containers complying with British Standard EN28317 of 1993 or British Standard 6652 republished in 1989 and certified by the British Standards Institution (SI 1994 No.1402); or
2    opaque or dark-tinted unit packages in the form of bubbles, blisters or other sealed units.

These products when for administration exclusively to children must be white and the contents of each container or pack of unit packages must not exceed 25. They can be flavoured.

The regulations do not apply to products which are (a) for export or not intended for retail sale; or (b) sold or supplied from a registered pharmacy under the supervision of a pharmacist on the prescription of a practitioner (which are subject to voluntary controls), or at the request of a patient or guardian in accordance with the pharmacist's judgment as to the treatment required; or (c) sold or supplied by a doctor or dentist to a patient of his/hers or to another doctor or dentist for a particular patient; or (d) sold or supplied for administration in accordance with the directions of a doctor or dentist at a hospital or health centre.

## Use of Fluted Bottles

A liquid medicinal product which is for external use (for definition see p.130) must be sold or supplied in a bottle the outer surface of which is fluted vertically with ribs or grooves recognisable by touch, if the product contains any of the substances listed below (SI 1978 No.40). This requirement applies to the following substances subject to the exemptions shown:

- Aconite, alkaloids of
- Adrenaline; its salts
- Amino-alcohols esterified with benzoic acid, phenylacetic acid, phenyl-propionic acid, cinnamic acid or the derivatives of these acids; their salts
- $p$-Aminobenzenesulphonamide; its salts; derivatives of
- $p$-Aminobenzenesulphonamide having any of the hydrogen atoms of the $p$-amino group or of the sulphonamide group substituted by another radical; their salts

- *p*-Aminobenzoic acid; esters of; their salts
- Ammonia except in medicinal products containing less than 5 per cent weight in weight of ammonia
- Arsenical substances, the following; arsenic sulphides, arsenates; arsenites; halides of arsenic; oxides of arsenic; organic compounds of arsenic
- Atropine; its salts
- Cantharidin; cantharidates
- Carbachol
- Chloral; its addition and its condensation products other than α-chloralose; their molecular compounds
- Chloroform except in medicinal products containing less than 1 per cent volume in volume of chloroform
- Cocaine; its salts
- Creosote obtained from wood except in medicinal products containing less than 50 per cent volume in volume of creosote obtained from wood
- Croton, oil of
- Demecarium bromide
- Dyflos
- Ecothiopate iodide
- Ephedrine, it salts, except in medicinal products containing less than the equivalent of 1 per cent weight in volume of ephedrine
- Ethylmorphine; its salts
- Homatropine; its salts
- Hydrofluoric acid; alkali metal bifluorides; potassium fluoride; sodium fluoride; sodium silicofluoride: except in mouth washes containing not more than 0.05 per cent weight in volume of sodium fluoride
- Hyoscine; its salts
- Hyoscyamine; its salts
- Lead acetates except in medicinal products containing lead acetates equivalent to not more than 2.2 per cent weight in volume of lead calculated as elemental lead
- Mercury, oxides of; nitrates of mercury; mercuric ammonium chloride; mercuric chloride; mercuric iodide, potassium mercuric iodide; organic compounds of mercury; mercuric oxycyanide; mercuric thiocyanate: except in medicinal products containing not more than 0.01 per cent weight in volume of sodium ethylmercurithiosalicylate as a preservative
- Nitric acid except in medicinal products containing less than 9 per cent weight in weight of nitric acid
- Opium
- Phenols (any member of the series of phenols of which the first member is phenol and of which the molecular composition varies from member to member by one atom of carbon and two atoms of hydrogen); compounds of phenol with a metal except in:

–    medicinal products containing one or more of the following: butylated hydroxytoluene, carvacrol, creosote obtained from coal tar, essential oils in which phenols occur naturally, tar (coal or wood, crude or refined), tert-butylcresol, *p*-tert-butyl-phenol *p*-tert-pentylphenol, *p*-(1,1,3,3-tetraethylbutyl) phenol, thymol
–    mouth washes containing less than 2.5 per cent weight in volume of phenols
–    any liquid disinfectant or antiseptics not containing phenol and containing less than 2.5 per cent weight in volume of other phenols
–    other medicinal products containing less than 1 per cent weight in volume of phenols

• Physostigmine; its salts
• Picric acid except in medicinal products containing less than 5 per cent weight in volume of picric acid
• Pilocarpine; its salts except in medicinal products containing less than the equivalent of 0.025 per cent weight in volume of pilocarpine.
• Podophyllum resin except in medicinal products containing not more than 1.5 per cent weight in weight of podophyllum resin
• Solanaceous alkaloids not otherwise included in this Schedule

## Other Exceptions to Fluted Bottle Requirements

The fluted bottle requirements do not apply where:

1   medicinal products are contained in bottles with a capacity greater than 1.14 litres;
2   a medicinal product is a Prescription Only Medicine containing a listed substance (fluted bottle requirements do apply to dispensed medicinal products or any other retail sale or supply);
3   medicinal products are packed for export for use solely outside the United Kingdom;
4   medicinal products are sold or supplied solely for the purpose of scientific education, research or analysis;
5   eye or ear drops are sold or supplied in a plastic container;
6   where the product licence, clinical trial certificate or animal test certificate otherwise provides.

## Summary

• There are detailed labelling requirements for relevant medicinal products for human use which includes all medicines which have been granted, or had renewed, marketing authorisations (product licences) since January

1994. These do not include those medicines dispensed against a prescription or official formula, or for research or trials.

- There are specific labelling requirements for relevant medicinal products for human use containing aloxiprin, aspirin and paracetamol, and additional requirements for Prescription Only Medicines.
- There are additional warning labels for paracetamol.
- There are modified labelling provisions for relevant medicinal products for human use which are in small containers, blister packs, homoeopathic products and for radiopharmaceuticals.
- Abbreviated labelling provisions exist for medicines dispensed against a prescription given by a practitioner.
- There are separate labelling requirements for ingredients, food and cosmetics, contract manufacture and assembly, chemist's nostrums, import and export, surgical materials, clinical trials, animal medicines, animal tests and animal feeding stuffs.
- Every container or package of relevant medicinal products must contain a patient leaflet. Detailed requirements exist for the contents of these leaflets.
- Similar requirements exist for leaflets for animal medicines.
- Special leaflets provisions exist for homoeopathic medicinal products.
- Special requirements apply to the sale of medicinal products in unit-dose form which contain aspirin or paracetamol. These products must be packed in child-resistant containers, i.e. opaque reclosable resistant containers or bubble/blister packs.
- There is a list of liquid medicinal products which are for external use which must be sold in bottles the outer surface of which is fluted with ribs or grooves recognisable by touch. These 'fluted' bottle requirements do not apply where medicinal products are contained in bottles greater than 1.14 litres, for export, for analysis or clinical trial, or which are eye or ear drops.

CHAPTER FIFTEEN

# Medicines Act 1968

# Pharmacopoeias and Other

# Publications

### European Pharmacopoeia

The *European Pharmacopoeia* is published under the direction of the Council of Europe (Partial Agreement) in accordance with the Convention on the Elaboration of a European Pharmacopoeia held in 1964.

In 1973 the standards in the *European Pharmacopoeia*, together with any amendments or alterations published in the *Gazette*, took precedence over the standards in other publications. The Health Ministers may publish amendments to the *British Pharmacopoeia* when necessary to give effect to the Convention but, should a difference exist at any time between the two pharmacopoeias, the standard of the *European Pharmacopoeia* would prevail (s.102).

A name is taken to be an approved synonym for a name at the head of a monograph in the *European Pharmacopoeia*, if, by a notice published in the *Gazette* and not subsequently withdrawn, it is declared to be approved by the Medicines Commission as a synonym for that name [s.65(8)].

### British Pharmacopoeia, Compendia, etc.

Until 1970 the *British Pharmacopoeia* was compiled by the General Medical Council under the Medical Act 1956 when the copyright was assigned to Her

Majesty (Medicines Act, s.98). A committee set up under section 4 of the Act, known as the British Pharmacopoeia Commission, has been established to prepare new editions of the *British Pharmacopoeia* and any amendments to such editions.

The *British Pharmacopoeia* comprises *relevant information*, i.e. information consisting of descriptions of, standards for, or notes or other matters relating to:

1    substances and articles (whether medicinal products or not) which are or may be used in the practice of medicine (other than veterinary medicine), surgery other than veterinary surgery, dentistry and midwifery; and
2    substances and articles used in the manufacture of substances and articles listed under 1.

In addition to the *British Pharmacopoeia*, compendia containing other relevant information may be published (s.99). Information relating to substances and articles used in veterinary medicine and surgery (whether veterinary drugs or not) is published in a separate compendium, the *British Pharmacopoeia (Veterinary)*.

The British Pharmacopoeia Commission is authorised to prepare lists of suitable names (British Approved Names) for substances and articles for placing at the head of monographs in the *British Pharmacopoeia* or in the compendia (s.100 and SI 1970 No.1256). The publication of any such lists supersedes any previously published list.

If the Medicines Commission so recommends, the *British Pharmacopoeia*, the compendia and the lists of names must be published and made available for sale to the public by the appropriate Ministers. Every copy must specify the date from which it is to take effect, and notice must be given in the *Gazette* not less than 21 days before that date (s.102). The Agriculture Ministers are responsible for the veterinary publication and the Health Ministers for the others (s.99).

Apart from the *British Pharmacopoeia* and the compendia, other publications containing relevant information may be prepared at the discretion of the Medicines Commission (s.101). These may be journals published periodically and made available to the public.

### British Pharmaceutical Codex and British Veterinary Codex

The *British Pharmaceutical Codex* (BPC), prepared and published by the Royal Pharmaceutical Society of Great Britain, first appeared in 1907. Successive editions were published, the last being in 1973. The requirements for drugs and dressings in the BPC have provided legally recognised standards which continue to be official standards under the Medicines Act. No analytical standards have been given in any codex published by the Royal Pharmaceutical Society of Great Britain since 1973.

The *British Veterinary Codex*, also prepared and published by the Royal Pharmaceutical Society, has similarly provided standards for medicines in veterinary use, which are now official standards under the Medicines Act.

The Medicines Commission has recommended that there should be only one source of published standard for medicines, namely the *British Pharmacopoeia*.

## Compliance with Official Standards

It is unlawful for any person, in the course of a business carried on by him/her: (a) to sell a medicinal product which has been demanded by the purchaser by, or by express reference to, a particular name; or (b) to sell or supply a medicinal product in pursuance of a prescription given by a practitioner in which the product required is described by, or by express reference, to a particular name; or (c) to sell or supply a medicinal product which, in the course of the business, has been offered or exposed for sale by, or by express reference to, a particular name; if that name is at the head of the relevant monograph in a specified publication, or is an approved synonym for such a name, and the product does not comply with the standard specified in that monograph (ss.65 and 67).

It is also an offence if the name in question is the name of an active ingredient of the product and, in so far as the product consists of that ingredient, it does not comply with the standard specified.

The publications to which these requirements extend are the *European Pharmacopoeia*, the *British Pharmacopoeia*, the *British Pharmaceutical Codex*, the *British Veterinary Codex* and any compendium published under Part VII of the Act.

For the purpose of complying with official standards the *relevant monograph* is ascertained thus:

1    If a particular edition of a particular publication is specified together with the name of the medicinal product, then the *relevant monograph* is (a) the monograph (if any) headed by that name in that edition of the publication; or (b) if there is no such monograph in that edition, the *appropriate current monograph* (if any) headed by that name.

2    If a particular publication, but not a particular edition, is specified, together with the name of the medicinal product, then the *relevant monograph* is (a) the monograph (if any) headed by that name in the current edition of the specified publication; or (b) if there is no such monograph in the current edition of the publication *the appropriate current monograph* headed by that name; or (c) if there is no *appropriate current monograph*, then the monograph headed by that name in the latest edition of the specified publication which contained a monograph so headed.

3    If no publication is specified together with the name of the medicinal product, the *relevant monograph* is *the appropriate current monograph*, if any [s.65(4)].

*Appropriate current monograph*, in relation to a particular name, means the monograph (if any) headed by that name, or by a name for which it is an approved synonym, in the current edition of: (a) the *European Pharmacopoeia*; or (b) the *British Pharmacopoeia*; or (c) a compendium published under section 99 of the Act; or (d) the *British Pharmaceutical Codex* or the *British Veterinary Codex,* taken in that order of precedence.

*Current* means current at the time when the medicinal product in question is demanded, described in a prescription, or offered or exposed for sale; and the current edition of a publication is the one in force at that time, together with any amendments, alterations or deletions. If the reference is to an edition previous to the current edition it must be taken as it was immediately before the time when it was superseded by a subsequent edition of that publication. Any monograph shall be construed in accordance with any general monograph, notice, appendix, note or other explanatory material applicable to the monograph which is contained in the relevant edition of the publication [s.65(5) and (6)].

## Specifications in Licences

When reference is made in a licence or certificate (Part II of the Act) to a publication specified in the Act, but no particular edition is mentioned, then it is to be construed as the current edition, that is, with any amendment, alteration or deletion made up to the date of issue of the licence or certificate (s.103). The publications specified are those mentioned above, that is the *European Pharmacopoeia*, the *British Pharmacopoeia*, the *British Pharmaceutical Codex*, the *British Veterinary Codex*, and compendia prepared under section 99 of the Act, and the lists of names prepared under section 100 of the Act, together with the *British National Formulary* (BNF) and the *Dental Practitioners' Formulary*.

These two formularies are published jointly by the British Medical Association and The Royal Pharmaceutical Society of Great Britain. The BNF is a standard formulary, with notes on drugs and other information for medical practitioners and pharmacists, which is recognised for use in the National Health Service. The *Dental Practitioners' Formulary* similarly provides standard formulae, notes and information relating to dental treatment pharmacopoeias and other publications.

## Summary

- The *British Pharmacopoeia* comprises information consisting of descriptions and standards for substances and articles which may be used in medicine other than veterinary medicine together with substances and articles used in the manufacture of medicinal products.

- The *European Pharmacopoeia*, where appropriate, takes precedence over the standards in other publications.
- It is an offence to sell, supply or dispense a medicinal product of a particular name, if that name is at the head of a monograph in a pharmacopoeia, and the product does not comply with the standard specified in that monograph.

# CHAPTER SIXTEEN

# Misuse of Drugs Act 1971

The Misuse of Drugs Act 1971 came into operation on 1 July 1973 (SI 1973 No.795 (C.20)). It consolidates and extends previous legislation and controls the export, import, production, supply and possession of dangerous or otherwise harmful drugs. The Act is also designed to deal with the control and treatment of addicts and to promote education and research relating to drug dependence. It extends to Northern Ireland (s.38).

In relation to drugs the Act is largely restrictive in its terms although it does provide for licences to be issued for importation and exportation (s.3). Apart from that, the general effect is to render unlawful all activities in the drugs which are controlled under the Act, except as provided in the regulations made under the Act. The extent to which these regulations relax the restrictions is dealt with later in this chapter.

## Advisory Council on Misuse of Drugs

The *Advisory Council* (s.1) was formally established from 1 February 1972 (SI 1971 No.2120 (C.57)) replacing the former Advisory Committee on Drug Dependence which had no statutory authority. It advises the *Ministers*, that is, the Secretary of State for the Home Department, and the Ministers responsible for Health and Education in England, Wales, Scotland and Northern Ireland.

The Council consists of not fewer than 20 members appointed by the Secretary of State after consultation with such organisations as s/he considers appropriate, including at least one person appearing to the Secretary of State to have wide and recent experience in each of the following:

1     the practice of medicine (other than veterinary medicine);
2     the practice of dentistry;
3     the practice of veterinary medicine;
4     the practice of pharmacy;
5     the pharmaceutical industry;
6     chemistry other than pharmaceutical chemistry;

together with persons appearing to the Secretary of State to have wide and recent experience of social problems connected with the misuse of drugs (Sch.1 to the Act). The Secretary of State appoints one of the members of the Advisory Council to be chairman of the Council, and the Council may appoint committees and include on them persons who are not members of the Council.

The Council is required to keep under review the situation in the United Kingdom with respect to drugs which are being, or appear to them likely to be, misused (s.1). If it considers that misuse could cause harmful effects which might constitute a social problem, it has a duty to advise the Ministers on the action to be taken. In particular it must advise on measures:

1     to restrict the availability of such drugs or to supervise the arrangements for their supply;
2     to enable persons affected by the misuse of such drugs to obtain proper advice, and to secure the provision of proper facilities and services for the treatment, rehabilitation and aftercare of such persons;
3     to promote co-operation between the various professional and community services which, in the opinion of the Council, have a part to play in dealing with social problems connected with the misuse of such drugs;
4     to educate the public (and in particular the young) in the dangers of abusing such drugs, and to give publicity to those dangers; and,
5     to promote research into, or otherwise to obtain information about, any matter which in the opinion of the Council is of relevance for the purpose of preventing the misuse of such drugs or dealing with any social problem connected with their misuse. The Secretary of State has authority to conduct or assist in conducting such research (s.32).

The Advisory Council also has a duty to advise on any matter relating to drug dependence or misuse of drugs which any of the Ministers may refer to it. In particular, the Council is required to advise the Secretary of State on communications relating to the control of any dangerous or otherwise harmful drug received from any authority established under a treaty, convention or other agreement to which HM Government is a party. Before any regulations are made under the Act the Advisory Council must be consulted [s.31(3)].

## Class A, Class B and Class C Drugs

The drugs subject to control are listed in Schedule 2 to the Act and the term *Controlled Drug* means any substance or product so listed. The Schedule is divided into three parts or classes largely on the basis of decreasing order of harmfulness: Part I (Class A); Part II (Class B); and Part III (Class C). This division into three classes is solely for the purpose of determining penalties for offences under the Act (s.25) (see Appendix 10).

Changes may be made to the list of Controlled Drugs subject to consultation with the Advisory Council. Amendment is made by an Order in Council which must be approved by an affirmative resolution of each House of Parliament (s.2).

It should be noted that the classification of Controlled Drugs for purposes of the regimes of control which must be applied to drugs when used for lawful purposes appears in the Schedules to the Misuse of Drugs Regulations. This classification is of importance to practitioners and pharmacists in their daily work and is set out in Appendix 11.

## Restrictions and Exemptions

The importation or exportation of Controlled Drugs is prohibited, except in accordance with a licence issued by the Secretary of State or when permitted by regulations (s.3). Certain activities are specifically declared to be unlawful, thus:

1   producing a Controlled Drug (s.4);
2   supplying or offering to supply a Controlled Drug to another person (s.4);
3   possessing a Controlled Drug (s.5);
4   cultivating any plant of the genus *Cannabis* (s.6).

*Producing* a Controlled Drug means producing it by manufacture, cultivation or any other method, and *supplying* includes distribution (s.37). For the purposes of the Act the things which a person has in his/her possession are taken to include anything subject to his/her control which is in the custody of another (s.37). *Cannabis* (except in the expression *cannabis resin*) means any plant of the genus *Cannabis* or any part of any such plant (by whatever name designated) except that it does not include cannabis resin or any of the following products after separation from the rest of the plant, namely:

1   mature stalk of any such plant;
2   fibre produced from mature stalk of any such plant; and
3   seed of any such plant (Criminal Law Act 1977, s.52).

Exemptions from these controls may be authorised by the Secretary of State. S/he may:

1     by regulations, exempt any specified Controlled Drug from any of the restrictions on import, export, production, supply or possession (s.7);
2     by regulations, make it lawful for persons to produce, supply or possess Controlled Drugs to the extent which s/he thinks fit (s.7);
3     permit by licence or other authority any of the activities in 2 and prescribe any conditions to be complied with (s.7).

The Secretary of State must exercise his/her powers to make regulations so as to secure appropriate exemptions for the possession, supply, manufacture or compounding of Controlled Drugs by practitioners, pharmacists and persons lawfully conducting retail pharmacy businesses, and for prescribing and administration by practitioners (s.7). The term *practitioner* (except in the expression 'veterinary practitioner') means a doctor, dentist, veterinary practitioner or veterinary surgeon (s.37).

If the Secretary of State considers that it is in the public interest for a drug to be used only for the purposes of research or other special purposes, s/he may make an order to that effect. It is then unlawful for a practitioner, pharmacist or a person lawfully conducting a retail pharmacy business to do anything in relation to that drug except under licence. In this connection *doing* things includes having things in one's possession. When making an order of this kind the Secretary of State must act on the recommendation of the Advisory Council or after consulting that Council (s.7). Licence fees are prescribed in SI 1986 No.416, as amended.

The 1999 Regulations (SI 1999 No.1404) list exempted products which means a preparation or other product consists of one or more parts any of which contains a Controlled Drug where:

1     the preparation or other product is not designed for administration of the Controlled Drug to a human being or animal;
2     the Controlled Drug in any component part is packaged in such a form or in combination with other active or inert substances in such a manner that it cannot be recovered by readily applicable means or in a yield which constitutes a risk to health;
3     no one component part of the product or combination contains more than 1 mg of the Controlled Drug or 1 μg in the case of lysergide or any other N-alkyl derivative of lysergamide.

These exemptions will apply for example to in vitro diagnostic devices or kits used by laboratories for the detection of drugs of misuse or for clinical diagnosis, or other products containing very small quantities of Controlled Drugs, e.g. radioactive research compounds. The provisions of the Act will apply to the possession of a stock of Controlled Drugs for the purpose of producing kits and other exempted products. The safe custody regulations will also apply to any stock of Schedule 1 and 2 Controlled Drugs and stocks of buprenorphine, diethylpropion, flunitrazepam and temazepam held for the propose of manufacture of the exempted products.

## Provisions for Preventing Misuse

The Secretary of State may make such regulations as appear to him/her necessary or expedient for preventing the misuse of Controlled Drugs (s.10). In particular s/he may make provisions that:

1    require precautions to be taken for the safe custody of Controlled Drugs;
2    impose requirements as to the documentation of transactions involving Controlled Drugs, and require copies of documents relating to such transactions to be furnished to the prescribed authority;
3    require the keeping of records and the furnishing of information with respect to Controlled Drugs and in such circumstances and in such manner as may be prescribed;
4    provide for the inspection of any precautions taken or records kept in pursuance of regulations under this section;
5    relate to the packaging and labelling of Controlled Drugs;
6    regulate the transport of Controlled Drugs and the methods used for destroying or otherwise disposing of such drugs when no longer required;
7    regulate the issue of prescriptions containing Controlled Drugs and the supply of Controlled Drugs on prescriptions, and require persons issuing or dispensing prescriptions containing such drugs to furnish to the prescribed authority such information relating to those prescriptions as may be prescribed;
8    require any doctor who attends a person who, s/he considers, or has reasonable grounds to suspect, is addicted (within the meaning of the regulations) to Controlled Drugs of any description to furnish to the prescribed authority such particulars with respect to that person as may be prescribed;
9    prohibit any doctor from administering, supplying and authorising the administration and supply to persons so addicted, and from prescribing for such persons, such Controlled Drugs as may be prescribed, except and in accordance with the terms of a licence issued by the Secretary of State in pursuance of the regulations.

In addition to making regulations about safe custody the Secretary of State may also, by notice in writing, require the occupier of any premises where Controlled Drugs are kept to take further precautions as specified in the notice (s.11).

## Information Concerning Misuse

Doctors, pharmacists and persons lawfully conducting retail pharmacy businesses in any area may be called upon to give particulars of the quantities of any dangerous or otherwise harmful drugs (not necessarily controlled under the Act) which have been prescribed, administered or supplied over a particular period of time. The Secretary of State may call for this information if it appears to him/her that a social problem exists in that area caused by a drug or drugs.

A notice in writing may be served on the persons concerned specifying the period, and requiring particulars of the drug to be furnished in such a manner and within such time as set out in the notice. Pharmacists may be required to give the names and addresses of the prescribing doctors but may not be required to identify the patients concerned. It is an offence to fail, without reasonable excuse, to give the information required or to give false information (s.17).

## Prohibitions on Possession, Prescribing and Supply

### Directions Following Convictions

Where a pharmacist or practitioner has been guilty of any offence under the Act or of any offence under the Customs and Excise Act 1952 or the Customs and Excise Management Act 1979 relating to the unlawful importation or exportation of Controlled Drugs, the Secretary of State may make a direction in respect of him/her. If s/he is a practitioner the direction will prohibit him/her from having in his/her possession, prescribing, administering, manufacturing, compounding and supplying, and from authorising the administration and supply of the Controlled Drugs specified in the direction. If s/he is a pharmacist the direction will prohibit him/her from having in his/her possession, manufacturing, compounding and supplying and from supervising and controlling the manufacture, compounding and supply of the Controlled Drugs specified in the direction (s.12).

A copy of any such direction given by the Secretary of State must be served on the person to whom it applies and notice of it must be published in the London, Edinburgh and Belfast *Gazettes*. A direction takes effect when a copy has been served on the person concerned and it is then an offence for him/her to contravene it. The Secretary of State may cancel or suspend any direction which s/he has given. S/he may also bring a suspended direction into force again by cancelling its suspension (ss.12, 13 and 16).

Conviction for an offence under the Act committed by a pharmacist or other person who is a director, officer or employee of a body corporate carrying on a retail pharmacy business renders that body liable to disqualification under Part IV of the Medicines Act 1968 (s.80) and consequent removal of its premises from the register of pharmacies (see Chapter 21).

## Prohibitions Affecting Doctors

If a doctor contravenes the regulations relating to notification of addicts or the prescribing of Controlled Drugs for addicts, s/he does not commit any offence under the Act. The Secretary of State may, however, make a direction prohibiting him/her from prescribing, administering or supplying or authorising the administration or supply of the Controlled Drugs specified in the direction. The doctor commits an offence if s/he contravenes that direction (s.13).

## Irresponsible Prescribing

If the Secretary of State is of the opinion that a practitioner has been prescribing, administering or supplying, or authorising the administration or supply of any Controlled Drugs in an irresponsible manner, s/he may give a direction in respect of the practitioner concerned prohibiting him/her from prescribing, administering and supplying or authorising the administration and supply of the Controlled Drugs specified in the direction (s.13).

## Tribunals, Advisory Bodies and Professional Panels

Before s/he gives a direction prohibiting a doctor or other practitioner from prescribing, administering or supplying Controlled Drugs the Secretary of State must, except when the direction is based on a conviction, follow the procedure set out in the Act (ss.14, 15 and 16). S/he must refer the case to a *tribunal* consisting of four members of the practitioner's profession and with a lawyer as chairman (Sch.3). The procedure to be followed before tribunals is in SI 1974 No.85 (L.1) and, for Scotland, SI 1975 No.459 (s.59). If, as a result of the tribunal's finding that the practitioner has been responsible for the contravention or conduct alleged, the Secretary of State then proposes to make a direction, the practitioner must be informed and given the opportunity to make representations in writing within 28 days. If the practitioner so does, then the case must be referred to an *advisory body* of three appointed persons, one being a member of the practitioner's profession. After receiving the advice of that body the Secretary of State may (a) advise that no further proceedings be taken; (b) refer the case back to the same, or another, tribunal; or (c) give a direction under section 13 as described above (s.14).

In a case of irresponsible prescribing, if the Secretary of State considers circumstances require that a direction be given with the minimum of delay, s/he may refer the matter to a *professional panel* consisting of three members of the practitioner's profession appointed by the Secretary of State. The panel must afford the practitioner an opportunity to appear before it and, after considering the circumstances of the case, must report to the Secretary of State whether or not it believes there are reasonable grounds for thinking that there has been conduct as alleged. If the panel considers there are such grounds, the Secretary of State may give a direction at once which is effective for a period of six weeks. S/he must also refer the case at once to a tribunal, in accordance with the procedures outlined above. The period of operation of the temporary direction may be extended from time to time by a further 28 days if the tribunal consents. After the tribunal, or the advisory body as appropriate, has considered the case, the Secretary of State may, if s/he thinks fit, make a permanent direction, if that is the advice given to him/her. If no such direction is given, the temporary prohibition will cease (s.15).

## Offences, Penalties and Enforcement

Schedule 4 to the Act is a tabulated summary of offences under the Act and the penalties applicable to them. The level of penalty for offences which concern a Controlled Drug varies according to the class (A, B or C) into which the drug falls, the generally more harmful drugs attracting greater penalties.

The occupier or manager of any premises commits an offence if s/he knowingly permits or suffers any of the following to take place on the premises:

1    producing or supplying, or attempting to produce or supply, or offering to supply any Controlled Drug in contravention of the Act;
2    preparing opium for smoking;
3    smoking cannabis, cannabis resin or prepared opium (s.8).

It is an offence for any person to:

1    smoke or otherwise use prepared opium; or
2    frequent a place used for the purpose of opium smoking; or
3    have in his/her possession:

   (a)    any pipes or other utensils made or adapted for use in connection with the smoking of opium, being pipes or utensils which have been used by him/her or with his/her knowledge and permission in that connection or which s/he intends to use or permit others to use in that connection; or
   (b)    any utensils which have been used by him/her or with his/her knowledge and permission in connection with the preparation of opium for smoking (s.9).

Other offences are described in some detail in Schedule 4. Those relating to contravention of regulations or of conditions of any licence, or of directions relating to safe custody of Controlled Drugs, are of special concern to practising pharmacists (ss.11 and 18).

A person commits an offence if in the United Kingdom s/he assists in or induces the commission in any place outside the United Kingdom of an offence punishable under the provisions of a corresponding law in force in that place (s.20).

*Corresponding law* means a law stated, in a certificate purporting to be issued by or on behalf of the government of a country outside the United

Kingdom, to be a law providing for the control and regulation in that country of the production, supply, use, export and import of:

1    drugs and other substances in accordance with the provisions of the Single Convention on Narcotic Drugs signed at New York on 30 March 1961; or
2    dangerous or otherwise harmful drugs in pursuance of any treaty, convention or other agreement or arrangement to which the government of that country and of the United Kingdom are parties (ss.20 and 36).

The unlawful import and export of Controlled Drugs is an offence under the Customs and Excise Management Act 1979, which provides penalties for improper importation or exportation or for fraudulent evasion of any prohibition or restriction affecting Controlled Drugs.

Attempting to commit an offence under any provision of the Act or inciting or attempting to incite another to commit such an offence are also offences. They attract the same penalty as the substantive offences (ss.19 and 25).

Where any offence under the Act committed by a body corporate is proved to have been committed with the consent or connivance of, or to be attributable to any neglect on the part of, any director, manager, secretary, or other similar officer of the body corporate, or any person purporting to act in any such capacity, s/he, as well as the body corporate, is guilty of the offence and is liable to be proceeded against accordingly (s.21).

Proof that the accused neither knew of nor suspected, nor had reason to suspect, the existence of some fact which it is necessary for the prosecution to prove, is a defence in connection with the offences of production, supply or possession of Controlled Drugs, cultivation of cannabis or possession of opium pipes and utensils. When it is necessary, in connection with any offence, to prove that a substance or product is a Controlled Drug the accused may prove that s/he believed it to be a different Controlled Drug. This, in itself, will not constitute a defence unless there could have been no offence had the drug been of that description (s.28).

It is also a defence for a person accused of unlawful possession of a Controlled Drug to prove that s/he took possession of it to prevent another person committing an offence, and that s/he took steps to destroy it as soon as possible, or that s/he took possession of the drug to hand it over to some authorised person as soon as possible (s.5).

A constable, or other person authorised by the Secretary of State, has power to enter any premises used for the production and supply of Controlled Drugs and inspect books and documents and any stocks of drugs. An inspector of the Royal Pharmaceutical Society of Great Britain is authorised by the Secretary of State to inspect books and documents. It is an offence to conceal any such books, documents or stock.

A constable may also, on the authority of a warrant, enter any premises named in the warrant, by force if necessary, and search them and any person found therein, seizing any Controlled Drug or any document relevant to the transaction, if s/he has reasonable grounds to consider that an offence under the Act has been committed (s.23).

A constable may arrest a person who has committed an offence under the Act, or whom s/he suspects has committed an offence, if that person's name and address are unknown to him/her or cannot be ascertained, or if s/he suspects the name and address are false, or if s/he has reasonable cause to think that the person may abscond unless arrested (s.24). S/he may detain for the purposes of search any person whom s/he has reasonable grounds to suspect is in unlawful possession of a Controlled Drug. S/he may also stop and search any vehicle or vessel for the same reason, and may seize anything which appears to be evidence of an offence under the Act (s.23).

It is an offence intentionally to obstruct a person exercising their powers of examination or search. Failure to produce any book or document without reasonable excuse is also an offence, and proof of the reasonableness of the excuse rests with the person offering it as a defence (s.23).

Upon a conviction anything relating to the offence may be forfeited and destroyed or otherwise dealt with by order of the court, subject to any person claiming to be the owner showing cause why the order should not be made (s.27). The Drug Trafficking Offences Act 1986 provides for the confiscation of the proceeds of drug trafficking received by convicted persons.

### Scheduled Substances – Precursors

*Scheduled substances* means those substances which are useful for the manufacture of Controlled Drugs.

Council Regulation 90/3677/EEC controls the import, export, recording and labelling of scheduled substances and the power to enter business premises to obtain evidence of irregularities. Records must be kept for two years. It also requires member states to adopt measures to enable them to obtain information on any orders for, or activities in, scheduled substances. There is a list of scheduled substances.

The EC regulation was implemented by the Criminal Justice (International Co-operation) Act 1990 (s.12) which created the offences of manufacturing or supplying scheduled substances knowing or suspecting they are to be used in or for the unlawful production of a Controlled Drug. Regulations made under the 1990 Act (s.13) enable the other requirements of the EC regulation to be investigated and enforced (SI 1991 No.1285, as amended).

Council Directive 92/109/EEC, which is complementary to the above EC regulation, applies to the manufacture and trade in scheduled substances within the European Union and is implemented in the United Kingdom by SI 1993 No.2166. It requires the person who manufactures or trades in these substances to be licensed and restricts the persons to whom supplies may be made. The 1993 United Kingdom regulations treat the provisions of Council Directive 92/109/EEC as if they were requirements of regulations made under section 13 of the 1990 Act.

## Powers of Secretary of State

The power of the Secretary of State to make regulations is exercised by statutory instruments (ss.7, 10, 22 and 31). Regulations may make provision for different cases and circumstances and for different Controlled Drugs and different classes of persons. The opinion, consent or approval of a prescribed authority or of any person may also be made material to a regulation, e.g. the approval of a chief officer of police is required in connection with certain safekeeping requirements for drugs (s.31). Any licence or other authority issued by the Secretary of State for the purposes of the Act may be made subject to such conditions as s/he thinks proper and may be modified or revoked at any time (s.30).

The application of any provision of the Act which creates an offence, and those provisions of the Customs and Excise Management Act 1979 which apply to the importation and exportation of Controlled Drugs (see p.165) may, in prescribed cases, be excluded by regulation. Similarly, any provision of the Act or any regulation or order made under it may, by regulation, be made applicable to servants and agents of the Crown (s.22).

Most of the regulations are designed to render lawful various activities in connection with Controlled Drugs which would otherwise be unlawful under the Act. For example, they are necessary to enable doctors, pharmacists and others to prescribe, administer, manufacture, compound or supply Controlled Drugs as appropriate to their particular capacities. They also govern such matters as the safekeeping of Controlled Drugs and their destruction, the notification of addicts and the supply of Controlled Drugs to addicts.

## Regimes of Control

The drugs controlled under the Act are classified in the Misuse of Drugs Regulations 1985 (SI 1985 No.2066, as amended) into five Schedules in descending order of control, the most stringent controls applying to drugs in Schedule 1. All the Schedules are set out fully in Appendix 11 and the controls applying to each are outlined below.

### Schedule 1

This Schedule reproduces the list of drugs in the Misuse of Drugs (Designation) Order 1977 (SI 1977 No.1379, as amended). These are Controlled Drugs which may not be used for medicinal purposes, their production and possession being limited, in the public interest, to purposes of research or other special purposes. Certain limited classes of persons have a general authority to possess these drugs in the course of their duties, e.g. constables, carriers, etc. (reg.6). Other persons may only produce, supply or possess the drugs within the authority of a licence issued by the Secretary of State. The requirements of the Misuse of Drugs Regulations relating to (a) documentation, (b) keeping of records, (c) preservation of records, (d) supply on prescription, (e) marking of containers and (f) procedure for destruction, apply in full to these drugs in Schedule 1.

## Schedule 2

This Schedule includes the opiates (such as heroin, morphine and methadone) and the major stimulants (such as the amphetamines). A licence is needed to import or export drugs in this Schedule, but they may be manufactured or compounded by a practitioner, or a pharmacist, or a person lawfully conducting a retail pharmacy business acting in their capacity as such, or a person holding an appropriate licence. A pharmacist may supply a Schedule 2 drug to a patient (or the owner of an animal) only on the authority of a prescription in the required form issued by an appropriate practitioner (regs.15 and 16).

The drugs may only be administered to a patient by a doctor or dentist, or by any person acting in accordance with the directions of a doctor or dentist (reg.7). Requirements as to safe custody in pharmacies and control over destruction apply to these drugs, and the provisions relating to the marking of containers and the keeping of records must also be observed (regs.18 and 19). A list of persons who may lawfully possess or supply them is given under the heading Possession and Supply (p.170 below).

## Schedule 3

This Schedule includes the barbiturates (except quinalbarbitone, which is a Schedule 2 Controlled Drug) and a number of minor stimulant drugs, such as benzphetamine, and other drugs which are not thought likely to be so harmful when misused as the drugs in Schedule 2. The controls which apply to Schedule 2 also apply to drugs in this Schedule, except that:

1   they may also be manufactured by persons authorised in writing by the Secretary of State;
2   there is a difference in the classes of persons who may possess and supply them;
3   the requirements as to destruction do not apply to retail dealers; and
4   entries in the register of Controlled Drugs need not be made in respect of these drugs but invoices or like records must be kept for a period of two years (see p.178).

## Schedule 4, Part I

This part of the Schedule contains the anabolic and androgenic steroids and derivatives, together with an andrenoceptor stimulant and polypeptide hormones. The restrictions applicable to Schedule 3 drugs apply to them with the following relaxations:

1    there is no restriction on the possession of any Schedule 4, Part I drug when contained in a medicinal product;
2    prescription and labelling requirements under the Misuse of Drugs Act do not apply, but the provisions of the Medicines Act do apply;
3    records need not be kept by retailers;
4    destruction requirements apply only to importers, exporters and manufacturers;
5    there are no safe custody requirements;
6    there is no restriction on imports or exports *provided* they are imported or exported:

   (a)    in the form of a medicinal product; *and*
   (b)    by a person for administration to him/herself.

## Schedule 4, Part II

This part of the Schedule contains the benzodiazepine tranquillisers. The restrictions applicable to Schedule 3 drugs apply to them with the relaxations as for Schedule 4, Part I drugs at 1, 2, 3, 4, and 5 above. There is no restriction on imports and exports.

## Schedule 5

This Schedule specifies those preparations of certain Controlled Drugs for which there is only negligible risk of abuse. There is no restriction on the import, export, possession or administration of these preparations, and safe custody requirements do not apply to them. A practitioner or pharmacist, acting in his/her capacity as such, or a person holding an appropriate licence, may manufacture or compound any of them.

No record in the register of Controlled Drugs need be made in respect of Schedule 3, 4 or 5 drugs obtained by a retail dealer but the invoice, or a copy of it, must be kept for two years. Producers and wholesale dealers must retain invoices of quantities obtained and supplied [reg.24(1)]. No authority is required to destroy these drugs, and there are no special labelling requirements, though Medicines Act labelling requirements apply. A *retail dealer* is defined as a person lawfully conducting a retail pharmacy business or a pharmacist engaged in supplying drugs to the public at a National Health Service health centre.

## Poppy Straw

Poppy straw, which includes poppy heads, is listed as a Controlled Drug in Schedule 2 to the Act, where it is defined as *all parts, except the seeds, of the opium poppy, after mowing*. It is not included in any of the Schedules to the regulations. Although a licence is required to import or export poppy straw its production, possession and supply are free from control (reg.4). *Concentrate of poppy straw,* which means the material produced when poppy straw has entered into a process for the concentration of its alkaloids, is included in Schedule 1 to the regulations to which apply the stringent controls described above.

## Import and Export

Controlled Drugs may only be imported or exported in accordance with the terms and conditions of a licence issued by the Secretary of State (s.3 of the Act) but drugs in Schedules 4 (Part II) and 5 are exempted from this requirement (reg.4). Drugs in Schedule 4, Part I are subject to certain restrictions (see p.168). Unlawful import or export is an offence under the Customs and Excise Management Act 1979 (see p.165).

## Possession and Supply

It is unlawful for any person to be in possession of a Controlled Drug unless:

1    s/he holds an appropriate licence from or is registered by the Secretary of State (reg.10); or,
2    s/he is a member of a class specified in the regulations and is acting in his/her capacity as a member of that class (regs.6 and 10); or
3    the regulations provide that possession of that drug or group of drugs is not unlawful. Possession of poppy straw or drugs in Schedule 5 and medicinal products in Schedule 4 are not controlled (reg.4).

The classes of persons who may possess or supply Controlled Drugs are given in Table 16.1, with an indication of the range of drugs they may possess and/ or supply. A person authorised to supply may supply only those persons authorised to possess, and such supply is subject to any provisions of the Medicines Act 1968 which apply to the drug being supplied.

**Table 16.1**  Possession and supply of Controlled Drugs

| | *Class of Person* | *Possession* | *Supply* |
|---|---|---|---|
| 1. | A person holding an appropriate licence from the Home Office | S1 S2 S3 S4 S5 | S1 S2 S3 S4 S5 |
| 2. | A constable when acting in the course of his/her duty | S1 S2 S3 S4 S5 | S1 S2 S3 S4 S5 |
| 3. | A person engaged in the business of a carrier when acting in the course of that business | S1 S2 S3 S4 S5 | S1 S2 S3 S4 S5 |

4.  A person engaged in the business of the Post Office when acting in the course of that business ............ S1 S2 S3 S4 S5    S1 S2 S3 S4 S5

5.  An officer of Customs and Excise when acting in the course of his/her duty as such ............................... S1 S2 S3 S4 S5    S1 S2 S3 S4 S5

6.  A person engaged in the work of any laboratory to which the drug has been sent for forensic examination when acting in the course of his/her duty as a person so engaged ........................... S1 S2 S3 S4 S5    S1 S2 S3 S4 S5
    [The supply of any Controlled Drug by any person in categories 1–6 above may only be to a person who may lawfully possess that drug]

7.  A person engaged in conveying the drug to a person authorised by the regulations to have it in his/her possession (see under Requisitions p.175) ...................... S1 S2 S3 S4 S5    S1 S2 S3 S4 S5

8.  A person possessing a drug for administration in accordance with the directions of a practitioner (for example, on a prescription) ................................................. S2 S3 S4 S5
    [The Home Office take the view that it is unlawful for a doctor to possess a Controlled Drug on the strength of a prescription issued by him/herself and naming him/herself as patient (*Pharm J* 8 October 1977 p.328)]

9.  A person authorised under a group authority ................................... S2 S3 S4 S5    S2 S3 S4 S5

10. A practitioner ............................... S2 S3 S4 S5    S2 S3 S4 S5

11. A pharmacist ............................... S2 S3 S4 S5    S2 S3 S4 S5

12. A person lawfully conducting a retail pharmacy business ........................... S2 S3 S4 S5    S2 S3 S4 S5

13. The person in charge or acting person in charge of a hospital or nursing home, which is wholly or mainly maintained by a public authority out of public funds or by a charity or by voluntary subscriptions (c.f. 24 below) may not supply if there is a pharmacist responsible for dispensing and supply of drugs ........................... S2 S3 S4 S5    S2 S3 S4 S5

14. The sister or acting sister for the time being in charge of a ward, theatre or other department in a hospital or nursing home as in 13, in the case of drugs supplied to him/her by a person responsible for the dispensing and supply of medicines at the hospital or nursing home (c.f. 25 below). *Sister or acting sister* includes any male nurse occupying a similar position. Supply subject to direction by doctor or dentist     S2 S3 S4 S5     **S2 S3 S4 S5**

15. A person who is in charge of a laboratory, the recognised activities of which consist in, or include, the conduct of scientific education or research and which is attached to a university, university college or a hospital as described in 13 or to any other institution approved for the purpose by the Secretary of State (c.f. 26 below)     S2 S3 S4 S5     **S2 S3 S4 S5**

16. A public analyst appointed under section 89 of the Food and Drugs Act 1955 or section 27 of the Food and Drugs (Scotland) Act 1956     S2 S3 S4 S5     **S2 S3 S4 S5**

17. A sampling officer within the meaning of the Food and Drugs Act 1955 or the Food and Drugs (Scotland) Act 1956     S2 S3 S4 S5     **S2 S3 S4 S5**

18. A sampling officer within the meaning of Schedule 3 to the Medicines Act 1968     S2 S3 S4 S5     **S2 S3 S4 S5**

19. A person employed or engaged in connection with a scheme for testing the quality or amount of the drugs, preparations and appliances supplied under the National Health Service Act 1946 or the National Health Service (Scotland) Act 1947 and the regulations made thereunder     S2 S3 S4 S5     **S2 S3 S4 S5**

20. A person authorised by the Royal Pharmaceutical Society of Great Britain for the purposes of sections 108 and 109 of the Medicines Act 1968     S2 S3 S4 S5     **S2 S3 S4 S5**

21. The owner or master of a ship (which is not carrying a doctor) for the purposes of complying with the Health and Safety at Work, etc. Act 1974 or the Merchant Shipping Acts. *Master of ship* includes every person (except a pilot) having command or charge of any ship     S2 S3 S4 S5     **S2 S3 S4 S5**

| | | |
|---|---|---|
| 22. | The master of a foreign ship in port in Great Britain possessing drugs as necessary for the equipment of his ship and authorised by the local medical officer of health | S2 S3 S4 S5 | |
| 23. | The installation manager of an offshore installation possessing drugs for the purpose of compliance with the Health and Safety at Work etc. Act 1974, or the Mineral Workings (Off-Shore Installations) Act 1971. S/he may supply to (a) any person who may lawfully supply the drug; (b) any person on the installation whether employed there or not; (c) any constable for destruction | S2 S3 S4 S5 | S2 S3 S4 S5 |
| 24. | The person in charge or acting person in charge of a hospital or nursing home (c.f. 13 above). May not supply if there is a pharmacist responsible for dispensing and supply of drugs | S3 S4 S5 | S3 S4 S5 |
| 25. | The sister or acting sister for the time being in charge of a ward, theatre or other department in a hospital or nursing home in the case of drugs supplied to him/her by a person responsible for the dispensing and supply of medicines at the hospital or nursing home (c.f. 14 above). Supply subject to direction by doctor or dentist | S3 S4 S5 | S3 S4 S5 |
| 26. | A person in charge of a laboratory the recognised activities of which consist in, or include, the conduct of scientific education or research (c.f. 15 above) | S3 S4 S5 | S3 S4 S5 |
| 27. | A person whose name is entered in a register maintained by the Home Office relating to Schedule 3 drugs | S3 S4 S5 | S3 S4 |
| 28. | A person authorised in writing by the Secretary of State | S5 | S5 |
| 29. | Registered practising midwives (see below for supply to midwives and administration) [reg.11].<br>Any Controlled Drug s/he may lawfully administer under the Medicines Act Regulations | see below | see below |
| 30. | A person licensed under the Wildlife and Countryside Act 1981 | S2 S3 | S2 S3 |

Other general authorities to possess and supply include:

1    Any person who is lawfully in possession of a Controlled Drug may supply that drug to the person from whom s/he obtained it.
2    Any person who is in possession of a Schedule 2, 3, 4 or 5 drug which has been supplied for him/her by, or on the prescription of, a practitioner may supply that drug to any doctor, dentist or pharmacist *for the purpose of destruction*.
3    Any person who is in lawful possession of a Schedule 2, 3, 4 or 5 drug which has been supplied by, or on the prescription of, a veterinary surgeon or veterinary practitioner for the treatment of animals may supply that drug to any veterinary surgeon, veterinary practitioner or pharmacist *for the purpose of destruction*.

## Midwives and Pethidine

A registered midwife who has, in accordance with the Nurses, Midwives and Health Visitors Act 1977, notified to the local supervising authority his/her intention to practise may, as far as is necessary for the practice of his/her profession or employment as a midwife, possess and administer any Controlled Drug which the Medicines Act 1968 permits him/her to administer. Supplies may only be made to him/her, or possessed by him/her, on the authority of a *midwife's supply order*, that is, an order in writing specifying the name and occupation of the midwife obtaining the Controlled Drug, the purpose for which it is required and the total quantity to be obtained (reg.11). It must be signed by the *appropriate medical officer*, which means:

1    a doctor who is for the time being authorised in writing for the purpose of regulation 11 by the local supervising authority for the region or area in which the Controlled Drug was, or is to be, obtained; or
2    a person appointed by that authority to exercise supervision over certified midwives within their area, e.g. a non-medical supervisor of midwives.

A midwife may surrender any stocks of Controlled Drugs in his/her possession which are no longer required by him/her to a doctor falling within category 1 above (reg.11) or to the person from whom s/he obtained them (reg.6).

The midwife must, on each occasion on which s/he obtains a supply of a Controlled Drug, enter in a book kept by him/her solely for this purpose: (a) the date, and (b) the name and address of the person from whom the drug was obtained, the amount obtained and the form in which it was obtained. When administering any Controlled Drug to a patient s/he must enter in the same book as soon as practicable the name and address of the patient, the amount administered and the form in which it was administered (reg.21).

A midwife's supply order must be retained for two years by the pharmacist who supplies the Controlled Drug and s/he must make an appropriate entry in his/her Controlled Drugs register (regs.19 and 22).

## Requisitions

A requisition in writing must be obtained by a supplier before s/he delivers any Controlled Drug except those in Schedules 4 and 5, poppy straw or any drug in Schedule 3 contained in or comprising a preparation which (a) is required for use as a buffering agent in chemical analysis, (b) has present both a substance in the Schedule and a salt of that substance, and (c) is pre-mixed in a kit (reg.14(7), as amended). A *supplier*, in this context, means any person who is not a practitioner supplying such a Controlled Drug, otherwise than on prescription, or by way of administration, to any of the following *recipients*:

1 a practitioner;
2 the person in charge or acting person in charge of a hospital or nursing home;
3 a person who is in charge of a laboratory;
4 the owner of a ship, or the master of a ship which does not carry a doctor among the seamen employed in it;
5 the installation manager of an off-shore installation;
6 the master of a foreign ship in a port in Great Britain [reg.14(4)].

The requisition must be signed by the recipient, must state his/her name, address and profession or occupation, and must specify the total quantity of the drug and the purpose for which it is required. A *wholesale dealer*, that is, a person who carries on the business of selling drugs to persons who buy to sell again, when supplying a pharmacist, does not require a requisition. The supplier must be reasonably satisfied that the signature is that of the person purporting to have signed the requisition and that s/he is engaged in the profession or occupation stated [reg.14(2)].

Where a supplier, who is not a practitioner, supplies a Controlled Drug for which a requisition is required s/he may not supply it to any person sent on behalf of the recipient to collect the drug unless that person: (a) is authorised to have the drug in his/her possession otherwise than as a messenger; or (b) produces to the supplier a statement in writing signed by the recipient to the effect that s/he is empowered by the recipient to receive the drug on his/her behalf, and the supplier is reasonably satisfied that the document is a genuine document [reg.14(1)].

Where a recipient is a practitioner who represents that s/he urgently requires a Controlled Drug for the purpose of his/her profession, the supplier, if s/he is reasonably satisfied that the practitioner requires the drug and is by reason of some emergency unable to furnish a written requisition, may deliver the drug on an undertaking by the practitioner to furnish a written requisition within the next 24 hours. Failure to do so is an offence on the part of the practitioner [reg.14(2)].

A requisition furnished by the master of a foreign ship must contain a statement signed by the proper officer of the port health authority or, in Scotland, the Medical Officer designated under section 14 of the National Health Service (Scotland) Act 1978 by the Health Board within whose jurisdiction the ship is, that the quantity of drug to be supplied is the quantity necessary for the equipment of the ship [reg.14(5)].

A requisition furnished by the matron or acting matron of a hospital or nursing home must also be signed by a doctor or a dentist employed or engaged in that hospital or nursing home [reg.14(5)].

A *sister* or *acting sister* for the time being in charge of any ward, theatre or other department of a hospital or nursing home who obtains a supply of a Controlled Drug from the person responsible for dispensing and supplying medicines at that hospital or nursing home must furnish a requisition in writing signed by him/her which specifies the total quantity of the drug required. S/he must retain a copy or note of the requisition. The person responsible for the dispensing and supply of medicines must mark the requisition in such a manner as to show that it has been complied with and must retain the requisition in the dispensary [reg.14(6)].

## Prescriptions for Controlled Drugs

*Prescription* means a prescription used by a doctor for the medical treatment of a single individual, by a dentist for the dental treatment of a single individual, or by a veterinary surgeon or veterinary practitioner for the purposes of animal treatment.

No prescription requirements are laid down for any Controlled Drug in Schedules 4 or 5 to the regulations. Neither are there any prescription requirements for the drug Temazepam (SI 1995 No.3244). In the case of other Controlled Drugs (i.e. those in Schedules 2 and 3) a prescription must not be issued unless it complies with the following requirements:

1    it must be in ink or otherwise indelible and be signed by the person issuing it with their usual signature and dated by them (it is unlikely that a carbon copy, even one bearing an original signature, would be sufficient to satisfy the indelibility requirement);

2    except in the case of a health prescription it must specify the address of the person issuing it;

3    it must have written thereon, if issued by a dentist, the words *for dental treatment only* and, if issued by a veterinary surgeon or a veterinary practitioner, a declaration that the Controlled Drug prescribed is for an animal under his/her care;

4    it must specify, in the handwriting of the person issuing it, the name and address of the person for whose treatment it is issued or, if it is issued by

a veterinary surgeon or veterinary practitioner, the name and address of the person to whom the Controlled Drug prescribed is to be delivered;

5    it must specify, in the handwriting of the person issuing it, the dose to be taken and:

(a)    in the case of a prescription containing a Controlled Drug which is a preparation, it must specify the form and, where appropriate, the strength of the preparation, and either the total quantity (in both words and figures) of the preparation or the number (in both words and figures) of dosage units, as appropriate, to be supplied;

(b)    in any other case, it must specify the total quantity (in both words and figures) of the Controlled Drug to be supplied;

6    in the case of a prescription for a total quantity intended to be dispensed by instalments, it must contain a direction specifying the amount of the instalments of the total amount which must be dispensed and the intervals to be observed when dispensing [reg.15(1)].

The requirement that the particulars in 4 and 5 above must be in the prescriber's own handwriting does not apply to a prescription containing no drug other than (a) phenobarbitone, (b) phenobarbitone sodium, or (c) either of those drugs. The requirement can also be waived by the Secretary of State who may approve prescribers for this purpose either personally or as a class. This provision is used to facilitate the issue of prescriptions from treatment centres for drug addiction [reg.15(2)].

A prescription issued for the treatment of a patient in a hospital or nursing home and written on the patient's bed card or case sheet need not specify the address of the patient [reg.15(3)].

When a drug is administered from stock held in the ward the prescription requirements do not apply.

A Controlled Drug, except those in Schedules 4 and 5 must not be supplied by any person on a prescription:

1    unless the prescription complies with the provisions set out above;
2    unless the prescriber's address on the prescription is within the United Kingdom;
3    unless the supplier is either acquainted with the prescriber's signature, and has no reason to suppose that it is not genuine, or has taken reasonably sufficient steps to satisfy him/herself that it is genuine;
4    before the date specified on the prescription;
5    later than 13 weeks after the date specified on the prescription [reg.16(1)].

Prescriptions (other than those for drugs in Schs.4 or 5) which contain a direction that specified instalments of the total amount may be supplied at stated intervals must not be supplied otherwise than in accordance with the directions. The first instalment must be supplied not later than 13 weeks after the date specified in the prescription, and the prescription must be marked with the date of each dispensing and retained for two years after the supply of the last instalment [reg.16(3)]. Repeat prescriptions as such are not provided for, in that the total quantity of drug prescribed must be stated on the prescription.

The date must be marked on a prescription for a Controlled Drug at the time each instalment is supplied. The prescription must be retained for two years (except for National Health Service or local health authority prescriptions) [regs.16(2) and 23(3)].

Nothing in the regulations relating to prescriptions (regs.15 and 16) has effect in relation to prescriptions issued for the purposes of a scheme for testing the quality and amount of the drugs, preparations and appliances supplied under the National Health Service, or to any prescriptions issued to sampling officers under the Food and Drugs (Scotland) Act 1956 or the Medicines Act 1968 (reg.17).

A person is not in lawful possession of a drug if s/he obtained it on a prescription which s/he obtained from the prescriber (a) by making a false statement or declaration, or (b) by not disclosing to the doctor that s/he was being supplied with a Controlled Drug by or on the prescription of another doctor [reg.10(2)].

### Marking of Containers

The container in which a Controlled Drug, other than a preparation, is supplied must be plainly marked with the amount of drug contained in it. If the drug is a preparation made up into tablets, capsules or other dosage units, the container must be marked with the amount of Controlled Drug(s) in each dosage unit and the number of dosage units in it. For any other kind of preparation, the container must be marked with the total amount of the preparation in it and the percentage of Controlled Drug(s) in the preparation [reg.18(1)]. These requirements do not apply to (a) poppy straw, (b) Controlled Drugs in Schedules 4 and 5, (c) Controlled Drugs supplied on the prescription of a practitioner or for administration in a clinical trial or a medicinal test on animals, or (d) any Schedule 3 drug in a preparation used as a buffering agent in chemical analysis, or which has present in it both a substance in that Schedule and a salt of that substance or is pre-mixed in a kit (reg.18(2), as amended).

### Registers and Records

An entry in a register of Controlled Drugs must be made in respect of every quantity of any drug in Schedules 1 and 2 which is obtained or supplied (whether by way of administration or otherwise). This requirement applies to any person authorised to supply those drugs except a sister or acting sister for the time being in charge of a ward, theatre or other department in a hospital or nursing home, or a person licensed to supply by the Secretary of State if the licence does not require a register to be kept (reg.19). A pharmacist or practitioner need not record any prescribed drug returned to him/her for destruction.

**Figure 16.1**   PART I: Entries to be made in case of obtaining Controlled Drugs

| Date on which supply received | NAME | ADDRESS | Amount obtained | Form in which obtained |
|---|---|---|---|---|
| | Of person or firm from whom obtained | | | |
| | | | | |

PART II: Entries to be made in case of supply of Controlled Drugs

| Date on which transaction was effected | NAME | ADDRESS | Particulars as to licence or authority of person or firm supplied to be in possession | Amount supplied | Form in which supplied |
|---|---|---|---|---|---|
| | Of person or firm supplied | | | | |
| | | | | | |

Entries in the register must be made in chronological sequence in the form specified in Schedule 6 to the regulations, as illustrated. *Register* means a bound book and does not include any form of loose-leaf register or card index.

A separate register or separate part of the register must be used in respect of each class of drugs, but the salts of any drug or any stereoisomeric form of the drug may be classed with the drug. Dexamphetamine, for example, may be entered under amphetamine, but a separate part of the register is required for methylamphetamine. Separate sections can be used, if desired, in respect of different drugs or different strengths of a drug falling within the same class (reg.19).

The class of drugs recorded must be specified at the head of each page of the register and entries must be made on the day of the transaction or the following day. No cancellation, obliteration or alteration of any entry may be made, and corrections must be by way of marginal notes or footnotes which must be dated. Every entry and correction must be in ink or be otherwise indelible (reg.20).

A register must not be used for any other purpose and must be kept at the premises to which it relates. A separate register must be kept in respect of each set of premises of the business. There may only be one such register for each premises unless the Secretary of State has approved the keeping of separate registers in different departments (reg.20).

Where a supply is made to a member of the crew of a ship or a person on an off-shore installation, an entry, specifying the drug, in the official log book or installation log book is a sufficient record. These books are required to be kept under the Merchant Shipping Acts. In the case of a ship which is not required to carry an official log book a report signed by the master of the ship is sufficient if it is delivered as soon as may be to the superintendent of a mercantile marine office.

For record-keeping requirements for midwives, see page 174.

### Furnishing of Information

Particulars of stocks, receipts and supplies of Controlled Drugs must be furnished on request to any person authorised in writing by the Secretary of State. The register, the stocks of drugs and other relevant books and documents must also be produced if requested (reg.25). Inspectors of the Royal Pharmaceutical Society are authorised for this purpose in relation to registered pharmacies.

Those required to furnish information are:

1   practitioners;
2   wholesale dealers;
3   retail dealers;
4   persons in charge of hospitals, nursing homes or laboratories;
5   persons authorised under the Act or regulations to produce, import or export any Controlled Drug;
6   persons authorised under regulation 9(4)(a) to supply drugs in Schedules 3 and 4.

Professional *personal records* relating to the physical or mental health of an individual are exempt.

### Preservation of Records

All registers and midwives' record books must be preserved for two years from the date on which the last entry is made therein. Every requisition, order or prescription (other than a health prescription) on which a Controlled Drug is supplied must be preserved for two years from the date on which the last delivery is made (reg.23).

For Controlled Drugs in Schedules 3 and 5 to the regulations it is sufficient if every invoice is preserved for two years from the date on which it is issued. Producers and wholesalers must keep invoices in respect of Schedule 3 and 5 drugs obtained or supplied by them, and retail dealers must keep invoices in respect of the drugs they obtain. Copies of invoices, e.g. on microfilm, may be retained in place of the original document (reg.24).

## Destruction of Controlled Drugs

Persons who are required to keep records in respect of Controlled Drugs in Schedules 1, 2, 3 or 4 may only destroy them in the presence of a person authorised by the Secretary of State either personally or as a member of a class. Among the classes of authorised persons for this purpose are police officers, inspectors of the Home Office and of the Royal Pharmaceutical Society of Great Britain and, for stock kept in a hospital, the Regional Pharmaceutical Officer or the Senior Administrative Officer employed on duties connected with the administration of the hospital concerned.

Particulars of the date of destruction and the quantity destroyed must be entered in the register of Controlled Drugs and signed by the authorised person in whose presence the drug was destroyed. The authorised person may take a sample of the drug which is to be destroyed, and destruction must be carried out according to his/her directions. A pharmacist or practitioner may destroy prescribed drugs returned by a patient or the patient's representative without making any record and without the presence of an authorised person.

The master of a ship or installation manager of an off-shore installation may not destroy any surplus drugs but may dispose of them to a constable or to a person who is lawfully entitled to supply them (that is, to any pharmacist or licensed dealer who could have supplied them to him/her) (reg.26).

## Addicts

There are separate regulations relating to addicts and the supply of certain Controlled Drugs to them (SI 1997 No.1001). A person is regarded as being addicted to a drug 'if, and only if, s/he has, as a result of repeated administration, become so dependent on a drug that s/he has an overpowering desire for the administration of it to be continued'. The expression drug in this context means those specified in the regulations namely:

1    cocaine, dextromoramide, diamorphine, dipipanone, hydrocodone, hydromorphone, levorphanol, methadone, morphine, opium, oxycodone, pethidine, phenazocine and piritramide;

2      any stereoisomeric form of a substance specified in paragraph 1 above, except dextrorphan;

3      any ester or ether of a substance specified in paragraph 1 or 2 above not being a substance for the time being specified in Part II of Schedule 2 to the Misuse of Drugs Act 1971 (see Appendix 11);

4      any salt of a substance specified in any of the paragraphs 1 to 3 above;

5      any preparation or other product containing a substance or product specified in any of paragraphs 1 to 4 above.

Except for the treatment of organic injury or disease or unless s/he is licensed so to do by the Secretary of State no doctor may administer or authorise the supply of cocaine, diamorphine or dipipanone or the salts of either, to an addicted person.

There is provision for addicts to receive daily supplies of cocaine, heroin, dextromoramide, dipipanone, methadone and pethidine on special prescription forms [FP(10) HP] issued by drug addiction clinics. There is also provision for supplies of all Schedule 2 Controlled Drugs for the treatment of addiction to be issued by general medical practitioners on special prescription forms [FP(10) MDA or in Scotland GP10]. These are administrative arrangements made under the National Health Service and do not form part of the Misuse of Drugs Regulations.

## Safe Custody of Controlled Drugs

The regulations relating to safe custody (SI 1973 No.798, as amended) apply to all Controlled Drugs except:

1      Any drug in Schedules 4 and 5.

2      Any liquid preparations, apart from injections, which contain any of the following:

   (a)    amphetamine
   (b)    benzphetamine
   (c)    chlorphentermine
   (d)    fenethylline
   (e)    mephentermine
   (f)    methaqualone
   (g)    methylamphetamine
   (h)    methylphenidate
   (i)    phendimetrazine
   (j)    phenmetrazine
   (k)    pipradol
   (l)    any stereoisomeric form of a substance specified in (a) to (k) above; and any salt of a substance specified in (a) to (l) above.

3    Any of the following:

(a)   cathine
(b)   ethchlorvynol
(c)   ethinamate
(d)   mazindol
(e)   meprobamate
(f)   methylphenobarbitone
(g)   methyprylone
(h)   pentazocine
(i)   phentermine
(j)   any 5,5-disubstituted barbituric acid
(k)   any stereoisomeric form of a substance specified in (a) to (j) above
(l)   any salt of a substance specified in (a) to (k) above; and any preparation or other product containing a substance or product specified in (a) to (l) above.

4    Quinalbarbitone.

The premises to which the safe custody requirements apply are:

1    any premises occupied by a retail dealer (see p.169) for the purposes of his/her business;
2    any nursing home within the meaning of Part VI of the Public Health Act 1936 or the Nursing Homes Registration (Scotland) Act 1938;
3    any residential or other establishment provided under or by virtue of section 59 of the Social Work (Scotland) Act 1968;
4    any mental nursing home within the meaning of Part III of the Mental Health Act 1959;
5    any private hospital within the meaning of the Mental Health (Scotland) Act 1960.

The occupier and every person concerned in the management of any of these premises must ensure that all Controlled Drugs (except those mentioned above) are, so far as circumstances permit, kept in a locked safe, cabinet or room which is so constructed and maintained as to prevent unauthorised access to the drugs (see also p.161).

This requirement does not apply in respect of any Controlled Drug which is for the time being constantly under the direct personal supervision of (a) a pharmacist in the premises of a retail dealer, e.g. when dispensing prescriptions; or (b) the person in charge of the premises or any member of his/her staff designated by him/her for the purpose in the case of other premises to which the regulations apply.

The relevant requirements which apply to safes, cabinets and rooms where Controlled Drugs are kept are in Schedule 2 to the regulations.

The owner of a pharmacy may, as an alternative, elect to apply to the police for a certificate that his/her safes, cabinets or rooms provide an adequate degree of security. Applications must be made in writing. After inspection by the police, and if the degree of security is found to be adequate, a certificate, renewable annually, may be issued. The certificate will specify conditions to be observed and may be cancelled if there is a breach of any condition, or if the occupier has refused entry to a police officer, or if there has been any change of circumstances lowering the degree of security.

Quite apart from these special requirements, which affect only certain classes of premises, a person having possession of any Controlled Drug to which the safe custody regulations apply must ensure that, as far as circumstances permit, it is kept in a locked receptacle which can be opened only by him/her or by a person authorised by him/her. This requirement does not apply to a carrier in the course of his/her business or to a person engaged in the business of the Post Office when acting in the course of that business, or to a person to whom the drug has been supplied on the prescription of a practitioner for his/her own treatment or that of another person or an animal.

## Summary

Table 16.2 summarises the Misuse of Drugs Regulations.

**Table 16.2**   Misuse of Drugs Regulations summarised

|  | Schedule 1 | Schedule 2 | Schedule 3 | Schedule 4 Part I & II | Schedule 5 |
|---|---|---|---|---|---|
| Administration | By licence only | To a patient by a doctor or dentist or by any person acting in accordance with the directions of a doctor or dentist | As for Schedule 2 | As for Schedule 2 | No restriction |
| Import and Export | By licence only | By licence only | By licence only | No restriction when contained in a medicinal product [Part I] No restriction [Part II] | No restriction |
| Possession | By licence only | See under Possession and Supply (p.170) | See under Possession and Supply (p.170) | No restriction | No restriction |
| Supply | By licence only | See under Possession and Supply (p.170) | See under Possession and Supply (p.170) | See under Possession and Supply (p.170) | See under Possession and Supply (p.170) |
| Emergency supply permitted | No | No | No except phenobarbitone for epilepsy | Yes | Yes |

*Table 16.2 contd.*

|  | Schedule 1 | Schedule 2 | Schedule 3 | Schedule 4 Part I & II | Schedule 5 |
|---|---|---|---|---|---|
| Production | By licence only | Licence holders, Pharmacists, Practitioners and Owners of pharmacies | Licence holders, Authorised persons, Pharmacists Practitioners and Owners of pharmacies | Licence holders, Authorised persons, Pharmacists, Practitioners and Owners of pharmacies | Licence holders, Pharmacists, Practitioners and Owners of pharmacies |
| Prescription requirements | By licensed person only | Yes | Yes except temazepam | Do not apply | Do not apply |
| Hand-written | Yes | Yes | Yes except phenobarbitone for epilepsy and temazepam | No | No |
| Records in Register | Yes | Yes | No register, but records to be kept by licensed and authorised persons. Invoices to be kept by retail dealers, wholesalers, hospitals, nursing homes and laboratories | No register, but licensed producers and authorised suppliers must keep records of imports and exports | No register, but licensed producers, wholesalers, and retail dealers must keep invoices |
| Labelling requirements | Yes | Yes | Yes | No | No |
| Destruction requirements | Yes | Yes, but do not apply to drugs returned by patients | Apply only to imports, exports, and licensed manufacturers | Apply only to imports, exports, and licensed manufacturers | Do not apply |
| Safe Custody required | Yes | Yes (except certain liquids, quinal-barbitone and temazepam) (see p.182) | No (except temazepam buprenorphine and diethylpropion) (see p.182) | No | No |

CHAPTER SEVENTEEN

# Poisons Act, List and Rules

The Poisons Act 1972 and the rules made under it, are concerned with the sale of poisons. Unlike the Medicines Act 1968 the Act does not extend to Northern Ireland.

A *poison* means a non-medicinal poison (rule 2) and is defined in the Act (s.11) as a substance which is included in Part I or Part II of the Poisons List made under the Act and which is neither a medicinal product as defined under section 130 of the Medicines Act 1968 nor a substance which is treated as a medicinal product by virtue of an order made under section 104 or 105 of the Medicines Act (see Chapter 1). In line with the Medicines Act the other definitions include *the board* (s.11); this means, in relation to a body corporate, persons controlling the body by whatever name it is called, e.g. the management committee of a co-operative society. The Act also follows the definitions of the Medicines Act for 'persons lawfully conducting a retail pharmacy business', and a 'registered pharmacy' (see Chapter 4). A more restricted meaning is given to 'sale by way of wholesale dealing'; in relation to poisons this means sale to a person who buys for the purpose of selling again (see Medicines Act definition, p.21).

## Poisons Board

The Act (s.1) provides for the continuation of an advisory committee first established under the Pharmacy and Poisons Act 1933 called the Poisons

Board. It consists of at least 16 members and the Secretary of State has powers to appoint up to three additional members if s/he thinks fit. The board must include five persons appointed by the Royal Pharmaceutical Society of Great Britain, one of whom is required to be engaged in the manufacture for sale by wholesale dealing of pharmaceutical preparations. Members of the Poisons Board hold office for three years and the Secretary of State appoints one of the members as the chair. The quorum is 11 and the Board has power to appoint replacements for casual vacancies. The Board makes its own regulations as to procedure, subject to the approval of the Secretary of State (s.1).

## Poisons List

The Poisons List is a list of substances treated as poisons for the purposes of the Act (s.2) and is set out in a Poisons List Order, as amended (SI 1982 No.218) (Appendix 12). After consultation with, or on the recommendations of, the Poisons Board the Secretary of State may amend or vary this list. This list is divided into two parts.

*Part I* consists of poisons the sale of which is restricted to persons lawfully conducting a retail pharmacy business (subsequently referred to as Part I poisons).

*Part II* consists of poisons which may only be sold either by a person lawfully conducting a retail pharmacy business or by a person whose name is entered in a local authority's list (subsequently referred to as Part II poisons). Except where provision is made to the contrary an unqualified reference to a poison includes a substance containing that poison.

N.B. Some substances in the Poisons List also have medicinal uses, e.g. arsenic, strychnine. When sold as medicinal products they are controlled under the Medicines Act 1968 (see p.1) but when sold for non-medicinal purposes they are subject to the Poisons Act 1972.

## Local Authorities' Lists

Every local authority is obliged to keep a list of the names and business addresses of persons, *listed sellers*, who are entitled to sell Part II poisons and must enter on the list all those persons who make application. A local authority has power (a) to refuse to enter a name if, in its opinion the person is not fit to be on the list, and (b) to remove a name for non-payment of the prescribed fee. A person aggrieved by such a decision can appeal to the Crown Court or, in Scotland, to the Sheriff (s.5).

A local authority's list, which is open to inspection without fee, must include particulars of the premises and of the names of the persons listed (Sch.9 and rule 24, see p.458).

The Act provides for the payment of reasonable fees as determined by the authority by a person making application for their name to be included on the list, and also for further annual payments of fees for having their name retained on the list [s.6(2), as amended].

If a person whose name is on a local authority's list is convicted of any offence, which in the opinion of the Court renders him/her unfit to have his/her name so listed, the Court may, as part of the sentence, order his/her name to be removed and disqualified from being on the list for a specified period. Any person whose name is on a local authority list may not use in connection with his/her business any title, emblem or description reasonably calculated to suggest that s/he is entitled to sell any poisons which s/he is not entitled to sell (s.6).

*Local authority* means: (a) in relation to England and Wales, the council of a county or London borough or the Common Council of the City of London; and (b) in relation to Scotland the council of a region or island area [s.11(2), as amended].

## Inspection and Enforcement

It is the duty of the Royal Pharmaceutical Society of Great Britain to take reasonable steps by means of inspection and otherwise to enforce the provisions of the Poisons Act and its rules. To do this, the Society must appoint as many inspectors as the Privy Council may direct. Nineteen have been appointed. Only a pharmacist can be appointed as an inspector, and every such appointment is subject to the approval of the Privy Council.

An inspector appointed by the Society, to ensure compliance by pharmacists and persons carrying on retail businesses has (a) power at all reasonable times to enter any registered pharmacy, and (b) power to enter any premises in which s/he has reasonable cause to suspect that a breach of the law has been committed in respect of any Part I poison. Whether in a retail pharmacy business or any other premises an inspector has power to make such examination and inquiry and do any other thing, including the taking of samples, as is necessary to ascertain that the Act and the rules are being complied with. (The Society's inspectors also have other duties under the Medicines Act 1968 and the Misuse of Drugs Act 1971.)

It is the duty of every local authority, by means of inspection and otherwise, to take all reasonable steps to secure compliance with the provisions of the Act and its rules, as far as they concern Part II poisons, (a) by persons not being persons conducting a retail pharmacy business, and (b) by any persons lawfully conducting a retail pharmacy business in so far as that business is carried on at premises which are not a registered pharmacy. Each local authority must appoint inspectors for these purposes.

An inspector appointed by the Society may, with the consent of the Society, also be appointed by a local authority to be an inspector for the purposes of this section of the Act (s.9).

For the purposes of enforcement an inspector appointed by a local authority has power at all reasonable times to enter any premises on the local authority's list and any premises where s/he has reasonable cause to suspect that a breach of the law has been committed in respect of any Part II poison (s.9). An inspector appointed by a local authority has power, with the consent of the authority, to institute proceedings before a court of summary jurisdiction, and to take any proceedings instituted by him/her, notwithstanding that s/he is not of counsel or a solicitor.

It is an offence for any person wilfully to delay or obstruct an inspector, to refuse to allow a sample to be taken, or to fail without reasonable excuse to give any information which the Act requires him/her to give to an inspector (s.9). It is specifically provided that nothing in the Act authorises an inspector to enter or inspect the premises of a doctor, a dentist, a veterinary surgeon, or a veterinary practitioner unless those premises are a shop (s.9).

A document purporting to be a certificate sent by a public analyst appointed under section 89 of the Food and Drugs Act 1955 or section 27 of the Food and Drugs (Scotland) Act 1956 or a person appointed by the Secretary of State (in Scotland the Lord Advocate) to make analyses for the purposes of the Poisons Act, is admissible in any proceedings under the Act as evidence of the matters stated therein, and either party may require the person who has signed the certificate to be called as a witness (s.8).

## Penalties and Legal Proceedings

Any person who contravenes or fails to comply with the Act, or any of the provisions made under the Poisons Rules, is liable on summary conviction to a fine not exceeding £2500, and for continuing offences to a further fine not exceeding £200 for every day subsequent to the day on which s/he is convicted of the offence (s.8 and the Criminal Law Act 1977). For the misuse of titles (s.6) and obstruction of an inspector (s.9) the maximum fine is £500.

In the case of proceedings against a person under the Act or rules for or in connection with the sale, exposure for sale or supply of a poison effected by an employee, it is not a defence that the employee acted without the authority of the employer and any material fact known to the employee is deemed to have been known to the employer (s.8).

Information in respect of any offence under the Act or rules must be laid within 12 months of the commission of the offence. There is an additional provision that the Secretary of State may institute proceedings within a period of three months after the date on which evidence sufficient in his/her opinion to justify a prosecution for an offence comes to his/her knowledge (s.8).

## Poison Rules

The Poisons Act (s.7) provides that the Secretary of State may, after consultation with or on the recommendation of the Poisons Board, make rules in respect of any of the following:

1    the sale, whether wholesale or retail, or the supply of poisons, by or to any persons or classes of persons and in particular but without prejudice to the generality of the foregoing provisions:

   (a)   for regulating or restricting the sale or supply of poisons by persons whose names are entered in a local authority's list and for prohibiting the sale of any specified poison or class of poisons by any class of such persons; and

   (b)   for dispensing with or relaxing with respect to any poisons of this Act relating to the sale of poisons;

2    the storage and labelling of poisons (but see pp.192 and 193);
3    the containers in which poisons may be sold or supplied;
4    the addition to poisons of specified ingredients for the purpose of rendering them readily distinguishable as poisons;
5    the compounding of poisons, and the supply of poisons on and in accordance with a prescription duly given by a doctor, a dentist, a veterinary surgeon or a veterinary practitioner;
6    the period for which any books required to be kept for the purpose of this Act are to be preserved;
7    the period for which any certificate for the purchase of a poison given under section 3 of the Act (see p.458) is to remain in force;
8    for prescribing anything which is by the Act to be prescribed by rules.

The Secretary of State may issue to the Poisons Board a direction that, before recommending rules under 1(a), 2, 3 and 4 above, the Board must first consult a body representative of persons engaged in the manufacture of poisons or preparations containing poisons.

The power to make rules or orders under the Act is exercised by Statutory Instrument. The current rules are set out in the Poison Rules 1982 (SI 1982 No.218, as amended) (Appendix 13). Apart from their general classification into Part I or Part II poisons, poisons may, in addition, be divided into classes by their inclusion in certain Schedules to the Poison Rules.

There are eight Schedules to the rules and they are described, briefly, below. More detailed reference is made later (see also Appendix 13).

*Schedule 1*: A list of poisons to which special restrictions apply relating to storage, conditions of sale, and keeping of sales records.
*Schedule 4*: A list of articles exempted from control as poisons (rule 8). It is in two groups: Group I comprises classes of articles which contain poisons but are totally exempt, e.g. builders' materials. Group II lists exemptions for certain poisons when in specified articles or substances, e.g. paraquat in pellet form containing not more than 5 per cent of salts of paraquat calculated as paraquat ion.
*Schedule 5*: Some Part II poisons may be sold by listed sellers only in certain forms. The details are given in this Schedule which also specifies certain poisons which may be sold by a person duly authorised, in

England or Wales, by the Minister of Agriculture, Fisheries and Food, only to persons engaged in the trade or business of agriculture or horticulture and for the purpose of that trade or business. In any other circumstances the sale of poisons in this Schedule is restricted to pharmacies.

*Schedule 8*: Form of application for inclusion in local authority's list of sellers of Part II poisons.

*Schedule 9*: Form of the list kept by a local authority of listed sellers of Part II poisons.

*Schedule 10*: Form of certificate for the purchase of a poison.

*Schedule 11*: Form of entry to be made in poisons book on sale of a Schedule 1 poison.

*Schedule 12*: Restriction of sale and supply of strychnine and other substances. Forms of authority required for certain of these poisons.

N.B. Schedules 2, 3, 6 and 7 were deleted by the Poisons Rules (Amendment) Order 1985 (SI 1985 No.1077). Packaging and labelling of poisons is now controlled under the Chemicals (Hazard Information and Packaging) Regulations 1994, as amended (see Chapter 18).

## Sale and Supply of Poisons

### General Requirements

Except in certain circumstances (see Sales Exempted by the Act, p.198) it is unlawful for a person to sell any substance which is a Part I poison unless:

1 s/he is a person lawfully conducting a retail pharmacy business;
2 the sale is effected on the premises which are a registered pharmacy;
3 the sale is effected by or under the supervision of a pharmacist (s.3).

It is unlawful for a person to sell any substance which is a Part II poison unless:

1 s/he is a person lawfully conducting a retail pharmacy business and the sale is effected on premises which are a registered pharmacy; or
2 his/her name is entered in a local authority list in respect of the premises on which the poison is sold (s.3).

As sales of poisons must be effected on registered or listed premises it is not lawful for sales to take place from door to door, although a sale through the post from registered or listed premises would appear to be lawful.

The conditions required for persons lawfully to conduct 'a retail pharmacy business' have been described in Chapter 4. Such persons may sell at a registered pharmacy any poison whether it is in Part I or Part II of the Poisons List. The sale of a Part I poison from retail premises must be made by or under the supervision of a registered pharmacist (s.3). Each sale, if not made by the pharmacist personally, must be effected under his/her supervision in the sense that s/he should be in a position to intervene to prevent the sale.

The opinion was expressed in the High Court (*Roberts* v. *Littlewoods Mail Order Stores* [1943] KB 269; see Chapter 26) that supervision could not be said to have been exercised if the pharmacist were in another part of the building from that at which the sales were effected. The sale, by a person lawfully conducting a retail pharmacy business, of a poison included in Schedule 1 (see p.193) must be effected by or under the supervision of a pharmacist even though it may be a Part II poison (rule 9).

Listed sellers may not sell any Part II poison which has, since being obtained by them, been subject to any form of manipulation, treatment or processing as a result of which the poison has been exposed, and in the case of any poison included in Schedule 1, unless the sale is effected by him/herself or by a responsible deputy (rule 10).

A *responsible deputy* means a person nominated as a deputy on the listed seller's form of application or any person substituted, by notice in writing to the local authority, for the person originally nominated. Not more than two deputies can be nominated at the same time in respect of one set of premises (rule 10).

A listed seller may not sell (rule 10):

1   any poison included in the first column of Part A of Schedule 5 (see p.454) unless the article or substance is in the form specified in the second column of that Part;
2   any poison included in Part B of Schedule 5 (see p.456) unless the purchaser is engaged in the trade or business of agriculture, horticulture or forestry and requires the poison for the purposes of that trade or business.

### Containers

Rule 20 of the rules which set out provision for containers has been repealed (SI 1992 No.2293). Provision for containers which have to bear tactile danger warnings are contained in the Chemicals (Hazard Information and Packaging for Supply) Regulations 1994 (see Chapter 18).

### Storage of Poisons

When a poison is included in Schedule 1 (see p.449) it must be stored in any retail shop or premises used in connection with a retail shop:

1   in a cupboard or drawer reserved solely for the storage of poisons; or
2   in a part of the premises which is partitioned off or otherwise separated from the remainder of the premises and to which customers are not permitted to have access; or
3   on a shelf reserved solely for the storage of poisons and no food is kept directly under the shelf.

Schedule 1 poisons used in agriculture, horticulture or forestry must not be stored on any shelf, or in any part of the premises where food is kept, or in any cupboard or drawer unless the cupboard or drawer is reserved solely for the storage of poisons to be used in agriculture, horticulture or forestry (rule 21).

## Labelling of Hydrogen Cyanide

It is an offence to sell or supply any compressed hydrogen cyanide unless the container is labelled with the words *Warning: This container holds poisonous gas and should only be opened and used by persons having expert knowledge of the precautions to be taken in its use* (rule 18). This does not apply to sale or supply of compressed hydrogen cyanide to be exported to purchasers outside the United Kingdom (rule 18).

## Labelling and Packaging of Poisons which are 'Chemicals'

Substances in the Poisons List are also subject to the Chemicals (Hazard Information and Packaging for Supply) Regulations 1994, as amended and must be labelled and packed in accordance with those regulations (see Chapter 18). The provisions of the Poisons Act and rules relating to labelling, containers and storage do not apply to these substances except:

1    the special warning label for compressed hydrogen cyanide (see above);
2    the storage requirements for poisons on retail premises (p.192).

## Schedule 1 Poisons

Sales of poisons included in Schedule 1 to the Poisons Rules are subject to requirements additional to those applying to Part I and Part II poisons.

### Knowledge of the Seller

The purchaser of a Schedule 1 poison must be either:

1    certified in writing in the prescribed manner, by a person authorised in the Poisons Rules to give such a certificate, to be a person to whom the poison may properly be sold; or
2    known by the seller, or by a pharmacist employed by him/her at the premises where the sale is effected, to be a person to whom the poison may properly be sold (s.3).

Any householder is a person authorised to give a certificate as in 1 above (rule 25). If the householder giving the certificate is not known to the seller to be a responsible person of good character then the certificate is required to be endorsed by a police officer in charge of a police station. N.B. The police officer certifies that the householder, not the purchaser, is a responsible person of good character. The form of the certificate is laid down in Schedule 10 (see p.458) and the certificate has to be retained by the seller (rule 25).

For certain sales or supplies of Schedule 1 poisons the requirement of knowledge of the purchaser by the seller is deemed to be satisfied if the purchaser is known by the person in charge of the premises in which the poison is sold, or of the department of the business in which the sale is effected, to be a person to whom the poison may properly be sold or supplied.

This relaxation applies to:

1    sales of Part II, Schedule 1 poisons made by listed sellers (rule 5);
2    supplies of commercial samples of Schedule 1 poisons (rule 6);
3    sales of Schedule 1 poisons exempted under section 4 of the Act (rule 6) (see also p.195).

### Records

The seller must not deliver a Schedule 1 poison until s/he has made, or caused to be made, the required entry in the Poisons Book and the purchaser has signed it (s.3). The entries must be made in the manner and form prescribed in Schedule 11 (rule 26, and see p.459). The particulars to be recorded are the:

1    date of the sale;
2    name and quantity of the poison supplied;
3    purchaser's name and address and their business trade or occupation;
4    purpose for which the poison is stated to be required;
5    date of certificate (if any);
6    name and address of persons giving certificate (if any).

The Poisons Book must be retained for two years from the date on which the last entry was made (rule 27). A signed order may be accepted in lieu of the purchaser's signature in certain circumstances (see below).

### Signed Orders

A person who requires a Schedule 1 poison for the purpose of their trade, business or profession may give the seller a signed order in lieu of his/her signature in the Poisons Book (rule 6). The seller must obtain, before completion of the sale, the order in writing signed by the purchaser stating:

1    their name and address;
2    their trade, business or profession;
3    the purpose for which the poison is required;
4    the total quantity of the poison to be purchased.

The seller must be reasonably satisfied that the signature is that of the person purporting to have signed the order and that that person carries on the trade, business or profession stated in the order being one in which the poison is used. The seller must make the entry in the Poison Book before delivery. S/he must include the words *signed order* in place of the signature and add a reference number by which the order can be identified.

When a person represents that s/he urgently requires a poison for his/her trade, business or profession the seller may, if s/he is reasonably satisfied that there is an emergency and the purchaser is unable to supply a signed order before delivery, supply the poison on an undertaking by the purchaser that the purchaser will supply a signed order within 72 hours. Failure to comply with an undertaking or the making of false statements in order to obtain Schedule 1 poisons without a signed order are contravention's of the Poison Rules (rule 6).

### Exemptions from Schedule 1 Requirements

The requirements described above as to the knowledge of the purchaser by the seller and entry in the Poisons Book with signature of the purchaser or supplier of a signed order do not apply to:

1 the sale of poisons to be exported to purchasers outside the United Kingdom;
2 the sale of any article by its manufacturer, or by a person carrying on a business in the course of which poisons are regularly sold by way of wholesale dealing if:

   (a) the article is sold or supplied to a person carrying on a business in the course of which poisons are regularly sold or regularly used in the manufacture of other articles; and
   (b) the seller or supplier is reasonably satisfied that the purchaser requires the article for the purpose of that business (rule 6);

3 the sale of nicotine, which is a Part II, Schedule 1 poison, in the form of agricultural or horticultural insecticides consisting of nicotine dusts containing not more than 4 per cent w/w of nicotine (rule 5);
4 the sale of articles containing barium carbonate or zinc phosphide and prepared for the destruction of rats or mice (rule 7).

### Schedule 1 Poisons Subject to Additional Restrictions (Rule 12)

All the Schedule 1 poisons mentioned below are subject to additional restrictions on sale or supply. They may only be sold or supplied:

1     by way of wholesale dealing; or
2     or export to purchasers outside the United Kingdom; or
3     to persons or institutions concerned with scientific education or research or chemical analysis for the purpose of that education research or analysis; or
4     in the circumstances described below under the name of each particular poison.

*Sodium and potassium arsenites* may only be sold for the purposes of 1, 2 and 3 above.
    *Strychnine* may be sold:

(a)    for the purposes of 1, 2 and 3 above; or
(b)    to a person producing a written authority, in the form set out in Part II of Schedule 12 (see p.461) issued in England or Wales, by a person duly authorised by the Minister of Agriculture, Fisheries and Food or, in Scotland, by a person duly authorised by the Secretary of State, authorising the purchase for the killing of moles. The quantity must not exceed 100 grams and the sale must be made within three months of the date of the written authority; or
(c)    to an officer of the Ministry of Agriculture, Fisheries and Food or, in Scotland, of the Department of Agriculture and Fisheries, producing a written authority in the form set out in Part III of Schedule 12 (see p.462) authorising the purchase by that officer for killing foxes in an infected area within the meaning of the Rabies (Control) Order 1974. The quantity must not exceed that stated in the authority and must be supplied within four weeks of the date of the written authority.

N.B. Since 1991 strychnine has also been controlled under the Control of Pesticides Regulations 1986 and may only be supplied to holders of an Authority to Purchase issued by the Ministry of Agriculture, Fisheries and Food (in Wales by the Welsh Office Agriculture Department and in Scotland by the Department of Agriculture and Fisheries). It must be labelled in an approved manner and supplied only in the original sealed package(s) and only in units of 2 grams or multiples thereof. Quantities of more than 8 grams may only be supplied to providers of a commercial service. These conditions are *in addition* to the possession of a strychnine permit under the Poisons Rules (see p.349).
    *Fluoroacetic acid, its salts or fluoroacetamide* may be sold for the purposes of 1, 2 and 3 above, or to a person producing a certificate in form 'A' or form 'B' as provided in Schedule 12 (see p.462). The quantity must not exceed that specified and must be sold or supplied within three months of the date on the certificate. The certificates must specify the quantity, certify that the substance is to be used as a rodenticide and identify the place where it is to be used which may be:

(a)    ships or sewers as indicated in the certificate; or

(b)    such drains as are identified in the certificate, being drains which are in restricted areas and wholly enclosed and to which all means of access are kept closed when not in use; or

(c)    such warehouses as are identified in the certificate which are in residential dock areas and to which all means of access are kept securely locked or barred when not in use.

Only the proper officer of a local authority or port health authority may issue form 'A' to employees of the authority for the purpose of purchasing rodenticide for use in (a), (b) or (c) above, or form 'B' to persons carrying on the business of pest control for the purpose of rodenticide for use in (a) and (b) above. For the purpose of rodenticide for use in (a) and (b) above form 'B' may also be issued by a person duly authorised in England or Wales by the Minister of Agriculture, Fisheries and Food or in Scotland by the Secretary of State.

*Salts of thallium* may be sold:

(a)    for the purposes of 1, 2 and 3 above; or

(b)    to a local authority or port health authority for the purpose of the exercise of its statutory powers; or

(c)    to a government department or an officer of the Crown, for the purpose of the public service; or

(d)    to a person producing a written authority in the form set out in Part V of Schedule 12 (see p.463) issued within the preceding three months, authorising the purchase of thallium sulphate for use by him/her or by the employees of the persons named in the authority, for the purpose of killing rats, mice or moles in the course of the business of pest control. Authorities are issued in Scotland by the Secretary of State; or

(e)    to a manufacturer who regularly uses them in the manufacture of articles for the purpose of his/her business; or

(f)    an ingredient in any article which is not intended for consumption by any person or animal.

The exemptions under (e) and (f) do not extend to thallium sulphate. *Port health authority* means in England or Wales the port health authority of the Port of London or a port health authority for the purposes of the Public Health Act 1936 and in Scotland a port health authority as constituted in the Public Health (Scotland) Act 1897.

*Zinc phosphide* may be sold:

(a)    for the purposes of 1, 2 and 3 above; or

(b)    to a local authority for the purpose of the exercise of its statutory powers; or

(c)    to a Government Department or an officer of the Crown, for the purpose of the public service; or

(d)    to a person, or persons carrying on a trade or business, for the purpose of that trade or business.

*Calcium, potassium and sodium cyanides* (rule 14) may only be sold in any of the circumstances described in section 4 of the Act (see Sales Exempted by the Act, below).

## Wholesale Dealing

See Sales Exempted by the Act, category 1 below.

## Sales Exempted by the Act

Section 4 of the Act exempts certain categories of sales of poisons from the provisions of the Act, except as provided by the Poisons Rules. The principal effect is that sales of poisons falling within these categories are not required to be made from pharmacies or the premises of listed sellers; and for Part I poisons, the supervision of a pharmacist is not required. Except as indicated the provisions as to labelling (p.193), containers (p.192) and Schedule 1 poisons (p.193) do apply to these exempted sales (rules 4, 6 and 2).

The exempted categories are:

1   Sales of poisons by way of wholesale dealing, that is, sales made to a person who buys for the purpose of selling again.

   N.B. 'Wholesale dealing' has a wider meaning in the Medicines Act 1968 (see p.21). A wholesaler who sells a Part I poison to a shopkeeper must have reasonable grounds for believing that the purchaser is a person lawfully conducting a retail pharmacy business. If not, then the wholesaler must obtain a statement signed by the purchaser, or a person authorised by the purchaser, to the effect that the purchaser does not intend to sell the poison on any premises used for or in connection with his/her retail business (rule 11).

2   Sales of poisons to be exported to purchasers outside the United Kingdom are exempted from the Act and rules.

3   The sale of an article to a doctor, dentist, veterinary surgeon or veterinary practitioner for the purposes of his/her profession.

4   The sale of an article for use in connection with any hospital, infirmary or dispensary or similar institution approved by an order of the Secretary of State.

5   The sale of an article by a person carrying on a business, in the course of which poisons are regularly sold either by way of wholesale dealing or for use by purchasers in their trade or business to:

   (a)   a government department or an officer of the Crown requiring the article for the public service, or any local authority requiring the article in connection with the exercise of any statutory powers; or

(b)   a person or institution concerned with scientific education or research, if the article is required for the purposes of that education or research; or

(c)   a person who requires the article for the purpose of enabling him/her to comply with any requirements made by or in pursuance of any enactment with respect to the medical treatment of persons employed by that person in any trade or business carried on by him/her; or

(d)   a person who requires the article for the purpose of his/her trade or business. A person can be said to be carrying on a business if s/he engages in full-time, or part-time, commercial activity with a view to profit. A sale of cyanide to a commercial fruit grower for killing wasps would be a *trade or business* sale but a sale for the same purpose to a householder for garden use would not. Sales in circumstances exempted by section 4 are the only sales of cyanides which are lawful (see p.198) so a sale made to a householder would be unlawful.

## Automatic Machines

It is unlawful for a poison to be exposed for sale in, or to be offered for sale by means of, an automatic machine (s.3) (see Automatic Machines p.62).

## Summary

- The Poisons Board advises the Secretary of State as to which substances should be in the Poisons List.
- The Poisons List is divided into two parts. Poisons in Part I may be sold only by authorised sellers of poisons, i.e. from retail pharmacies by or under the supervision of a pharmacist, whereas Part II poisons can be sold from retail pharmacies and other shopkeepers who are listed with the local authority.
- There are eight active Schedules. Schedule 1 contains poisons to which special restrictions apply relating to sale, storage and the keeping of records. The seller must have special knowledge of the purchaser and record the transaction and obtain the purchaser's signature in a 'Poisons register'. Special provisions are made for signed orders in lieu of the purchaser's signature and for storage of poisons (away from the public).
- Special conditions apply to the sale of strychnine. It may only be sold by way of wholesale, or to persons or institutions concerned with education or research, for export, or to a person who has obtained a written

authority from the appropriate agricultural authority in England, Scotland or Wales. The format of the written authority is set out in Schedule 12.

• Various specific additional conditions apply to sodium and potassium arsenites, fluoroacetic acid and its salts, thallium, zinc phosphide, and the cyanides.

## Further Reading

*Medicines, Ethics and Practice*, published annually. The Royal Pharmaceutical Society of Great Britain.
(Lists of poisons are included.)

CHAPTER EIGHTEEN

# Dangerous Substances and Consumer Protection

The way in which certain chemicals are classified, packaged and labelled is now controlled under the Chemical (Hazard Information and Packaging for Supply) Regulations 1994 (SI 1994 No.3247, as amended). They are known collectively as the CHIP regulations. The regulations, made under the Health and Safety at Work etc. Act 1974 and the European Communities Act 1972, implement within Great Britain the European Community Directives regulating and controlling the classification, packaging and labelling of dangerous substances (Council Directive 67/548/EEC, as amended, and Council Directive 88/379/EEC).

Chemicals classified under the CHIP regulations as being harmful to health are also subject to control under the Control of Substances Hazardous to Health Regulations 1999 (COSHH) (see p.208).

## Definitions

*Substances dangerous to supply* means a substance listed in Part 1 of an approved supply list.

*Approved supply list* means the list approved by the Health and Safety Commission entitled 'Information Approved for the Classification and Labelling of Substances and Preparations Dangerous for Supply' (6th ed.) (SI 2000 No.2381).

*Preparations* means mixtures or solutions of two or more substances and *preparation dangerous to supply* means a preparation which is in one or more categories of danger in Schedule 1 to the Chemical (Hazard Information and Packaging for Supply) Regulations 1994 (SI 1994 No.3247, as amended).

*Supply*, in relation to a substance or preparation, means supply by way of:

1    sale or offer for sale;
2    commercial sample;
3    transfer from a factory, warehouse or other place of work and its curtilage to another place of work whether or not in the same ownership.

### Application of the Regulations and Exceptions

The regulations apply to the classification, packaging and labelling of any substance or preparation which is dangerous for supply except:

1    a substance which is either:

   (a)    a medicinal product; or
   (b)    a substance specified in an order made under sections 104 or 105 of the Medicines Act 1968;

2    Controlled Drugs;
3    animal feeding stuffs;
4    cosmetic products;
5    pesticides approved under the Food and Environmental Act 1985 (N.B. a preparation intended for use as a pesticide is classified as dangerous to supply and must comply with the regulations unless it is approved under the 1985 Act);
6    radioactive substances;
7    substances and preparations intended for use as food;
8    substances intended for export to a country which is not a member state of the European Union;
9    munitions, including fireworks;
10    waste materials;
11    substances and preparations which are dangerous by reason that they contain disease-producing micro-organisms;
12    a substance transferred from a factory, warehouse, or other place of work to another place of work in the same ownership and in the immediate vicinity;
13    a substance to which the Notification of New Substances Regulations 1982 apply and is labelled in accordance with such regulations;
14    a substance imported and still under Customs control.

Most of the substances controlled as dangerous substances in the approved supply list are chemicals and only a few are likely to be encountered in pharmacy. A selection of the substances taken from the approved supply list is given in Appendix 14. It comprises:

1    those dangerous substances which are also controlled by the Poisons Act 1972 (see Chapter 17);
2    other dangerous substances which may be held in stock in a pharmacy.

A pharmacy dealing with a request for any chemical not shown in Appendix 14 should refer to the approved supply list and regulations, or seek advice from the Royal Pharmaceutical Society of Great Britain. It should be borne in mind that substances sold as medicinal products or pesticides are not subject to the labelling requirements of the Chemical (Hazard Information and Packaging for Supply) Regulations 1994 (SI 1994 No.3247).

## Inspection and Enforcement

The provisions are enforced as if they were health and safety regulations made under the Health and Safety at Work etc. Act 1974.

Where a dangerous substance is supplied in or from a registered pharmacy the enforcing authority is the Royal Pharmaceutical Society of Great Britain. The enforcing authority in relation to supplies made in any shop, market stall or other retail outlet is the local weights and measures authority and in all other cases the Health and Safety Executive (reg.16).

## Classification

Substances or preparations which are dangerous to supply have to be classified by the manufacturer. The manufacturer must decide what kind of danger the chemical presents and allocate to it a phrase describing the general nature of the risk attached to it (a *risk phrase*).

Each substance or preparation is classified in the approved list as to its category of danger:

1    *Physico-chemical properties*: explosive, extremely flammable, highly flammable or flammable, and oxidising;
2    *Health effects*: very toxic, toxic, harmful, irritant, corrosive, sensitising, carcinogenic, mutagenic and toxic for reproduction;
3    *Dangerous to the environment.*

All substances and preparations which are classified as carcinogenic, mutagenic or toxic for reproduction, together with certain solvents, e.g. chloroform and carbon tetrachloride, have to be labelled *Restricted for professional users* and thus cannot be sold to the general public.

Pharmacists will normally not have to classify dangerous substances or preparations as this will have been done by the supplier. However, if a pharmacist still produces preparations to his/her own formulation then s/he will have to classify the dangers.

Each classification of danger will carry with it indications of danger, particular risks, and safety precautions which will be required when such substances or preparations are labelled and sold.

## Indications of Danger

There are ten categories of indications of danger. Each category has its own symbol which must be in black on an orange/yellow background. The symbols (see Appendix 14) are:

1    Explosive – an exploding bomb.
2    Extremely flammable, highly flammable – a flame.
3    Very toxic, toxic – a skull and cross-bones.
4    Corrosive – a hand and a piece of metal being dissolved by liquid dropping from two test tubes.
5    Oxidising – a flame over a circle.
6    Irritant, harmful – a St Andrew's cross.
7    Dangerous to the environment – a tree and a fish.

## Indication of Particular Risks

Each dangerous substance or preparation is classified in the approved list as to the indications of particular risks with which the receptacle must be labelled. These include, for example: *reacts violently with water*; *irritating to the eyes*; *harmful if swallowed*; *explosive when mixed with a combustible material*; *sensitising*; *carcinogenic*, etc. (see Appendix 14).

## Indication of Safety Precautions Required

Each dangerous substance or preparation is classified in the approved list as to the indication of safety precautions with which the receptacle must be labelled. These include (see Appendix 14) for example: *keep out of the reach of children*; *wear suitable protective clothing*; *never add water to this product*.

## Packaging

It is unlawful to supply any person with a substance or preparation dangerous to supply unless it is in a receptacle which is designed, constructed, maintained and closed so as to prevent its escape when subjected to the stresses and strains of normal handling. This does not prevent the fitting of a suitable safety device (reg.8).

When the receptacle is fitted with a replaceable closure the latter must be so designed so that the receptacle can be repeatedly reclosed without the contents escaping.

The packaging must be made of materials which are neither adversely affected by the substance nor liable in conjunction with that substance to produce another substance which is a risk to the health and safety of the public (reg.8).

*Receptacle* means a vessel or the innermost layer of packaging which is in contact with the substance and which is liable to be individually handled when the substance is used and includes any closure or fastener.

*Package* means the package in which a substance or preparation is supplied and which is liable to be individually handled during the course of the supply and includes the receptacle containing the substance or preparation and any other packaging associated with it and any pallet or other device which enables more than one receptacle containing a substance or preparation to be handled as a unit, but does not include:

1    a freight container (other than a tank container), a skip, a vehicle or other article of transport equipment; or
2    in the case of supply by way of retail, any wrapping such as a paper or plastic bag into which the package is placed when presented to the purchaser.

## Child-Resistant Closures

Child-resistant closures must be used on certain products when sold to the general public. These substances or preparations include those that are classified as *Toxic, Very Toxic,* or *Corrosive* and methanol above 3 per cent (reg.12).

## Tactile Danger Warnings

In order to aid the blind and partially sighted a tactile danger warning (EN ISO 11683) (SI 2000 No.2381), such as a raised triangle, must be used on packaging when products classified as *Harmful, Highly Flammable, Extremely Flammable, Toxic, Very Toxic* and *Corrosive* are sold to the general public (reg.12).

## Labelling for Supply

Labelling for supply must be in English, unless supply is to another member state of the European Community when it has to be in the language of that state. It must be clearly and indelibly marked on a part of the package reserved for that purpose and securely fixed with its entire surface in contact with the package. Where it is impracticable to attach a label in this way, because the package is an awkward shape or is too small, then it may be attached in some other appropriate manner.

The colour and nature of the markings on the label must be such that the symbols required (see below) stand out from the background so as to be readily noticeable and the wording be of such a size and spacing as to be easily read (reg.11).

The package must be labelled so that the particulars can be read horizontally when the package is set down normally (reg.11).

The dimensions of the label must be in accordance with Table 18.1.

**Table 18.1**   Label dimensions for supply

| *Capacity of Package* | *Dimensions of Label* |
| --- | --- |
| (a)  3 litres or less | if possible at least 52×74 mm |
| (b)  exceeding 3 litres but not exceeding 50 litres | at least 74 × 105 mm |
| (c)  exceeding 50 litres but not exceeding 500 litres | at least 105 × 148 mm |
| (d)  exceeding 500 litres | at least 148 × 210 mm |

Any symbol required to be shown must be printed in black on an orange/yellow background and its size, including the orange/yellow background, must be at least equal to one-tenth of the area of a label and in any case shall not be less than 100 mm$^2$ (reg.11).

Where because of the size of the label it is not reasonably practicable to provide safety phrases on the label, that information may be given on a separate label or on a sheet accompanying the package (reg.9).

No *dangerous substance* may be supplied unless it is in a package which clearly shows the following particulars [reg.9(2)]:

1   the name and full address and telephone number of a person in a member state who is responsible for supplying the substance, whether s/he is the importer, manufacturer, or distributor;

2   the name of the substance;

3   the following particulars:

   (a)   the indication(s) of danger and the corresponding symbol(s) (if any);

   (b)   the risk phrases (set out in full);

   (c)   the safety phrases (set out in full);

   (d)   the EEC number and, in the case of a substance dangerous for supply which is listed in Part 1 of the approved supply list the words *EC label* or *EEC label*;

4   certain substances which are specified in Schedule 6 to the regulations and which are classified as carcinogenic, mutagenic or toxic for reproduction have to be labelled *Restricted for professional users.*

N.B. The risk and safety phrases need not be shown on packages of 125 ml or less except if the substance is classified as *Flammable, Highly Flammable, Oxidising* or *Irritant.*

No *dangerous preparation* may be supplied unless it is in a package which clearly shows the following particulars [reg.9(3)]:

1    the name and full address and telephone number of a person in a member state who is responsible for supplying the preparation whether s/he is the importer, manufacturer, or distributor;
2    the trade name or other designation of the preparation;
3    the following particulars:

    (a)    the identification of the constituents of the preparation which result in the preparation being classified as dangerous to supply;
    (b)    the indication(s) of danger and the corresponding symbol(s) (if any);
    (c)    the risk phrases (set out in full);
    (d)    the safety phrases (set out in full);
    (e)    in the case of a preparation intended for sale to the public, the nominal quantity;

4    certain preparations which are specified in Schedule 6 to the regulations and which are classified as carcinogenic, mutagenic or toxic for reproduction have to be labelled *Restricted for professional users.*

**Figure 18.1**   Example of a label

| Mineralised Methylated Spirits | |
| --- | --- |
| | Highly flammable<br>Toxic by inhalation and if swallowed<br>Keep locked up and out of reach of children<br>Keep container tightly closed<br>Keep away from sources of ignition - no smoking |
| | Avoid contact with skin<br>In case of accident or if you feel unwell, seek medical advice immediately and show label where possible |
| EEC 250 659 6 | |
| Tel: 0101 1111 | A.N.Other MRPharmS<br>1 High Street<br>Blanktown      500 ml |

## Data Sheets

Safety data sheets have to be provided when substances and preparations which are subject to the regulations are supplied for the first time in connection with work, e.g. a supply to a doctor for use in his/her practice, to a health centre, to factories, etc. This is to ensure that the recipient can take any necessary precautions relating to the protection of health and safety at work and relating to the protection of the environment.

The supplier must ensure that the data sheet is kept up to date and revise it in line with any new health or safety information. A revised data sheet must be supplied to a customer who has received a supply within the last 12 months.

Data sheets do not have to be given when supplies are made to the general public for their private use.

The data sheet must contain the following headings: identification of the substance/preparation; composition/information on the product; supplier's name; hazard identification; first-aid measures; fire-fighting measures; accidental release measures; handling and storage; exposure controls and personal protection; and, physical and chemical properties.

## Control of Substances Hazardous to Health (COSHH)

The Control of Substances Hazardous to Health Regulations 1999 (SI 1999 No.437), made under the Health and Safety at Work Act, impose duties on employers to protect employees and other persons who may be exposed to substances hazardous to health and impose certain duties on employees concerning their own protection in the work place. The regulations implement a number of European Directives and are consistent particularly with Council Directive 80/1107/EEC which provides for protection of workers from risks related to exposure from chemical, physical and biological agents.

The regulations apply to any place of work including hospital or community pharmacies, pharmaceutical laboratories or administrative offices. They cover virtually any substance (except those subject to specific legislation such as asbestos, ionising radiation) but are particularly relevant to pesticides, chemicals, harmful micro-organisms and medicines. Persons consuming medicines are not covered by the regulations.

COSHH requires that an assessment of risk is made of substances used and procedures operated in the workplace.

*Risk* means the likelihood of harm in the actual circumstances of use and depends on, for example, how the substance is used, who is using it, how much substance is involved, how long the exposure and what precautions are taken. A high-level hazard could arise from mis-handling a low-risk substance; e.g. licking the fingers while handling metallic mercury. The level of hazard is usually greater following ingestion and becomes progressively less through inhalation to skin contamination due to leakage and spillage.

Every employer must ensure that the exposure of their employees to substances hazardous to health is either prevented or, where this is not reasonably practicable, is adequately controlled. *Substances hazardous to health* are those as defined in the Chemicals (Hazard Information and Packaging for Supply) Regulations 1994 (see p.201).

Every employer must not carry out work which is liable to expose their employees to any hazardous substance unless they have made a suitable and sufficient assessment of the risks created by that work and the steps needed to avoid risk as set out in the regulations. Where employees are exposed to risk the employer must ensure that they are under suitable health surveillance.

Manufacturers of substances which may be hazardous to health must provide full details (e.g. labels, leaflets, data sheets, instruction manuals) of the precautions to be taken when handling the substance.

Employers must take measures to train and inform staff of the dangers, to prevent or minimise exposure where possible and, if necessary, monitor exposure and implement a health surveillance programme for all those exposed. Risk can be reduced by avoiding the substance altogether, using a safer substance or the same substance in a safer form, by enclosing the process and extracting the by-products, by improving ventilation or hygiene facilities, by instituting safer handling procedures or by introducing personal protective equipment such as gloves, masks and respirators. In cases of difficulty, advice should be sought from the local area office of the Health and Safety Executive or from the local authority environmental health officer.

## Summary

- The CHIP regulations, as amended, require that all substances and preparations defined as dangerous to supply must be classified, usually by the supplier, as to the kind of danger the chemical presents and allocate to it a phrase describing the general nature of the risk.
- All substances and preparations defined as dangerous to supply must be supplied in packages which comply with the standards set out in the regulations including child-resistant closures and tactile warnings.
- All packages must be labelled with the appropriate symbols of danger, the relevant risk phrases and safety precautions.
- The COSHH regulations impose duties on employers to protect employees and other persons who may be exposed to substances hazardous to health and impose certain duties on employees concerning their own protection in the workplace.
- Employers must take measures to train and inform staff of the dangers, to prevent or minimise exposure where possible and, if necessary, monitor exposure and implement a health surveillance programme for all those exposed.

## Further Reading

COSHH: *The New Brief Guide for Employers*, 9/98 INDG 136 (rev). Health and Safety Executive.

*Medicines, Ethics and Practice*, published annually. The Royal Pharmaceutical Society of Great Britain.

*The Complete Idiot's Guide to CHIP 2000*. Health and Safety Executive.

# The Royal Pharmaceutical Society of Great Britain

N.B. In June 1999, the government passed the Health Act 1999 which provided powers to change the regulation of health professions and health professionals and to amend National Health Service law. The consequences of implementing this Act were not complete at the time of going to press and may affect the workings of the Society, its charter and bye-laws. Where possible, an indication of probable changes is given (see The Future p.220).

The Royal Pharmaceutical Society of Great Britain, the professional body for pharmacy, was founded in 1841 and incorporated by Royal Charter in 1843. A Supplemental Charter granted in 1953 lays down the main objects of the Society which are:

1   to advance chemistry and pharmacy;
2   to promote pharmaceutical education and the application of pharmaceutical knowledge;
3   to maintain the honour and safeguard and promote the interests of the members in the exercise of the profession of pharmacy;
4   to provide relief for distressed persons, being:
    (a)   members;
    (b)   persons who at any time have been members or have been registered as pharmaceutical chemists or as chemists and druggists;
    (c)   widows, orphans, or other dependants of deceased persons who were at any time members or registered aforesaid;
    (d)   students.

The original Charter of 1843 was revoked by the Supplemental Charter 1953 except in so far as it incorporated the Society and authorised it to have a common seal and to sue and be sued.

The Supplemental Charter gave the Society power to take and hold personal property and from time to time purchase, acquire, take or hold land. It requires that there shall be a Council of the Society consisting of 21 members nominated and elected as laid down in the bye-laws. The current bye-laws are set out in full in Appendix 15. In practice these 21 Council members are elected by the total membership of the Society by postal single transferable vote. Seven members retire annually in rotation and are eligible for re-election. The bye-laws require these 21 Council members to be registered pharmaceutical chemists. Three additional members of Council, not necessarily pharmacists, are nominated by the Privy Council under the Pharmacy Act 1954 (s.15), making a total of 24 members.

The Supplemental Charter gives the Council power to make bye-laws for all or any of the purposes for which bye-laws may, by the express provisions of the Charter, be made, and such other bye-laws as seem to the Council to be necessary for the management and regulation of the affairs and property of the Society and its chartered objects (see Appendix 15). Parts of the 1953 Charter have since been overlaid by statute. In particular, those relating to the power to make bye-laws and to provide relief for distressed persons can now be found in the Pharmacy Act 1954 (ss.16 and 17).

No bye-law, and no alteration or revocation of any bye-law, can have effect until not less than 60 days' notice has been given to members and until it has been confirmed and approved by the Privy Council. No bye-law may exceed the powers laid down in the Charter or Pharmacy Acts or otherwise be in conflict with the laws of the land. The extent of the Society's powers under its Royal Charter and its powers and duties under the Pharmacy Acts have been considered by the High Court in *Jenkin* v. *Pharmaceutical Society of Great Britain* [1921] 1 Ch 392 and by the House of Lords in *Pharmaceutical Society of Great Britain* v. *Dickson* [1968] 2 All ER 686 (see p.226 and Chapter 26).

The Charter requires that there shall be a president, vice-president and treasurer of the Society appointed in such a manner and with such powers as are laid down in the bye-laws. Although the powers of the Society are mainly contained in the 1953 Charter, additional powers and duties have been conferred and/or imposed by various Acts of Parliament. One of the principal duties under statute is that the Council of the Society must appoint 'a fit and proper person' as registrar (Pharmacy Act 1954, s.1). It is the duty of the registrar to maintain the Register of Pharmaceutical Chemists under the Pharmacy Act 1954 (s.2) and the Register of Premises (registered pharmacies) under the Medicines Act 1968 (s.75).

The Society also has law enforcement duties under various sections of the Medicines Act 1968 and the Animal Health and Welfare Act 1984 (see Chapter 1) and the Poisons Act 1972 (see Chapter 17). The other major statutory power conferred upon the Society relates to the exercise of professional discipline through the work of the Statutory Committee (see Chapter 21).

## Organisation

The Council has full power to manage the Society's affairs but cannot dispose of or mortgage any 'land, tenement or hereditament' belonging to the Society without the consent of a special general meeting of members. In addition, a special general meeting of the Society can be requisitioned for any specified purpose by not fewer than 30 members. This power was last exercised with regard to the supervision of medicines (*Pharm J* 15 April 1989 p.438).

The Council has a duty to manage the Society's affairs and, subject to the provision of the bye-laws, has power to regulate the conduct of proceedings at meetings of the Council and its committees and subcommittees. The Council exercises its powers through a number of committees, three of which are particularly relevant to this book, namely the Law and Ethics Committee, the Infringements Committee, and the Animal Medicines Committee.

The Law and Ethics Committee deals with policy matters involving professional conduct and the legal aspects of the Society's affairs. It is responsible for the interpretation of the Code of Ethics (see Chapter 20 and Appendix 18) and for advising the Council on any question of professional conduct that may arise.

The Infringements Committee considers alleged breaches of the legislation which the Society enforces, e.g. the Medicines Act 1968 and the Poisons Act 1972, and alleged infringements of standards of professional conduct.

The Animal Medicines Committee deals with registration matters concerning agricultural merchants and saddlers, infringements of the relevant Codes of Practice and policy relating to the Animal Medicines Division of the Law Department (see Chapter 12).

The management of the Scottish and Welsh Executives were under consultation at the time of writing as part of the measures to implement the Health Act 1999. The bye-laws currently provide that the Society has a Scottish Department governed by the Scottish Executive acting under the authority of the Council. The president and vice-president of the Society and such members of the Council as are resident in Scotland are ex-officio members of the Scottish Executive; the others are elected annually by the members of the Society resident in Scotland. The Executive elects from among its members a chairman and vice-chairman. The chairman has charge of the funds voted for the use of the Department, and the Executive reports to the Council of the Society in London. The Society's Council appoints a resident secretary of the Scottish Department, based in Scotland.

The Society has a Welsh Executive responsible under the authority of the Council for the implementation of its policies in Wales. The president and vice-president of the Society and such members of Council as are resident in

Wales are ex-officio members of the Welsh Executive; the others are elected from and by the members of the Society resident in Wales. The Executive elects from among its members a chairman and vice-chairman. The Council appoints a resident secretary of the Welsh Executive, based in Wales.

The Society has laboratories at York Place in Edinburgh under the control of the director of the Professional Affairs in London. The work done in the laboratories includes pharmaceutical investigation and formulation, and pharmaceutical analysis. One analytical laboratory examines formal samples which are taken under the Scottish drug testing scheme of the National Health Service. The Society undertakes much of the analysis of the samples taken by the Medicines Inspectorate under the Medicines Act 1968.

## Branches and Regions

In 1922 the Council of the Society set up branches throughout Great Britain. These, with their own officers, function at local level and at present number 136. They organise local meetings of members and pharmacy students on topics of common interest and provide a medium for members to take an active part in the Society's affairs. In 1968 the Society set up a regional organisation in England and Wales, each region being based on a school of pharmacy. In 1975 the boundaries were revised to become coterminous with the then regions of the National Health Service and one of the resulting Society regions has two schools of pharmacy within its boundaries. The regions are intended to supplement the branch structure and help the smaller branches. In addition the regions are intended to improve communication between the Council and the membership.

## Membership Groups

The Council has authority under the bye-laws to establish and determine the constitution of special groups of members based on the nature of their occupation or special interests. The function of any such group must be the discussion of matters of a professional and technical character of common interest to the members of the group.

In 1965 an Agricultural and Veterinary Pharmacy Group was established to promote the study of agricultural and veterinary pharmacy. Membership is open to any pharmacist engaged in 'the preparation and supply of agricultural chemicals, veterinary medicines and allied products'.

An Industrial Pharmacists Group was formed in 1972 for all those members engaged within the pharmaceutical industry. In 1975 a Hospital Pharmacists Group and in 1990 an Academic Group were also formed. In 1995 a Community Pharmacists Group was formed to consider issues relating to community pharmacy and to work to promote knowledge and standards of practice in this field. During 1999 the Society consulted on the future of special interest groups and a number of new groups and changes to existing groups, particularly in relation to primary care practice, were proposed *(Pharm J* 2 October 1999 p.517). These proposals are now likely to be taken together with consultation on the changes needed to implement the Health Act 1999.

## Membership and Registration

The membership of the Society consists of members and fellows. Membership is restricted to those persons registered as pharmaceutical chemists under the Pharmacy Act 1954. Every person registered as a pharmaceutical chemist pays an annual retention fee and is a member of the Society. If s/he ceases to be registered s/he ceases to be a member.

Fellows of the Society (who are also members) can be divided into several categories:

1    All members registered as pharmaceutical chemists on or before 1 February 1951 were designated as fellows. Until the Pharmacy Act 1953 came into force there were two qualifications. The Chemist and Druggist examination led to the basic qualification and membership of the Society. Those who took a further examination (the 'Major') after a further year's study were known as pharmaceutical chemists. The Registers of Chemists and Druggists and of Pharmaceutical Chemists were merged following the 1953 Act which was later replaced by the Pharmacy Act 1954. All chemists and druggists were then designated pharmaceutical chemists and those pharmaceutical chemists who had passed the old 'Major' examination were then, on application, designated as fellows.

2    Members of not less than five years' standing who have made outstanding original contributions to the advancement of pharmaceutical knowledge, or who have attained exceptional proficiency in a subject embraced by or related to the practice of pharmacy, may be designated as fellows by the Council.

3    A member of not less than 20 years' standing who has made outstanding original contributions to the advancement of pharmaceutical knowledge or who has obtained distinction in the science, practice, profession or history of pharmacy, may be designated as a fellow by a panel of fellows appointed by the Council for that purpose.

Members designated as fellows only remain so designated as long as they remain members. Both designated fellows and ordinary members are registered pharmaceutical chemists and they pay the same annual retention fee.

Persons who have rendered distinguished service to the Society or to pharmacy can be elected honorary members. A person who is nominated by the Privy Council to serve as a member of the Society's Council is an honorary member while holding that position. The Council also has power to elect as honorary fellows such persons as scientific workers who have distinguished themselves in any branch of knowledge which embraces the educational objects of the Society, or other persons eminent in national life. Honorary members and Honorary fellows are not registered pharmacists.

### Registration as a Pharmaceutical Chemist

The Pharmacy Act 1954 (s.4) and the bye-laws provide that any person who has obtained a degree in pharmacy at one of the United Kingdom universities approved by the Council or passed the Pharmaceutical Chemist Qualifying examination shall be registered as a Pharmaceutical Chemist provided that: s/he has attained the age of 21 years; has paid the prescribed registration fee; and has produced to the registrar of the Society evidence that s/he is of good character, in good health, both physically and mentally, and a declaration that subsequent to passing the final degree examination the applicant has satisfactorily performed, under the direct personal supervision of a pharmacist and as his/her sole pupil, a course of training of not less than one year in one or more of the following:

1   a community pharmacy approved for the purpose by the Council;
2   the pharmaceutical department of a hospital or similar institution, approved by the Council for the purpose;
3   a pharmaceutical industrial establishment approved by the Council for the purpose;
4   a school of pharmacy.

At least 26 weeks must be spent in community or hospital pharmacy. The person concerned must also pass a registration examination after completing their course of training.

Full details of the requirements for such pre-registration training and the examination are given in section XX of the bye-laws (see Appendix 15).

### EEC Recognition of Pharmaceutical Qualifications

An order made under the European Communities Act 1972 (SI 1987 No.2202) amended the Pharmacy Act 1954 to give effect to the Council Directives 85/432/EEC and 85/433/EEC relating to the mutual recognition of diplomas, to the right of establishment of pharmacists, and to their freedom to provide pharmaceutical services. The Royal Pharmaceutical Society of Great Britain and the Pharmaceutical Society of Northern Ireland are the competent authorities for certifying matters relating to the registration of pharmacists in Great Britain and Northern Ireland respectively. Section XIX of the bye-laws (see Appendix 15) sets out the full registration requirements.

Any pharmacist who is a national, or is entitled to be treated no less favourably than a national (SI 1996 No.1405), of a member state in the

European Economic Area (which includes the European Community, European Union and the European Free Trade Association Areas) and has a recognised qualification awarded in a member state, or has acquired rights under the Directives, has the right to be registered as a pharmacist in the United Kingdom. Before registration such a pharmacist must produce to the registrar evidence that s/he is of good character and in good health, both mentally and physically. Pharmacists from all member states have the right of establishment, although they cannot be in personal control of a pharmacy which has been open for less than three years.

## Reciprocal Registration

The bye-laws provide that the Council may by resolution enter into reciprocal agreements with a pharmaceutical authority that is empowered to grant certificates of qualification to practice pharmacy in any states outside the United Kingdom. At present such reciprocal agreements exist with Northern Ireland, New Zealand, in Australia with New South Wales, Queensland, South Australia, Victoria, Western Australia and Tasmania, and in South Africa for persons registered in South Africa before 31 March 1968. For Northern Ireland the provision for reciprocity is to be found in the Pharmacy Act 1954.

Under these reciprocal arrangements registration as a pharmaceutical chemist in the United Kingdom may take place without examination provided the applicant is resident in the United Kingdom, can produce evidence of their identity, can prove that s/he has passed a qualifying examination specified in the reciprocal agreement, and can prove that s/he is registered and is in good standing with the pharmaceutical registration authority of the state concerned (see Appendix 15).

A person who has been granted a certificate of qualification in an Australian State or in New Zealand after 31 March 1968, must also:

1   produce a certificate from the registrar of the Pharmacy Board concerned that s/he has completed, normally within their jurisdiction, a period of one year's employment in pharmacy as a registered pharmacist;
2   produce evidence satisfactory to the Council that s/he has completed in Great Britain a period of four weeks' employment in a pharmacy under the direct personal control and supervision of a pharmacist registered in Great Britain; and
3   produce a declaration in accordance with the Statutory Declarations Act 1835 that s/he has studied the laws governing the practice of pharmacy and the sale of medicines and poisons in Great Britain.

All applicants for reciprocal registration are required to pay a registration fee.

## Recognition by Adjudication

A person with a degree or diploma in pharmacy granted by a university or body outside the United Kingdom which is not covered by reciprocal arrangements may nevertheless apply for registration in Great Britain. S/he must produce evidence that s/he holds a degree or diploma in pharmacy granted by a university or body of comparable academic status in a country outside the United Kingdom, that s/he is registered or qualified to be registered in that country and is of good character and in good health, both mentally and physically. S/he must then satisfy an adjudicating committee appointed by the Council of the Society as to the content and standard of the course and examination in pharmacy that s/he has taken, and as to his/her knowledge of pharmacy as practised in the United Kingdom.

If English is not his/her mother tongue s/he must demonstrate his/her knowledge of the English language. S/he may also be required by the adjudicating committee to take certain examinations and s/he must complete a period of employment in the practice of pharmacy in Great Britain under conditions laid down by the committee. Two certificates of character satisfactory to the Council and given by British subjects must be submitted. If these conditions are complied with the Council may, by resolution, authorise registration of the applicant as a pharmaceutical chemist in Great Britain on payment of a registration fee (see Appendix 15).

## Registration Without Examination

The Council has power under the Pharmacy Act 1954 (s.4) to make bye-laws providing for registration of persons who satisfy the Council that they have sufficient skill and knowledge to practise and who are either persons registered as pharmaceutical chemists of Northern Ireland, or qualified military dispensers, or certified assistants to apothecaries under the Apothecaries Act 1815. However, this power has not been fully exercised and the bye-laws do not provide either for the registration of qualified military dispensers or of certified assistants to apothecaries. Northern Ireland pharmacists can register under the reciprocal arrangements (see above).

## The Register and Registration Certificates

The registrar is obliged under the Pharmacy Act 1954 (s.2) to publish annually a Register of Pharmaceutical Chemists in the form prescribed in section XXI of the bye-laws (see Appendix 15).

The Act places a duty on the Council to issue on the demand of any registered pharmaceutical chemist, without fee, a certificate of registration signed by the registrar and countersigned by either the president of the Society or two members of the Council (s.5).

A further certificate may be issued to a person to whom a certificate has already been issued if that person satisfies the registrar that the original has been lost or destroyed. The fee prescribed in the bye-laws for the supply of such a further certificate must be paid.

A certificate of registration is admissible as evidence that the person named thereon is a registered pharmaceutical chemist. Similar provisions as to evidence apply to the printed *Annual Register of Pharmaceutical Chemists* (s.6).

## Annual Retention Fees

In addition to the initial registration fee, a pharmacist must also pay an annual retention fee as prescribed in the bye-laws in order to retain his/her name on the Register. Different fees are prescribed in respect of different classes of members. Reduced fees are payable by pharmacists aged over 65 who are not employed in any occupation, pharmacists not gainfully employed in any occupation for more than 13 weeks in a year (part-time), and pharmacists not ordinarily resident in Great Britain. A pharmacist who on 30 December 1933 was a life member in accordance with the bye-laws then in force pays no retention fee.

The registrar is empowered to send a demand for a fee by registered post or recorded delivery addressed to the pharmacist at his/her address on the Register. If a pharmacist does not pay his/her fee within two months of having received such a demand, the registrar must inform the Council and the Council may direct the registrar to remove the name of the pharmacist from the Register (Pharmacy Act 1954, s.12). If, before the expiry of the year or such longer period as the Council may allow, the fee plus an additional sum by way of penalty is paid, the registrar has a duty to restore the name to the Register (Pharmacy Act 1954, s.12).

## Students

In 1978 the Society formed a section of the Society entitled 'The British Pharmaceutical Students Association', membership of which was open to all pharmaceutical students. Membership is also open to those members of the Society who have been registered initially for not more than 12 months. The Association, which is jointly financed by the Society, is recognised by the Council to be the representative body for the students. The Association is administered, in accordance with its constitution, by an elected Executive.

## Health Problems

During the early 1990s, the Society set up a scheme to assist pharmacists who have alcohol, drug or stress-related problems. This is now in two parts: the

Listening Friends Scheme and the Pharmacists Health Support Scheme. Both provide telephone support and referral facilities for pharmacists who are under stress and/or need help to manage dependence on alcohol or drugs. In this way the Society has sought to discharge its benevolent support role for pharmacists as well as its duties to protect the public from pharmacists who transgress through dependence and other problems (see p.211).

## Standards Tribunal

At the end of 1995, the Society announced its intention to set up a Standards Tribunal to consider any case in which the Council alleges that the member named has failed to meet the professional standards required of him/her in respect of standards set out in the Society's Code of Ethics and Appendix, as amended from time to time and generally adopted by the profession as applying to the systems for hygiene, control and professional intervention in the storage and supply of medicinal products and in respect of the fabric, equipment, decoration and repair of pharmacy premises. New draft bye-laws (s.XXVI) were published (*Pharm J* 16 December 1996 p.861) giving further details on the powers and sanctions of the Tribunal. In February 1996, draft rules of procedure for the Tribunal were published *(Pharm J* 17 February 1996 p.229) and submitted to the Privy Council. Due to the proposals for amendments to the disciplinary procedures and the enactment of the Health Act 1999 the creation of a standards tribunal is now likely to be subsumed in the consultations on the implementation of that Act.

## Pharmacists (Fitness to Practise) Act 1997

In November 1996 a Pharmacists (Fitness to Practise) Bill was introduced as a private members bill into the House of Commons to give the Society powers to set up a committee to consider allegations against pharmacists of unfitness to practise due to ill health, either physical or mental, and to impose practising conditions on, or suspend from registration, those pharmacists whose ability to practise it finds seriously impaired (*Pharm J* 11 January 1997 p.49). The Act, which amends the Pharmacy Act 1954, received the Royal Assent on 19 March 1997. **Draft** proposed regulations under the Act were received just prior to preparing this book for press and are set out in Appendix 21.

## The Future

In 1998 the Society set up a disciplinary working party which produced a consultation paper for the reform of the Society's disciplinary procedures (*Pharm J* 2 May 1998). However due to the wide powers to amend legislation in the field of professional regulation provided by the Health Act 1999 the

Society widened the remit of the disciplinary working party and renamed it the Health Act working party. Subsequently the Health Act working party has issued three consultation papers to the membership.

The first consultation paper related to measures to ensure professional competence and lifetime learning (*Pharm J* 11 March 2000 p.400 and insert) (see also Chapter 20 p.230).

A second preliminary consultation paper has been published to the membership seeking views on the composition of the Council and election of Council members *(Pharm J* 22 April 2000 p.116 and insert). This is likely to result in an increase in the numbers on the Council to accommodate wider representation at least of those affected by pharmacy and possibly representation of educational, political, sectoral and geographical factors. In addition, changes may be needed to reflect the devolution of political control, particularly of health matters, to Scotland and Wales.

A third and final consultation paper was issued and sought the profession's views on ensuring the competence of pharmacy support staff and, in particular, whether there is a need for a more robust regulatory framework for support staff and, if so, who should regulate and what form this should take (*Pharm J* 15 July 2000 p.88 and insert).

The responses to the three consultation papers are to be collated and a formal consultation document, together with the amended disciplinary reforms, was issued in the autumn of 2000 (*Pharm J* 17 February 2001 p.220 and insert).

In July 2000 the government published a blueprint for the National Health Service in England (The NHS Plan) which proposes the establishment of a UK Council of Health Regulators to co-ordinate and act as a forum for relevant bodies in areas such as complaints against practitioners. The Society is included in these proposals.

## Summary

- The Society derives its powers from two Royal Charters, 1843 and 1953, and the Pharmacy Act 1954.
- The Society exercises its powers principally through bye-laws which cover the management of the Society and the achievement of the Charter objects.
- The Council comprises 21 elected pharmacists plus three additional members appointed by the Privy Council (subject to consultations under the Health Act 1999).
- A president, vice-president and treasurer of the Council must be appointed annually; the Council also appoints a registrar to maintain the registers of pharmacists and pharmacies.
- The committees of Council which are concerned with law and ethical matters are: the Law and Ethics Committee, the Infringements Committee, and the Animal Medicines Committee.

- Members of the Society are assigned to 136 geographical branches, falling within 12 regions – not the same as the National Health Service regions (see Chapter 23).
- There are membership groups for pharmacists in agricultural and veterinary, hospital, industrial and community pharmacy practice.
- The bye-laws specify requirements for pre-registration training, registration and retention on the Registers and make provisions for fellowship and honorary membership of the Society.
- The bye-laws allow, subject to detailed conditions, for admission to the Register of pharmacists from other countries.
- Changes are likely in the arrangements for regulation of support staff following consultations under the Health Act 1999.
- The Society has a section for membership of students.
- The Society runs a help-line for pharmacists with alcohol, drug or stress-related problems.

Only those aspects of the Society's work that relate to law and ethics have been explained in this chapter.

# CHAPTER TWENTY

# Professional Conduct

N.B. In June 1999, the government passed the Health Act 1999 which provided powers to change the regulation of health professions and health professionals and to amend National Health Service law. The consequences of implementing this Act were not complete at the time of going to press and may affect the scope of the Society's powers to enforce standards of professional conduct. Where possible, an indication of probable changes is given.

The term 'profession' was formerly applied only to the church, the law and medicine – the three 'learned' professions. The meaning of the term is now broader as is apparent from the definition in the *Oxford English Dictionary*: *a vocation in which a professed knowledge of some department of learning is used in its application to the affairs of others, or in the practice of an art founded upon it.* In modern usage it seems that almost all occupations that require some measure of intellectual training can be described as professions.

But an organised profession requires more than the mere existence of an intellectual discipline. The essence of professionalism is the relationship of trust which exists between the practitioner and the person who receives his/her advice or services. The recipient, relying entirely on the knowledge of the practitioner, must be able to have complete trust in his/her services and the impartiality of his/her advice. It follows that there must be an established minimum standard of knowledge for practitioners, and that there must be agreement amongst them about standards of behaviour in their professional work. This means that there must be a body which determines the standard of education and establishes the code of conduct, and that this body must be representative of practitioners and be subject to their collective control.

## The Profession of Pharmacy

If the characteristics described are accepted as the elements of a profession, then pharmacy meets the essential requirements, which are four in number as follows:

1    *An Intellectual Discipline and a Standard of Knowledge*: Pharmacy is of ancient origin. In Great Britain it was never clearly separated from medicine until the formation of the Pharmaceutical Society of Great Britain in 1841. Membership of the Society was, from the first, by examination, but it was not until the Pharmacy Act 1868 that all newcomers to the profession who wished to practise were required to pass a qualifying examination, whether or not they intended to become members of the Society. Today a university degree in pharmacy followed by a period of practical training is required before registration as a pharmaceutical chemist (see Chapter 19).

2    *A Representative Body of Practitioners*: The representative body of the profession is the Royal Pharmaceutical Society of Great Britain. The Council of the Society is elected by the members and its functions include control over educational standards for pharmaceutical chemists. It also guides the profession in establishing and interpreting a code of conduct. All registered pharmaceutical chemists are, by statute, members of the Society (see Chapter 19). *Pharmacist* means a registered pharmaceutical chemist (Medicines Act 1968, s.132).

3    *Standards of Conduct*: There are accepted standards of conduct known throughout the profession. Many of these are expressed in the Code of Ethics, a document which represents the collective views of members of the Royal Pharmaceutical Society and which has been approved at a general meeting of members. The Council of the Society, through its Law and Ethics Committee and its Infringements Committee, interprets the Code and gives guidance on any matter concerning professional conduct. The disciplinary committee of the Society – the Statutory Committee – takes into account the Code of Ethics when considering complaints of misconduct, but is not bound by it (see Chapter 21).

4    *Service and Advice*: Pharmacists are mainly concerned with the supply to the public of medicines, which may be prescribed by a medical practitioner, prescribed by the pharmacist himself, or sold over the counter in a pre-packed form. In all these cases the pharmacist should give whatever advice is necessary in the interest of the patient or customer. S/he may, for example, advise against the purchase of a medicinal product which

conflicts with one already prescribed, advise against the taking of any medicine at all, or, in appropriate cases, advise that a doctor be consulted.

The existence of a body of independent private practitioners has been held to be essential if an occupation is truly to be regarded as a profession. The argument is that only the relationship between an independent practitioner and his/her client is a fully professional one, and an employed practitioner must inevitably be subject to external pressures, either consciously or unconsciously, according to the conditions of his/her employment. No pharmacist, whether employed in public service or in the service of a body corporate engaged in retail pharmacy, would accept that his/her standards or his/her judgment are in any way affected by the fact that s/he is an employee. Indeed, some might argue that a pharmacist in public service is free from some of the commercial pressures which may influence the judgment of the independent practitioner. Even so, there is some force in the argument that the existence of a number of independent practitioners is indispensable for the full development of the profession.

## Trade and Profession

There is a deep-rooted feeling that trading and professional activities are incompatible. But what is the difference between making a living from selling one's professional services and from the buying and selling of goods? The professional person might have some difficulty in explaining his/her objections to commerce without casting doubts on the integrity of the tradesperson. Although there is an element of snobbery in it, there is undoubtedly a difference between the trading outlook and the professional outlook. The tradesperson, however honest, is principally concerned with the profitability of his/her business. His/her main object is to achieve as large a financial return as possible. S/he holds his/her customers to be the best judges of what they want and s/he seeks to satisfy their demands. The old common law maxim applicable to trade was *let the buyer beware.*

Professional people working in their special field of knowledge where their advice is crucial must be the judges of what is best for their clients or customers. If they do this according to the standards of their profession, then the advice they give must, at times, be to the practitioners' own financial disadvantage. It is recognition of this essential trust by the public which confers any special status the professional person may have.

Some pharmacists, such as those who work in hospitals or in teaching, do not engage in trade, although within the context of the National Health Service (see Chapter 23) they are increasingly involved in marketing their services and operating within budgets and business constraints similar to those applied in retailing. However, the majority of pharmacists in retail pharmacy businesses practise pharmacy in a trading environment. In addition to the supply of medicines and the provision of other professional services they sell many other goods. Theirs is a *trading profession*, a description applied by Lord Wilberforce in the *Dickson* case (see below and Chapter 26).

Not surprisingly, pharmacists are often misunderstood in their attempts to apply professional principles in a commercial world. If it is hard for the proprietor pharmacist, it is even harder for the employed superintendent pharmacist of a company or other body corporate which is controlled by non-pharmacist directors or shareholders. The fact that the control of the pharmacy is given by statute to the pharmacist is sometimes found irksome to the owners, and the restrictions pharmacists place on ordinary commercial practices because of their profession are not understood. For this reason the Royal Pharmaceutical Society has found it necessary to incorporate statements setting out the duties and responsibilities of a superintendent pharmacist in the Code of Ethics and Professional Standards (see Appendix 18).

## The *Dickson* Case

The conflict between professional and commercial methods in pharmacy has its origin in the economic need for most pharmacists to engage in ordinary trade as well as pharmacy, together with the fact that any corporate body which complies with certain requirements has the legal right to establish a retail pharmacy business (see Chapter 4). As might be expected, the Royal Pharmaceutical Society, as the professional body, has throughout its history resisted any pressures of the commercial world that have appeared to be adverse to the profession. The *Dickson* case is the most recent example of a clash of this kind.

For a fuller understanding of the events leading to the case it is necessary to read the Report on the General Practice of Pharmacy published by the Society in 1963 *(Pharm J* 20 April 1963). Whether or not one agrees with the recommendations in the report, it is a succinct review of the state of retail pharmacy at that time. The report was adopted by the Council and accepted by a meeting of Branch Representatives of the Society. It was suggested in paragraph 19 of the report that it was undesirable for non-professional business to predominate in a pharmacy, and that the extension of this kind of business in pharmacies should be controlled. An attempt to incorporate this principle into the then Statement Upon Matters of Professional Conduct was challenged and led to the *Dickson* case, which is discussed in some detail in Chapter 26.

The Society was unable during the hearing of this case to satisfy the courts, on the evidence presented, that the professional side of a pharmacy business was adversely affected by other activities. As it was not shown that the public suffered any harm, the proposed restraints were held to be unjustified, and an injunction was granted preventing the proposed addition to the Statement

Upon Matters of Professional Conduct. The House of Lords upheld the decision of the lower courts.

In the course of the case the practice of pharmacy in Britain was subjected to searching examination and discussion, with the result that the judgment brought clarity to a situation which had tended to become uncertain. It was made plain that the Society could make rules affecting the non-professional as well as the professional activities of pharmacists, but only if the rules could be shown to be in the interest of the public and the profession. The following extracts illustrate the point:

> 'The restraints upon professional men are justifiable in law for they are not only necessary in the interests of the profession but of the public who trust to the peculiarly high standing and integrity of a profession to serve it well.'
>
> (Lord Upjohn)

> 'I have no doubt that there could be some trading activities which it would be undesirable for pharmacists to undertake in conjunction with their professional activities as pharmacists. '
>
> (Lord Morris)

> 'I have no doubt that it would be within the competence of the Society as a body concerned for the honour and well-being of those engaged in the profession of pharmacy, to lay down rules concerning non-professional (as well as professional) activities to professional standards and behaviour. But that would have to be proved. In agreement with the Court of Appeal, I do not think that it was proved in this case. It will normally be for a profession itself to decide in regard to its standards and its codes of behaviour and the mere fact that certain rules are laid down which are severely restrictive will not warrant attack upon them if the interests of members and in the public interest such rules are reasonable. '
>
> (Lord Morris)

## Professional Ethics

Ethics is the science of morals, or moral philosophy. The principles, written or unwritten, which are accepted in any profession as the basis for proper behaviour are the ethics of the profession. Rules of law and rules of ethics are commonly held to differ because law is enforced by the state while ethical rules are only morally binding. But law and ethics are not opposites. The law itself has a basis in ethics; in general it reflects the moral standards of the community. Criminal law comprises those rules of conduct which the community (through Parliament) has decided must be observed on pain of a penalty, such as a fine or imprisonment. Criminal law therefore includes the Medicines, Poisons and Misuse of Drugs Acts, where transgression may result in prosecution.

Other parliamentary legislation creates administrative law, which gives power to public bodies to regulate certain activities. The National Health Service Terms of Service (see p.307) being an example. A breach may result in an administrative sanction such as appearance before the Pharmaceutical Disciplinary Committee of the local Health Authority.

Moral obligations are also recognised by the state through common law, which essentially enshrines certain duties which individuals owe to one another. Breach of these duties may result in action through the civil law courts to seek compensation for a 'civil wrong'. The most familiar of these is probably an action alleging negligence on the part of a health practitioner. Negligence is just one of a range of *torts* or civil wrongs and is discussed in more detail later in this chapter (see p.233). Other torts which might arise in pharmacy practice are breach of confidentiality and defamation.

Pharmacists, as they become integrated into the health care team, will increasingly come into possession of sensitive information and will be expected to observe strict confidentiality over the use and disclosure of such information and refrain from using it in ways which may lower the standing of the subject in the eyes of the community (i.e. defamation).

But the state does not attempt to enforce every rule of social behaviour, nor does it interfere in those matters which are by common consent left to the consciences of individuals, e.g. religious observance nor those standards which are agreed amongst a profession provided they can be seen to be necessary for the further protection of the public.

## Code of Ethics

Ever since the foundation of the Pharmaceutical Society in 1841 there has been concern about the need to maintain and improve standards of conduct in pharmacy. The advantage of having a written code was recognised, but nothing positive emerged until the changes made by the Pharmacy and Poisons Act 1933 gave the Society wider authority, including the power to take disciplinary action and to remove names from the Register of Pharmaceutical Chemists (see Chapter 21).

A proposal for a code of ethics made by the Tees-side branch of the Society in 1937 was widely discussed, but it was found difficult to strike the right balance between a general description of good behaviour and the expression of specified principles in clear-cut terms. The document which was finally accepted by the profession was the first attempt at a written code. An amended version of this 'Statement upon Matters of Professional Conduct' was later published in *Pharm J* 17 June 1944.

Other amendments led to the publication of revised versions in 1953, 1964, 1970, 1984 and 1992. In each case a revised code was presented to the membership for approval and ratification at the Annual General Meetings in May.

In September 1999, the Society published a consultation document on a new code of ethics *(Pharm J* 18 September 1999 p.416 and insert), initially with the aim of adoption at the May 2000 Annual General Meeting. The intention of the revision was to devise a new code to take account of the changing expectations of government, other health professionals and the public in the area of professional self-regulation. Moreover, the new code had to reflect the requirements of the Health Act 1999 and be sustainable against challenge under the Competition Act 1998 (see Chapter 25 p.341). This process proved lengthy and could not be completed within the original timescale.

The 1992 Code of Ethics was therefore not replaced in total but was significantly amended in May 2000. The preface was replaced by 'Part 1: Pharmacists' ethics' and Principle Four (confidentiality), Principle Five and Standard 7 (competence and keeping up to date) were replaced by 'Part 2: Standards of professional performance'. The remaining Code and Appendix was termed 'Part 3'.

The Code of Ethics now comprises:

> Part 1 Pharmacists' ethics including the key responsibilities of a pharmacist.
> Part 2 Standards of professional performance.
> Part 3 The residue of seven *principles* supplemented by more detailed *obligations*. The substantive principles and obligations are supplemented by *guidance* which is intended to help in the interpretation of the Code.

Further revisions are planned for the Annual General Meeting in 2001 which will be intended to replace Part 3, namely the residual parts of the 1992 Code.

Disreputable behaviour, a breach of professional responsibility or requirement identified in the Code could form the basis of a complaint of misconduct. The Council and the Statutory Committee, in considering whether or not action should follow, take into consideration the circumstances of an individual case and do not regard themselves as being limited to those matters which are mentioned in the Code.

For ease of reference a brief summary of the effect of these amendments is given below. The full text became available as this book went to print and appears in Appendix 18.

## Part 1: Pharmacists' Ethics

Part 1 covers an outline of the process of ethical decision making, the exercise of professional judgement and the key responsibilities of a pharmacist as, briefly, being knowledgeable, competent and up to date in his/her field of practice, respectful of and sensitive to patients' rights and needs and behaving with integrity and probity.

## Part 2: Standards of Professional Performance
## (amended – see Appendix 18)

A. PROFESSIONAL COMPETENCE
This covers the process of continuous professional development, evidence of the undertaking of a minimum of 30 hours per year of such development, the provision of information and advice to patients, the public and prescribers and responding to adverse drug reactions. (As part of implementing the Health Act, responses to consultation paper No.1 will inform the measures

planned to ensure professional competence and lifelong learning, *Pharm J* 11 March 2000 p.400 and insert.) (See also Chapter 19 p.220.)

B. CONFIDENTIALITY

This covers detailed requirements for protection of information acquired in the course of pharmacy practice and the safeguards which must be exercised over disclosure. (See also the requirements of data protection legislation, Chapter 25 p.352.)

### Part 3. Residual Principles, Obligations, Guidance and Standards from the 1992 Code (amended – see Appendix 18)

1   A pharmacist's prime concern must be for the welfare of both the patient and other members of the public.

2   A pharmacist must uphold the honour and dignity of the profession and not engage in any activity which may bring the profession into disrepute.

3   A pharmacist must at all times have regard to the laws and regulations applicable to pharmaceutical practice and maintain a high standard of professional conduct. A pharmacist must avoid any act or omission which would impair confidence in the pharmaceutical profession. When a pharmaceutical service is provided, a pharmacist must ensure that it is efficient.

4   Replaced by Part 2B, above.

5   Replaced by Part 2A, above.

6   A pharmacist must neither agree to practise under any conditions which compromise professional independence or judgment nor impose such conditions on other pharmacists.

7   A pharmacist or pharmacy owner should, in the public interest, provide information about available professional services. Publicity must not claim or imply any superiority over the professional service provided by other pharmacists or pharmacies, must be dignified and must not bring the profession into disrepute.

8   A pharmacist offering services directly to the public must do so in premises which reflect the professional character of pharmacy.

9   A pharmacist must at all times endeavour to co-operate with professional colleagues and members of other health professions so that patients and the public may benefit.

### Standards of Good Professional Practice

An obligation in the 1992 Code of Ethics (1.14) states:

'A pharmacist must conform to the obligations in the Standards of Good Professional Practice and with other guidelines appropriate to the relevant field of work.'

These standards appear as an appendix to the Code and are expressed as *standards* supplemented by *guidance*. Failure to meet the standards could form the basis of a complaint of misconduct. The standards are applicable to all aspects of pharmacy practice although the detail is most relevant to community or hospital pharmacy. A summary of the standards is given below; the full text appears in Appendix 18. Since 1995 the number of Standards has risen to 19. It is likely that revisions aimed for adoption in May 2001 will incorporate some of these standards into Part 2: Standards for Professional Performance. For the latest text see Appendix 18.

1   Standards for premises – appearance, safety, condition, tidiness, environment, size and hygiene.
2   Standards for dispensary design and equipment – suitability, work surfaces, shelves, flooring, water supply, dispensing equipment and reference sources.
3   Standards for procurement and sources of materials – responsibilities, sources of supply, safe systems of work and requirements for medical gases.
4   Standards of manufacturing and quality assurance – good manufacturing practice, quality assurance, quality control, batch numbers, manufacturing formulae, documentation and equipment.
5   Standards for dispensing procedures – sources of supply, supervision, counselling/information and advice, containers, reuse of medicines, labels, storage, defective medicines, hygiene and forged prescriptions.
6   Standards for professional indemnity – personal and establishment insurance.
7   Standards for education, training and development – competency, self-assessment, changes in legal, ethical and practice requirements and new services.
8   Standards for relationships with patients and the public.
9   Standards for relationships with other health care professionals.
10   Standards for administration and management.
11   Standards for community pharmacists providing a repeat medication service.
12   Standards for the sale of non-prescribed medicines.
13   Standards for pharmacists providing services to nursing and residential homes.
14   Standards for pharmacists providing instalment dispensing services.
15   Standards for the home delivery of medicines.
16   Standards for pharmacists providing domiciliary oxygen services.
17   Standards for pharmacists providing needle and syringe exchange schemes.
18   Standards for the collection and disposal of pharmaceutical waste by community pharmacies.
19   Standards for the provision of on-line pharmacy services.

20   Standards for the supply of emergency hormonal contraception as a
Pharmacy Medicine.

## Council Statements and Other Advice

Modifications to the Code of Ethics are made from time to time in response to
changing activity in pharmacy practice. The Council of the Royal Pharmaceutical Society gives advice to pharmacists on particular topics of current
importance by way of statements published in *The Pharmaceutical Journal.*
The Council also publishes a consolidated version of the Code and supplementary statements and advice on practice, once a year in *Medicines, Ethics
and Practice.* The profession is asked to endorse these additions and amendments at the Annual General Meeting held in May every year.

For example, at the Annual General Meeting in 1998, further requirements
or guidance were agreed for dealing with and noting instances where patients
had received a substandard quality of pharmaceutical care, for dealing with
surplus stocks of medicines and donating medicines to third-world countries
or disaster areas, for collection points for dispensed medicines, for needle
and syringe exchange schemes, for security of computer-held data, on obligations of superintendent pharmacists, on advertising in GP literature, on
definitions of carers, on standards for dispensary design and equipment and
the details of 'new' Standards numbered 13 to 18 (see above) (*Pharm J* May
1998 p.624).

Of special importance were Council Statements subsequently incorporated
in a modified form into the Code of Ethics (*Pharm J* 14 December 1996
p.884) which have the effect of providing an alternative interpretation of
*supervision* (see Chapters 5, 21 and 26), as follows:

> 'There should be a written protocol in each pharmacy covering the procedure to be
> followed in that pharmacy when a medicine is supplied or advice on treatment of a
> medical condition is sought. A superintendent pharmacist or pharmacist owner of a
> business has a professional responsibility to ensure that all members of staff whose work
> regularly includes the sale of medicines must have completed an accredited training
> course for counter assistants, or are undergoing such a course.'

Such an interpretation better reflects the modern pharmacy where many
hundreds of Pharmacy Only Medicines must be supervised by the pharmacist.
This can realistically be achieved only by delegating simpler parts of the
process to assistants who have received specified training and who then work
within protocols which allow for referral to the pharmacist where appropriate. As the scope of pharmacy increasingly moves away from the simple
supply of medicines into provision of services, it is likely that more protocols
will be developed to define the contribution made by trained support staff and
that made personally by the pharmacist.

## Clinical Governance

During 1999, following publication of the government's white paper *A First Class Service*, the concept of clinical governance has been applied to all health care provision, especially by those within or contracted to the National Health Service. The concept essentially makes all health care professionals and their staff accountable for their standards of patient care. Clinical governance requires a continuous commitment to measuring and improving those standards. As the quality of patient care to be expected becomes more transparent, then the expectations of 'a reasonably competent practitioner' as used in determining negligence and Statutory Committee cases will become higher.

## Negligence

The inability of a pharmacist to carry out his/her duties because of a mental or physical disability does not normally amount to misconduct. Whether or not actions arising solely out of mere incompetence can be regarded as misconduct is doubtful, although the Statutory Committee has dealt with such a case (see Chapter 21). Certainly, in most cases considered by the Statutory Committee (see Chapter 21), there has always been some additional factor such as an indifference to the consequence of errors which amounts to a dereliction of duty.

A pharmacist is not normally likely to find him/herself charged with misconduct merely because s/he has made one mistake, although in 1985 one pharmacist was so charged before the Statutory Committee and was found guilty of misconduct and reprimanded (see p.257 and *Pharm J* 11 May 1985 p.600).

Until 2000, a pharmacist was equally unlikely to be charged with criminal sanctions in respect of a dispensing error. However, this position may change following charges of manslaughter brought that year against a pharmacist and a pre-registration graduate who failed to prevent a fatal dispensing error when preparing a mixture for an infant. The mixture was erroneously compounded using concentrated instead of double-strength chloroform water. When the case came to court, the crown prosecution service agreed to drop the charges of manslaughter and to substitute prosecutions under section 64 of the Medicines Act (see Chapter 1 p.10) for supplying a medicine not of the nature and quality demanded *(Pharm J* 4 March 2000 p.356, 11 March 2000 pp.389–392, 18 March 2000 p.427).

A pharmacist is more likely, however, to be faced with an action for negligence in the civil courts. The essence of the tort of negligence is that there is on the part of the defendant a legal duty to take care which s/he has failed to meet, as a result of which the plaintiff has suffered damage. The duty to take care was described in the case of *Donoghue* v. *Stephenson* [1932] AC 562 at 580 thus:

'You must take reasonable care to avoid acts or omissions which you can reasonably foresee would be likely to injure your neighbour. Who, then, in law is my neighbour? The answer seems to be . . . persons who are so closely and directly affected by my act that I ought reasonably to have them in contemplation as being so affected when I am directing my mind to the acts or omissions which are called in question.'

The law imposes a duty to take care in a variety of circumstances. As sellers of goods, retail pharmacists have a duty to take reasonable care to warn customers of any potential dangers arising from them. Quite apart from this general duty on all vendors of goods, there is a special relationship between pharmacists and their customers in respect of transactions involving pharmaceutical knowledge. Reliance is placed upon the special skill and knowledge of the pharmacist when selling, dispensing or prescribing medicinal products. The law would expect him/her to exercise that degree of competence which the average member of the profession is required to possess.

A pharmacist occupying a special position in any branch of pharmacy would be expected to have a degree of ability commensurate with that position. Pharmacists consistently, and with good reason, press for recognition as experts upon drugs and medicines, and for the right to take a greater part in the health services. Every right has its correlative duty, and pharmacists, as they achieve greater recognition, must expect the law to require from them a higher degree of skill. It is probable that they will as a consequence be more liable to actions for professional negligence.

Three High Court decisions illustrate this point well. A woman who suffered gangrene in both feet, requiring extensive surgery, as a result of receiving an overdose of Migril prescribed for migraine was awarded £100 000 damages *(Pharm J* 20 February 1982 p.205). The owner of the pharmacy, who admitted negligence, was held liable for 45 per cent of the damages awarded. The judge, Mr Justice Stuart-Smith, in making the award said that the pharmacist owed a duty to the patient to ensure that drugs were correctly prescribed and that the pharmacist should have spotted the doctor's error and queried the prescription with the prescriber.

It is clear from the judgment that a pharmacist must not be deterred in querying prescriptions with the prescriber by any adverse response on the part of the prescriber who may resent his/her decisions being questioned. The legal and professional responsibility of the pharmacist to verify and question prescriptions has been highlighted and established by this case.

In another case in 1988 a patient had gone to his doctor for his regular prescription for inhalers and tablets. At the same time he was prescribed Amoxil for a chest infection. When he took the prescription to the pharmacy, the pharmacist misread Amoxil as Daonil and the patient suffered irreversible brain damage.

Mr Justice Auld in awarding £139 000 damages (75 per cent against the pharmacist: 25 per cent against the doctor) said that even assuming that the prescription was unclear, the pharmacist should have been alerted to the fact that Daonil was being recommended in the wrong dosage and quantity. He should also have noticed that the man who collected the drugs did not claim exemption from paying for the Daonil, although diabetics were entitled to free drugs. It was not enough for pharmacists to blindly dispense drugs without giving thought to what they were doing.

Giving the decision in the High Court, Mr Justice Auld held that a doctor had a duty to his/her patient to write a prescription sufficiently legibly so as to reduce the likelihood of its being misread by a busy or careless pharmacist. But the pharmacist, in turn, was under a duty to give some thought to the prescriptions s/he was dispensing. If there was an ambiguity in the prescription s/he should not dispense a drug without first satisfying him/herself that it was the correct one *(Pharm J* 26 March 1988 p.404).

That apportioned liability is now an accepted principle in dispensing negligence cases was much more recently demonstrated in a settlement in the High Court in Manchester on 28 February 2000. The claim arose from a negligently written prescription, in November 1999, for Epilim 500 mg tablets where the strength, and hence the dosage and administration instructions were incorrect. The pharmacy's professional indemnity insurer agreed to pay 25 per cent of the settlement (£225 000 plus costs) for the pharmacist's failure to detect and correct the error. The prescribing GP was held liable for the remaining 75 per cent of the compensation paid to the patient (*Chemist and Druggist* 4 March 2000 p.5).

## Summary

- Pharmacy is regarded as a profession because its members must belong to a professional body which determines their standard of education and establishes a code of conduct – the Code of Ethics.
- Most pharmacists are engaged in trading in goods as well as the provision of services and advice; this has led to the development of detailed guidance on how to avoid conflict between these two areas.
- The *Dickson* case established that the Society could make rules affecting the non-professional as well as the professional activities of pharmacists, but only if the rules could be shown to be in the interest of the public and the profession.
- Pharmacists' activities are subject to criminal law, administrative law, civil law and the Code of Ethics.
- The Code of Ethics comprises statements on pharmacists' ethics and key responsibilities, standards of professional performance and service standards.
- The Code is supplemented by guidance and practice advice published in *The Pharmaceutical Journal* and the *Medicines, Ethics and Practice Guide*.
- Several cases now demonstrate the duty of care owed by pharmacists to their clients.

## Further Reading

Appelbe G. E. 'Pharmacy – Profession or Trade', *Irish Pharmacy J* October 1995 p.289.

Barber N., O'Neill, R. 'Suggestions for a New Code of Ethics', *Pharm J* 26 June 1999 pp.923–925.

Brazier M. (1992). *Medicine, Patients and the Law*, 2nd edn. London: Penguin Books.

Carey (1998). *Medical Negligence Litigation*. Birmingham: CLT Professional Publishing.

Gillon R., ed. (1994). *Health Care Ethics*. Chichester: John Wiley & Sons.

Mason J. K., McCall Smith R. A. (1994) *Law and Medical Ethics*, 5th edn. London: Butterworths.

Smith M., Strauss, S., eds (1991). *Pharmacy Ethics*. New York: Pharmaceutical Products Press. (Covers American pharmacy practice but still relevant.)

Wingfield J. 'Pharmacy and Advertising – The Pendulum Swings', *Pharm J* 5 May 1990 p.542.

# CHAPTER TWENTY-ONE

# The Statutory Committee of the Royal Pharmaceutical Society

N.B. In June 1999, the government passed the Health Act 1999 which provided powers to change the regulation of health professions and health professionals and to amend National Health Service law. The consequences of implementing this Act were not complete at the time of going to press and may affect the constitution, powers and operation of the Statutory Committee. In addition, the Society itself proposed changes to its disciplinary machinery in 1998 and it is likely that these will be reflected in the consultations on a new framework for professional self-regulation (*Pharm J* 22 April 2000 p.616) (see also Chapter 19 p.211). Reference is made to the possible effect of these proposals, made in 1998, which appear in full in Appendix 17.

The Statutory Committee, which is a committee of the Royal Pharmaceutical Society of Great Britain, exercises the disciplinary powers of the Society. The provisions relating to pharmacists are to be found in the Pharmacy Act 1954 (ss.7 and 8) and the constitution of the Committee appears in the first Schedule to that Act. New provisions may be made under the Health Act 1999 (see p.298). The provisions relating to bodies corporate are in the Medicines Act 1968 (ss.80 to 83).

## Constitution

The Committee comprises a chairman and five members. The chairman is appointed by the Privy Council, and has to be a person *having practical legal experience*. In practice the Committee has always had as its chairman an eminent member of the legal profession.

The five members are appointed by the Council of the Royal Pharmaceutical Society of Great Britain. They need not all necessarily be pharmacists, although one must be a pharmacist resident in Scotland. However, it has always been the practice to appoint as members of the Committee pharmacists of wide experience. A lay member was appointed to the Committee for the first time in 1998 *(Pharm J* 27 June 1998 p.942) thus implementing one of the proposed changes set out in Appendix 17. A member of the staff of the Royal Pharmaceutical Society of Great Britain normally acts as secretary of the Committee.

The quorum of the Committee is three, one of whom must be the chairman. The Committee makes decisions by a majority vote of its members present and where necessary the chairman has a casting vote. A decision to remove a name from the Register, however, can be taken only with the consent of the chairman. The Committee has power to make its own regulations as to procedure, but they must be approved by the Privy Council (see Appendix 16). Proposals for change appear in Appendix 17.

**Procedure**

The secretary of the Committee must submit a report to the chairman whenever s/he receives information from which it appears that:

1    any of the following *persons* has been convicted of a criminal offence or has been guilty of misconduct (Pharmacy Act 1954, s.8):

   (a)    a registered pharmaceutical chemist or a person employed by him/her in his/her business;

   (b)    a member of the board or an officer or an employee of a body corporate which is carrying on a retail pharmacy business;

   (c)    a representative (see Chapter 4) or an employee of a representative in a retail pharmacy business;

   (d)    a person applying for registration as a pharmaceutical chemist;

   (e)    a person whose name has been removed from the Register under section 12(1) of the Pharmacy Act 1954, or a business employee of such a person.

2    a *body corporate* which is carrying on a retail pharmacy business has been convicted of an offence under the Pharmacy Acts, the Misuse of Drugs Act 1971 or the Medicines Act 1968.

It will be noted that for *corporate bodies* only offences under the Pharmacy Acts, the Medicines Act 1968 and the Misuse of Drugs Act 1971 need be reported to the Statutory Committee; but for any of the *persons* listed from (a) to (e) above, *any* criminal offence is relevant.

The chairman can deal with the information received from the secretary in any of the following ways:

1   If s/he considers that the case is not within the jurisdiction of the Committee, or that the complaint is frivolous, or that because of lapse of time or other circumstances that complaint may properly be disregarded, s/he must decide that the case will not proceed further.

2   If s/he considers that the conviction or misconduct alleged is not serious or is for any other reason of such a character that the matter can be disposed of without any inquiry, s/he can after consultation orally or by letter with the other members of the Statutory Committee decide that the case shall not proceed further. S/he may, however, direct the secretary to send a reprimand to the person affected and caution that person as to their future conduct.

3   In any other case s/he must direct the secretary to take steps for an inquiry to be held. The procedure for an inquiry is specified in the regulations of the Committee (Appendix 16). A notice of the charge must be sent to the affected person at least 28 days before the hearing takes place. The hearing must open in public, and must continue in public unless the Committee otherwise directs.

In 1999, the chairman clarified three circumstances in which a hearing might be in private: where there was evidence involving a person's medical history, especially if it was intimate; where there was evidence involving a young child; and where the evidence involved serious allegations against a third party who was unaware of the allegation and unable to rebut it (*Pharm J* 4 September 1999 p.347).

At the hearing a statement of the case against the person affected is given first, usually by a solicitor representing the body or person who has made the complaint. Then the person affected, or their counsel or solicitor, replies to the charges. Evidence may be received by the Committee orally, in a written or signed statement, or by means of a statutory declaration.

Witnesses may be examined and cross-examined at the hearing. A Crown Court subpoena can be issued to ensure attendance of witnesses, but there is no power to administer oaths, or to deal with contempt of court.

The chairman must announce in public the decision of the Committee. If the decision, or any part of it, is postponed, the chairman must announce such postponement and state the terms, if any, on which it is made. The secretary must then communicate the decision of the Committee in writing to the person affected.

## Jurisdiction

The Committee's authority, as will have been seen, extends to five classes of persons and to corporate bodies.

In a case affecting a *registered pharmaceutical chemist*, the Committee can adopt one of the following courses (proposals for change appear in Appendix 17):

1    direct that no further action be taken;
2    give an admonishment or caution as to the pharmaceutical chemist's future conduct;
3    postpone their decision generally or on approved terms; or
4    direct that the registrar remove the pharmaceutical chemist's name from the Register. Such a direction requires the consent of the chairman.

In a case of a person applying to be registered the Committee can direct that the person's name shall not be registered or shall not be registered until the Committee otherwise directs. Although this last power is most usually exercised following removal of a pharmacist's name from the Register, it can also be invoked when considering an initial application for registration.

A pre-registration graduate who had convictions for actual bodily harm, failed to surrender to custody and who attempted to deceive the Society in regard to details about his pre-registration training was refused admittance to the Register on the grounds that:

'. . . the Register should only be entered upon by persons of good character.'
(*Pharm J* 20 July 1996 p.91)

Similarly, admittance was refused in the case of an overseas pharmacist involved in a benefit fraud (*Pharm J* 24 June 2000 p.947). Conversely, a case involving the provision of untruthful information about pre-registration training, but lacking in evidence of an intention to deceive, resulted in eventual permission to seek registration *(Pharm J* 6 September 1997 p.367).

A person aggrieved by a direction of the Committee may at any time within three months appeal to the High Court. A direction for removal from the Register does not take effect until three months after the giving of notice of the direction or, if there is an appeal to the High Court, until the appeal is determined or withdrawn.

In a case affecting a *body corporate* the Committee may decide to:

1    take no further action;
2    admonish or caution;
3    adjourn a hearing for a set amount of time, usually 12 months;
4    direct the registrar to remove from the Register all those premises at which the body corporate carries on a retail pharmacy business, or such of them as may be specified; or
5    direct that the body corporate be disqualified for the purposes of the Medicines Act 1968, i.e. unable to conduct retail pharmacy businesses. If a direction is given to disqualify then the Committee must direct the registrar to remove from the Register all those premises at which the body corporate carries on a retail pharmacy business.

A direction under 4 or 5 may, if the Committee thinks fit, be given so as to have effect for a limited period.

Sanctions can also be applied against a body corporate if any member of the board, or any officer or person employed by that body, has committed an offence or has been guilty of misconduct, and if the offence or misconduct is such as in the opinion of the Statutory Committee renders him/her, or would if s/he were a pharmacist have rendered him/her, unfit to be on the Register.

The words *in the opinion of the Statutory Committee* in the Pharmacy Act 1954 (s.8) leave the Committee completely unfettered in its discretion. It is not bound by its previous decisions. Further, as it is a Committee of the Royal Pharmaceutical Society and not of the Council of the Society, it is completely independent of the Council, even though the Council appoints all the Committee members except the chairman. A number of references to the Committee's independent status were made in the case of *Pharmaceutical Society of Great Britain* v. *Dickson* (p.363).

## Enquiries Following Criminal Convictions

So far as pharmacists are concerned, the Committee has jurisdiction in all cases of criminal conviction, whether they arise from offences under the Medicines Act or from offences of a general nature, e.g. theft. The jurisdiction was challenged in 1979 when it was argued before, and accepted by, the Committee that the facts leading to the imposition by the Courts of conditional discharge orders could not be adduced before the Committee (*Pharm J* 24 March 1979 p.245). The Society applied successfully to the Divisional Court for the decision to be quashed (*R* v. *Statutory Committee and Others, ex parte the Pharmaceutical Society of Great Britain* [1981] All ER 805, *Pharm J* 15 November 1980 p.272).

From time to time various chairmen have stressed that the directions given by the Committee are not given by way of punishment. For example, in 1953 one chairman said:

> '. . . a man who had already suffered punishment had to come before the Committee not for the purpose of considering additional punishment but for the purpose of considering whether in the interests of the public it was right that he should remain on the Register.'
>
> (*Pharm J* 10 October 1953 p.297)

In 1990, the chairman said:

> 'Parliament set up this Committee for the purposes of taking care of three dimensions . . . the protection of the public, next comes the honour and dignity of the profession and the third dimension is the best interest of the pharmacist.'
>
> (*Pharm J* 14 April 1990 p.488)

The Committee has always placed public safety and the reputation of the profession as its prime concerns and has limited scope for dealing with the rehabilitation of an offending pharmacist (but see proposals for change in

Appendix 17). To address this need, the Society introduced the Sick Pharmacists Schemes in the early 1990s (see p.219).

Nevertheless, the Committee has played its part in requiring rehabilitation by imposing certain conditions on the respondent pharmacist before consideration will be given to an application for restoration to the Register. In a case in which the name of a pharmacist was erased following abuse of Heminevrin, amphetamine and alcohol, the Committee specified that, before application for restoration could be made, he should be alcohol- and drug-free for two years, that he should receive appropriate medical care for those two years and should confirm compliance with these conditions by reports from a consultant psychiatrist and from persons in charge of his accommodation (*Pharm J* 2 February 1991 p.154).

More recently, a pharmacist who had stolen and consumed Dexedrine tablets over a significant period had become 'drug-free' following support from the Sick Pharmacists Scheme. The Committee considered that he was unfit to be on the Register but given these *unusual* circumstances, the more appropriate disposal was a reprimand (*Pharm J* 2 July 1994 p.18). Further examples of 'conditional' orders following alcohol-related convictions are given on page 252.

The majority of Statutory Committee inquiries arise following criminal convictions relating to pharmaceutical offences. Most common are those in which the sale or dispensing of medicinal products that are required by law to be supervised by a pharmacist take place in the absence of a pharmacist. The Committee has always taken the view that supervision is of paramount importance. Inquiries are also held relating to other criminal offences, not all of which are connected with a pharmacist's professional work, for example, motoring offences, theft, receiving stolen goods, forgery, indecent assault and other sexual offences, offences against the Misuse of Drugs Act or the Food and Drugs Act, procuring abortion, firearms offences and labelling offences under the Medicines Act 1968.

In a case in which a pharmacist had been convicted of firearms offences the chairman said:

> '. . . ought a professional man, such as a pharmacist, who has been convicted of an offence of this character be allowed to remain on the Register? The test is whether the offence of which the accused pharmacist stands convicted is an offence which, in the opinion of the Committee, rendered him unfit to have his name on the Register. So we are not really concerned with the particular motive or behaviour of the particular man. We are concerned with the nature of the offence of which he has been convicted.'
>
> (*Pharm J* 15 April 1972 p.344)

This view was confirmed in 1982 in the appeal case *Re Harari* (see p.268), involving an unlawful eviction. Since then, pharmacists have appeared before the Committee for trading unlawfully in written-off cars (*Pharm J* 20 April 1985 p.511), making false statements to collect insurance monies (*Pharm J* 7 August 1993 p.189), making untrue endorsements on passport applications (*Pharm J* 13 December 1997 p.965), impersonating a GP (*Pharm J* 29 June

1991 p.811), paedophilia *(Pharm J* 15 August 1998 p.234) and false imprisonment and assault *(Pharm J* 27 November 1999 p.853).

Most Statutory Committee cases, however, deal directly with a pharmacist's professional and legal responsibilities and are related to his/her professional work.

The jurisdiction of the Committee also applies to offences committed outside the United Kingdom, e.g. drug offences committed in Canada *(Pharm J* 1 December 1984 p.695) and convictions under Jersey's state law *(Pharm J* 3 December 1988 p.727). Moreover, there is no time limit which removes the possibility of inquiry; in 1999 a pharmacist was removed from the Register by the Committee in relation to child abuse offences which were committed 20 years previously *(Pharm J* 10 July 1999 p.51).

## Enquiries Following Allegations of Misconduct

In 1947 the chairman made clear the jurisdiction of the Committee in relation to allegations of misconduct:

> 'The jurisdiction is not limited to acts which constitute criminal offences. Indeed, in a very large number of cases we are not considering criminality but conduct which pharmacists ought not to pursue.'
>
> *(Pharm J* 26 July 1947 p.60)

Nearly all the complaints to the Committee alleging professional misconduct are made by the Council of the Royal Pharmaceutical Society but there have been exceptions. In the 'Care Chemist' case *(Pharm J* 16 November 1974 p.473 and 14 December 1974 p.575), the 'Boots Scribbling Diary' case *(Pharm J* 11 February 1978 p.126) and the 'Boots Times Advertisement' case *(Pharm J* 4 January 1992 p.13) the complainants were individual members of the Society and not the Council. Although the Committee deals with allegations of professional misconduct, the question of what is good conduct for a professional person is a matter for the profession itself (see Chapter 20). Nevertheless, one Statutory Committee chairman said in an address to students in 1953:

> 'With regard to the code of ethics, the actual decision as to what conduct is misconduct which justified removal from the Register is one which can be made only by the Statutory Committee, and the Committee is not bound by any code formulated by the Pharmaceutical Society.'
>
> *(Pharm J* 4 April 1953 p.238)

Whilst this is strictly true, the Committee has in practice used as a guideline the Code of Ethics, issued by the Council of the Royal Pharmaceutical Society and amended from time to time (see Chapter 20) as reflecting standards of professional practice.

Support for this view may be found in a 1987 case when the chairman began his judgment thus:

' . . . it is well known that this Committee is not bound by the Code . . . but nevertheless [it represents] in clear terms the views of the most senior members of the profession and they have been approved by the profession as a whole, they are expressed in terms which are easy to understand and this Committee attaches great importance to them.'

(*Pharm J* 21 November 1987 p.633)

Notwithstanding the above, there is no specific reference in any Code of Ethics suggesting that it is wrong to be in charge of a pharmacy when drunk or to make a dispensing error. Such things are self-evident and implicit in the duty of pharmacists to have in mind at all times their responsibilities to the general public, although these duties have now been made more explicit (see Chapter 20 p.228).

### Applications for Restoration to the Register

Applications for restoration to the Register are also considered by the Committee (see Appendix 16). Such an application is considered in public unless the chairman grants a specific application for a private hearing. It must be supported by a statutory declaration made by the applicant, and also by at least two certificates as to the applicant's identity and good character. One of the certificates must be given by a registered pharmaceutical chemist; the other can be given by a registered pharmaceutical chemist, a Justice of the Peace, a fully registered medical practitioner or a legally qualified holder of a judicial office (reg.31). The secretary must notify the applicant in writing of the Committee's decision.

If the High Court has dismissed an appeal against a decision that a name be removed from the Register, then a direction of the Committee authorising restoration cannot take effect unless it is approved by the Privy Council.

### Statutory Committee Cases

Analysis of the work of the Statutory Committee taken from the first author's doctoral thesis shows that 75 per cent of all convictions leading to reference to the Statutory Committee fell into five clearly defined areas: supervision; theft of cash; theft of drugs; unlawful sale of Prescription Only Medicines; and Controlled Drug offences. Similarly, cases involving misconduct largely fall into five categories: unsatisfactory conduct; unsatisfactory premises; excessive or uncontrolled supply of substances of abuse; dispensing mistakes; and advertising. Although an inordinate amount of the Committee's time has been spent on this last topic, it has only once resulted in the erasure of a pharmacist's name and that was associated with other aspects of misconduct (*Pharm J* 14 October 1972 p.373). Some cases have bridged both conviction and misconduct, such as drink-driving offences linked to erratic behaviour in the pharmacy. It has been necessary to be selective over the cases quoted and only brief reference is made to advertising cases. Interested readers will find earlier examples in previous editions of this work. What follows is a selection of cases exemplifying the kinds of activity or behaviour which have resulted in sanctions by the Statutory Committee.

## Supervision

The Committee has always been concerned with cases which involve the lack of supervision of the sale of Pharmacy Medicines and of dispensing. The cases illustrate the Committee's attitude to supervision. For example in a case in 1971 the chairman, referring to large departmentalised pharmacies, said:

> '... it is vitally important to ensure that the drug counter and the dispensary are adequately covered by a qualified pharmacist at all times of the day with a real 100% cover.'
>
> (*Pharm J* 23 January 1971 p.72)

Much more recently in a case of unsupervised sales, the chairman stated that:

> '... to be on the shop floor looking after the public was essential to the pharmacist's role.'
>
> (*Pharm J* 30 August 1997 p.322)

and in the following year, the Committee removed a pharmacist from the Register for attempting to supervise by telephone from 19 miles away (*Pharm J* 2 May 1998 p.625).

Permanent or temporary absence is equally culpable. Late arrival in the pharmacy on three occasions led to pharmacist being reprimanded (*Pharm J* 22 January 2000 p.128). A locum pharmacist who failed to fulfil his engagement was reprimanded in the following terms:

> 'we can point out that the sale of these medicines without any supervision by a pharmacist is a matter that is not only serious, but the cause of great possible and potential danger to the public.'
>
> (*Pharm J* 25 May 1985 p.662)

Failure on the part of a pharmacist proprietor, about to holiday in New Zealand, to act when he knew that a locum had cancelled a booking led to the unsupervised dispensing of over 200 prescriptions and an unknown number of unsupervised sales before the inspector intervened. The pharmacist was removed from the Register (*Pharm J* 1 February 1997 p.166). Erasure in a very similar case, arising when the proprietor was on holiday in India, followed failure to arrange adequate locum cover in his absence (*Pharm J* 3 June 2000 p.840).

Inquiries have resulted from attempts to run two pharmacies with only one pharmacist, to do without the services of a pharmacist at quiet times like Saturday afternoons (*Pharm J* 26 June 1999 p.915), Sundays (see below) or Bank Holidays (*Pharm J* 18 February 1995 p.221) or to leave businesses in the charge of a range of unqualified persons. In 1990 a pharmacist had paid a visit to his 'other shop' following which the chairman commented:

'. . . The fact that dispensing is left to the hands of experienced staff we will not receive as mitigation. Such staff should never be regarded as a substitute for what the Act requires . . .'

*(Pharm J* 18 August 1990 p.220)

Later the same year, a pharmacy had had no regular pharmacist for seven months and sales of Pharmacy Medicines were in the hands of a 15-year-old girl. The company owning both pharmacies was disqualified following the chairman's general statement:

'The signal we send out to the profession is, "if you cannot get proper cover then the pharmacy has to be closed" . . . There are no half measures.'

*(Pharm J* 29 September 1990 p.436)

In two cases in 1991 the chairman was even more forceful:

'Parliament does not offer a choice, such as "I would like to run this pharmacy without proper cover, because it helps those around and in the district". There is no alternative – the pharmacy has to close and that is the end of the matter.'

*(Pharm J* 19 January 1991 p.89)

and, following an attempt to operate a partial service on a Sunday:

'. . . a point arose as to whether or not the shop was open . . . A sale can take place whether the premises are open or not . . . it is the opinion of the Committee that the shop was willing to take casual trade . . . and customers would be dealt with . . . as and when they came in.'

*(Pharm J* 27 July 1991 p.136)

The reasons for the Committee's position are clear:

'. . . medicines can be ill-used, ill-advisedly, by members of the public when they are uninstructed by a pharmacist . . . Sales have to be under the supervision of a pharmacist, not for any fanciful notion, but because the law requires it for the safety of the public.'

*(Pharm J* 17 August 1991 p.224)

In 1994 the chairman felt it necessary to issue a general warning to the profession:

'. . . pharmacists need to be particularly alert towards certain categories of unqualified persons whose standing may lead them into usurping the pharmacist's role . . . One is employers; another is long service employees whose over familiarity with practices in the pharmacy may lead them to transgress; and the third category . . . is the unqualified relative.'

*(Pharm J* 29 January 1994 p.154)

The chairman went on to say that the subject of supervision should be routinely discussed from time to time with such individuals to ensure the meaning of the prohibition on their activities was *brought home and fully understood.*

To the above list should be added the dispensing assistant (*Pharm J* 3 May 1997 p.622) and the pre-registration graduate, who does not assume the privileges or responsibilities of a pharmacist either in the sale of Pharmacy Medicines (*Pharm J* 8 October 1994 p.496) or in dispensing (*Pharm J* 17 May 1997 p.697) until registration. In the last case, the chairman said:

'It is very important indeed to make sure that those persons you leave behind know precisely what they can do and what they cannot do ... ultimately the pharmacist is there to serve the public safely. The pharmacist should not put the public at risk for the sake of his own private profit.'

*(Pharm J* 17 May 1997 p.697)

Although the interpretation of *supervision* by the Council has been modified (see p.232), this is unlikely to be reflected in cases before the Committee which almost exclusively reflect situations where the pharmacist was simply not present, rather than any failure to ensure supervisory procedures were carried out.

## Theft and Handling Stolen Goods

Cases of theft are always treated by the Committee very seriously on the grounds that the pharmacist is in a position of trust particularly when the theft is from an employer.

In one case the pharmacist had stolen money from his employer over a period of some 12 months. The chairman, in giving the decision of the Committee, said:

'I should point out that if a pharmacist steals from his employer, and if he continues in that wrongdoing over a period of time ... he cannot possibly complain if this Committee decides that his name should be removed from the Register.'

*(Pharm J* 25 May 1986 p.662)

In another case the chairman said:

'It is just one more incident of a tale so often told of a man who falls from his earlier position of honour because, he says, he has got into financial difficulties and in that process he lets down those who have trusted him, not only his employers but his wife and children as well and, of course his profession ... insofar as professional conduct is concerned this Committee has no doubt at all that he was guilty of gross professional misconduct.'

*(Pharm J* 24 January 1987 p.108)

In 1998, a pharmacist who drew cheques to purchase goods on stolen cheque books and cards was described as demonstrating:

'... disgusting behaviour ... he himself does the very thing that he is on the lookout to stop other people doing ... [and shows] ... irresponsibility, a cavalier attitude and a lack of sensitivity towards other persons.'

*(Pharm J* 25 July 1998 p.118)

The theft by an employee of a substantial sum accumulated through 'Air Miles' by over-purchasing dispensary stock paid for by the employer was considered a very serious breach of trust towards Mr X's employer and the pharmacist's name was erased from the Register *(Pharm J* 9 January 1999 p.47).

Repeatedly, the Committee's decisions reflect the view that pharmacists who breach their position of trust in such a way are unfit to be on the Register:

'Honesty, integrity and honourable behaviour are at the core of all professional people ... dishonesty and professionalism never go together. Secondly [a feature of this case] is a breach of trust. Mr X has been placed ... in a position of trust as the manager ... How does he repay that trust? He repays it by acting dishonestly ... Our conclusion is that there [is] no place for a pharmacist who behaves like this on the Register ...'

*(Pharm J* 22 May 1993 p.704)

### Theft and Unlawful Possession of Drugs

Until the 1980s few pharmacists were involved with theft of drugs and their consumption. However, this situation has changed.

In 1984 the chairman commented on the potential danger to the public of a pharmacist who is addicted to drugs:

'He became so irrational that not only did he steal from his employers but also deceived his friend ... This illustrates the dangers inherent in addiction in the case of a pharmacist upon whom the lives and the well-being of his customers or patients may depend ...'

*(Pharm J* 24 March 1984 p.358)

and in 1993 on the public danger which results from the pharmacist's efforts to disguise the theft of Controlled Drugs:

'It involved substitution of Epsom salts in three tubs (formerly containing cocaine), which could have jeopardised the comfort and assistance that cocaine may have given to other patients ...'

*(Pharm J* 10 July 1993 p.58)

and again in 1995, in a case where the pharmacist had stolen diamorphine, replaced it with tragacanth powder and abused the stolen diamorphine himself:

'... three years of dispensing in a pharmacy while taking diamorphine, with its euphoric and distorting effects, and while there was no-one to check him, correct him or monitor him, meant that there was the chance of a mistake.'

*(Pharm J* 19 August 1995 p.246)

Such activities clearly bring the profession into disrepute and, as with theft of money, represent a breach of trust:

'The public [is] content that ... pharmacists [shall be the custodians of these dangerous drugs] ... because ... pharmacists can be trusted to behave responsibly and professionally. Thus when a pharmacist behaves irresponsibly, taking drugs out of his own custody, either for his own use, or, in particular, for pushing them on the street, the Committee must take a very stern view.'

*(Pharm J* 26 October 1991 p.578)

For a report of a more recent case, involving cocaine, see *Pharm J* 9 November 1996 p.669.

### Deception

The Committee has dealt severely with pharmacists who have been convicted of obtaining a pecuniary advantage by deception, usually by means of defrauding the National Health Service.

In a case which involved a submission of claims for payment on National Health Service prescriptions, which had been altered by the addition of extra items after the original prescription had been dispensed, the chairman, in directing the removal of a name from the Register, said:

'The submission of prescriptions for payment is a very important part of the carrying on of the business of a pharmacy and is one where the complete honesty of a pharmacist is paramount. It is the pharmacist . . . who submits the claim. In our view Mr X has failed lamentably to comply with the high standard of honesty required in the practice of this profession . . .'

*(Pharm J* 20/27 December 1986 p.846)

Erasures resulted in a similar case in 1998 *(Pharm J* 24 January 1998 p.116); in a case where a pharmacist had made false claims for rota payments and false endorsements relating to non-resident claims and false pack sizes (*Pharm J* 7 March 1987 p.312); where false declarations of exemption were made when submitting prescriptions for payment (*Pharm J* 24 November 1990 p.702); for falsely claiming urgent dispensing fees on non-urgent prescriptions (*Pharm J* 5 March 1994 p.323); falsely claiming extemporaneous fees *(Pharm J* 10 June 2000 p.876); making false endorsements (*Pharm J* 3 June 2000 p.841); and claiming for prescriptions not dispensed (*Pharm J* 22 January 2000 p.128). A reprimand was administered for substituting medicines on a prescription without the prescriber's consent (*Pharm J* 31 October 1998 p.698).

An attempt to deceive the Society by forging a certificate of professional indemnity resulted in erasure from the Register (*Pharm J* 4 December 1999 p.896).

## Unlawful Supplies of Prescription Only Medicines

Few cases following convictions have arisen in recent years. Legislation, particularly under the Misuse of Drugs Act 1971, has lagged behind fashion in drug abuse, and those drugs which featured in cases in the mid-1980s – diethylpropion, barbiturates and Heminevrin – are now replaced by the benzodiazepines, buprenorphine and dihydrocodeine.

In 1991, a pharmacist who illicitly manufactured amphetamine sulphate was sentenced to eight years' imprisonment and:

'. . . forfeited for ever any right to be registered again as a pharmacist.'

*(Pharm J* 23 November 1991 p.705)

An erasure was ordered in 1992 in the case of a pharmacist who supplied medicines, mainly Temgesic in tablet and ampoule form, to Greek persons, mainly in Greece, without any legal prescriptions. More recently a pharmacist was removed from the Register following a conviction for unlawful supplies of anabolic steroids (*Pharm J* 9 May 1998 p.658); however, such activity is more often brought as a complaint of misconduct (see p.243).

A persistent 'misuse' of medicines involves the use of steroid creams for 'skin lightening'. Investigation by the media resulted in a complaint leading to erasures for pharmacists who unlawfully made supplies of Dermovate without prescription in 1997 (*Pharm J* 12 July 1997 p.57) and, following convictions, again in 2000 (*Pharm J* 19 February 2000 p.290–291).

## Controlled Drugs

The majority of convictions relating to Controlled Drugs have related to inadequate record keeping (e.g. *Pharm J* 22 November 1997 p.835 and 20 June 1998 p.897). The importance of keeping proper records was summed up in a case in 1990 when the chairman listed four important reasons:

> 'One is that it is essential to know where dangerous drugs are. [Secondly], where one is dealing with a drug commonly supplied to addicts, one is playing with fire if records are not kept. Such people, in order to feed their habit, frequently lie, sell part of the drugs they are given, horde drugs and forge prescriptions . . . it is . . . extremely important that records are kept right up to date, scrupulously and accurately. [Thirdly] . . . it is for the greater protection of the pharmacist himself that he keeps records in that fashion . . . his records would help to avoid any false accusations being made against him . . . [Fourthly] Controlled Drugs have to be locked away . . . sometimes those cabinets are broken into and the drugs stolen. It therefore becomes very, very important for the proper authorities to know precisely what had been in the cabinet before the commencement of their inquiries.'
>
> (*Pharm J* 4 August 1990 p.158)

The Committee administered a reprimand to a pharmacist who failed to store Controlled Drugs securely in a misguided attempt to foil persistent burglars (*Pharm J* 4 February 1995 p.151) but where a similar offence had been compounded by re-issue of dispensed medicines returned by patients and the selling on of free condoms included with the local needle and syringe exchange scheme, the Committee ordered erasure of the pharmacist's name from the Register (*Pharm J* 11 December 1993 p.251).

## Supply of Dangerous Chemicals

In 1991 two different pharmacists appeared before the Committee following convictions for the supply to a 17-year-old youth of sodium cyanide in one case and strychnine hydrochloride, potassium permanganate and glycerol in the second. The young man accidentally caused an explosion with the combination of the chemicals and both pharmacists received reprimands (*Pharm J* 23 March 1991 p.371 and *Pharm J* 21 November 1991 p.608).

## Disposal of Dangerous Waste

Implementation of environmental protection laws has led to a number of convictions of pharmacists. In 1987 a pharmacist entrusted some 20 plastic sacks of trade and domestic waste to an outside contractor. These contained a small number of Prescription Only Medicines which eventually surfaced on the waste ground where the contractor had illegally dumped the sacks (*Pharm J* 27 June 1987 p.798). The following year a pharmacist was reprimanded following a conviction for herself placing sacks of unwanted medicines in a skip at a local authority tip (*Pharm J* 23 July 1988 p.128).

Reprimands followed in three later cases. A pharmacist had cleared out stock from a pharmacy he had just acquired and caused sacks containing Prescription Only Medicines and Controlled Drugs to be left in a skip outside the premises. The chairman concluded that the pharmacist had made no inquiries at all about what the refuse sacks contained and added:

'. . . by that carelessness, led the public to be exposed to dangerous substances.'

(*Pharm J* 2 February 1991 p.154)

Two years later, irresponsible dumping by a pharmacist of waste containing potassium dichromate and other dangerous material caused a fire in the dustcart that tried to dispose of it (*Pharm J* 9 January 1993 p.50) and, more recently, a pharmacist simply left sacks of obsolete medicines in the garden of his old house (*Pharm J* 22 January 2000 p.129).

## Parallel Imports

The advent of European Community imports led to a spate of cases in the late 1980s in which pharmacists had failed to check that imported medicines were properly licensed and complied with United Kingdom labelling requirements. A conviction under the latter regulations led to a reprimand for a pharmacist who, despite previous warnings, had continued to remove legitimately imported tablets from their blister packaging into a larger plastic pot as a stock bottle, thus mixing tablets from different production runs and losing details of batch numbers and expiry dates (*Pharm J* 21 March 1992 p.387).

When two pharmacists knowingly had in their possession a substantial quantity of unlicensed medicines the Committee regarded the matter as one of the utmost seriousness and in reprimanding the pharmacists the chairman said:

'We view with growing concern developments that have brought (this case) here today . . . in cases of this kind, the Committee is of a mind to direct the erasure of persons who have shown themselves to be unfit to be on the Register by reason of convictions like these.'

(*Pharm J* 25 January 1992 p.113)

In a later case involving the possession and dispensing of unlabelled and unlicensed imported medicinal products the chairman, in reprimanding the pharmacist, commented that the pharmacist had not sufficiently asked himself what was meant by the words for 'export only' on the invoice and why the medicines had been invoiced that way and not itemised. He added:

'Why, for goodness sake, is the name of the supplier removed so that any enquiry is thwarted as to who supplied these products? Why is it that the labelling of the products he receives is deficient? Is it not suspicious that medicines are supplied in plastic see-through bags without any labelling? How is such a good discount to be achieved? We would like it to be known that such features ought to strike home to any pharmacist worth his salt and ring bells so loud and clear that a pharmacist in performing properly his duty would never have anything to do with such a product . . .'

(*Pharm J* 2 January 1993 p.17)

The events in the 1980s led to more explicit statements and guidance in the 1992 Code of Ethics (Obligation 1.4 and Guidance) so that stiffer sanctions were administered in 1996 when a series of inquiries into what became known as the *Schaffer* cases came before the Committee. Mr Schaffer, who was never a pharmacist, was an unlicensed wholesaler who was convicted in 1994 of seven offences relating to unlicensed importing, trading and supplying of medicinal products. Most of these were purported to be 'parallel imports' from Europe but in fact originated from India and Mexico.

In every case, there were features which should have alerted the pharmacists who obtained medicines from Mr Schaffer that something was wrong. For example:

'. . . very high discounts . . . that Mr Schaffer appeared to deal from the back of his car . . . always wanted cash . . . a "remarkable lack" of invoices . . . that some of the medicines were described as "shoddy and dirty" . . .'

(*Pharm J* 2 March 1996 p.301)

In all, 18 pharmacists appeared before the Statutory Committee as a consequence of Mr Schaffer's activities; the names of 15 pharmacists were ordered to be removed from the Register, the other three were reprimanded. Notwithstanding, in a later but unrelated case, another pharmacist was erased for dealings in unlicensed Turkish Zantac (*Pharm J* 3 May 1997 p.622).

## Unsatisfactory Conduct

Until the 1990s, cases which could be classified under this heading would principally be situations where a pharmacist's personal or professional conduct was compromised by alcoholism. Today, transgressions which reflect lack of professional competence or application of proper standards for whatever reason have become more common and they frequently arise from a *course of conduct* rather than a single event.

Early in 1972 the Committee considered complaints against a pharmacist alleging that he kept irregular hours and absented himself without due cause at times when the pharmacy was open. It was further alleged that his general appearance was unclean and unkempt, that he frequently smelt of drink, that he constantly borrowed money which he did not repay, and that he made dispensing errors. Further, his general conduct in the pharmacy was alleged to be totally unsatisfactory. It was alleged that his course of conduct over a period of years had shown that members of the public were put at risk and that he had acted in a manner calculated to bring pharmacy into disrepute. The chairman stressed the duty of the Committee to the public in the following words:

'If we are to discharge our duty in protecting the public and protecting the fair name of pharmacy there is only one step we can take, which with the utmost regret we do take, and that is to direct that his name be removed from the Register.'

(*Pharm J* 15 April 1972 p.343)

The Committee has taken a strong line with pharmacists who have been found incapable of carrying out their duties as a pharmacist due to the influence of alcohol and has used its limited powers to introduce measures which approximate to both suspension from the Register and the imposition of conditions before re-admission (proposals to change this situation are in Appendix 17).

For example, in 1999, after ordering the removal of her name from the Register, the chairman said:

'[this case] gives rise to a clear indication that she has a drink problem, is going to be a danger if she works in a pharmacy . . . we regard alcoholism . . . as an illness which needs treatment . . . there is a scheme available in this profession which will extend help to her if she is willing to receive it.'

He directed that Mrs X would not be restored to the Register until she could show that she had been free from alcohol abuse for at least 12 months, supported by references to that effect from psychiatrists, doctors and others who knew her (*Pharm J* 30 January 1999 p.153).

This latter case arose from driving convictions which can sometimes lead to erasure (*Pharm J* 18 December 1999 p.979), reprimand (*Pharm J* 21 November 1998 p.804) or admonition (*Pharm J* 27 November 1999 p.854) depending on the circumstances.

A range of sanctions have been administered for other forms of unsatisfactory conduct which generally include *failure to adopt safe practices*. In the first case of its kind, a pharmacist was erased from the Register principally for failure to maintain his professional indemnity insurance cover for a period of at least 40 months. In this case, the chairman was also critical of how long it took the Society's Council to bring the complaint forward pointing out that it would have been dreadful to imagine '*an uninsured patient*' having a claim for personal injuries and uncovering that the Society knew all about it (*Pharm J* 17 May 1997 p.698) (see also Appeals Against Decisions p.269 and Table 21.1 p.271).

Pharmacists have been removed from the Register for other unsafe practices such as using an open and unlocked Controlled Drugs cabinet, the presence of unlabelled pre-packs on the dispensary shelves, the presence of plastic measures containing unidentified tablets recovered from monitored dosage system trays, and an intention to re-use tablets of which the pharmacist had no knowledge of either batch number or expiry date (*Pharm J* 8 January 2000 p.52).

Following three reprimands at earlier hearings, a pharmacist was erased for *failure to achieve proper standards*, namely, failure to produce evidence of professional indemnity insurance cover, trading as a pharmacy when the premises were not registered, reuse of patient returned medicines, sale of restricted medicines in the absence of a pharmacist, lack of personal control, poor physical standards of the premises (such as stock stored in the toilet area, heavily frosted refrigerator and no segregation of waste medicines) and unacceptable practices in relation to handling medicines (such as handling tablets with bare hands and preparing food in a room used for dispensing) (*Pharm J* 27 November 1999 p.852).

An erasure also followed a case of *pharmaceutical incompetence* where the supply of medicines to residential homes was so chaotic that monthly requests were being made for prescriptions which bore amounts for two and three months duration, some patients were supplied with two years supply of medicines in six months, prescriptions had been requested for a deceased patient and 30 outstanding prescriptions had never been dispensed (*Pharm J* 17 May 1997 p.597).

A reprimand was given to a pharmacist who removed batch numbers and expiry dates from medicines (*Pharm J* 26 September 1998 p.482) but, in another case, when accompanied by the re-use of patients' returned medicines and deliberate 'popping' of tablets from their original blister packaging, such behaviour led to an erasure (*Pharm J* 22 August 1998 p.264).

A reprimand was given to a pharmacist who had claimed for items not dispensed and allowed himself to be duped into giving credit to a bogus doctor (*Pharm J* 10 June 2000 p.876) and to a pharmacist who kept a stock of blank prescription forms to fill in on behalf of prescribers (*Pharm J* 26 June 1999 p.914), but where this practice was linked to deliberate sale of blank forms to drug misusers the pharmacist's name was erased from the register (*Pharm J* 24 June 2000 p.947).

### Unsatisfactory State of Pharmacy Premises

Allegations about pharmacists conducting pharmacies in such a state as to be a potential hazard to the public are now relatively rare. This follows enforcement of the Guide to Good Dispensing Practice, which in 1979 set minimum environmental standards for pharmacies as part of the Code of Ethics and the incorporation of a more rigorous set of Standards of Practice into the Code of Ethics in 1992. However, the Committee continues to deal with a few cases where the conditions are still unacceptable.

For example, in 1993, a pharmacist was reprimanded for conditions in his pharmacy described as:

'. . . the floor covering [was] dirty and split, constituting a hazard to the public . . . the shelves [were] dirty and dusty. There had been insufficient work surfaces, and these had been cluttered, leaving little usable space. The sink had been dirty and the surfaces around it had been cluttered with old medicine bottles and rubbish.'

and, on a later date:

'The refrigerator was dirty, had no maximum/minimum thermometer and water was running out of the bottom. Some of the stock was found to be wet.'

(*Pharm J* 31 July 1993 p.162)

In a 1994 case, similar conditions led to the dispensing of a mixture containing the remains of insects and a consequent reprimand for the pharmacist (*Pharm J* 17 June 1995 p.840) and in 1997 a pharmacist's name was erased for allowing the pharmacy to be contaminated with food debris and to be poorly maintained (*Pharm J* 2 August 1997 p 195).

### Excessive or Uncontrolled Supplies of Substances of Abuse

The fact that the sale of certain substances is not unlawful does not permit the pharmacist to abrogate his professional responsibility as custodian of the nation's medicines, nor to ignore his specialised knowledge of chemicals and other harmful material. The names of many pharmacists have been erased from the Register in connection with selling excessive quantities of medicines likely to be abused or for being unable to account, other than by way of sale, for large discrepancies between the amount of such medicines purchased and supplies made on prescription. Although a complaint of misconduct may be associated with supply of chemicals (see above p.250), it more commonly follows irresponsible supply of abused medicines such as those containing codeine, morphine, methadone, ephedrine, cyclizine and antihistamines or anabolic steroids.

The distinctions between what is and is not considered to be irresponsible can be fine. In the 1980s the chairman made it clear that a pharmacist should not supply adjuvants such as cyclizine to drug misusers saying:

'. . . he dealt with these potentially dangerous medicines (cyclizine), knowing them to be dangerous, with complete recklessness and a complete disregard for the health of those to whom he supplied.'

(*Pharm J* 9 January 1988 p.62 and see also *Pharm J* 25 July 1987 p.104)

Commenting on a more recent case, involving the supply, over a six-month period, of 39 000 Valoid tablets to a single customer the chairman commented:

'It was startling to the point of disbelief if he did not know that Valoid was [cyclizine] . . . [the pharmacist] had demonstrated a complete lack of expertise, the public had been put at risk, no check had been made on the customer or on the use of the tablets, and no warning had been given.'

(*Pharm J* September 2, 2000 p.326)

However in June 2000, steps were underway to include the provision of another adjuvant, citric acid, as part of the support services for drug misusers, at least in Scotland (*Pharm J* 24 June 2000 p.950).

Five cases involving the supply of hundreds of litres of codeine linctus in the Glasgow area were considered by the Committee between 1987 and 1989. In defence the pharmacists often gave as the explanation for supplying such large quantities that they were trying to help the addict. The chairman rejected this argument in round terms:

'. . . in the existing climate which appertains to drug abuse these days, we think it would be a dereliction of our duty to take a charitable view of the wilful, deliberate omission to take action, which was carried out over the period in question to his own profit and to the detriment, the serious detriment, of members of the public.'

*(Pharm J* 10 March 1990 p.307)

In a later case, involving failure to account satisfactorily for 725 g ephedrine hydrochloride powder, 59.5 litres ephedrine hydrochloride elixir, 541.5 litres of Phensedyl linctus, 1857.9 litres of codeine linctus, 9432 tablets of codeine phosphate 30 mg and 5600 tablets of codeine phosphate 60 mg the chairman declared that the pharmacist's duty of care could not be avoided even under duress and added:

'Even if those threats were made, which we do not accept, we were invited . . . to consider the balance of the Code of Ethics . . . and . . . the law . . . against the threat of violence to himself, to his children and to his livelihood . . . and, upon striking that balance, to determine that what he did was right and the only alternative a professional man could follow. We emphatically reject that suggestion and anything approaching that. A professional man does not see things in that way at all. It is not a question of balance. A professional man does not act illegally, neither does he deliberately act in a flagrant breach of the Code . . . What he does is to face up to threats and temptations as part of his professional responsibilities.'

The chairman continued:

'It is no way for a professional man to behave, to feed secretly the addiction of drug addicts, having given in to the temptation of supplying their demands, and to allow seepage of drugs of abuse and addiction onto the street where they can be absorbed into the black market and into the wrong hands . . . We have decided . . . that Mr X, by behaving in such an utterly irresponsible way, must reasonably expect that he may have forfeited forever his right to practise as a pharmacist.'

*(Pharm J* 28 September 1991 p.445)

Despite these clear warnings, two pharmacists were removed from the Register in 1999 for making excessive sales of codeine linctus (*Pharm J* 30 January 1999 p.152) and similarly in relation to kaolin and morphine mixture (*Pharm J* 10 July 1999 p.50).

The dangers of too close a relationship with drug misusers was dramatically demonstrated in a case where a pharmacist had allowed her pharmacy to be used by a substantial number of recreational drug users, giving rise to drug dealing on the premises, brawls and the dumping of used needles and syringes in the vicinity. The pharmacy had been christened a 'drug den' and 'Smack Street' by local residents and had attracted drug users far beyond the local population; in short, it was 'a honey pot for illicit trading in drugs'. The chairman said that a pharmacist could not dispense a prescription simply because a doctor had written it and added that:

'The pharmacist is there to check, to monitor, to counsel, to use his informed judgement, to use experience, to sniff out mistakes. If one is asked to do something which is unlawful, or which is highly likely to be, then one should challenge it and confront the prescriber.'

*(Pharm J* 29 November 1997 p.888)

Such sentiments are reflected in the 1992 Code of Ethics (Guidance on Obligation 1.7) thus:

'A pharmacist should not attempt on his own to control a misuser's habit, but should liaise with bodies such as drug misuse clinics in any local initiatives to assist misusers.'
(*Pharm J* 25 April 1992 p.547)

## Dispensing Mistakes

It has been rare for dispensing errors to lead to removal from the Register unless there are particularly worrying circumstances. In December 1973 the Committee heard a complaint alleging that a pharmacist had made a series of dispensing mistakes over a period of three weeks. Moreover, the same pharmacist had been before the Committee two years earlier on a very similar charge. Directing erasure from the Register the chairman said:

'. . . it was quite properly impressed upon us that we ought to view the whole matter cumulatively, without putting the microscope on each particular item in isolation . . . we [cannot] resist the conclusion that the cumulative effect of all these individual matters, coupled with the history of what had taken place before, amounted to misconduct. We have borne very much in mind that our prime duty is to see that the public is protected. This is an important duty, for one can hardly imagine anybody who could be more dangerous to the public than a pharmacist who is liable to make errors in dispensing what may be dangerous drugs.'
(*Pharm J* 5 January 1974 p.11)

However, in a much later case, a series of dispensing errors ultimately (after a year's adjournment) resulted in a reprimand for a pharmacist who was dispensing nearly twice the national average of prescriptions without dispensing assistance and in the knowledge that he had impaired eyesight. The chairman commented that Mr X should have backed up his practice with protocols and double-checks so that even if he had blurred vision, mistakes were picked up. He added

'Pharmacists must not act without safety nets.'
(*Pharm J* 5 June 1999 p.804)

Later the same year, another pharmacist was reprimanded for making dispensing errors whilst being grossly overworked (*Pharm J* 21 August 1999 p.270).

Confirmation that a single dispensing error *could* constitute misconduct arose in a 1985 case and was later confirmed by the High Court (see p.271). A patient was prescribed by his doctor pethidine in the form of a 'Brompton' mixture. The doctor intended the mixture of 50 mg of pethidine per 1 ml to be diluted to 15 ml. The mixture dispensed was not diluted to 15 ml and was in fact 15 times the strength intended by the doctor. The patient died, death being due to pethidine poisoning (*Pharm J* 11 May 1985 p.600). Any error which results in death, notwithstanding that all could, is likely to be referred to inquiry by the Committee.

Any error which demonstrates lack of competence is also likely to result in an inquiry. In 1992, a pharmacist who did not understand the difference between Oramorph Concentrate and Oramorph Solution supplied a medicine which was ten times as strong as it should have been. The patient survived but the pharmacist was erased from the Register (*Pharm J* 6 June 1992 p.746).

A case in 1998 provided the opportunity for the chairman to give advice on what to do, or rather what not to do, when a dispensing mistake is discovered. A pharmacist discovered that a supply of atenolol had inadvertently been given to the wrong patient but did nothing active to try and remedy the mistake. The chairman did not accept that the pharmacist could simply expect the patient to realise the mistake and return to the pharmacy. In fact it took 28 days before the wrong recipient of the atenolol was identified. Listing all the things that could have been done when a mistake is discovered, the chairman said:

'Forget personal dignity and reputation. The patient comes first. If it needs to be disclosed to the whole world that one has made a mistake, so be it . . . Let the profession know that this particular pharmacist . . . sat on her hands and waited for the tablets to turn up. Pharmacists should not do that; they should get on the rooftop and shout.'

(*Pharm J* 27 February 1999 p.288)

## Advertising

In the past, many cases of alleged professional misconduct in relation to advertising came before the Committee. Most notable were the cases involving the Boots organisation, all of which related to the advertising of professional services, in particular the advertising of dispensing (*Pharm J* 4 June 1949 p.411; 8 July 1950 p.26; 16 May 1959 p.361), the 'Scribbling Diary' case in 1977 (*Pharm J* 11 February 1978 p.126) and *The Times* newspaper advertisement for their monitored dosage system (*Pharm J* 4 January 1992 p.13), together with the 'Care Chemist' campaign launched by Independent Chemists Marketing Ltd, a company sponsored by the National Pharmaceutical Union (as it then was) (*Pharm J* 16 November 1974 p.473 and 14 December 1974 p.575). A full account of these cases appears in earlier editions of *Pharmacy Law and Ethics*.

The provision of information, i.e. advertising, about professional services is now positively encouraged by the Code of Ethics as being in the public interest. However, it should not be thought that there are *no* limits on the form that such advertising may take. Such material must, among other things, be factual, dignified and restrained and must not disparage the professional services of other pharmacists or pharmacies, nor make claims of superiority, either expressed or implied, in this respect. Moreover, the series of cases involving Boots demonstrates the paramount importance of the superintendent pharmacist in controlling the professional activities of a corporate body which owns retail pharmacy businesses.

### Responsibility of the Superintendent Pharmacist

In 1971 the Committee considered the responsibility of a superintendent pharmacist particularly in circumstances where the effective proprietors of the business are not pharmacists. The relevant section of the decision reads:

> 'The proper course if it were necessary for him to absent himself would have been to close the business. In that it is the superintendent pharmacist's responsibility to control the whole of the running of the pharmacy, it is for him to say if the business is to be closed and it is for nobody else to say that. I make that remark because there was some suggestion that his better judgement was overborne by the proprietors of the business; but I do want him and indeed any other superintendent pharmacist to whom my words may come, to appreciate that it is the superintendent pharmacist's responsibility and nobody else's. He is responsible for the whole of the conduct of the pharmacy. The Committee is left in no doubt that his behaviour did in the circumstances amount to gross misconduct on the part of Mr. X.'
>
> (*Pharm J* 30 January 1971 p.107)

Conflicts with employers still arise. In 1995, the Committee ordered the removal from the Register of a superintendent pharmacist whose conduct had appalled the Committee. The non-pharmacist sole director of the company which owned the pharmacy was also arraigned. The Committee heard that the director had insisted that the superintendent pharmacist should only work for four of the eight hours a day that the pharmacy was open and that no other pharmacist had been present at other times. When the Society's inspectors made test purchases to demonstrate the absence of a pharmacist, the superintendent could not return to the unsupervised pharmacy because he was employed on a regular basis at another pharmacy.

Making reference to the Code of Ethics (Guidance to Principle 6), *The superintendent may carry total responsibility if, as a result of his neglect or inactivity, a director is permitted to exercise functions which are the superintendent pharmacist's own responsibility*, the chairman said:

> '[the superintendent pharmacist should have been] obliged to resign. He cannot lend his name to an operation to be carried on in the pharmacy in flagrant defiance of either the law or the ethics of the profession ... It is the superintendent pharmacist who must insist on things being done as he wishes and as he requires, being informed pharmaceutically as to what is right and proper ... The employer should not be ... allowed to do [just] what he wishes. A superintendent pharmacist should be firm and robust with his employer and exercise his own professional integrity and insist ... that things are done properly.'
>
> (*Pharm J* 25 February 1995 p.255)

In a case involving a young female pharmacist the chairman said she had been unable to stand up to the pressure put on her by a non-pharmacist director who was effectively in day-to-day control of the business. For two or three years the pharmacy had been run without a pharmacist between 3.00 p.m. and 6.00 p.m. on Saturday afternoons and Ms X ought to have known such a thing was happening because it was 'her job to find out'. The chairman set out a very clear summary of the duties of a superintendent:

'A superintendent pharmacist . . . was in charge of seeing that the premises were run in a proper manner – legally, pharmaceutically and ethically. A superintendent pharmacist had to insist on things being done properly even when they may be contrary to the company's interests. Furthermore . . . a superintendent pharmacist had to take responsibility for any acts or omissions by the company or its directors which were within the scope of the superintendent's responsibilities.'

Noting that Ms X became superintendent at the age of 23 or 24, the chairman commented that it was 'simply outrageous' for the *Pharmaceutical Journal* to have accepted an advertisement for a superintendent which included the words 'suitable for a newly qualified pharmacist'. Given the responsibilities set out above, the chairman considered that, having entered the role at 'a young age and in a vulnerable frame of mind', the fact that the non-pharmacist director had run the pharmacy since 1981 was pertinent to the case (*Pharm J* 23 August 1997 p.283). In the accompanying editorial, the Editor did not agree, and also questioned the fairness of the judgment in which the name of the pharmacist was erased from the Register but the employing company was only reprimanded.

An example of the **right** approach by a superintendent pharmacist, and indeed by a locum pharmacist, can be found in a case reported in 2000 in which a locum went to lunch and returned to find that the director, a former pharmacist struck off three years earlier, had dispensed seven prescriptions in her absence. She immediately closed the premises, contacted the superintendent and took steps to trace all the patients involved. Several dispensing errors had been made by the non-pharmacist director.

The superintendent pharmacist had contacted the Society, told the non-pharmacist to leave the premises and ordered the locks on the pharmacy to be changed. The chairman congratulated the superintendent for acting in a way that was a model for all superintendent pharmacists (*Pharm J* 24 June 2000 p.948).

### Personal Control of a Pharmacy

The Medicines Act 1968 (s.71) requires that in respect of each set of premises the business must, as concerned the retail sale of drugs, be under the *personal control* of a pharmacist. The requirement that medicinal products not on the General Sale List must be *supervised* by the pharmacist is an additional provision. The more general requirement of personal control by the pharmacist extends to all medicinal products, including those on the General Sale List.

A case in 1966 concerned a pharmacist who had made a habit of not arriving before 10 a.m. each morning although the pharmacy opened at 9 a.m. In that case the chairman said:

'. . . to leave his pharmacy unattended from 9 a.m. till 10 a.m. every morning is in itself a breach of the regulations, and if he persists in doing that another complaint will be made against him which may not be treated so leniently.'

(*Pharm J* 2 April 1966 p.311)

A complaint was made to the Statutory Committee in 1970 alleging that a pharmacist had not been complying with the Pharmacy and Poisons Act 1933 in that he had left his premises on several occasions for long periods without a pharmacist in personal control. There was no question of sales of poisons having been made as the pharmacist had put them into the dispensary and the dispensary had been locked in his absence.

In giving the Committee's decision, the chairman discussed the matter of personal control as follows:

'It must be plain that a question of degree is involved. I would not for my part say that the pharmacist ceased to be in personal control of his premises because he slipped out for a few minutes even if he went down the street to make some purchases in some other shops. At the other end of the scale, it is equally clear that a pharmacist cannot claim to be in personal control of the premises if he has exercised what may be described as remote control and has put in only an occasional appearance. Somewhere between these two extremes a line has to be drawn. I think it is probably fair to say that the question is whether the attendance of the pharmacist at the premises is such as to give him substantial personal control over the business for a substantial part of the time. Wherever the line is drawn this much I think, is clear – Mr. X fell on the wrong side of it . . . If a pharmacist wishes to carry on while making absences of that sort then either, as I see it, he must obtain the services of a locum pharmacist to take his place and to act for him in his absence, or the premises must be closed . . .'

(*Pharm J* 12 September 1970 p.286)

In 1982 the Committee considered a case where a company conducted a pharmacy for substantial periods of each week when there was no pharmacist on the premises. Sales of General Sale List medicines had taken place in the absence of the pharmacist and it was alleged that when these were made the business was not under the personal control of a pharmacist. The superintendent pharmacist maintained that despite these facts he was capable of being reached by telephone and therefore the conduct of the business was under his personal control. In giving the decision of the Committee the chairman said:

'. . . it will come as no surprise to the persons in this matter . . . that we do not propose to try and lay down strict lines which have got to be toed to achieve personal control . . . We have considered the facts of this matter. We are faced with a deliberate course of conduct involving the absence of a pharmacist for substantial periods of each day, one to one and a half hours during the week days and anything up to six hours over the weekend . . . it was pointed out to us that the pharmacist who did attend during those periods in the evening and at the weekend was a man who unfortunately had no appreciation that General Sale List medicines needed the control of a pharmacist . . . we . . . have come to the conclusion that in our view such a course of control of this pharmacy could not amount to its being under the personal control of a pharmacist during the relevant periods. In the circumstances it means that the business was not being run as a retail business in accordance with the Acts.'

(*Pharm J* 4 December 1982 p.664)

The Committee had little difficulty in determining that the facts amounted to misconduct and issued a reprimand to the pharmacist.

Further support for the view that a pharmacy cannot simply revert to behaving as though it were a *drugstore* when the pharmacist is absent comes in a case in 1994. Two pharmacists allowed for a period of about three years their pharmacy to be open on Saturday afternoons without a pharmacist present and, more recently, on Thursday afternoons as well. Quoting sections 69 and 70 of the Medicines Act 1968 (on personal control of pharmacies), the chairman looked at the mischief which the Act sought to avoid:

> 'Any premises which sold more than just GSL medicines was holding itself out as a specialist in medicinal products. It was only to be expected that such specialist premises – i.e. a pharmacy – would be under a pharmacist's personal control and that what was done there impliedly had his approval whatever the range of products involved.'

At one point, one of the pharmacists had been in the USA and the other not on the premises and there was no procedure whereby either could be contacted. Commenting further the chairman said:

> 'What could be more fundamental in exercising personal control than to make yourself available should you be needed and so instruct the staff so that they know how to contact you?'

The Committee regarded as totally misconceived the defence that if pharmacists could be away for a lunchtime period then in some way this clothed their absence for three or four hours with legitimacy. Such practices neither conformed with the spirit of the Act nor protected the public. Nor were they fair to the public. This was an irresponsible way of carrying on a business which was far removed from personal control. Describing the reprimands as *lenient*, the chairman issued a warning to the profession that:

> '. . . on future occasions, if they turn out to be as bad as this [we could] disqualify a company . . . from trading.'
>
> *(Pharm J* 3 September 1994 p.308)

Despite these precedents, a pharmacist was reprimanded in 1997 for, when the shop opened at 9.00 a.m., 'a pattern of . . . turning up at 10.00 a.m. or later' (*Pharm J* 1 February 1997 p.166).

### 'Quackery' or Unprofessional Claims

Two cases of an unprecedented nature came before the Committee in the late 1990s. In the first, a five-day inquiry resulted in an unusual order to the superintendent of Signalysis Ltd, a company which provided 'Spagyrik Therapy'. Adjourning the case till later that year, the superintendent was advised that she would be reprimanded if she had resigned from the company by that time; if not, her name would be removed from the Register. An order was also made immediately to remove all the premises at which the company conducted a retail pharmacy business to be removed from the Register.

Spagyrik Therapy was said to consist of a treatment of the patient's own body fluids in such a way that they became the remedy for that patient. Such activity was not accepted as a therapy either by the Medicines Control Agency or the Centre for Complementary Health Studies at the University of Exeter.

Conducting such activity from registered pharmacy premises under the supervision of a pharmacist might lead potential customers to believe that the therapy enjoyed some recognition within the profession, which it did not (*Pharm J* 16 August 1997 p.250).

The following year, a pharmacist who had made misleading and unprofessional claims for products which were not licensed medicines was reprimanded by the Committee. Despite a warning from the Society, the pharmacist had continued to lend her name to advertising material from a company called NutriHealth Ltd which suggested that certain products could be 'fat eliminators', could reduce mood swings, reduce cholesterol, relieve symptoms of poor bowel function, reduce risk of bowel cancer and many similar medicinal claims. The Committee was impressed by the pharmacist's sincerity but said she had overstepped the mark.

> 'This profession has won the reputation that if it says something then it really is true . . . and these claims from a pharmacist are likely to be believed totally . . . We should be very careful when we appeal to the public's greed and vanity . . .'
>
> (*Pharm J* 24 October 1998 p.663)

## Appeals Against Decisions

It has been explained that a direction for erasure from the Register does not take effect until the expiration of three months from the giving of notice of such a direction. During that three months a person who is aggrieved by a direction of the Committee has a right of appeal against that direction to the Queen's Bench Division of the High Court. This right is provided for pharmacists in the Pharmacy Act 1954 (s.10) and for bodies corporate in the Medicines Act 1968 (s.82). A High Court decision is final and there is no further right of appeal.

The number of appeals against a direction for erasure heard by the High Court since the Statutory Committee was established in 1933 has been relatively small. Those establishing major points of principle are set out in some detail below.

## Re Lawson

The first appeal from a decision of the Statutory Committee was heard in the King's Bench Divisional Court in February 1941 before the Lord Chief Justice Viscount Caldicote and Mr. Justice Humphreys (see also p.366).

The Council of the Pharmaceutical Society had complained to the Statutory Committee that the appellant, a member of the Society, had distributed to a member or members of the public, and without invitation or request, a printed pamphlet of an objectionable or indecent nature and that he had been guilty of such misconduct as could render him unfit to be on the Register. The pamphlet had consisted of an advertisement for certain drugs which were described as 'Hormonal Treatment for Impotence and Sexual Debility in Men, and Frigidity and Apathy in Women'. In giving the decision of the Committee in 1940 the chairman had said:

'The second rule in the Statement on Matters of Professional Conduct is that advertisements of medicines should not be issued to the public referring to sexual weakness. Quite clearly, this pamphlet issued by a man who is on the Register contravenes that rule of professional conduct which ought to guide its members. Even if such a rule did not exist we should have had no hesitation in saying that for a chemist to issue this pamphlet broadcast to members of the public is misconduct which renders him unfit to be on the Register of Pharmacists.'

There were several grounds of appeal and each was considered unfounded. One of the main grounds was that the offence was not of sufficient gravity as to justify removal of a name from the Register. In dismissing the appeal both judges commented on the weight which should be placed on decisions of the Statutory Committee. The Lord Chief Justice said:

'Arguments have been addressed to us that that decision was a harsh one, and that, having regard to similar publications which have been going on for a number of years of which the appellant was well aware and of which the Council must be taken to be aware also, it was a very harsh measure that the appellant's name should have been removed from the Register. As to that matter, I observe that the intention of the Act seems to me to make, as one might say, the Council of the Pharmaceutical Society, as representing the profession as it has been called, masters in their own house. They were to have a Statutory Committee composed of members of the Society,* and the Statutory Committee was to undertake such inquiries as have been conducted in this case and to give such directions as have been given in this case so as to maintain, and perhaps improve, the standard of the members of the Society as the members of a respectable and honourable profession. Although I do not say for a moment that the mere fact that the Statutory Committee have come to this decision that it is right to remove the appellant's name from the Register is conclusive, if they have evidence upon which they may act I say that the opinion is entitled to the greatest possible respect, because they know what is the standard of requirement of the profession to which they belong and which, as I read the Act of Parliament, they are directed to take into consideration. One cannot shut one's eyes to the fact, which indeed was mentioned by learned counsel on behalf of the appellant in opening this case, that the Act of 1933 was intended, as I think he said in substance, to elevate this business into the status of a profession which is to be part managed and controlled by members of the Society to which all persons carrying on the business or exercising the profession must belong. While I agree with the decision to remove the appellant's name from the Register, I go further and say that the view which the Statutory Committee have formed they themselves, being members of the Society, is one which should carry, and does carry, great weight with me in the decision which I have formed.'

Mr Justice Humphreys said:

'There are various powers given to the Statutory Committee, one of which we are told in certain cases they do exercise. It is the power of reserving their judgement for a time and giving the person against whom the allegation is made an opportunity of mending his ways, and then inquiring after the lapse of time, and hearing evidence as to what has happened since their original decision. That is a very useful power, and one which they exercise, although it is for the Statutory Committee to decide in which cases they should exercise that power, and in what cases they should decide that the penalty stated by the

---

* This is not strictly so (see p.237).

Act should be imposed. For my own part I should be very loath indeed to interfere seeing that I am not a pharmaceutical chemist, and cannot be as well acquainted with the ethics and proper way of carrying on business by such a person as the members of this Statutory Committee are. I should be extremely loath to interfere with their discretion in the matter, assuming I had power to do so.'

(*Pharm J* 22 February 1941 p.60, report and leading article)

The appeal was dismissed with costs.

## Re Sims

This was an appeal from a decision of the Statutory Committee which had directed that a pharmacist's name be removed from the Register following a conviction for the unlawful sale of drugs (Dexedrine tablets). The appeal was dismissed. The Lord Chief Justice (Lord Parker), sitting with Mr Justice Ashworth and Mr Justice McKenna, said:

'It will be seen therefore that, so far as the present case is concerned, it had to be shown that he had been guilty of a criminal offence. That was shown. The Statutory Committee had then to be satisfied that the criminal offence was of a kind that rendered the convicted person unfit to have his name on the Register. That they so found, and there is no challenge to their finding. Thirdly, they have had to inquire into the matter and having reached that conclusion, to decide whether it was a case in which they should direct the Registrar to remove the chemist's name. It is only against their decision to remove the appellant's name that he now appeals . . . As I conceive it the principle upon which this Court can act is this, that only in a very extreme case would they interfere with the penalty which the professional body concerned has inflicted for a very good reason, that it is the intention of Parliament that they should be the judges of the case because they are the people who can judge best the need for a particularly drastic penalty in the circumstances prevailing. The matter was dealt with on that basis in the case of the Statutory Committee under the Pharmacy and Poisons Act 1933 in the case *Re Lawson* [1941] 57 TLR 315 (p.146) and words to the same effect were used by Lord Goddard in connection with the Disciplinary Committee of the Law Society in the case *Re a Solicitor* [1956] 3 AFR 516. Lord Goddard there said at p.517: "If a matter were one of professional misconduct, it would take a very strong case to induce this Court to interfere with the sentence passed by the disciplinary committee, as obviously the disciplinary committee are the best possible people for weighing the seriousness of professional misconduct." '

(*Pharm J* 3 February 1962 p.89)

## Re Levy and Pharmaceutics (M/C) Ltd

Disciplinary proceedings in this case had originally begun in March 1966 following a prosecution against the company under the Pharmacy and Poisons Act 1933 for sales of poisons not under the supervision of a pharmacist. The Committee had adjourned the case until April 1966 to allow the defendant to attend. At that hearing judgment had been postponed for 12 months. In May 1967 the defendant had not appeared and the Committee had adjourned the case further until November 1967.

Immediately before the November hearing the company had again been prosecuted for a similar offence. At the Statutory Committee hearing the name of the pharmacist had been ordered to be erased from the Register and a direction had been made that the company ceased to be an authorised seller of poisons for a period of 12 months.

The appeal was heard before the Lord Chief Justice (Lord Parker), who sat with Mr Justice Waller and Mr Justice Fisher. Lord Parker commented:

> 'It is not the nature of the offence, but the fact that it disclosed a casual attitude, also indicated by the fact that he did not appear before the Committee. The Statutory Committee in April 1966 gave what was in effect a conditional discharge. They decided not to sentence him in any way, but the chairman gave him a pretty severe warning. The Committee had adjourned the matter for 12 months and instructed an inspector to make visits to the premises. He then had a clear warning of what would happen if he did anything of the sort again. Unfortunately in November 1967 the company had been fined over the sale of Veganin. Mr. Levy had come before the Committee a month later, where it had been pointed out to him that he had had his chance, and the Committee had made their direction . . . It is equally clear that this Statutory Committee has been put in charge and entrusted with the affairs of the profession and this court would rarely interfere. This seems to me to be a case in which the Committee were almost forced to act as they did as a result of this man being given a conditional discharge and getting into trouble again. So far as sentence was concerned, the Committee had only two alternatives. One was to do nothing and give a conditional discharge and the other was to direct removal from the Register . . . In this case they decided, after postponing the matter time and time again to give him every chance, to strike his name off.'
>
> (*Pharm J* 25 May 1968 p.615)

The appeal was dismissed.

### Re Eyre

In October 1975 the Committee had directed the removal of the name of a pharmacist from the Register following his conviction on 21 offences involving the forging of documents purporting to be National Health Service prescriptions with intent to defraud. The basis of the offences was that the pharmacist had used blank both signed and unsigned National Health Service prescription forms which had been left with him by doctors to make entries for medicines not supplied by him in order to obtain payment from the National Health Service. This he had claimed had been done with the agreement of several local doctors. It was alleged that the doctor would come into the pharmacy and obtain toothpaste, toiletries and other goods such as contraceptives and would charge them up to an account which was later satisfied by means of the bogus prescriptions.

The pharmacist had appealed against the direction of the Committee and in the High Court Mr Justice Croom-Johnson sitting with the Lord Chief Justice (Lord Widgery) and Mr Justice May said in dismissing the appeal:

> 'The effect of all this was that really the people who seemed to get the most financial benefit out of this course of conduct were the doctors concerned, and there was some profit but not a great deal of profit which came to Mr. X. This court has to consider whether the Statutory Committee was justifiably to come to the conclusion which it did. It is quite clear that it considered that the convictions at the Central Criminal Court in this fashion were of a nature as to render the appellant unfit to have his name on the Register. The committee had to consider this fact that, although little profit was accruing to Mr. X what was being done was that the standing of the pharmaceutical profession as

a whole was being gravely affected by the fact that the National Health Service was being defrauded systematically over a period of several years, and that the defrauding was being made possible by Mr. X in his capacity as a pharmaceutical chemist facilitating the doctors in getting their money and their goods in this way. He was, in other words, consenting to be used as a tool for the fraud on the National Health Service even though it may be that he was not actually getting much of the money into his own pocket. He also of course had a motive in assisting the doctors in this way because he was afraid that if he did not fall in with what they wanted him to do they could do, as it were, financial damage to his practice.

This court, although it has power to review the decision of statutory committees and statutory bodies which control the discipline of the various professions, such as this, is loath to interfere with those decisions unless it is clear that the decision which was come to was a wrong one. For my part I am quite unable to say on the facts of this case, by Mr. X going in for a course of conduct over a number of years in this way and in a way which makes the National Health Service wide open to frauds of this kind if they are practised by anything, that in coming to the conclusion that it did that the Statutory Committee was wrong. In those circumstances I should be in favour of dismissing this appeal.'

(*Pharm J* 24 July 1976 p.69)

## Re Fletcher and Lucas

In September 1976 the Committee had directed that the names of the two appellants be removed from the Register following allegations of excessive sales of amyl nitrite (*Pharm J* 6 November 1976 p.430).

The appeal was heard before the Lord Chief Justice (Lord Widgery), sitting with Mr Justice Milmo and Mr Justice Tudor Evans, Mr Justice Milmo giving judgment said:

'Basically what was being alleged against the appellants was [that they] were selling to the public large quantities of Amyl Nitrite ampoules knowing, or deliberately shutting their eyes to two facts (1) that the bulk of these were being sold to people who were going to use them for an improper purpose and, (2) that such use could be injurious to health . . . The first ground [of appeal] is that the Committee misdirected itself on the burden of proof . . . I find that contention is without substance . . . It is said as a second ground that there is no evidence that either of the appellants had himself made a sale to any purchaser . . . In my judgement there was abundant evidence . . . to find that very substantial quantities of this drug were being sold to individual members of the public in the full knowledge of the appellants that the persons in question were going to use the drugs so supplied for an improper purpose . . . The third ground is what has been described as the "Martindale" point . . . The appellants now complain that this textbook was introduced into the case in the judgement without reference to the defence . . . I cannot see that there would be any valid objection to their [the Committee] refreshing, or confirming, their professional knowledge and experience by reference to a standard textbook, but it is apparent from the judgment that in the present case they went very much further. The reference to the difficulty and anxiety, which they experience satisfies me that this particular point was not covered by their professional knowledge and that they were driven to extraneous sources to acquire the knowledge which they lacked. In the result they reached a decision on the strength of evidence which had not been adduced at the hearing . . . for this reason I would allow the appeal.'

(*Pharm J* July 1978 p.93)

## Re Harari

In this case the pharmacist had appeared before the Statutory Committee after being convicted of offences which had no connection with his professional work. They included assault, motor offences, and convictions under the Protection from Eviction Act 1977. A direction was given for the erasure of his name from the Register and he appealed.

In dismissing the appeal Lord Justice May, sitting with Mr Justice Stephen Brown, said:

'... in the course of that enquiry witnesses were called to speak to the facts which had given rise to the convictions ... He [Mr Harari] submits that the Statutory Committee in following that procedure effectively re-presented the prosecution material that was before the criminal courts by which he was convicted ... In my judgement it is quite clear from the decision of this court in *Shutt and Others* ([1981] 2 All ER 805; see p.241) ... that the Statutory Committee was entirely correct in the procedure which they followed ... Indeed the circumstances in which the chemist came to be convicted, and so give rise to the enquiry, are matters which the Statutory Committee must have available to it in a way in which it can be, if necessary, challenged by the chemist. That is not to say however that the fact that the chemist was convicted of the offences alleged can itself be challenged ... the Divisional Court has made it quite clear in these and other cases that it is loath to interfere with decisions of domestic tribunals of this nature unless it is clear that they are decisions that are wrong ... it is the tribunals themselves who actually see the witnesses involved, and even more importantly, in addition to the legally qualified chairman, comprise members of the relevant profession who have specialist knowledge of and opinions on the issues raised in these sort of disciplinary hearings. Consequently this court should not lightly disturb any such decision.'

Dealing with the question of the severity of the penalty his Lordship continued:

'Mr. Harari stresses that the conduct, of which complaint was made, related in no way to his activity, experience or business as a pharmaceutical chemist. But I am sure that Mr. Harari would be the first person, upon cool reflection when this matter is completed, to accept that it is not only conduct directly related to pharmacy and pharmacists of which the Statutory Committee is entitled and should properly take cognisance. When one is dealing with the activities of professional men and women it must be realised that there can be conduct on their part which although in no way directly referable to their profession, nevertheless, in the view of right minded members of that profession, renders them unsuitable to continue to be members of the profession ... Once again the decisions of this court in other cases relating to pharmaceutical chemists and, indeed other professional bodies, have made it clear that the principle that it will only interfere where the tribunal below has clearly gone wrong applies with greater force in relation to any penalties imposed by the domestic tribunal than to the actual decision on the merits. That must follow from the professional composition of the Statutory Committee, who have to decide on the suitability of the particular defendant before them to continue to carry on practising as a pharmaceutical chemist.'

(*Pharm J* 1 May 1982 p.509)

## Re Whitechurch

In 1997 the Statutory Committee considered the case of a pharmacist who had failed to maintain professional indemnity insurance contrary to the

Society's Code of Ethics (see p.228). It was alleged that this conduct demonstrated a lack of professional responsibility which could have had serious consequences for members of the public using his pharmacy and any locum pharmacists working there. The Committee found the alleged misconduct proved and directed that the pharmacist's name be removed from the Register (*Pharm J* May 1997 p.698). The pharmacist appealed to the High Court on the basis (1) that he was partially insured and (2) that the penalty was too severe.

In dismissing the appeal Mr Justice Schiemann, sitting with Mr Justice Mitchell, said in relation to the first leg of the appeal:

'. . . the insurance which he had was manifestly not designed to cover a pharmacist's liability to the public arising out of his activities as a pharmacist with the heavy obligations for those imposed . . . [and] the Committee clearly regarded his failure to insure himself promptly, once the matter was drawn to his attention, as significant misconduct . . . in my judgement they were right to do so.'

On the second ground for appeal Mr Justice Schiemann said:

'The right approach for this Court . . . is set out in the case of *Alnazir Thobani* v. *The Royal Pharmaceutical Society of Great Britain* in January 1990. In that case Watkins LG said "the function of this Court when reviewing a sentence of the Society, as has been said on many previous occasions, is not to impose its own view in substitution for a view taken by the Committee unless it comes to the conclusion that the decision of the Committee was plainly wrong or unless of course the Committee has, in reaching its conclusion, misdirected itself". Having read all the material before the Committee and now before me I am convinced that the penalty, which they imposed on the material before them, was amply justified and this Court should not interfere with it.'
(*Whitechurch* v. *Royal Pharmaceutical Society of Great Britain* (1998) 41 BLMR 46, QBD)

## Re Korsner

In 1998 the Committee considered the case of a pharmacist, who arranged for patients of a private doctor to go on the list of an National Health Service doctor as well (see also p.249). When patients received a private prescription, they would take it to the pharmacist, who would let them have the drugs but would not receive payment from the patients. The pharmacist would then send to the National Health Service doctor a list of medicines for which National Health Service prescriptions were required for that patient and would then add further items to the prescriptions to compensate for the National Health Service charges he had not received. The pharmacist was also making declarations of exemption from National Health Service charges on behalf of these patients.

The Committee directed that Mr Korsner's name be removed from the register (*Pharm J* 24 January 1998 p.116). Mr Korsner appealed on the grounds that he was prejudiced by a failure to give him a fair hearing and to observe minimum standards of procedural fairness. This was said to be because he had not had the chance to agree, or not, to the submission of certain statements submitted to the Statutory Committee.

Declining to make a finding on this point, Lord Justice Brooke in dismissing the appeal, said that even if the evidence in the disputed statements was put to one side there was ample evidence on which the Committee was entitled to make the findings that it did (*Pharm J* 30 January 1999 p.147 and 27 February 1999 p.277).

However, the judges criticised the Society's procedures, saying that the regulations under which they operated, contained in a 1978 Order in Council, bore a 'rather dated air' and needed modernising, especially in the light of the Human Rights Act 1998 (brought into force October 2000). Thus the need for change to the constitution and operation of the Statutory Committee is recognised by the High Court (see Appendix 17).

## Other Appeals

For completeness the other appeals are listed in Table 21.1 below, together with the type of 'offence' which led to erasure and whether the appeal by the pharmacist was successful or not.

**Table 21.1**  Other appeals

| | |
|---|---|
| *Re Zygmunt (Chemists) Ltd (Pharm J* 4 April 1966 p.324) <br> Conviction/Pharmacy and Poison Act 1933 | Appeal won |
| *Re Robinson (Pharm J* 19 April 1975 p.19) <br> Conviction/Misuse of Drugs Act 1971 | Appeal lost |
| *Re Jobson (Pharm J* 22 November 1980 p.589) <br> Conviction/Misuse of Drugs Act 1971 | Appeal lost |
| *Re Rajabali (Pharm J* 7 February 1981 p.136) <br> Misconduct/Excessive sale of drugs liable to misuse | Appeal lost |
| *Re Kuperberg (Pharm J* 29 January 1983 p.97) <br> Misconduct/Excessive sale of drugs liable to misuse | Appeal lost |
| *Re Riley (Pharm J* 2 March 1985 p.282) <br> Conviction/Theft Act 1968 | Appeal won |
| *Re Tenbrook Ltd (Pharm J* 13 July 1985 p.61) <br> Conviction/Medicines Act 1968 | Appeal lost |
| *Re Leach* (unreported, July 1985) <br> Conviction/Misuse of Drugs Act 1971 | Appeal lost |
| *Re Patel* (unreported, January 1986) <br> Conviction/Medicines Act 1968 | Appeal lost |
| *Re Sowood (Pharm J* 6 December 1986 p.754) <br> Conviction/Medicines Act 1968 | Appeal lost |
| *Re Smith (Pharm J* 3 January 1987 p.17) <br> Misconduct/Under influence of drink | Appeal lost |

| | |
|---|---|
| *Re Singh* (*Pharm J* 28 March 1987 p.416)<br>Convictions/Misuse of Drugs Act 1971 and others | Appeal lost |
| *Re Parkin* (*Pharm J* 2 April 1988 p.451)<br>Misconduct/Unsatisfactory pharmacy premises | Appeal lost |
| *Re Shah* (*Pharm J* 7 May 1988 p.607)<br>Conviction/Theft Act 1968 | Appeal won |
| *Re Sabir* (*Pharm J* 19 November 1988 p.665)<br>Conviction/Misuse of Drugs Act 1971 | Appeal lost |
| *Re Thobani* (*Pharm J* 3 February 1990 p.122)<br>Offences/Theft Act 1968 | Appeal lost |
| *Re Kansal* (*Pharm J* 27 July 1996 p.111)<br>Offences of dishonesty | Appeal lost |
| *Re Mistry* (unreported)<br>Forged certificate of professional indemnity | Appeal lost |

## Judicial Review

A reprimand is not considered to be a direction against which there is a right of appeal (see p.240) hence a pharmacist reprimanded by the Statutory Committee seeking redress may only do so by way of the legal remedy of judicial review.

In December 1982 a company, its superintendent pharmacist and a pharmacist manager in charge of one of the company's pharmacies applied by way of judicial review in the High Court to have reprimands, which each had received, quashed. The reprimands had been administered by the Statutory Committee (*Pharm J* 15 May 1982 p.557) following an advertising feature which had appeared in a local newspaper. Mr Justice Woolf, in quashing the reprimands, said that it was not disputed that the feature had contravened the Society's guidelines on advertising or that the company had been a party to the advertising appearing but the company had argued that it had done its best to prevent the feature appearing in the form it did and therefore had done everything to prevent the guidelines being broken. If the company's account of what happened was accepted by the Statutory Committee then it could not have found them guilty of misconduct. It appeared that the Statutory Committee disbelieved the pharmacists' account when it came to its decision, but Mr Justice Woolf said that there was absolutely no evidence to indicate that the superintendent's account was incorrect and therefore the reprimand in his case was unjustified. Because the decision in the case of the superintendent was clearly wrong the whole decision was unsafe and the reprimands against all the applicants were set aside (*Pharm J* 1 and 8 January 1983 p.13).

In 1986 another pharmacist, Mr Sokoh, applied to the High Court for judicial review following a reprimand which had been administered to him by the Statutory Committee. The case concerned the dispensing of a 'Brompton mixture' and the facts are summarised on page 257. Counsel for Mr S argued that the decision was wrong and that the Committee had failed to direct itself that a single considered exercise of professional judgement, without more, even if wrong, could not amount to professional misconduct.

Professional misconduct, he said, involved an act or omission deserving of moral condemnation by the profession. His Lordship rejected the submission that misconduct necessarily carried moral censure commenting that *misconduct* meant no more than incorrect or erroneous conduct of any kind of a serious nature. As to the submission that the Committee failed to direct itself that one error could not constitute misconduct, Mr Justice Webster said:

> 'One error is in my judgement, as a matter of law, capable of constituting misconduct if it is sufficiently serious, though whether it in fact constitutes misconduct or misconduct such as to render the person unfit to be on the Register must depend on the precise evidence taken as a whole and on the Committee's view of that evidence.'

In discussing the Court's primary function in judicial review, Mr Justice Webster, in dismissing the application, said:

> 'If in [the Court's] judgement conduct occurred which was capable of constituting misconduct then in the absence of a material misdirection or a decision which no reasonable Committee could reach if it had properly directed itself [the Court] cannot interfere with the Committee's findings.'
>
> (*Pharm J* 13 December 1986 p.797)

A unique situation arose in January 1996 when the Statutory Committee failed to reach a unanimous judgment. The case involved a Council complaint against Boots The Chemists Ltd and its superintendent in relation to two collection and delivery services in rural areas formerly served by dispensing doctors, namely Durrington in Wiltshire and Winterton in South Humberside. The Council had decided in June 1993 that a pharmacy operating a prescription collection and delivery service should discontinue such a service if a new pharmacy opened in the area, although this decision appeared only in the monthly report of Council and was not promulgated as a new ethical requirement. Both services had been initiated at the request of local GPs and residents after National Health Service contracts had been awarded to new pharmacies in the villages. In the case of Durrington, the residents arranged for the collection of the prescriptions, the return of the dispensed medicines and undertook the transport themselves. Boots argued that these services were patient-driven and widened choice and that the Council's position was a restraint of trade. The Council argued that the continuance of a collection and delivery service in these circumstances could deprive patients of a full pharmaceutical service, in particular the absence of direct face to face contact between patient or carer and the pharmacist. The hearing lasted two days and judgment was deferred (*Pharm J* 21 October 1995 p.533 and 28 October 1995 p.571).

When judgment was given, the majority of the Committee (in this case three pharmacists) found misconduct proved but decided that it was not serious enough to warrant any further action. The chairman, a Queen's Counsel, gave a dissenting judgment. Almost the full text of the majority decision was reported in *Pharm J* 20 January 1996 (pp.89–93) and this should be referred to for a full account of the reasoning of the pharmacists on the Committee. The dissenting decision of the chairman was somewhat truncated and the best understanding of his reasoning may be obtained from the two passages below which did not appear in the *Pharmaceutical Journal* report but appear in the transcript:

> 'It is simply not right to say that Boots' activities could deprive local people of a full pharmaceutical service. The villagers are deprived of nothing. It really is impossible to describe as serious misconduct the provision of a doctor approved delivery and collection service which the patient chose to use, rather than use the village pharmacy. In fact what Boots were providing was an **additional** service and not one that compelled the patients to take their service in substitution for the village pharmacy.
>
> It is very disturbing to read the statements of mature witnesses who as patients are exasperated by the notion that is implicit in the Society's case that the choice of where they are to obtain their dispensing services is not theirs to make. Some of the patients' views are expressed with vehemence and I would have thought it unwise not to have proper regard to what patients really feel . . . In these days of consumer choice I am not at all surprised that Boots feel that they should respond if it is lawfully possible to do what their patients actually want.'

On this basis, Boots applied for judicial review. As reported in *Pharm J* 14 February 1997, the High Court quashed the finding of misconduct and said that the Committee's decision making process had been 'fundamentally tainted'. The Court did not attempt to adjudicate on whether the Council's position on collection and delivery services was correct but considered that the finding of misconduct had not been justified on the evidence. In further (unreported) comments, Justice Ognall said the pharmacist members of the Committee should have heeded more closely the admonitions which appeared in the judgment of the legally qualified chairman. The test was the same as in Sokoh (above), that 'misconduct can be any incorrect or erroneous conduct **provided it is of a serious nature**'. He held that the pharmacist members of the Committee had failed to address whether the undoubted knowing and continuing breach of the promulgated policy was of such quality as to constitute serious misconduct.

Since this case, medicines have become available over the Internet and the Society has taken steps to produce guidelines for pharmacies which wish to undertake such a service (Appendix 18). These aim to provide a measure of protection where the patient elects not to seek face to face contact but to exercise more fully their right to choice as a consumer.

## Summary

- The Statutory Committee exercises the disciplinary powers of the Society.
- Its constitution, procedures, jurisdiction and sanctions are laid down in regulations made under the Pharmacy Act 1954.

- The Committee comprises a legally experienced chairman and five members who have until very recently all been pharmacists.
- The Committee may discipline pharmacists, pharmacists' representatives and employees of pharmacy businesses and persons applying for admission or restoration to the Register.
- When making their decisions, the Committee may take no action, admonish or caution (usually a reprimand), postpone their decision or direct erasure of a pharmacist's name from the Register. Additionally, for a company, the Committee may disqualify it from conducting retail pharmacies, or remove any or all of their premises from the Register.
- The Committee may consider all convictions against pharmacists; for pharmacy businesses, its jurisdiction is limited to those Acts relating to Pharmacy, Poisons, Medicines, and Misuse of Drugs.
- The Committee's jurisdiction extends to offences committed outside the United Kingdom and is not subject to any time limits.
- The Committee uses, but is not bound by, the Code of Ethics when considering whether there has been such misconduct as renders a pharmacist unfit to be on the Register.
- Examples of cases are given under the following headings: Supervision; Theft; Theft and unlawful possession of drugs; Deception; Unlawful supplies of POM medicines; Controlled drugs; Supply of dangerous chemicals; Disposal of dangerous waste; Parallel imports; Unsatisfactory conduct; Unsatisfactory state of pharmacy premises; Excessive or uncontrolled supplies of substances of abuse; Dispensing mistakes; Advertising; Responsibility of the superintendent pharmacist; Personal control of a pharmacy; and Quackery.
- Appeals establishing major points of principle are discussed: *Re Lawson*; *Re Sims*; *Re Levy and Pharmaceutics (M/C) Ltd*; *Re Eyre*; *Re Fletcher and Lucas*; *Re Harari*, *Re Whitechurch*; and *Re Korsner*. A summary of all others is given.
- Three judicial reviews are discussed where the Committee's decisions were not considered to be subject to appeal.

### Further Reading

Appelbe G. E., Harrison I. H. 'The Statutory Committee: Convictions', *Pharm J* 23 October 1993 p.565.

Appelbe G. E., Harrison I. H. 'The Statutory Committee: Major Misconduct', *Pharm J* 1 January 1994 p.22.

Appelbe G. E., Harrison I. H. 'The Statutory Committee: Advertising and Sundry Misconduct', *Pharm J* 8 January 1994 p.56.

Appelbe G. E., Harrison I. H. 'The Statutory Committee', *Pharm J* 7 August 1994 p.197.

Soothill K., Sharp D. 'Discipline and Punishment: Reflections on the Disciplinary procedures of the Royal Pharmaceutical Society', *Pharm J* 12 February 2000 pp.266–267.

Wingfield J. 'Misconduct and the Pharmacist' (Parts 1 and 2), *Pharm J* 27 October 1990 pp.531, 572.

# CHAPTER TWENTY-TWO

# Organisation of other Professions

N.B. In June 1999, the government enacted the Health Act 1999 which provided powers to change by order the regulation of health professions and health professions. At the time of going to press no changes affecting the health professions have taken place. Where possible, an indication of probable changes is given.

Various classes of professional persons are mentioned in the statutes relating to poisons, medicinal products and Controlled Drugs. Pharmacists are principally concerned with supplies made to, or to the order of, medical practitioners, veterinary surgeons and dentists, and some knowledge of the statutory registration requirements of these and other related professions is desirable.

## The Medical Profession

N.B. The government has been concerned for some time regarding the competence of doctors and dentists. Comments have been made that mandatory professional development or some form of 're-certification' will be introduced. Commentary has also been made that the General Medical Council may be replaced by another body comprising a majority of lay persons.

The Acts at present regulating the medical profession are the Medical Act 1983 and the Medical (Professional Performance) Act 1995.

### The General Medical Council

The General Medical Council (GMC), which is the sole registering authority in the United Kingdom, was established by the Medical Act 1858. The Council consists of elected members, appointed members and nominated members, the number of elected members exceeding the number of appointed and nominated members (Sch.1 to the 1983 Act).

The nominated members, the majority of whom must be without any registerable medical qualification, are nominated by the Privy Council. The electoral scheme for elected members is made by the GMC with the approval of the Privy Council. The Act provides for four constituencies, that is to say:

1    England, the Channel Islands, and the Isle of Man;
2    Wales;
3    Scotland;
4    Northern Ireland.

The universities and other bodies which appoint members to the GMC are designated in an Order in Council. Persons who are fully registered, provisionally registered or registered with limited registration are eligible for election, subject to certain restrictions for those with limited registration. The GMC has power to regulate medical education and to provide advice for members of the medical profession on standards of professional conduct or on medical ethics.

### The Register and Registration

The registrar of the GMC is appointed under Schedule 1 to the 1983 Act but the procedures for registration and the maintenance of the registers are dealt with in Part IV of the Act and the regulations made thereunder.

There are two registers: the *Register of Medical Practitioners* and the *Register of Medical Practitioners with Limited Registration*.

The main register kept under the Act is known as the *Register of Medical Practitioners*. It comprises the *Principal List*, the *Overseas List*, the *Visiting Overseas List* and the *Visiting EEC Practitioners List*.

The *Principal List* contains the names of those doctors who are *fully registered*, i.e. those with United Kingdom qualifications and those doctors who hold primary European qualifications and who are nationals of a European Community member state, together with those doctors who are *provisionally registered*.

The *Overseas List* comprises those doctors who hold a qualification recognised by the GMC, granted in an overseas country, and who satisfy the requirements as to good character, professional experience and proficiency in English.

The two *Visiting Lists* relate to those doctors visiting the United Kingdom temporarily, usually for specialised activities. The provision of medical services of a specialist nature on a temporary basis is subject to providing proof of the applicant's qualifications to the registrar and a declaration about the services s/he intends to provide (s.27).

The *Medical Register*, which must be published each year, contains in alphabetical order the names, addresses and registered qualifications of all persons fully or provisionally registered in the Principal List as at 1 January of the year of publication (s.34).

Fully or provisionally registered practitioners who reside outside the United Kingdom, the Republic of Ireland, the Channel Islands and the Isle of Man and other member states of the European Community may apply to have their names transferred to the Overseas List. An asterisk marks each entry which relates to a provisionally registered practitioner. The GMC may publish the *Overseas Register.*

The registrar is also required to prepare and keep a Register of Medical Practitioners with Limited Registration (s.22). Practitioners must pay registration fees and annual retention fees.

In any enactment the expression *legally qualified medical practitioner*, or *duly qualified medical practitioner*, or any expression implying a person recognised by law as a medical practitioner or members of the medical profession means a fully registered person. Similarly, any reference (however expressed) to a person registered under the Medical Act or as a medical practitioner means a fully registered person registered under the 1983 Act. A prescription for a Controlled Drug or a Prescription Only Medicine may lawfully be dispensed even though the prescriber's name is in the Overseas List.

Section 60 of the Medicines Act 1968 provides that specified medicinal products may be prescribed only by a practitioner who holds a certificate issued for that purpose from the appropriate Minister (see Chapter 7) and a licence from the Secretary of State is required in respect of certain Controlled Drugs (see Chapter 16). Apart from these restrictions there is no limitation on the prescribing of a fully registered practitioner, unless s/he is the subject of a direction by the Secretary of State under the Misuse of Drugs Act 1971 in respect of named Controlled Drugs (see Chapter 16).

Only fully registered persons may hold certain appointments as physicians, surgeons or other medical officers (e.g. in the naval, military or air services or in the prison service), or recover in any court of law any charge made for medical or surgical advice or attendance. A certificate required by law to be from a physician, surgeon, licentiate in medicine and surgery, or other medical practitioner, is not valid unless the person signing it is fully registered.

Any person who wilfully and falsely pretends to be or takes or uses the name or title of physician, doctor of medicine, licentiate in medicine and surgery, bachelor of medicine, surgeon, general practitioner or apothecary, or any name, title, addition or description implying that s/he is registered under any provision of the 1983 Act, or that s/he is recognised by law as such, commits an offence (s.49). Nothing in the Act prejudices or in any way affects the lawful occupation, trade or business of chemists and druggists, or of dentists, so far as they extend to selling, compounding and dispensing of medicines (s.54).

### Visiting EEC Practitioners List

An applicant can also be registered as a *visiting EEC practitioner*, although s/he may render medical services temporarily without first being registered. The registrar is required to enter the names of such practitioners on a list of visiting EEC practitioners which forms part of the Register of Medical Practitioners (s.18). Visiting EEC practitioners will be issued with certificates of registration by the GMC.

Pharmacists may lawfully supply Prescription Only Medicines (POM) and Controlled Drugs (see Chapter 16) against a prescription issued by a visiting practitioner only if that practitioner is in fact registered in the United Kingdom in accordance with the Act.

### Provisional Registration

A person who holds a qualification which entitles him/her to be registered but has not completed the requirements as to experience is entitled to be provisionally registered. While s/he is completing these requirements s/he is deemed to be fully registered so far as is necessary to enable him/her to be engaged in employment in a resident medical capacity in one or more approved hospitals or institutions, but not further (s.15).

The effect is that s/he may issue prescriptions for Controlled Drugs or for Prescription Only Medicines only if required to do so as part of his/her duties in that resident medical post. S/he may not order or prescribe such drugs or medicinal products in any other circumstances, e.g. for his/her own use or for the use of his/her own private patients.

### Limited Registration

There is also provision in the Act (ss.22–25) for the limited registration of practitioners having *acceptable overseas qualifications*, i.e. qualifications granted outside the United Kingdom, which are accepted by the GMC as furnishing a sufficient guarantee of possession of the knowledge and skill required for the practise of medicine under the supervision of a fully registered medical practitioner. An applicant for limited registration must, in addition to holding an *acceptable overseas qualification*:

1    satisfy the registrar that s/he has been selected for employment in the United Kingdom or Isle of Man as a medical practitioner in one or more approved hospitals or institutions;
2    that s/he has the necessary knowledge of English;
3    that s/he is of good character; and

4    that s/he has the knowledge and skill and has acquired the experience
     which is necessary for practise as a medical practitioner appropriate in
     his/her case.

A direction for limited registration is for a specified period only; the total
aggregate period in which limited registration is permitted is five years, except
for doctors who have held temporary registration. In relation to employment
covered by his/her limited registration and to things done or omitted to be
done in the course of it, and to any other thing incidental to his/her work in
that employment which may not lawfully or validly be done except by a fully
registered person, a doctor holding limited registration is treated as being fully
registered but not otherwise (s.22).

  S/he may, therefore, only issue prescriptions for Controlled Drugs and
Prescription Only Medicines in connection with employment to which his/her
limited registration relates. The names of practitioners with limited registration are not included in any published register. Any inquiries about such
practitioners should be made to The Registrar, General Medical Council, 24
Gosfield Street, London W1P 8BP.

### Professional Conduct and Fitness to Practise

The functions of the Council in respect of professional conduct and fitness to
practise are performed by six committees known as:

1    The Professional Conduct Committee.
2    The Health Committee.
3    The Preliminary Proceedings Committee.
4    The Committee on Professional Performance.
5    The Assessment Referral Committee.
6    The Interim Orders Committee.

The first three committees are constituted as provided by the GMC by rules
made under the Medical Act 1983, the fourth and fifth on 1 January 1997,
under the Medical (Professional Performance) Act 1995 and the sixth under
the 1983 Act on 3 August 2000.

THE PROFESSIONAL CONDUCT COMMITTEE
If any fully registered person is found by the Professional Conduct Committee
to have been convicted of a criminal offence in the British Isles, or convicted
elsewhere of an offence which would constitute an criminal offence in the
England and Wales (SI 2000 No.1803) or judged by the Committee of having
been guilty of serious professional misconduct, the Committee may direct that
his/her name be erased from the register, or that his/her registration shall be
suspended for a specified period not exceeding 12 months or that his/her

registration shall be conditional on compliance with requirements imposed by the Committee for the protection of members of the public and in his/her own interests (s.36).

Regulations have been made increasing the period of time that a person who has been erased from the Register, or in respect of whom a prohibition has been imposed, must wait before being able to apply for restoration, or termination of the prohibition, from ten months to five years (SI 2000 No.1803). The same regulations have also increased the time which must elapse between each application for restoration, or termination of a prohibition, to 12 months. In addition before restoring a name or terminating a prohibition the applicant must satisfy the Committee as to his/her fitness to practise with regard to good character, professional competence and health.

THE HEALTH COMMITTEE

Where the fitness to practise of a fully registered person is judged by the Health Committee to be seriously impaired by reason of his/her physical or mental condition, the Committee may direct, if they think fit, that his/her registration shall be suspended for a specified period not exceeding 12 months or that his/her registration shall be conditional on compliance with such requirements as the Committee may think fit to impose for protection of members of the public or in his/her own interests (s.37).

THE COMMITTEE ON PROFESSIONAL PERFORMANCE

Where the standard of professional performance of a doctor is found by the Committee to have been seriously deficient, the Committee may direct that the registration of the doctor be suspended during a period not exceeding 12 months or that his/her registration be conditional upon him/her complying with specific requirements (1995 Act).

The practitioner's registration may be suspended forthwith if the Professional Conduct Committee, the Committee on Professional Performance or the Health Committee is satisfied that it is necessary to do so for the protection of members of the public or in the best interests of the practitioner (s.38).

Any period of suspension imposed by the Professional Conduct Committee, the Committee on Professional Performance or the Health Committee may be further extended by a subsequent direction of that Committee or may be extended indefinitely. If suspended indefinitely it must be reviewed when requested to do so by the suspended doctor, but not before two years has elapsed after the direction takes effect and not more than once in any two years.

During the period of suspension, the practitioner's name is not removed from the register but s/he is treated as not being registered.

Appeals from the Professional Conduct Committee, the Committee on Professional Performance and the Health Committee lie to the Judicial Committee of the Privy Council. The person concerned is not permitted to practise during the time allowed for an appeal to be made or whilst any such appeal is being disposed of.

### THE PRELIMINARY PROCEEDINGS COMMITTEE

This committee has the duty of deciding whether any case referred to them for consideration ought to be referred for inquiry to the Professional Conduct Committee or the Health Committee, as appropriate. In giving a direction designating the committee which is to inquire into the case, the Preliminary Proceedings Committee may make an order of interim suspension or interim conditional registration in respect of the practitioner concerned. The period specified in such an order shall not exceed six months, and the Professional Conduct Committee or the Health Committee, as appropriate, may revoke or vary the order or make an order for interim suspension or conditional registration where required to protect the public or the interest of the doctor concerned (s.42, as amended).

### THE ASSESSMENT REFERRAL COMMITTEE

The GMC may make rules authorising the giving of directions by the committee requiring an assessment of the standard of a doctor's competence to be carried out. Such rules may specify the manner in which complaints about standards of professional performance are handled (1995 Act).

### THE INTERIM ORDERS COMMITTEE

This Committee was established by the Medical Act 1983 (Amendment) Order 2000 (SI 2000 No.1803). Where the Interim Orders Committee is satisfied that it is necessary for the protection of the public, or in the interests of the doctor, for registration of the doctor to be suspended, or made subject to conditions, the Committee may make an order suspending registration for up to 18 months or that registration may continue conditional on compliance, during a period not exceeding 18 months, with such requirements as the Committee think fit.

The Committee must review the order within six months of the order being made and every three months subsequently as long as the order remains in force or where new evidence becomes available.

The Committee, the Professional Conduct Committee, the Health Committee or the Committee on Professional Performance may revoke the order, or any condition, or vary any condition, if it is satisfied to do so is necessary for the protection of, or in the interest of, the public or the doctor and replace it with an interim suspension order for the remainder of the term. The GMC may apply to the Courts for any order to be extended and the Courts may further extend an order for up to 12 months.

### VOLUNTARY ERASURE FROM THE REGISTER

Provisions have been made for a doctor to request that his name be removed from the Register. The Registrar shall remove the name unless he is aware that any proceedings are pending or have been started against the doctor (SI 2000 No.2033).

DISCLOSURE OF INFORMATION

Regulations give power to persons authorised by the GMC to require disclosure of information that would assist them in carrying out their functions in respect to fitness to practise and professional conduct.

In addition the GMC is obliged to notify specified persons when formal proceedings are initiated against a doctor in respect of his/her fitness to practise or professional conduct where they consider it in the public interest so to do. Those specified persons include the Secretary of State, Scottish Ministers, the National Assembly of Wales and any person in the United Kingdom of whom the Council is aware by whom the doctor concerned is employed in any area of medicine (SI 2000 No.1803).

## The Veterinary Profession

N.B. Under a proposed major agricultural plan the Veterinary Medicines Directorate is to undertake a review of the provisions of the Veterinary Surgeons Act 1966. No further details were available at the time of going to press.

### Royal College of Veterinary Surgeons

The Veterinary Surgeons Act 1966 is the principal statute dealing with the management of the veterinary profession in relation to registration, education and professional conduct. The Council of the Royal College of Veterinary Surgeons, the controlling body, includes 24 persons elected by the members, four appointed by the Privy Council and two appointed by each university in the United Kingdom that grants a veterinary degree recognised by the Privy Council. Degrees of Irish universities are also recognised by the Privy Council.

*Veterinary surgery* means the art and science of veterinary surgery and medicine and includes: the diagnosis of diseases in, and injuries to, animals including tests performed on animals for diagnostic purposes; the giving of advice based upon such diagnosis; the medical or surgical treatment of animals; and the performance of surgical operations on animals (s.27).

### The Register

The registrar of the college, who is appointed by the Council, maintains the register. It is published as often as the Council thinks fit, but in any year in which a full register is not produced, alterations to it must be published instead (s.9). It comprises four lists (s.2), as amended by SI 1980 No.1951, namely:

1    *The General List* of persons entitled to be registered as graduates in veterinary surgery of universities recognised by the Privy Council (s.3) or as students of other universities who have passed the examinations held

by the Royal College of Veterinary Surgeons (s.4) or persons from the European Community who hold recognised European qualifications (s.5a).

2   *The Commonwealth List* of persons entitled to be registered as holding some Commonwealth qualification (s.6).

3   *The Foreign List* of persons entitled to be registered as holding some foreign qualification (s.6).

4   *The Temporary List* of persons registered to practise veterinary surgery temporarily, subject to such restrictions as to place and circumstances as the Council may specify (e.g. persons who have passed the examinations for a degree but have not yet formally graduated, or the holders of Commonwealth or foreign qualifications not otherwise registerable). It is not lawful for a temporarily registered person to practise except in accordance with the restrictions specified in the Council's direction.

An applicant for registration on lists 2 and 3 must satisfy the Council that s/he has the requisite knowledge and skill to practise veterinary surgery in the United Kingdom.

In addition to these lists there is a *Supplementary Register* (first established under the Veterinary Surgeons Act 1948) of persons known as *veterinary practitioners*. The 1948 Act restricted the practice of veterinary surgery by unqualified persons as from 30 July 1949. Those persons whose principal means of livelihood, for seven out of ten years before that date, had been the diagnosing of diseases of animals were included in the Supplementary Register. Certain licensed employees of societies and institutions providing free treatment for animals were also transferred to the Supplementary Register under the 1966 Act, but are subject to such restrictions as the Council may impose.

## Professional Discipline

Names may be removed from the register for crimes or 'disgraceful conduct in any professional respect'. There is a preliminary investigation committee and a disciplinary committee. The disciplinary procedure is similar to that of the medical profession and there is provision for suspension of registration as well as complete removal from the register (ss.15 and 17). Appeals against a direction are made to the Privy Council.

## Restrictions on Practice and Use of Titles

No one may practise, or hold themselves out as practising, or being prepared to practise, veterinary surgery unless they are registered as a veterinary surgeon or are in the supplementary register as a veterinary practitioner (s.19). It is an offence for an unregistered person to use the titles 'veterinary surgeon' or 'veterinary practitioner' or any name, title, addition or description implying that s/he is qualified to practise veterinary surgery (s.20).

The Act provides some limited exceptions for students of veterinary surgery, for medical practitioners and dentists in certain circumstances, and for the carrying out of minor treatment in terms of exemption orders made under the Act. Examples include orders allowing treatment by physiotherapists at veterinarians' request, blood sampling for the brucellosis eradication scheme, vaccinations of poultry against certain diseases, use of epidural anaesthesia (SIs 1973 No.308, 1982 No.1267, 1983 No.6, as amended, and 1990 No.2217).

Exemption is also provided in Schedule 3 to the Act, as amended by SI 1988 No.526 for the following treatments and operations to be given or carried out by unqualified persons:

1   Any minor medical treatment given to an animal by its owner, by another member of a household of which the owner is a member, or by a person in the employment of the owner.

2   Anything given, otherwise than for the reward, to an animal used in agriculture, as defined in the Agriculture Act 1947, by the owner of the animal or by a person engaged or employed in caring for animals so used.

3   The rendering in an emergency of first-aid for the purpose of saving life or relieving pain.

4   The performance by any person aged 18 or more of any of the following operations:

   (a)   castration of a male animal or caponising of an animal, whether by chemical means or otherwise (except the castration of a horse, pony, ass or mule; of a bull, boar or goat which has reached the age of two months; or of a ram which has reached the age of three months; the spaying of a cat or dog);

   (b)   the docking of the tail of a lamb;

   (c)   the amputation of the dew claws of a dog before its eyes are open; or

   (d)   the disbudding of a calf subject to certain conditions.

5   Any medical treatment or minor surgery (not involving entry into the body cavity) to a companion animal by a veterinary nurse provided the animal is under the care of a veterinary surgeon, the treatment is carried out under his/her direction, and the veterinary surgeon is the employer, or acting on behalf of the employer, of the nurse (SI 1991 No.1412).

## The Dental Profession

### The General Dental Council

The practice of dentistry is controlled by the Dentists Act 1984 through the General Dental Council, whose constitution and functions in respect of education, registration and discipline are similar to those of the General Medical Council.

The practice of dentistry is deemed to include the performance of any such operation and the giving of such treatment, advice or attendance as is usually performed or given by dentists, and any person who performs any operations or gives any treatment, advice or attendance on or to any person as preparatory to or for the purpose of or in connection with the fitting, insertion or fixing of dentures, artificial teeth or other dental appliances is deemed to have practised dentistry within the meaning of the Act (s.37).

### The Dentists Register

The *Dentists Register* is required to be published each year (s.22). It is kept by the registrar appointed by the General Dental Council in the manner prescribed by the Council's regulations (ss.14 and 19). The following are entitled to be registered:

1    any person who is a graduate or licentiate in dentistry of a dental authority;
2    any person who is a national of an European Community member state and holds an appropriate European diploma;
3    any person who holds a recognised overseas diploma.

An applicant must satisfy the registrar as to his/her identity, good character, and good physical and mental health. An overseas applicant under 3 above must also satisfy the registrar that s/he has the necessary skill and knowledge, and a knowledge of English which, in the interests of him/herself and patients, is necessary for the practice of dentistry in the United Kingdom.

The holder of a recognised overseas diploma may, without meeting any additional requirements, be temporarily registered in the Dentists Register for a specified period for the purpose of practising dentistry in a specified hospital or institution. The register must include a note of the restriction.

The names of all dentists who are entitled to practise are, therefore, included in the published register and there is no provisional registration as is the case with the medical profession. It is not lawful for a temporarily registered dentist to practise except as indicated in the register.

Serious professional misconduct or conviction in the United Kingdom for a criminal offence may lead to removal of a dentist from the register. There is a Preliminary Proceedings Committee and a Disciplinary Committee. The disciplinary procedure closely resembles that of the medical profession.

### Titles and Descriptions

Only registered dentists and medical practitioners may use the titles dentist, dental surgeon, or dental practitioner. It is an offence for other persons to use such titles. Similarly, no person, including a medical practitioner, may use the term *registered dentist* unless s/he is so registered (s.39). Dentists, however, have no legal right or title to be registered under the Medical Act 1983 and may not assume any title implying a right to practise medicine or general surgery (s.7).

The practice of dentistry is restricted to registered dentists and medical practitioners (s.38). It is no longer lawful for a pharmaceutical chemist to extract a tooth in the case of emergency.

### The Business of Dentistry

A person is treated as carrying on the business of dentistry if, and only if, s/he or a partnership of which s/he is a member receives payment for services rendered in the course of the practice of dentistry by him/her or by a partner of his/hers, or by an employee of his/hers or of the partnership (s.40). A lay person cannot employ dentists for the purpose of carrying on a business of dentistry (s.41) but there is an exception for individuals who were carrying on the business of dentistry on 21 July 1955. That was the date of the introduction into Parliament of the Bill for the Dentists Act 1956, which was subsequently absorbed into the Dentists Act 1984. Bodies corporate which were in the business of dentistry on that date are also exempted if the majority of the directors are dentists and all the operating staff are dentists or dental auxiliaries.

The Act provides for the establishment of classes of dental auxiliaries and for regulations, made by the General Dental Council, to prescribe qualifications for such auxiliaries and the dental work they undertake. The Council may entrust to the Dental Auxiliaries Committee all matters relating to ancillary dental services, including enforcement of standards of conduct (Part V of the Act).

## Nurses, Midwives and Health Visitors

N.B. In a report in 1999 *The Regulation of Nurses, Midwives and Health Visitors: Report on a review of the Nurses, Midwives and Health Visitors Act 1997*, the government made it clear that the United Kingdom Central Council for Nurses, Midwives and Health Visitors (UKCC) would be replaced by a single UK-wide body to regulate nurses, midwives and health visitors. On 1 August 2000 the government published its proposals to reform the ways of working. The new Nursing and Midwifery Council (NMC) will be required to treat the health and welfare of patients as paramount, collaborate and consult with key stakeholders and to be open and pro-active in accounting to the public and the professions for its work.

Key objectives to reform the structure and functions will be by:

- giving wider power to deal effectively with individuals who present unacceptable risks to patients;
- creating a smaller Council, comprising directly elected practitioners, and a strong lay input, charged with strategic responsibility for setting and

monitoring standards of professional training, performance and conduct;
- streamlining the professional register;
- providing explicit powers to link registration with evidence of continuing professional development.

Health visitors will continue to have a separate register and representation within the new Council. A three-month consultation process was underway when this book went to press. The new Council will be UK-based.

The present situation is as follows. The Nurses, Midwives and Health Visitors Act 1997 consolidated all previous legislation relating to these professions. It provides for a United Kingdom Central Council for Nursing, Midwifery and Health Visiting and National Boards for each of the four parts of the United Kingdom; i.e. England, Wales, Scotland, and Northern Ireland.

## The Central Council

The membership of the Council shall not exceed 60. Two-thirds of the members of the Council are appointed by the Secretary of State on being elected under an electoral scheme. Additional appointments may be made from nurses, midwives, health visitors, registered medical practitioners or persons who have such qualifications and experience in education or other fields as will be of value to the Council. There is a need to ensure in such appointments that each part of the United Kingdom is represented, as are those experienced in the teaching of nursing, midwifery and health visiting.

The principal functions of the Council are to establish and improve standards of training and professional conduct in the three professions. The Council must ensure that the standards of training meet any European Community obligations of the United Kingdom and, by means of rules, determine conditions of training and the kind of standard of training to be undertaken with a view to registration. The rules may also make provision for further training to be available to persons already registered.

The Council has power to provide advice to the professions on standards of professional conduct and has done so; e.g. the *Code of Professional Conduct for the Nurse, Midwife and Health Visitor*. It is required, in the discharge of its functions, to have a proper regard for the interests of all groups within the professions, including those with minority representation.

It is required to prepare and maintain a register, the *Professional Register*, of qualified nurses, midwives, and health visitors. Provision is made for the registration of European Union nurses and midwives.

## The National Boards

Each Board consists of members of the three professions, who must be in the majority, or persons who have such qualifications or experience in education or other fields who will be of value to the Board. Such members are appointed by the Secretary of State. The Secretary of State may, by order, make different provision in relation to the different Boards.

The Boards must carry out their functions in accordance with, and subject to, any rules of the Council. They must approve institutions in relation to the provision of courses of training to enable persons to qualify for registration, and for courses of further training for those already registered. They must also hold, or arrange for others to hold, qualifying examinations to enable persons to register and also to obtain additional qualifications. They must also perform such functions in relation to the three professions which by order the Secretary of State may prescribe.

### Standing Committee – Midwifery

The Secretary of State is specifically required to establish a Midwifery Committee of the Council. The majority of the members of the Midwifery Committee must be practising midwives.

The making of rules as to midwifery practice is assigned to the Midwifery Committee of the Council. The rules may, in particular, deal with the attendance of courses of instruction, suspension from practice, and with notification to local supervising authorities by midwives of the intention to practice.

The local supervising authorities are: in England and Wales, the health authorities; and in Scotland and Northern Ireland the health boards. Local supervising authorities exercise general supervision over midwives, have power to suspend a midwife from practice in accordance with the Council's rules, and to report alleged misconduct to the Council.

### The Professional Register

The register is divided into parts, indicative of different qualifications and standards of training, and the Council may make rules relating to admission to the register, its maintenance, and any fees to be paid. The Council also makes rules relating to the circumstances in which a person may be removed from the register for 'misconduct or otherwise'.

A Committee of the Council hears and determines proceedings for a person's removal or suspension from, or restoration to, the register. Cautions as to future conduct may also be given. The conduct of disciplinary proceedings is prescribed in the Act (Sch.2).

### Offences by Unqualified Persons

Except in a case of sudden or urgent necessity, or a person undergoing training with a view to becoming a midwife or doctor, it is an offence for any person other than a registered midwife or a registered medical practitioner to attend a woman in childbirth. It is also an offence for any person, with intent to deceive, falsely to represent him/herself to be registered or to possess qualifications in nursing, midwifery or health visiting. The deception may be by words or in writing or by the assumption of any name or description, or by the wearing of any uniform or badge or by any other kind of conduct.

## Opticians

The Opticians Act 1989 is the statute which regulates the practice of opticians and the conduct by bodies corporate of their business as opticians.

### General Optical Council

The General Optical Council, established under the Act (s.1), has the general function of promoting high standards of professional education and professional conduct among opticians. Its members include elected representatives of ophthalmic opticians and dispensing opticians, together with medical practitioners nominated by the College of Ophthalmologists, persons nominated by the Privy Council, and the examining bodies including the British College of Optometrists. The Council must appoint an Education Committee (s.2), and a Companies Committee to advise on matters relating to bodies corporate (s.3). The Council has an Investigation Committee (s.4) and a Disciplinary Committee (s.5). The Council has power to approve institutions for the purpose of training opticians and to approve of qualifications (s.12).

### Registers of Opticians

The Council is required to maintain two registers (s.7) of *ophthalmic opticians*: namely, those engaged in the testing of sight and the fitting and supply of optical appliances; and those engaged in the testing of sight only. In addition the Council must maintain a register of *dispensing opticians*: namely, persons who are engaged in the fitting and supply of optical appliances.

Those persons entitled to be included in any of the health service ophthalmic lists at the time of establishment of the General Optical Council in 1959 were entitled to be registered, as also were other persons who in 1961 satisfied the Council as to their qualifications. Subsequently, only applicants holding qualifications approved or recognised by the Council may be accepted for inclusion in the appropriate register (s.8).

The register must be published by the Council (s.11). The Council is also required to maintain and publish lists of bodies corporate carrying on businesses as ophthalmic opticians or carrying on businesses as dispensing opticians (s.9). A body corporate is entitled to be included in any of the following circumstances:

1    if the majority of its directors are registered opticians; or
2    if it was included in one of the National Health Service ophthalmic lists on 20 November 1957; or

3      if the greater part of its business consists of activities other than the testing of sight and the fitting and supply of optical appliances; or

4      if it is a society registered under the Industrial and Provident Societies Act 1965.

In 3 and 4 the business of testing sight or the fitting or supply of optical appliances must be under the management of a registered ophthalmic optician or a registered optician as is appropriate.

## Professional Discipline

The General Optical Council has an Investigating Committee (s.4) and a Disciplinary Committee (s.5) to deal with any disciplinary case. The Disciplinary Committee may direct the removal of a name from the register or list (s.17). The name of a registered optician may be suspended or removed from the register following a conviction in the United Kingdom for any criminal offence or following a judgment of the Disciplinary Committee that s/he has been guilty of serious professional misconduct. A financial penalty can also be imposed, either on its own or together with a suspension or erasure. The name of an enrolled body corporate may be removed following a conviction of the body corporate for an offence under the Act, or aiding, abetting, counselling or inciting another person to commit an offence, or following a finding of the Disciplinary Committee that the conditions for enrolment of the body corporate are no longer satisfied.

The Disciplinary Committee may also direct the suspension or erasure of a name from the list or register on grounds of fraud or error (s.19); for a contravention of any rule of the Council made under section 31 (e.g. advertising); or for carrying on a practice or business without the supervision of a registered ophthalmic or dispensing optician as appropriate (s.17).

## Offences under the Opticians Act 1989

Subject to certain exceptions, it is unlawful for any person who is not a registered medical practitioner or registered ophthalmic optician to test the sight of another person (s.24). It is also unlawful to sell any optical appliance, that is an appliance designed to correct, remedy or relieve a defect of sight, unless the sale is effected by or under the supervision of a registered medical practitioner or a registered optician (s.27). This does not apply to certain types of sales, e.g. sales to an optician or to medical practitioners, hospitals or government departments; neither does it apply to the sale to a person over 16 of 'reading glasses', subject to limitation on spherical power, to correct presbyopia (s.27). It is a defence to prove that an appliance was sold as an antique.

The Sale of Optical Appliances Order of Council 1984 (SI 1984 No.1778), which is applicable to the new Act, also exempts from the supervision requirements the sale of spectacles provided such sales are made against a prescription written by a registered medical practitioner or registered optician.

The exemption does not apply to the sale or supply of contact lenses or spectacles for those aged under 16.

It is an offence for any person or body corporate to use any of the titles ophthalmic optician, dispensing optician, registered optician or ancillary optician if that person is not registered or, in the case of a body corporate, enrolled. It is also an offence to use any name, title, addition or description falsely implying registration or enrolment (s.28).

## Professions Supplementary to the Medicines Act 1960

N.B. The government published proposals on 1 August 2000 for the establishment of a new Council for the professions allied to medicine – The Health Professions Council – which will replace the present Council for Professions Supplementary to Medicine. The Council will be required to treat the health and welfare of patients as paramount, collaborate and consult with key stakeholders and be open and pro-active in accounting to the public and the professions for its work.

Key objectives to reform the structure and functions will be by:

- giving wider power to deal effectively with individuals who present unacceptable risks to patients;
- creating a smaller Council, comprising directly elected practitioners, and a strong lay input, charged with strategic responsibility for setting and monitoring standards of professional training, performance and conduct;
- providing explicit powers to link registration with evidence of continuing professional development;
- providing stronger protection of professional titles;
- enabling an extension of regulation to new groups.

A three-month consultation process was underway when this book went to press. The new Council will be UK-based.

The current position is as follows. The 1960 Act provides a system, similar to that in the Opticians Act, for the regulation of the smaller professions related to medicine. A Board governs each of the professions of *chiropodists, dieticians, medical laboratory science officers, occupational therapists, physiotherapists,* and *radiographers. Prosthetists and orthotists* (SI 1997 No.504) and *arts therapists* (SI 1997 No.1121) were added in 1997. Three more professions were added in 1999, each with their own board – *paramedics* (SI 1999 No.1853), *clinical scientists* (SI 1999 No.1854), and *speech and language therapists* (SI 1999 No.1855).

The Boards have the general function of promoting high standards of professional education and professional conduct among the members of their respective professions. General supervision over the Boards is exercised by a Council which is itself subject to the conditions of the Privy Council. Boards for additional professions may be established, or existing Boards may be amalgamated or cease to exist, but the total number must not exceed 12. On each Board the number of members who represent the profession must exceed the number of the other members of the Board by one.

The Council for Professions Supplementary to Medicine co-ordinates and supervises the activities of the Boards, and there is on the Council a member representative of each profession from the Boards. The remaining members are appointed, some by the Privy Council, some by Secretaries of State, and some by various medical bodies. The number of medical practitioners on the Council must equal the number of representatives of the relevant professions.

The Council makes rules dealing with the keeping of the registers maintained by the Boards. The Council must submit to the Privy Council any application it receives from a Board for the approval of any course, qualification or institution. Each Board must prepare and maintain in the prescribed manner a register of all those entitled to be registered therein. It must have the register printed, published and put on sale, and must deposit a copy with the Council for Professions Supplementary to Medicine whose duty is to keep all the registers and lists of corrections open for inspection by the public.

The registers, when first established, included all those persons qualified in accordance with the National Health Service (Medical Auxiliaries) Regulations 1954 (SI 1954 No.55, now revoked), together with other persons who satisfied the Boards as to their qualifications and experience. Subsequently only applicants holding qualifications approved or recognised by the appropriate Board may be registered. Each Board approves education institutions and is responsible for the supervision of approved institutions and for the conduct of examinations.

### Professional Discipline

Each Board must appoint an Investigating Committee, which conducts preliminary investigations into any disciplinary case and decides whether or not to refer the case to a second committee, a Disciplinary Committee, for final determination. The membership of the two committees must be different (s.8).

A Disciplinary Committee may, if it thinks fit, direct that the name of a registered person shall be removed from the register on account of a criminal conviction, or is judged by the Disciplinary Committee to be guilty of infamous conduct in any professional respect, or where that person's name has been fraudulently entered on the register (s.9). Appeal from a direction of a Disciplinary Committee lies to the Privy Council. Each Disciplinary Committee is required to prepare and to send by post to each member on the register a statement as to the kind of conduct which the Committee considers to be infamous conduct in a professional respect, but this does not preclude the Committee from judging other conduct to be infamous.

*Titles, etc.*

A registered person is entitled to use the title of state registered chiropodist, state registered dietician (and similarly for the other professions). It is an offence for any person to take or use, alone or in conjunction with other words, the title state registered chiropodist, state chiropodist or registered chiropodist (and similarly for the other professions) if s/he is not so registered, or to take or use any name, title, addition or description falsely implying, or otherwise to pretend, that his/her name is on a register established under the Act (s.6).

Only registered persons may be employed by health authorities within the National Health Service unless they were employed in their specific capacity prior to the registration requirements applying to their profession. Apart from these restrictions there is no prohibition on practice by unregistered persons.

## Hearing Aid Council Act 1968

The main Act was amended by the Hearing Aid Council (Amendment) Act 1989. The Hearing Aid Council has the general function of securing adequate standards of competence and conduct among persons engaged in dispensing hearing aids. It is required to draw up standards of competence for dispensers of hearing aids and codes of trade practice for adoption by such dispensers and by persons employing them (s.1). The Hearing Aid Extension Act 1975 extended the Act to Northern Ireland.

The Council is appointed partly from persons representing persons registered under the Act and partly from persons representing the interests of persons with impaired hearing. The Council is required to maintain for public inspection a register of dispensers of hearing aids, and a register of persons (including bodies corporate) employing such dispensers (s.2).

A *dispenser of hearing aids* means an individual who conducts or seeks to conduct 'oral negotiations' with a view to effecting the supply of a hearing aid, whether by him/her or another, to or for the use of a person with impaired hearing. An *employer of dispensers* includes any person who enters into any arrangement with an individual whereby that individual undertakes for reward or anticipation of reward to act as a dispenser with a view to promoting the supply of hearing aids by that person (s.14).

*Professional Discipline*

The Council must also establish an Investigating Committee (s.5) and a Disciplinary Committee (s.6) comparable with those under the Professions Supplementary to Medicine Act 1960. A registered person may have his/her name suspended or removed from the register for any criminal conviction or if judged by the Disciplinary Committee to be guilty of serious misconduct in connection with the dispensing of hearing aids or the training of persons to act as dispensers of hearing aids (s.7, as amended by the 1989 Act). A financial penalty may also be imposed. Appeals against a direction lie to the High Court. It is an offence for any person whose name is not in the appropriate register to act as a dispenser of hearing aids or to employ such a dispenser.

## The Future

The government has announced that it has a plan to establish a single National Health Service disciplinary body covering all professions, including doctors and nurses. At the same time ministers are considering a more radical plan to create a single regulatory body which would include doctors and nurses together with dentists, physiotherapists and pharmacists (*Independent* 17 July 2000).

## Further Reading

Appelbe G.E., Harrison I. 'Professional Self-Regulation: Pharmacy and the Other Health Professions', *Pharm J* 14 May 1994 p.679.
*Code of Best Practice for Members*. UKCC.
*Nurses, Midwives and Health Visitors – Standards for Education and Practice* EL(95)(36). NHS Executive.

CHAPTER TWENTY-THREE

# National Health Service Acts

N.B. In June 1999, the government passed the Health Act 1999 which provided powers to change the regulation of health professions and health professionals and to amend National Health Service law. The consequences of implementing this Act were not complete at the time of going to press but, for the National Health Service, the changes are now largely in place and appear in this chapter.

## History

The National Health Service Act 1946 made it the duty of the Minister of Health (now the Secretary of State for Health) in England, and the Secretary of State for Wales (SI 1968 No.1699):

> 'to promote the establishment in England and Wales of a comprehensive health service designed to secure improvement in the physical and mental health of the people of England and Wales and the prevention, diagnosis and treatment of illness . . .'
>
> (s.1)

For that purpose a number of services specified in the Act were to be provided. Generally, they were to be free of charge unless otherwise expressly provided in the Act (s.1). In Scotland a similar health service was established by the National Health Service (Scotland) Act 1947, the Minister responsible being the Secretary of State for Scotland. Following the implementation of the 1946 Act in July 1948, the National Health Service (NHS) was organised into three distinct parts which were managed and financed separately. These were the hospital service, the local health authority service (community health services), and the general practitioner (GP) service (which included the doctors and the chemists). The service was reorganised into a single management structure in England and Wales by the National Health Service Reorganisation Act 1973 (now revoked) and in Scotland by the National Health Service (Scotland) Act 1978.

In 1977 the provisions of the 1946 Act and most of the provisions of the 1973 Act, including those affecting the pharmaceutical service, were consolidated into the National Health Service Act 1977. The principal duty set out in section 1 of the 1946 Act was repeated in the 1977 Act (s.1). Under the 1997 Act, the NHS is essentially split into two different systems. The first (Part I services) relates to the provision of health care in hospital and those provided in the community by district nurses, midwives, health visitors and the schools services. The second group (Part II services) could be called the 'NHS in the High Street' comprising services from general practitioners (GPs), dentists, optometrists and pharmacists. Each of these is in contract with the NHS according to the relevant national contract and Terms of Service. Part II services are often called Family Health Services.

Overall, the Secretary of State or the appropriate ministers are required to provide, to such an extent as they believe necessary to meet reasonable requirements:

1    hospital accommodation;
2    other accommodation for the purpose of any service provided under the Act;
3    medical, dental, nursing and ambulance services;
4    facilities for the care of expectant and nursing mothers and young children;
5    facilities for the prevention of illness, the care of persons suffering from illness, and the aftercare of persons who have suffered from illness;
6    services for the diagnosis and treatment of illness;
7    a family planning service.

The Secretary of State or Ministers are also required to appoint Health Service Commissioners to investigate complaints about the operation of the service (s.106). The remit of the Health Service Commissioner (Ombudsman) was extended in April 1996 to include clinical matters and complaints involving practitioners (see Discipline Committees and Tribunals p.309). In July 1999, the first complaint involving a dispensing error by a community pharmacist was investigated by the Ombudsman (*Chemist and Druggist* 3 July 1999 p.5)

## The Organisation of the NHS

The NHS is highly sensitive to political change and the advent of a Labour government in 1997 changed the tenor of the service from a competitive internal market of purchasers and providers to one of co-operation and partnership. This was not a complete change, however, since the government's aim was to 'keep what works and discard what fails'. Thus the legislative framework is complicated by retention of parts of earlier (pre-Labour) legislation overlaid by the new. Moreover, in 1999, power to manage health matters in Scotland and Wales passed to the Scottish Parliament and the Welsh Assembly respectively. This means that the operation of the NHS in the three countries is now diverging and each jurisdiction is developing its own body of NHS legislation and management guidance. The account below therefore applies primarily to England; later sections in this chapter point to differences which will be apparent in Wales and Scotland. The overall approach to health service planning remains largely the same.

## National Health Service and Community Care Act 1990

The 1990 Act paved the way for the creation of an internal market by transforming the then District Health Authorities into purchasers with power to use contracts or service agreements with providers. It enabled the setting up of self-governing trusts and GP fundholders as providers and removed Crown immunity from hospital premises, so allowing equal competition with other providers. GP fundholders were abolished by the 1999 Health Act.

A Trust is an NHS body which is permitted, initially by individual orders made under the 1990 Act, to assume responsibility for the ownership and management of hospitals and certain other facilities, such as ambulance or local community health services. (Later, under the 1999 Health Act, primary health services are also included.) A Trust is run by a Board, which may engage its own staff and set their rates of pay and may borrow capital and dispose of assets. However, this freedom is constrained in that the staff remain NHS employees and the premises remain NHS property. Moreover, the Secretary of State may require that certain services are provided, e.g. accident and emergency facilities, regardless of the wishes of the Trust Board. Within four years of the passing of this Act, Trusts accounted for well over 90 per cent of hospital and community health services. Until 1999, NHS Trust meant an NHS body concerned with Part I services. However, the advent of the Health Act 1999 means that Trusts will also exist for the commissioning and delivery of primary health care (Part II) services.

## Health Authorities Act 1995

The Health Authorities Act 1995 formalised the purchasing of both *secondary* (hospital and community) and *primary* (GP-based) health care with the creation of Health Authorities (HAs) across England and Wales whose function is to identify the health needs of patients in their locality and secure services to meet those needs. Wherever possible, the geographical boundaries of the Health Authorities were redrawn to be co-terminous with those of the local authority which commissioned social services. This process created 100 HAs in England and five in Wales, with statutory recognition from 1 April 1996. Health Authorities were required to enter into arrangements with NHS Trusts (i.e. hospitals) for the provision of hospital and community (Part I) health services and with family health practitioners for family health (Part II) services.

## National Health Service (Primary Care) Act 1997

This Act introduced a new option for the delivery of two of the family health services, namely, those from GPs and dentists. In additional to the national contracts for general medical services (GMS) and for general dental services (GDS), schemes known as personal medical services (PMS) and personal dental services (PDS) were put in place with individual Health Authorities. Originally set up as 'pilots' using Part I NHS funding, the 1997 Act makes provision for these schemes to be permanent.

## Health Act 1999

This Act gave the powers needed by the government to deliver its plans for managing the NHS. These plans were set out in 1998 in a series of white papers and consultation documents: in England, *The New NHS* (Cm.3807), *A First Class Service* (HSC 1998/113) and *Partnership in Action* (published by Department of Health September 1998) together with companion documents for Wales and Scotland. The 1999 Act makes ten major changes:

1    Abolition of GP fundholding.
2    Enabling the establishment of Primary Care Trusts in England and Wales and NHS Trusts in Scotland to take on additional functions.
3    Amending the NHS and Community Care Act to change the purposes and financing of NHS Trusts.
4    Introduction of a statutory duty of quality on NHS bodies and services (*clinical governance*).
5    Creation of the Commission for Health Improvement to monitor and improve the quality of health care.
6    Introduction of a requirement for family health practitioners to hold approved indemnity cover.
7    Introduction of a statutory duty of co-operation within the NHS and between NHS bodies and local authorities in England and Wales.
8    Introduction of measures to control fraud.

9    Enabling powers to set maximum prices for medicines supplied to the NHS.

10   Enabling powers to regulate health care professions.

Thus the 1999 Act has a profound effect on the way pharmacy interacts with the NHS by creating a powerful local focus for health services in the Primary Care Trust and by requiring a commitment to quality and co-operation in achieving health improvement for local populations. Measures to control costs, tackle fraud and overhaul the self-regulation of health professionals also have an impact on pharmacy.

The National Health Service Act 1977, the National Health Service and Community Care Act 1990, the Health Act 1995, the National Health Service (Primary Care) Act 1997 and the Health Act 1999 **all** now form the legal basis for the NHS in England and Wales, plus further enactments post-1999 which apply to Wales only. The National Health Service (Scotland) Act 1978 together with the relevant parts of the pre-1999 legislation covers Scotland, to which should now be added its own post-1999 Scottish enactments.


## The Future

In July 2000 the government published a further blueprint for the NHS in England, *The NHS Plan* (Cm.4818-1) setting out proposals for a number of changes significant to pharmacy.

The Plan predicts a 'shift away from (pharmacies) being paid mainly for dispensing of individual prescriptions towards rewarding overall service'. The Plan proposes to extend the Personal Medical Services arrangements (see p.298) to allow 'alternative' contracting for community pharmacy services such as medicines management and repeat prescribing.

Other proposals include ordering prescriptions via NHS Direct; extending delivery to the patient's door; electronic prescribing by 2004; reviewing the availability of out-of-hours pharmacy services; and bringing pharmacists into 'one-stop' premises with other health care professionals. The Plan also proposes to abolish Community Health Councils and replace them with a Patient Advocacy and Liaison Service (PALS) in every Trust.

In September 2000, further details, including a significant number of potential changes to NHS legislation, were clarified in a government document setting out a strategy for pharmacy in England entitled *Pharmacy in the Future: Implementing the NHS Plan. A Programme for Pharmacy*. Similar documents were expected for Scotland and Wales.

Legislation is likely in the following areas:

*   Facilitation of repeat dispensing arrangements for Prescription Only Medicines, possibly through group directions or rules amending the use of FP10 forms.
*   Changes to the particulars which must appear on a prescription for a Prescription Only Medicine to include 'electronic signatures'.

- Changes to the awarding of contracts to dispense NHS prescriptions to include virtual e-pharmacies operating over the Internet, to recognise patient demand in major retail developments and 'one-stop primary care centres' for out-of-hours dispensing.
- Changes to existing NHS contracts for dispensing to include clinical quality, speed and efficiency, standards of premises and private consultation areas, record keeping and information, continuing professional development, and clinical governance.
- Introduction of an alternative contract for local pharmaceutical services, which could include dispensing along with medicines management, health promotion, and disease prevention components.
- Inclusion of pharmacists, initially in the managed service, in a list of appropriate practitioners who are able to authorise a prescription for a Prescription Only Medicine.

(*Pharm J* 16th September 2000 pp.384 and 397)

## NHS Structure in Great Britain

The biggest change achieved by the 1999 Act has been in the commissioning of primary health care services. It is here that the structures vary significantly in England, Wales and Scotland. Since April 1999, all GPs in England have been obliged to be brought together in what are technically subcommittees of the Health Authorities, namely *Primary Care Groups*, with a view to eventual transition to autonomous bodies called *Primary Care Trusts*. In Scotland, the transition took place immediately on 1 April 1999. In Wales, the primary care group is termed a *Local Health Group* and these seem likely to remain as subcommittees of the Welsh Health Authorities. In England therefore, the local commissioning may be undertaken by either the HA in conjunction with a Primary Care Group (PCG) or by a Primary Care Trust (PCT) alone; the transition from PCG to PCT is expected to be completed in perhaps three years from 1999.

## England

### The NHS Executive and Regional Offices

The NHS Executive has a central unit in Leeds and eight regional offices, each with a regional director. Their functions, primarily, are to be accountable to government for the performance of the NHS, to set strategy and allocate resources, and to co-ordinate certain functions, such as education and research, which are not best planned at local levels. Because the NHS Executive does not have an operational role, there are no statutory arrangements for the provision of pharmaceutical or other professional advice at regional level. However, most regional offices have appointed persons with

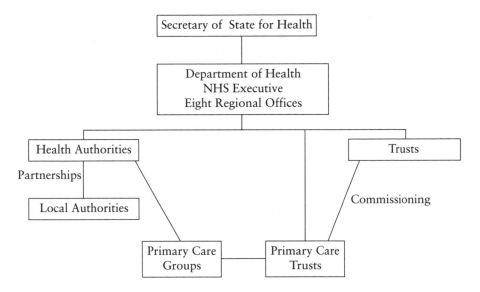

**Figure 23.1**   NHS structure in England

both medical and nursing practice experience to their policy boards and have taken steps to secure pharmaceutical advice. The latter may well be on a part-time consultancy basis or through specific contracts with centres of excellence such as university academic practice units. The English regional offices are: Northern and Yorkshire; Trent; Eastern; London; South East; South West; West Midlands and North West.

### Health Authorities

Health Authorities have been established in England and in Wales since 1 April 1996 under the Health Authorities Act 1995. Each authority consists of a chairman appointed by the Secretary of State and 'a prescribed number of persons (not being officers of the Health Authority) appointed by the Secretary of State and a prescribed number of officers of the Health Authority' (Sch.1 to the 1995 Act).

Regulations (SI 1996 No.707) stipulate that, in addition to the chairman, there shall be a maximum of seven *non-officer members* (usually referred to as non-executive directors) and a maximum of five *officer members* of the HA (reg.2). Of the five officers, three must be the Chief Executive, the Director of Finance and the Director of Public Health (regs.4 and 5). Certain roles may be prescribed for the non-executive directors: for example, one such member is charged with managing the arrangements for dealing with NHS complaints (see p.309). Further regulations (SI 2000 No.696) deal with the consequences of establishing PCTs which will take over some of the functions of the HA.

Health Authorities must ensure that they receive *appropriate advice* to enable them effectively to carry out functions conferred or imposed on them

(Sch.1 to the 1995 Act) but no specific place is reserved for nominations from the practitioner professions to the HAs. However, in an NHS Executive Circular, *Ensuring the Effective Involvement of Professionals in Health Authority Work* (HSC (95) 11, 30 June 1995), amplifying the requirements of Schedule 1, a range of sources for pharmaceutical advice to HAs is suggested. These include: the employment of a pharmaceutical adviser; the development of locality teams; partnerships with providers; service review groups which include local pharmacists; and pharmaceutical advice from an individual on a consultancy or secondment basis.

Further regulations specify the functions of the HA (SI 1996 No.708) and establish procedures for dealing with complaints about family health care practitioner services (SI 1996 No.698) (see also p.309).

Each HA awards contracts, administers the conditions applying to the contract (the Terms of Service, see below), operates statutory disciplinary arrangements and makes arrangements for persons in its own locality to be supplied with 'pharmaceutical services', namely:

1     proper and sufficient drugs and medicines and listed appliances which are ordered for those persons by a medical practitioner in pursuance of his/her functions in the Health Service;
2     listed drugs and medicines which are ordered for those persons by a dental or nurse practitioner in pursuance of such functions; and
3     such other services as may be prescribed by order (added by the 1990 Act).

The pharmaceutical services are provided by community pharmacists, or their employers, who are under contract to the local HA, and are legally known as *chemists* or more usually as *chemist contractors*.

## Primary Care Groups and Primary Care Trusts

Four hundred and eighty-one PCGs were established in England in April 1999. As subcommittees of their local HA, their constitution and functions are set out, not in legislation, but in Health Service Circulars (HSCs), the internal communications on management issues from the Department of Health and NHS Executive to NHS bodies. The boards of PCGs are predominantly composed of local GPs, supplemented by up to two community or practice nurses, one social services nominee, one lay member, one HA non-executive director and the PCG's chief executive. The role of the PCG is to improve the health of their local community, to develop primary and community health care services and to commission secondary (hospital) health services (HSCs 1998/065, 1998/139 and 1998/228).

PCGs may operate at four levels; Levels Three and Four require the establishment of a PCT:

•     Level One: act in an advisory capacity to the HA.
      Level Two: take responsibility from the HA to manage the budget for primary health care in the area.

- Level Three: become a free-standing body accountable to the HA for **commissioning** community care.
- Level Four: as level three, with added responsibility for the **provision** of community services for the local population.

Details of the transition process from PCG to PCT may be found in HSCs 1999/167, 207, 244 and 246 and in separate NHS Executive guidance, *Primary Care Trusts: Establishment, the preparatory period and their functions*, published in February 2000.

Several statutory instruments under the Health Act have formalised the membership, procedure and administration arrangements for PCTs, the composition of their executive committees and their functions (SI 2000 No.89 and subsequent Directions, and SI 2000 No.695). Although the statutory input of pharmacists to local health planning, lost in 1990, has not been formally replaced, the PCT executive retains places for up to three 'community professionals' (other than GPs and nurses) who are providing or performing health services for the population served by the PCT. Community pharmacists should have a strong case for appointment to a PCT executive.

The first PCTs in England were established in April 2000. More were established in September 2000 and it is anticipated that others will follow in April 2001 and in subsequent years.

### NHS Direct, NHS Walk-in Centres

During 1999, NHS Direct, a 24 hour nurse-led telephone help-line on health matters, was set up in England. It was planned to cover the whole of England by the end of 2000 and was extended to Scotland in mid-2000. The service has also been developed into a published and on-line self-care guide and to interactive 'kiosks' in public places such as surgeries, pharmacies, accident and emergency departments, libraries and post offices.

A number of pilot NHS walk-in centres were established during 1999 and 2000. Again led by nurses, these aim to improve access to primary health care services. Legally they are equivalent to NHS hospital outpatient units so that supplies of medicines and collection of prescription charges may be made on the spot to patients who use the centres. If appropriately trained, nurse prescribers in walk-in centres may also issue NHS prescriptions for products in the nurse prescribers' formulary (see Chapter 7 p.66) (SIs 2000 No.121 and 2000 No.122).

### Community Health Councils

The Community Health Council is established to represent, to the HA, the public interest in the health service. It keeps under review the provision of health service in its locality, has statutory rights to the provision of relevant information and can make recommendations for improvements to local health services and also provides general information to the public. From April 1996, greater emphasis has been placed on the role of the Council in developing relationships with providers such as Trusts and GPs in PCGs and PCTs, with local authority social services departments and on involvement in complaints procedures as a means of giving feedback on the local health service.

The Councils are funded from a national budget held by the NHS Executive and contracts of employment for Community Health Council staff are held by one or two HAs within the regional office area. Support services and the administration of procedures for appointing members on behalf of the Secretary of State are provided by the regional office of the NHS Executive. The membership comprises representatives of the local authorities, voluntary organisations and persons appointed by the Secretary of State (SI 1996 No.640).

## Local Pharmaceutical Committees

Local Pharmaceutical Committees (LPCs), recognised by the Act (s.44), consist of nine or 15 persons, as may be decided locally, all of whom must be engaged in providing *Part II* pharmaceutical services in the area.

In a nine-person Committee there must be at least six representatives elected by the chemists in the area, together with one employee pharmacist employed by a chemist and elected by the employee pharmacists in the area. In addition, if a member of the Company Chemists' Association and/or a co-operative society has a pharmacy in the area, then they are entitled to nominate representatives. If not, the places are filled by chemists' representatives.

In a 15-person Committee the chemist representatives number nine, the employee pharmacists three, the company chemist nominees two, and the co-operative society one. Following the merging of authorities to form unified Health Authorities, about half of the existing LPCs were reconstituted to reflect new geographical boundaries from 1 April 1996. In most cases these new Committees adopted a constitution which limited the number of employee representatives to two per employer.

Each Committee appoints its own secretary and the appointment has to be notified to the Secretary of State, to the HA, and to the Pharmaceutical Services Negotiating Committee. The terms of office for members of the Committee is four years and the Committee has power of co-option for casual vacancies. A person ceases to be a member of the Committee if s/he ceases to be engaged in the section of the NHS which s/he represents. His/her seat must be declared vacant if s/he has been absent from three consecutive meetings of the Committee without reasonable cause.

The functions of an LPC include:

1    consultations with the HA on such occasions and to such an extent as may be prescribed by the Secretary of State, and exercising such other functions as may be prescribed by the Secretary of State;

2    establishing effective liaison with other NHS bodies in the area;

3    appointing representatives to the HA Discipline Committee and to any other Committee appointed by the HA on which pharmaceutical representation is required;

4    appointing representatives to conferences called by the Pharmaceutical Services Negotiating Committee;

5    advising any chemist who needs help or assistance on NHS matters;

6    considering any complaint made by a chemist against another chemist carrying on a business in the area and involving any question of the efficiency of the pharmaceutical services;

7    making representations to the HA and to the Pharmaceutical Services Negotiating Committee on matters of importance to chemists.

The Committee must prepare an annual report and accounts, and must circulate them to the electors in the area and to the Pharmaceutical Services Negotiating Committee. The expenses of LPCs may be met by contributions made by the chemists in the area.

## Pharmaceutical Services Negotiating Committee

The Pharmaceutical Services Negotiating Committee (PSNC) negotiates terms and conditions of service for chemists. The Committee is composed of 25 pharmacists engaged in the provision of pharmaceutical services, elected on a geographical basis in England, a member elected from the contractors in Wales, five nominated by the Board of Management of the National Pharmaceutical Association, four nominated by the Company Chemists Association, and one nominated by the Co-operative Wholesale Society.

## Prescription Pricing Authority

The Prescription Pricing Authority is a special HA established under the Act to exercise functions in relation to the checking and pricing of prescriptions on behalf of the HAs. It consists of eight members, of which one must be a pharmacist providing pharmaceutical services under the Act (SI 1990 No.1718).

## Provision of Pharmaceutical Services

The arrangements for the provision of pharmaceutical services are in the National Health Service (Pharmaceutical Services) Regulations 1992 (SI 1992 No.662). These incorporate, among other things, provisions to enable any person to receive such drugs, medicines and appliances as are ordered, and include the terms of service for chemists. The regulations were amended by the 1995 Act to reflect the creation of HAs.

Each HA is required to prepare a list, *a pharmaceutical list* of the names and addresses, together with the terms of business, of all those chemists who have undertaken to provide pharmaceutical services in the area (reg.4). Any chemist who wishes to be included in the list must apply to the HA in the prescribed form. Other than for a minor relocation of an existing pharmacy the application is only granted if the HA is satisfied that a service is necessary or it is desirable to grant the application in order to provide in its locality adequate pharmaceutical services (reg.4).

The HA must remove from the list the name of any chemist who has died or has ceased to be a chemist. Provision is made for representatives of a deceased chemist who comply with the provisions of the Medicines Act (s.71) (see Chapter 4) and who agree to be bound by the terms of service to remain on the list (reg.17). If a chemist fails to provide pharmaceutical services over a period of six months, the HA may remove the chemist's name from the list. The chemist must, however, be given 28 days' notice of the intention, and s/he must be given the opportunity to make representations. In addition, the Local Pharmaceutical Committee must be consulted (reg.17).

THE DRUG TARIFF

The Drug Tariff, compiled and published by the Secretary of State, includes (reg.18):

1    the list of appliances approved by the Secretary of State;
2    the list of chemical reagents approved by the Secretary of State;
3    the list of drugs approved by the Secretary of State;
4    the prices on the basis of which the payment for drugs and appliances ordinarily supplied is to be calculated;
5    the method of calculating the payment for drugs not mentioned in the Drug Tariff;
6    the method of calculating the payment for containers and medicine measures;
7    the dispensing or other fees payable in respect of the supply of drugs and appliances and other supplemental services;
8    arrangements for claiming fees, allowances and remuneration for the provision of pharmaceutical services;
9    the method by which a claim may be made for compensation for financial loss in respect of oxygen equipment.

DIRECTED SERVICES

From 1992, chemists could claim payments for *supplemental services*, namely:

1    a regular supply of medicines to persons in residential homes and the giving of advice on the safe-keeping and administration of those medicines and the keeping of records in relation to visits made to the homes;
2    the keeping of records in connection with medicines supplied to patients in circumstances where the nature of the medicine is such that in the opinion of the pharmacist the same medicine is likely to be prescribed regularly on future occasions, i.e. *Patient Medication Records* (reg.16, as amended).

In 1996, the second of these services was incorporated into the requirements for the payment of a professional allowance (SI 1996 No.698) (see p.309). Further, in April 1999, regulations amending the original 1992 Terms of Service allowed Health Authorities to re-direct payments for residential homes services to any persons (whether chemists or not) who were carrying them out (SI 1999 No.696). This latter process is referred to as removing the 'ring-fencing' of this money for chemist contractors and the services became 'directed services', directed by the HA.

### Chemists' Terms of Service

The basic requirements of the chemists' terms of service are as follows. A chemist must provide pharmaceutical services at the place or places of business and during the hours specified in his/her application form for contract. At each place of business s/he is required to exhibit a notice, provided by the HA, showing his/her hours of contract. At times when the business is not open the contractor must exhibit, in such a manner as to be legible to the public from outside the premises, a notice listing the addresses of the other contractors in the *pharmaceutical list*, together with the hours of opening of their premises for the supply of medicines.

A chemist may supply pharmaceutical services only against a prescription form signed by a doctor or dentist, or a nurse prescriber (see Chapter 7 p.66). *Prescription* is defined as a form supplied by a HA (e.g. FP10, FP14, etc.). The chemist must supply any drugs except those covered by the Selected List Scheme. This list, introduced in 1985, is popularly known as the *Black List* and, as its name suggests, comprises medicines in certain categories which cannot be prescribed for supply against NHS prescriptions. The categories were originally indigestion remedies, laxatives, analgesics for mild to moderate pain, bitters and tonics, vitamins, and the benzodiazepine tranquillisers and sedatives. The current control is under the National Health Service (General Medical Services) Regulations 1992 (SI 1992 No.635, as amended) and the list now includes many other medicines, more recently, so-called 'lifestyle' drugs such as Viagra and Propecia. A full list of the drugs affected is to be found in Part XVIIIA of the Drug Tariff or in the appropriate Schedule to the National Health Service (General Medical Services) Regulations 1992 (SI 1992 No.635, as amended).

All supplies must be made with *reasonable promptness*. However, when a doctor, by telephone or in writing, requests the chemist to dispense a medicine in a case of urgency without a signed prescription, the chemist may dispense the medicine provided that the doctor is personally known to him/her, and has undertaken to supply a signed prescription within 72 hours. Provision is made for the supply of original packs, calendar packs, etc. which are different in quantity from that ordered, e.g. sterile products, effervescent or hygroscopic tablets, oral contraceptives, etc.

A chemist must supply medicines in a *suitable container* which, subject to any regulations made under the 1977 Act, must be supplied free of charge. A suitable container for tablets or capsules means an airtight container made of glass, aluminium or rigid plastic. Cardboard containers must not be used for ointments or creams; they must be used only for foil or strip packed tablets. Eye, ear and nose drops must be supplied in a dropper bottle or with a separate dropper. When an oral liquid medicine is dispensed, a 5 ml measuring spoon or oral syringe must be provided unless the patient already possesses one.

A chemist must not give, promise or offer any person any gift or reward (whether by way of a share of or dividend on the profits of the business, or by way of discount, rebate or otherwise) as an inducement for prescriptions to be presented to a particular pharmacy.

The dispensing of medicines must be performed either by or under the direct supervision of a registered pharmaceutical chemist. The chemist must, on request of the HA, give the name of the registered pharmaceutical chemist employed in the dispensing of medicines at any set of premises.

Subject to any regulations under the Act (s.77) no charge may be made for medicines or appliances under the NHS except those set out in the regulations. Currently, all medicines (except oral contraceptives) and all trusses and appliances (except elastic hosiery) carry a fee per item when ordered on an NHS prescription. Fees payable may be altered by regulation. All fees are collected by the chemist who is later debited with them when his/her prescriptions are submitted for pricing.

In certain circumstances no fees are payable, but to qualify for exemption the patient or their representative, or, in the case of a young child, the parent or guardian, must sign a declaration on the back of the prescription form. The patient or representative must also sign a declaration stating the amount which has been paid, if the patient is not exempt. The categories exempted from fees are of four types (full details are to be found in Part XVI of the Drug Tariff):

1    Exemption on age grounds.
2    Holder of exemption certificate.
3    Receiver of or partner of someone receiving, state benefits.
4    Receiver of no-charge contraceptives.

In 1999, as part of a concerted government attack on fraud in the NHS, chemists were required to implement *point of dispensing checks* by asking patients or their representatives for evidence of their exemption (other than on the grounds of age) from paying prescription charges. If no such evidence is available, the chemist must endorse the prescription accordingly. Later regulations extended these arrangements to checking for evidence of exemption on the grounds of age (SI 1999 No.2563). A reward system for the detection of fraud was also introduced (HSC 1999/133 and SI 1999 No.696) as was the power for responsible authorities to recover penalty fees from patients who evade charges (SI 1999 No.2794).

In 1993, amending regulations (SI 1993 No.2451) made arrangements for the HA to pay for *additional professional services* (new reg.16A), which became known as the *professional allowance*. This allowance depends upon the chemist dispensing a threshold number of prescriptions per month, publishing a practice leaflet, displaying health promotion leaflets as agreed between the HA and the LPC and, from 1996, the maintenance of patient medication records.

Further amending regulations in 1995 (SI 1995 No.644) provided for HAs to determine the local service level requirement and rates of remuneration for out-of-hours service and professional advice to residential and nursing homes. This has to be done in consultation with LPCs. The regulations also clarified the distinction between normal opening hours and additional hours which would fall to be negotiated locally. *Normal* working hours are thus defined as between 9 a.m. and 5.30 p.m. on working days (or 9 a.m. to 1 p.m. on early closing days; i.e. those working days when most shops in the neighbourhood are habitually closed after the hour of 1 p.m.). Working days are then further defined as 'Monday to Saturday excluding a Good Friday, Christmas Day or a bank holiday which falls on any such day' (Sch.2). Later regulations in 1999 allowed HAs to make arrangements for out-of-hours 'on-call' services from a chemist, subject to appropriate consultation and payment (SI 1999 No.696).

From 1 April 1996, further amendments to the chemists' terms of service (SI 1996 No.698) required the institution of a complaints procedure in every pharmacy, together with an obligation to give the procedure publicity and co-operate with the HA in any investigations it may make following a complaint from a recipient of pharmaceutical services. The 1996 regulations also extend the power of the NHS Tribunal (see below) to suspend or declare unfit a chemist to prevent their involvement in the provision of pharmaceutical services.

All these regulations, the Drug Tariff, and the National Health Service (Service Committees and Tribunal) Regulations 1992 (SI 1992 No.664, as amended), which relate to investigations of questions between chemists and persons receiving pharmaceutical services, and other investigations made by the Pharmaceutical Discipline Committee, form part of the terms of service.

## Discipline Committees and Tribunals

Discipline (formerly Service) Committees and Tribunals under the NHS are governed by the National Health Service (Service Committees and Tribunal) Regulations 1992 (SI 1992 No.664), which have been substantially amended by 1996 regulations (SI 1996 No.703). These amendments implement the recommendations of the Wilson Report (*Acting on Complaints*, Department of Health (1995)) on the handling of complaints throughout the NHS. Principally aimed at Trusts and GP practices, the recommendations advocate a positive and constructive approach to complaints which should be used as information to improve and develop the NHS to reflect more closely the wants and needs of patients.

Complaints about practitioners (such as chemists) should be dealt with firstly at 'practice' (i.e. pharmacy) level and only if this fails, may be considered by the HA. These processes are termed Local Resolution and Independent Review respectively and guidance on what they should involve is given in an NHS Executive booklet (see p.314).

Where a complaint is made by a patient, the HA must ensure that an opportunity has been given to resolve the complaint through the above processes first. If, however, the complaint is withdrawn or abandoned by the patient and the HA has information which it considers could amount to an allegation that a chemist has failed to comply with his/her terms of service, then disciplinary proceedings may be instituted. In such a case the HA becomes the complainant and the matter is referred to another HA for investigation (regs.4 and 5).

Every HA is required to establish a Pharmaceutical Discipline Committee which consists of a chairman, no more than three lay members appointed by the HA and no more than three pharmacists appointed by the HA from a list of nominees provided by the LPC. The chairman must be a solicitor or barrister appointed by the HA and the lay members must not be, or have been, a doctor, dentist, pharmacist or optometrist (Sch.2).

The HA is also required to establish a Joint Discipline Committee consisting of a chairman as above and ten other persons, two of whom must be lay members appointed by the HA, and two appointed by and from each of the respective professional discipline committees (Sch.2). Such a Committee would deal with matters involving, for example, a doctor and a pharmacist. When an HA decides to refer a matter to the Pharmaceutical Discipline Committee, it must do so within 28 days of the allegation having ceased to be the subject of a complaint which is being investigated. If the matter has not been the subject of a complaint, the HA must refer it within 13 weeks of the event which is the subject of the allegation (reg.6).

The procedure of the Pharmaceutical Discipline Committee is governed by the regulations (Sch.4). After the procedure has been followed, a report is prepared for the HA, including details of material evidence given to it, its findings on all relevant questions of fact, its inferences, its reasons for drawing such inferences and its recommendations for action. The HA, which must accept as conclusive the Discipline Committee's findings of facts and infer-ences, may determine to take the recommended action, or to take no action or action other than that recommended in the report. In the last two cases, the HA must give reasons for its decision. Where the HA has determined that the chemist has failed to comply with any of his/her terms of service it may:

1    recover from the chemist an amount of money by way of deduction from his/her remuneration;

2    warn the chemist to comply more closely with their terms of service in future.

All decisions have to be notified in writing to all parties who have a right of appeal to the Secretary of State. The procedure for appeals is set out in the regulations (reg.9).

If the HA, or any other person, considers that the continued inclusion of a chemist on the pharmaceutical list would be prejudicial to the efficiency of the service, it may make representations to that effect to the NHS Tribunal constituted under section 46 of the 1977 Act. The constitution of the Tribunal, together with its procedure, is set out in the 1992 regulations (Part III).

## Wales

### NHS Organisation

In Wales, the strategy for health care is set out in *Putting Patients First* (Cm.3841), *Quality Care and Excellence* and *Partnership for Improvement*, all published in 1998. Instead of Primary Care Groups, as in England, the NHS in Wales established, in April 1999, *Local Health Groups* (LHGs) coterminous with local authority boundaries. LHGs bring together GPs, other family health service practitioners (a place is provided for a community pharmacist), nurses, local authority officials and other local interests to advise HAs and to plan services. LHGs are subcommittees of the five Welsh Health Authorities and the Welsh Assembly has yet to decide whether LHGs will eventually become Primary Care Trusts as in England and Scotland. A pharmacist who advises on pharmaceutical matters, usually called the Director of Pharmaceutical Public Health, is normally appointed to each HA, but there is no statutory place on the HA. The public interest in the NHS is vested in local Community Health Councils as in England.

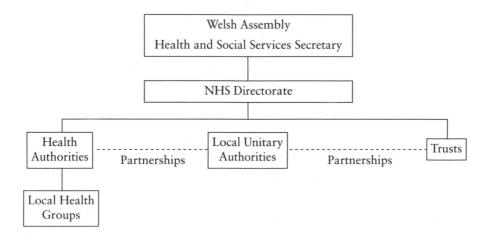

**Figure 23.2** NHS structure in Wales

*Pharmacy Organisation*

The Prescription Pricing Authority has a unit in Wales which deals with payments for prescriptions dispensed in Wales. Negotiation on reimbursement and national service payments are undertaken by the Welsh Central Pharmaceutical Committee (WCPC), now separate from the Pharmaceutical Services Negotiating Committee which previously dealt with negotiations for England and Wales. The constitution of the WCPC has not yet been formalised.

From 1999, the Welsh assembly has had powers to make its own NHS regulations, for example on the nature of the Terms of Service or the level of the prescription charge, but at the time of writing, these have followed the changes made in England.

## Scotland

*NHS Organisation*

The NHS in Scotland has always operated separately from the service in England and Wales. The principal Act is the National Health Service (Scotland) Act 1978 as amended. The function of the HAs in England is undertaken in Scotland by Health Boards. These Boards are directly responsible through the NHS Executive to the Scottish Parliament and are responsible for strategy and planning. The Scottish white paper *Designed to Care* (Cm.3811) published in 1997, planned the creation, throughout Scotland from April 1999, of Primary Care Trusts (PCTs) with responsibility for primary and community health care. The PCTs are largely coterminous with Health Boards except for the islands which share services and have been established by regulations under the Health Act 1999 (see p.298). In October 1999, PCTs took over operational management and responsibility for the awarding of NHS contracts for pharmaceutical services from the Health Boards (SI 1999 No.57).

In addition to PCTs, Local Health Care Co-operatives (LHCCs) have been formed on a voluntary basis to involve local GPs and other family health practitioners in planning the provision of primary health care services. To represent the interest of the public in the health service in Scotland, *Local Health Councils* had been established earlier in 1974. Their role and function is as that for Community Health Councils in England and Wales.

Each Health Board has the services of a pharmacist, called variously a 'Consultant' or 'Specialist in Pharmaceutical Public Health', who provides strategic pharmacy advice to the Board. In addition all Boards have an *Area Pharmaceutical Committee*. These Committees comprise pharmacists who work in both the hospital and community sectors, and are representative of the professionals working in the area. The chairman is elected from the membership, and the secretary (who need not be a member) is elected at the first meeting. The pharmacist adviser to the Health Board is normally invited to attend all meetings of the Committee.

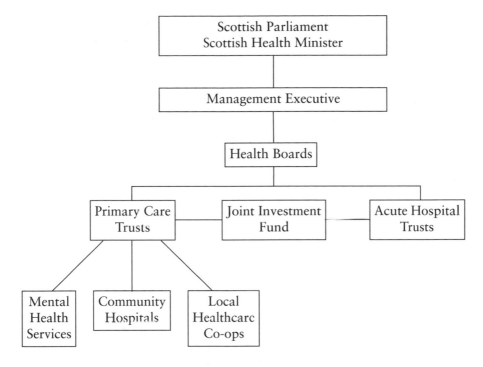

**Figure 23.3**  NHS structure in Scotland

The Primary Care Trusts have the services of a 'Trust Chief Pharmacist' one of which, in Glasgow, has the title Director of Pharmacy. These appointments are not statutorily required.

## Pharmacy Organisation

The Pharmacy Practices Division deals with payments for NHS prescriptions in Scotland, which has a separate Drug Tariff from England and Wales. Negotiations on reimbursement and national service payments are undertaken by the *Scottish Pharmaceutical General Council*. This comprises 42 representatives elected by the 15 Area Chemist Contractors Committees, together with two representatives elected by the Company Chemists Association and one elected by the co-operative societies. In addition, there are three pharmacists appointed by the Council after consultation with the Royal Pharmaceutical Society's Scottish Executive, the Scottish Pharmaceutical Federation and the Pharmaceutical Contractors Committee in Northern Ireland. (The NHS Terms of Service adopted by the Northern Ireland chemists are, with minor amendments, those agreed in Scotland.)

*Area Pharmacy Contractor Committees* have been set up in each of the 15 Health Board areas. Their functions include negotiating with their own Health Boards the local service agreements for the chemists in the area. In addition, they establish liaison with other organisations within the NHS and elect representatives to the Scottish Pharmaceutical General Council. The committees have power to co-opt any pharmacist who in their opinion could assist the work of the committee.

The *Terms of Service* for chemists in Scotland are laid down in the National Health Service (Pharmaceutical Services) (Scotland) Regulations [SI 1995 No.414 (S.28), as amended] (see Appendix 20). Amendments include adoption of procedures for the handling of complaints and the establishment of discipline committees [SIs 1996 No.840 (S.95) and 1996 No.938 (S.103)], and the adoption of point of dispensing checks for evidence of exemption [SI 1998 No.3031 (S.174)].

Arrangements for disciplinary service committees and tribunals parallel those in England and Wales with authority for implementation in respect of chemists being passed to Primary Care Trusts (SIs 1992 No.434 and 1999 No.53).

## Summary

- The statutory framework for NHS services differs between England, Scotland and Wales although the objectives are similar.
- The NHS is a mixed market of commissioning and provision of services by a range of health service bodies, overseen by civil service departments reporting to governments.
- Health Authorities in England and Wales secure the provision of pharmaceutical services through contracts with local owners of pharmacies; in Scotland this activity has passed to the Primary Care Trusts.
- These NHS contracts are limited in number and impose numerous conditions on the chemist as set out in the NHS chemists' terms of service.
- Specifications for the amount and conditions which apply to payments under the NHS chemists' terms of service are set out in the Drug Tariff.
- Negotiations for payments take place nationally through the Pharmaceutical Services Negotiating Committee, the Welsh Central Pharmaceutical Committee or the Scottish Pharmaceutical General Council and locally through the Local Pharmaceutical Committees or Area Pharmacy Contractor Committees.
- The public interest in the NHS is represented by the local Community Health Council (Local Health Council in Scotland).

## Further Reading

*Complaints Listening . . . Acting . . . Improving* (Guidance for community pharmacists and other providers of NHS Pharmaceutical Services) (February 1996). NHS Executive.

Merrills J, Fisher J. (1997). *Pharmacy Law and Practice*, 2nd edn. Oxford: Blackwell Science Ltd.
Wellards (2000/2001) *NHS Handbook*. NHS Confederation. Tonbridge: JMH Publishing.

## Websites

All legislation: http://www.hmso.gov.uk/stat.htm
Health Service Circulars in England: http://tap.ccta.gov.uk/doh/coin4.nsf/
NHSE guidance on PCTs in England: http://www.doh.gov.uk/pricare/pcts.htm
NHS England: http://www.doh.gov.uk/
NHS Scotland: http://www.show.scot.nhs.uk/
NHS Wales: http://www.wales.gov.uk/ (click on policy and information)
*Pharmacy in the Future: Implementing the NHS Plan*: http://www.doh.uk/medicines.htm
*The NHS Plan* Cmnd 4818-1: http://www.doh.uk/nhsplan

CHAPTER TWENTY-FOUR

# Spirits and Methylated Spirits

The law relating to spirits and methylated spirits is contained mainly in the Customs and Excise Management Act 1979 and in the Alcoholic Liquor Duties Act 1979 and in various regulations and notices.

The term *spirits* means 'spirits of any description and includes all liquor mixed with spirits and all mixtures, compounds or preparations made with spirits but does not include methylated spirits'.

*Intoxicating liquor* means spirits, wine, beer, cider and any other fermented, distilled or spirituous liquor, but (apart from cider) does not include any liquor for the sale of which by wholesale no excise licence is required.

### Retail Sales of Intoxicating Liquor

Intoxicating liquor may be sold only by a person holding an appropriate justice's licence granted in England and Wales by licensing justices or in Scotland by a licensing court. The justices have an absolute discretion in the granting of such licences.

The justice's licence may be granted to authorise sales for consumption either on or off the premises. Sales of intoxicating liquor may be made only during permitted hours and these hours are usually fixed by the licensing justice. The holder of a licence requires to have painted on or affixed to his/her premises in a conspicuous place his/her name and, after the name, the word 'licensed', followed by words sufficient to express the business for which the licence is granted.

The maximum quantity of intoxicating liquor which may be sold by retail to any one person is: in the case of spirits, wine, or made wine nine litres or one case; in the case of beer or cider 21 litres or two cases.

N.B. A licence is not required for the sale by retail of spirits made up in a medicine by a pharmacist or a sale to a trader for the purpose of that trade.

## Spirits Duty

Spirits and all goods containing spirits imported into the United Kingdom are liable to a customs duty, and all spirits made in the United Kingdom by a licensed distiller are liable to an excise duty (Customs and Excise Management Act 1979). Exemption from customs and excise duty exists for spirits used in making methylated spirits (see below).

A *reduced rate of duty* is payable if any person can prove to the Commissioner of Customs and Excise that s/he has used spirits, upon which the full duty has been paid, solely for the purpose of manufacturing or preparing any article recognised by the Commissioner as being used for medical or scientific purposes. This concession is granted subject to any conditions which the Commissioner may impose by means of regulations. The guidelines have been made and are contained in the Spirits Regulations 1952 (SI 1952 No.2229, as amended) (see below).

A person wishing to claim repayment of a portion of the duty must comply with the following (as set out in Part VIII of the regulations): s/he must not *receive* at his/her premises any spirits except (a) spirits accompanied by a permit or certificate, or (b) spirits which, if not required to be accompanied by a permit or certificate on removal, are accompanied by an invoice or similar document containing particulars of the spirits and the duty paid, and the name and address of the supplier (reg.63).

A claimant must *store* separately: (a) spirits recovered from spirits in respect of which s/he has or intends to make a claim; (b) any other recovered spirits; (c) any other spirits (reg.65). S/he is not allowed to mix spirits recovered from spirits, in respect of which s/he has or intends to make a claim, with any other spirits except for use in the manufacture or preparation of a medicine which is recognised as such by the Commissioners, or for scientific purposes (reg.65). On each container in which s/he stores spirits or recovered spirits the claimant must permanently and legibly mark the capacity of the container. Each container has to be stored to give convenient access to a Customs and Excise officer (reg.64).

The claimant is required to keep a *stock book* in an approved form (reg.66) and is required to make immediate entries in respect of:

1    spirits received at the premises, brought back into stock for use or recovered on the premises;
2    spirits or recovered spirits intended to be delivered from, or to be used on, the premises;
3    any article made with spirits (reg.67).

The pharmacist both in retail and hospital is mainly concerned with spirits other than recovered spirits. Separate accounts must be kept for spirits and recovered spirits in a stock book. Specimen stock-book rulings are illustrated in Figures 24.1 and 24.2.

If a person uses spirits in the *manufacture or preparation of any recognised medicine*, e.g. homoeopathic medicine, entries must be made in a stock book recording:

1    all spirits received at his/her premises;
2    all spirits and mixtures brought back into stock for use in the manufacture or preparation of a recognised medicinal article, being spirits or mixtures previously entered in the stock book as having been used and in respect of which s/he has in accordance with the Alcoholic Liquor Duties Act 1979 refunded any duty repaid;
3    all spirits delivered from his/her premises;
4    all spirits used on his/her premises, the purposes for which they are used and the quantities used for each purpose;
5    the name and quantity of each recognised medical article made;
6    the name and quantity of any other article made;
7    any other use of the spirits (reg.66).

**Figure 24.1**   Spirits received

| DATE | PERMIT NO. | NAME AND ADDRESS OF SUPPLIER | QUANTITY RECEIVED | STRENGTH O.P. |
|------|-----------|------------------------------|-------------------|---------------|
|      |           |                              |                   |               |

**Figure 24.2**   Spirits used or sold

| REPAYMENT OF DUTY NOT CLAIMED PLUS SALES | | | REPAYMENT OF DUTY CLAIMED | | | | |
|---|---|---|---|---|---|---|---|
| DATE | QUANTITY | STRENGTH | DATE | QUANTITY | STRENGTH | RECOGNISED ARTICLE MADE | |
| | | | | | | NAME | QUANTITY |
| | | | | | | | |
| | | | | | | | |
| | | | | | | | |
| | | | | | | | |
| | | | | | | | |

Separate particulars are required for spirits used for scientific purposes (reg.66).

It is an offence for a claimant to cancel, obliterate or, except with the permission of a Customs and Excise officer, alter any entry in the book (reg.68). The book must be left on the premises while in use and for 12 months following the final entry, together with all books, invoices and other trade documents containing any information on which entries in the book are based. The claimant must at all reasonable times allow an officer to inspect the book, invoices and documents, and take extracts therefrom or make entries in the book (reg.69). Unless the Commissioners permit otherwise, the claimant, if not a rectifier, must take stock and balance the account of spirits in his/her stock book at the end of each month (reg.70) or when required to do so by an officer.

A claimant must not deliver from his/her premises or use for any purpose other than manufacture or preparation of a recognised medicinal article or for a scientific purpose any spirits in respect of which s/he has made or intends to make a claim (reg.71). Claims for recovery of duty must be made on the approval form obtainable from a Customs and Excise officer. The claim must be signed by the claimant or a person duly authorised by the claimant, and must be made within three months of the date on which the spirits were used. Claims cannot be made more frequently than twice a month in respect of spirits used on any one set of premises (reg.73).

When in doubt concerning any provisions of the spirits regulations, pharmacists are advised to consult the local officer of Customs and Excise.


## Methylated Spirits

Methylated spirits are spirits which are mixed with other substances in accordance with regulations made by the Commissioners under the Alcoholic Liquor Duties Act 1979.

There are three types of methylated spirits but the pharmacist is generally concerned only with two, namely mineralised methylated spirits and industrial methylated spirits. The regulations giving particulars for the methylation of spirit, and governing the supply, receipt, sale, storage, etc. of all types of methylated spirits are to be found in the Methylated Spirits Regulations (SI 1987 No.2009), although the provisions for licensing and inspection are to be found in the Act itself. In addition, the Commissioners issue notices for guidance and these can be obtained from local Customs and Excise offices. No person may methylate, or wholesale, methylated spirits of *any type* unless they hold a licence as a methylator from the Commissioners authorising them to do so.

The local Customs and Excise officer may enter and inspect in the daytime the premises of any person authorised by the regulations to receive methylated spirits, and may inspect and examine any of the methylated spirits stored there. The local officer is empowered to take samples of methylated spirits and any goods containing methylated spirits, provided a reasonable price is paid for the sample.

It is unlawful:

1    to prepare, attempt to prepare, or sell any methylated spirits for use as a beverage or mixed with a beverage;
2    to use methylated spirits in the preparation of any article capable of being used as a beverage or as a medicine for internal use;
3    to sell or possess any such article;
4    to purify or attempt to purify any methylated spirits, or recover or attempt to recover the alcohol therein, by means of distillation, condensation or in any other manner unless permitted to do so by the Commissioners.

Nothing in the statute prevents the use of methylated spirits in the making for external use only of any article sold or supplied in accordance with regulations.

If required to do so by the Commissioners the retailer must keep an account, in a prescribed form, of his/her stock of methylated spirits (reg.27). The retailer is required to keep methylated spirits under proper control or under the control of a responsible person appointed by the retailer and held under lock or otherwise stored to the satisfaction of the local officer.

On the closure or transfer of a business, or on the death of the retailer, the stock of methylated spirits must be disposed of in an approved manner and within a reasonable time to the satisfaction of the Commissioners (reg.26).

## Industrial Methylated Spirits

The regulations require that industrial methylated spirits must consist of 95 parts by volume of spirits together with 5 parts by volume of wood naphtha (reg.15).

A person lawfully conducting a retail pharmacy business cannot receive industrial methylated spirits for sale by him/her or for export unless s/he has made application to the proper officer in the required form which is available from the local office of Customs and Excise, and has supplied such information as may be required. The proper officer may make the certificate of authority subject to conditions (reg.25) and restrict it to the receipt of methylated spirits for certain purposes only. Pharmacists *must* comply with the conditions of the certificate. The certificate of authority may be revoked or varied for any reasonable cause at any time (reg.24). The authorised uses for which it may be sold are set out in HM Customs and Excise Notice No.474 dated March 1993.

The proper officer may authorise a pharmacist to receive industrial methylated spirits and:

1  use them to make any article approved by the proper officer;
2  dispense them, or articles made from them, on a prescription;
3  sell or supply them, other than on a prescription, for medical or scientific purposes.

Sales of industrial methylated spirits may be made:

1  to any person authorised to receive them in any quantity not exceeding 20 litres provided that a written statement is received from the user that s/he is authorised to receive them;
2  in any quantity not exceeding 3 litres to a doctor, dentist, nurse, chiropodist, veterinary surgeon or any other person entitled by law to provide medical or veterinary services in the United Kingdom, provided that a written order signed by such a person is received;
3  of not more than 20 litres to persons outside the United Kingdom;
4  for medical or veterinary purposes on a prescription or order of a medical practitioner, dentist or veterinary surgeon or practitioner.

Similarly, a pharmacist may supply or sell articles:

1  which have been manufactured by that pharmacist using industrial methylated spirits in accordance with the conditions imposed in the certificate of authority; or
2  which are so manufactured in accordance with the certificate of authority and are sold or supplied on a prescription.

Industrial methylated spirits must be purchased from an authorised methylator in quantities of not less than 20 litres. Alternatively, not more than 20 litres at a time can be obtained from an authorised user, e.g. a wholesale chemist.

An authorised user, such as a pharmacist, must keep records of his/her dealings with industrial spirits in accordance with any conditions imposed by the proper officer who must be allowed to inspect such records at any reasonable time. An annual return of all industrial methylated spirits received and used or supplied must be made to the proper officer on request. Records must be kept for two years.

All stocks must be kept under lock and key under the control of the pharmacist. The local Customs and Excise may require a pharmacist to comply with special storage requirements.

All bottles and other containers in which industrial methylated spirits or articles containing it are supplied must be labelled in accordance with the Chemicals (Hazard Information and Packaging for Supply) Regulations (see Chapter 18 and pp.205–207). If supplied or dispensed for medical use it must also be labelled *For External Use, Not To Be Taken,* or words to the same effect.

A specimen form of account is shown in Figure 24.3.

**Figure 24.3**  Specimen form of account for guidance of pharmacists when selling industrial methylated spirits otherwise than on prescription

| Received or set aside as a separate stock for sale | | | Sold | | |
|---|---|---|---|---|---|
| Date | Whence received | Quantity | Date | Whether sold on requisition or for use of a doctor etc., on written order | Quantity |
|  |  |  |  |  |  |

## Mineralised Methylated Spirits

The regulations require that mineralised methylated spirits must consist of 90 parts by volume of spirits together with 9.5 parts by volume of wood naphtha and 0.5 part of crude pyridine. To every 1000 litres of the mixture must be added 3.75 litres of petroleum oil and not less than 1.5 g by weight of powdered aniline dye (methyl violet).

Mineralised methylated spirits can be purchased from a methylator or, in small quantities, from a wholesaler. No restrictions are placed on the retailing of mineralised methylated spirits in England and Wales other than that they cannot be sold between 10 p.m. on Saturday and 8 a.m. on the following Monday (Revenue Act 1889). The local officer of Customs and Excise visits the premises to satisfy him/herself as to the suitability of the premises for the storage of mineralised methylated spirits.

## Scotland: Sale of Mineralised Methylated Spirits and Surgical Spirits

For many years there were additional restrictions on the retail sale of methylated spirits and surgical spirits in Scotland. These included the need for sellers to register, keep records and additional labelling requirements. These restrictions were removed in 1998 by the Deregulation (Methylated Spirits Sale by Retail) (Scotland) Regulations [SI 1998 No.1602 (S.87)].

The requirements in Scotland are now similar to those in England and Wales. However it remains an offence to sell mineralised methylated spirits to a person under 14 years of age.

# CHAPTER TWENTY-FIVE

# Miscellaneous Legislation Affecting Pharmacy

The principal statutes concerning drugs, medicines and poisons have been explained in Chapters 1 to 18. The organisation and regulation of the profession of pharmacy have been described in Chapters 19 to 21, followed by a brief account of other health professions in Chapter 22. The organisation of the National Health Service, with particular reference to pharmacy, was outlined in Chapter 23.

There remain several enactments, and other measures, which are relevant to pharmacy. Some are of general application; others may apply only to one of the branches of pharmacy practice, namely: (a) community (or retail) pharmacy; (b) hospital pharmacy; (c) agricultural and veterinary pharmacy; or (d) industrial pharmacy. Separate chapters are devoted to spirits and methylated spirits (Chapter 24), and European matters (Chapter 28). This chapter comprises notes on the remaining statutes and regulations. The law is as it applies in England and Wales. Where the law in Scotland differs it is described, e.g. jury service.

The notes are grouped under appropriate subject headings, as follows:

- Pharmacy Ownership
- Pharmacy Employment
- Pharmacy Premises
- Trade Descriptions and Competition
- Consumer Protection

- Weights and Measures
- Environment
- Merchant Shipping – Medical Scales
- Protection of Animals and Birds
- Data Protection
- Jury Service

## Pharmacy Ownership

A full explanation has been given in Chapter 4 of the controls applied by the Medicines Act 1968 to the conduct of 'retail pharmacy businesses'. As such a business can be owned by an individual pharmacist, a partnership of pharmacists, or a body corporate (that is, a company), it is desirable that the legal status of partnerships and companies should be understood. Only a brief explanation can be given here and any pharmacist contemplating ownership should seek legal advice.

### Partnerships

A partnership is defined in the Partnership Act 1890 as the relationship which exists between persons carrying on a business in common with a view of profit. In contrast to a company (see below), a partnership, or *firm*, is simply a number of individuals each of whom has a responsibility for the affairs and the liabilities of the firm as a whole.

In England and Wales a partnership (firm) does not have a legal status of its own as does a company. This means that the private assets of each partner can be called upon to satisfy any of the firm's debts. All the partners are liable for any debts incurred by one partner acting on behalf of the firm.

In Scotland a partnership has a status similar to that of a body corporate, i.e. it *is a legal person distinct from the partners of whom it is composed*. It is for this reason that in a partnership owning a retail pharmacy in England and Wales all the partners must be pharmacists, whereas in a Scottish partnership only one partner need be a pharmacist (see Chapter 4).

A partnership can arise in either of two ways: by express agreement, or by implied agreement between two or more persons. A partnership can be implied if two or more persons work together in such a way as to fall within the definition as set out in the Act. Generally, if they share in the management of the business and share the profits, then the law will recognise them as partners.

When a partnership is formed to run a retail pharmacy it is invariably a partnership of express agreement, and the conditions of the partnership are set out in a partnership contract or articles. The articles can be altered at any time with the consent of all the partners, whether this is express or implied. The only exception is where the articles restrict the right to vary, e.g. that no change may be made for two years.

A partnership can be formed where one of the partners may limit their responsibility for the firm's debts, leaving the other partners to share the unlimited liability. This partner is often referred to as a *sleeping partner*, as s/he takes no part in the management of the firm. Partnerships of this type are not common and are governed by the Limited Partnerships Act 1907. If a person wishes to limit their liability in this way today they are more likely to invest in a limited company. Once again, it is stressed that before contemplating forming a partnership pharmacists should take legal advice and have any partnership contract drawn up by a solicitor.

### Companies

A company – or corporation aggregate – is a body of persons combined or incorporated for some common purpose. The most common example is a registered trading company, that is, a company which has been incorporated under the Companies Act 1985. This Act is a consolidation of the law relating to companies contained in a number of earlier statutes, including certain sections of the European Communities Act 1972. The notes given here can only outline the general principles of company law, with some special reference to certain aspects which particularly affect pharmacy businesses.

Incorporation as a company enables a group of people to act and to trade in the same way as an individual owner. It also enables them to trade with limited liability to the individual shareholder. Once incorporated a company is *a legal person* and quite distinct from its members. It can own property, employ persons, and be a creditor or debtor just like a human being. This is the fundamental principle of company law.

The promoters of a company must file the following documents with the Register of Companies:

1   memorandum of association;
2   articles of association;
3   list of directors and name of secretary;
4   statement of the nominal share capital;
5   notice of the address of the registered office;
6   declaration by a solicitor or a person named in the articles as a director or secretary that all the requirements of the Companies Acts in respect of registration have been complied with.

If all the documents are in order the registrar will issue a certificate of incorporation which is conclusive evidence that the company has been registered and that the requirements of the Act have been complied with.

There are at least three types of company: a public company; a private limited company; and a private unlimited company. Most pharmacists will be concerned with the private company, whether limited or not.

A *private company* needs only one director but if there is a sole director s/he cannot also be the company secretary. Shares and debentures in a private company cannot be offered to the public.

An *unlimited company* is one where there is no limit on the members' liability to contribute to the assets in order to satisfy the company's debts.

## Memorandum of Association

The memorandum of association regulates the external affairs of the company and must include five clauses, namely, those relating to the name, registered office, objects, liability and capital of the company. It must be signed by each subscriber.

The name of a private limited company must end with the word *limited*. For a public limited company the last words must be *public limited company* or *plc*.

There is a general freedom of choice of the company name, but a company cannot be registered under the Act by a name which includes, otherwise than at the end of its name, the word *limited, unlimited* or *public limited company* or the Welsh equivalents, e.g. *cfyngedig*. Where *cfyngedig* is used, the fact that the company is a limited company must be stated in English and in legible characters on all official company stationery and publications, and in a notice conspicuously displayed in every place where the company's business is carried on.

No name may be used which the registrar considers offensive, or which, if used, would constitute a criminal offence. In the latter category would fall a retail company which is not conducting a retail pharmacy business and which wished to use the title *chemist*.

Certain words and expressions may only be used in company or business names with the approval of the Secretary of State or other relevant body specified in regulations (SI 1981 No.1685, as amended). For the word *chemist* the Royal Pharmaceutical Society of Great Britain is the relevant body, but, when *chemist* or *chemistry* is used in an industrial sense, it is the Royal Society of Chemistry. Similarly, for the word *apothecary* the relevant body in England and Wales is the Worshipful Society of Apothecaries and in Scotland, the Royal Pharmaceutical Society of Great Britain.

## Articles of Association

The articles regulate the internal affairs of the company, i.e. the rights of shareholders and the manner in which the business of the company is conducted. A model set of articles is set out in regulations made under the Act. It may be used by a company as it is, or adapted as required. If no articles are submitted with the application for registration the statutory ones will apply. The articles of a company are freely alterable by special resolution, subject to certain safeguards.

The legal effect of the memorandum and articles is that they bind the company and its members as if they had been signed and sealed by each individual member and contained covenants on the part of each member to observe all the provisions of the memorandum and articles.

## Directors

The first directors of a company are usually appointed in accordance with the articles; if not they are appointed by the original subscribers to the company. Subsequent appointments are usually governed by a procedure laid down in the articles. It must be stressed that a pharmacist becoming a director should be fully aware of the contents of the memorandum and articles of association of the company s/he joins. Directors must exercise their powers as directors for the benefit of the company. A director has a duty to the company to exercise such skill and care as s/he possesses. If appointed in a specific capacity calling for a particular skill, e.g. a pharmacist who is a director of a body corporate, s/he must exercise that skill in a reasonable manner for the benefit of the company. Directors are not bound to give continuing and unremitting attention to the company's affairs and are justified in trusting the officers of the company to perform their duties honestly.

A pharmacist who becomes superintendent chemist of a company will almost invariably be appointed a director, and a knowledge of the powers and duties of directors is essential. For example, if a company fails to make its annual return then the company and/or any of its officers or directors is liable to a default fine. A pharmacist who resigns as a superintendent chemist should ensure that s/he also resigns as a director. Instances have occurred where a pharmacist, some years after having resigned as a superintendent chemist, has been prosecuted for failing to make an annual return as s/he had remained a director of the company.

## Business Names Act 1985

A *business name* is a name used by a business which is other than: (a) for a sole trader, his/her surname; (b) for a partnership, the surnames or corporate names of all members of the partnership, or (c) for a corporate business, the names of the company concerned. Certain additions are permitted, e.g. forenames or initials.

Where a business name is used the true name(s) and address(es) of the owner(s) must appear on all business stationery and that information must be prominently displayed at the business premises. The use of certain types of business names require the written approval of the Secretary of State and regulations may specify certain words or expressions which may only be used with the approval of a Government Department or some other relevant body.

## Pharmacy Employment

Difficulties and misunderstandings frequently arise between employer and employee because the terms of the employment have not been put into writing. It is advisable for every pharmacist, whether employer or employee, to ensure that all the conditions of service are set out either in an exchange of letters or in a formal contract. In the absence of such written agreement, the terms of the Employment Protection (Consolidation) Act 1978, as amended by the Employment Act 1980 and 1982, together with the Trade Union Reform and Employment Rights Act 1993 apply.

All practising pharmacists experience the effects of this Act whether as an employer or employee. An *employee* for the purpose of this Act is defined as 'an individual who has entered into, or works under (or, where the employment has ceased, worked under), a contract of employment'.

Many of the Act's provisions do not apply to persons on fixed-term contracts, nor does it apply where the employee is the father, mother, husband, wife, sons or daughter of the employer.

## Written Particulars of Employment

An employer is required to give an employee, not later than eight weeks after commencement of employment, a written statement identifying the parties, specifying the date of commencement of employment and giving among other particulars details as to the scale or rate of remuneration; terms and conditions relating to hours of work; holiday and sickness entitlement; and the length of notice which the employee is obliged to give and is entitled to receive in order to terminate his/her employment. Each statement must specify the person to whom an employee can apply for the purpose of seeking redress of any grievance relating to his/her employment and give details of any disciplinary rules which apply to him/her.

The statement may, for any of the particulars required, refer the employee to a document to which s/he has ready access or which s/he has reasonable opportunity of reading in the course of his/her employment. An employer may insert into the statement a power of search but this is not a legal requirement. There is no requirement to give a written statement if the employee normally works less than 16 hours per week. N.B. The written statement is *not* a contract of employment.

Changes in the terms of employment have to be notified in writing by the employer to the employee within one month of such a change, or the employee must be referred to a document to which s/he has reasonable access. If a statement is not given by an employer, or any particulars are queried, the employee may refer the matter to an industrial tribunal.

If the name or identity of the employer is changed and this does not entail any change in the terms of employment other than the names of the parties, the new employer is not required to issue new statements to the employees.

## Minimum Period of Notice

The amount of notice an *employer* must give to terminate the contract of employment of a person who has been continuously employed for one month or more varies with the period of continuous employment and is shown in Table 25.1:

**Table 25.1**  Minimum periods of notice by employer

| Continuous employment | Notice |
| --- | --- |
| less than 2 years | 1 week |
| not less than 2 years but less than 12 years | 1 week for each year of continuous employment |
| 12 years or more | 12 weeks |

Notice required to be given by an *employee* who has been in continuous employment for one month or more is one week, unless different terms are stated in the contract of employment. It is generally accepted that a professional person, such as a pharmacist, should give at least one month's notice to their employer if they wish to terminate their employment. Apart from any contractual requirement, a registered pharmacist has a professional obligation not to leave the pharmacy for which s/he is responsible without giving adequate notice.

Either party can waive their right to notice. The Act does not affect the right of either party to treat the contract as being ended without notice by reason of the conduct of the other party, e.g. theft by the employee, but there are provisions against unfair dismissal (see below).

The Trade Union Reform and Employment Rights Act 1993, as amended, additionally gives rights to pregnant employees whether full-time or part-time. Such maternity rights include:

1    All pregnant employees must be given paid time off to attend antenatal clinics and other antenatal care. The employer should include proper pregnancy risk assessment in line with the COSHH regulations (see Chapter 18).

2    Such an employee has the right to statutory maternity pay from her employer and the right to return to her employment on terms and conditions no less favourable than those which would have applied had she not be pregnant.

3    She is entitled to 18 weeks maternity leave with all contractual rights except pay. This entitlement is irrespective of length of service or contracted hours worked. If she is dismissed because of her pregnancy then she is automatically deemed to have been *unfairly dismissed* (see Unfair Dismissal, below).

4    Women who have been employed for more than two years at the beginning of the 11th week before the expected date of delivery may return to work at any time during the period beginning at the end of her maternity leave period and ending 29 weeks after the week of the birth. Any existing benefits which are better remain unaffected by the Act.

The employer must allow the employee to return, if she so wishes at any time before the end of a period of 29 weeks from the date of confinement. The right is to return to the same job as before on conditions and terms no less favourable than those which would have applied had her employment not been interrupted.

During the period of maternity leave the employee is eligible for *statutory maternity pay* under the Social Security Act 1986, provided that the conditions set out in the Act are satisfied. *Statutory maternity pay* is a combination of maternity pay and social security maternity allowance. It is payable by the employer who then recovers the sum from the state.

## Sick Pay

Statutory Sick Pay (SSP) is payable to all staff between 16 and 65 years of age who earn more than the lower earnings limit for National Insurance contributions. SSP cannot be claimed until the employee has been absent for more than three days. For further information on this and the National Joint Industrial Council scheme see the NPA Leaflet *Absence due to Sickness*.

## Unfair Dismissal

The concept of fair and unfair dismissal received recognition in the Industrial Relations Act 1971 and is now to be found in the Employment Act 1989. In every employment to which the Act applies every employee has the right not to be unfairly dismissed by their employer, and accordingly it is an 'unfair industrial practice' for an employer to dismiss an employee unfairly. A number of grounds for dismissal which are considered as *fair* are listed in the Act. These include giving notice to an employee on the grounds:

1   that s/he is incapable of or lacks the qualifications for doing the job for which s/he was employed;
2   of certain forms of conduct on his/her part;
3   of redundancy;
4   that to continue in work the employee would contravene an enactment;
5   of sickness.

Any employee who is dismissed with or without notice has the right to apply within three months to an industrial tribunal alleging unfair dismissal and claiming compensation. The tribunal will take all relevant factors into account and, if dismissal was for misconduct, one fact will be whether or not the employee had been warned about his/her conduct before s/he was dismissed. The conduct of the employer may also be considered.

If it is found that the dismissal was fair then no further action will be taken except possibly an award of costs against the employee. If the tribunal finds that the dismissal was unfair it can recommend that the person be re-instated or it may award compensation. The employer can refuse re-instatement but such refusal will be taken into consideration when the tribunal awards compensation.

The amount of compensation is 'such amount as the tribunal considers just and equitable in all the circumstances having regard to the loss sustained by the aggrieved party'. Compensation is subject to a maximum allowed by regulations – at present £50 000 (SI 1999 No.2830) except in cases involving health and safety issues or public interest disclosure, i.e. whistle blowing. Compensation will be granted only if the employee can show s/he has suffered a loss and s/he is under a duty to offset that loss by attempting to find employment. For example, a pharmacist was held to have been unfairly dismissed but as he had found another job immediately no compensation was awarded as he had suffered no loss.

Disciplinary rules and a written disciplinary procedure for employees are now obligatory and should be strictly followed, especially the giving of warnings, and an employee must be given every opportunity to state his/her case. Tribunals are now concerned with the manner as well as the reasons for dismissal.

An employee with less than one year's continuous service cannot claim for unfair dismissal unless the dismissal related to membership of a trade union or on the grounds of race, sex or disability when there is no qualifying period. Certain other classes of employees are excluded from the unfair dismissal provisions, and if proper notice is given may still be dismissed without the question of compensation arising. These include the wife or husband of the employer, an employee working less than 16 hours per week, employees on fixed-term contracts of one year or more, e.g. pre-registration graduates and staff who have reached retirement age.

If an employee steals s/he may be dismissed and the risk of an unfair dismissal charge is remote, particularly if criminal proceedings follow. Pharmacists have been involved in proceedings before industrial tribunals both as employers and employees. In 1977 it was held that a female pharmacy assistant who had taken an overdose of drugs, properly obtained on a prescription, was fairly dismissed from her employment as a result of taking that overdose (*Pharm J* 18 March 1978 p.247). Two years later an industrial tribunal dismissed a complaint of unfair dismissal brought by a pharmacist who, as a regional manager for a company conducting retail pharmacies, had been dismissed for employing as a pharmacist *locum tenens* a man who was not a registered pharmaceutical chemist (*Pharm J* 12 July 1980 p.36).

Pharmacists are advised to seek legal advice if they consider they have been unfairly dismissed, and pharmacist employers should exercise caution before deciding to dismiss an employee, particularly if summary dismissal is contemplated.

## Vicarious Liability

The term *vicarious liability* in this context signifies the liability which an employer may incur to a customer for damage caused by an employee in the course of his/her employment. This in legal terms is the relationship between *master* and *servant* and means that the 'master' can not only order or require *what* must be done, but also *how* it shall be done.

All employee pharmacists should have a contract of employment (see p.329) but in many areas pharmacists themselves will decided *how* a task should be performed and this will often be a matter for the pharmacist's own professional judgement. Thus, if an employee pharmacist makes a mistake or is so careless as to cause *damage* (e.g. injury, fear, anxiety, etc.) to a patient or customer, the employer would probably be liable. However, if the act or omission fell into the realm of professional judgement, the pharmacist may also incur additional personal liability and might be accountable to the Society and/or to his/her employer to justify his/her actions.

This is why pharmacists are advised to carry their own professional indemnity insurance or ensure that they practise only in an establishment which is covered by such insurance (see pp.253 and 268 and Appendix 18).

## Sex Discrimination

The Sex Discrimination Acts 1975 and 1986 render unlawful discrimination on the grounds of sex or marriage in the fields of employment, education, and provision of goods, facilities and services, and in the disposal and management of premises. Individuals have the right of direct access to the courts and to industrial tribunals to redress any unlawful discrimination. Complaints related to employment are made to industrial tribunals. The Act established a Commission – the Equal Opportunities Commission – with the function of working towards the elimination of discrimination and promoting equality of opportunity between men and women generally. The Act applies to discrimination against both men and women, and references to the rights of women to equal treatment with men include the rights of men to equal treatment with women.

A person discriminates against a woman if on the grounds of sex she is treated less favourably than a man would be or has applied to her a condition that she cannot meet because she is a woman.

Although the Act covers various kinds of discrimination, the pharmacist will be affected in particular by the provisions relating to employment and advertising for staff. Employment is defined as employment under a contract of service or apprenticeship, or a contract personally to execute work or labour. It is unlawful for the employer, when recruiting staff, to discriminate in the arrangements s/he makes for deciding who should be offered the post, in relation to any terms offered (e.g. salary, holiday pay, leave, etc.) and/or by refusing or deliberately omitting to offer a woman employment. An employer may not discriminate against a woman by refusing or deliberately omitting to afford access to opportunities for promotion, transfer, training or other benefits.

It is not unlawful for an employer to afford special treatment to women employees in connection with pregnancy or childbirth and in any provision s/he makes to cover death or retirement (e.g. as to what age an employee retires).

There is a further exemption where a person's gender is a 'genuine occupation qualification' for the job, e.g. where considerations of decency or privacy require the job to be held by a woman (or man) or where the job is one of two which are to be held by a married couple. It is unlikely that a pharmacist recruiting staff could claim exemption under this section. Other exemptions apply to certain categories of employment, e.g. police, prison service, armed forces, etc.

Unless an exemption is provided in the Act, no person may publish or place for publication any advertisement which indicates or might reasonably be taken to indicate an intention to do an act which is unlawful discrimination. A job advertised which uses a job description with a sexual connotation such as 'salesgirl' is taken as an indication of discrimination.

The Act covers many other facts of discrimination which do not necessarily affect the pharmacist. Explanatory leaflets on the subject published by the Equal Opportunities Commission are available from the Commission at Overseas House, Quay Street, Manchester M3 3HN, and from Citizens Advice Bureaux. Advice generally on the Act may be sought from the Commission.

### Equal Pay

The Equal Pay Act 1970 requires that a woman shall not be treated less favourably than a man in the same employment in respect of pay and other terms of her contract of employment where she is employed on the same or similar work as a man. A complaint of less favourable treatment in relation to payment of money regulated by a contract of employment is dealt with under this Act. If the less favourable treatment does not relate to money, whether or not it is in a contract, it is dealt with under the Sex Discrimination Act 1975 (see above). A guide to the Equal Pay Act 1970 is available from local offices of the Department of Employment.

### Race Discrimination

The Race Relations Act 1976 makes it an offence to discriminate against any person on grounds of colour, race, nationality or ethnic origins. Its provisions extend to recruitment, terms and conditions of employment, benefits, promotion, etc. There is a Commission for Race Equality which has powers to issue a non-discrimination notice against any person when it is satisfied that person has contravened the Act. The Commission has issued a Code of Practice for the elimination of racial discrimination and the promotion of equality in employment. Although not penal the Code's provisions are taken into account by industrial tribunals.

### Disability Discrimination

The Disability Discrimination Act 1995 outlaws discrimination against disabled people in both employment practice and service provision. It established the National Disability Council to advise the government in this area. In this context, *disability* means 'a physical or mental impairment which has a substantial and long-term adverse effect on a person's ability to carry out normal day-to-day activities'. *Day-to-day activities* involve mobility, manual dexterity, physical co-ordination, ability to lift, carry or move ordinary objects, speech, hearing or eyesight, memory or ability to concentrate, learn, understand, or perceive physical danger.

Thus the definition includes those with hearing or visual impairment, those with learning disabilities or mental illness and those with long-term illnesses such as severe arthritis, HIV infection, multiple sclerosis and muscular dystrophy. Certain conditions are excluded, notably, addiction to alcohol, nicotine or non-therapeutic drugs.

A Disability Rights Commission was established in July 1998 and it advises and assists disabled people to secure their rights under the Act, i.e. conciliation and/or formal investigations. An aggrieved person can also seek civil proceedings, citing the relevant Code of Practice established in October 1999 as the standard to be expected. Practical steps applying to pharmacy practice are discussed in *Pharm J* 6 September 1997 p.381 and 31 July 1999 p.149. Implementation of the Act in National Health Service bodies is set out in HSC 1999/156.

## Pharmacy Premises

### Conditions of Employment

Previous legislation, e.g. the Shops Acts and the Offices, Shops and Railway Premises Act 1963, had provided certain rights for shop employees concerning their working hours, tea breaks, half days, time off in lieu of Sunday working, etc. These provisions have to some extent been replaced by the Employment Acts.

The Sunday Trading Act 1994 permits trading on Sundays and removed many of the earlier restrictions. Small shops (less than 280 m$^2$) may open at any time on a Sunday. Shops over 280 m$^2$ may open for a continuous six hours between 10 a.m. and 6 p.m. and a few types of large shops may trade all day. The large shops permitted to open for six hours are not allowed to open on Easter Day or when Christmas falls on a Sunday. Retailers have to register their intent with the local authority.

Those large shops permitted to open all day on a Sunday include pharmacies open for the sale of medicines and airport shops.

The Act allows shop workers to refuse to work on Sundays. Should they do so they have the right not to be dismissed, made redundant or subjected to any other prejudicial action by the employer. These rights apply irrespective of age, sex or length of service.

In 1993 Council Directive 93/104/EEC was issued to deal with, amongst other things, a minimum level of safety and health requirements for the organisation of the working day and contains provisions for minimum periods of daily rest, annual leave and breaks. These provisions have been implemented in the Working Time regulations.

### Working Time

The Working Time Regulations 1998 (SI 1998 No.1833) came into force on 1 October 1998 and require employers to consult with their employees, and set up procedures, to monitor and record working hours. This may be done either individually or collectively via employee representatives. There are three types of agreements.

1  collective agreements which are between employer and a trade union;
2  workforce agreements where an employer negotiates modification of the rules with an elected member representing the employees; and,
3  relevant agreements between the employer and an individual member of staff.

Most pharmacists, if they wish to modify the rules, will probably have a relevant agreement with their employer. Such agreement has to be in writing, its duration may be specified and the employee has the right to terminate the agreement giving seven days' notice.

The regulations provide for a maximum working week of 48 hours which can be waived by the employee. The 48 hours is averaged over a period of 17 weeks which can be extended to 26 weeks in special cases and to 52 weeks in the case of collective/workforce agreements. In the case of annual leave, sickness and maternity leave the 17-week period must be extended by an equivalent number of days. The employee has the right to 'opt out' of the 48-hour week by agreeing in writing to exclude the limit but has the right to 'opt in' on giving notice to the employer.

Any person over the age of 18 years must have a rest period of at least 11 hours in any 24-hour period and a 24-hour rest period (15 to 18 years, 48 hours) in a seven-day period. Aged 15 to 18 years the rest period is 12 hours. This may also be waived by the employee.

If the working day exceeds six hours the employee is entitled to at least a 20-minute unpaid break. However the employee can choose not to take the break to which he/she is entitled. This rest break must be taken away from the work place.

All employees must be provided with paid annual leave after three months' service This entitlement is three weeks paid annual leave rising to four weeks after November 1999. Such leave must be taken within the year it is earned; it cannot be carried over to subsequent years. The annual leave provisions are mandatory in that they must be taken and cannot be waived.

All working hours, leave, holidays, etc. have to be recorded by the employer, monitored by him/her and the records preserved for two years.

The regulations make special provisions for employees under the age of 18 years and for night workers. Doctors in training are excluded from the rights provided by the regulations and, according to Department of Trade and Industry guidance, the exclusion could also apply to all National Health Service training grades, e.g. pre-registration pharmacy graduates.

The regulations also exclude 'managing executives or others with autonomous decision making powers' but not professional staff who work core hours plus additional hours as required.

### Health and Safety

The Health and Safety at Work etc. Act 1974 requires:

1 the provision of a comprehensive system for securing the health, safety and welfare of persons at work; and
2 the protection of the health and safety of the public against the risks to health arising from work activities.

The Act applies to all people who are working, including employers, employees, and the self-employed. Persons carrying out any work activities must exercise a duty of care towards the public in respect of matters affecting health and safety. For example, an employer must ensure that the public, as well as his/her employees, are protected from the consequences of work taking place at his/her premises. No one may intentionally or recklessly interfere with or misuse anything provided for the health, safety and welfare of persons affected by this Act.

It is the duty of every employer to ensure as far as is reasonably practicable the health, safety and welfare of their employees. The employer's duties include the adequate maintenance of plant and systems of work so that, as far as is reasonable, they are safe and free from risk to health. Arrangements must be made to ensure the safe use, handling, storage and transport of articles and substances. In addition, the employer must provide such information, together with instruction, training and supervision, as is necessary to ensure the safety and health of their employees. S/he is required to prepare a written statement of his/her general policy in relation to the health and safety of employees; thus, each proprietor pharmacist must provide such a statement for the benefit of his/her employees, but there is an exemption for employers with less than five employees (see Control of Substances Hazardous to Health (COSHH), Chapter 18).

The employer must conduct his/her business in such a way that people not in his/her employ, e.g. the general public, are not exposed to risk to their health or safety. It is the duty of each person who has control of premises to ensure that means of access to and from such premises which are available for use by the public are safe and without risk to health.

Each *employee* while at work has a duty to take reasonable care of him/herself and not to endanger the health and safety of other persons who may be affected by his/her acts or omissions. In addition, s/he is required to cooperate with his/her employer to enable the employer to carry out their duties under the Act.

Each *self-employed person* (e.g. a locum pharmacist) must conduct their business in such a way so as to ensure that s/he and other persons not his/her employees are not exposed to risks to their health or safety.

The Health and Safety Commission and the Health and Safety Executive have been established under the Act. The Health and Safety Commission is responsible to the Secretary of State for Employment for making any arrangements it considers proper for the purposes of the Act. It assumes responsibility for health and safety at work in all industry except agriculture and in 1975 took over responsibility for the existing legislation concerned with health and safety. The Commission has a specific duty to arrange for the provision of information and advice and for the conduct of research. It has issued a series of booklets, which are available from The Stationery Office, on the Acts and their effects on employers and employees.

The Health and Safety Executive gives effect to any Directives which are given to it by the Commission. It has an enforcement role and for this purpose has the power to appoint inspectors. The inspectors can serve improvement notices and prohibition notices, and can deal with any article or substance by way of destruction or otherwise which they have reasonable cause to believe capable of causing severe personal injury.

The Secretary of State may by means of regulations give local authorities an enforcement role under the Act. The Commission may also arrange for other government departments to exercise some functions on its behalf, including certain enforcement roles.

The Secretary of State has power to make health and safety regulations and the Commission may submit proposals for providing practical guidance. The Commission may approve and issue codes of practice, whether prepared by itself or not. It may also approve codes of practice which have been issued by outside bodies, e.g. a particular industry. Before approving any code of practice the Commission must obtain the consent of the Secretary of State after consulting those interested organisations which it considers appropriate. Approved codes of practice may be used in criminal proceedings as evidence that the statutory provisions have been contravened. The status of these codes is similar to that of the Highway Code in relation to the Road Traffic Act.

The first-aid provisions are now dealt with under the Health and Safety (First Aid) Regulations 1981 (SI 1981 No.917).

The Workplace (Health, Safety and Welfare) Regulations 1992 (SI 1992 No.3004) replaced much of the old legislation regarding the conditions in the workplace. They deal with four areas, namely working environment, safety, facilities and matters of general housekeeping:

1    Working environment:

    (a)    The temperature shall be 'reasonable' without the need for special clothing and should normally be at least 16°C. Where the work is highly physical, e.g. unloading in a warehouse, the temperature should be at least 13°C.

    (b)    There should be adequate ventilation to allow an exchange of air.

(c)    Good lighting should be provided so that staff may use the facilities and move around safely.

(d)    Workplaces should have enough free space to allow staff to move around with ease. Eleven cubic metres is the minimum work space.

(e)    Seating should be provided for staff and workstations should be at a suitable height and equipment within easy reach to avoid undue bending or stretching.

2    Safety:

(a)    The shop area of the pharmacy should allow staff and customers to circulate safely.

(b)    Where windows (or other translucent surfaces) are part of a wall they must be robust. Any clear or translucent surface should be marked to make it apparent to customers and staff. All windows and skylights should be so designed as to be easily cleanable and when open should not present a risk to customers.

(c)    All floors should be free from holes and unevenness, be non-slippery and regularly maintained. Leakages and spillages should be dealt with immediately. Stair-rails should be fitted where necessary and floors kept free from obstructions.

(d)    To prevent falls, all step ladders and kick-steps should be properly sited and kept in good repair. Special precautions should be given to trap doors (if any).

3    Facilities:

(a)    There must be sufficient sanitary and washing facilities to enable everyone at work to use them without undue delay (see Table 25.2).

**Table 25.2**    Minimum sanitary and washing facilities

| No. of people at work | No. of water closets | No. of wash basins |
|---|---|---|
| 1–5 | 1 | 1 |
| 6–25 | 2 | 2 |
| 26–50 | 3 | 3 |
| 51–75 | 4 | 4 |
| 76–100 | 5 | 5 |

Special provision should be made for the disabled. Water closets must be connected to a suitable drainage system and provided with effective means of flushing. Toilet paper in a holder and a coat hook should be provided. In water closets used by women suitable means of disposal of sanitary towels must be provided. Wash basins must have hot and cold running water and be large enough to enable effective washing of the hands, face and forearms. The employer must ensure adequate privacy for the user and the whole area must be adequately ventilated so as to disperse odours.

(b) An adequate supply of drinking water must be available. This should normally be obtained by a tap on a pipe direct from the mains supply.

(c) A clean, dry, ventilated place should be available for staff to hang their clothes, each having a separate hook.

(d) Seats must be provided for staff to rest during breaks. In new premises there must be a separate rest room.

4     General housekeeping matters:

(a) The workplace, including furnishing and fittings, must be maintained in a good state of repair and equipment therein in efficient order. *Efficient* in the regulations means efficient in the sense of health, safety, and welfare, not productivity or economy.

(b) Waste material must be stored in a suitable receptacle.

## Trade Descriptions and Competition

### Trade Descriptions

The Trade Descriptions Act 1968 provides control for the false and misleading descriptions of goods and services in the course of trade or business. It makes separate provision for goods and services. A *trade or business* includes a retailer, wholesaler or manufacturer. It is generally accepted that a *business* is a wider term than a *trade* and there is some legal authority for the term *business* to include a profession.

A trade description is an indication, direct or indirect, and by whatever means given, of certain matters with respect to any goods including:

1     quantity and size;
2     production process, or method of production;
3     composition;
4     strength performance;
5     any physical characteristics not included in the preceding paragraphs;
6     place or date of manufacture, production, processing;

and generally speaking any other description applied to goods whether they are sold, supplied, or offered for sale or supply.

A person applies a trade description to goods when s/he affixes any mark to the goods or to anything in, on or with the goods, or when s/he uses a mark in any way where it can be taken as referring to the goods, e.g. in an advertisement. An oral statement may also amount to a trade description, and it is important, therefore, for pharmacists and their assistants to be fully aware of these provisions as both are liable under the Act.

If goods are supplied in response to a specific request it is important to ensure complete compliance with that request, as the person supplying the goods is deemed to have applied that trade description to the goods. For example, any wrongful supply, or quantity or substitution on a prescription could amount to a false trade description. An employee can be liable under the Act as well as the employer, according to who has applied such a description.

Where a description is applied during the course of a service, it is an offence knowingly to make a false statement or make such a statement recklessly without regard to its accuracy. A statement made regardless of whether it is true or false is deemed to be made recklessly whether or not the person making it had reasons for believing that it might be false.

Offences under the Act are of *strict liability*, but there are defences. These include the defences of: mistake; reliance on information supplied; the act or default of another person; or an accident or some other cause beyond the control of the seller. The defence most commonly used is that of 'due diligence', where it is argued that all reasonable precautions had been exercised to avoid the commission of the offence either by the defendant or any person under his/her control. It is a defence for the person charged to prove that s/he did not know, and could not with reasonable diligence have ascertained, that the goods did not conform to the description that had been applied to them.

The Act also covers services and care should be taken to ensure that any description of services provided to consumers is accurate and not misleading.

A duly authorised officer of the local authority has the power, at all reasonable times, to enter any premises not wholly used as residential premises and to inspect and seize any goods or documents. It is an offence wilfully to obstruct an officer or wilfully to fail to comply with any requirement properly made by him/her.

## Competition

The Competition Act 1998 reflects a worldwide trend to open up markets, stimulate competition and establish transparent and fair marketing arrangements. It is having far-reaching effects upon previously familiar and entrenched financial and ethical constraints on pharmacy practice. The Act broadly aims to foster competition, to prevent the abuse of a dominant position in the market, to facilitate investigation across Europe into 'fair trading' and to establish ground rules for what that means in relation to the supply of services. It came into force in March 2000.

Most significant for community pharmacy business is the repeal by the Competition Act of the Restrictive Practices Court and Trade Practices Acts of the mid-1970s which allowed Resale Price Maintenance (RPM) to apply to the retail sale of medicines. At the time of writing, the Director General of Fair Trading, under the 'old' legislation, was seeking to abolish RPM on medicines whereby manufacturers or suppliers are able to fix the price at which their products may be sold by retail. Should the action succeed, RPM will be brought to an end. If the action fails, then there is a five-year transitional period before the Competition Act requires that RPM is terminated.

Overall, the Competition Act aims to outlaw 'agreements between under-takings, decisions by undertakings or concerted practices' which 'affect trade within the United Kingdom' and 'have as their object or effect the prevention, restriction or distortion of competition within the United Kingdom'. Examples of such measures include those which 'directly or indirectly fix purchase or selling prices' which clearly covers RPM on medicines (*Pharm J* 16 August 1997 p.236; 25 October 1997 p.676).

The second major implication of this Act affects all of pharmacy practice. The rules of trade associations and professional bodies are covered by the anti-competitive prohibitions in the Act, unless they are specifically exempted in Schedule 4. For historical reasons, pharmacy was not included in Schedule 4 (although some other health professions were) and the Code of Ethics for pharmacy must comply with the provisions of the Act. Since the current Code contains several restraints, in the public interest, on the promotion and supply of medicines, further work is needed to ensure that the Code is not challenge-able under the Competition Act (see Chapter 20 p.229).

## Consumer Protection

Note that the Disability Discrimination Act 1995 provides protection for disabled consumers as well as employees (see p.334).

The Consumer Protection Act 1987 deals with a variety of issues, including product liability, safety of goods, and misleading prices.

### Product Liability

The Act creates liability without fault on the part of the producer for damage caused by a defect in their product. Four classes of person may face liability for a defective product: the manufacturer, the importer, any person who holds themself out as the manufacturer, and, in the event of none of the above being identified, the person supplying the product to the victim. The first three groups have a primary liability, whereas the supplier has a secondary liability based upon their inability to identify a primary producer.

When medicines might be the subject of an action in the Courts (there have been very few cases brought under the Act), the primary producer will normally be the product licence holder. The supplying pharmacist should therefore ensure that s/he has adequate systems and records to ensure that s/he can identify with certainty the licence holder/manufacturer of the medicines s/he supplies. Liability probably does not arise from re-packing licensed medicines or from supplying them against a prescription, provided the source is known.

The supplying pharmacist will carry full liability for 'own-branded' goods in which the pharmacist's name and address are affixed to containers of medicines made up elsewhere and not so identified and when s/he prepares his/her own remedies for a patient under section 10 of the Medicines Act (see p.26). In these circumstances it is advisable to maintain full manufacturing records so that the producer of the ingredients can always be identified. Claims may be made up to three years after the 'relevant date' – when the victim becomes aware of the facts – subject to a maximum of ten years from the date of putting the product into circulation.

## Safety of Goods

Any consumer goods must be reasonably safe. In considering what would be reasonably safe the Courts will probably consider (a) any warnings or instructions given with respect to the goods, (b) any published safety standards in respect of the goods, and (c) any means by which the goods could be safer with regard being given to cost. The Act covers not only the goods but also their containers and packaging and provides for the enforcement authorities to prohibit the sale of unsafe goods by way of prohibition notices.

## Price Controls

The Act has replaced the earlier provision under the Trade Descriptions Act as to misleading prices for goods. The offence is one of giving, by whatever means, an indication which is *misleading* as to the price at which goods, services, accommodation or facilities are available. Unlike the earlier legislation, it now additionally provides for misleading prices in respect of *services* offered.

Where advertising material is concerned it is important to ensure that it is always updated and amended as prices change in order that no consumer is mislead as to the price of the goods or services offered.

Any pharmacist involved in retailing should be aware of the contents of the *Code of Practice for Traders on Price Indications*. The enforcement of the Act and the code is in the hands of the local Weights and Measures Authority (Trading Standards Department). The Price Marking Order 1999 (SI 1999 No.3042) made provision for the display of prices in retail premises. Pharmacists should be aware that the price of all goods sold from retail premises should be indicated to the customer. Methods of indicating the price include: on the goods, a price list adjacent to the goods, shelf edge display, etc. There is also a requirement to display the unit price (cost per litre/kg) for certain goods. The unit price controls do not apply to medicines. In pharmacy, cosmetics, toiletries, and food supplements are the items most likely to be affected. The unit price controls only apply in larger (over 280 m$^2$) stores. The controls are complex and being frequently updated. Advice should be sought from local trading standards departments.

**Weights and Measures**

The Weights and Measures Act 1985 and the regulations made thereunder control the manner in which goods should be weighed or measured and the quantity indicated on packaging. Enforcement of the Act rests with local government authorities, usually through their consumer protection or trading standards departments. All the equipment used by pharmacists for the buying or selling of goods must comply with the provisions of the Act. If in doubt a pharmacist should consult his/her local government authority's department.

An inspector under the Acts may at all reasonable times inspect and test any weighing or measuring equipment which is, or which s/he has reasonable cause to believe is, used for trade, or is in the possession of any person or upon any premises for such use. S/he may enter any premises, other than premises used solely as a dwelling house, at which s/he has reasonable cause to believe that an offence may be committed. S/he may at any time seize or detain any article which is liable to forfeiture under the Act, or any document or goods which may be required as evidence in proceedings under the Act. S/he may also make test purchases.

Any person who, in selling or purporting to sell any goods by weight or other measurement, or by numbers (e.g. goods supplied on private prescriptions), delivers to the buyer a lesser quantity than that purported to be sold or than corresponds with the price charged, may be guilty of an offence. Similarly, a misrepresentation by word of mouth or otherwise as to the quantity of the goods, or any act calculated to mislead a person buying as to the quantity of the goods, is an offence. It is also an offence to sell pre-packed goods marked with a quantity on the container where the quantity is less than that stated. When charged a person may have a defence under warranty or if the misrepresentation is the fault of a third person.

Where an offence has been committed by a body corporate and it is proved to be attributable to the negligence or committed with the connivance or consent of any director, manager, secretary or similar officer of the body corporate, then that person shall be deemed guilty of the offence.

Much of the detailed legislation relating to weights and measures appears in a range of regulations issued under the 1985 Act or the European Communities Act 1972. These control, amongst other things:

1   the material of which weights, measures and weighing instruments may be made;
2   the type, shape, form and markings of weights; the construction of weighing instruments;
3   the obliteration or defacement of stamps;
4   the inspection, testing and confirmation of fitness for use in trade and the stamping of weights and measures and general provisions regarding packaging; and
5   the marking, making up, checking and testing of packaging.

*Liquid capacity measures* must be made of certain materials only, e.g. glass, enamelled metal, aluminium alloys and stainless steel. All liquid capacity measures must be marked with the maximum purported volume and glass measure graduations must be clearly marked and stamped.

*Weights* must be made entirely of metal (but not of lead or other soft metal). Details are set as to type of metal, shape, size, etc., depending on the weight value. Weights must have their purported values conspicuously, legibly and durably marked either in full or by means of the permitted abbreviations, e.g. kg, mg, etc.

*Weighing instruments* used in retail transactions, including those used in the preparation of medicines, must be balances (or instruments other than balances) which fall within the requirements of the Non-automatic Weighing Machine Regulations 1995 (SI 1995 No.1907).

Equipment for weighing or measuring must be passed by an inspector of weights and measures as fit for such use, and must bear a verification mark or stamp either of the inspector or the mark applied under the European Community verification system.

Transactions in drugs, by way of sale, supply or dispensing, must be carried out in the metric system. The 1985 Act lists those units of measurement which may, and may not, be used in trade and it is now unlawful to use apothecary weights and measures (SI 1986 No.1082).

The Weights and Measures (Packaged Goods) Regulations 1986 (SI 1986 No.2049) made under the Act implement European Community provisions and anyone involved in packaging goods should consult the 'Code of Practice Guidance for Packers and Importers', available from The Stationery Office.

## Environment

The Environmental Protection Act 1990 introduced a *duty of care* which applies to all persons who import, produce, carry, keep, treat or dispose of controlled waste. This therefore applies to pharmacists who necessarily handle waste or unwanted medicines in the course of their practice. An exemption is given to householders (s.26) but this is not extended to those accepting waste from a private householder, for example, when a pharmacy agrees to take back returned medicines from a patient or patient's relative. The duty of care lies on all holders of waste at every stage in its history, such that a pharmacist having held controlled waste may only pass it on to an *authorised person*, such as a registered carrier, a licensed waste manager or a waste collection or regulation authority. Further, s/he must transfer with the waste such a written description of the waste – a transfer note – as will enable others to avoid committing an offence under the Act.

The removal of National Health Service Crown immunity in 1991 means that all National Health Service and governmental incinerators must meet the full provisions of environmental protection legislation and a substantial number were substandard in relation to temperature of operation, load limits, smoke emission, warning systems, etc. Anyone consigning medicines or other controlled waste to hospital facilities for disposal must discharge the full duty of care as set out above.

Details of the duty of care are set out in a code of practice, reissued in 1996 (available from The Stationery Office) and principally require that the handler shall prevent the escape of controlled waste, shall ensure its transfer to an authorised person and that it is described in a transfer note, to provide an audit trail, such that the nature of the risk involved is adequately conveyed to another person.

### Controlled and Special Waste

The Controlled Waste Regulations 1992 (SI 1992 No.588) define *clinical waste* as, amongst other things, 'waste arising from . . . pharmaceutical or similar practice . . .' and describes clinical waste which arises from a private dwelling or residential home as household waste, as distinct from that from any other source which becomes industrial waste. This is significant because the local waste collection authority has a duty to collect household waste, albeit for a fee, but producers of industrial waste are more likely to have to use private contractors for this purpose.

It is unlawful to deposit controlled waste in, or keep it on, any land, or knowingly cause or permit such waste to be deposited unless a waste management licence authorising the deposit is in force under the Environmental Protection Act 1990. The Water Resources Act 1991 prohibits a person from causing or knowingly permitting any noxious poisonous, or polluting matter to enter any controlled inland waters.

A pharmacist whose actions give rise to controlled waste, including a decision to discard such material, is fully bound under the legislation as a producer of controlled waste and carries the corresponding duty of care, including where medicines are returned by patients. A clear interpretation as to how the code of practice should be applied to medicines returned by patients is not available. It is clearly wise to contact the local office of the Environment Agency (or equivalent in Scotland) for specific guidance on compliance with the code.

The special restrictions on the destruction of Controlled Drugs under the Misuse of Drugs Act 1971 were considered in Chapter 16. Controlled Drugs returned by patients are subject to the same considerations described above for other returned medicines and advice should be sought from the relevant Environment Agency. Unwanted stocks of Controlled Drugs are still subject to the requirement for witnessed destruction on the site of their production but disposal via the sewage system does not comply with the Water Resources Act. Accordingly, the practice has developed that the pharmacist will arrange with the relevant Environment Agency for the drugs to be subject to a process of denaturing. The resultant product and its container is then treated as a special waste.

*Controlled waste* includes household, industrial and commercial waste of any kind, whether conventionally thought of as polluting or not.

The Special Waste Regulations 1996 (SI 1996 No.972, as amended) made under the Act provide that waste falling within certain descriptions should be designated as *special waste* and subject to more extensive documentation than is required for non-special waste before it may be removed from premises. Most consignments of special waste require prior notice being given to the waste regulation authorities, namely the Environment Agency in England and Wales and the Scottish Environmental Protection Agency in Scotland; fees are payable.

*Special waste* means controlled waste containing substances listed in Schedule II to the regulations and which has specified hazardous properties (set out in the regulations) or is a Prescription Only medicinal product.

The responsibility for enforcing the provisions of the Act lies with the waste regulations authorities. Local authorities have a responsibility for physical collection and disposal of controlled waste in their capacities as water collection, and waste disposal authorities.

Where an offence has been committed by a body corporate and it is proved to have been committed with consent or connivance, or attributable to any neglect on the part of a director, manager, secretary or other similar officer of the body corporate, including a member concerned with management where the affairs are managed by its members (e.g. a co-operative society), then that person is also guilty of the offence. Thus, pharmacist directors of companies, and, indeed, individual pharmacists, could be liable under this Act for wrongful disposal, without notice, of medicinal products and non-medicinal poisons. This is particularly pertinent when a pharmacy closes down and old stocks of, for example arsenicals and mercurials, are being destroyed.

In March 1997, the Producer Responsibilities Obligations (Packaging Waste) Regulations 1997 (SI 1997 No.648) set obligations for the recovery and recycling of packaging waste. From 1 January 2000, businesses handling more than 50 tonnes of packaging waste per year and with a turnover of more than £1m must comply. A 'shared producer responsibility' may be adopted whereby each part of the supply chain undertakes a share of the recovery targets. Businesses must register with the Environment Agency or its Scottish equivalent, pay a fee, provide data on the packaging passing through their business and certify that they reached their targets each year. Special waste packaging, which includes packaging immediately in contact with Prescription Only Medicines is not covered by the regulations, but must be included in the calculations. An article on the practical implications for pharmacy practice appears in *Pharm J* 2 August 1997 p.186.

The Carriage of Dangerous Goods (Classification, Packaging and Labelling) Regulations 1996 (SI 1996 No.2092) require carriers of what is termed *health care waste* under proposed Health and Safety Executive guidelines to use new containers for such waste and different containers for *health care risk waste*, which may include pharmaceutical waste. Carriers can be expected to pass on these new requirements to their customers and expect the latter to change their methods as to how they separate, pack and label their waste.

The Food and Environment Protection Act 1985 is concerned, amongst other matters, with the reduction of pollution of the environment by pesticides. Subject to certain exemptions, the Control of Pesticide Regulations 1986 (SI 1986 No.1510, as amended) prohibit the advertisement, sale, supply, storage and use of pesticides unless in accordance with an approval and consent given by the Ministry of Agriculture, Fisheries and Food. Any breach of the regulations may result in seizure and disposal of the offending pesticide and any material treated with it, and an order for remedial action.

*Pesticide* is defined as 'products used for the control of rats and mice, flies and other garden pests, cyanide, strychnine, wood and masonry treatments, and pesticides used in public health maintenance'. Additional restrictions are placed on *pesticides approved for agricultural use*. These apply to all crop protection products such as herbicides, fungicides and insecticides, plus some soil sterilants and fumigants. The regulations and consents are supplemented by two codes of practice; one dealing with sale, supply and storage and the other covering use.

Failure on the part of any person to follow the guidance given in the codes does not of itself render that person liable to proceedings, but such failure is admissible in evidence in any criminal proceedings brought under the Act.

Anyone stocking in excess of 200 litres or 200 kg of *pesticides approved for agricultural use* must comply with parts of the code dealing with the physical construction, design and maintenance of sites used for the storage of any pesticide. A person in charge of a store or a salesperson who advises on the use of these products must be in possession of the appropriate Ministry certificate.

Anyone offering a commercial service for the use of pesticides must possess Ministry certification, and any persons using pesticides must be instructed as to such matters as storage and transport on the farm, application techniques and disposal and record keeping.

The effect of all these provisions is to impose the following obligations upon anyone selling, supplying or storing pesticides:

1   They and their staff must be provided with such instructions and guidance as is necessary to enable them to be competent for the duties they are called upon to perform.

2   All reasonable precautions must be taken, especially with regard to storage and transport, to protect the health of human beings and creatures, and to safeguard the environment.

3   The pesticide must be sold or supplied in the container supplied by the manufacturer of the pesticide and under the label approved by the Ministry.

*Strychnine*

Under the pesticide legislation strychnine must be labelled with an approved label, supplied in original containers, and supplied only to holders of an authority to purchase issued by the appropriate department of the Ministry of Agriculture, Fisheries and Food (see also Schedule 1 Poisons Subject to Additional Restrictions p.195).

## Merchant Shipping – Medical Scales

The Merchant Shipping and Fishing Vessels (Medical Stores) Regulations 1995 (SI 1995 No.1802), as amended, implement Council Directive 92/29/EEC and make for the minimum safety and health requirements for improved medical treatment so far as the Directive relates to the carriage of medicines and other medical stores. They cover the carrying of appropriate medical stores on board ships, including fishing vessels. A *ship* in this context means a United Kingdom ship other than pleasure vessels used for non-commercial purposes and not manned by professional crews and ships employed in inland navigation.

The master of any ship which does not carry a doctor is required to make arrangements for securing medical attention on board ship to be given by himself or by some other person appointed by him/her for the purpose. There are minimum requirements for the medicines and medical stores to be carried before a ship may put to sea and the scale of medicines to be carried depends upon whether or not there is a duly qualified medical practitioner in the ship's complement.

The various scales are provided for in the 1995 regulations and in Merchant Shipping Notices M.1607 and M.1608. The regulations also specify requirements for the packaging, labelling, and storage of medicines and other medical items, e.g. disinfectants.

The containers must be labelled amongst other things with:

1    the name of the medicine, in English, as indicated in the respective scale;
2    the expiry date, where appropriate;
3    any storage requirements;
4    name and address of supplier, product licence number and batch number;
5    any further information required by the notices.

The containers of capsules and tablets must be capable of reclosure so as to prevent the ingress of moisture.

A ship in the United Kingdom may be detained if a person empowered under the Act to inspect the medical stores is not satisfied that the required stores are being carried.

Orders made under the Misuse of Drugs Act 1971 and the Medicines Act 1968 permit the owner or master of a ship which does not carry a doctor as part of its complement, to obtain certain Controlled Drugs (see p.172) and any other Prescription Only Medicines (see p.90) which are necessary for the treatment of persons on the ship. The medical scales issued under the Merchant Shipping Act are minimum requirements only.

## Protection of Animals and Birds

The Animal (Scientific Procedures) Act 1986 makes provision for the protection of animals used for experimental or scientific procedures. A *protected animal* for the purposes of the Act means *any living vertebrate other than man*. Any experimental or other scientific procedure applied to a protected animal which may have the effect of causing that animal pain, suffering, distress, or lasting harm is known as a *regulated procedure*. The Act provides for a system of (a) personal licences, (b) project licences and (c) scientific establishment licences. Before issuing any licence the Secretary of State must consult one of the inspectors appointed under the Act (s.9). The breeding and sale of animals for experimental purposes is also controlled.

The Act specifies the type of programmes for which project licences may be issued including, amongst other things, the prevention, diagnosis or treatment of disease, certain educational purposes, and forensic enquiries. Projects may only be carried out by licensed persons on licensed scientific establishments. The Act deals specifically with humane methods of killing experimental animals. The Animals Procedures Committee has the duty of advising the Secretary of State on matters concerned with the Act. S/he may consult the Committee on the question of licences and on the preparation of codes of practice.

Where under the Animal (Cruel Poisons) Act 1962 the Secretary of State has specified that a poison cannot be used for destroying animals without causing undue suffering, and that other suitable methods of destroying them exist, s/he may, by regulations, prohibit or restrict the use of that poison for destroying animals or animals of a particular description.

Regulations have been made (SI 1963 No.1278) which prohibit the use of yellow phosphorus and red squill for the destruction of animals. The regulations also prohibit the use of strychnine for killing any animals except moles. The supply of these substances for prohibited purposes could constitute aiding and abetting an offence under the Act.

N.B. Where the Minister of Agriculture, Fisheries and Food believes or suspects that rabies exists in any area s/he may by an order made under the Rabies Act 1974 declare that area to be an *infected area* for purposes connected with the control and eradication of that disease. S/he may also take steps to secure destruction of foxes in an *infected area* and an officer of the Ministry of Agriculture, Fisheries and Food and any person authorised in writing by the Minister may enter any land for the purpose of carrying out such destruction. Where the Minister exercises this power, methods of destruction may be used (e.g. the use of strychnine) which would apart from these provisions be unlawful (The Rabies (Control) Order 1974 (SI 1974 No.2212)). For restrictions on the sale of strychnine under poisons legislation see Chapter 17.

The Protection of Animals Act 1911 provides that it is unlawful wilfully to administer, or cause or procure to be administered, to any animal a poisonous or injurious drug or substance. Similarly, it is unlawful to sell or offer or expose for sale any grain or seed which has been rendered poisonous except for *bona fide* use in agriculture. It is also an offence to place upon any land or in any building any poison or any fluid or edible matter (not being seed or grain) which has been rendered poisonous.

It is a defence to prove that the poison was placed for the purpose of destroying insects and other invertebrates where it is found necessary in the interest of public health or agriculture, or to preserve other animals, and that adequate precautions have been taken to prevent injury to dogs, cats, other domestic animals and wild birds (Protection of Animals (Amendment) Act 1927).

A defence also exists where a person uses poisonous gas in a rabbit hole, or places in a rabbit hole a substance which by evaporation or any contact with moisture generates poisonous gas, e.g. Cymag (Prevention of Damage by Rabbits Act 1939). These defences are not valid where the poison concerned is prohibited by the Animal (Cruel Poisons) Act 1962 (see above). It is also a defence under the Wildlife and Countryside Act 1981 to prove that what was done was performed in accordance with a licence granted under that Act.

In relation to wildlife, the Wildlife and Countryside Act 1981 prohibits certain methods of killing or taking of wild birds and wild animals including the laying of 'any poisonous, poisoned or stupefying substance'. The prohibition does not apply to anything done under or in accordance with the terms of a licence granted by the appropriate authority. The appropriate authority varies according to the purpose of the licence, e.g. if the licence is issued for the purpose of preventing the spread of disease then the appropriate authority is the Agriculture Minister.

Such a licence may be issued by Agriculture Ministers for the killing or taking of certain wild birds, e.g. feral pigeons, house sparrows, etc., using the chemical alpha-chloralose. Alpha-chloralose can be sold to local authorities and to *bona fide* pest control companies who have had issued to them by the Agriculture Minister a licence which allows them to compound and use their own bait. Farmers have been known to make approaches to pharmacists for supplies of alpha-chloralose and although the pharmacist may lawfully supply this chemical under poison legislation a supply made for the purpose of stupefying birds could be an offence under the Wildlife and Countryside Act 1981. Pharmacists receiving requests for alpha-chloralose or stupefying bait should, before supplying, contact the Royal Pharmaceutical Society of Great Britain for further details.

## Data Protection

The Data Protection Act 1998 came into force on 1 March 2000 and regulates the 'processing' of 'personal data'. *Personal data* means any information whereby a living individual can be identified; *processed* means virtually any activity such as obtaining, recording or holding the data, carrying out operations or sets of operations on the data, organisation, adaptation or alteration of the data, retrieval, consultation or use of the data and alignment, combination, blocking, erasure or destruction of the data. Unlike the earlier Act of 1984, which applied only to 'computerised' data, the 1998 Act additionally covers paper records and filing systems and, indeed, any storage system structured so that data relating to a living individual can be retrieved.

The person to whom the data relates is called the *data subject*. The person who determines how and for what purposes the personal data is processed is called the *data controller*; anyone else who actually processes the data is called a *data processor* (s.1). The 1998 Act also imposes additional controls on *sensitive personal data* which includes any information, including opinion, relating to the physical or mental health or condition of the data subject (s.2).

The Act is administered by the Data Protection Commissioner (formerly the Registrar) who maintains a register of *registrable particulars* notified by data controllers who pay an annual fee (s.18). Data controllers must comply with the eight *data protection principles* set out in the Act (Sch.1). These principles have the force of law. Briefly, the principles require that personal data shall be:

1    obtained and processed fairly and lawfully and shall not be processed at all unless certain conditions are met (see below);
2    obtained and processed for, or in ways compatible with, one or more lawful purpose;
3    adequate, relevant and not excessive in relation to that purpose or purposes;
4    accurate and kept up to date;
5    kept for no longer than necessary;
6    processed in accordance with the rights of data subjects under the Act (see below);
7    protected against unauthorised or unlawful processing and against accidental loss, destruction or damage;
8    not transferred (with certain exceptions) outside the European Economic Area unless the recipient country operates the same controls on data protection as applies within the European Economic Area.

The Commissioner may refuse to register notification if s/he considers that these principles will be contravened (s.22). Processing personal data without notification is a criminal offence (s.21).

The Act imposes conditions which must be met even before processing of personal data can be contemplated (see principle 1 above). Generally, no personal data may be processed at all unless either the data subject has given consent or one of a series of other conditions has been met. These include 'the need to pursue the legitimate interests of the controller' *provided* these are not prejudicial to the interests of the data subject (Sch.2). This condition should be applicable to all uses of personal data in pharmacy practice. In addition, where the data is also *sensitive* personal data, either *explicit consent* must be obtained from the data subject or such consent may not be needed if the processing is 'necessary for medical purposes and is undertaken by:

1    a health professional, or
2    a person who in the circumstances owes a duty of confidentiality which is equivalent to that which would arise if that person were a health professional.'

*Medical purposes* includes the purposes of preventative medicine, medical diagnosis, medical research, the provision of care and treatment and the management of health care services (Sch.3).

Thus virtually all personal data used in pharmacy practice is 'sensitive' but 'explicit consent' (which implies a written explanation, a consent form and a decision freely made in appreciation of all its consequences) is not deemed necessary for patient medication records at least, provided **all** personnel who may process such data are bound by the health professional's duty of confidentiality. The definition of *health professional* in the Act includes pharmacists (s.69).

The Act sets out explicit rights of data subjects and others (see principle 6 above). Data controllers must, on receipt of a written request accompanied by a fee:

1    inform the data subject if personal data is being processed;
2    give data subjects a description of the data which is being processed, for what purposes and to whom it will be disclosed;
3    provide data subjects with that information in an intelligible form within 40 days of the request (s.7).

Data subjects also have a right to prevent processing of their data for marketing purposes (s.11) and to be notified if 'automated' decisions are taken in relation to, for example, work performance, creditworthiness, reliability or conduct (s.12). Rights are also conferred to allow data subjects to claim compensation from the data controller for failure to comply with any of the requirements of the Act or to fail to rectify, block, erase or destroy any inaccurate data (s.14).

There are exemptions allowing the data controller to exclude information relating to an individual other than the data subject, to allow some latitude where provision of copy records is very difficult or impossible to achieve, to protect trade secrets (s.8) and to withhold data if it is likely to cause substantial damage or distress to the data subject or any other person (s.10). Regulations made under section 7 also allow data controllers to decline to disclose data if it would be likely to cause serious harm to the physical or mental health or condition of the data subject or any other person. Information should not normally be disclosed without data subject consent unless it has been established that the data subject is incapable of managing his own affairs and the person requesting disclosure has been appointed by a court to manage those affairs (SI 2000 No.413).

Parents, guardians or carers may seek disclosure of information about data subjects other than themselves for whom they undertake parental or carer responsibility. If the data subject is a child or anyone else who is likely to understand fully his or her rights to confidentiality, then consent should be established if at all possible. The maximum fee for arranging access to automated health records is £10, although £50 is the maximum if paper records are included (SI 2000 No.191).

A further condition for the processing (which includes disclosure) of sensitive personal data is in accordance with circumstances specified by the Secretary of State (para.10, Sch.3 of the Act). This could therefore include disclosure where it is necessary for the prevention or detection of crime or for protecting the public against dishonesty, malpractice, incompetence or mismanagement where seeking the consent of the data subject would prejudice those purposes (SI 2000 No.417).

The requirements of the Caldicott Report on security of data information transfer in the National Health Service have been implemented in National Health Service bodies through HSC 1999/012 and MEL (Scotland) (1999) No.19.

### Access to Health Records

Most of the provisions of the Access to Health Records Act 1990 are now within the Data Protection Act 1998, but the 1990 Act continues to provide that a personal representative of a deceased person or anyone who has a claim arising out of a patient's death can also claim access to 'sensitive personal data' maintained in health records.

Generally speaking, the requirements of data protection legislation do not apply to any information which relates to a data subject who has died (but see above) nor to data which has been 'anonymised', i.e. has been detached from any details or any links whatsoever which could identify a living individual. A series of legal cases have been brought to clarify the limits on the use of anonymised data when derived from patient medication records held by community pharmacists. Details are given in Chapter 26 (p.371).

### Jury Service

All persons normally resident in the United Kingdom and aged between 18 and 65 who are registered as parliamentary or local government electors are with certain exceptions liable for jury service. Electoral rolls no longer differentiate the names of persons liable for jury service. The legislation is set out in England and Wales in the Juries Act 1974 and in Scotland in the Law Reform (Miscellaneous Provisions) (Scotland) Act 1980.

Certain classes of persons are not liable for jury service as follows:

1    Persons who are *ineligible*: these include members of the judiciary, solicitors, barristers, justices' clerks, police officers, clergy, etc.

2    Persons who are *disqualified*: these include persons who have served a term of imprisonment of five years or more.

3    Persons who are *excusable as of right*: these include members of the Houses of Lords and Commons, members of the armed forces, and members of medical and allied professions.

Pharmacists are not automatically exempt but can claim exemption, *after* a jury summons has been issued, provided they are actually practising their profession and registered. A written application for exemption should be made to the Court giving reasons for the claim. If a pharmacist is in doubt as to whether s/he can claim to be *actually practising* their profession s/he should set out in their application for exemption the nature of their work or employment. A person summoned for jury service must attend for the number of days required in the summons but the appropriate officer of the Court may withdraw a summons at any time before the day named in the summons. A person who serves as a juror is entitled to payment for travel and subsistence and for financial loss where this has occurred as a consequence of his/her attendance in Court. The rates and conditions for these payments are set out in the Juror's Allowances Regulations 1978 (SI 1978 No.1579).

In Scotland pharmacists are now eligible for exemption from jury service. Exemption is not automatic and the pharmacist who wishes to be excused must give written notice to the clerk of the Court from whom the citation is received, indicating his/her right and desire to be so excused.

## Further Reading

*A Guide to Working Time Regulations* (September 1998). Department of Trade and Industry.
*Clinical Waste Code of Practice*. The Stationery Office.
Health and Safety Executive booklets:
    *Good Health to Good Business – Employers Guide*
    *Health and Safety in Small Firms*
    *Help on Work Related Stress*
    *Working Times Regulations*
    *Working with VDUs*
    *Workplace Health, Safety and Welfare*
*Information Pack on Disability Discrimination Act*. Department for Education and Employment
    pamphlets:
    DL 60 (definitions)
    DL70 (employment)
    DL80 (services)

National Pharmaceutical Association leaflets on relevant topics including:
> *Absence Due to Sickness*
> *The Contract of Employment* (No.1A)
> *The Workplace (Health, Safety and Welfare) Regulations*
> *Unfair Dismissal* (No.1B)

*Sunday Trading Act 1994 – New Employment Rights for Shop Workers.*
> (Available at Job Centres and Citizens Advice Bureaux.)

*Weights and Measures Code of Practice Guidance for Packers and Importers.* The Stationery Office.

# CHAPTER TWENTY-SIX

# Legal Decisions Affecting Pharmacy

The decisions in important cases in the Courts which have directly affected pharmacy are brought together in this chapter. Although Acts of Parliament take precedence over all other law, the meaning of any statute is subject to interpretation by the Courts. Consequently, most of the cases outlined here are about the meaning of terms, or of individual words, used in the statutes. Some arise from the application of a statute in particular circumstances. A few are concerned with general principles. *Jenkin* v. *The Pharmaceutical Society* and *The Pharmaceutical Society* v. *Dickson* deal with the extent of the Society's powers under its Charter; the authority of the Statutory Committee is considered in *Re Lawson*; whilst *The Pharmaceutical Society* v. *Boots Cash Chemists (Southern) Ltd* has a bearing on the law of contract.

The cases are set out individually, or in groups, under headings which indicate the subject or the point at issue. Where appropriate some explanatory comment is added.

Given below is a list of the cases together with references to the pages on which the relevant points at issue are explained.

## The Meaning of 'acting in accordance with the directions of a practitioner'

### Roberts v. Coombs *(1949)*

The Penicillin Act 1947 read:

> '. . . no person shall sell or otherwise supply any substance to which this Act applies or any preparation of which any such substance is an ingredient or part unless (a) he is a duly qualified medical practitioner, a registered dental practitioner or a registered veterinary surgeon, or a person acting in accordance with the directions of any such practitioner or surgeon, and the substance or preparation is sold or supplied for the purposes of treatment by or in accordance with the directions of that practitioner or surgeon; or (b) he is a registered pharmacist or an authorised seller of poisons, and the substance or preparation is sold or supplied under the authority of a prescription signed and dated by any such practitioner or surgeon as aforesaid.'

A shopkeeper, who was not an authorised seller, sold penicillin ointment to customers who presented prescriptions signed and dated by a medical practitioner. The shopkeeper was charged with selling ointment containing penicillin contrary to section 1(1) of the Act, he not being one of the qualified persons mentioned in that subsection. The magistrates dismissed the summonses on the grounds that, although the shopkeeper was not a practitioner, he was a person acting in accordance with the directions of a duly qualified medical practitioner.

On appeal to the High Court it was held that *a person acting in accordance with any such practitioner or surgeon* was a person in the employment of a doctor or in some way actually under the direct orders of the doctor. A prescription signed and dated by a medical practitioner could be made up only by a registered pharmacist or an authorised seller of poisons.
[1949] 2 All ER 37; *Pharm J* 14 May 1949 p.356.

Comment: The Penicillin Act 1947 was later replaced by the Therapeutic Substances Act 1956. The wording was subsequently retained in section 58(2)(b) of the Medicines Act 1968 which also repealed the 1956 Act.

## The Meaning of 'by a doctor or dentist to a patient of his' under the Medicines Act 1968

### Pharmaceutical Society v. Wright *(1981)*

The Medicines Act requires that no person shall sell a Prescription Only medicinal product except in accordance with a prescription given by an appropriate practitioner. However, the Act provides that this provision does not apply to the sale or supply of a medicinal product to a patient of his/hers by a doctor or dentist who is an appropriate practitioner.

Once a week Dr Wright ran a slimming clinic and those attending were given a medicinal product which was on the Prescription Only list. Many of the persons attending the clinic were patients of other doctors in the town and only attended the clinic, which was supervised by a nurse, for slimming purposes. The issue turned upon whether or not there was a doctor/patient relationship between the attendees and Dr Wright.

Mr Justice Bingham said:

> '... if a doctor acting as such, treats or gives advice to a person and assumes responsibility for that treatment or advice, that person may very well be his patient ... in determining whether the relationship does exist it is not ... of primary importance whether the person is a patient of another doctor as well nor whether the treatment or advice is given by the doctor's staff under his supervision rather than the doctor himself. Nor ... whether the relationship is a short-lived or long-lived. Nor ... need it be of primary importance whether the doctor takes less care in giving the advice or treatment than he should ...'

(1981) Unreported.

Comment: In dismissing the appeal brought by the Society, Lord Donaldson, who sat with Mr Justice Bingham, said that it was for the Society to prove there was no doctor/patient relationship not for Dr Wright to prove there was.

### The Meaning of 'person'

### Pharmaceutical Society of Great Britain v. London and Provincial Supply Association Ltd (1880)

The Pharmacy Act 1868 (s.1) provided:

> 'From and after 31 December, 1868 it shall be unlawful for any person to sell or keep open shop for retailing ... poisons ... unless such person shall be a pharmaceutical chemist, a chemist and druggist ... and be registered under this Act ...'

Section 15 provided penalties for offences under section 1.

A company had sold poisons by retail from its shop. The Society took legal proceedings against the company, contending that a body corporate was a 'person' in law and that section 1 applied to it. The High Court had supported that view but the Court of Appeal had not.

On appeal to the House of Lords it was held that in the context of the Act the word *person* in sections 1 and 15 meant a natural person and did not include a body corporate.

5 App. Cases 857; *Pharm J* 31 July 1880 p.83.

Comment: This decision enabled a company to keep open shop for the sale of poisons provided the other conditions in the Act were met. The Poisons and Pharmacy Act 1908 and subsequent statutes took account of the decision and required a body corporate to appoint a superintendent to conduct and manage the keeping, retailing and dispensing of poisons.

## The Meaning of 'personal control'

### Hygienic Stores Ltd *v.* Coombes *(1937)*

The Pharmacy and Poisons Act 1933 (s.9) read:

> 'A body corporate carrying on a business which comprises the retail sale of drugs shall be an authorised seller of poisons if the following conditions are complied with: (a) the business must, so far as concerns the keeping, retailing, dispensing and compounding of poisons, be under the management of a superintendent who must be a registered pharmacist . . . and; (b) in each set of premises the business must, so far as concerns the retail sale of drugs, if not under the personal control of the superintendent, be carried on subject to the direction of the superintendent, under the personal control of a manager or assistant who is a registered pharmacist.'

Section 18(1) provided, amongst other things, that it is unlawful for any person to sell poisons in Part I of the Poisons List unless s/he is an authorised seller of poisons.

A company carried on retail business at 16 shops. At three of the shops pharmacists were employed, but at one of these the pharmacist did not attend full time. At the other 13 shops, where there were no pharmacists, proprietary medicines and some non-poisonous drugs were sold. The company was prosecuted under section 18(1) of the Act in respect of the sale of Part I poisons at two of the pharmacies. The magistrates found the case proved in that the company was not an authorised seller of poisons. The medicines sold at the 13 shops were drugs. There were no pharmacists in personal control of those shops, and at one of the pharmacies there was a pharmacist present only for part of the time the business was open. Consequently, the company did not fulfil the requirements for an authorised seller of poisons laid down in section 9. On appeal to the High Court the magistrates' decision was upheld and the appeal by the company dismissed.

[1938] 1 All ER 63; *Pharm J* 18 December 1937 p.664.

Comment: The Pharmacy and Poisons Act 1933 (s.9) has been replaced by the Medicines Act 1968 (s.71) (see Chapter 4). The requirements for bodies corporate remains unchanged. The meaning of *personal control* has also been considered by the Statutory Committee of the Royal Pharmaceutical Society (see Chapter 21).

## Powers of the Royal Pharmaceutical Society

### Jenkin *v.* Pharmaceutical Society of Great Britain *(1921)*

The Society's Charter of Incorporation 1843 had, as one of its objects, *the protection of those who carry on the business of chemists and druggists.*

In 1919 the Council of the Society took part in promoting an Industrial Council for the drug trade. The objects of the proposed body included, among others, the regulation of wages, hours and working conditions, and of production and employment. Mr Jenkin, who was a member of the Society and, prior to the case, a member of the Council of the Society, sought an injunction in the High Court (Chancery Division) to prevent the Society from sponsoring the Industrial Council on the grounds that the functions proposed were not within the scope of the Society's powers.

It was held by the Court that a member was entitled to obtain an injunction restraining the commission of acts outside the scope of the Charter. The Society could not carry on a business of general insurance, even though limited to members, as it would not benefit members as a whole. Nor could it legalise by its Charter a combination in restraint of trade and so convert itself into a trade union as defined in the Trade Union Act 1876 (s.16).

The Court declared that it was not within the power or purposes of the Society to take part in, or expend any of its funds in the formation, establishment, maintenance or work of the Industrial Council, or to undertake or perform the following matters:

1    to regulate the hours of business of members of the Society; or
2    to regulate the wages and conditions of employment as between masters and their employees who were members of the Society; or
3    to regulate the prices at which members should sell their goods; or
4    to insure and to effect insurance of members of the Society against errors, neglect and misconduct of employees, and against fire, burglary, damage to plate glass and generally against insurable risks.

[1921] 1 Ch 392, *Pharm J* 23 October 1920 p.386 and 30 October 1920 p.405.

Comment: As a result of this decision a separate body, the Retail Pharmacists' Union (later called the National Pharmaceutical Association) was established to carry out various functions including those denied to the Society. No action was taken by the Society to carry on any of the other activities which had been proposed for the Industrial Council and which had not been declared to be outside the Society's powers. They were:

1    the provision and maintenance of an employment register and a register of unsatisfactory employees;
2    the auditing of accounts, the collection of debts, and the taking of stock for its members;
3    the provision and supply of information to the commercial standing of persons and firms with whom members of the Society wish to transact business; and
4    the provision of legal advice to members.

In the Supplemental Charter of 1953 (see Chapter 19) the objects of the Society were amended. The wording *the protection of those who carry on the business of chemists and druggists* was replaced by *to maintain the honour and safeguard and promote the interests of the members in the exercise of the profession of pharmacy.*

In the *Dickson* case (see below) reference was made to the decision in the *Jenkin* case to the change of emphasis in the chartered objects of the Society from *business* to *profession*.

### Pharmaceutical Society of Great Britain v. Dickson (1968)

This was an appeal by the Society to the House of Lords against an Order of the Court of Appeal ([1967] All ER 558; *Pharm J* 4 February 1967 p.113), which upheld a judgment of the High Court (Chancery Division) ([1966] 3 All ER 404; *Pharm J* 2 July 1966 p.22).

The background to the case was as follows. Arising out of a recommendation of the Report on the General Practice of Pharmacy (*Pharm J* 20 April 1963) a motion was put to the Annual General Meeting of the Pharmaceutical Society in 1965 in the following terms:

'New pharmacies should be situated only in premises which are physically distinct, and should be devoted solely to:

(i) professional services, as defined,
(ii) non-professional services, as defined . . . and
(iii) such other services as may be approved by the Council; and the range of services as may be approved by the Council; and the range of services in existing pharmacies, or in pharmacy departments of larger establishments should not be extended beyond the present limits except as approved by the Council.'

Owing to the large attendance at the Annual General Meeting no vote could be taken and a special general meeting to consider the recommendation was held at the Royal Albert Hall on 25 July 1965. Mr R. C. M. Dickson (a director of Boots Pure Drug Co. Ltd) sought an injunction to restrain the holding of the meeting. He also claimed that the motion:

1    was outside the scope of the Society's powers; and
2    if implemented, would be a restraint upon trade.

Application for an injunction was refused by the High Court an undertaking being given by the Society that the motion would not be made effective until after the judgment in the action to determine whether or not the object of the motion was within the Society's powers. At the Albert Hall meeting a motion supporting the recommendation was passed by 5020 votes to 1336.

The order of the High Court declared:

'That it is not within the powers, purposes or objects of the Pharmaceutical Society of Great Britain . . . to enforce or carry out or attempt to enforce or carry out the provisions of the motion . . . on the ground that the said provisions are in restraint of trade.'

The Court of Appeal dismissed an appeal by the Society against the order. On further appeal to the House of Lords the order given by the High Court was affirmed. It was held that:

1     The proposed restriction, although intended to be binding in honour only, might be a basis for disciplinary action. The Courts had the power and the duty to determine its validity.
2     It was not within the powers or purposes of the Society to control selling activities which did not interfere with the proper performance of professional pharmaceutical duties. The only relevant object in the Society's Charter was 'To maintain the honour and safeguard and protect the interests of the members in their exercise of the profession of pharmacy', and the proposed rules of conduct had too slender a connection or link with that object.
3     The proposed restrictions were beyond the powers of the Society as they were in restraint of trade and had not been shown to be reasonable.

[1968] 2 All ER 686; *Pharm J* 1 June 1968 p.651.

Comment: This decision did not affect the Society's powers to regulate professional conduct in pharmacy (see Chapter 20).

## Substances Containing Poisons

### Pharmaceutical Society of Great Britain v. Piper and Co.*(1893)*

[1893] 1 QB 686; *Pharm J* 11 February 1893 p.656 and 18 February 1893 p.669.

### Pharmaceutical Society of Great Britain v. Delve *(1893)*

[1893] 1 QB 71; *Pharm J* 4 November 1893 p.378.

### Pharmaceutical Society of Great Britain v. Armson *(1894)*

[1894] 2 QB 720; *Pharm J* 28 April 1894 p.902.

Comment: These three cases concerned the interpretation of certain sections of the Pharmacy Act 1868 (now repealed). The principal point at issue was the meaning of the word *poison* as used in the Act. It was held by the High Court that a compound containing a poison, as well as the actual poison, was subject to the Act.

## The Meaning of 'sale by way of wholesale dealing'

### Oxford v. Sanger (1964)

The Pharmacy and Poisons Act 1933 (s.18) provided that poisons in Part I of the Poisons List could be lawfully sold only by authorised sellers of poisons. An exemption from this requirement was given in section 20(1) of the Act in respect of sales of poisons by way of wholesale dealing. Section 29 defined *sale by way of wholesale dealing* as 'sale to a person who buys for the purposes of selling again'.

Sanger Ltd (wholesalers) had on five occasions sold Part I poisons to a retail shopkeeper who had subsequently sold the poisons (tablets) to the public by retail. The shopkeeper was not an authorised seller of poisons.

The wholesaler was charged with selling Part I poisons contrary to section 18 of the Act. It was contended for the prosecution that the company could not claim the benefit of the exemption for wholesale dealing as the poison had been sold to a shopkeeper who could not lawfully sell again. The magistrate dismissed the information, and an appeal to the High Court against that decision was also dismissed.

It was held in the High Court that the word *lawfully* could not be read into the definition of *wholesale dealing*. Section 20 did not lay any duty upon a wholesaler to ascertain that the retailer to whom he sold was lawfully entitled to resell. If it was desired to control wholesalers, it could and must be done by rule.

[1965] 1 All ER 96; *Pharm J* 12 December 1964 p.599.

Comment: Rule 11 of the Poisons Rules made under the Poisons Act 1972 now requires wholesalers who sell Part I poisons to be satisfied that their shopkeeper customers who order such poisons are authorised sellers of poisons, or that they do not intend to sell the poisons by way of retail trade. The Medicines Act 1968 (s.61) provides for similar regulations to be made in respect of medicinal products (SI 1980 No.1923).

## The Meaning of 'shop'

### Greenwood v. Whelan (1966)

[1967] All ER 294; *Pharm J* 3 December 1966 p.575.

Comment: This case turned on the meaning of the word *shop* in the Pharmacy and Medicines Act 1941. In *Greenwood v. Whelan* the Lord Chief Justice, referring to the Shops Act 1950, pointed out that retail trade or business could be carried out in three different ways, firstly from a shop, secondly, from a place that is not a shop, e.g. a stall, and thirdly from a barrow or itinerant van, in a way where there is no fixed place. The stall in that case, notwithstanding the regularity of the business, the permanence of the site, and the type of the structure, was a *place not being a shop*. The 1941 Act was repealed by the Medicines Act 1968 which now refers to *premises* not *shops* (s.53). Medicinal products may only be sold from premises which the occupier can 'close so as to exclude the public' (see Chapter 6).

## Functions of the Statutory Committee

### Re Lawson *(1941)*

Mr Lawson's appeal against the direction of the Statutory Committee of the Pharmaceutical Society of Great Britain that his name should be removed from the Register of Pharmaceutical Chemists was dismissed. Extracts from this judgment and other appeal cases are given in Chapter 21.
[1941] 57 LT 315; *Pharm J* 22 February 1941 p.60.

## The Meaning of 'supervision'

### Roberts *v.* Littlewoods Mail Order Stores Ltd *(1943)*

The Pharmacy and Poisons Act 1933 (s.18) provided: '. . . it shall not be lawful for a person to sell any poison in Part I of the Poisons List unless . . . the sale is effected by, or under the supervision of, a registered pharmacist.' Similar wording is now in the Medicines Act (s.52) (see Chapter 5).

A sale of a Part I poison was made at the company's pharmacy to one of the Society's inspectors while the sole pharmacist was in a stockroom upstairs and unaware that the sale was being made by an unqualified assistant. The magistrates found that the sale, though not effected by the pharmacist, was effected sufficiently under his supervision. His actual presence was not reasonably required.

The decision was reversed in the High Court where it was held that the sale had not been supervised. Lord Caldecote said:

> '. . . the man who was upstairs might have been a person who was exercising personal control of a business, but I do not think that, while he was upstairs and therefore absent, he could be a person who was supervising a particular sale. It has been suggested that a man can supervise a sale without being bodily present. I do not accept that contention . . . each individual sale must be, not necessarily effected by the qualified person, but something which is shown by the evidence to be under his supervision in the sense that he must be aware of what is going on at the counter, and in a position to supervise or superintend the activities of the young woman by whom each individual sale is effected.'

[1943] 1 All ER 271; *Pharm J* 30 January 1943 p.38.

## Pharmaceutical Society of Great Britain v. Boots
## Cash Chemists (Southern) Ltd *(1953)*

This was a case arising under the Pharmacy and Poisons Act 1933 (s.18) (see also *Roberts* v. *Littlewoods Mail Order Stores Ltd*, above). It was an appeal by the Pharmaceutical Society against a judgment of the Lord Chief Justice in the High Court.

A Boots pharmacy was arranged on a 'self-service' system. A customer could select goods, including Part I poisons, from the shelves, place them in a wire basket and take them to the cash desk. Before the cashier accepted payment a pharmacist at the cash desk could, if he thought fit, prevent a sale. It was suggested by the Society that a purchase was completed when a customer took an article and put it in the basket so that the pharmacist could not later intervene. That suggestion had not been accepted in the High Court by the Lord Chief Justice, who had said that self-service was no different from the normal transactions in a shop. He had continued:

'. . . the mere fact that a customer picks up a bottle of medicine from the shelves in this case does not amount to an acceptance of an offer to sell. It is an offer by the customer to buy . . . By using the words the sale is effected by, or under the supervision of, a registered pharmacist, it seems to me the sale might be effected by somebody not a pharmacist. If it be under the supervision of a pharmacist, the pharmacist can say: "You cannot have that. That contains poison". In this case I decide . . . that there is no sale until the buyer's offer to buy is accepted by the acceptance of the money, and that takes place under the supervision of a pharmacist . . .'

The Court of Appeal upheld this decision and dismissed the appeal by the Society.
[1953] 1 All ER 482; *Pharm J* 14 February 1953 p.115.


## R v. Family Health Services Appeal Authority,
## ex parte Elmfield Drugs Ltd, Selles Dispensing
## Chemists Ltd, and E Moss (Chemists) Ltd *(1998)*

The Pharmacy companies appealed against a judicial review judgment that three health authorities were correct in allowing dispensing contracts to doctors who intended to delegate dispensing of medicines to their staff. The case was based on the wording of s.55(1)(a) of the Medicines Act 1968 which reads:

'The restrictions imposed by s.52 (supervision) do not apply to the sale or offer for sale of a medicinal product:

(a)    *by a doctor or dentist to a patient of his . . .*'

The companies contended that that the words meant that the exemption for a doctor required the doctor to sell or supply the medicinal product **personally** and did not authorise him to delegate the sale or supply to another person. The state maintained that applying the general principles of agency and the normal principles of construction there was no requirement for the doctor to hand over medicines to his patients personally.

At the earlier hearing for judicial review the companies failed to convince the judges of their argument and Owen J said:

> 'I have no hesitation in finding that if Parliament had intended doctors to be guilty of an offence in the factual situation described by the pharmacists it would have said so.'
>
> (*Pharm J* 18 October 1997 p.634).

In dismissing the appeal Stuart-Smith LJ said:

> 'Whatever the reason I can see no basis for imposing a far stricter regime on doctors who *ex hypothesi* have prescribed or ordered medicine for their patients, by requiring them not merely to supervise the supply, as in the case of pharmacists, but actually to perform the mechanical act of delivery in person.'

The judge agreed with counsel for the respondents that the solution to the problem was to be found in the general principles of agency and the ordinary principles of statutory construction. i.e. '. . . *prima facie what a person can do himself he can do by an agent.*'
*Pharm J* 1 August 1998 p.146, *The Times* 16 September 1998.

Comment: The judge said that if he had ruled in favour of the pharmacy companies he would have been making doctors criminals. It would have been criminalising something that has been widely adopted, particularly in rural areas, for many years.

## Use of Titles and Descriptions

### Norris v. Weeks (1970)

The Pharmacy Act 1954 (s.19) read: 'it shall not be lawful for any person, unless he is a registered pharmaceutical chemist . . . (b) to take or use, in connection with the sale of goods by retail, the title of chemist.'

A notice, about 1 ft high × 2.5 ft wide was displayed at Mr Weeks' drug store over goods intended for retail sale. It bore the wording on three lines, *Wyn's/Chemist/Sundries*. The word 'chemist' was in larger script than the other words and in a different colour. The magistrate dismissed a summons under section 19(1)(b) on the ground that, having regard to the articles displayed, the word *chemist* was merely descriptive of the type of goods sold.

The High Court dismissed an appeal against this decision. It was held that an offence is committed only if a person asserts that they are a chemist or takes to themself the title 'chemist'. It could not be said that an offence is committed whenever the word 'chemist' appears.
*Pharm J* 14 March 1970 p.268; *The Times* 6 March 1970.

## Definitions of 'a sample'

### Mistry v. Norris (1985)

This case concerned the sale of a bottle of medicine containing Phenobarbitone without the authority of a prescription issued by a medical practitioner, as required by the Medicines Act 1968 (s.58). The appellant argued that, as the sale had been made to an enforcement officer under the Act, it was a sample subject to section 112. Therefore, the evidence of analysis of the contents of the medicine was not admissible as the mixture had not been divided, and a portion left with the appellant, in accordance with the sampling requirements under the Act.

The appeal was dismissed by the High Court. It was held that the inspector was not acting as a sampling officer but making an ordinary purchase as any member of the public has the right to do.

*The Times* 16 October 1985 p.27.

## Sale of Prescription Only Medicines – Offence of Strict Liability

### Pharmaceutical Society of Great Britain v. Storkwain Ltd (1986)

Section 58 of the Medicines Act 1968 provides for orders to be made specifying those medicinal products which may only be sold by retail in accordance with the prescription of an appropriate practitioner. Storkwain Ltd supplied quantities of Physeptone ampoules, Ritalin tablets and Valium tablets, all of which are Prescription Only Medicines, on the authority of two 'prescriptions' which were, in fact, forgeries. In 1984 the Pharmaceutical Society prosecuted the company for unlawfully selling those medicines contrary to section 58(2)(a) of the Act. It was submitted for Storkwain Ltd that they were unaware that the 'prescriptions' were not genuine. In the absence of any guilty knowledge (*mens rea*) of the forgeries on the part of the company the magistrates dismissed the charges. The Society successfully appealed to the Court of Appeal who held that an offence under section 58(2)(a) was one of strict liability and directed the magistrates to convict.

On further appeal by Storkwain Ltd, the House of Lords confirmed the decision of the Court of Appeal. It was held that guilty knowledge (*mens rea*) was a required ingredient of offences under certain sections of the Act, but section 58 was not one of those sections. That view was supported by the construction of section 58(4) and (5) and by section 121. The wording of the Prescriptions Only Order also conformed with that construction of the statute. An offence under section 58(2)(a) is, therefore, one of strict liability.

[1986] 2 All ER 635; *Pharm J* 28 June 1986 p.829.

## Is Dispensing a Medicine on a National Health Service Prescription a 'sale'?

### Appleby v. Sleep *(1968)*

A woman obtained a National Health Service prescription for Penidural syrup and took it to the pharmacy for dispensing. A few days later she found a sliver of glass in the medicine. The pharmacy was charged with selling a medicine not of the quality demanded under the Food and Drugs Act 1955. The magistrates dismissed the case and ruled there was no *sale*. The Executive Council appealed to the High Court.

In dismissing the appeal Lord Parker CJ said that:

> 'In *Pfizer Corporation v. Ministry of Health* [1965] AC 512 it was held that there was no *sale* of a medicine to a person presenting a National Health Service prescription and that was clearly the case because, even if there was a prescription charge, the patient was not paying for the medicine itself. The sole question was whether the contract between the pharmacy and the Executive Council was a contract of sale. A chemist . . . undertook to perform services . . . for those services he was remunerated by the Executive Council . . . not only a sum to cover the basic price of the medicine but for his general services . . . the property did not pass to the Executive Council and it was not a contract of sale . . .'

[1968] 2 All ER 265.

Comment: The provisions of the Food and Drugs Act 1955 as they applied to medicines have since been replaced by similar provisions in the Medicines Act 1968 (s.64) (see p.6).

## Importation of Medicinal Products from the European Community

### R v. Royal Pharmaceutical Society of Great Britain, ex parte Association of Pharmaceutical Importers and Others *(1989)*

The Society had adopted a provision in its Code of Ethics which, amongst other things, prohibited a pharmacist from substituting, except in an emergency, any other medicine for the medicine specifically ordered on a prescription, even if he believed that the quality and therapeutic effect were identical. In 1986 the Society had published a statement to the effect that this rule applied to imported medicines as well as to UK-licensed medicines. The Association, who represented companies who were involved in importing medicines from the European Community, maintained that the Society's rule infringed the provisions of the Treaty of Rome on the basis that its effect was to impose a quantitative restriction on their importing medicines – *parallel imports* – from the Community.

The European Court of Justice held that in the absence of any Community legislation regulating the doctor/pharmacist relationship, and in particular the doctor's freedom to prescribe any medicine he chose, it was for each member state to decide, within the limits of the Treaty, the degree to which they wish to protect the health of their people and how that was to be achieved. It was said that there was no evidence that the Society's rule went beyond what was necessary to achieve the objective, which was to leave the entire responsibility for the treatment of the patient in the hands of the doctor treating him/her. It followed therefore that the rule could also be justified under the Treaty on the grounds of the protection of public health.

[1989] 2 All ER 758; *Pharm J* 27 May 1989 p.613.

## Sale of Prescription Data – Breach of Confidentiality?

### R v. Department of Health, ex parte Source Informatics Ltd (2000)

Source Informatics Ltd proposed a scheme whereby after they, Source Informatics, had obtained the prescribers' consent, pharmacists, for a fee, would supply anonymised information contained on National Health Service prescriptions for the purposes of market research. The Department of Health in a policy document entitled *The Protection and Use of Patient Information* had made clear that under common law and the Data Protection Act principles the general rule was that information given in confidence may not be disclosed without the consent of the provider of the information, i.e. doctor or pharmacist. It also stated that anonymisation, with or without aggregation did not remove the duty of confidence towards patients who are the subject of the data, namely details on their prescriptions written by the doctor and dispensed by the pharmacist. The High Court ([1999] 4 All ER 185) agreed with the Department of Health. The Court of Appeal on judicial review reversed the decision and Simon Brown LJ said:

> '. . . the patient has no proprietorial claim to the prescription form or to the information it contains. . . [he has] no right to control its use provided only and always that his privacy is not put at risk . . .'

He concluded by saying:

> 'Participation in Source's scheme by doctors and the pharmacists would not in my judgment expose them to any serious risk of successful breach of confidence proceedings by a patient.'

*The Times* 18 January 2000.

Comment: This case was not appealed and it would seem that the Data Protection Act does not normally cover data which have been anonymised, i.e. detached from any details which could identify a living individual.

## Further Reading

*Dale and Appelbe's Pharmacy Law and Ethics*. London: The Pharmaceutical Press.
    (Other pharmaceutical cases of historical interest are outlined in earlier editions.)

# CHAPTER TWENTY-SEVEN

# Hospitals, Trusts and Health Authorities

With the removal of Crown immunity from the National Health Service hospitals in April 1991 the major statutes concerning medicines (including Controlled Drugs) and related matters now apply to National Health Service hospitals as well to hospitals and nursing homes that are privately owned.

Similarly, as a consequence of the change in overall structure of the National Health Service, hospitals have had to redefine the legal position under which the main statutes apply to them and the formal contracting between Trusts for the cross-boundary supply of services.

In addition, it is now relatively common for a hospital or Trust to register the hospital dispensary or pharmacy department with the Royal Pharmaceutical Society as a *registered pharmacy* (see Chapter 4), thus enabling it to engage in over-the-counter sales and a limited amount of wholesale dealing (licence exempted, see Chapter 9).

Trusts now relate directly to the National Health Service Executive and are legally responsible for the activities they manage. Litigation against Trusts and Health Authorities is increasing and it is important that pharmacists employed in these sectors of pharmacy understand not only the legislation but also the criteria against which accepted standards of care may be judged.

The common law principles of negligence and contributory negligence (see p.233) and the concepts of professional responsibility also apply to these pharmacists, who should be aware of the differences between managerial responsibility (master/servant relationship) and professional responsibility.

In National Health Service hospitals the statutory provisions are often supplemented by the recommendations of a number of Official Reports and by advice in notes and circulars issued mainly by the Department of Health and Social Security or the National Health Service Management Executive. These are listed under the various headings in this chapter.

## Misuse of Drugs Act 1971

(See Chapter 16.)

The reports and the circulars quoted below give additional advice on the ordering and transportation of Controlled Drugs in hospitals; supply to hospitals without a pharmacist; the keeping of records; the destruction and security of Controlled Drugs and all drugs likely to be misused or abused.

The Aitken Report recommended that the sister or acting sister in charge of a ward, theatre or other department of a hospital or nursing home should keep a register. Although it is not a requirement of the Misuse of Drugs Regulations, the keeping of records is contained in the general nursing policy recommendations within the National Health Service and the accreditation of units for training under the UKCC would be withheld if records were not kept.

Destruction of ward stocks of Controlled Drugs can be carried out in the ward by the 'sister in charge' but, in his/her own interest, it is advisable that such destruction be witnessed, preferably by a pharmacist.

The *sister or acting sister in charge* (because there are now a significant number of male nurses, the term more commonly used is that of *charge nurse*) is the person appointed in that capacity by the employing authority and there is no requirement that s/he should have any specific qualification. In practice, of course, a sister normally has a nursing qualification and the Gillie Report recommended that, if an Enrolled Nurse were appointed as sister in charge, then the hospital authorities should ensure that s/he has received instructions and is proficient in such duties.

Controlled Drugs in a theatre are the responsibility of the sister in charge and operating department assistants (ODAs) have no authority to possess Controlled Drugs.

Documents

*The Aitken Report 1958: Control of Dangerous Drugs and Poisons in Hospitals*

Joint Sub-Committee of the Standing Medical, Nursing, and Pharmaceutical Advisory Committees.

*The Gillie Report 1970: Measures for Controlled Drugs on the Wards*

Joint Sub-Committee of the Standing Medical, Nursing, and Pharmaceutical Advisory Committees.

*The Misuse of Drugs Regulations 1973, as amended, the Misuse of Drugs (Safe Custody) Regulations 1973, as amended, and Security of Drugs Liable to Misuse*
HC(77)16, May 1977.

*Guide to the Misuse of Drugs Act 1971 and to certain Regulations made under the Act*
Department of Health, Welsh Office and SHHD (1989), ISBN1 85197 412 1.

*Misuse of Drugs Regulations 1985. Written authorities under Regulations 25(1) and 26(1) and confidential enquiries*
EL(91)62 NHS Management Executive, April 1991.

*Destruction of Controlled Drugs, as amended*
EL(97)22 NHS Executive.

## Medicines and the Medicines Act 1968

(See Chapters 1 to 15.)

The brief notes given here, under headings, indicate where advice on any particular subject appears. National Health Service documents are listed below. Hospital pharmacists should, of course, refer to the original documents for details.

### Manufacture

Guidelines are available from the Medicines Control Agency (MCA) concerning whether or not licences for manufacture and/or assembly are required (see p.31). The Medicines Inspectorate visit hospitals with a view to ensuring parity between standards of manufacture in hospitals and commercial manufacturers bearing in mind the requirements of the Medicines Act and the guidelines laid down in the Guide to Good Manufacturing Practice (see pp.19–20). The Medicines Control Agency gave specific guidance to hospitals on the licensing requirements in September 1992 and the Department of Health gave advice on aseptic dispensing under section 10 in 1994 (see p.376).

Hospitals undertaking manufacturing and/or assembly should seek a *specials licence* (see p.30) or rely on the exemption for pharmacists in section 10 of the Medicines Act (see p.26).

### Ordering of Medicines

The Aitken Report recommended that hospital pharmacists should be responsible for the ordering and storage of all medicines.

### Supply for Ward Stock

The Aitken and Roxburgh Reports dealt at some length with the question of ward stocks. The established practice is for each ward to have lists of medicines agreed with the pharmacist, usually a standard stock list, and a smaller special list of medicines peculiar to the work of the ward, e.g. cardiac ward.

The Aitken Report suggested that ward stock supplies should be obtained from the pharmacy on printed requisition forms signed by the sister in charge of the ward and this is a method still in use in some hospitals. In other hospitals a modified system, for which the pharmacist is responsible, has now been adopted. Requisitions for ward stock are completed by members of the pharmacy staff and running totals are kept to ensure adequate stock control. It is understood that some hospitals are now receiving direct supply to wards from outside the pharmacy department of the hospital.

### Prescriptions for Medicinal Products

For in-patients, most hospitals require that medicines should not be administered to a patient without a written authority from a doctor on the prescription sheet. The Aitken Report recommended that this should be standard practice.

### Patient Group Directions

The details of the use of Patient Group Directions is set out for pharmacists in Chapter 7 and for Health Bodies and other professionals in Chapter 8.

### Labelling

There is useful advice on labelling in the Aitken Report but the statutory provisions now apply (see Chapter 14 and below).

### Containers

Health authorities have been requested to arrange for solid dose preparations containing aspirin and paracetamol to be dispensed in reclosable child-resistant containers. On medicines for outpatients or discharge patients most hospitals follow the Royal Pharmaceutical Society's guidance and supply child-resistant containers with most medicines.

### Storage

The Aitken and Roxburgh Reports both recommended storage cupboards that should be lockable and the keys of which should be kept by the sister in charge of the ward. The siting of cupboards and refrigerated storage are also dealt with. The Gillie Report, in contrast to the Aitken Report, recommended, in addition to cupboards, the use of ward trolleys, subject to suitable safety precautions when they were not in use.

Documents

*The Roxburgh Report 1972 and 1979(GEN)11*
A report on 'Control of Medicines in Hospital Wards and Departments' (Scottish Home and Health Department).

*The Breckenbridge Report 1976*
The report on the addition of drugs to intravenous infusion fluids (HC(76)9 Department of Health).

*Application of the Medicines (Labelling) Regulations 1976 to Hospital Pharmaceutical Departments*
HN (76)205, November 1976.

*Duthie Report 1988: Guidelines for the Safe and Secure Handling of Medicines*
Joint Sub-Committee of the Standing Medical, Nursing and Midwifery, and Pharmaceutical Advisory Committees.

*Guidance to the NHS on the Licensing Requirements of the Medicines Act 1968*
Medicines Control Agency, September 1992.

*Parenteral administration of Prescription Only Medicines (POMs) by extended trained ambulance paramedics*
HSG(93)33 NHS Management Executive, July 1993.

*Aseptic Dispensing in NHS Hospitals*
PL/CPhO(96)2 and EL(96)95 NHS Executive.

*The Supply of Unlicensed Relevant Medicinal Products for Individual Patients – Specials*
Medicines Control Agency, February 2000.

*Patient Group Directions (England Only)*
HSC 2000/026.


### Supply of Medicines to Hospital Staff

Supply of medicines to hospital staff, including medical staff, is governed by circulars issued by the Department of Health (or its former equivalent). These include:

Documents

*Hospital Staff – Prescription Charges*
HN (56) 86, October 1956.

*Prescription forms EC10 (HP)*
HN (64) 74, September 1964.

*Irregularities in the Use of Prescription Forms EC10 (HP)*
G/P72/2C, December 1967, as amended.

These circulars in effect stated that members of hospital staff should obtain any drugs they need for their own treatment or their families in the same way as other members of the public. Hospital authorities are reminded that if drugs from the hospital need to be supplied on hospital premises as part of immediate treatment to staff who sustain an accident or who become ill on duty then no charge should be made.

Hospital medical staff who prescribe for themselves should be asked to pay the full cost of the drugs unless the hospital authority is satisfied that they are obtained to cover emergency illness.

## Poisons Act 1972

(See Chapters 17 and 18.)

Most hospitals will deal with poisons and hazardous substances. Details are set out in Chapters 17 and 18 and in the National Health Service document below.

DOCUMENT
*Poisons: Supply and Storage in Health Service Premises*
   HN (78)21, February 1978.

## Health and Safety at Work etc. Act 1974

The practical effect for hospital pharmacists is that the Chemical (Hazard Information and Packaging for Supply) Regulations (CHIP) and the Control of Substances Hazardous to Health Regulations (COSHH) made under the Act (see Chapter 18) apply to persons in the public service of the Crown in addition to the general provisions of the Act (see Chapter 25). Earlier advice drew the attention of Health Authorities in England and Wales and Health Boards in Scotland to the need for policy statements to be prepared in the knowledge that the legal requirements are binding on health authorities.

## Security

The National Association of Health Authorities and Trusts has issued a manual giving guidelines to Health Authorities and Trusts regarding the security of equipment, medicines and premises and to develop a security strategy. It also covers, amongst other matters, the return of medicines for destruction (NHS Security Manual, Chapter 9).

DOCUMENT
*NHS Security Manual, 1992*
   National Association of Health Authorities and Trusts.

**Miscellaneous**

Attention is drawn to other aspects of law and practice of which hospital pharmacists should be mindful. These include legislation affecting employment and consumer protection (Chapter 25), disposal of special waste including medicines (Chapter 25), spirits and methylated spirits (Chapter 24), data protection and access to health records plus employment legislation (Chapter 25) and dangerous substances and preparations (Chapter 18). Professional conduct is dealt with in Chapters 20 and 21.

DOCUMENTS

*Implementation of New Complaints Procedures*
  EL(96)19 NHS Management Executive.

*Disability Discrimination Act: Implications for NHS Trusts and Authorities*
  EL(96) 70 NHS Executive.

*Implementing s.21 of the Disability Discrimination Act 1995 Across the NHS*
  HSC 1999/156.

*Data Protection Act*
  HSC 2000/009.

*Continuing Professional Development: Quality in the New NHS*
  HSC 1999/154.

*Management and Control of Hospital Infection*
  HSC 2000/002.

*NHS Direct and Primary Care – Liability Issues*
  HSC 1999/235.

*The Public Interest Disclosure Act 1998*
  HSC 1999/198.

*Legislation – Human Rights Act, Working Time regulations, Maternity Leave, etc*
  HSC 2000/05.

*Statement of Principles and Standards of Good Practice for Hospital Pharmacy*
  in *Medicines, Ethics and Practice* Royal Pharmaceutical Society of Great Britain, July 2000.

# CHAPTER TWENTY-EIGHT

# The European Community

In 1957 six member states signed the Treaty of Rome which established the European Economic Community – now the European Union. The United Kingdom acceded to the Treaty in 1973, along with Denmark and Ireland; Greece acceded in 1981 and Portugal and Spain followed in 1986. With the addition of Sweden, Finland and Austria in 1996 the number of member states is now 15.

The Single European Act 1987 was designed to expedite a single internal market and to remove all the remaining barriers which exist to the free movement of people, goods, services, and capital. It is the object of the Community to ensure that there is no impediment to these 'four freedoms' and, if there is, to remove it. Harmonisation is one method by which such obstacles can be overcome and this is shown in many of the Directives which have affected the production and distribution of pharmaceuticals.

## European Law

The primary source of Community law is the Treaty of Rome. The legislation implementing the Treaty is formulated by the Council of Ministers in four basic forms:

1   *Regulations*. These have a direct effect and are binding on all member states and on individuals.

2   *Directives*. These are binding as to their objectives but leave to member states the method of implementation. Such implementation may be legislative or administrative.
3   *Decisions*. These are binding on those to whom they are addressed and are often of an administrative nature.
4   *Recommendations*. These are self-evident.

Most of the current United Kingdom law which applies to pharmacy practice derives from European legislation in the form of *Directives* although recently *regulations* have been made concerning the marketing authorisation of medicinal products (see p.14).

## The Institutions

There are five main institutions of the Community.

### The Council of Ministers

This is composed of representatives of each member state and in practice the Minister attending changes according to the item under discussion. The Council is supported by working parties which include civil servants from each state and which study proposals put forward by the Council or the Commission. The working party reports are sent to the Committee of Permanent Representatives (COREPER), which makes the decision whether or not to put the proposal forward to a Council meeting.

### The Commission

This comprises 20 Commissioners, each with responsibilities for a particular area of interest, e.g. agriculture, internal affairs, environment, etc. It has been called the Civil Service of the Community and proposes, executes, and polices the policies of the Community as promulgated by the Council. Discussions between a Commissioner's department and interested parties can lead to the formation of draft proposals. These are discussed by the Commission as a whole which then decides on the form of any final proposal to be laid before the Council.

### The Parliament

This is a directly elected chamber of members from the 15 states; member state representation is related directly to population size. It has three main functions: control over the Community's budget, power of censure over the Commission, and scrutiny of the legislative process. The latter function has been of importance in the promulgation of Directives affecting pharmacy upon which the Parliament must be consulted. The detailed work is done by Standing Committees who have a *rapporteur*, responsible for preparing the draft response of the Committee and presenting it to the plenary session of the Parliament.

## The Economic and Social Committee

This comprises representatives of economic and social groups in the member states. It is divided into three groups: employers, workers (trade unions), and a variety of interest groups which includes the professions. The Committee has to be consulted before any final decision can be taken on proposed legislation. The work is mainly done in various specialist sections, e.g. agriculture, transport, etc. Within each section there are study groups which deal with specific proposals. The section produces an Opinion which is presented to a plenary session of the Committee before being forwarded to the Council.

## The European Court of Justice

This settles legal disputes involving Community legislation and its judgments are binding on each member state. Much of its work now involves giving preliminary rulings on questions referred by the courts of the member states. An example was a case involving the parallel importation of medicinal products (*R* v. *Royal Pharmaceutical Society of Great Britain, ex parte Association of Parallel Importers and Others* (see p.370)).

## Free Movement of Pharmacists

### Council Directives 85/432/EEC and 85/433/EEC

In 1985 the Council of Ministers introduced two Directives concerned with the free movement of pharmacists. Directive 85/432/EEC dealt with the education and training of the pharmacist and Directive 85/433/EEC dealt with a pharmacist's right to establishment within the member states. Each member state is obliged to recognise, without impediment, the list of degrees (or equivalent) laid down in the Directives. Registration as a pharmaceutical chemist in the United Kingdom is recognised. The competent authorities within the member states deal with the procedure and those authorities in the United Kingdom are the Royal Pharmaceutical Society of Great Britain and its equivalent in Northern Ireland.

In order for a pharmacist to move freely throughout the Community s/he must produce evidence from his/her own competent authority to the corresponding one in the host member state that s/he:

1　is a national of a member state of the Community or treated as such;

2　(a)　possesses a university degree (or equivalent) which was obtained following a course of study of not less than five years, at least four years of which comprised theoretical and practical training in a university, together with at least six months in-service training in a community or hospital pharmacy; or

(b)  has for at least three consecutive years during the previous five years been effectively and lawfully engaged in regulated pharmaceutical activity, e.g. a community pharmacy, hospital pharmacy, etc. This is known as the *acquired rights* provision for those who cannot comply with (a) above.

and, where required in the host member state:

3    is in good physical and mental health; and
4    is of good character.

The pharmacy degrees in the United Kingdom together with the pre-registration year and the 'A'-level at university entrance are considered to be equivalent to the total five-year requirement.

The Directives have been implemented in Great Britain by means of the Pharmaceutical Qualifications (European Community) Order 1987 (SI 1987 No.2202, as amended) and by section XIX(5) of the bye-laws of the Royal Pharmaceutical Society of Great Britain (see pp.482–483 and Appendix 14). Pharmacists seeking free movement should contact the Society.

In addition to the two Directives, an accompanying Decision established an Advisory Committee on Pharmaceutical Training whose task is 'to help to ensure a comparably high standard of pharmaceutical training in the Community' (Decision 85/434/EEC).

## Production and Distribution of Medicinal Products for Human Use

Council Regulation 2309/93/EEC laid down Community procedures for the authorisation and supervision of medicinal products for human and veterinary use and established the European Agency for the Evaluation of Medicinal Products (EMEA).

Directive 65/65/EEC states that the primary purpose of controls on the production and distribution of medicinal products is to safeguard public health. A number of amending Directives have been issued, but the 'parent' Directive is that of 1965. This Directive defined a medicinal product and established that before a medicine could be put on the market it must possess a licence or marketing authorisation which had been granted on the basis of safety, quality, and efficacy. In addition, the Directive covered the labelling of medicines.

The amending Directives are:

1    *Directive 75/319/EEC* established the Committee for Proprietary Medicinal Products (CPMP) which is responsible for giving opinions as

to whether a medicinal product complies with the provisions of Directive 65/65/EEC, as amended. It also created the position of the 'qualified person' who, with minimum conditions of qualifications, is responsible for the supervision and control of the manufacture of medicinal products. This Directive exempted vaccine and sera, blood products, radiopharmaceuticals, and homoeopathic medicines from control (see below).

2  *Directive 83/570/EEC* introduced an increased number of product characteristics which had to be included in any application for a marketing authorisation and stated that such an authorisation was valid for five years.

3  *Directive 87/21/EEC* added further amendments to the requirements for application of marketing authorisations.

4  *Directive 89/341/EEC,* together with other amendments, introduced the legal requirement for a manufacturer to comply with the principles and guidelines of Good Manufacturing Practice (GMP). Indeed, the Commission issued a Directive in 1991 laying down the principles and guidelines of Good Manufacturing Practice (Directive 91/356/EEC).

5  *Directive 89/342/EEC* made the provisions of Directive 65/65/EEC, as amended, applicable to vaccines, toxins, and sera.

6  *Directive 89/343/EEC* made the provisions of Directive 65/65/EEC, as amended, applicable to radiopharmaceuticals.

7  *Directive 89/381/EEC* made the provisions of Directive 65/65/EEC, as amended, applicable to medicinal products derived from human blood and human plasma.

8  *Directive 93/39/EEC* made further amendments to Directives 65/65/EEC, 75/318/EEC and 75/319/EEC.

9  *Directive 91/356/EEC* lays down the principles and guidelines for Good Manufacturing Practice for medicinal products.

10  *Directive 92/26/EEC* sets out the requirements for the classification of medicinal products for human use and lays down the criteria for those medicinal products whose supply should only be available against a medical prescription.

In 1975 the Pharmaceutical Committee, comprising *senior experts in public health matters,* was set up to examine questions relating to the application of the Directives on medicinal products and is consulted on such matters by the Commission (Decision 75/320/EEC).

Council Regulation 2309/93/EEC, Directive 65/65/EEC and all the amendments have been implemented in the United Kingdom under the provisions of the Medicines Act (see Chapter 2 and Appendices 1–9).

## Analytical, Toxicological and Clinical Standards for Medicines for Human Use

Directive 75/318/EEC set up standards and protocols for the analysis, and toxicological and pharmacological tests which had to be applied to medicinal products. The Directive also covered the conduct of clinical trials. It has been amended by Directives 83/570/EEC, 87/19/EEC and 91/507/EEC. All have been incorporated into United Kingdom legislation under the Medicines Act.

## High Technology Medicinal Products for Human and Animal Use

Directive 93/41/EEC repealed Directive 87/22/EEC and set up procedures to deal with applications for marketing authorisations involving high technology medicinal products, in particular those derived from biotechnology.

## Homoeopathic Medicinal Products

Directive 92/73/EEC amends Directives 65/65/EEC and 75/319/EEC and is concerned with the authorisation for marketing and the labelling of homoeopathic medicinal products for human use. It also provides for a special simplified registration procedure for those traditional homoeopathic medicinal products which are placed on the market without therapeutic indications in a pharmaceutical form and dosage which do not present a risk to the public.

Directive 92/74/EEC is the companion to Directive 92/73/EEC and relates to homoeopathic medicinal products for veterinary use. United Kingdom legislation implementing both these Directives came into force in 1994 (see Chapter 2).

## Advertising, Labelling and Leaflets

Directive 92/27/EEC deals with the labelling of medicinal products and the availability of package leaflets aimed at the public. It requires that 'information supplied to users should provide a high degree of consumer protection in order that medicinal products may be used correctly on the basis of full and comprehensible information'. This was implemented in the United Kingdom on 1 January 1994 (see Chapter 14).

Directive 92/28/EEC deals with the advertising of medicinal products for human use both to the general public and to health professionals. It also deals with the question of hospitality related to sales promotion, samples, medical representatives, etc. (see Chapter 3).

## Wholesale Distribution

Directive 92/25/EEC covers the control of wholesale distribution of medicinal products for human use in the European Community. It requires that such distribution should be subject to the possession of an authorisation to engage in the activity as a wholesaler in medicinal products and lays down the conditions for such an authorisation. Such activity is subject to licensing in the United Kingdom (see Chapter 9).

## Colouring of Medicinal Products

Directive 78/25/EEC controls the colouring agents which can, and those which cannot, be added to medicinal products.

## Production of Medicinal Products for Animal Use

Directive 81/851/EEC established provisions for marketing authorisations for medicinal products for animal use and created the Committee on Veterinary Medicinal Products (CVMP). It has been amended by Directives 90/676/EEC and 90/677/EEC.

Directive 91/412/EEC introduced a legal requirement for a manufacturer of medicinal products for animal use to comply with the principles and guidelines of Good Manufacturing Practice.

Directive 81/852/EEC set up standards and protocols for the analysis, and toxicological tests which had to be applied to medicinal products for animal use. It has been amended by Directives 87/20/EEC and 92/18/EEC which extended its application to biological products such as vaccines.

Regulation 90/2377/EEC lays down procedures to establish maximum residue limits for animal medicines in foodstuffs of animal origin.

All these Directives have been implemented in the United Kingdom under the Medicines Act.

## Data Protection

Council Directive 95/46/EEC extends data protection to all data maintained manually and effect the way in which patient medication records are stored. This Directive was implemented in the United Kingdom by way of the Data Protection Act 1998 which came into force on 1 March 2000. All data, both electronic and manual, are now controlled under the 1998 Act (see p.352).

## The Future

### Medicinal Products: Human and Animal

In 1996 the Commission produced documents for the recasting and consolidation of the Directives in the pharmaceutical field, both for human and animal medicines namely:

1    *Codifying and Recasting Community Legislation – Animal Use.* Working document of the Commission Services, April 1996.
2    *Recasting of the Community Pharmaceutical Legislation – Human Section.* Working document of the Commission Services, October 1996.

Both documents aimed to be a consolidation exercise but minor amendments were being considered and areas where there was ambiguity were being clarified. It is understood that these recasting documents have been withdrawn and a simple consolidation will take place sometime in the future. At the time of going to press no further information was available.

## Further Reading

Louis, Jean-V. *The Community Legal Order.* Luxembourg: Office for Official Publications of the European Communities.
*Rules Governing Medicinal Products for Human Use in the European Community* vol. 1. The Stationery Office.
*Rules Governing Medicinal Products for Animal Use in the European Community* vol. Va. The Stationery Office.

# Medicines Act 1968

# Medicinal Products

Various articles and substances are treated as medicinal products (see Chapter 1) by virtue of orders made under the Act, as follows:

## Section 104(1) Orders

Orders made under section 104(1) of the Act can extend the application of specified provisions of the Act to articles and substances which are not medicinal products as defined in section 130 of the Act but which are manufactured, sold, supplied, imported or exported for use wholly or partly for a medical purpose. Two orders under this section are still extant:

1.  THE MEDICINES (RADIOACTIVE SUBSTANCES) ORDER 1978 (SI 1978 No.1004) extends the application of the provisions relating to the holding of licences to the following articles and substances:

    (a)  Interstitial and intracavity appliances (other than nuclear powered cardiac pacemakers) which contain or are to contain a radioactive substance sealed in a container (otherwise than solely for the purpose of storage, transport or disposal) or bonded solely within material and including the immediate container or bonding that are designed to be inserted into the human body or body cavities.

    (b)  Surface applicators, that is to say plates, plaques and ophthalmic applicators which contain or are to contain a radioactive substance sealed in a container (otherwise than solely for the purpose of storage, transport or disposal) or bonded solely within material and including the immediate container or bonding that is designed to be brought into contact with the human body.

(c)   Any apparatus capable of administering neutrons to human beings when the neutrons are administered in order to generate a radioactive substance in the person to whom they are administered for the purpose of diagnosis or research.

(d)   Other substances or articles (not being an instrument, apparatus or appliance) which consist of or contain or generate a radioactive substance and which:

(i) consist of or contain or generate that substance in order, when administered, to utilise the radiation emitted therefrom; and

(ii) are manufactured, sold or supplied for use wholly or mainly by being administered to one or more human beings solely by way of a test for ascertaining what effects it has when so administered.

The meaning of *administer* in relation to any apparatus in paragraph (c) above is modified to include the exposure of the body or any part of the body to the neutrons issued by the apparatus. The order also enables regulations to be made under section 60 prohibiting sale, supply and administration except by certain practitioners (see p.71).

2.   THE MEDICINES (CYANOGENETIC SUBSTANCES) ORDER 1984 (SI 1984 No.187) extends to *cyanogenetic substances* the application of those provisions of the Act relating to dealings with products (including sale, supply or importation), the packaging and promotion of products and miscellaneous and supplementary provisions. Licensing requirements are not applied.

*Cyanogenetic substances* means preparations which:

(a)   are presented for sale or supply under the name of, or as containing, amygdalin, laetrile or Vitamin B17; or

(b)   contain more than 0.1 per cent by weight of any substance having the formula either α-Cyanobenzyl-6-Oβ-D-glucopyrosol-D-glucopyranoside or α-Cyanobenzyl-Oβ-D-glucopyranosiduronic acid.

## Section 105(1)(a) Orders

Orders made under section 105(1)(a) of the Act extend the application of specified provisions of the Act to certain substances which are not medicinal products but which are used in the manufacture of medicinal products. Two orders under this section have been made:

1.   THE MEDICINES (CONTROL OF SUBSTANCES FOR MANUFACTURE) ORDER 1971 (SI 1971 No.1200) controls the substances set out below. The terms used are defined in detail in Schedule 2 (not here reproduced). The order makes those substances subject to certain provisions of the Act concerning the holding of licences and certificates; the regulation of dealings; offences and penalties; labelling, leaflets and containers; and certain miscellaneous matters. The substances affected, and the circumstances in which they are affected are as follows:

(a)   When manufactured, assembled, sold, supplied, imported or exported for use as an ingredient in a medicinal product *for parenteral injection* into human beings or animals, the following:

amphotericin B, bacitracin, capreomycin, colistin, erythromycin, gentamicin, heparin, hyaluronidase, kanamycin, neomycin, nystatin (added by SI 1985 No.1403), penicillin, polymyxin B, preparations of the pituitary (posterior lobe), streptomycin, the lincomycins, the rifamycins, the tetracyclines, vancomycin, viomycin.

(b)     When manufactured, assembled, sold, supplied, imported or exported for use as an ingredient in a medicinal product which is to be administered to human beings or animals by means *other than parenteral injection*, the following:

gentamicin\*, neomycin\*, nystatin\*, oxytetracycline, tetracycline.
(\* added by SI 1985 No.1403)

(c)     When manufactured, assembled, sold, supplied, imported or exported for use as ingredients of *dextran injection* for human or animal use, the following:

dextrans.

(d)     When manufactured, assembled, sold, supplied, imported or exported for use as an ingredient in a *medicinal product for human or animal use,* the following:

antigens, antisera, antitoxins, chorionic gonadotrophin, corticotrophin, follicle-stimulating hormone, insulin, sera, streptodornase, strepto-kinase, toxins, vaccines.

(e)     When manufactured, assembled, sold, supplied, imported or exported for use as an ingredient in a medicinal product *for human use,* the following:

preparations of blood.

(f)     When manufactured, assembled, sold, supplied, imported or exported for use as an ingredient in a medicinal product *for administration to animals,* the following:

plasma; any substances wholly or partly derived from animals not being substances specifically mentioned in any of the above paragraphs.

## Section 105(1)(b) and (2) Orders

Orders made under section 105(1)(b) and (2) of the Act extend the application of specified provisions of the Act to substances which, if used without proper safeguards, are capable of causing damage to the health of the community, or of causing danger to the health of animals generally or of one or more species of animals. One order has been made under this section:

THE MEDICINES (EXTENSION TO ANTIMICROBIAL SUBSTANCES) ORDER 1973 (SI 1973 No.367) extends certain specified provisions of the Act concerning such matters as the holding of licences; the provision of information; the commission of offences; the prohibition of sale, supply or importation; and the promotion of sales to the following classes of substances:

Substances which are not medicinal products, which are or contain:

(1)     any of the substances commonly known as *antibiotics* being:

(a)     substances synthesised by bacteria, fungi or protozoa which have antimicrobial properties, and derivatives of such substances possessing such properties;
(b)     substances which are synthesised in any other way and are identical with any substances described in sub-paragraph (a), of this paragraph;
(c)     any salt of any of the substances described in sub-paragraphs (a) and (b), of this paragraph;

(2)     any other substances *which possess antigenic properties* similar to the antigenic properties of any of the substances described in paragraph 1 above;

(3)   sulphanilamide (being *p*-aminobenzene sulphonamide) or any derivative of sulpha-nilamide which possesses antimicrobial properties, and any salt of any such sub-stance; or

(4)   any derivative of the *nitrofurans* which possesses antimicrobial properties, and any salt of any such derivative.

## European Communities Act 1972 Orders

Orders made under section 2 of the European Communities Act extend the application of certain provisions of the Act to other products not originally covered by Council Directive 65/65/EEC.

The Medicines 1968 (Amendment) Regulations 1992 (SI 1992 No.604) extend the scope of Council Directives 65/65/EEC and 75/319/EEC and makes licensable under the Act certain products for human use as follows:

(1)   immunological products;

(2)   medicinal products based on human blood or blood constituents; and

(3)   medicinal products based on radioactive isotopes (other than isotopes which are sealed sources).

APPENDIX TWO

# Medicines Act 1968

# Prohibition of Non-Medicinal

# Antimicrobial Substances

Antimicrobial substances were brought within the control of the Act by an order under section 105 (see Appendix 1).

The Medicines (Prohibition of Non-Medicinal Antimicrobial Substances) Order 1977 (SI 1977 No.2131) prohibits, subject to certain exceptions, the sale or supply of the antimicrobial substances set out below. The prohibition applies whether or not the substance is contained in any other substance or article, unless it is a medicinal product or an animal feeding stuff.

PROHIBITED SUBSTANCES

PART I

| | | |
|---|---|---|
| Amphomycin | Furazolidone | Oleandomycin |
| Bacitracin | Fusidic acid | Paromomycin |
| Candicidin | Griseofulvin | Spectinomycin |
| Capreomycin | Hachimycin | Spiramycin |
| Chloramphenicol | Nalidixic acid | Tylosin |
| Cycloserine | Nitrofurantoin | Vancomycin |
| Erythromycin | Nitrofurazone | Viomycin |
| Framycetin | Novobiocin | Virginiamycin |
| Furaltadone | Nystatin | |

N.B. In this Part:

(a)    a reference to any substance, other than furaltadone, shall be construed as a reference to the substance for which such name is shown in the current edition of the list of names prepared and published under section 100 of the Act; and

(b)    *furaltadone*    means    (±)-5-morpholino-methyl-3-(5-nitrofurylideneamino)-2-
      oxazolidine.

Part 2

| Class of substance | Meaning |
|---|---|
| Amphotericins | Antimicrobial substances or mixtures of such substances produced by *Streptomyces nodosus*. |
| Cephalosporins | Antimicrobial substances containing in their chemical structure a fused dihydrothiazine β-lactam nucleus. |
| Gentamicins | Any antimicrobial basic substance or mixture of such substances produced by the strain *Micromonospora purpurea* which on 1 September 1967 was numbered NRRL 2953 in the culture collection of the Northern Utilisation Research and Development Branch of the United States Department of Agriculture. |
| Kanamycins | Any antimicrobial substance or mixture of such substances produced by *Streptomyces kanamyceticus*. |
| Lincomycins | Antimicrobial substances produced by *Streptomyces lincolnensis* (var. *lincolnensis*). These substances are the basic amides of hygric acid or of a substituted hygric acid with 6-amino-6,8-dideoxy-1-thiogalacto-octopyranose or with substituted 6-amino-6,8-dideoxy-1-thiogalacto-octopyranose. |
| Neomycins | Antimicrobial substances or mixtures of such substances produced by *Streptomyces fradiae* which are complex organic bases and which yield on hydrolysis with mineral acids the base neamine. |
| Penicillins | Any antimicrobial acid which contains in its structure a fused thiazolidine β-lactam nucleus. |
| Polymixins | Any antimicrobial substance produced by any strain of *Bacillus polymyxa*. |
| Rifamycins | A group of related antimicrobial macrolactams produced by the growth of *Streptomyces mediterranei* and containing the chemical structure of 11-acetoxy-7,9,15-trihydroxy-13-methoxy-2,6,8,10,12-penta-methyl-pentadeca-2,4,14-trienoic acid amide attached by the nitrogen atom and by the oxygen atom in the 15- position respectively to the 7- and 2- positions of a 5,6,9-trioxygenated 2,4-dimethyl-1-oxonaphtho-(2,1-b)-furan. |
| Ristocetins | Antimicrobial substances produced by a strain of a *Nocardia* species referred to as *Nocardia lurida*. |
| Streptomycins | Any antimicrobial complex organic base or mixture of such bases produced by *Streptomyces griseus* which:<br>(a) yields on hydrolysis with mineral acids the base streptidine (meso-1-3-diguanidocyclohexane-2,4,5,6-tetraol); and<br>(b) yields on hydrolysis by a 4 per cent solution of sodium hydroxide the substance maltol (3-hydroxy-2-methyl-8-pyrone) |
| Sulphanilamide | Sulphanilamide being *p*-aminobenzenesulphonamide, having any of the hydrogen atoms of either or both nitrogen atoms substituted by an equal number of univalent atoms or radicals. |
| Tetracyclines | Antimicrobial bases which contain the chemical structure naphthacene-2-carboxamide, hydrogenated to any extent and having each of the positions 1, 3, 10, 11, 12 and 12α substituted by a hydroxyl or an oxo group. |

## Permitted sales or supplies

Sale or supply of prohibited substances is permitted in the circumstances described below:

(a)    Where a sale by way of wholesale dealing is made to:

    (i) a veterinary surgeon or veterinary practitioner;

    (ii) a person lawfully conducting a retail pharmacy business;

    (iii) a holder of a manufacturer's licence granted under Part II of the Act; or

    (iv) a person carrying on the business of selling by way of wholesale dealing.

(b)    Where the sale or supply is to any of the following:

    (i) a public analyst appointed under section 89 of the Food and Drugs Act 1955, section 27 of the Food and Drugs (Scotland) Act 1956 or section 31 of the Food and Drugs Act (Northern Ireland) 1958;

    (ii) an agricultural analyst appointed under section 67 of the Agriculture Act 1970;

    (iii) a person duly authorised by an enforcement authority under sections 111 and 112 of the Act;

    (iv) a sampling officer within the meaning of Schedule 3 to the Act;

    (v) universities, other institutions concerned with higher education or institutions concerned with research.

(c)    Griseofulvin. When sold or supplied in a fungicide for horticultural purposes and containing other ingredients in such a quantity as to render the product unfit for any medicinal purpose and unpalatable to such a degree as to prevent consumption by human beings.

(d)    Streptomycins as for Griseofulvin plus when used, sold or supplied for use as a preservative in a product used in the artificial breeding of animals.

(e)    Sulphanilamide. When, as the derivative sulphaquinoxaline (not exceeding 0.5 per cent), it is sold or supplied in a product for the destruction of rats or mice, or for the manufacture of such a product. The product must also contain warfarin, or its sodium or triethanolamine derivative.

(f)    Sulphonamide. When, as the derivative methyl-4-aminobenzenesulphonyl carbamate, it is sold or supplied for use in the manufacture of herbicides, or contained in a product used as a herbicide for agricultural, horticultural or forestry purposes or for use in or near water or on uncultivated land.

(g)    Amphotericins, gentamicins, kanamycins, lincomycins, nystatin, tylosin, penicillins, and spectinomycin when used, sold or supplied for use as a preservative in a product used in the artificial breeding of animals.

# Medicines Act 1968

# Applications for Marketing

# Authorisations

### Relevant Medicinal Products for Human Use

The Medicines for Human Use (Marketing Authorisations, etc.) Regulations 1994 (SI 1994 No.3144) together with Council Directive 65/65/EEC, Council Directives 75/318/EEC and 75/319/EEC and Council Directives 89/342/EEC and 89/343/EEC, as amended by Council Directive 93/39/EEC, prescribe the form and manner in which applications for marketing authorisations for medicinal products for human use are to be made. These provisions also apply to medicinal products consisting of vaccines, toxins and/or sera and allergens together with radiopharmaceuticals and blood products.

### Applications for Marketing Authorisations for Relevant Medicinal Products for Human Use

Any application must be made in writing, and signed by or on behalf of the applicant, and be accompanied by any fee which may be payable. Twenty-six copies of the application shall be supplied to the licensing authority in English. Where any material has been translated from another language then a copy in the original language must be supplied.

An application shall indicate what legal category the medicinal product falls into namely Prescription Only, Pharmacy Only, or General Sale.

An application for a marketing authorisation shall be accompanied by the following particulars and documents:

1. The name or corporate name of and the permanent address of the person responsible for placing the product on the market and, where applicable, the name and address of the manufacturer.

2.  The name of the medicinal product (brand name, or common name) together with a trade mark or name of manufacturer, or scientific name together with a trade mark or name of manufacturer.

3.  The qualitative and quantitative particulars of all the constituents of the product in usual terminology, but excluding empirical chemical formulae, with the mention of the international non-proprietary name recommended by the World Health Organization where such a name exists.

4.  A brief description of the method of preparation.

5.  Particulars of the therapeutic indications, contra-indications and side-effects.

6.  Posology, pharmaceutical form, method and route of administration and expected shelf-life. If applicable, the reasons for any precautionary and safety measures to be taken for the storage of the medicinal product, its administration to patients and for the disposal of waste products, together with an indication of any potential risks presented by the product for the environment.

7.  Description of the control methods employed by the manufacturer – qualitative and quantitative analysis of the constituents and of the finished product, special tests, e.g. sterility tests, tests for the presence of pyrogenic substances and for the presence of heavy metals, stability tests, biological and toxicity tests, and controls carried out at an intermediate stage of the manufacturing process.

8.  Results of:

    (a)   physico-chemical, biological or microbiological tests,
    (b)   pharmacological and toxicological tests,
    (c)   clinical trials.

However, and without prejudice to the law relating to the protection of industrial and commercial property:

    (a)   The applicant shall not be required to provide the results of pharmacological and toxicological tests or the results of clinical trials if:

          (i)   either the product is essentially similar to a product authorised in the country concerned by the application and that the person responsible for the marketing of the original product has consented to the pharmacological, toxicological or clinical references contained in the file on the original medicinal product being used for the purpose of examining the application in question; or
          (ii)  by detailed references to published scientific literature presented in accordance with the second paragraph of Article 1 of Directive 75/318/EEC that the constituent(s) of the medicinal product have a well established use, with recognised efficacy and an acceptable level of safety; or
          (iii) the medicinal product is essentially similar to a product which has been authorised within the Community, in accordance with Community provisions in force for not less than six years (ten years for high technology products) and is marketed in the member state for which an application is made; this period shall be extended to ten years in the case of high technology medicinal products within the meaning of Directive 87/22/EEC (Part A of Annex) or a medicinal product within the meaning of that Directive (Part B of Annex).

    Furthermore, a member state may also extend this period to ten years by a single decision covering all products marketed on its territory where it considers this necessary in the interest of public health. Member states are at liberty not to apply the six-year period beyond the date of expiry of the patent protecting the original product.

However, where the medicinal product is intended for a different therapeutic use from that of the other medicinal products marketed or to be administered by different routes or in different doses the results of appropriate pharmacological and toxicological tests and/or of appropriate clinical trials must be provided.

(b) In the case of new medicinal products containing known constituents not hitherto used in combination for therapeutic purposes, the results of pharmacological and toxicological tests and of clinical trials relating to the combination must be provided, but it is not necessary to provide references relating to each individual constituent.

9. A summary of the product characteristics (see below), one or more mock-ups of the sales presentation of the product, together with a package leaflet where one is to be enclosed.

10. A document showing that the manufacturer is authorised in his own country to produce medicinal products.

11. Copies of any authorisation obtained in another member state or a third country to place the medicinal product on the market, together with a list of those member states in which an application for authorisation submitted in accordance with this Directive is under examination. Copies of the summary of product characteristics proposed by the applicant in accordance with this Directive (see below) or approved by the competent authorities of the member state concerned. Copies of the package leaflet proposed in accordance with Directive 92/27/EEC or approved by the competent authorities of the member state concerned. Details of any decision to refuse authorisation, whether in the Community or a third country and the reasons for such a decision.

This information must be updated on a regular basis.

N.B. Member states must take all appropriate measures to ensure that the documents and particulars listed in points 7 and 8 above are drawn up by experts with the necessary technical or professional qualification before they are submitted to the competent authorities.

### Summary of the Product Characteristics

The summary of product characteristics must contain the following information:

(a) name of the medicinal product;
(b) its qualitative and quantitative composition in terms of the active ingredients and constituents of the excipient, knowledge of which is essential for proper administration of the product, the international non-proprietary names recommended by the World Heath Organization must be used where such names exist, or, failing this, the usual common name or chemical description;
(c) pharmaceutical form;
(d) pharmacological properties and, in so far as this information is useful for therapeutic purposes, pharmacokinetic particulars;
(e) clinical particulars covering:

(i) therapeutic indications;
(ii) posology and method of administration for adults and, where necessary, for children;

   (iii) contra-indications;
   (iv) special precautions for use;
   (v) undesirable effects (frequency and seriousness);
   (vi) interaction with other medicaments and other forms of interaction;
  (vii) use during pregnancy and lactation;
 (viii) effects on ability to drive and to use machines;
   (ix) special warnings;
   (x) overdose (covering symptoms, emergency procedures and antidotes).

(f)    Pharmaceutical particulars covering:

    (i) major incompatibilities;
   (ii) shelf life, when necessary after reconstitution of the product or when the container is opened for the first time;
  (iii) special precautions for storage;
  (iv) nature and contents of container;
   (v) special precautions for disposal of unused products or waste materials derived from such products, if appropriate;
  (vi) name or style and permanent address or registered place of business of the holder of the marketing authorisation.

When the marketing authorisation has been issued, the competent authority of the member state must inform the person responsible for placing the product on the market that the summary of product characteristics has been approved. The competent authority must send a copy of the marketing authorisation together with the summary of product characteristics to the European Agency for the Evaluation of Medicinal Products.

### Immunologicals, Radiopharmaceuticals and Blood Products

Council Directives 89/342/EEC, 89/343/EEC and 89/381/EEC amended Directives 65/65/EEC, 75/318/EEC and 75/319/EEC so that they now apply to immunologicals, radiopharmaceuticals and blood products. The documents and particulars (see applications for marketing authorisations, above) apply but there are additional requirements.

These additional requirements are:

#### Blood Products

1.    Where the name of the product derived from human blood or human plasma is expressed, the common or scientific name of the active constituents must also be included, at least once (though they may be abbreviated in other references).

2.    The statement required by Article 4a of Council Directive 65/65/EEC shall:

   (a)    as respects quantitative composition, be expressed by mass, by international units or by units of biological activity as appropriate to the product concerned;

   (b)    qualitative and quantitative particulars of constituents must include particulars relating to biological activity and qualitative and quantitative composition shall include the composition of the product expressed in terms of biological activity.

#### Vaccines, Toxins, Sera, or Allergen Products

1.    Whenever the name of the product is expressed, the common or scientific name of the active constituents must also be included.

2.    The statement required by Article 4a of Council Directive 65/65/EEC shall:

(a)   in respect to quantitative composition, be expressed by mass, by international units or by units of biological activity as appropriate to the product concerned;

(b)   qualitative and quantitative particulars of constituents must include particulars relating to biological activity or to protein content and qualitative and quantitative composition shall include the composition of the product expressed in terms of biological activity or of protein content.

3.   The particulars must include any special precautions to be taken by persons handling the immunological product and persons administering the product to patients, together with any precautions to be taken by the patient.

### Radiopharmaceuticals

Authorisations are required for generators, kits, precursor radiopharmaceuticals and industrially prepared pharmaceuticals.

The particulars shall include:

(a)   full details of internal radiation dosimetry;

(b)   additional detailed instructions for extemporaneous preparation and quality control of such preparation and, where appropriate, maximum storage time during which any intermediate preparation such as an eluate or the ready to use pharmaceutical will conform with its specifications; and

(c)   if the application is in respect of a radiopharmaceutical which is a generator:

(i)   a general description of the system together with a detailed description of the components of the system which may affect the composition or quality of the daughter nuclide preparation; and

(ii)   qualitative and quantitative particulars of the eluate or the sublimate.

### An Application for the Issue of a Clinical Trial Certificate

Particulars relating to the applicant, the certificate holder and the activities to which the certificate relates must include:

1.   The name and address of the applicant, and, where the applicant is not the proposed certificate holder, the name and address of the proposed certificate holder.

2.   The period for which the certificate is desired, where it is for less than two years.

3.   A statement of the activities to which the certificate is to relate, and in respect of each medicinal product which is the subject of the application, whether it is one or more of the following:

(a)   to sell or supply the medicinal product for the purpose of a clinical trial;

(b)   to procure the sale or supply of the medicinal product for the purpose of a clinical trial;

(c)   to procure the manufacture or assembly of the medicinal product for sale or supply for the purpose of the clinical trial and whether or not in addition to the purpose specified in sub-paragraphs (a) or (b) of this paragraph.

(d)   to import into the United Kingdom the medicinal product for the purpose of a clinical trial.

4.   Whether in respect of each medicinal product which is the subject of the application it is to be sold or supplied for the purposes of the trial:

(a)   to practitioners;

(b)    to persons engaged in providing hospital services; or

(c)    otherwise.

5.    (a)    The name and address of any person in the United Kingdom other than the proposed certificate holder taking part in the manufacture or assembly of each medicinal product; and

(b)    in the case of an imported medicinal product, the name and address of the manufacturer or assembler of the medicinal product in the form in which it is to be imported; and

(c)    a statement of the relevant manufacturing or assembling operations; and

(d)    the address of the place or proposed place of manufacture or assembly.

## Applications for Certificates of Registration for Homoeopathic Products

An application for special, simplified registration submitted by a person responsible for placing the product on the market relates to homoeopathic medicinal products and may cover a series of homoeopathic medicinal products derived from the same homoeopathic stock or stocks.

The application must be in writing and be accompanied by the following material and information (SI 1994 No.105, as amended):

1.    The name or corporate name of and the permanent address of:

(a)    the person responsible for placing the product on the market in the United Kingdom;

(b)    the manufacturers and the sites involved in the different stages of the manufacture including the manufacturer of the finished product and the manufacturers of the homoeopathic stock or stocks; and

(c)    where relevant, the importer.

2.    Details of the scientific name or other name given in a pharmacopoeia of the homoeopathic stock or stocks.

3.    A statement of the various routes of administration, pharmaceutical form and degree of dilution to be registered.

4.    A dossier describing how the homoeopathic stock or stocks is or are to be obtained and controlled and justifying its or their homoeopathic nature.

5.    A manufacturing and control file for each pharmaceutical form and a description of the method of dilution and potentisation.

6.    A copy of the manufacturer's licence or corresponding authorisation granted by a member state other that the United Kingdom in respect of the product.

7.    Copies of any registrations or authorisations obtained for the same product in member states other than the United Kingdom.

8.    One or more specimens of mock-ups of the sales presentation of the product to be registered.

9.    Data concerning the stability of the product.

## Medicinal Products for Animal Use

The Marketing Authorisations for Veterinary Medicinal Products Regulations 1994 (SI 1994 No.3142, as amended) together with Council Directives 81/851/EEC and 81/852/EEC prescribe the form and manner in which applications for marketing authorisations for animal use are to be made. The particulars required in applications for marketing authorisations are thus:

Any application must be made in writing, and signed by or on behalf of the applicant, and be accompanied by any fee which may be payable. Four copies of the application shall be supplied to the licensing authority in English, plus a further twenty-two copies if requested. Where any material has been translated from another language then a copy in the original language must be supplied.

## Application for a Marketing Authorisation for a Medicinal Product for Animal Use

An application for a marketing authorisation shall be accompanied by the following particulars and documents:

1.  The name or business name and the permanent address or registered place of business of the person responsible for placing the product on the market and, if different, of the manufacturer(s) involved and of the sites of manufacture.

2.  The name of the veterinary medicinal product (brand name, non-proprietary name), with or without trade mark or name of manufacturer, or scientific name or formula with or without a trade mark or name of the manufacturer.

3.  The qualitative and quantitative particulars of all the constituents of the product using the usual terminology, but not empirical chemical formulae, also giving the international non-proprietary name recommended by the World Health Organization where such a name exists.

4.  A description of the method of preparation.

5.  Therapeutic indications, contra-indications and side-effects.

6.  Dosage for the various species of animal for which the product is intended, its pharmaceutical form, method and route of administration and proposed shelf life.

7.  If applicable the reasons for any precautionary and safety measures to be taken when the product is stored, when it is administered to animals and when the waste therefrom is disposed of, together with an indication of any potential risks the product might pose to the environment and the health of humans, animals and plants.

8.  Indication of the withdrawal period necessary between the last administration of the product to animals under normal conditions of use and the production of foodstuffs from such animals in order to ensure that such foodstuffs do not contain residues in quantities in excess of the maximum limits laid down. Where necessary the applicant must propose and justify a tolerance level for residues which may be accepted in foodstuffs without risk for the consumer, together with routine analysis methods which could be used by the competent authorities to trace residues.

9.  Description of the control testing methods employed by the manufacturer – qualitative and quantitative analysis of the constituents and of the finished product, special tests, e.g. sterility tests, tests for the presence of pyrogens, for the presence of heavy metals, stability tests, biological and toxicity tests, and tests on intermediate products.

10. Results of:

    (a)    physico-chemical, biological or microbiological tests;

(b) pharmacological and toxicological tests;

(c) clinical trials.

However, and without prejudice to the law relating to the protection of industrial and commercial property:

(a) The applicant shall not be required to provide the results of pharmacological and toxicological tests or the results of clinical trials if:

(i) either the product is essentially similar to a product authorised in the country concerned by the application and that the person responsible for the marketing of the original product has agreed to the pharmacological, toxicological or clinical references contained in the file on the original medicinal product may be used for the purpose of examining the application in question; or

(ii) by detailed references to the scientific literature presented in accordance with the second paragraph of Article 1 of Directive 81/852/EEC that the constituent(s) of the medicinal product have a well-established medicinal use, with recognised efficacy and an acceptable level of safety; or

(iii) the veterinary medicinal product is essentially similar to a product which has been authorised within the Community, in accordance with Community provisions in force for not less than six years and is marketed in the member state for which an application is made; this period shall be extended to ten years in the case of high technology medicinal products within the meaning of Directive 87/22/EEC (Part A of Annex) or a medicinal product within the meaning of that Directive (Part B of Annex).

Furthermore a member state may also extend this period to ten years by a single decision covering all products marketed on its territory where it considers this necessary in the interest of public health. Member states are at liberty not to apply the six-year period beyond the date of expiry of the patent protecting the original product.

(b) In the case of new medicinal products containing known constituents not hitherto used in combination for therapeutic purposes, the results of pharmacological and toxicological tests and of clinical trials relating to the combination must be provided, but it is not necessary to provide references relating to each individual constituent.

11. A summary of the product characteristics, one or more mock-ups of the sales presentation of the product, together with a package leaflet where one is to be enclosed.

12. A document showing that the manufacturer is authorised in his own country to produce medicinal products.

13. Any authorisation to place the relevant product on the market obtained in another member state or in a third country together with a list of those countries to which an application for authorisation to place the product on the market has been made and explanation of the reasons for which the member state or third country has refused to grant authorisation for the product concerned.

N.B. Member states must take all appropriate measures to ensure that the documents and particulars listed in points 8, 9 and 10 are drawn up by experts with the necessary technical or professional qualification before they are submitted to the competent authorities.

The summary of product characteristics is similar to that for human medicinal products (see p.396) with the added requirement as to the target species and withdrawal periods.

# Medicines Act 1968

## Prescribed Conditions for

## Manufacturers' Undertakings

In dealing with applications for licences for the importation of medicinal products the licensing authority may require the production of an undertaking to comply with prescribed conditions. Those conditions are in the schedule to the Medicines (Manufacturers' Undertakings for Imported Products) Regulations 1977 (SI 1977 No.1038, as amended by SI 1992 No.2845), and are set out below.

For the purpose of these regulations *medicinal product* includes a relevant medicinal product within the meaning of the Medicines for Human Use (Marketing Authorisations etc.) Regulations 1994 (SI 1994 No.3144).

1. The manufacturer shall provide and maintain such staff, premises, and plant as are necessary for the carrying out in accordance with the relevant product licences of such stages of the manufacture and assembly of the medicinal products to which the relevant product licences relate as are undertaken by him.

2. The manufacturer shall provide and maintain such staff, premises, equipment and facilities for the handling, storage and distribution of the medicinal products to which the relevant product licences relate which he handles, stores or distributes as are necessary to avoid deterioration of the medicinal products.

2A. In relation to medicinal products for human use, the manufacturer shall provide and maintain a designated quality control department having authority in relation to quality control and being independent of all other departments.

3. The manufacturer shall conduct all manufacture and assembly operations in such a way as to ensure that the medicinal products to which the relevant product licences relate conform with the standards of strength, quality and purity applicable to them under the relevant product licences.

3A. In relation to medicinal products for human use, the manufacturer shall maintain an effective pharmaceutical quality assurance system involving the active participation of the management and personnel of the different services involved.

4. Where animals are used in the production of any medicinal product and the relevant product licences contain provisions relating to them, the manufacturer shall arrange for the animals to be housed in premises of such a nature and to be managed in such a way as will facilitate compliance with such provisions.

5. The manufacturer shall make such adequate and suitable arrangements as are necessary for carrying out in accordance with the relevant product licences any tests of the strength, quality or purity of the medicinal products to which the licences relate.

6. The manufacturer shall inform the holder of the relevant product licences of any material alteration in the premises or plant used in connection with the manufacture or assembly of the medicinal products to which the relevant product licences relate or in the operations for which such premises or plant are used and of any change, since the granting of the relevant product licences, in respect of any person:

(a)    responsible for supervising the production operations; or
(b)    responsible for quality control of the medicinal products to which the relevant product licences relate; or
(c)    in charge of the animals from which are derived any substance used in the production of the medicinal products to which the relevant product licences relate; or
(d)    responsible for the culture of any living tissues used in the manufacture of the medicinal products to which the relevant product licences relate.

7. The manufacturer shall keep readily available for inspection by a person authorised by the licensing authority durable records of the details of manufacture and assembly of each batch of every medicinal product to which each relevant product licence relates and of the tests carried out thereon in such a form that the records will be easily identifiable from the number of the batch as shown in each container in which the medicinal product is exported from the country where it has been manufactured or assembled; the manufacturer shall permit the person authorised to take copies of or make extracts from such records. Such records shall not be destroyed:

(a)    in relation to medicinal products for human use, for a period of five years from the date of release of the relevant batch, or for a period of one year after the expiry date of the relevant batch, which ever expires later;
(b)    in any other case.

7A. In relation to medicinal products for human use to which a product licence relates, the manufacturer shall keep readily available for examination by a person authorised by the licensing authority, samples of:

(a)    each batch of finished products for at least a period of one year after their expiry date; and
(b)    starting materials (other than solvents, gases or water) for at least a period of two years after release of the medicinal product of which the relevant starting materials formed part;

except where the manufacturer is authorised by the licensing authority to destroy such samples earlier.

7B. (1) The manufacturer shall implement a system for recording and reviewing complaints in relation to medicinal products for human use to which a product licence relates together with an effective system for recalling promptly and at any time the medicinal products in the distribution network.

(2) The manufacturer shall record and investigate all complaints described in sub-paragraph (a) of this paragraph and shall immediately inform the licensing authority of any defect which could result in a recall from sale, supply or exportation or is an abnormal restriction on such sale, supply or exportation.

8. The manufacturer shall inform the holder of the relevant product licence of any material change since the date upon which such licence was granted in respect of:

(a)     the facilities and equipment available at each of the premises of the manufacturer for carrying out any stage of the manufacture or assembly of the medicinal products to which the relevant product licences relate; or

(b)     the facilities and equipment available in each of the premises of the manufacturer for the storage of the medicinal products to which the relevant product licences relate on, and distribution of the products from or between, such premises; or

(c)     any manufacturing operations, not being operations in relation to the medicinal products to which the relevant product licences relate, which are carried on by the manufacturer on or near any of the premises on which such medicinal products are manufactured or assembled and the substances or articles in respect of which such operations are carried on; or

(d)     the arrangements for the identification and storage of materials and ingredients before and during manufacture of the medicinal products to which the relevant product licences relate and the arrangements for the storage of the medicinal products after they have been manufactured or assembled; or

(e)     the arrangements for ensuring a satisfactory turnover of stocks of medicinal products to which the relevant product licences relate; or

(f)     the arrangements for maintaining production records and records of analytical and other testing procedures applied in the course of manufacture or assembly of the medicinal products to which the relevant product licences relate; or

(g)     the arrangements for keeping reference samples of materials used in the manufacture of any medicinal products to which the relevant product licences relate and reference samples of such medicinal products.

# Medicines Act 1968

## Standard Provisions and Obligations for Marketing Authorisations

The standard provisions and obligations relating to marketing authorisations for human medicines are set out in SI 1994 No.3144 and in Council Directives 65/65/EEC, 75/318/EEC, 75/319/EEC, 89/342/EEC, 89/343/EEC, 89/381/EEC, 92/27/EEC and 93/39/EEC.

### Definitions

*Allergen product* means any product which is intended to identify or induce a specific acquired alteration in the immunological response to an allergising agent.

*Expiry date* means the date after which the medicinal product should not be used.

*Good manufacturing practice* means the part of quality assurance which ensures that medicinal products are consistently produced and controlled to the quality standards appropriate to their intended use, the principles and guidelines of which are specified in Chapter II of Commission Directive 91/356/EEC (O.J. No.L193 17.7.91).

*Relevant period* means the period of five years from the date of certification of the relevant batch referred to in paragraph 16(3)(b) of Schedule 2 to the Regulations or the period of one year from the expiry date of the relevant batch, whichever expires later.

*Adverse reaction* means a reaction which is harmful and unintended and which occurs at doses normally used in man for the prophylaxis, diagnosis or treatment of disease or the modification of physiological function.

*Serious adverse reaction* means an adverse reaction which is fatal, life-threatening, disabling, incapacitating, or which results in or prolongs hospitalisation.

*Unexpected adverse reaction* means an adverse reaction which is not mentioned in the summary of product characteristics.

*Serious unexpected adverse reaction* means an adverse reaction which is both serious and unexpected.

### Obligations on Holders of Marketing Authorisations for Relevant Medicinal Products for Human Use

The Licensing Authority in this context can mean either the member state competent authority, e.g. the Medicines Control Agency in the United Kingdom, or the European Agency for the Evaluation of Medicinal Products.

1. The person responsible for placing the product on the market must inform the Licensing Authority of any new information which might entail the amendment of the particulars and documents referred to in his application for a marketing authorisation or in the summary of product characteristics (see Appendix 3). In particular he must inform the Licensing Authority, the Commission and the member states of any prohibition or restriction imposed by a competent authority of any country in which the medicinal product is placed on the market and any other new information which might influence the evaluation of the benefits and risks of the medicinal product concerned (Regulation 2309/93/EEC).

2. The holder of a marketing authorisation shall comply with all the obligations which relate to him by virtue of the relevant Community provisions including in particular obligations relating to providing or updating information, making changes, to applying to vary the authorisation, to pharmacovigilance, and to labels and package leaflets (SI 1994 No.3144).

3. The holder of a marketing authorisation shall maintain a record of reports of which he is aware of suspected adverse effects in accordance with the relevant Community provisions, which shall be open to inspection by a person authorised by the Licensing Authority, who may take copies of the record and, if the Licensing Authority so directs, the authorisation holder shall furnish the Licensing Authority with a copy of any such reports of which he has a record or of which he is or subsequently becomes aware (SI 1994 No.3144).

4. The holder of a marketing authorisation shall keep such documents as will facilitate the withdrawal or recall from sale or supply any relevant medicinal product to which the authorisation relates (SI 1994 No.3144).

5. The person responsible for placing the product on the market must notify the Licensing Authority forthwith of any action taken by him to suspend the marketing of a product, or withdraw a product from the market, together with the reasons for such action if the latter concerns the efficacy of the product or the protection of public health (Directive 75/319/EEC).

6. The person responsible for placing the product on the market must, in respect of methods of production and control take account of technical and scientific progress and make any amendments that may be required to enable the product to be manufactured and checked by means of generally accepted scientific methods. These changes shall be subject to approval of the Licensing Authority (Regulation 2309/93/EEC).

7. In exceptional circumstances a marketing authorisation may be granted subject to certain specific obligations to be reviewed annually including:

(a)   the carrying out of further studies following the granting of the authorisation;
(b)   the notification of adverse reactions to the medicinal product (Directive 65/65/EEC).

8. The person responsible for placing the product on the market must have permanently and continuously at his disposal an appropriately qualified person responsible for pharmacovigilance.

That qualified person shall be responsible for:

(a) the establishment and maintenance of a system which ensures that information about all suspected adverse reactions which are reported to the personnel of the company, and to medical representatives, is collected and evaluated and collated so that it may be accessed at a single point within the Community;

(b) the preparation of the reports for the competent authorities in accordance with the requirements of Regulation 93/2309/EEC;

(c) ensuring that any request from the competent authorities for the provision of additional information necessary for the evaluation of the benefits and risks afforded by a medicinal product is answered fully and promptly, including the provision of information about the volume of sales or prescriptions of the medicinal product concerned (Regulation 2309/93/EEC).

9. The person responsible for placing the product on the market shall be required to record and to report all suspected serious adverse reactions, which are brought to his attention by a health care professional, to the Licensing Authority immediately and in any case within 15 days of their receipt at the latest (Regulation 2309/93/EEC).

10. The person responsible for placing the product on the market must be required to maintain detailed records of all other suspected adverse reactions which are reported to him by a health care professional. These records shall be submitted to the competent authorities immediately upon request or at least every six months during the first two years following authorisation and once a year for the following three years. Thereafter the records shall be submitted every five years together with the renewal of the authorisation or immediately upon request. They shall be accompanied by a scientific evaluation (Regulation 2309/93/EEC).

## Additional Obligations for Holders of Marketing Authorisations Relating to Blood Products and Immunological Medicinal Products

### Blood Products

1. The holder of a marketing authorisation shall take all necessary measures to ensure that the manufacturing and purifying processes used in the preparation of blood products to which the licence relates:

(a) are properly validated;

(b) attain batch-to-batch consistency;

(c) guarantee, in so far as the state of technology permits, the absence of specific viral contamination;

and shall take all necessary measures to ensure that appropriate records relating to relevant control measures are:

(i) signed by the qualified person referred to in paragraph 16 of Schedule 2 to these Regulations;

(ii) kept for the relevant period; and

(iii) if so requested, submitted to the competent authority.

2. The manufacturer shall notify the competent authority of the method or methods used to reduce or eliminate pathogenic viruses liable to be transmitted by blood products.

### Immunological Products

3. The holder of a marketing authorisation shall take all necessary measures to ensure that the processes used in the production of vaccines, toxins, sera or allergen products to which the licence relates:

(a)    are properly validated; and

(b)    attain batch-to-batch consistency;

and shall take all necessary measures to ensure that appropriate records relating to control measures are:

> (i)    signed by the qualified person referred to in paragraph 16 of Schedule 2 to these Regulations;
>
> (ii)    kept for the relevant period; and
>
> (iii)    if so requested by the Licensing Authority, submitted to the Licensing Authority.

## Standard Provisions for Clinical Trials

The provisions are in the Medicines (Standard Provisions for Licences and Certificates) Regulations 1971 (SI 1971 No.972, as amended).

1. The certificate holder shall forthwith report to the Licensing Authority any change in his name and address and in any address at which there is carried on a business to which the clinical trial certificate relates.

2. The certificate holder shall forthwith inform the Licensing Authority of any information received by him that casts doubt on the continued validity of the data which was submitted with, or in connection with, the application for the clinical trial certificate for the purpose of being taken into account in assessing the safety, quality or efficacy of any medicinal products to which the certificate relates for the purpose for which the certificate holder proposed that it may be used.

3. The certificate holder shall forthwith inform the Licensing Authority of any decision to discontinue the trial of any medicinal product to which the certificate relates and shall state the reason for the decision.

4. The clinical trial in respect of which the clinical trial certificate has been issued shall be carried out in accordance with the outline of the clinical trial contained in the application for that certificate subject to any changes thereto which the Licensing Authority may from time to time approve.

5. (1) The medicinal product to which the clinical trial certificate relates shall be administered only by or under the direction of a doctor or dentist named in the application for that certificate or by or under the direction of a doctor or dentist approved by the Licensing Authority for this purpose.

(2) Where the medicinal product to which the clinical trial certificate relates is to be administered by or under the direction of a doctor or dentist who has not been named in the application for the certificate or where it is intended that there shall be a change of the doctor or dentist so named, the certificate holder shall seek the approval of the Licensing Authority and for this purpose shall notify the Licensing Authority in writing of the name, address and qualifications of the doctor or dentist in question.

(3) In the event of any doctor or dentist ceasing to participate in the clinical trial in respect of which the clinical trial certificate has been issued, the certificate holder shall as soon as is reasonably possible inform the Licensing Authority and shall give the reason for such cessation.

6. Before any administration of the medicinal product to which the clinical trial certificate relates takes place, the certificate holder shall communicate the provisions of that certificate to each and every doctor or dentist who, in the course of the clinical trial in respect of which that certificate has been issued, is to administer or to direct the administration of that medicinal product.

## Standard Provisions for Animal Test Certificates

The provisions are in the Medicines (Standard Provisions for Licences and Certificates) Regulations 1971 (SI 1971 No.972, as amended).

1. The certificate holder shall forthwith report to the Licensing Authority any change in his name and address and in any address at which there is carried on a business to which the animal test certificate relates.

2. The certificate holder shall forthwith inform the Licensing Authority of any proposed change in the arrangements for the supervision of the performance of the medicinal test on animals to which the certificate relates.

3. The certificate holder shall forthwith furnish the Licensing Authority with any information received by him that casts doubt on the continued validity of the data which was submitted with, or in connection with, the application for the animal test certificate for the purpose of being taken into account in assessing the safety, quality or efficacy of any medicinal product to which the certificate relates for the purpose for which the certificate holder proposed that it may be used.

4. The certificate holder shall maintain a record of any report received by him of adverse effects in any animal or animals associated in the report with the use of any medicinal product to which the certificate relates, which shall be open to inspection by a person authorised by the Licensing Authority, who may take copies thereof, and the certificate holder, unless requested by the Licensing Authority not to do so, shall forthwith furnish the Licensing Authority with a copy of any such reports that have been received by him.

5. The certificate holder shall keep readily available for inspection by a person authorised by the Licensing Authority durable records of his arrangements:

(a)    for procuring the sale, supply, manufacture, assembly or importation of any medicinal product to which the certificate relates; and

(b)    for obtaining materials for the purpose of the manufacture or assembly by him, or on his behalf, of any medicinal product to which the certificate relates; and

(c)    for tests to be carried out on the materials used for manufacture or assembly of any medicinal products and on any medicinal products to which the certificate relates;

and shall permit the person authorised to take copies or to make extracts from such records. Such records shall not, without the consent of the Licensing Authority, be destroyed for a period of one year from the date of the expiry of the last certificate for the medicinal test on animals to which such records relate.

6. The certificate holder shall forthwith notify the Licensing Authority of any decision to discontinue the test of any medicinal product to which the certificate relates and shall inform the Licensing Authority of the reason for the decision.

7. The medicinal test on animals in respect of which the animal test certificate has been issued shall be carried out in accordance with the outline of the medicine test on animals contained in the application for that certificate subject to any changes thereto which the Licensing Authority may from time to time approve.

8. (1) The medicinal product to which the animal test certificate relates shall be administered only by, or under the direction of, the person named in the application for that certificate as the person to whom it was proposed that the medicinal test on animals should be carried out by or under the direction of such other person approved by the Licensing Authority for this purpose.

(2) Where the medicinal product to which the animal test certificate relates is to be administered by, or under the direction of, a person who has not been named in the application for that certificate or where it is intended that there shall be a change of the person so named, the certificate holder shall seek the approval of the Licensing Authority and for this purpose shall notify the Licensing Authority in writing of the name, address and qualifications of the person in question.

(3) In the event of any such named or approved person ceasing to participate in the medicinal test on animals in respect of which the animal test certificate has been issued, the certificate holder shall as soon as is reasonably possible inform the Licensing Authority and shall give the reason for such cessation.

9. (1) The medicinal test on animals in respect of which the animal test certificate has been issued shall be carried out only at the location specified in the application for that certificate.

(2) Where the medicinal test on animals to which the animal test certificate relates is to be carried out at a location that has not been specified in the application or where it is intended that there shall be a change in the location so specified, the certificate holder shall seek the approval of the Licensing Authority and for this purpose shall notify the Licensing Authority in writing of the location in question.

10. Before any administration of the medicinal product to which the animal test certificate relates takes place, the certificate holder shall arrange that the particulars relating to the administration of that medicinal product together with any relevant safety precautions be communicated to each and every person who, in the course of the medicinal test on animals in respect of which that certificate has been issued, is to administer or to direct the administration of that medicinal product.

### Standard Provisions for a Manufacturer's Licence for Medicinal Products for Human Use

These are laid down in Council Directive 75/319/EEC and SI 1971 No.972, Schedule 2, as amended. Council Directive 91/356/EEC lays down the principles and guidelines of Good Manufacturing Practice (GMP) which are applicable to all activities relating to manufacture. The provisions are as follows.

1. The licence holder shall provide and maintain such staff, premises and plant as are necessary for the carrying out in accordance with his licence and the relevant product licences of such stages of the manufacture and assembly of the medicinal products as are undertaken by him, and he shall not carry out any such manufacture or assembly except at the premises specified in his manufacturer's licence.

2. The licence holder shall provide and maintain such staff, premises, equipment and facilities for the handling, storage and distribution of the medicinal products which he handles, stores or distributes under his licence as are necessary to avoid deterioration of the medicinal products and he shall not use for such purposes premises other than those specified in the licence or which may be approved from time to time by the Licensing Authority.

3. The licence holder shall conduct all manufacture and assembly operations in such a way as to ensure that the medicinal products conform with the standards of strength, quality and purity applicable to them under the relevant product licences and, in relation to medicinal products for human use, shall conduct all such operations in accordance with the principles and guidelines of good manufacturing practice.

3A. The licence holder shall, in relation to medicinal products for human use, establish and implement an effective pharmaceutical quality assurance system involving the active participation of management and personnel of the different services involved.

4. The licence holder, where animals are used in the production of any medicinal products and the relevant product licences contain provisions relating to them, shall arrange for the animals to be housed in premises of such a nature and to be managed in such a way as will facilitate compliance with such provisions.

5. The licence holder, in relation to medicinal products other than for human use, shall either:

(a)     provide and maintain such staff, premises and plant as are necessary for carrying out in accordance with the relevant product licences any tests of the strength, quality or purity of the medicinal products that he manufactures under his manufacturer's licence as required by those product licences, and when animals are used for such tests they shall be suitably housed and managed; or

(b)    make arrangements with a person approved by the Licensing Authority for such tests to be carried out in accordance with the relevant product licences on his behalf by that person.

5A. (1) The licence holder shall, in relation to medicinal products for human use:

(a)    provide and maintain a designated quality control department having authority in relation to quality control and being independent from all other departments in the exercise of that authority; and

(b)    place the quality control department under the authority of the person notified to the Licensing Authority in accordance with paragraph 7(2) of Schedule 1 to the Medicines (Applications for Manufacturer's and Wholesale Dealer's Licences) Regulations 1971 as being responsible for quality control.

(2) Subject to 5B of this Schedule, the licence holder shall, in order to support the quality control department, provide and maintain such staff, premises and plant as are necessary for carrying out:

(a)    such tests of the strength, quality and purity of the medicinal products which he manufactures for human use under the manufacturer's licence as are required by the relevant product licences; and

(b)    any tests or controls which relate to the conditions of production and in-process controls.

(3) Any animals used for the tests referred to in sub-paragraph (2) of this paragraph shall be suitably housed and managed.

(4) The licence holder shall ensure that the quality control department, in determining whether finished medicinal products for human use are to be released for sale or distribution, takes into account, in addition to analytical results:

(a)    the conditions of production;
(b)    the results of in-process controls;
(c)    the examination of production documents;
(d)    the conformity of products to the specification in the relevant product licence.

5B. A licence holder need not himself provide and maintain staff, premises and plant as are necessary for carrying out such tests as are specified in paragraph 5A(2) of this Schedule provided that he makes arrangements with a person approved by the Licensing Authority to carry out such tests on his behalf in accordance with paragraph 5A(2) and (3) of this Schedule.

6. The licence holder shall provide such information as may be requested by the Licensing Authority for the purposes of the Act, about the products currently being manufactured or assembled under his licence and of the operations being carried out in relation to such manufacture and assembly.

7. The licence holder shall inform the Licensing Authority before making any material alteration in the premises or plant used under his licence, or in the operations for which they are used, and he shall inform the Licensing Authority of any change that he proposes to make in any personnel named in his licence as respectively:

(a)    responsible for supervising the production operations; or

(b)    responsible for quality control of the medicinal products being manufactured or assembled including the person named as the qualified person for the purposes of paragraphs 16 or 17, as the case may be, of this Part of this Schedule; or

(c)    in charge of the animals from which are derived any substances used in the production of the medicinal products being manufactured or assembled; or

(d)    responsible for the culture of any living tissues used in the manufacture of the medicinal products being manufactured or assembled.

8. The licence holder shall keep readily available for inspection by a person authorised by the Licensing Authority durable records of the details of manufacture and assembly of each batch of every medicinal product being manufactured or assembled under his licence and of the tests carried out thereon, including any register or other record referred to in paragraph 16(3)(b) or 17(3)(b), as the case may be, of this Schedule, in such a form that the records will be easily identifiable from the number of the batch as shown on each container in which the medicinal product is sold, supplied or exported, and he shall permit the person authorised to take copies or make extracts from such records. Such records shall not be destroyed without the consent of the Licensing Authority:

(a)    in relation to a medicinal product for human use, for the relevant period;
(b)    in any other case, for a period of five years from the date when the manufacture or assembly of the relevant batch occurred.

8A. The licence holder shall keep readily available for examination by a person authorised by the Licensing Authority, samples of each batch of finished medicinal products for human use manufactured or assembled under his licence for at least a period of one year from their expiry date and shall retain samples of starting materials (other than solvents, gases or water) for at least a period of two years from the date of the release of the relevant batch of which the relevant starting materials formed part, except where the licence holder is authorised by the Licensing Authority to destroy any such sample earlier.

8B. The licence holder shall make suitable arrangements to ensure that any record or sample referred to in paragraph 8 or 8A above relating to a medicinal product for human use is retained for the relevant period.

9. The licence holder shall, in relation to medicinal products other than for human use, keep such documents as will facilitate the withdrawal or recall from sale, supply or exportation of any such medicinal products to which the licence relates.

9A. (1) The manufacturer shall implement a system for recording and reviewing complaints in relation to medicinal products for human use manufactured or assembled under his licence, together with an effective system for recalling promptly and at any time such medicinal products in the distribution network.

(2) The manufacturer shall record and investigate all complaints described in sub-paragraph (1) of this paragraph and shall immediately inform the Licensing Authority of any defect which could result in a recall from sale, supply or exportation or in an abnormal restriction on such sale, supply or exportation.

10. Where the licence holder has been informed by the Licensing Authority that any batch of any medicinal product to which his licence relates has been found not to conform as regards strength, quality or purity with the specification of the relevant product or with the provisions of the Act or of any regulations under the Act that are applicable to the medicinal product, he shall, if so directed, withhold such batch from sale, supply or exportation, so far as may be reasonably practicable, for such a period not exceeding six weeks as may be specified by the Licensing Authority.

11. The licence holder shall ensure that any tests for determining conformity with the standards and specifications applying to any particular product used in the manufacture shall, except so far as the conditions of the relevant product licence may otherwise provide, be applied to samples taken from the medicinal product after all manufacturing processes have been completed, or at such earlier stage in the manufacture as may be approved by the Licensing Authority.

12. (1) The licence holder who is not the holder of a product licence in respect of the medicinal product to which the manufacturer's licence relates, shall comply with any provisions of such a product licence that relates to the sale of that medicinal product and shall, by means of a label or otherwise, communicate the particulars of such provisions as relate to mode of sale, or restrictions as to sale, to any person to whom the licence holder sells or supplies that medicinal product.

(2) Where the manufacturer's licence relates to the assembly of a medicinal product, and the licence holder sells or supplies that medicinal product at such a stage of assembly that

does not fully comply with the provisions of the relevant product licence that relates to labelling, that licence holder shall communicate the particulars of those provisions to the person to whom that medicinal product has been so sold or supplied.

13. Where in his application for a manufacturer's licence the licence holder had specified a general classification of medicinal products in respect of which that licence was required or had given particulars of manufacturing operations and of substances or articles in accordance with paragraph 6 of Schedule 1 to the Medicines (Applications for Manufacturer's and Wholesale Dealer's Licences) Regulations 1971 and there has been, or it is proposed that there shall be, a change in such general classification or such particulars, the licence holder shall forthwith notify the Licensing Authority in writing of such change or proposed change.

14. Where the manufacturer's licence relates to the assembly of a medicinal product and that medicinal product is not manufactured by the licence holder, and where particulars as to the name and address of the manufacturer of, or of the person who imports, that medicinal product have been given by the licence holder to the Licensing Authority, the licence holder shall forthwith notify the Licensing Authority in writing of any changes in such particulars.

15. The licence holder, for the purpose of enabling the Licensing Authority to ascertain whether there are any grounds for suspending, revoking or varying any licence or certificate granted or issued under Part II of the Act, shall permit, and provide all necessary facilities to enable, any person duly authorised in writing by the Licensing Authority, on production if required of his credentials, to carry out such inspection or to take such samples or copies, in relation to things belonging to, or any business carried on by, the licence holder, as such person would have the right to carry out or take under the Act for the purpose of verifying any statement contained in an application for a licence or certificate.

16. (1) Subject to sub-paragraph (5) below, the licence holder shall at all times have at his disposal the services of a person who as respects qualification and experience satisfies the provisions of Articles 23 and 24 of the Second Council Directive, to carry out the functions specified in sub-paragraph (3) below (*qualified person*). For the purposes of this paragraph, but without prejudice to sub-paragraph (4) below, the licence holder may regard a person as satisfying the provisions of the said Article 24 as respects formal qualifications if he produces evidence that he is a member of the Royal Pharmaceutical Society or of the Royal Society of Chemistry or of such other body as may appear to the Licensing Authority to be an appropriate body for the purpose, and that he is regarded by the body of which he is a member as so satisfying those provisions.

(2) The licence holder shall at all times provide and maintain such staff, premises, equipment and facilities as will enable the qualified person who is at his disposal to carry out the said functions.

(3) The functions to be carried out by the qualified person shall be as follows:

(a)   to ensure that each batch of the medicinal product to which the licence relates has been manufactured or assembled and checked in compliance with the provisions of the Act and regulations made thereunder, the provisions of the licence and the provisions of the product licence which relates to the product;

(aa)  where there is in relation to the product which has been manufactured or assembled, a certificate of registration, to ensure that each batch of the product has been manufactured or assembled and checked in compliance with that certificate and the provisions of the Medicines (Homoeopathic Medicinal Products for Human Use) Regulations 1994;

(b)   to certify in a register, or other record appropriate for the purpose, whether each production batch of the medicinal product to which the licence relates satisfies the requirements set out in (a), or, as the case may be, (aa) above and to ensure that such register or other record is regularly maintained, in particular that the appropriate entries in such register or other record are made as soon as practicable after each such batch has been manufactured.

(4) Where, after giving the licence holder and the person acting as a qualified person the opportunity of making representations to them (orally or in writing), the Licensing Authority are of the opinion that the person so acting does not satisfy the provisions of the said Articles 23 and 24 of the Second Council Directive as respects qualifications and experience, or that he is failing to carry out the functions specified in sub-paragraph (3) above, and have notified the licence holder accordingly in writing, the licence holder shall not permit that person to act as a qualified person so long as the said notification has not been withdrawn by the Licensing Authority.

(5) The provisions of this paragraph shall not apply in relation to veterinary drugs.

(6) The provisions of this paragraph shall also not apply where the licence relates to manufacturing activity which:

(a)     is limited to medicinal products to which Article 2 of the Medicines (Exemption from Licences) (Special and Transitional Cases) Order 1971 as amended applies, and consists solely of mixing together medicinal products and ingredients, other than active ingredients, on premises of which the licence holder is the occupier and which he is able to close so as to exclude the public; or

(b)     is limited to assembly only, where all the products to be assembled are for sale or supply in the course of a business and are supplied, without any recommendation, for the purpose of administration to a particular person after the licence holder has been requested by or on behalf of that person, and in that person's presence, to use his judgement as to the treatment required.

(7) The provisions of this paragraph shall not have effect until 22 November 1977 in relation to a licence which has been granted before the coming into operation of these Regulations.

## Standard Provisions for Manufacturer's Licences Relating to Vaccines for Human Use (SI 1971 No.972, Part I, Schedule 4, as amended)

1. Revoked by SI 1992 No. 2846.

2. The licence holder shall provide separate premises or separate parts of premises for the activities specified in the following sub-paragraphs, namely:

(a)     the production and the testing involved in the production of cell cultures for use in the production of vaccine;

(b)     the production and the testing involved in the production of vaccine prepared from viruses; and

(c)     the production and the testing involved in the production of vaccine prepared from micro-organisms or detoxified microbial toxins;

and shall ensure that only persons necessary to each activity as aforesaid shall have access to the separate premises or separate parts of premises provided for that activity.

3. The licence holder shall ensure that any procedure which, in the course of any of the activities specified in the preceding paragraph, involves or might involve:

(a)     the presence of transmissible agents; or

(b)     the use of cell cultures, animal tissues or micro-organisms, other than those from which the vaccine is produced;

shall not be carried out in the separate premises or separate parts of premises as aforesaid.

4. The licence holder shall ensure that no person who has been in contact with transmissible agents or experimental animals other than those connected with the vaccine being produced in the separate premises or separate parts of premises as aforesaid shall

enter those premises or separate parts of premises on the same day that the contact as aforesaid has been made.

5. Before an animal is used in the production of vaccine the licence holder shall take all reasonable steps to ensure that it is free from disease and to this end shall keep the animal in quarantine and under observation for such period as the Licensing Authority may direct.

6. (1) The licence holder shall ensure that animals used in the production of vaccine are isolated and shall provide separate premises (not being the premises or parts of premises referred to in paragraph 2 above) for this purpose.

(2) The licence holder shall ensure that only persons engaged in the production and testing of vaccine or in the maintenance of animals or premises shall have access to the separate premises in which the animals are isolated.

7. The licence holder shall provide a special room capable of being washed and disinfected in the separate premises referred to in paragraph 6 above for the purpose of:

(a)     the inoculation of animals; and
(b)     the collection of material to be used in the preparation of vaccine.

8. Without prejudice to any other requirements to keep records, where vaccines contain or might contain micro-organisms or microbial toxins the licence holder shall keep a durable record, readily available for inspection by a person authorised by the Licensing Authority, of the origin, properties and characteristics of the cell cultures used in the production of those vaccines and shall ensure that the said record is not destroyed for a period of five years from the date when the relevant production occurred.

## Standard Provisions for Manufacturer's Licences Relating to Smallpox (SI 1971 No.972, Part II, Schedule 4, as amended)

1. (1) The licence holder shall ensure that animals used in the production of smallpox vaccine:

(a)     shall only be inoculated on a part of the skin that has been depilated and cleansed and which cannot be soiled by urine or faeces; and
(b)     are kept under observation for 28 days after the collection of the vaccinal material.

(2) Should any animal during the 28 days as aforesaid be found to be suffering from any infection other than vaccinia or show serious or persistent signs of ill health, vaccinal material obtained from that animal shall not be used in the production of smallpox vaccine.

2. Where it is necessary for an animal which has been inoculated as aforesaid to be killed, the licence holder shall ensure that:

(a)     the vaccinal material is collected immediately after the animal has been killed;
(b)     if the Licensing Authority so direct, a post-mortem examination of the carcass of the animal is made by a person with experience of the diseases of the particular animal so killed;
(c)     a durable record of the examination is kept readily available for inspection by a person authorised by the Licensing Authority;
(d)     the said record is not destroyed for a period of five years from the date when the animal was killed; and
(e)     where the examination indicates that the animal was suffering from diseases other than vaccinia, no vaccinal material obtained from that animal shall be used in the production of smallpox vaccine.

### Standard Provisions for Manufacturer's Licences Relating to BCG Vaccine (SI 1971 No.972, Part III, Schedule 4, as amended)

1. The licence holder shall provide separate premises or separate parts of premises for the production of BCG vaccine and shall ensure that only persons necessary to the production and testing of that vaccine shall have access to those separate premises or separate parts of premises.

2. The licence holder shall ensure that any procedure which involves or might involve:

(a)    the presence of transmissible agents other than BCG; or

(b)    the use of microbial cultures other than BCG, shall not be carried out in the separate premises or separate parts of premises referred to in paragraph 1 of this Part of this Schedule.

3. The licence holder shall ensure that all media, glassware and other apparatus issued in the production of BCG vaccine shall be kept and prepared for use in the separate premises or separate parts of premises referred to in paragraph 1 of this Part of this Schedule.

4. The licence holder shall not permit animals to be in the separate premises or separate parts of premises referred to in paragraph 1 of this Part of this Schedule and where it is necessary to use animals for testing BCG vaccine, the tests shall not be carried out in those separate premises or separate parts of premises.

5. (1) The licence holder shall arrange for all persons engaged in the production of BCG vaccine to be examined clinically by a doctor and where appropriate, radiologically and bacteriologically, at least every twelve months and whenever such a person shows signs of ill health.

(2) The licence holder shall ensure (as far as sub-paragraph (c) below is concerned, in so far as is reasonably practicable), that persons falling within the following descriptions shall not engage in the production of BCG vaccine, that is to say:

(a)    persons examined as aforesaid who are found to be suffering from active or potentially active tuberculosis lesions;

(b)    persons who show a negative reaction when tested with tuberculin; or

(c)    persons who are in close contact with a person who is suffering from any active form of tuberculosis.

(3) If on examination as aforesaid a person engaged in the production of BCG vaccine is found to be suffering from active or potentially active tuberculosis lesions, then, after that person has been removed from the separate premises or separate parts of premises referred to in paragraph 1 of this Part of this Schedule, the licence holder shall make arrangements for those separate premises or separate parts of premises and all equipment used in the production of BCG vaccine to be treated in such a manner as to remove the risk of contamination of the vaccine and shall cease to use any unsealed cultures of BCG and all current preparations of BCG vaccine which may have become contaminated with other *Mycobacterium tuberculosis* organisms.

6. The licence holder shall ensure that no person who has been in contact with transmissible agents other than BCG vaccine shall enter the separate premises or separate parts of premises referred to in paragraph 1 of this Part of this Schedule on the same day that the contact as aforesaid has been made.

### Standard Provisions for Manufacturer's Licences Relating to Toxins (SI 1971 No.972, Part IV, Schedule 4, as amended)

1. Revoked by SI 1992 No.2846.

2. The licence holder shall provide separate premises or separate parts of premises for the production and the testing involved in the production of toxins and shall ensure that only

persons necessary to the production and testing of toxins (or related toxoids) shall have access to the separate premises or separate parts of premises as aforesaid.

3. The licence holder shall ensure that any procedure which in the course of the production and testing referred to in the previous paragraph involves or might involve the presence of micro-organisms, plants or animals other than those from which the toxins are to be produced, shall not be carried out in the separate premises or separate parts of premises as aforesaid.

### Standard provisions for Manufacturer's Licences Relating to Sera (SI 1971 No.972, Part V, Schedule 4, as amended)

1. Revoked by SI 1992 No.2846.

2. The licence holder shall ensure that blood used in the production of any serum shall only be collected from living animals in separate premises which:

(a)   are used for no other purpose;
(b)   have impervious walls and floors; and
(c)   are capable of being washed and chemically disinfected.

3. The licence holder shall ensure that an adequate system of manure removal is in operation in the separate premises referred to in paragraph 2 of this Part of this Schedule.

4. Before an animal is used in the production of any serum, the licence holder shall take all reasonable steps to ensure that it is free from disease and to this end shall keep the animal in quarantine and under observation for such period as the Licensing Authority may direct.

5. The licence holder shall notify the Licensing Authority if any animal which has been used in the production of any serum is found to be suffering from an infection other than an infection produced by living organisms against which it is being immunised or shows serious or persistent signs of ill health not attributable to the process of immunisation and shall withhold any serum obtained from that animal from sale, supply or exportation until he has obtained the consent of the Licensing Authority in writing to its release.

6. The licence holder shall notify the Licensing Authority if any post-mortem examination on any animal indicates that any other animals used in the production of any serum are or are likely to be unhealthy, and the licence holder shall not use those animals for the production of any serum until either he has obtained the consent of the Licensing Authority in writing or has complied with any requirements the Licensing Authority may consider necessary in the interest of safety.

7. The licence holder shall ensure that laboratories in which any serum is processed are separate from premises in which animals are housed.

8. The licence holder shall provide such number of sterilisers as are necessary for the sterilisation of all glassware and other apparatus used in the production of sera as aforesaid.

9. Without prejudice to any other requirements to keep records, the licence holder shall keep the following durable records relating to the production of sera readily available for inspection by a person authorised by the Licensing Authority and shall ensure that the said record is not destroyed for a period of five years from the date when the relevant production occurred:

(a)   as to the cultures used:

(i) the source from which the culture was obtained;
(ii) the nature of the material from which the culture was isolated;
(iii) the date of the isolation; and
(iv) evidence of the identity and specificity of the culture;

(b)   as to the procedure used in the immunising of animals:

(i) the method of preparing the culture or antigen used for immunisation;

(ii) the dosage and methods employed in administering the culture or antigen;

(iii) the time in the course of immunisation at which blood is withdrawn for preparation of the serum;

(c)    the results of any tests which may have been applied to the serum to determine its content of specific antibodies or its specific therapeutic potency.

## Standard Provisions for Wholesale Dealer's Licences (Council Directive 92/25/EEC and SI 1971 No.972, Schedule 3, as amended)

1. The licence holder shall provide and maintain such staff, premises, equipment and facilities for the handling, storage and distribution of the medicinal products which he handles, stores or distributes under his licence, as are necessary to avoid deterioration of the medicinal products and he shall not use for such purposes premises other than those specified in the licence or which may be approved from time to time by the Licensing Authority.

2. The licence holder shall provide such information as may be requested by the Licensing Authority concerning the type and quantity of any medicinal product which he currently handles, stores or distributes.

3. The licence holder shall inform the Licensing Authority of any proposed structural alterations to, or discontinuance of use of, premises to which the licence relates or premises which have been approved from time to time by the Licensing Authority.

4. The licence holder shall keep such documents relating to his transactions by way of the sale of medicinal products to which the licence relates as will facilitate the withdrawal or recall from sale or exportation of such products.

4A. Where the licence relates to products to which Chapters II to V of the 1965 Directive apply, the licence holder shall institute an emergency plan which ensures effective implementation of any recall from the market which is either:

(a)    ordered by the Licence Authority or the competent authority of a member state other than the United Kingdom; or

(b)    carried out in co-operation with the manufacturer or the holder of the product licence or of the marketing authorisations granted by the competent authority of a member state other than the United Kingdom in respect of the products.

4B. (1) Where the licence relates to products to which Chapters II to V of the 1965 Directive apply, the licence holder shall keep records, which may be in the form of invoices or on computer or in any other form giving the following information in respect of such products which have been received or despatched:

(a)    the date of receipt and of despatch;

(b)    the name of the medicinal products;

(c)    the quantity of the medicinal products received or despatched;

(d)    the name and address of the person from whom or to whom the products are sold or supplied as appropriate.

N.B. The licence holder may only sell medicinal products to persons who hold authorisations or who are entitled to sell to the public. The licence holder may only purchase from a person who possesses an authorisation.

(2) The record referred to in sub-paragraph (1) above shall be made available for inspection by any person duly authorised in writing by the Licensing Authority for a period of five years after the date of receipt or despatch.

5. Where the licence holder has been informed by the Licensing Authority or by the holder of the product licence that any batch of any medicinal product to which the wholesale dealer's licence relates has been found not to conform as regards strength, quality

or purity with the specification of that product or with the provisions of the Act or of any regulations under the Act that are applicable to the medicinal product, he shall, if so directed, withhold such batch from sale or exportation, so far as may be reasonably practicable, for such period not exceeding six weeks as may be specified by the Licensing Authority.

6. (1) Subject to the provisions of sub-paragraph (2) of this paragraph, no medicinal product to which the wholesale dealer's licence relates shall be sold or offered for sale by way of wholesale dealing by virtue of that licence unless there has been granted in respect of that medicinal product a product licence or certificate of registration which is for the time being in force and any sale or offer for sale shall be in conformity with the provisions of such product licence or certificate of registration.

(2) The provisions of the preceding sub-paragraph of this paragraph shall not apply where:

(a) by virtue of any provisions of the Act or of any order made thereunder, the sale (other than sale by way of wholesale dealing) of the medicinal product to which the wholesale dealer's licence relates is not subject to the restrictions imposed by section 7(2) of the Act; or

(b) the sale or offer for sale by way of wholesale dealing is of a medicinal product the dealings in which, at the time of its acquisition by the licence holder, were not subject to the said restrictions imposed by section 7(2) of the Act; or

(c) at the time of such sale or offer for sale, the licence holder does not know, or could not by reasonable diligence and care have known, that such sale or offer for sale is of a medicinal product, or believes, on reasonable grounds, that the provisions of sub-paragraph (2)(i) or (2)(ii) of this paragraph apply in relation to such sale or offer for sale.

7. The licence holder, for the purpose of enabling the Licensing Authority to ascertain whether there are any grounds for suspending, revoking or varying any licence or certificate granted or issued under Part II of the Act, shall permit, and provide all necessary facilities to enable any person duly authorised in writing by the Licensing Authority, on production if required of his credentials, to carry out such inspection or to take samples or copies, in relation to things belonging to, or any business carried on by, the licence holder, as such person would have the right to carry out or take under the Act for the purpose of verifying any statement contained in an application for a licence or certificate.

7A. (1) Where the licence relates to products to which Chapters II to V of the 1965 Directive apply, the licence holder shall at all times have at his disposal the services of a person (in this paragraph called a *responsible person*) who possesses in the opinion of the Licensing Authority:

(a) knowledge of the activities to be carried out and of the procedures to be performed under the licence which is adequate for performing the functions of the responsible person; and

(b) experience in those activities and procedures which is adequate for those purposes.

(2) The functions of the responsible person shall be to ensure that the conditions under which the licence has been granted have been, and are being, complied with and that the quality of the products is maintained in accordance with the requirements of the appropriate product licence.

(3) The provisions of sub-paragraphs (5) and (6) of paragraph 8 of this Schedule shall apply in relation to a responsible person as they apply to a qualified person within the meaning of that paragraph but as though the references to:

(a) the provisions of Articles 23 and 24 of the Second Council Directive as respects qualifications and experience were to the provisions of sub-paragraph (1) and (2) of this paragraph; and

(b) sub-paragraph (3) of paragraph 8 were to sub-paragraph (2) of this paragraph.

7B. (1) Where the licence relates to products to which Chapters II to V of the 1965 Directive apply, the licence holder shall obtain supplies of such products only from:

(a)     any person who is the holder of a manufacturer's licence or a wholesale dealer's licence which relates to those products; or

(b)     any person who holds an authorisation granted by the competent authority of a member state other than the United Kingdom authorising the manufacture of such products or the distribution by way of wholesale dealing of such products.

7C. (1) Where the licence relates to products to which Chapters II to V of the 1965 Directive apply, the licence holder shall distribute them by way of wholesale dealing only to:

(a)     the holder of a wholesale dealer's licence which relates to those products;

(b)     the holder of an authorisation granted by the competent authority of a member state other than the United Kingdom authorising the supply of such products by way of wholesale distribution; or

(c)     any person who may lawfully sell those products by retail or may lawfully supply them in circumstances corresponding to retail sale; or,

(d)     any person who may lawfully administer those products.

(2) where supply is made pursuant to paragraph (1)(c) above the licence holder shall enclose with the products a document which makes it possible to ascertain:

(a)     the date on which the transaction took place;
(b)     the name and pharmaceutical form of the products;
(c)     the quantity of the products supplied;
(d)     the names and addresses of the persons from whom the products were supplied.

8. (1) Subject to sub-paragraphs (7), (7A) and (8) below, where the licence relates to imported proprietary products the licence holder shall at all times have at his disposal the services of a person who as respects qualifications and experience satisfies the provisions of Articles 23 and 24 of the Second Council Directive to carry out the functions specified in sub-paragraph (3) below (*qualified person*). For the purposes of this paragraph, but without prejudice to sub-paragraph (6) below, the licence holder may regard a person as satisfying the provisions of the said Article 24 as respects formal qualifications if he produces evidence that he is a member of the Royal Pharmaceutical Society or of the Royal Society of Chemistry or of such other body as may appear to the Licensing Authority to be an appropriate body for the purpose, and that he is regarded by the body of which he is a member as so satisfying those provisions.

(2) The licence holder shall at all times provide and maintain staff, premises, equipment and facilities as will enable the qualified person who is at his disposal to carry out the said functions.

(3) The functions to be carried out by the qualified person shall be as follows:

(a)     to ensure that each production batch of any imported proprietary product to which the licence relates has undergone a full qualitative analysis, a quantitative analysis of at least all the active ingredients and all other tests or checks necessary to ensure that the quality of the product imported satisfies the requirements of the product licence which relates to the product; or

(aa)    where there is in relation to the imported proprietary product, a certificate of registration, to ensure that each batch of the product has been tested in accordance with the manufacturing and control file submitted with the application for that certificate;

(b)     to certify in a register or other record appropriate for the purpose whether each batch of the imported proprietary product to which the licence relates satisfies the requirements set out in (a) or (as the case may be) (aa) above and to ensure that such register or other record is regularly maintained.

Provided that the above functions shall be deemed to be carried out in respect of a batch which had entered the territory of another member state prior to its importation if there is available evidence in writing, signed by a person carrying out the functions of a qualified person in that member state, that the batch in question satisfies the requirements set out in (a) above.

(4) The licence holder shall keep the said register or other record readily available for inspection by a person authorised by the Licensing Authority and such register or other record shall not be destroyed for a period of five years from the date of the certification referred to in sub-paragraph (3)(b) above.

(5) The licence holder shall notify the Licensing Authority of the name and address and degrees, diplomas or qualifications and experience of the person who will carry out the functions of a qualified person and shall notify the Licensing Authority of any change as to the qualified person and shall not permit any person to act as a qualified person except the person named in his licence as the qualified person for the purposes of this paragraph or, subject to the provisions of paragraph (6) below, any other such person whose name is notified to the Licensing Authority.

(6) Where, after giving the licence holder and the person acting as a qualified person the opportunity of making representations to them (orally or in writing), the Licensing Authority are of the opinion that the person so acting does not satisfy the provisions of the said Articles 23 and 24 of the Second Council Directive as respects qualifications and experience, or that he is failing to carry out the functions specified in sub-paragraph (3) above, and have notified the licence holder accordingly in writing, the licence holder shall not permit that person to act as a qualified person so long as the said notification has not been withdrawn by the Licensing Authority.

(7) The provisions of this paragraph shall not apply where the imported proprietary product that is to be sold or offered for sale or in any other way distributed has been in the possession of a person in the course of his business who is the holder of a wholesale dealer's licence which relates to imported proprietary products of the same description in circumstances by virtue of which that licence holder is required to comply with the provisions of this paragraph.

(7A) The provisions of this paragraph shall also not apply where the imported proprietary product is an exempt imported product.

(8) The provisions of this paragraph shall also not apply where the licence holder handles the imported proprietary product:

(a)    in the course of the provision of facilities solely for the transport of the medicinal product; or

(b)    in the course of a business carried on by him as an import agent where he imports the medicinal product solely to the order of another person who intends, in the course of a business carried on by him, to sell, or offer for sale the medicinal product by way of wholesale dealing or in any other way intends to distribute the medicinal product.

(9) The provisions of this paragraph shall not have effect until 22 November 1977 in relation to a licence which has been granted before the coming into operation of these regulations.

8A. (1) Where the licence relates to imported proprietary products, the licence holder shall in relation to medicinal products for human use:

(a)    ensure that all manufacture and assembly operations have been carried out by a duly authorised manufacturer or assembler and that the products have been manufactured or assembled in accordance with the principles and guidelines of good manufacturing practice;

(b)    keep readily available for examination by a person authorised by the Licensing Authority, samples of each batch of finished medicinal products for at least one year after their expiry date except where the licence holder is authorised by the Licensing Authority to destroy any such samples earlier;

(c) implement a system for recording and reviewing complaints relating to the medicinal products to which his licence relates, together with an effective system for recalling promptly and at any time any such medicinal product in the distribution network; and

(d) record and investigate all such and immediately inform the Licensing Authority of any defect which could result in a recall from sale, supply or exportation or is an abnormal restriction on such sale, supply or exportation.

8B. (1) Where the licence relates to exempted imported products, the licence holder shall only sell or supply such products in response to a bona fide unsolicited order to fulfil special needs, formulated in accordance with the specification of a doctor or dentist and for use by his individual patients on his direct personal responsibility and where the provisions set out in sub-paragraphs (2) to (9) are complied with.

(2) No later than 28 days prior to each importation of an exempted imported product, the licence holder shall give written notice to the Licensing Authority stating his intention to import that medicinal product and stating the following particulars:

(a) the name of the medicinal product, being the brand name or the common name, or the scientific name, and any name, if different, under which the medicinal product is to be sold or supplied in the United Kingdom;

(b) any trademark or name of the manufacturer of the medicinal product;

(c) in respect of each active constituent of the medicinal product, any international non-proprietary or British approved name or monograph name or where that constituent does not have an international non-proprietary name, a British approved name or monograph name, the accepted scientific name or any other name descriptive of the true nature of the constituent;

(d) the quantity of the medicinal product which is to be imported which shall not exceed the quantity specified in sub-paragraph (6); and

(e) the name and address of the manufacturer or assembler of that medicinal product in the form in which it is to be imported and, if the person who will supply that medicinal product for importation is not the manufacturer or imported, the name and address of such supplier.

(3) Subject to sub-paragraph (4), the licence holder shall not import the exempt imported product if, before the end of 28 days from the date on which the Licensing Authority sends or gives the licence holder an acknowledgement in writing by the Licensing Authority that they have received the notice referred to in sub-paragraph (2) above, the Licensing Authority have notified him in writing that the product should not be imported.

(4) The licence holder may import the exempted imported product referred to in the notice where he has been notified in writing by the Licensing Authority before the end of the 28 day period referred to in sub-paragraph (3), that the exempted import product may be imported.

(5) Where the licence holder sell or supplies exempted imported product he shall in addition to those records mentioned in 4B of this Schedule make and maintain written records relating to:

(a) the batch number of the batch of the product from which the sale or supply was made; and

(b) details of any adverse reaction to the product sold or supplied of which he becomes aware.

(6) Where the licence holder shall import no more on anyone occasion than such an amount as is sufficient for 25 single administrations, or 25 courses of treatment where the amount imported is sufficient for a maximum of three months' treatment and on any such occasion shall not import more than the quantity notified to the Licensing Authority under sub-paragraph (2)(d).

(7) the licence holder shall inform the Licensing Authority forthwith of any matter coming to his attention which might reasonably cause the Licensing Authority to believe

that the medicinal product can no longer be regarded either as a product which can safely be administered to human beings or as a product which is of satisfactory quality for such administration.

(8) The licence holder shall not issue an advertisement, catalogue, price list or circular relating to the exempted imported product or make any representations in respect of that product.

(9) The licence holder shall cease importing or supplying an exempt imported product if he has received a notice in writing from the Licensing Authority directing that, as from a date specified in that notice, a particular product or class of products shall no longer be imported or supplied.

(10) In this paragraph:

*British approved name* means the name which appears in the current edition of the list prepared by the appropriate body in accordance with section 100 of the Act and published by the Ministers on the recommendation of the Medicines Commission and *current* in this definition means current at the time the notice is sent to the Licensing Authority.

*Common name* means the international non-proprietary name or, if one does not exist, the usual common name.

*International non-proprietary name* means the name which has been selected by the World Health Organization as a recommended international non-proprietary name and in respect of which the Director-General of the World Health Organization has given notice to that effect in the *World Health Organization Chronicle*.

*Monograph name* means the name or approved synonym which appears at the head of a monograph in the current edition of the *British Pharmacopoeia*, the *British Pharmaceutical Codex*, the *European Pharmacopoeia* or a foreign or international compendium of standards and *current* in this definition means current at the time the notice is sent to the Licensing Authority.

APPENDIX SIX

# Medicines Act 1968

# Particulars Required in Data

# Sheets

The Medicines (Data Sheet) Regulations 1972 (SI 1972 No.2076, as amended) prescribe the form of data sheets and the particulars to be contained in them which holders of marketing authorisations are required, unless there is a summary of product characteristics, to send or deliver to practitioners in connection with any advertisement or representation. The regulations are described briefly in Chapter 3.

Schedule 1 to the regulations sets out the requirements as to shape, weight, colour and typesetting with which data sheets must comply. Schedules 2 and 3, the substance of which is reproduced below, set out the particulars required in data sheets relating to medicinal products for human use (Schedule 2) and for administration to animals (Schedule 3). The required data sheet headings are shown in *italics*, followed by specifications for the particulars to appear under each heading.

## Products for Human Use

Schedule 2 requires data sheets for products *for human use* to include the following:

1.  *Name of Product*: Name of the medicinal product and, if the medicinal product has an approved name, the approved name.

2.  *Presentation*: Description of appearance and pharmaceutical form of the medicinal product together with the following information that is to say:

    (a)  where the medicinal product contains active ingredients all of which can be definitively identified:

        (i)  a list of such ingredients, each described by its approved name or monograph name or, where it has no approved name or monograph name, any other descriptive application; and

(ii) the quantity of each such ingredient contained in each unit or dose of the medicinal product or, where there is no such unit or dose, the percentage of each such ingredient contained in the medicinal product;

(b) where the medicinal product contains any active ingredient that cannot be definitively identified:

(i) the information as required under (a) above in respect of each identifiable active ingredient (if any); and

(ii) a description of the material to which the activity of any other ingredient is ascribed and, where appropriate, a statement of the activity or potency of the medicinal product;

(c) where there are no active ingredients in the medicinal product, a statement indicating the material of which that medicinal product consists.

3. *Uses*: Principal action (if any) of the medicinal product and the purposes for which it is recommended to be used.

4. *Dosage and Administration*: Where the medicinal product is recommended for administration only to adults, the dosage (if any) for adults stating, unless it is otherwise apparent, that the medicinal product is not recommended for administration to children and, where the medicinal product is recommended for administration only to children, the dosage (if any) for children stating, unless it is otherwise apparent, that it is not recommended for administration to adults and, where it is recommended for administration to both adults and children, both such dosages (if any) and in each case the methods and routes of administration and, where appropriate, recommendations as to diluents.

5. *Contra-indications, Warnings, etc.*: Contra-indications, warnings, precautions and action to be taken in the event of overdosage, relating to the medicinal product and main side-effects and adverse reactions likely to be associated therewith and, where there are no such particulars to be given, a statement to that effect shall be made; where required in the interests of safety, the antidote or other appropriate action to be taken.

6. *Pharmaceutical Precautions*: Special requirements for the storage of medicinal products and, where appropriate, pharmaceutical precautions including recommendations as to excipients, diluents and other additives and as to suitable containers, or, where there are no such requirements or no such precautions, a statement to that effect shall be made.

7. *Legal Category*: References to statutory provisions relating to sale or supply of the medicinal product.

8. *Package Quantities*: Quantity or amount of the medicinal product in each size of package or container for retail sale, or supply in circumstances corresponding to retail sale.

9. *Further Information*: Such further information (if any) as may be necessary to assist the practitioner in the proper understanding, recognition, administration and use of the medicinal product provided that such information shall not cover more than one-tenth of the total surface of the data sheet.

10. *Product Licence Numbers, Names and Addresses*: Product licence number of the medicinal product and (a) name and address of the holder of the marketing authorisation/product licence, or (b) the business name and address of the part of his business that is responsible for its sale and supply, or (c) the name and address of a

person named in the product licence as being responsible for, or permitted to participate in, its sale and supply, unless, as respects the name and address in the case of a product information compendium, data sheets are grouped together by references to any name falling within either (a), (b), or (c) of this paragraph and the name and address appears either at the head of that group or in the first data sheet of that group.

11.    *Date of Preparation or Last Review*: Date of preparation of the data sheet or, where since such preparation there has been a review or revision of the data sheet, the date of the last such review or revision.

## Products for Administration to Animals

Schedule 3 requires data sheets for products for administration to animals to contain the same particulars as data sheets for products for human use, except the following are substituted:

4.    *Dosage and Administration*: Dosage (if any), for the medicinal product together with methods and routes of administration according to species and categories within species and, where appropriate, recommendations as to diluents.

5.    *Contra-indications, Warnings, etc.*: Contra-indications, warnings, precautions, and action to be taken in the event of overdosage, relating to the medicinal product and main side-effects and adverse reactions likely to be associated therewith including, where necessary, measures for the protection of:

(a)    operators; and
(b)    consumers of the whole or any part of a carcase or any produce of an animal to which the medicinal product has been administered, including withdrawal periods, if any; and
(c)    livestock, wildlife and others; and

where there are no such particulars to be given a statement to that effect shall be made; where required in the interests of safety, the antidote or other appropriate action to be taken.

## Summary of Product Characteristics

See Appendix 3, pages 396–397.

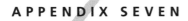

APPENDIX SEVEN

# Medicines Act 1968
# Certificates of Analysis

Certificates of analysis of samples taken under the Act are required to be in the form set out in the Schedule to The Medicines (Certificates of Analysis) Regulations 1977 (SI 1977 No.1399). There are three forms of certificate. The form in Part I of the Schedule applies to samples submitted to a public analyst by a person who has purchased a medicinal product but who is not a 'sampling officer'. When a sample is submitted by a sampling officer to a public analyst the form in Part II applies. When such a sample is submitted to a person having the management or control of a laboratory which is used by arrangement with an enforcement authority then the form in Part III applies.

## Forms of Certificates of Analysis or Examination

PART I
CERTIFICATE OF ANALYSIS OF SAMPLE

This certificate is issued under section 115(6) of the Medicines Act 1968 by me, the undersigned, public analyst for the[1]

I hereby certify that I received on the        day of        20  ,. from[2]
, *[to whom the sample had been submitted
by[3]        ] one part of a sample of[4]
for analysis; which was undamaged, duly sealed and
fastened up and marked[5]        ; and that the said part has
been analysed by me or under my direction. I further certify the results of analysis to be as
follows:[6]

and I am of the opinion that[7].

day of                 20   .

(Signature and address of analyst)

*Delete words in square brackets if not required.

---

NOTES

These notes and the numbers referring to them are for guidance only and do not form part of and need not appear on the certificate.

(1)   Here insert the name of the local authority.
(2)   Here insert, as appropriate, the name of the person who submitted the sample for analysis or the name of the public analyst to whom the sample was originally submitted.
(3)   Here insert the name of the person who originally submitted the sample for analysis.
(4)   Here insert the name or description of the substance or article.
(5)   Here insert the distinguishing mark on the sample and the date of sampling shown thereon.
(6)   Here insert relevant results as appropriate, e.g. physical characteristics, impurities microbial or chemical, cross-contamination with other medicines, uniformity of dosage, conformance with specification or label claims.
(7)   Here enter whether the sample complies with the appropriate monograph standard (if any), or other appropriate interpretation of the results.

PART II
CERTIFICATE OF ANALYSIS OF SAMPLE

This certificate is issued under section 19(61) of Schedule 3 to the Medicines Act 1968 by me, the undersigned, public analyst for the[1]

I hereby certify that I received on the                 day of                 19   , from[2]
                 ,   *[to   whom   the   sample   had   been   submitted   by[3]
] one part of a sample of[4]                                          for
analysis;   which   was   undamaged,   duly   sealed   and   fastened   up   and   marked[5]
                 ; and that the said part has been analysed by me or under my direction. I
further certify the results of anlaysis to be as follows:[6]

and I am of the opinion that[7]

day of                 20   .

(Signature and address of analyst)

*Delete words in square brackets if not required.

NOTES

These notes and the numbers referring to them are for guidance only and do not form part of and need not appear on the certificate.
(1)   Here insert the name of the local authority.
(2)   Here insert the name of the sample officer who submitted the sample for analysis, or the name of the public analyst to whom the sample was originally submitted.
(3)   Here insert the name of the sampling officer who submitted the sample for analysis.
(4)   Here insert the name or description of the substance or article.
(5)   Here insert the distinguishing mark on the sample and the date of sampling shown thereon.
(6)   Here insert the relevant results as appropriate, e.g. physical characteristics, impurities microbial or chemical, cross-contamination with other medicines, uniformity of dosage, conformance with specifications or label claims.
(7)   Here enter whether the sample complies with the appropriate monograph standard (if any), or other appropriate interpretation of the results.

PART III

CERTIFICATE OF ANALYSIS OR EXAMINATION OF SAMPLE

This certificate is issued under paragraph 19(2) of Schedule 3 to the Medicines Act 1968 by me, the undersigned, *[having the management or control] [being a person appointed for the purpose of issuing this certificate by[1],
the person having the management or control] of the[2]
with which arrangements have been made in pursuance of the provisions of the Medicines Act 1968. I hereby certify that *[I] [the said[1]]
received on the            day of                20  , from[3]
one part of a sample of[4]                          for *[analysis] [examination]; which was undamaged, duly sealed and fastened up and marked[5]                          and that the said part has been *[analysed] [examined] *[by me] [by the said[1]                          ] [under the direction of the said[1]]
I further certify the results of *[analysis] [examination] to be as follows:[6]


and I am of the opinion that[7]

        day of                20  .



(Signature and address of the person who issues the certificate)
*Delete words in square brackets if not required.

---

NOTES

These notes and the numbers referring to them are for guidance only and do not form part of and need not appear on the certificate.
(1)   Here insert the name of the person having the management or control of the laboratory.
(2)   Here insert the name of the laboratory.
(3)   Here insert the name of the sampling officer who submitted the sample.
(4)   Here insert the name or description of the substance or article.
(5)   Here insert the distinguishing mark on the sample and the date of sampling shown thereon.
(6)   Here insert relevant results as appropriate, e.g. physical characteristics, impurities microbial or chemical, cross-contamination with other medicines, uniformity of dosage, conformance with specification or label claims.
(7)   Here enter whether the sample complies with the appropriate monograph standard (if any), or other appropriate interpretation of the results.

APPENDIX EIGHT

# Medicines Act 1968

# Patient Group Directions (PGD)

**Classes of Individuals by Whom Prescription Only Medicines may be Supplied or Administered**

Pharmacists
Registered nurses
Registered midwives
Registered health visitors
Registered ophthalmic opticians
State registered chiropodists
Registered orthoptists
Registered physiotherapists
Registered radiographers
Individuals who hold a certificate of proficiency in ambulance paramedic skills issued by the Secretary of State or state registered paramedics

**Particulars to be Included in a Patient Group Direction**

(a)   the period during which the Direction shall have effect;
(b)   the description or class of Prescription Only Medicine to which the Direction applies;
(c)   whether there are any restrictions on the quantity of medicine which may be supplied on any one occasion, and, if so, what restrictions;
(d)   the clinical situations which Prescription Only Medicines of that description or class may be used to treat;

(e)    the clinical criteria under which the person shall be eligible for treatment;

(f)    whether any class is excluded from treatment under the Direction and, if so what class of person;

(g)    whether there are any circumstances in which further advice should be sought from a doctor or dentist and if so what circumstances;

(h)    the pharmaceutical form or forms in which Prescription Only Medicines of that class or description are to be administered;

(i)    the strength, or maximum strength, at which Prescription Only Medicines of that description or class are to be administered;

(j)    the applicable dosage or maximum dosage;

(k)    the route of administration;

(l)    the frequency of administration;

(m)    any minimum or maximum period of administration applicable to Prescription Only Medicines of that description or class;

(n)    whether there are any relevant warnings to note and, if so, what warnings;

(o)    whether there is any follow up action to be taken in any circumstances and, if so, what action and in what circumstances;

(p)    arrangements for referral for medical advice;

(q)    details of the records to be kept of the supply, or the administration, of medicines under the Direction.

APPENDIX NINE

# Medicines Act 1968

## Veterinary Drugs: Pharmacy and Merchants List (PML)

The Medicines (Exemptions for Merchants in Veterinary Drugs) Order 1998 (SI 1998 No.1044, as amended) permits the retail sale of certain categories of veterinary drugs which are listed by the Minister. This list is open to inspection at the office of the Veterinary Medicines directorate and copies will be publicly available and published regularly (see Chapter 12). The Minister's list includes such products specified only by their product licence number and name.

The vast majority of pharmacies do not regularly handle these listed medicines which are used in the commercial husbandry of livestock. For the convenience of pharmacists, the details of the listed cat, dog and horse wormers are set out below. They are all PML.

### Veterinary Drugs Saleable by Pharmacists, Merchants and Saddlers

#### Cat and Dog Wormers

| Marketing Authorisation No. | Name of Product |
| --- | --- |
| Vm 00010/4113 | Bayer Dog Wormer Tablets |
| Vm 00010/4115 | Bayer Multi-Worm for Dogs |
| Vm 00715/4071 | Bob Martins Easy to use Wormer Granules |
| Vm 00010/4102 | Drontal Puppy Suspension |
| Vm 11188/4003 | Granofen Wormer for Cats and Dogs |
| Vm 15476/4059 | Panacur Pet Paste |
| Vm 11990/4014 | Zerofen 22% Granules for Cats and Dogs |

**Horse Wormers**

| Marketing Authorisation No. | Name of Product |
| --- | --- |
| Vm 00057/4131 | Equitac |
| Vm 0025/4069 | Eqvalan Paste for Horses and Donkeys |
| Vm 00242/4038 | Furexel |
| Vm 0844/4207 | Multiwurma |
| Vm 0286/4039 | Oxfendazole Horse Paste |
| Vm 15476/4060 | Panacur Equine Guard |
| Vm 15476/4053 | Panacur Paste |
| Vm 00086/4158 | Panacur 22% Granules Horse Wormer |
| Vm 15476/4009 | Panacur 10% Suspension |
| Vm 12597/4013 | Pyratape-P Horse Wormer |
| Vm 00057/4060 | Strongid-P Granules |
| Vm 00057/4062 | Strongid-P Paste |
| Vm 05869/4151 | Systamex Horse Paste Wormer |
| Vm 00242/4013 | Telmin |
| Vm 00242/4026 | Telmin B |
| Vm 00242/4014 | Telmin Paste |
| Vm 00015/4052 | Verdisol |
| Vm 11990/4017 | Zerofen 22% Equine Granules |

# Misuse of Drugs Act 1971

## Controlled Drugs Classified for Level of Penalties

Schedule 2 to the Act classifies Controlled Drugs into three lists (Class A, Class B, and Class C) for the purpose of the level of penalties for offences under the Act. The penalties are given in Schedule 3 (not reproduced here).

Since the Act came into force numerous additions have been made, by Orders, to the original list of drugs in Schedule 2. In this appendix a date shown against any drug indicates the year it was added to the list.

For the Schedules to the Misuse of Drugs Regulations, which classify Controlled Drugs according to the relevant regimes of control, see Appendix 11.

### Schedule 2

### Part I: Class A Drugs

1(a). The following substances and products, namely:

Acetorphine
Alfentanil (1984)
Allylprodine
Alphacetylmethadol
Alphameprodine
Alphamethadol
Alphaprodine
Anileridine
Benzethidine
Benzylmorphine (3-benzylmorphine)

Betacetylmethadol
Betameprodine
Betamethadol
Betaprodine
Bezitramide
4-Bromo-2,5-dimethoxy-α-
    methylphenethylamine (1975)
Bufotenine
Cannabinol, except where contained in
    cannabis or cannabis resin

Cannabinol derivatives, not being Dronebenol or its stereoisomers

Carfentanil (1986)

Clonitazene

Coca leaf

Cocaine

4-Cyano-2-dimethylamino-4,4-diphenylbutane

4-Cyano-1-methyl-4-phenylpiperidine

Desomorphine

Dextromoramide

Diamorphine

Diampromide

Diethylthiambutene

N,N-Diethyltryptamine

Difenoxin (1-(3-cyano-3,3-diphenylpropyl)-4-phenylpiperidine-4-carboxylic acid) (1975)

Dihydrocodeinone O-carboxymethyloxime

Dihydromorphine

Dimenoxadole

Dimepheptanol

Dimethylthiambutene

2,5-Dimethoxy-α,4-dimethylphenethylamine

N,N-Dimethyltryptamine

Dioxaphetyl butyrate

Diphenoxylate

Dipipanone

Drotebanol (3,4-dimethoxy-17-methylmorphinan-6β,14-diol) (1973)

Ecgonine, and any derivative of ecgonine which is convertible to ecgonine or to cocaine

Ethylmethylthiambutene

Eticyclidine (1984)

Etonitazene

Etorphine

Etoxeridine

Etryptamine (1998)

Fentanyl

Furethidine

Hydromorphinol

Hydromorphone

Hydroxypethidine

N-Hydroxy-tenamphetamine (1990)

Isomethadone

Ketobemidone

Levomethorphan

Levomoramide

Levophenacylmorphan

Levorphanol

Lofentanil (1986)

Lysergamide

Lysergide and other N-alkyl derivatives of lysergamide

Mescaline

Metazocine

Methadone

Methadyl acetate

Methyldesorphine

Methyldihydromorphine (6-methyldihydromorphine)

4-Methylaminorex (1990)

2-Methyl-3-morpholino-1,1-diphenylpropanecarboxylic acid

1-Methyl-4-phenylpiperidine-4-carboxylic acid

Metopon

Morpheridine

Morphine

Morphine methobromide, morphine N-oxide and other pentavalent nitrogen morphine derivatives

Myrophine

Nicomorphine (3,6-dinicotinoyl-morphine)

Noracymethadol

Norlevorphanol

Normethadone

Normorphine

Norpipanone

Opium, whether raw, prepared or medicinal

Oxycodone

Oxymorphone

Pethidine

Phenadoxone

Phenampromide

Phenazocine

Phencyclidine (1979)

4-Phenylpiperidine-4-carboxylic acid ethyl ester

Phenomorphan

Phenoperidine

Piminodine

Piritramide

Poppy-straw and concentrate of poppy-straw

Proheptazine

Properidine (1-methyl-4-phenylpiperidine-4-carboxylic acid isopropyl ester)

Psilocin

Racemethorphan

Racemoramide

Racemorphan

Rolicyclidine (1984)

Sufentanil (1983)

Tenocyclidine (1984)

Thebacon

Thebaine

Tilidate (1983)

Trimeperidine

(b)+   any compound (not being a compound for the time being specified in sub-paragraph (a) above) structurally derived from tryptamine or from a ring-hydroxy tryptamine by substitution at the nitrogen atom of the sidechain with one or more alkyl substituents but no other substituent.

(c)+   any compound (not being methoxyphenamine or a compound for the time being specified in sub-paragraph (a) above) structurally derived from phenethylamine, an N-alkylphenethylamine, α-methylphenethylamine, an N-alkyl-α-methyl-phenethyl-amine, α-ethyl-phenethylamine, or an N-alkyl-α-ethyl-phenethylamine by substitution in the ring to any extent with alkyl, alkoxy, alkylenedioxy or halide substituents, whether or not further substituted in the ring by one or more other univalent substituents.

[Note +: sub-paragraphs (b) and (c) added by SI 1977 No.1243.]

(d) *   any compound (not being a compound for the time being specified in sub-paragraph (a) above) structurally derived from fentanyl by modification in any of the following ways, that is to say:

   (i)   by replacement of the phenyl portion of the phenethyl group by any hetero-monocycle whether or not further substituted in the heterocycle;
   (ii)   by substitution in the phenethyl group with alkyl, alkenyl, alkoxy, hydroxy, halogeno, haloalkyl, amino or nitro groups;
   (iii)   by substitution in the piperidine ring with alkyl or alkenyl groups;
   (iv)   by substitution in the aniline ring with alkyl, alkoxy, alkylenedioxy, halogeno or haloalkyl groups;
   (v)   by substitution at the 4- position of the piperidine ring with any alkoxycarbonyl or alkoxyalkyl or acyloxy group;
   (vi)   by replacement of the N-propionyl group by another acyl group;

(e) *   any compound (not being a compound for the time being specified in sub-paragraph (a) above) structurally derived from pethidine by modification in any of the following ways, that is to say:

   (i)   by replacement of the 1-methyl group by an acyl, alkyl whether or not unsaturated, benzyl or phenethyl group, whether or not further substituted;
   (ii)   by substitution in the piperidine ring with alkyl or alkenyl groups or with a propano bridge, whether or not further substituted;
   (iii)   by substitution in the 4-phenyl ring with alkyl, alkoxy, aryloxy, halogeno or haloalkyl groups;
   (iv)   by replacement of the 4-ethoxycarbonyl by any other alkoxycarbonyl or any alkoxyalkyl or acyloxy group;
   (v)   by formation of an N-oxide or of a quaternary base.

2. Any stereoisomeric form of a substance for the time being specified in paragraph 1 above not being dextromethorphan or dextrorphan.

3. Any ester or ether of a substance for the time being specified in paragraph 1 or 2 above, not being a substance for the time being specified in Part II of this Schedule.

4. Any salt of a substance for the time being specified in any of paragraphs 1 to 3 above.

5. Any preparation or other product containing a substance or product for the time being specified in any of paragraphs 1 to 4 above.

6. Any preparation designed for administration by injection which includes a substance or product for the time being specified in any of paragraphs 1 to 3 of Part II of this Schedule.

[Note *: sub-paragraphs (d) and (e) added by SI 1986 No.2230.]

## Part II: Class B Drugs

1.(a) The following substances and products, namely:

Acetyldihydrocodeine
Amphetamine
Cannabis and cannabis resin
Codeine
Dihydrocodeine
Ethylmorphine (3-ethylmorphine)
Glutethimide (1985)
Lefetamine (1986)
Mecloqualone (1984)
Methaqualone (1984)
Methcathinone (1998)
Methylamphetamine

Methylphenidate
Methylphenobarbitone (1984)
Nicocodine
Nicodicodine (6-nicotinoyldihydrocodeine) (1973)
Norcodeine
Pentazocine (1985)
Phenmetrazine
Pholcodine
Propiram
Zipeprol (1998)

(b) any 5,5- disubstituted barbituric acid.

2. Any stereoisomeric form of a substance for the time being specified in paragraph 1 of this Part of this Schedule.

3. Any salt of a substance for the time being specified in paragraph 1 or 2 of this Part of this Schedule.

4. Any preparation or other product containing a substance or product for the time being specified in any of paragraphs 1 to 3 of this Part of this Schedule, not being a preparation falling within paragraph 6 of Part I of this Schedule.

## Part III: Class C Drugs

1.(a) The following substances, namely:

Alprazolam
Aminorex (1998)
Benzphetamine
Bromazepam (1985)
Brotizolam (1998)
Camazepam (1985)
Cathine (1986)
Cathinone (1986)
Chlordiazepoxide (1985)
Clorphentermine
Clobazam (1985)
Clonazepam (1985)
Clorazepic acid (1985)
Clotiazepam (1985)
Cloxazolam (1985)
Delorazepam (1985)
Dextropropoxyphene (1983)
Diazepam (1985)
Diethylpropion (1984)
Estazolam (1985)
Ethchlorvynol
Ethinamate (1985)
Ethyl loflazepate (1985)
N-Ethylamphetamine
Fencamfamin (1986)
Fenethylline (1986)
Fenproporex (1986)
Fludiazepam (1985)
Flunitrazepam (1985)
Flurazepam (1985)

Halazepam (1985)
Haloxazolam (1985)
Ketazolam (1985)
Loprazolam (1985)
Lorazepam (1985)
Lormetazepam (1985)
Mazindol (1985)
Medazepam (1985)
Mefenorex (1985)
Mephentermine
Meprobamate (1985)
Mesocarb (1998)
Methyprylone (1985)
Midazolam (1990)
Nimetazepam (1985)
Nitrazepam (1985)
Nordazepam (1985)
Oxazepam (1985)
Oxazolam (1985)
Pemoline (1989)
Phendimetrazine
Phentermine (1985)
Pinazepam (1985)
Pipradol
Prazepam (1985)
Pyrovalerone (1986)
Temazepam (1985)
Tetrazepam (1985)
Triazolam (1985)

2. Any stereoisomeric form of a substance for the time being specified in paragraph 1 of this Part of this Schedule, not being phenylpropanolamine.

3. Any salt of a substance for the time being specified in paragraph 1 or 2 of this Part of this Schedule.

4. Any preparation or other product containing a substance for the time being specified in any of paragraphs 1 to 3 of this Part of this Schedule, Part IV.

5. The following substances:

| | |
|---|---|
| Atamestane | Metribolone |
| Bolandiol | Mibolerone |
| Bolazine | Nandrolone |
| Boldenone | Norboletone |
| Bolenol | Norclostebol |
| Calusterone | Norethandrolone |
| 4-Chloromethandienone | Ovandrotone |
| Clostebol | Oxabolone |
| Drostanolone | Oxandrolone |
| Enestebol | Oxymesterone |
| Epitiostanol | Oxymetholone |
| Ethyloestrenol | Prasterone |
| Fluoxymesterone | Propetandrol |
| Formebolone | Quinbolone |
| Furazabol | Roxibolone |
| Mesbolone | Silandrone |
| Mestanolone | Stanozolol |
| Mesterolone | Stenbolone |
| Methandienone | Testosterone |
| Methandriol | Thiomesterone |
| Methenolone | Trenbolone |
| Methyltestosterone | |

6. Any compound (not being Trilostane or a compound for the time being specified in paragraph 5 above) structurally derived from 17-hydroxyandrostan-3-one or from 17-hydroxy-estran-3-one by modification in any of the following ways:

(a)　by further substitution at position 17 by a methyl or ethyl group;

(b)　by substitution to any extent at one or more positions 1, 2, 4, 6, 7, 9, 11, or 16, but at no other position;

(c)　by unsaturation in the carbocyclic ring system to any extent, provided that there are no more than two ethylenic bonds in any one carbocyclic ring;

(d)　by fusion of ring A with a heterocyclic system.

7. Any substance which is an ester or ether (or, where more than one hydroxyl function is available, both an ester and an ether) of a substance specified in paragraph 5 above or described in paragraph 6 above.

8.

| | |
|---|---|
| Chorionic Gonadotrophin (HCG) | Somatotropin |
| Clenbuterol | Somatrem |
| Non-human chorionic gonadotrophin | Somatropin |

## Meaning of Certain Expressions Used in This Schedule

For the purposes of this Schedule the following expressions (which are not among those defined in section 37(1) of this Act) have the meanings hereby assigned to them respectively, that is to say:

*cannabinol derivatives* means the following substances, except where contained in cannabis or cannabis resin, namely tetrahydro derivatives of cannabinol and 3-alkyl homologues of cannabinol or of its tetrahydro derivatives;

*coca leaf* means the leaf of any plant of the genus Erythroxylon from whose leaves cocaine can be extracted either directly or by chemical transformation;

*concentrate of poppy-straw* means the material produced when poppy-straw has entered into a process for the concentration of its alkaloids;

*medicinal opium* means raw opium which has undergone the process necessary to adapt it for medicinal use in accordance with the requirements of the British Pharmacopoeia, whether it is in the form of powder or is granulated or is in any other form, and whether it is or is not mixed with neutral substances;

*poppy-straw* means all parts, except the seeds, of the opium poppy, after mowing;

*raw opium* includes powdered or granulated opium but does not include medicinal opium.

# Misuse of Drugs Regulations 1985 (as Amended)

## Classification of Controlled Drugs for Regimes of Control

The five Schedules of Controlled Drugs appended to the Misuse of Drugs Regulations 1985 (SI 1985 No.2066, as amended) are reproduced in this appendix. It should be used in conjunction with Chapter 16 and the tabulated summary on pp.184–185 at the end of that chapter. They provide a full explanation of the regulations, and how they affect the drugs in the various Schedules.

### Schedule 1

Controlled Drugs subject to the requirements of Regulations 14, 15, 16, 18, 19, 20, 23, 25 and 26.

1. The following substances and products, namely:

(a)   4-Bromo-2,5-dimethoxy-α-methylphenethylamine
Bufotenine
Cannabinol: not being Dronebenol or its stereoisomers
Cannabinol derivatives
Cannabis and cannabis resin
Cathinone
Coca leaf
Concentrate of poppy-straw
N,N-Diethyltryptamine

2,5-Dimethoxy-α,4-dimethylphenethylamine
N,N-Dimethyltryptamine
Eticyclidine
Etryptamine (1998)
N-Hydroxy-tenamphetamine
Lysergamide
Lysergide and other N-alkyl derivatives of lysergamide
Mescaline
Methcathinone (1998)
4-Methylaminorex
Psilocin
Raw opium
Rolicyclidine
Tenocyclidine

(b)    any compound (not being a compound for the time being specified in sub-paragraph (a) above) structurally derived from tryptamine or from a ring-hydroxy tryptamine by substitution at the nitrogen atom of the sidechain with one or more alkyl substituents but no other substituents;

(c)    any compound (not being methoxyphenamine or a compound for the time being specified in sub-paragraph (a) above) structurally derived from phenethylamine, an N-alkylphenethylamine, α-methylphenethylamine, an N-alkyl-α-methyl-phenethylamine, α-ethylphenethylamine, or an N-alkyl-α-ethylphenethylamine by substitution in the ring to any extent with alkyl, alkoxy, alkylenedioxy or halide substituents, whether or not further substituted in the ring by one or more other univalent substituents;

(d)    any compound (not being a compound for the time being specified in Schedule 2) structurally derived from fentanyl by modification in any of the following ways, that is to say:

    (i)   by replacement of the phenyl portion of the phenethyl group by any hetero-monocycle whether or not further substituted in the heterocycle;

    (ii)  by substitution in the phenethyl group with alkyl, alkenyl, alkoxy, hydroxy, halogeno, haloalkyl, amino or nitro groups;

    (iii) by substitution in the piperidine ring with alkyl or alkenyl groups;

    (iv) by substitution in the aniline ring with alkyl, alkoxy, alkylenedioxy, halogeno or haloalkyl groups;

    (v)  by substitution at the 4- position of the piperidine ring with any alkoxy-carbonyl or alkoxyalkyl or acyloxy group;

    (vi) by replacement of the N-propionyl group by another acyl group.

(e)    any compound (not being a compound for the time being specified in Schedule 2) structurally derived from pethidine by modification in any of the following ways, that is to say:

    (i)   by replacement of the 1-methyl group by an acyl, alkyl whether or not unsaturated, benzyl or phenethyl group, whether or not further substituted;

    (ii)  by substitution in the piperidine ring with alkyl or alkenyl groups or with a propano bridge, whether or not further substituted;

    (iii) by substitution in the 4-phenyl ring with alkyl, alkoxy, aryloxy, halogeno or haloalkyl groups;

    (iv) by replacement of the 4-ethoxycarbonyl by any other alkoxycarbonyl or any alkoxyalkyl or acyloxy group;

    (v)  by formation of an N-oxide or of a quaternary base.

2. Any stereoisomeric form of a substance specified in paragraph 1.

3. Any ester or ether of a substance specified in paragraph 1 or 2.

4. Any salt of a substance specified in any of paragraphs 1 to 3.

5. Any preparation or other product containing a substance or product specified in any of paragraphs 1 to 4, not being a preparation specified in Schedule 5.

## Schedule 2

Controlled Drugs subject to the requirements of Regulations 14, 15, 16, 18, 19, 20, 21, 23, 25 and 26.

    1. The following substances and products, namely:

Acetorphine
Alfentanil
Allylprodine
Alphacetylmethadol
Alphameprodine
Alphamethadol
Alphaprodine
Anileridine
Benzethidine
Benzylmorphine (3-benzylmorphine)
Betacetylmethadol
Betameprodine
Betamethadol
Betaprodine
Bezitramide
Carfentanil
Clonitazene
Cocaine
4-Cyano-2-dimethylamino-4,4-diphenylbutane
4-Cyano-1-methyl-4-phenylpiperidine
Desomorphine
Dextromoramide
Diamorphine
Diampromide
Diethylthiambutene
Difenoxin
Dihydrocodeinone O-carboxymethyloxine
Dihydromorphine
Dimenoxadole
Dimepheptanol
Dimethylthiambutene
Dioxaphetyl butyrate
Diphenoxylate
Dipipanone
Dronabinol
Drotebanol
Ecgonine, and any derivative of ecgonine
    which is convertible to ecgonine or to
    cocaine
Ethylmethylthiambutene
Etonitazene
Etorphine
Etoxeridine
Fentanyl
Furethidine
Hydrocodone

Hydromorphinol
Hydromorphone
Hydroxypethidine
Isomethadone
Ketobemidone
Levomethorphan
Levomoramide
Levophenacylmorphan
Levorphanol
Lofentanil
Medicinal opium
Metazocine
Methadone
Methadyl acetate
Methyldesorphine
Methyldihydromorphine
    (6-methyldihydromorphine)
2-Methyl-3-morpholino-
    1,1-diphenylpropanecarboxylic acid
1-Methyl-4-phenylpiperidine-4-carboxylic
    acid
Metopon
Morpheridine
Morphine
Morphine methobromide, morphine N-oxide
    and other pentavalent nitrogen morphine
    derivatives
Myrophine
Nicomorphine
Noracymethadol
Norlevorphanol
Normethadone
Normorphine
Norpipanone
Oxycodone
Oxymorphone
Pethidine
Phenadoxone
Phenampromide
Phenazocine
Phencyclidine
Phenomorphan
Phenoperidine
4-Phenylpiperidine-4-carboxylic acid ethyl
    ester
Piminodine

Piritramide
Proheptazine
Properidine
Quinalbarbitone
Racemethorphan
Racemoramide
Racemorphan

Sufentanil
Thebacon
Thebaine
Tilidate
Trimeperidine
Zipeprol (1998)

2. Any stereoisomeric form of a substance specified in paragraph 1 not being dextromethorphan or dextrorphan.

3. Any ester or ether of a substance specified in paragraph 1 or 2, not being a substance specified in paragraph 6.

4. Any salt of a substance specified in any of paragraphs 1 to 3.

5. Any preparation or other product containing a substance or product specified in any of paragraphs 1 to 4, not being a preparation specified in Schedule 5.

6. The following substances and products, namely:

Acetyldihydrocodeine
Amphetamine
Codeine
Dextropropoxyphene
Dihydrocodeine
Ethylmorphine (3-ethylmorphine)
Fenethylline
Glutethamide
Lefetamine
Mecloqualone

Methaqualone
Methylamphetamine
Methylphenidate
Nicocodine
Nicodicodine (6-nicotinoyldihydrocodeine)
Norcodeine
Phenmetrazine
Pholcodine
Propiram
Quinalbarbitone (1988)

7. Any stereoisomeric form of a substance specified in paragraph 6.

8. Any salt of a substance specified in paragraph 6 or 7.

9. Any preparation or other product containing a substance or product specified in any of paragraphs 6 to 8, not being a preparation specified in Schedule 5.

## Schedule 3

Controlled Drugs subject to the requirements of Regulations 14, 15, 16, 18, 22, 23, 24, 25 and 26.

1. The following substances, namely:

(a)    Buprenorphine (1989)
Cathine
Chlorphentermine
Diethylpropion
Ethchlorvynol
Ethinamate
Flunitrazepam (1998)
Mazindol
Mephentermine

Meprobamate
Methylphenobarbitone
Methyprylone
Pentazocine
Phendimetrazine
Phentermine
Pipradrol
Temazepam

(b)    any 5,5- disubstituted barbituric acid, not being quinalbarbitone.

2. Any stereoisomeric form of a substance specified in paragraph 1, not being phenylpropanolamine.

3. Any salt of a substance specified in paragraph 1 or 2.

4. Any preparation or other product containing a substance specified in any of paragraphs 1 to 3, not being a preparation specified in Schedule 5.

## Schedule 4: Part I

Controlled Drugs excepted from the prohibition on possession when in the form of a medicinal product; excluded from the application of offences arising from the prohibition on importation and exportation when imported or exported in the form of a medicinal product by any person for administration to himself; and subject to the requirements of Regulations 22, 23, 25 and 26.

1. The following substances and products, namely:

| | |
|---|---|
| Atamestane | Methyltestosterone |
| Bolandiol | Metribolone |
| Bolasterone | Mibolerone |
| Bolazine | Nandrolone |
| Bolenol | Norboletone |
| Bolmantalate | Norclostebol |
| Calusterone | Norethandrolone |
| 4-Choromethandienone | Ovandrotone |
| Clostebol | Oxandrolone |
| Drostanolone | Oxymesterone |
| Enestebol | Oxymetholone |
| Epitiostanol | Prasterone |
| Ethyloestrenol | Propetandrol |
| Fluoxymesterone | Quinbolone |
| Formebolone | Roxibolone |
| Furazabol | Silandrone |
| Mebolazine | Stanolone |
| Mepitiostane | Stanozolol |
| Mestanolone | Stenbolone |
| Mesterolone | Testosterone |
| Methandienone | Thiomesterone |
| Methandriol | Trenbolone |
| Methenolone | |

2. Any compound (not being Trilostane or a compound for the time being specified in paragraph 1 of this part of this Schedule) structurally derived from 17-hydroxyandrostan-3-one or from 17-hydroxyestran-3-one by modification in any of the following ways:

(a)    by further substitution at position 17 by a methyl or ethyl group;

(b)    by substitution to any extent at one or more positions 1, 2, 4, 6, 7,9, 11 or 16, but at no other position;

(c)    by unsaturation in the carbocyclic ring system to any extent, provided that there are no more than two ethylenic bonds in any one carbocyclic ring;

(d)    by fusion of ring A with a heterocyclic system.

3. Any substance which is an ester or ether (or, where more than one hydroxyl function is available, both an ester and an ether) of a substance specified in paragraph 1 or described in paragraph 2 of this Part of the Schedule.

4. The following substances:

| | |
|---|---|
| Chorionic gonadotrophin (HCG) | Somatotropin |
| Clenbuterol | Somatrem |
| Non-human Chorionic gonadotrophin (HCG) | Somatropin |

5. Any stereoisomeric form of a substance specified or described in any of paragraphs 1 to 4 of this Part of this Schedule.

6. Any salt of a substance specified or described in any of paragraphs 1 to 5 of this Part of this Schedule.

7. Any preparation of other product containing a substance or product specified or described in any of paragraphs 1 to 6 of this Part of the Schedule, not being a preparation specified in Schedule 5.

## Schedule 4: Part II

Controlled Drugs excepted from the prohibition on importation, exportation and, when in the form of a medicinal product, possession and subject to the requirements of Regulations 22, 23, 25 and 26.

1. The following substances and products, namely:

Alprazolam
Aminorex (1998)
Bromazepam
Brotizolam (1998)
Camazepam
Chlordiazepoxide
Clobazam
Clonazepam
Clorazepic acid
Clotiazepam
Cloxazolam
Delorazcpam
Diazepam
Estazolam
Ethyl loflazepate
N-Ethylamphetamine
Fencamfamin
Fenproporex
Fludiazepam
Flurazepam
Halazepam

Haloxazolam
Ketazolam
Loprazolam
Lorazepam
Lormetazepam
Medazepam
Mefenorex
Mesocarb (1998)
Midazolam
Nimetazepam
Nitrazepam
Nordazepam
Oxazepam
Oxazolam
Pemoline
Pinazepam
Prazepam
Pyrovalerone
Tetrazepam
Triazolam

2. Any stereoisomeric form of a substance specified in paragraph 1.

3. Any salt of a substance specified in paragraph 1 or 2.

4. Any preparation or other product containing a substance or product specified in any of paragraphs 1 to 3, not being a preparation specified in Schedule 5.

## Schedule 5

Controlled Drugs excepted from the prohibition on importation, exportation and possession and subject to the requirements of Regulations 24 and 25.

1. (1) Any preparation of one or more of the substances to which this paragraph applies, not being a preparation designed for administration by injection, when compounded with one or more other active or inert ingredients and containing a total of not more than 100 milligrams of the substance or substances (calculated as base) per dosage unit or with a total concentration of not more than 2.5 per cent (calculated as base) in undivided preparations.

(2) The substances to which this paragraph applies are acetyldihydrocodeine, codeine, dihydrocodeine, ethylmorphine, nicocodine, nicodicodine (6-nicotinoyldihydrocodeine), norcodeine, pholcodine and their respective salts.

2. Any preparation of cocaine containing not more than 0.1 per cent of cocaine calculated as cocaine base, being a preparation compounded with one or more other active or inert ingredients in such a way that the cocaine cannot be recovered by readily applicable means or in a yield which would constitute a risk to health.

3. Any preparation of medicinal opium or of morphine containing (in either case) not more than 0.2 per cent of morphine calculated as anhydrous morphine base, being a preparation compounded with one or more other active or inert ingredients in such a way that the opium or, as the case may be, the morphine, cannot be recovered by readily applicable means or in a yield which would constitute a risk to health.

4. Any preparation of dextropropoxyphene, being a preparation designed for oral administration, containing not more than 135 milligrams of dextropropoxyphene (calculated as base) per dosage unit or with a total concentration of not more than 2.5 per cent (calculated as base) in undivided preparations.

5. Any preparation of difenoxin containing, per dosage unit, not more than 0.5 milligrams of difenoxin and a quantity of atropine sulphate equivalent to at least 5 per cent of the dose of difenoxin.

6. Any preparation of diphenoxylate containing, per dosage unit, not more than 2.5 milligrams of diphenoxylate calculated as base, and a quantity of atropine sulphate equivalent to at least 1 per cent of the dose of diphenoxylate.

7. Any preparation of propiram containing, per dosage unit, not more than 100 milligrams of propiram calculated as base and compounded with at least the same amount (by weight) of methylcellulose.

8. Any powder of ipecacuanha and opium comprising:

    10 per cent opium, in powder

    10 per cent ipecacuanha root, in powder, well mixed with

    80 per cent of any other powdered ingredient containing no Controlled Drug.

9. Any mixture containing one or more of the preparations specified in paragraphs 1 to 8, being a mixture of which none of the other ingredients is a Controlled Drug.

# The Poisons List Order 1982

Non-medicinal poisons are listed in the Schedule to this order (SI 1982 No.217, as amended) made under the Poisons Act 1972. Those substances in Part I of the list may not be sold by retail except by a person lawfully conducting a retail pharmacy business. Those in Part II of the list may only be sold by a person lawfully conducting a retail pharmacy business or by a person whose name is entered in a local authority's list.

## The Poisons List: Part I

Aluminium phosphide
Arsenic; its compounds, other than those
    specified in Part II of this list
Barium, salts of, other than barium sulphate
    and the salts of barium specified in Part II
    of this list
Bromomethane
Chloropicrin
Fluoroacetic acid; its salts, fluorocetamide
Hydrogen cyanide; metal cyanides, other than
    ferrocyanides and ferricyanides
Lead acetates; compounds of lead with acids
    from fixed oils
Magnesium phosphide
Mercury, compounds of, the following:
    nitrates of mercury; oxides of mercury;
    mercuric cyanide oxides; mercuric
    thiocyanate; ammonium mercuric

chlorides; potassium mercuric iodides;
organic compounds of mercury which
contain a methyl group directly linked to
the mercury atom
Oxalic acid
Phenols
    (phenol; phenolic isomers of the
    following: cresols, xylenols,
    monoethylphenols) except in substances
    containing less than 60 per cent, weight in
    weight, of phenols; compounds of phenol
    with a metal, except in substances
    containing less than the equivalent of 60
    per cent, weight in weight, of phenols
Phosphorus, yellow
Strychnine; its salts, its quaternary
    compounds
Thallium, salts of

## The Poisons List: Part II

Aldicarb
Alpha-chloralose
Ammonia
Arsenic, compounds, of; the following:
  Calcium arsenites
  Copper acetoarsenite
  Copper arsenates
  Copper arsenites
  Lead arsenates
Barium, salts of; the following:
  Barium carbonate
  Barium silicofluoride
Carbofuran
Cycloheximide
Dinitrocresols (DNOC); their compounds
  with a metal or a base
Dinoseb; its compounds with a metal or a
  base
Dinoterb
Drazoxolon; its salts
Endosulfan
Endothal; its salts
Endrin
Fentin, compounds of
Formaldehyde
Formic acid
Hydrochloric acid
Hydrofluoric acid; alkali metal bifluorides;
  ammonium bifluoride; alkali metal
  fluorides; ammonium fluoride; sodium
  silicofluoride
Mercuric chloride; mercuric iodide; organic
  compounds of mercury except compounds
  of mercury which contain a methyl ($CH_3$)
  group directly linked to the mercury atom

Metallic oxalates
Methomyl
Nicotine; its salts; its quaternary
  compounds
Nitric acid
Nitrobenzene
Oxamyl
Paraquat, salts of
Phenols (as defined in Part I of this List)
  in substances containing less than 60
  per cent, weight in weight, of
  phenols; compounds of phenols with
  a metal in substances containing less
  than the equivalent of 60 per cent,
  weight in weight, of phenols
Phosphoric acid
Phosphorus compounds, the following:
  Azinphos-methyl, chlorfenvinphos,
  demephion, demeton-S-methyl,
  demeton-S-methyl sulphone, dialifos,
  dichlorvos, dioxathion, disulfoton,
  fonofus, mecarbam, mephosfolan,
  methidathion, mevinphos, omethoate,
  oxydemeton-methyl, parathion,
  phenkapton, phorate, phosphamidon,
  pirimiphos-ethyl, quinalphos,
  schradan, sulfotep, thiometon,
  thionazin, triazophos, vamidothion
Potassium hydroxide
Sodium hydroxide
Sodium nitrate
Sulphuric acid
Thiofanox
Zinc phosphide

*13*

# The Poisons Rules 1982

The Poison Rules 1982 (SI 1982 No.218, as amended), made under the Poisons Act 1972, are described in Chapter 17. In this appendix are set out eight of the Schedules to the rules. N.B. Schedules 2, 3, 6 and 7 were deleted by the Poisons Rules (Amendment) Order 1985 (SI 1985 No.1077).

## Schedule 1

### Rules 5, 6, 7, 9, 10(1), 17(2) and 21(2)

Poisons included in the Poisons List to which special restrictions apply unless exempted by Rule 7 (see pp.190 and 193–198).

Aldicarb
Alpha-chloralose
Aluminium phosphide
Arsenic; its compounds, except substances containing less than the equivalent of 0.0075 per cent of arsenic (As)
Barium, salts of (other than barium sulphate)
Bromomethane
Carbofuran
Chloropicrin
Cycloheximide
Dinitrocresols (DNOC); their compounds with a metal or a base; except winter washes containing not more than the equivalent of 5 per cent of dinitrocresols
Dinoseb; its compounds with a metal or a base
Dinoterb

Drazoxolon; its salts
Endosulfan
Endothal: its salts
Endrin
Fentin, compounds of
Fluoroacetic acid; its salts, fluoroacetamide
Hydrogen cyanide except substances containing less than 0.15 per cent, weight in weight, of
  hydrogen cyanide (HCN); metal cyanides, other than ferrocyanides and ferricyanides, except
  substances containing less than the equivalent of 0.1 per cent, weight in weight, of hydrogen
  cyanide (HCN)
Lead, compounds of, with acids from fixed oils
Magnesium phosphide
Mercuric chloride; except substances containing less than 1 per cent of mercuric chloride;
  mercuric iodide except substances containing less than 2 per cent of mercuric iodide: nitrates
  of mercury except substances containing less than the equivalent of 3 per cent, weight in
  weight, of mercury (Hg); potassio-mercuric iodides except substances containing less than the
  equivalent of 1 per cent of mercuric iodide; organic compounds of mercury except substances,
  not being aerosols, containing less than the equivalent of 0.2 per cent, weight in weight, of
  mercury (Hg)
Methomyl
Nicotine; its salts; its quaternary compounds
Oxamyl
Paraquat, salts of
Phosphorus compounds, the following:
  Azinphos-methyl
  Chlorfenvinphos
  Demephion
  Demeton-S-methyl
  Demeton-S-methyl sulphone
  Dichlorvos
  Dioxathion
  Disulfoton
  Fonofos
  Mecarbam
  Mephosfolan
  Methidathion
  Mevinphos
  Omethoate
  Oxydemeton-methyl
  Parathion
  Phenkapton
  Phorate
  Phosphamidon
  Pirimiphos-ethyl
  Quinalphos
  Thiometon
  Thionazin
  Triazophos
  Vamidothion
Strychnine; its salts; its quaternary compounds; except substances containing less than 0.2 per
  cent of strychnine
Thallium, salts of
Thiofanox
Zinc phosphide

**Schedule 4**

**Rule 8**

Articles exempted from the provisions of the Act and Rules (see p.186)

*Group I*

*General Exemptions*
Adhesives; anti-fouling compositions; builders' materials; ceramics; cosmetic products; distempers; electrical valves; enamels; explosives; fillers; fireworks; fluorescent lamps; flux in any form for use in soldering; glazes; glue; inks; lacquer solvents; loading materials; matches; medicated animal feeding stuffs; motor fuels and lubricants; paints other than pharmaceutical paints; photographic paper; pigments; plastics; propellants; rubber; varnishes; vascular plants and their seeds.

*Group II*

*Special Exemptions*

| *Poison* | *Substance or article in which exempted* |
|---|---|
| Ammonia | Substances not being solutions of ammonia or preparations containing solutions of ammonia; substances containing less than 5 per cent, weight in weight, of ammonia (NH3); refrigerators |
| Arsenic; its compounds | Pyrites ores or sulphuric acid containing arsenic or compounds of arsenic as natural impurities; in reagent kits or reagent devices supplied for medical or veterinary purposes, substances containing less than 0. 1 per cent, weight in weight, of arsanilic acid |
| Barium, salts of | Witherite other than finely ground witherite; barium carbonate bonded to charcoal for case hardening; fire extinguishers containing barium chloride; sealed smoke generators containing not more than 25 per cent, weight in weight, of barium carbonate |
| Bromomethane | Fire extinguishers |
| Carbofuran | Granular preparations |
| Drazoxolon; its salts | Treatments on seeds |
| Fenaminosulf | Granular preparations |
| Formaldehyde | Substances containing less than 5 per cent, weight in weight, of formaldehyde (H.CHO); photographic glazing or hardening solutions |
| Formic acid | Substances containing less than 25 per cent, weight in weight, of formic acid (H.COOH) |
| Hydrochloric acid | Substances containing less than 10 per cent, weight in weight, of hydrochloric acid |
| Hydrogen cyanide | Preparations of wild cherry; in reagent kits supplied for medical or veterinary purposes, substances containing less than the |

| *Poison* | *Substance or article in which exempted* |
|---|---|
| | equivalent of 0. 1 per cent, weight in weight, of hydrogen cyanide |
| Lead acetate | Substances containing less than the equivalent of 2.5 per cent, weight in weight, of elemental lead |
| Mercuric chloride | Batteries |
| Mercuric chloride | Treatments on seeds or bulbs |
| Mercuric iodide | Treatments on seeds or bulbs |
| Mercury organic, compounds of | Treatments on seeds or bulbs |
| Mercury, oxides of | Canker and wound paints (for trees) containing not more than 3 per cent, weight in weight, of yellow mercuric oxide |
| Methomyl | Solid substances containing not more than 1 per cent, weight in weight, of methomyl |
| Nicotine; its salts; its quaternary compounds | Tobacco; in cigarettes, the paper of a cigarette (any part of that paper forming part of or surrounding a filter), where that paper in each cigarette does not have more than the equivalent of 10 milligrams of nicotine; preparations in aerosol dispensers containing not more than 0.2 per cent, weight in weight, of nicotine; other liquid preparations, and solid preparations with a soap base containing not more than 7.5 per cent, weight in weight, of nicotine |
| Nitric acid | Substances containing less than 9 per cent, weight in weight, of nitric acid ($HNO_3$) |
| Nitrobenzene | Substances containing less than 0.1 per cent of nitrobenzene |
| Oxalic acid; metallic | Laundry blue; polishes; cleaning powders or scouring oxalates products containing the equivalent of not more than 10 per cent of oxalic acid dihydrate |
| Oxamyl | Granular preparations |
| Paraquat, salts of | Preparations in pellet form containing not more than 5 per cent of salts of paraquat calculated as paraquat ion (see p.190) |
| Phenols | Creosote obtained from coal tar; liquid disinfectants or antiseptics containing phenol less than 0.5 per cent phenol and containing less than 5 per cent of other phenols (as defined in the Poisons List); motor fuel treatments not containing phenol and containing less than 2.5 per cent of other phenols; in reagent kits supplied for medical or veterinary purposes; solid substances containing less than 60 per cent of phenols; tar (coal or wood), crude or refined; in tar oil distillation fractions containing not more than 5 per cent of phenols |

| *Poison* | *Substance or article in which exempted* |
|---|---|
| Phenylmercuric salts | Antiseptic dressings on toothbrushes; in textiles containing not more than 0. 01 per cent of phenylmercuric salts as bacteriostat and fungicide |
| Phosphoric acid | Substances containing phosphoric acid, not being descaling preparations, containing more than 50 per cent, weight in weight, of ortho-phosphoric acid |

Phosphorus compounds, the following:

| | |
|---|---|
| Chlorfenvinphos | Treatments on seeds; granular preparations |
| Dichlorvos | Preparations in aerosol dispensers containing not more than 1 per cent, weight in weight, of dichlorvos; materials impregnated with dichlorvos for slow release; granular preparations; ready for use liquid preparations containing not more than 1 per cent, weight in volume, of dichlorvos |
| Disulfoton | Granular preparations |
| Fonofos | Granular preparations |
| Oxydemeton-methyl | Aerosol dispensers containing not more than 0. 25 per cent, weight in weight, of oxydemeton-methyl |
| Parathion | Granular preparations |
| Phorate | Granular preparations |
| Pirimiphos-ethyl | Treatments on seeds |
| Thiazophos | Granular preparations |
| Thionazin | Granular preparations |
| Potassium hydroxide | Substances containing the equivalent of less than 17 per cent of total caustic alkalinity expressed as potassium hydroxide; accumulators; batteries |
| Sodium fluoride | Substances containing less than 3 per cent of sodium fluoride as a preservative |
| Sodium hydroxide | Substances containing the equivalent of less than 12 per cent of total caustic alkalinity expressed as sodium hydroxide |
| Sodium nitrite | Substances other than preparations containing more than 0. 1 per cent of sodium nitrite for the destruction of rats or mice |
| Sodium silicofluoride | Substances containing less than 3 per cent of sodium silicofluoride as a preservative |
| Sulphuric acid | Substances containing less than 15 per cent, weight in weight, of sulphuric acid ($H_2SO_4$); accumulators; batteries and sealed containers in which sulphuric acid is packed together with car batteries for use in those batteries; fire extinguishers |
| Thiofanox | Granular preparations |

In Group II in this Schedule the expression *granular preparation* in relation to a poison means a preparation:

(a)    which consists of absorbent mineral or synthetic solid particles impregnated with the poison, the size of the particles being such that not more than 4 per cent, weight in weight, of the preparation is capable of passing a sieve with a mesh of 250 microns, and not more than 1 per cent, weight in weight, a sieve with a mesh of 150 microns;

(b)    which has an apparent density of not less than 0.4 grams per millilitre if compacted without pressure; and

(c)    not more than 12 per cent, weight in weight, consists of one or more poisons in respect of which an exemption is conferred by this Schedule in relation to granular preparations.

## Schedule 5

### Rule 10(2)

*Part A*

Form to which the poisons specified are restricted when sold by listed sellers of Part II poisons (see p.192)

| *Poison* | *Form to which sale is restricted* |
|---|---|
| Aldicarb | Preparations for use in agriculture, horticulture or forestry |
| Alpha-chloralose | Preparations intended for indoor use in the destruction of rats or mice and containing not more than 4 per cent, weight in weight, of alpha-chloralose, preparations intended for indoor use in the destruction of rats or mice and containing not more than 8.5 per cent, weight in weight, of alpha-chloralose, where the preparation is contained in a bag or sachet which is itself attached to the inside of a device in which the preparation is intended to be so used and the device contains not more than 3 grams of the preparation |
| Arsenic, compounds of; | Agricultural, horticultural and forestal insecticides or fungicides |
| Calcium arsenites | Agricultural, horticultural and forestal insecticides or fungicides |
| Copper acetoarsenite | Agricultural, horticultural and forestal insecticides or fungicides |
| Copper arsenates | Agricultural, horticultural and forestal insecticides or fungicides |
| Copper arsenites | Agricultural, horticultural and forestal insecticides or fungicides |
| Lead arsenates | Agricultural, horticultural and forestal insecticides or fungicides |
| Barium carbonate | Preparations for the destruction of rats or mice |
| Carbofuran | Preparations for use in agriculture, horticulture or forestry |
| Cycloheximide | Preparations for use in forestry |
| Dinitrocresols (DNOC); their compounds with a metal or a base | Preparations for use in agriculture, horticulture or forestry |
| Dinosam; its compounds with a metal or a base | Preparations for use in agriculture, horticulture or forestry |

| Poison | Form to which sale is restricted |
|---|---|
| Dinoseb; its compounds with a metal or a base | Preparations for use in agriculture, horticulture or forestry |
| Drazoxolon; its salts | Preparations for use in agriculture, horticulture or forestry |
| Endosulfan | Preparations for use in agriculture, horticulture or forestry |
| Endothal; its salts | Preparations for use in agriculture, horticulture or forestry |
| Endrin | Preparations for use in agriculture, horticulture or forestry |
| Fentin, compounds of | Preparations for use in agriculture, horticulture or forestry |
| Mercuric chloride | Agricultural, horticultural and forestal fungicides, seed and bulb dressings, insecticides |
| Mercuric iodide | Agricultural, horticultural and forestal fungicides, seed and bulb dressings |
| Mercury, organic compounds of | Agricultural, horticultural and forestal fungicides, seed and bulb dressings, solutions containing not more than 5 per cent, weight in volume, of phenylmercuric acetate for use in swimming baths |
| Metallic oxalates other than potassium quadroxalate | Photographic solutions or materials |
| Methomyl | Preparations for use in agriculture, horticulture or forestry |
| Nitrobenzene | Agricultural, horticultural and forestal insecticides |
| Oxamyl | Preparations for use in agriculture, horticulture or forestry |
| Paraquat, salts of | Preparations for use in agriculture, horticulture or forestry |
| Phosphorus compounds, the following: | Preparations for use in agriculture, horticulture or forestry |

    Azinphos-methyl
    Chlorfenvinphos
    Demephion
    Demeton-S-methyl
    Demeton-S-methyl sulphone
    Dialifos
    Dichlorvos
    Dioxathion
    Disulfoton
    Fonofos
    Mecarbam
    Mephosfolan
    Methidathion
    Mevinphos
    Omethoate
    Oxydemeton-methyl
    Parathion
    Phenkapton
    Phorate
    Phosphamidon
    Pirimiphos-ethyl
    Quinalphos

| *Poison* | *Form to which sale is restricted* |
|---|---|
| Thiometon | |
| Thionazin | |
| Triazophos | |
| Vamidothion | |
| Thiofanox | Preparations for use in agriculture, horticulture or forestry |
| Zinc phosphide | Preparations for the destruction of rats or mice |

### Part B

Poisons which may be sold by listed sellers of Part II poisons only to persons engaged in the trade or business of agriculture, horticulture or forestry and for the purpose of that trade or business.

Aldicarb
Arsenic, compounds of
  Calcium arsenites
  Copper acetoarsenite
  Copper arsenates
  Copper arsenites
  Lead arsenates
Carbofuran
Cyclohexamide
Dinitrocresols (DNOC); their compounds with a metal or a base; except winter washes containing not more than the equivalent of 5 per cent of dinitrocresols
Dinosam; its compounds with a metal or a base
Dinoseb; its compounds with a metal or a base
Dinoterb
Drazoxolon; its salts
Endosulfan
Endothal; its salts
Endrin
Fentin; compounds of
Mercuric chloride; mercuric iodide; organic compounds of mercury, except solutions containing not more than 5 per cent, weight in volume, of phenylmercuric acetate for use in swimming baths
Methomyl
Oxamyl
Paraquat, salts of
Phosphorus compounds, the following:
  Azinphos-methyl
  Chlorfenvinphos
  Demephion
  Demeton-S-methyl
  Demeton-S-methyl sulphone
  Dialifos
  Dichlorvos
  Dioxathion
  Disulfoton
  Fonofos
  Mazidox
  Mecarbam
  Mephosfolan

Methidathion
Mevinphos
Mipafox, except in the form of a cap on a stick or wire
Omethoate
Oxydemeton-methyl
Parathion
Phenkapton
Phorate
Phosphamidon
Pirimiphos-ethyl
Quinalphos
Thiometon
Thionazin
Triazophos
Vamidothion
Thiofanox

## Schedule 8

### Rule 24(1)

Form of application for entry in the list kept by a local authority under section 5 of the Act (see p.191)

POISONS ACT 1972
(1972 c.66)

*Form of application by a person to have his name entered in a local authority's list of persons entitled to sell non-medicinal poisons included in Part II of the Poisons List.*

To the Chief Executive of ....................................................................................................................
 I,.......................................................................................................................................................
being engaged in the business of.........................................................................................................
hereby apply to have my name entered in the list kept in pursuance of section 5 of the above Act
in respect of the following premises, namely,......................................................................................
.............................................................................................................................................................
.............................................................................................................................................................
.............................................................................................................................................................
as a person entitled to sell from those premises non-medicinal poisons included in Part II of the
Poisons List.
 I hereby nominate ..........................................................................................................................
.............................................................................................................................................................
to act as my deputy (deputies) for the sale of non-medicinal poisons in accordance with Rule
10(1) of the Poisons Rules 1982
                    Signature of applicant ...........................................................................
                                Date................................................................................
*This space is for the use of the local authority.*
.............................................................................................................................................................
.............................................................................................................................................................
.............................................................................................................................................................
.............................................................................................................................................................
.............................................................................................................................................................

## Schedule 9

### Rule 24(2)

Form of the list to be kept by a local authority in pursuance of section 5(1) of the Act (see p.191)

POISONS ACT 1972

(1972 c. 66)

*List of persons entitled to sell non-medicinal poisons in Part II of the Poisons List*

| Full name | Address of premises | Description of business carried on at the premises | Name of deputy (or deputies) permitted to sell |
|---|---|---|---|
|  |  |  |  |

## Schedule 10

### Rule 25

Certificate for the purchase of non-medicinal poison (see pp.191 and 195–198)

For the purposes of section 3(2)(a)(i) of the Poisons Act 1972 I, the undersigned, a householder occupying (a) ..................................................................................................
hereby certify from my knowledge of (b) ..................................... of (a) ...............................
that he is a person to whom (c) ................................................. may properly be supplied.
  I further certify that (d) .................................................. is the signature of the said (b) ........................................................

........................................................
Signature of the householder giving
certificate
Date
(a) Insert full postal address.
(b) Insert full name of intending purchaser.
(c) Insert name of poison.
(d) Intending purchaser to sign his name here.

*Endorsement required by Rule 25 of the Poisons Rules 1982 to be made by a police officer in charge of a police station when, but only when, the householder giving the certificate is not known to the seller of the poison to be a responsible person of good character.*
I hereby certify that in so far as is known to the police of the district in which * resides he is a responsible person of good character.

Signature of Police Officer...............................
Rank.................................................................
In charge of Police Station at ...........................
Date.................................................................

Office Stamp of
Police Station.

*Insert full name of householder giving the certificate.

## Schedule 11

### Rule 26

*Form of entry to be made in a book to be kept by sellers of poisons in accordance with section 3(2)(b) of the Act* (see p.194)

| Date of Sale | Name and quantity of poisons supplied | Purchaser's | | | Purpose for which the poison stated to be required | Date of certificate (if any) | Name and address of person giving certificate (if any) | Signature of purchaser or, where a signed order is permitted by the Poisons Rules 1982 the date of the signed order |
|---|---|---|---|---|---|---|---|---|
| | | Name | Address | Business, trade or occupation | | | | |
| | | | | | | | | |

## Schedule 12

### Rule 12

Restriction of sale and supply of strychnine and certain other poisons (see pp.191 and 195–198)

*Part I*

*Cases of sale or supply to which provisions of Rule 12 do not apply*

1. The provisions of Rule 12 shall not apply in the case of the sale of substance to be exported to purchasers outside the United Kingdom.

2. The provisions of Rule 12 shall not apply in the case of the sale of a substance to a person or institution concerned with scientific education or research or chemical analysis, for the purposes of that education or research or analysis.

3. The provisions of Rule 12 shall not apply in the case of the sale of a substance by way of wholesale dealing.

4. The following provision of Rule 12 namely, paragraph (1) (strychnine, etc.), shall not apply in the case of the sale of a substance to a person producing a written authority in the form set out in Part II of this Schedule issued, in England by a person duly authorised by the Minister of Agriculture, Fisheries and Food, or, in Scotland, or Wales, by a person duly authorised by the Secretary of State, authorising the purchase of the substance for the purpose of killing moles; so, however, that the authority in question has been issued within the preceding three months and the quantity sold does not exceed the quantity, not being more than 100 grams, specified therein.

5. The following provisions of Rule 12, namely, paragraph (1) (strychnine, etc.), shall not apply in the case of the sale of a substance to:

(a)     an officer of the Ministry of Agriculture, Fisheries and Food who produces a written authority in the form set out in Part III of this Schedule issued by a person duly authorised by the Minister of Agriculture, Fisheries and Food; or

(b)     an officer of the Department of Agriculture and Fisheries for Scotland or the Welsh Office who produces a written authority in the form set out in Part III of this Schedule issued by a person duly authorised by the Secretary of State, authorising the purchase by that officer of the substance for the purpose of killing foxes (other than foxes held in captivity) in an infected area within the meaning of the Rabies (Control) Order 1974 (SI 1974 No. 2212); so, however, that the authority in question has been issued within the preceding four weeks and the quantity sold does not exceed specified therein.

6. (1) The following provision of Rule 12, namely, paragraph (2) (fluoroacetic acid, etc.), shall not apply in the case of the sale of a substance:

(a)     to a person producing a certificate in form 'A' of the forms set out in Part IV of this Schedule issued by the proper officer of a local authority or port health authority certifying that the substance is required for use as a rodenticide by employees of that local authority or port health authority being such use:

　　　(i) in ships or sewers in such places as are identified in the certificate; or
　　　(ii) in such drains as are identified in the certificate, being drains which are situated in restricted areas and wholly enclosed and to which all means of access are, when not in actual use, kept closed; or
　　　(iii) in such warehouses as are identified in the certificate, being warehouses which are situated in restricted dock areas and to which all means of access are, when not in actual use, kept securely locked or barred; or

(b)     to a person producing a certificate in form 'B' of the said forms issued by the proper officer of a local authority or port health authority certifying that the substance is required for use as a rodenticide by such person or by the employees of such body of persons, carrying on a business of pest control, as is named in the certificate, being such use as is mentioned in sub-paragraph (1)(a)(i) or (ii) of this paragraph; or

(c)     to a person producing a certificate in form 'B' of the said forms issued, in England by a person duly authorised by the Minister of Agriculture, Fisheries and Food or, in Scotland or Wales, by a person duly authorised by the Secretary of State certifying that the substance is required for use as a rodenticide by officers of the Ministry of Agriculture, Fisheries and Food or of the Department of Agriculture and Fisheries for Scotland, or the Welsh Office being such use as is mentioned in sub-paragraph (1)(a)(i) or (ii) of this paragraph;

　　　　　so, however, that the certificate in question has been issued within the preceding three months and the quantity sold does not exceed the quantity specified therein.

(2) In this paragraph the following expressions have the meanings hereby respectively assigned to them, that is to say:

*dock area* means an area in the vicinity of a dock as defined in section 57(1) of the Harbours Act 1964;

*drain* and *sewer* have the meanings respectively assigned to them by section 343(1) of the Public Health Act 1936;

*local authority* in Greater London means the Common Council of the City of London or the council of a London borough, elsewhere in England or Wales means the council of a county or a district and, in Scotland, means an islands or district council;

*port health authority* means, in England or Wales, the port health authority of the Port of London or a port health authority for the purposes of the Public Health Act 1936 and, in

Scotland, a port health authority as constituted in terms of section 172 of the Public Health (Scotland) Act 1897;

*restricted* in relation to any area, means controlled in such manner that access to the area by unauthorised persons is in normal circumstances prevented.

7. (1) The following provisions of Rule 12, namely, paragraph (3) (salts of thallium), shall not apply in the case of the sale of a substance:

(a)    to a local authority or a port health authority for the purpose of the exercise of its statutory powers; or
(b)    to a government department or an officer of the Crown, for the purposes of the public service; or
(c)    other than thallium sulphate, to a person, or body of persons, carrying on a business in the course of which salts of thallium are regularly used in the manufacture of other articles, for the purposes of that business; or
(d)    other than thallium sulphate, as an ingredient in any article, not being an article intended for internal consumption by any person or animal.

(2) The following provision of Rule 12, namely paragraph (3) (salts of thallium) shall not apply as regards thallium sulphate in the case of the sale of a substance to a person producing a written authority in the form set out in Part V of this Schedule issued, in England or Wales, by a person duly authorised by the Minister of Agriculture, Fisheries and Food, or, in Scotland, by a person duly authorised by the Secretary of State, authorising the purchase of salts of thallium for use by him or by the employees of such body of persons as is named in the authority for the purpose of killing rats, mice or moles in the course of a business of pest control; so, however, that the authority in question has been issued within the preceding twelve months.

(3) In this paragraph the expressions *local authority* and *port health authority* have the meanings assigned to them by paragraph 6(2) of this Part of this Schedule.

8. (1) The following provision of Rule 12, namely, paragraph (4) (zinc phosphide) shall not apply in the case of the sale of a substance:

(a)    to a local authority for the purpose of the exercise of its statutory powers; or
(b)    to a government department or an officer of the Crown, for the purposes of the public service; or
(c)    to a person, or body of persons, carrying on a trade or business, for the purposes of that trade or business.

(2) In this paragraph the expression *local authority* has the meaning assigned to it by paragraph 6(2) of this Part of this Schedule.

## Part II

*Form of authority for the purchase of strychnine or a salt or quaternary compound thereof for killing moles*

For the purposes of Rule 12(1) of the Poisons Rules 1982 and of paragraph 4 of Part I of Schedule 12 thereto I hereby authorise ...............................................................................................................
to purchase within three months from the date hereof ........................... of .................................
for the purpose of killing moles.

.................................................................

A person authorised by [the Minister of Agriculture Fisheries and Food] [the Secretary of State for Scotland] [the Secretary of State for Wales]

Date.......................................................

*Part III*

*Form of authority for the purchase of strychnine or a salt or quaternary compound thereof for killing foxes*

For the purposes of Rule 12(1) of the Poisons Rules 1982 and of paragraph 5 of Part I of Schedule 12 thereto I hereby authorise ..................................................................................................
(an officer of [the Ministry of Agriculture, Fisheries and Food] [the Department of Agriculture and Fisheries for Scotland]) [the Welsh Office] to purchase within four weeks of the date hereof
.............................. of .............................. for the purpose of killing foxes (other than foxes held in captivity) in the following infected area (within the meaning of the Rabies (Control) Order 1974), namely the infected area in ........................................ (locality).

.................................................................

A person authorised by [the Minister of Agriculture, Fisheries and Food] [the Secretary of State for Scotland] [the

Date ...................................................  Secretary of State for Wales]

*Part IV*

*Forms of certificate authorising the purchase of fluoroacetic acid, a salt thereof or fluoroacetamide as a rodenticide*

FORM A

*Certificate authorising the purchase of fluoroacetic acid, a salt thereof or fluoroacetamide as a rodenticide for use by employees of a local authority or a port health authority (in Scotland, a port local authority or joint port authority)*

For the purposes of Rule 12(2) of the Poisons Rules 1982 and of paragraph 6 of Part I of Schedule 12 thereto, I hereby certify that ....................................................................................................
of ........................................ is required for use by employees of ...............................
as a rodenticide in [ships] [sewers]situated at ......................................................................
[the following warehouses] viz......................................................................................................
situated in the restricted dock area at......................................................................................
being warehouses to which all means of access are, when not in actual use, kept securely locked or barred.
[the following drains] viz ............................................................................................................
situated in the restricted area at................................................................................................
being drains which are wholly enclosed and to which all means of access are, when not in actual use, kept closed.

.................................................................

The officer appointed for this purpose by

Date ........................................................  .................................................................

FORM B

*Certificate authorising the purchase of fluoroacetic acid, a salt thereof or fluoroacetamide as a rodenticide for use by a person, or the employees of a body of persons, carrying on a business of pest control or for use by officers of the Ministry of Agriculture, Fisheries and Food or of the Department of Agriculture and Fisheries for Scotland or of the Welsh Office*

For the purposes of Rule 12(2) of the Poisons Rules 1982 and of paragraph 6 of Part I of Schedule 12 thereto, I hereby certify that ...............................................................................................................
of ...................................................... is required for use by [ ...........................................................
...................................................] [employees of] ...........................................................................
[officers of the Ministry of Agriculture, Fisheries and Food/Department of Agriculture and Fisheries for Scotland/Welsh Office] as a rodenticide in:
   [ships] [sewers] situated at ...................................................................................................
   [the following drains] viz ....................................................................................................
   situated in the restricted areas at.........................................................................................
   being drains which are wholly enclosed and to which all means of access are, when not in actual, use, kept closed.

...................................................
[The officer appointed for this purpose by]

...................................................
[A person authorised by the Minister of Agriculture, Fisheries and Food]
[A person authorised by the Secretary of State for Scotland]
[A person authorised by the Secretary of of State for Wales]

Date ..............................................................

## Part V

*Form of authority for the purchase of salts of thallium for killing rats, mice or moles*

For the purpose of Rule 12(3) of the Poisons Rules 1982 and of paragraph 7 of Part I of Schedule 12 thereto I hereby authorise.........................................................................................................
to purchase salts of thallium within twelve months from the date hereof for the purpose of killing rats, mice or moles.

...................................................
A person authorised by [the Minister of Agriculture, Fisheries and Food] [the Secretary of State for Scotland] [the Secretary of State for Wales]

Date ..............................................................

# Substances and Preparations Dangerous to Supply

The Chemicals (Hazard Information and Packaging for Supply) Regulations 1994 (SI 1994 No.3247, as amended) made under the Health and Safety at Work etc. Act 1974 are described in Chapter 18. An Authorised and Approved List of Dangerous Substances is set out in *Information Approved for the Classification and Labelling of Substances Dangerous for Supply* (3rd edn, January 1996, HMSO). There are five parts to the list:

Part I:     List of Dangerous Substances and Articles
Part II:    List of Substances Dangerous for Supply (Solvents)
Part III:   List of Substances Dangerous for Supply (paints, varnishes, printing inks, adhesives and similar products)
Part IV:    List of Risk Phrases
Part V:     List of Safety Phrases

The classification of and symbols for substances dangerous for supply are set out in Schedule 1 to the Regulations.

## Part I

### List of 'Dangerous Substances'

N.B. This is a selection only (see above).

| Name of substance | Indication of general nature of risk. (The references in this column are references to the relevant entry in Schedule 1) 1 | Indication of particular risks. (The references in this column are references to the relevant entry in Part IV) 2 | Indications of precautions required. (The references in this column are references to the relevant entry in Part V) 3 |
|---|---|---|---|
| Acetic acid more than 90% | Corrosive | 10, 35 | 2, 23, 36 |
| Acetone | Highly Flammable | 11 | 2, 9, 16, 23, 33 |
| Ammonia more than 10% | Corrosive | 34, 37 | 1/2, 7, 26, 45 |
| Ammonia 5–10% | Irritant | 36/37/38 | 1/2, 7, 26, 45 |
| Amyl acetate | Flammable | 10 | 23 |
| Carbon tetrachloride more than 1% | Carcinogenic Toxic, dangerous for the environment | 23/24/25, 40, 48/23, 59 | 1/2, 23, 36/37, 45, 59, 61 |
| Chlorfenvinphos | Toxic | 26/27/28 | 26/27/28 |
| Chloroform | Carcinogenic Harmful | 22, 38, 40, 48/20/22 | 2, 36/37 |
| Copper sulphate | Harmful | 22, 36/38 | 22 |
| Dichlorvos | Toxic | 23/24/25 | 2, 13, 44 |
| Ephedrine, salts of | Harmful | 22 | 22, 25 |
| Ethanol (Ethyl alcohol) | Highly flammable | 11 | 7, 16 |
| Ethylene glycol | Harmful | 22 | 2 |
| Fluoroacetates, soluble salts | Toxic | 28 | 1/2, 20, 22, 26, 45 |
| Formaldehyde solution, | Carcinogenic | | |
| more than 25% | Toxic | 23/24/25, 34, 40, 43 | 1/2, 26, 36/37, 45 |
| 5–25% | Harmful | 20/21/22, 36/37/38, 40, 43 | 51 (all) |
| 1–5% | Harmful | 40, 43 | |
| Hydrochloric acid, more than | | | |
| 25% | Corrosive | 34, 37 | 1/2, 26, 45 |
| 10–25% | Irritant | 36/37/38 | 1/2, 26, 45 |
| Hydrogen peroxide | | | |
| more than 60% | Oxidizing | 8 | 1/2, 3, 28, 36/39 |
| 20–60% | Corrosive | 34 | 45 (all) |
| 5–20% | Irritant | 36/38 | |
| Mercurous chloride | Harmful | 22 | 2 |
| Methylated spirits | | | |
| more than 20% | Highly flammable | 11, 23/25 | 1/2, 7, 16, 24, 45 |
| 3–20% | Harmful | 20/22 | 1/2, 7, 16, 24, 45 |
| Mevinphos | Toxic | 26/27/28 | 1, 13, 28, 45 |
| Oxalic acid | Harmful | 21/22 | 2, 24/25 |
| Paraquat, and salts of | Toxic | 26/27/28 | 1, 13, 45 |
| Potassium chlorate | Oxidizing, Harmful | 9, 20/22 | 2, 13, 16, 27 |
| Potassium permanganate | Oxidizing, Harmful | 8, 22 | 2 |
| Sodium chlorate | Oxidizing and Harmful | 9, 20/22 | 2, 13, 16, 27 |
| Sodium hydroxide | | | |
| more than 5% | Corrosive | 35 | 1/2, 26, 37/39, 45 |
| 2–5% | Corrosive | 34 | 1/2, 26, 37/39, 45 |
| 0.5–2% | Irritant | 36/38 | 1/2, 26, 37/39, 45 |
| Strychnine, salts of | Toxic | 26/28 | 1, 13, 28, 45 |
| Sulphuric acid | Irritant | 36/38 | 2, 26 |

**Part IV**

### Indication of particular risks

| | |
|---|---|
| 1: | Explosive when dry |
| 2: | Risk of explosion by shock, friction, fire or other sources of ignition |
| 3: | Extreme risk of explosion by shock, friction, fire or other sources of ignition |
| 4: | Forms very sensitive explosive metallic compounds |
| 5: | Heating may cause an explosion |
| 6: | Explosive with or without contact with air |
| 7: | May cause fire |
| 8: | Contact with combustible material may cause fire |
| 9: | Explosive when mixed with combustible material |
| 10: | Flammable |
| 11: | Highly flammable |
| 12: | Extremely flammable |
| 13: | Extremely flammable liquefied gas |
| 14: | Reacts violently with water |
| 15: | Contact with water liberates highly flammable gases |
| 16: | Explosive when mixed with oxidizing substances |
| 17: | Spontaneously flammable in air |
| 18: | In use, may form flammable/explosive vapour-air mixture |
| 19: | May form explosive peroxides |
| 20: | Harmful by inhalation |
| 21: | Harmful in contact with skin |
| 22: | Harmful if swallowed |
| 23: | Toxic by inhalation |
| 24: | Toxic in contact with skin |
| 25: | Toxic if swallowed |
| 26: | Very toxic by inhalation |
| 27: | Very toxic in contact with skin |
| 28: | Very toxic if swallowed |
| 29: | Contact with water liberates toxic gas |
| 30: | Can become highly flammable in use |
| 31: | Contact with acids liberates toxic gas |
| 32: | Contact with acids liberates very toxic gas |
| 33: | Danger of cumulative effects |
| 34: | Causes burns |
| 35: | Causes severe burns |
| 36: | Irritating to eyes |
| 37: | Irritating to respiratory system |
| 38: | Irritating to skin |
| 39: | Danger of very serious irreversible effects |
| 40: | Possible risk of irreversible effects |
| 41: | Risk of serious damage to eyes |
| 42: | May cause sensitisation by inhalation |
| 43: | May cause sensitisation by skin contact |
| 44: | Risk of explosion if heated under confinement |
| 45: | May cause cancer |
| 46: | May cause heritable genetic damage |
| 47: | May cause birth defects |
| 48: | Danger of serious damage to health by prolonged exposure |

## Combination of particular risks

| | |
|---|---|
| 14/15: | Reacts violently with water, liberating highly flammable gases |
| 15/29: | Contact with water liberates toxic, highly flammable gas |
| 20/21: | Harmful by inhalation and in contact with skin |
| 20/21/22: | Harmful by inhalation, in contact with skin and if swallowed |
| 20/22: | Harmful by inhalation and if swallowed |
| 21/22: | Harmful in contact with skin and if swallowed |
| 23/24: | Toxic by inhalation and in contact with skin |
| 23/24/25: | Toxic by inhalation, in contact with skin and if swallowed |
| 23/25: | Toxic by inhalation and if swallowed |
| 24/25: | Toxic in contact with skin and if swallowed |
| 26/27: | Very toxic by inhalation and in contact with skin |
| 26/27/28: | Very toxic by inhalation, in contact with skin and if swallowed |
| 26/28: | Very toxic by inhalation and if swallowed |
| 27/28: | Very toxic in contact with skin and if swallowed |
| 36/37: | Irritating to eyes and respiratory system |
| 36/37/38: | Irritating to eyes, respiratory system and skin |
| 36/38: | Irritating to eyes and skin |
| 37/38: | Irritating to respiratory system and skin |
| 42/43: | May cause sensitisation by inhalation and skin contact |

## Part V

### Indication of safety precautions required

| | |
|---|---|
| 1: | Keep locked up |
| 2: | Keep out of reach of children |
| 3: | Keep in a cool place |
| 4: | Keep away from living quarters |
| 5: | Keep contents under . . . (appropriate liquid to be specified by the manufacturer) |
| 6: | Keep under . . . (inert gas to be specified by the manufacturer) |
| 7: | Keep container tightly closed |
| 8: | Keep container dry |
| 9: | Keep container in a well ventilated place |
| 12: | Do not keep the container sealed |
| 13: | Keep away from food, drink and animal feeding stuffs |
| 14: | Keep away from . . . (incompatible materials to be indicated by the manufacturer) |
| 15: | Keep away from heat |
| 16: | Keep away from sources of ignition – No Smoking |
| 17: | Keep away from combustible material |
| 18: | Handle and open container with care |
| 20: | When using do not eat or drink |
| 21: | When using do not smoke |
| 22: | Do not breathe dust |
| 23: | Do not breathe gas/fumes/vapour/spray (appropriate wording to be specified by manufacturer) |
| 24: | Avoid contact with skin |
| 25: | Avoid contact with eyes |
| 26: | In case of contact with eyes, rinse immediately with plenty of water and seek medical advice |
| 27: | Take off immediately all contaminated clothing |
| 28: | After contact with skin, wash immediately with plenty of . . . (to be specified by the manufacturer) |

| | |
|---|---|
| 29: | Do not empty into drains |
| 30: | Never add water to this product |
| 33: | Take precautionary measures against static discharges |
| 34: | Avoid shock and friction |
| 35: | This material and its container must be disposed of in a safe way |
| 36: | Wear suitable protective clothing |
| 37: | Wear suitable gloves |
| 38: | In case of insufficient ventilation, wear suitable respiratory equipment |
| 39: | Wear eye/face protection |
| 40: | To clean the floor and all objects contaminated by this material use . . . (to be specified by the manufacturer) |
| 41: | In case of fire and/or explosion do not breathe fumes |
| 42: | During fumigation/spraying wear suitable respiratory equipment (appropriate wording to be specified) |
| 43: | In case of fire, use . . . (indicate in the space the precise type of fire-fighting equipment. If water increases the risk, add – Never use water) |
| 44: | If you feel unwell, seek medical advice – show the label where possible |
| 45: | In case of accident or if you feel unwell, seek medical advice immediately – show the label where possible |
| 46: | If swallowed seek medical advice immediately and show this container or label |
| 47: | Keep at temperature not exceeding . . . degrees C (to be specified by the manufacturer) |
| 48: | Keep wetted with . . . (appropriate material to be specified by the manufacturer) |
| 49: | Keep only in the original container |
| 50: | Do not mix with . . . (to be specified by the manufacturer) |
| 51: | Use only in well ventilated areas |
| 52: | Not recommended for interior use on large surface areas |

### Combination of safety precautions required

| | |
|---|---|
| 1/2: | Keep locked up and out of reach of children |
| 3/7/9: | Keep container tightly closed, in a cool well ventilated place |
| 3/9: | Keep in a cool, well ventilated place |
| 3/19/14: | Keep in a cool, well ventilated place away from . . . (incompatible materials to be indicated by the manufacturer) |
| 3/9/14/49: | Keep only in the original container in a cool, well ventilated place away from . . . (incompatible materials to be indicated by the manufacturer) |
| 3/9/49: | Keep only in the original container in a cool, well ventilated place |
| 3/14: | Keep in a cool place away from . . . (incompatible materials to be indicated by the manufacturer) |
| 7/8: | Keep container tightly closed and dry |
| 7/9: | Keep container tightly closed and in a well ventilated place |
| 20/21: | When using do not eat, drink or smoke |
| 24/25: | Avoid contact with skin and eyes |
| 36/37: | Wear suitable protective clothing and gloves |
| 36/37/39: | Wear suitable protective clothing, gloves and eye/face protection |
| 36/39: | Wear suitable protective clothing and eye/face protection |
| 37/39: | Wear suitable gloves and eye/face protection |
| 47/49: | Keep only in the original container at temperature not exceeding degrees C (to be specified by the manufacturer) |

## Schedule 1 to the Regulations

### Indication of Danger

 Toxic or Very Toxic

 Dangerous for the Environment

 Corrosive

 Explosive

 Oxidizing

 Harmful

 Highly or Extremely Flammable

 Irritant

The above symbols shall be in black on an orange-yellow background.

# Bye-laws of the Royal Pharmaceutical Society of Great Britain

## Confirmed and Approved by the Privy Council January 2001

### Section I: Preliminary

1. All the bye-laws heretofore passed are hereby revoked, and these bye-laws shall be the bye-laws of the Society.

2. In these bye-laws, unless the context otherwise requires, the following expressions have the meanings hereby respectively assigned to them, that is to say:

*The Council* means the Council of the Society.

*Member* means a member of the Society other than an honorary member.

*Pharmacist* means a pharmaceutical chemist.

*Pre-registration Trainee* means a graduate with a degree granted in respect of pharmacy that has been approved by the Council or a student undertaking a pharmacy degree sandwich course approved by the Council who is engaged in pre-registration training approved by the Council.

*Register* means the register of pharmaceutical chemists.

*Registered* means, in relation to a pharmacist, duly registered in the register.

*Registrar* means the Registrar appointed under section 1 of the Pharmacy Act 1954.

*Registration examination* means the examination for the purpose of section 3 of the Pharmacy Act 1954.

*Retention fee* means the retention fee referred to in section 2(3) of the Pharmacy Act 1954.

*The Society* means the Royal Pharmaceutical Society of Great Britain and any reference to the Pharmaceutical Society of Great Britain in any Act of Parliament or other legislative instrument shall be so construed.

*Student* means a student of the Society, who is an undergraduate student at a school of pharmacy in Great Britain reading for a degree granted in respect of pharmacy that has been approved by the Council for the purpose of registration as a pharmaceutical chemist in Great Britain, or a graduate who has been awarded such a degree, who is not registered as a pharmaceutical chemist and who is undertaking postgraduate research or studies leading to a higher degree, or who is undertaking a period of pre-registration training in Great Britain.

In these bye-laws, unless the context otherwise requires, words importing the singular number only shall include the plural number and *vice versa*, words importing the masculine gender only shall include the feminine gender and *vice versa*.

## Section II: Members

1. No person who is not registered as a pharmacist shall be a member.

2. The retention fee payable annually by a pharmacist in respect of the retention of his name on the register shall be £142* provided that:

(i) A pharmacist who on 30 December 1933, was a life member in accordance with the bye-laws then in force shall pay no retention fee.

(ii) A pharmacist not being entitled under (i) above to pay no fee, who holds the position of superintendent of a body corporate carrying on a retail pharmacy business shall pay the fee of £142* and shall not be eligible to pay any of the lower fees specified in (iii) to (v) of this bye-law.

(iii) A pharmacist who when paying his retention fee declares in writing in the form set out in the fourth schedule to these bye-laws that he will not during the year for which the fee is payable be gainfully employed in any occupation for more than 13 weeks or the equivalent thereof shall pay a retention fee of £80*. If a pharmacist who has made such a declaration is subsequently gainfully employed in any occupation for more than 13 weeks or the equivalent thereof in the year for which the declaration has been made he shall forthwith without demand remit to the Registrar the balance of £62*.

(iv) A pharmacist who when paying his retention fee declares in writing in the form set out in the fourth schedule to these bye-laws that he has attained his 65th birthday and that he will not during the year for which the fee is payable be gainfully employed in any occupation, shall pay a retention fee of £20*.

    (a) If a pharmacist who has made such a declaration is subsequently gainfully employed in any occupation for up to 13 weeks or the equivalent thereof in the year for which the declaration has been made, he shall forthwith without demand remit to the Registrar a further sum of £62*; and

    (b) If a pharmacist who has made such a declaration is subsequently gainfully employed in any occupation for more than 13 weeks or the equivalent thereof in the year for which the declaration has been made he shall forthwith without demand remit to the Registrar a further sum of £62* to bring the total paid to £142*.

(v) A pharmacist who has not attained his 65th birthday and who satisfies the Registrar that he is not engaged in the practice of pharmacy in, and is not ordinarily resident in, Great Britain, shall pay a retention fee of £67*.

3. Every retention fee shall be due and payable on the first day of January in each year in respect of which such fee is payable.

4. The Registrar may send to any pharmacist who has not paid his retention fee on the first day of January in the year in respect of which such fee is payable a demand for payment thereof, which demand shall be by registered or recorded delivery letter addressed to the pharmacist at his address in the register.

5. A demand made pursuant to paragraph 4 hereof shall be deemed to have been made on the day following the day on which the letter containing the demand was posted.

6. If any pharmacist shall not have paid his retention fee within two months of the making of a demand therefore as aforesaid the Registrar shall inform the Council of such failure and the Council may direct the Registrar to remove the name of such pharmacist from the register.

7. A person paying his fee in accordance with section 12(2) of the Pharmacy Act 1954, for the restoration of his name to the register shall pay an additional sum of £306* by way of penalty.

* Fees are reviewed annually by the Council.


### Section III: Fellows

1. All members registered as pharmaceutical chemists on or before the first day of February, 1951, shall be designated fellows of the Society.

2. The Council may designate as a fellow of the Society any member who before 1st February, 1955, either (a) was registered as a pharmaceutical chemist with the provisions of the Pharmacy Act 1852, or (b) is registered as a pharmaceutical chemist in accordance with the provisions of the Pharmacy Act 1954, and who but for the passing of that Act would have been registered as a pharmaceutical chemist in accordance with the provisions of the Pharmacy Act 1852, provided, in either case, that he was eligible for registration as an apprentice or student before 1st June, 1948, and that he commenced in or before the session 1951/52 a recognised course of study of at least two years for a final examination in pharmacy or being registered as a chemist and druggist commenced in or before that session the last year of such a course.

3. The Council may designate as fellows of the Society such members of the Society of not less than five years' standing as in the opinion of the Council have made outstanding original contributions to the advancement of pharmaceutical knowledge or have attained exceptional proficiency in a subject embraced by or related to the practice of pharmacy.

A member desiring to be designated a fellow under this bye-law shall apply in writing, enclosing the evidence on which he bases his application. The application shall be considered by assessors appointed for the purpose by the Council. The assessors may at their discretion call the applicant for interview and examine him upon his work either orally or in writing. The assessors shall report to the Education Committee of the Council who shall submit the report to the Council with or without a recommendation.

4. Notwithstanding the provisions of the last preceding bye-law the Council may appoint a panel of fellows not being members of Council who shall have power to designate as a fellow a member of not less than 20 years' standing who in their opinion has made outstanding original contributions to the advancement of pharmaceutical knowledge or attained distinction in the science, practice, profession or history of pharmacy.

5. Designation under the two preceding bye-laws shall take place only at the June or December meeting of Council in any year.

6. Members designated as fellows of the Society shall be so designated only so long as they remain members.


### Section IV: Honorary Fellows and Honorary Members

1. The Council may at their discretion elect as honorary fellows such scientific workers as have distinguished themselves in any of the branches of knowledge embraced in the educational objects of the Society and persons who are eminent in the national life.

2. The Council may at their discretion elect as honorary members such persons as have rendered distinguished service to the Society or to pharmacy.

3. A person who is nominated by the Privy Council to be a member of Council, under the provisions of the Pharmacy Act 1954, shall, if not registered as a pharmacist, be an honorary member while so holding office.

4. The Council may from time to time determine the number of persons to be honorary fellows and honorary members, other than members of Council nominated by the Privy Council. A member of the Society may suggest the names of persons for election as honorary fellows or honorary members by writing to the Secretary, providing biographical information on the person nominated. At the meeting of the Council held in April of each year, the Secretary shall report in confidence the names of those so nominated and provide to the Council biographical details of the persons concerned. The Council, at its meeting in June of each year, shall consider the names proposed and may select persons to be elected honorary fellows and honorary members respectively.

## Section V: Students

1. There shall be a section of the Society entitled *The British Pharmaceutical Students' Association*, membership of which shall be open to all students. Additionally, the Executive of the Association may include members of the Society who have been registered initially for not more than twelve months.

2. The Association shall be regarded by the Council as the representative body for students. It shall act within the policies of the Council, but may make recommendations to the Council.

3. The Association shall be administered by an elected Executive and in accordance with a constitution to be decided jointly by the Association and the Society.

4. The Association shall be jointly financed by the Society and the membership of the Association. The subscription to be paid by the membership shall be decided by the Council, following consultation with the Executive of the Association.

5. There shall be an annual meeting between representatives of the Council and the Executive, and regular discussions between the Executive and officials of the Society.

6. The Association shall be able to participate in the Branch Representatives' Meeting and shall be permitted to send up to two representatives, to submit up to three motions directly related to students, and, at the President's discretion, to participate in the discussion of other motions directly related to students.

7. Members of the Association shall be eligible to receive The Pharmaceutical Journal and The Journal of Pharmacy and Pharmacology at special subscription rates, to be decided by the Council.

8. Members of the Association shall be permitted to serve as coopted members on the committees of the Society's Branches and Regions.

9. All students, whether or not members of the Association, shall:

(a)    be able to attend meetings of the Society's Branches and Regions;
(b)    be eligible to receive assistance from the Benevolent Fund.

## Section VI: Annual and Special General Meetings

1. The annual general meeting of members shall be held in each year in the month of May on such date and at such time and place as the Council may determine.

2. The Council shall prepare a report of their proceedings in respect of each calendar year, which together with the financial statement prepared by the Council, with the Auditors' report thereon, shall be presented at the annual general meeting held in the next subsequent

calendar year and the said report of the Council's proceedings and a summary of the financial statement shall be sent to members to arrive not less than 10 days before the day appointed for the said meeting.

3. A member may raise any matter or move any motion at any annual general meeting of which he has given the Secretary notice in writing not later than the 20th day of April in the year in which the said meeting is to be held. The Rules of Procedure for debating such motions shall be proposed by the Council and presented for adoption at each annual general meeting at which such a motion is to be moved.

4. The Council shall meet previous to each annual general meeting and arrange the order of business to be transacted thereat.

5. Special general meetings of members shall be held on such dates and at such times and places and for such purposes as the Council may determine. Upon the requisition in writing of not less than 30 members requiring the Council to convene a special general meeting for the purpose specified in the requisition, such meeting shall accordingly be convened within such reasonable time as the Council shall think fit.

6. All general meetings shall be summoned by the Secretary by notice published in The Pharmaceutical Journal not less than 10 clear days before the day thereby appointed for the meeting, or by notice sent by prepaid post not less than 10 clear days before the day thereby appointed for the meeting and addressed to each member at his address in the register. Any such notice shall specify the general nature of the business to be transacted at the meeting.

7. Notwithstanding the provisions of the last preceding bye-law, any special general meeting to be convened for the purpose of considering whether to confirm any alteration, amendment or addition to the Supplemental Charter granted to the Society on 31st December 1953 shall be summoned in all respects as though the references in the said bye-law to 10 clear days were each of them to 40 clear days.

8. At all general meetings the President or in his absence the Vice-President or in the absence of the President and the Vice-President such member of the Council as shall be elected by the members present at the meeting shall preside, or if there be no such member of the Council present then such other member of the Society as shall be elected to preside by the members present.

9. Every member shall have one vote and no more at a general meeting and such vote shall be given personally and not by proxy.

10. Any question to be decided by a general meeting, if not resolved on without a division, shall be decided by a simple majority of votes and subject to a demand for a ballot the voting shall be by show of hands.

11. In any case of an equality of votes the chairman shall have a second or casting vote.

12. The chairman of any general meeting may adjourn such meeting from time to time and from place to place, but no such adjournment shall extend beyond a period of four days. It shall not be necessary to give members notice of such adjourned meeting, but no business shall be transacted thereat other than the business left unfinished at the meeting from which the adjournment took place.

13. The proceedings of any general meeting shall be considered perfect in themselves without the necessity of reading or confirming the minutes of the preceding general meeting.

### Section VII: Council and Meetings of Council

1. The Council shall consist of the persons nominated by the Privy Council in accordance with the provisions of section 15 of the Pharmacy Act 1954, and for the time being holding office as members of the Council, and 21 members of the Society elected by the members of the Society in accordance with the provisions of these bye-laws.

2. The Council shall meet not less than four times in each calendar year, at such day and hour as may from time to time be decided by the Council. Such further meetings of the Council shall be held as are notified by the Secretary upon direction of the President or any eight members of Council in writing under his or their hands.

3. Members of Council shall be entitled to receive a fee which shall be determined by the Council from time to time by resolution but not exceeding £200 for each day or part of a day for attending any meeting of the Council or any meeting of a committee of the Council or subcommittee of such a committee or on such other occasions as the Council may from time to time by resolution determine.

4. A member of Council who personally incurs expenditure in employment of a pharmacist to take personal control of registered pharmacy premises in order to comply with the requirements of the Medicines Act 1968 whilst a member of Council is engaged on Council business shall be entitled to reimbursement of sums expended not exceeding £200 per day.

5. Members of the Council shall be entitled to be reimbursed for expenditure on travel incurred on business of the Society and for costs for accommodation and subsistence up to limits to be determined by resolution of the Council and reported to the Annual General Meeting each year.

6. Eight members shall constitute a quorum, and without that number being present no business shall be transacted. Before other business is entered on, the minutes of the preceding monthly and of any subsequent meeting shall be confirmed.

7. All meetings of the Council shall be summoned by the Secretary by notice left at the place of business or residence of, or sent by prepaid post addressed to the place of business or residence of, the person summoned not less than four clear days before the day thereby appointed for the meeting. Any such notice shall specify the general nature of the business to be transacted at the meeting.

8. The President shall preside at all meetings of the Council, or in his absence the Vice-President. If the President and Vice-President are both absent, a chairman shall be chosen by the members present. In any case of an equality of votes, the chairman of the meeting shall have a second or casting vote.

9. The Council may, from time to time, frame and adopt standing orders for the regulation of their procedure, but the chairman may, notwithstanding the standing orders, require any ordinary motion or proposition to be in writing and signed by the proposer and seconder. Any member of the Council desirous of bringing any special motion or proposition before the Council shall give written notice to the Secretary of the terms of the motion at least six clear days before the ordinary meeting of the Council, and in default of such notice the motion may be postponed or adjourned by the chairman until the next ordinary meeting. A ballot may be demanded by any member of the Council on any motion put from the chair.

10. Subject to the provisions of these bye-laws, all resolutions carried at the meetings of the Council shall be acted upon without confirmation.

11. The Council may, from time to time, in their discretion appoint from amongst their members or otherwise such committees as shall appear expedient, and may from time to time modify or dissolve any committee. The President and Vice-President shall be ex officio members of all committees.

12. Nothing in this section shall apply to the Statutory Committee appointed in accordance with section 7 of the Pharmacy Act 1954.

## Section VIII: Casual Vacancies in the Council

1. If any elected member of the Council shall cease to be a member of the Society, he shall thereupon cease to be an elected member of the Council. Any elected member of the Council may at any time resign his office by giving notice in writing of his resignation to the Secretary.

2. In the event of any casual vacancy occurring in the elected members of Council, the Council shall appoint a member of the Society to fill the place of such elected member of Council and the member so appointed shall hold office for such period as the person whom he has replaced would have held office.

3. The Secretary shall report any casual vacancy in the elected members of Council, and the cause thereof, to the next ensuing meeting of the Council, and shall also report the same if time shall permit in the notice summoning the said meeting.

4. At the meeting of Council next following that at which the casual vacancy is reported nominations of persons to fill the vacancy shall be made, and at the meeting of the Council held next following the meeting at which nominations are made the Council shall proceed to the election of a member to fill the casual vacancy except that if the meeting of the Council at which the vacancy is reported is the March meeting, the Council may, if they so decide, disregard the May meeting for the purpose of this procedure.

## Section IX: Officers of the Society

1. The Council shall at their first meeting held after each annual general meeting elect from among their number who are pharmacists a President, a Vice-President and a Treasurer and they together with the Immediate Past President shall be designated as the Officers of the Society.

2. The President, Vice-President and Treasurer shall hold office until the first meeting of the Council held after the next following annual general meeting and they or any one or more of them shall be eligible for re-election.

3. If any President, Vice-President or Treasurer shall cease to be a member of Council, he shall thereupon cease to be President, Vice-President or Treasurer, as the case may be. The President, Vice-President or Treasurer may at any time resign his office by giving notice in writing of his resignation to the Secretary. If the Immediate Past President ceases to be a member of the Council, he shall thereupon cease to be designated Officer of the Society within the terms of paragraph 1. Until the next election under the terms of paragraph 1 above, his place as an Officer will be taken by the person who preceded him in the office as President and who continues to serve on the Council.

4. In the event of any vacancy occurring in the office of President, Vice-President or Treasurer, the Secretary shall report the same, and the cause thereof, to the next meeting of the Council, and shall also report the same if time shall permit in the notice summoning the said meeting, and the Council shall at that or the next subsequent meeting proceed to elect one of their number to fill such vacant office. Any person so elected shall hold office for such period as the person whom he has replaced would have held office.

5. It shall be the duty of the Treasurer to take charge of all moneys, to pay such accounts as the Council may order by resolution, and to render his account at each monthly meeting.

## Section X: Secretary

1. The Council shall at their first meeting held after each annual general meeting appoint a person who shall be a pharmacist to be Secretary of the Society.

2. The Secretary shall hold office until the first meeting of the Council held after the next following annual general meeting, and shall be eligible for reappointment.

3. The Secretary shall have such powers, duties and obligations as, subject to the provisions of these bye-laws, may be determined by the Council.

4. The Secretary shall be under a duty to superintend and administer the affairs of the Society under the direction of the Council and committees. He shall conduct the correspondence, and issue all summonses and notices, take the minutes of all meetings for business and read them, and make a report of all matters that come under his cognisance for the

information of the Council and committees. He shall consult and act on the instructions of the President or Vice-President on any business requiring attention between the various meetings, and be responsible for the safe custody of all the documents and property belonging to the Society which shall be under his control. He shall receive all subscriptions, fees and donations, and give a printed receipt for the same, and no other, except where payment is received by cheque in which case the issue of a receipt, unless specifically requested by the payer, shall be in his discretion. He shall promptly pay to the Society's bankers on behalf of the Treasurer the amount of moneys so received by him. He shall receive such a sum in advance for current expenses as the Council may order, and account for the same to the Council.

5. If at any time more than one person is appointed to be Secretary of the Society, the Council shall assign all the powers, duties and obligations referred to in paragraph 4 hereof to one of such persons.

6. In the event of a casual vacancy occurring in the office of Secretary, the President or Vice-President shall appoint some person, pro tempore, to fulfil the duty of the office, and shall report the same and the cause thereof to the next meeting of the Council, and shall also cause the same, if time shall permit, to be reported in the notice summoning the said meeting. At the said meeting the Council shall take appropriate action with a view to filling the vacancy and at some subsequent meeting shall appoint a person to fill the vacancy. The person so appointed shall hold office for such period as the person whom he has replaced would have held office.

7. If at any time more than one person is appointed to be Secretary of the Society, the provisions of the last preceding bye-law shall be deemed to refer only to the Secretary to whom all the powers, duties and obligations referred to in paragraph 4 hereof have been assigned.

### Section XI: Auditors

1. Every third year five members other than members of Council shall be elected as Auditors of the accounts of the Society in accordance with the provisions of these bye-laws.

2. The Auditors shall hold office until the Auditors are elected in the next succeeding election, and they or any one or more of them shall be eligible for re-election.

3. If any Auditor shall cease to be a member of the Society, or shall become a member of Council, he shall thereupon cease to be an Auditor. Any Auditor may at any time resign his office by giving notice in writing of his resignation to the Secretary.

4. In the event of any casual vacancy occurring in the office of Auditor, the Council shall appoint a member other than a member of Council to fill the place of such Auditor, and the member so appointed shall hold office for such period as the person whom he has replaced would have held office.

5. The Secretary shall report any casual vacancy in the office of Auditor, and the cause thereof, to the next ensuing meeting of the Council, and shall also report the same, if time shall permit, in the notice summoning the said meeting, and the Council shall at that or the next subsequent meeting appoint a person to fill such a vacancy.

6. The Auditors shall meet previous to the annual general meeting, and at such a time as will enable them to carry out their duties under this bye-law. It shall be their duty to inspect the accounts of the Society, and the financial statement prepared for them by the Council, which, when approved, must be certified and signed by the Auditors present at the audit, and presented to the Council not later than at its ordinary meeting in May.

### Section XII: Election of Council and Auditors

1. Seven of the elected members of the Council shall go out of office in every year, and the vacancies shall be filled by election, the retiring members being eligible for re-election if duly

nominated for that purpose. The seven members who so go out shall be the elected members of the Council who have been longest in office without re-election.

2. The retiring members of the Council shall be ascertained by, and recorded on the minutes of, the Council at the monthly meeting held in February of every year.

3. All members are entitled to vote for the election of members of the Council and Auditors. A member shall only be eligible for election to the Council or as an Auditor if he is normally resident in Great Britain, the Isle of Man or the Channel Islands. If in the opinion of the Council any elected member of the Council or any Auditor ceases to be normally resident in Great Britain, the Isle of Man or the Channel Islands, he shall cease to be a member of the Council or an Auditor as the case may be. In the election of members of the Council any 10 members of whom at least five must be from the branch of the member nominated, desirous of nominating any other member for election as a member of the Council shall, on or before the 18th day of March in each year, give a notice signed by them to the Secretary with the name and address of the nominee. In the election of Auditors any four members desirous of nominating any other member for election as an Auditor, shall on or before the 18th day of March in an election year, give a notice signed by them to the Secretary with the name and address of the nominee. The Secretary shall on or before the 20th day of March then instant address and send by post to each nominee a notice of his having been nominated, and inquiring whether he will accept office, if elected, and in default of a written reply from such nominee being received on or before the 31st day of March then instant, declaring his readiness to accept office, if elected, such nominee shall not be deemed eligible or willing to be elected; provided that no member shall be eligible for election or entitled to vote who has failed to pay on or before the 10th day prior to the day on which the annual general meeting of the Society is held any retention fee or penalty then due and payable by him to the Society.

4. The Council shall at its monthly meeting, held in April of every year, prepare a list of all members nominated for election and willing to be elected members of Council; and at its monthly meeting in April in each year that an election of Auditors is to be held prepare a list of all members nominated for election and willing to be elected as Auditors. No nominations shall be received or made after the 18th day of March, except such as may be made by the Council in the manner and under the circumstances hereinafter stated at the monthly meeting in April.

5. If the number of members nominated and willing to accept office is less than the number of vacancies, the Council shall nominate as many as may be required to form a complete list of members willing to fill all the vacancies in the Council and a complete list of five Auditors; the members named in the lists so formed shall at the annual general meeting be declared by the chairman to have been elected. If the number of members nominated and willing to accept office is equal to the number of vacancies, such members shall at the annual general meeting be declared by the chairman to have been elected.

6. Except in the circumstances for which provision is made in the last preceding bye-law, the Secretary shall issue to every member, not less than 10 days prior to the annual general meeting, voting papers giving the names and addresses, in alphabetical order by surname, of the members willing to serve if elected.

7. In the election of members of Council and in the election of Auditors, each member shall have a single transferable vote. The quota for election shall be determined by dividing the total number of valid votes by one more than the number to be elected, ignoring the remainder, and increasing the result by one. Candidates (if any) with totals of votes in excess of the quota shall, commencing with the largest, have their surpluses transferred in turn in accordance with next available preferences, and the candidates with fewest votes shall be excluded in turn, and their votes likewise transferred until the required number of members nominated has secured election.

8. The completed voting papers shall be sent by post to such appropriate body (hereinafter referred to as 'the appointed body') as the Council shall from time to time appoint to count the votes.

9. The appointed body shall count the votes and shall make to the Secretary a signed return of the names of the members nominated who have secured election as members of Council and as Auditors, together with result sheets disclosing the number of votes given at each stage of the count to each member nominated.

10. The Secretary shall announce by a notice published in The Pharmaceutical Journal not later than the Saturday preceding the Council meeting in June, the report of the election received from the appointed body and shall declare elected those named therein as having secured election.

## Section XIII: Common Seal

1. The common seal of the Society shall consist of the armorial bearings, crest, and motto, registered in Her Majesty's College of Arms.

2. The said seal shall be deposited in the custody of the Secretary.

3. The common seal may be set or affixed to any deed, instrument, or writing, only in pursuance of an order or minute of the Council, entered in their minute book, which shall be laid on the table at each monthly Council meeting. The affixing of the common seal shall be recorded in a seal register, and be certified by the persons present.

4. The affixing of the common seal shall be attested by the President, or Vice-President, or two members of Council.

## Section XIV: Funds and Property

1. The whole property of or under the control of the Society shall be subject to the management, direction and control of the Council, and may, under the direction of the Council (but subject always to any special trusts upon which any particular fund may be held), be invested:

(1)  in or upon any investments authorised by Part 1 or II of the first Schedule to the Trustee Investments Act 1961, as amended from time to time; or

(2)  in or upon any of the securities of the government of the United Kingdom or of any of the countries mentioned in paragraph 2 of this bye-law or of the government of any province or state within any such country that has a separate legislature; or

(3)  in or upon any mortgages or other securities of any municipality, county or district council or local or public authority or board in any country mentioned in the last preceding subparagraph or in any province or state within any such country that has a separate legislature; or

(4)  in or upon any mortgages or other securities the capital whereof or a minimum rate of interest or dividend whereon is guaranteed by the government of any country mentioned in subparagraph (2) above or of any province or state within any such country that has a separate legislature; or

(5)  in or upon the bonds or mortgages or the fully paid guaranteed or preference or ordinary stock or shares or ordinary preferred or deferred or other stock or shares of any company incorporated either by Royal Charter or under any general or special Act of the United Kingdom Parliament or any general or special enactment of the legislature of any country mentioned in subparagraph (2) above having an issued and paid up share capital of at least £1 000 000 or its equivalent at current rates of exchange, being stocks or shares which are quoted upon a recognised stock exchange within any such country, and so that in the case of a company having shares of no par value such paid up capital shall be deemed to include the capital sum (other than capital surplus) appearing in the company's accounts in respect of such shares. Provided always that no investment shall be made in any ordinary stocks or shares

unless in each of the four years immediately preceding the calendar year in which the investment is made, the company shall have paid a dividend and that the total amount at any time standing invested in investments authorised by this subparagraph as shown by the books of the Society shall not exceed 75 per centum of the total amount at such time standing invested in any of the investments hereby authorised as appearing by such books. For the purpose of this subparagraph a company formed to take over the business of another company or other companies, or for either of those purposes, shall be deemed to have paid a dividend in any year in which such a dividend has been paid by the company or all the other companies. For the purpose of valuing the investments authorised by this subparagraph and held by the Society the minimum price to be taken for each security shall be the cost price thereof to the Society; or

(6)   in the purchase of freehold ground rents or freehold or leasehold land, messuages, tenements and hereditaments within England and Wales provided that as regards leaseholds, the term thereof shall have at least 60 years to run; or in the purchase of lands or house property, feu duties or ground annuals, in Scotland; or

(7)   upon the security of freehold property, freehold ground rents, land charges or rent charges in England and Wales or upon heritable security in Scotland, by way of first mortgage or bond, up to the limit of two-thirds of the value.

2. This bye-law shall authorise investment in the securities of countries situated outside the United Kingdom only of the following: Australia, Austria, Belgium, Canada, Denmark, France, Federal Republic of Germany, Italy, Japan, Luxembourg, Netherlands, New Zealand, Norway, Portugal, Republic of South Africa, Spain, Sweden, Switzerland, United States of America.

3. The property and funds of the Society, other than moneys from time to time in the hands of the Secretary, shall not be disposed of, or otherwise dealt with, except in pursuance of an order of the Council.

### Section XV: Benevolent Funds

1. There shall be a fund known as *the Benevolent Fund* consisting of donations and subscriptions and such grants as may from time to time be made by the Council from the general funds of the Society and the investments for the time being in respect of the said fund.

2. Such subscriptions, donations, grants and interest on investments as are not required for current needs shall be invested.

3. The whole of the Benevolent Fund, both as to capital and interest, shall be applicable, in the discretion of the Council, towards the relief of distressed persons being:

(1)   members;

(2)   persons who at any time have been members or have been registered as pharmaceutical chemists or as chemists and druggists;

(3)   widows, orphans or other dependants of deceased persons who were at any time members or registered as aforesaid; or

(4)   students.

4. There shall be a fund known as *the Orphan Fund*, and the provisions of paragraphs 1, 2 and 3 hereof shall apply to the said fund as though references in the said bye-laws to the Benevolent Fund were references to the Orphan Fund, save that the Orphan Fund shall be applicable towards the relief of distressed persons who are the orphan children of deceased persons who were at any time members and not otherwise.

5. There shall be a fund known as *the Birdsgrove House Fund*, and the provisions of paragraph 1, 2 and 3 hereof shall apply to the said fund as though references in the said bye-laws to the Benevolent Fund were references to the Birdsgrove House Fund, save that the Birdsgrove House Fund shall be applicable towards the establishment and maintenance of convalescent homes for the relief of distressed persons being:

(1)    members;

(2)    persons who at any time have been members or have been registered as pharmaceutical chemists or as chemists and druggists; or

(3)    widows, orphans or other dependants of deceased persons who were at any time members or registered as aforesaid.

### Section XVI: Branches and Branch Representatives' Meetings

1. The Council shall establish and maintain a system of local Branches of the Society.

2. Each local Branch shall be constituted and governed in such manner and have such functions as may be determined by the rules for the time being in force in respect of that Branch. The rules of each Branch shall be based upon the model rules set out in the second schedule to these bye-laws with such modifications in respect of any Branch as the Council may from time to time approve.

3. The Council shall arrange the holding from time to time and from place to place of meetings of members representative of the local Branches. The number of Representatives of each local Branch, the mode of their appointment, and the procedure to be adopted at the meetings of Representatives, shall be determined by the Council.

4. The functions of the meetings of Representatives shall be to inform the Council of the views of the Branches on matters of concern to the Society, to inform the Representatives of the Council's activities or proposed activities and the reasons therefore, and to ascertain the views of the Branches upon the said activities or proposed activities.

### Section XVII: Memberships Groups

1. The Council may from time to time establish and determine the constitution of special groups of members based on the nature of their occupations or special interests. The function of any such group shall be the discussion of matters of a professional and technical character of common interest to the members of the group.

### Section XVIII: Meetings for the Reading of Papers

1. Meetings of the Society may be held for the reading of papers and discussion of subjects relating to the objects of the Society.

2. Notice of such meetings shall be given in The Pharmaceutical Journal.

### Section XIX: Registration of Overseas Pharmacists

1. The Council may by resolution enter into a reciprocal agreement with the Pharmaceutical Society of Northern Ireland, for the registration as a pharmaceutical chemist under the Pharmacy Act 1954, of a person registered as a pharmaceutical chemist in Northern Ireland who is able to satisfy the Registrar that he registered in Northern Ireland after qualifying in pharmacy in the United Kingdom or by virtue of holding an appropriate European diploma as specified in Schedule 1A to the Pharmacy Act 1954.

2. Persons making application for registration pursuant to an agreement entered into in accordance with the provisions of the preceding bye-law shall:

(a)     produce evidence to satisfy the Registrar:

>    (i) as to his identity;
>    (ii) that he is of good character;
>    (iii) that he is in good health, both physically and mentally;
>    (iv) that he is registered as a pharmaceutical chemist in Northern Ireland within the terms of such agreement; and

(b)     pay to the Registrar a fee of £141*;

whereupon, subject to the Registrar being satisfied that all conditions have been complied with, he shall be registered.

3. The Council may by resolution enter into a reciprocal agreement with a pharmacists registration authority in any country or state outside the United Kingdom, other than a Member State of the European Community, for the registration as a pharmaceutical chemist under the Pharmacy Act 1954, of any person who is able to satisfy the Registrar that he complies with the conditions specified in the following bye-law.

4. A person making application for registration pursuant to an agreement entered into in accordance with the provisions of the preceding bye-law shall:

(a)     produce evidence to satisfy the Registrar:

>    (i) that he is resident in the United Kingdom;
>    (ii) as to his identity;
>    (iii) that he is of good character;
>    (iv) that he is in good health, both physically and mentally;
>    (v) that he has passed a qualifying examination specified in such agreement;
>    (vi) that he is registered as a pharmacist in the country or state, as the case may be, in which he passed that examination and is in good standing with the pharmacists registration authority of the country or state concerned;

(b)     produce a declaration made in accordance with the Statutory Declarations Act 1935, that he is the person referred to in the documents produced by him and that they are his property;

(c)     in the case of a person who was granted a certificate of qualification to practise pharmacy in any State of the Commonwealth of Australia or in New Zealand after March 31, 1968:

>    (i) produce a certificate from the Registrar of the pharmacists registration authority concerned that, subsequent to the date of his statutory registration, he completed, normally within the jurisdiction of that authority, a period of one years' employment in pharmacy as a registered pharmacist;
>    (ii) produce evidence satisfactory to the Registrar that he has completed in Great Britain a period of four weeks' experience in the practice of pharmacy in a pharmacy or pharmacy department of a hospital under the direct personal control and supervision of a pharmacist registered in Great Britain; and
>    (iii) produce a declaration made in accordance with the Statutory Declarations Act 1835, that he has studied the laws affecting the practice of pharmacy and the current Code of Ethics (as amended) and Notes for Guidance; and

(d)     pay to the Registrar a fee of £141*;

whereupon subject to the Registrar being satisfied that all conditions have been complied with, he shall be registered.

5. The Council, shall authorise the registration as a pharmaceutical chemist under the Pharmacy Act 1954, of a national from a Member State of the European Community other than the United Kingdom who:

(a) produces evidence to satisfy the Registrar:

    (i) as to his identity;

    (ii) that he is of good character;

    (iii) that he is in good health, both physically and mentally; and

    (iv) that he holds an appropriate European diploma as specified in Schedule 1A to the Pharmacy Act 1954; and

(b) pays to the Registrar a fee of £141*;

whereupon, subject to the Registrar being satisfied that all conditions have been complied with, he shall be registered.

6. The Council may by resolution authorise the registration as a pharmaceutical chemist under the Pharmacy Act 1954, of a person who:

(a) produces evidence to satisfy the Registrar

    (i) as to his identity;

    (ii) that he is of good character;

    (iii) that he is in good health, both physically and mentally;

    (iv) that he holds a pharmaceutical qualification or qualifications comparable with an approved degree in pharmacy awarded in the United Kingdom but granted by a University, or a body of comparable academic status, outside the United Kingdom; and

    (v) that he is registered or is qualified to be registered as a pharmacist in the country, state or province in which the university or body is situated, or is registered as a pharmacist in another country;

(b) satisfies an adjudicating committee appointed by the Council as to the content and standard of the course and examination in pharmacy taken by him, his knowledge of pharmacy in relation to current practice in Great Britain and of the English language if that is not his mother tongue;

(c) subsequently produces evidence to satisfy the adjudicating committee:

    (i) that he has completed a period of employment in Great Britain in the practice of pharmacy under conditions laid down by the adjudicating committee; and

    (ii) that he has satisfied the examiners in such part or parts of an examination or examinations approved by the Council for the purposes of this bye-law as may be required by the adjudicating committee and if the committee requires passing of the registration examination, he will be treated as if he was a preregistration trainee in accordance with paragraphs 27, 28 and 29 of Section XX;

(d) pays the Registrar the fee prescribed in paragraph 26 of Section XX of the bye-laws; and

(e) pays to the Registrar:

    (i) a fee of up to £210* in respect of the examination of the evidence produced under (a); and

    (ii) a fee of £379* in respect of the inquiry under (b); and

    (iii) a fee of £141* in respect of registration;

whereupon, subject to the Registrar being satisfied that all conditions have been complied with, he shall be registered.

* Or such other amounts as the Privy Council may approve

### Section XX: Registrar and Registrations

1. In the event of a vacancy occurring in the office of Registrar, the President or Vice-President shall appoint some person, pro tempore, to fulfil the duty of the office, and shall

report the same, and the cause thereof to the next meeting of the Council, and shall also cause the same if time shall permit to be reported in the notice summoning the said meeting. At the said meeting the Council shall take appropriate action with a view to filling the vacancy and at some subsequent meeting shall appoint a person to fill the vacancy.

1A. The subjects for the registration examination shall include: The Practice of Pharmacy including the implementation in practice of laws governing pharmacy and the application in practice of the Code of Ethics and Standards of Professional Practice of the Royal Pharmaceutical Society of Great Britain.

1B. The Council, under the terms of the Supplemental Charter of 1953, hereby delegates to the Education Committee appointed by the Society's Officers its duties and responsibilities set out in paragraphs 2, 4, 5, 6, 7, 12, 18, 18A, 19 and 22 of this section of the bye-laws but reserves to itself the consideration of withdrawal of approval of a pharmacy degree course, previously approved within the terms of Paragraph 2.

2. A person who holds a degree of a University of the United Kingdom or of the Council for National Academic Awards, granted in respect of pharmacy at the conclusion of a course of study undertaken in the United Kingdom and in accordance with European Community obligations and provisions, and approved by the Council, need not be examined in the latin language, botany, materia medica, pharmaceutical chemistry and general chemistry and need not be granted the certificate mentioned in section 3(5) of the Pharmacy Act 1954 and shall be eligible to be registered as a pharmaceutical chemist provided he produces evidence to satisfy the Registrar:

   (i) as to his identity;
  (ii) that he has attained the age of 21 years;
 (iii) that he has obtained the appropriate degree;
  (iv) in the case of a pharmacy trainee who commenced Preregistration training after June 30, 1992, or a pharmacy student in a pharmacy degree sandwich course approved by the Council who commenced his 27th week of preregistration training after that date, that he has passed a registration examination;
   (v) that he is of good character;
  (vi) that he is in good health, both physically and mentally;
 (vii) by a declaration upon an official form obtainable from the Registrar that he has satisfactorily undergone a period of preregistration training in accordance with this section;
(viii) that in the event of his having obtained the degree at a date when the degree was not recognised by the Council, he has complied with such other requirements as may be prescribed by the Council;
  (ix) that he has not failed an examination set by the Pharmaceutical Society of Northern Ireland for registration as a pharmacist in Northern Ireland.

3. A person making application for registration in accordance with bye-law 2 of this section shall pay to the Registrar a fee of £142*, whereupon, subject to the Registrar being satisfied that all conditions have been complied with, he shall be registered.

4. Preregistration training shall be gained in not more than two of the following pharmaceutical establishments in Great Britain approved by the Council for these purposes, subject to the provisions of bye-laws 13 to 20 of this section:

(a)    a community pharmacy, or up to three community pharmacies owned by a pharmacist, partnership, or corporate body provided no period of less than 10 consecutive weeks is spent in any one pharmacy;
(b)    the pharmaceutical department of a hospital or similar institution or more than one pharmaceutical department within a group of hospitals;
(c)    a pharmaceutical industrial establishment;
(d)    a school of pharmacy;
(e)    a registered pharmacy engaged solely in the supply of animal and agricultural products.

Unless the Council otherwise determines in any particular case, establishments referred to in (a) and (e) shall be required to have been a registered pharmacy for at least one year before the commencement of a period of preregistration training.

5. Except in the case of schools of pharmacy, applications from registered pharmaceutical chemists for the approval of pharmaceutical establishments for the purposes of preregistration training shall be made on forms provided by the Council and shall be considered by the Council, in accordance with aims, objectives and guidance agreed by resolution of the Council as to the training and the establishment in which it is to be undertaken and if necessary following inspection by a member of the Society appointed by the Council. Approval for these purposes shall normally be given for a period of five years. Approval will be given without further consideration by the Council to any school of pharmacy offering a course leading to a degree in pharmacy approved by the Council for the purposes of registration as a pharmaceutical chemist in Great Britain, and the conditions of preregistration training in a school of pharmacy shall be agreed by resolution of the Council.

6. In an application for the approval of a pharmaceutical establishment a registered pharmacist shall be named as the preregistration tutor who, except in circumstances approved by the Council, shall ensure that during any period of preregistration training, each preregistration trainee is under the supervision of a registered pharmacist. In an approved establishment at any time there must be no more preregistration trainees and pharmacy students working in the premises than pharmacists, except for periods totalling 13 weeks or less in any year corresponding with a trainee's full 52 weeks' preregistration training, or for periods totalling seven weeks or less in any period corresponding with a trainee's engagement in a lesser number of weeks' preregistration training, in partial fulfilment of the total training requirement.

7. The preregistration tutor shall have practised for at least three years as a registered pharmaceutical chemist in the aspect of pharmacy with which the establishment is concerned, shall undertake to provide the training required by the Council, and shall fulfil such other requirements as may be resolved by the Council from time to time.

8. In any period of training in one approved establishment, the preregistration tutor shall be engaged full time in the same premises as the trainee, except in those programmes of training within an approved establishment where preregistration trainees move from one premises to another to undertake the full range of training, in which case the preregistration tutor shall undertake to meet each trainee in the place of employment at least once a month.

9. In a school of pharmacy each preregistration trainee shall have a different preregistration tutor, who shall be a member of staff and a registered pharmacist. The head of the school may be one of the preregistration tutors if he is a registered pharmacist, and will be expected to co-ordinate the arrangements within the school.

10. If for any reason the preregistration tutor ceases to occupy the position mentioned in the pharmaceutical establishment concerned, the preregistration trainee concerned shall be permitted to complete the period of preregistration training under the supervision of the registered pharmacist who succeeds the preregistration tutor, without a further application for approval of the establishment. For the remainder of the five-year approval period, the establishment shall only be acceptable for preregistration training if a pharmacist who fulfils the necessary requirements for preregistration tutors undertakes in writing to the Society to provide the training described in the original application.

11. The Council, at its discretion, may decide that any pharmaceutical establishment is unacceptable for this purpose, either upon application or if, during a period of approval, the training gained therein or the facilities provided are found to be no longer satisfactory.

12. The Council may approve any establishment, other than those mentioned above, if satisfied that it is suitable for this purpose.

13. The total duration of preregistration training shall be full-time employment, for at least 52 weeks, including the normal holiday entitlement for the establishment concerned and public holidays. The Registrar shall be informed of any sick leave exceeding the

equivalent of one week's full-time employment and any allowance for sick leave or for other reasons will be at the discretion of the Registrar.

14. It will be acceptable for a 52-week period to be undertaken in either an approved community pharmacy or hospital pharmaceutical department.

15. Experience in two approved establishments shall be acceptable, provided each 52-week programme contains:

(i) at least one period of not less than 26 weeks in a community pharmaceutical department; and

(ii) no more than one period in either an industrial establishment, a school of pharmacy or a registered pharmacy engaged solely in the supply of animal and agricultural pharmaceutical products.

16. The periods of training in two establishments may vary in length, provided at least 26 weeks is undertaken in a community pharmacy or hospital pharmaceutical department.

17. When the two periods are of equal duration and are in community and hospital pharmacy practice, the 52-week programme shall be lodged with the Society in advance.

18. When only one of two periods is in community or hospital pharmacy practice the 52-week programme of training shall be approved by the Council in advance.

18A. With the prior approval of the Council, up to 13 weeks of the total period of preregistration training may be undertaken in a pharmacy establishment in another member state of the European Union, provided the placement overseas is continuous, takes place within or for the duration of the period between the 13th and 26th week of the total period and is an integral part of a complete programme which meets the Council's requirements and includes a single placement of at least six months' duration in a community or hospital pharmacy in Great Britain.

19. When two separate periods of acceptable training are undertaken, the second shall be completed within three years immediately following the end of the first, except in circumstances specifically approved by the Council.

20. Within a 52-week programme undertaken in one establishment it shall be permissible, with the mutual agreement of the preregistration tutor and the preregistration trainee, to include up to four weeks' training in another approved establishment, and up to a total of one weeks' experience, normally in another aspect of practice or for a specific training purpose, in a pharmaceutical establishment or establishments which need not be approved by the Council for this purpose.

21. For the purposes of these bye-laws, a person wishing to undertake preregistration training shall, prior to the commencement of each period:

(a) inform the Registrar on the prescribed form of the name and address of the establishment concerned, the name of the preregistration tutor and the date of commencement of the period;

(b) pay a fee of £77* to the Society for a 52-week period, or, where applicable, a proportion of that amount for any shorter or additional period.

22. The preregistration tutor and the preregistration trainee concerned shall complete the assessment procedure approved by the Council and the trainee shall attend appropriate study days when necessary to complete the required training.

23. Preregistration training shall not be acceptable in an establishment in which the preregistration trainee has a controlling interest.

24. The Registrar shall have discretion to accept, as an exceptional circumstance, a period of preregistration training which does not comply with the bye-laws or with the guidance approved by the Council, but which fulfils the aims and objectives of the Council to his satisfaction.

25. Periods of preregistration training shall commence normally between July 1st and August 15th. The commencement date of preregistration training may be between the last day of the final term of the pharmacy degree course and the date that the Registrar is

informed by the appropriate authority that the graduate has successfully completed the examinations of an approved pharmacy degree. In these circumstances, training will only be acceptable from that date if the Registrar is subsequently informed by the appropriate authority that the applicant has successfully completed the degree examinations held during that term.

26. Subject to a satisfactory appraisal report by the preregistration tutor after at least 39 weeks of preregistration training have been undertaken, and in the case of a pharmacy degree sandwich course student after the final degree examinations have been taken, a preregistration trainee shall be eligible, after payment of an examination fee of £75\* to the Registrar not later than six weeks before the examination, or after payment of a late-entry fee of £151\* to the Registrar not later than four weeks before the examination, and after completion of at least 45 weeks of preregistration training, to sit the registration examination within eighteen months of such completion.

27. After payment of a fee of £47\* a preregistration trainee who:

(a)    fails to pass the registration examination at the first attempt may take the examination again within the following 18 months;

(b)    fails to pass the examination at the second attempt shall be required to complete a period of six months' employment acceptable to the Registrar in a community or hospital pharmacy notified in advance to the Registrar, and may take the examination for a third time within 12 months of satisfactory completion of such period of employment.

28. A preregistration trainee who:

(a)    does not sit the registration examination within 18 months of satisfactory completion of preregistration training; or

(b)    fails to pass the registration examination at the first attempt and does not resit the examination within 18 months; or

(c)    fails to pass the registration examination at the second attempt and does not resit the examination within 12 months of completing his period of employment as required under paragraph 27(b) shall be required to fulfil such requirements as are specified by the Registrar before being eligible for registration as a pharmaceutical chemist.

29. A person who fails the registration examination at the third attempt will not normally be eligible for registration as a pharmaceutical chemist. In circumstances considered by the Council to be exceptional, the Council may specify conditions under which it is prepared to permit a preregistration trainee to sit the examination on one further occasion.

30. On completion of the period of preregistration training the applicant shall submit to the Registrar:

(1)    a declaration:

(a)    that a period or periods of preregistration training of 52 weeks total duration have been completed at the establishment or establishments named in the declaration, stating the dates of commencement and the completion of each period;

(b)    that in the opinion of the preregistration tutor for the full period or second period as the case may be, the applicant is able to apply in practice the knowledge of the law relating to the practice of pharmacy gained during the degree course and is a fit and proper person to be registered as a pharmaceutical chemist;

(2)    a report, in a prescribed form, on each period of preregistration training.

The declaration and the report shall be signed by the preregistration tutor for each approved establishment.

31. A person who satisfies the Registrar that his original certificate of registration has been lost or destroyed shall be issued with a replacement certificate on payment of a fee to be determined by the Council.

\* Or such other amounts as the Privy Council may approve.

## Section XXI: The Register of Pharmaceutical Chemists

1. Each entry in the Register of Pharmaceutical Chemists shall include the full name of the person concerned, his address, a distinguishing registration number, the date of registration, and particulars of such person's qualification for registration.

2. The entries in the said Register shall be arranged in alphabetical order according to the surnames.

3. Each Annual Register of Pharmaceutical Chemists shall contain the particulars and be in the form set forth in the third Schedule to these bye-laws.

4. The entries in each annual Register of Pharmaceutical Chemists shall be arranged in alphabetical order according to the surnames.

## Section XXII: Certificates of Registration

1. The period referred to in paragraph 9 of the second Schedule to the Pharmacy Act 1954 (being the period during which a certificate of registration as a chemist and druggist is deemed to be a certificate of registration as a pharmaceutical chemist), shall be a period of five years commencing the 1st day of January, 1954.

## Section XXIII: Scottish Department

1. The Scottish Department of the Society shall consist of those members of the Society whose addresses in the Register are in Scotland and shall be governed by a body to be called *the Executive of the Scottish Department* and hereinafter called *the Executive* acting under the authority of the Council.

2. The Executive shall consist of the President, the Vice-President and such other members of Council as may be resident in Scotland, *ex officio*, and, in addition, 18 members of the Society elected from and by members whose addresses in the Register are in Scotland.

3. Six of the elected members shall go out of office in each year, and the vacancies shall be filled by election, the retiring members being eligible for re-election. The six elected members who go out of office shall be the elected members who have been longest in office without re-election.

4. The elections shall be conducted upon such dates and in such manner as may be determined by the Executive. Casual vacancies occurring in the elected members shall be filled in such manner and subject to such conditions as the Executive may determine.

5. The Executive shall elect from among their number a Chairman and a Vice-Chairman to hold office for such period as may be determined by the Executive.

6. There shall be a Secretary of the Scottish Department of the Society resident in Scotland whose duties shall be determined by the Council and who shall be appointed by the Council after considering any recommendation of the Executive.

7. The functions of the Executive will include the implementation in Scotland of the policies of the Society, the management of the Society's House in Edinburgh, the arrangement of meetings in Scotland for the advancement of the objects of the Society, the organisation and supervision of the local Branches of the Society in Scotland, and the making of recommendations to the Council upon any matters affecting the Society and their members.

8. The Executive may appoint from their members such committees or subcommittees as may be necessary to assist them in carrying out their functions. Persons not being members of the Executive may be coopted in an advisory capacity to any such committee or subcommittee.

9. The Secretary shall submit to the Secretary of the Society a report of each of the meetings of the Executive and such reports upon the Scottish Department of the Society as he may be requested by the Council to submit.

10. Members of the Executive shall be entitled to receive such fee and reimbursement of expenditure incurred on travel, accommodation and subsistence as they may by resolution from time to time determine, but not exceeding the fee and sums for reimbursement of expenses incurred payable to members of Council, for attendance at meetings of the Scottish Department Executive or any meeting of a committee of the Executive or subcommittees of such a committee.

### Section XXIV: Welsh Executive

1. The Welsh Executive, acting under the authority of the Council, shall consist of the President, the Vice-President and such other members of Council as may be resident in Wales, *ex officio*, and, in addition, 12 members of the Society elected from and by members whose addresses in the Register are in Wales.

2. Four of the elected members shall go out of office in each year, and the vacancies shall be filled by election, the retiring members being eligible for re-election. The four elected members who go out of office shall be the elected members who have been longest in office without re-election.

3. The elections shall be conducted upon such dates and in such manner as may be determined by the Executive. Casual vacancies occurring in the elected members shall be filled in such manner and subject to such conditions as the Executive may determine. The member so appointed shall hold office for such period as the person whom he has replaced would have held office.

4. The Executive shall elect from among their number a Chairman and a Vice-Chairman to hold office for one year and be eligible for re-election.

5. There shall be a Secretary of the Welsh Executive resident in Wales and based in the Society's headquarters in Cardiff whose duties shall be determined by the Council and who shall be appointed by the Council after considering any recommendation of the Executive.

6. The full title in English of the Welsh Executive shall be: 'Royal Pharmaceutical Society of Great Britain – Welsh Executive' and the full title in Welsh shall be: *Cymdeithas Fferyllol Frenhinol Prydain Fawr – Gweithgor Cymru.*

7. The Executive shall be responsible under the authority of the Council for the implementation in Wales of the policies of the Society, the organisation and supervision of the local Branches of the Society in Wales, and the making of recommendations to the Council upon matters affecting the Society and its members.

8. The Executive may appoint from their members such committees or subcommittees as may be necessary to assist them in carrying out their functions. Persons not being members of the Executive may be coopted in an advisory capacity to any such committees or subcommittees.

9. The Secretary shall submit to the Secretary of the Society a report of each of the meetings of the Executive and such other reports upon the Welsh Executive as may be requested by the Council.

10. Members of the Executive shall be entitled to receive such fee and reimbursement of expenditure incurred on travel, accommodation and subsistence as they may by resolution from time to time determine, but not exceeding the fee and sums for reimbursement of expenses incurred payable to members of Council, for attendance at meetings of the Welsh Executive or any meeting of a committee of the Executive or subcommittees of such a committee.

### Section XXV: Journal and Transactions

1. The Pharmaceutical Journal shall be edited, printed and published in such manner as the Council shall from time to time direct.

2. The transactions of the Society required to be published shall be inserted in the said Journal, and all notices shall be considered duly given if inserted therein.

### Section XXVI: Museum

1. The Society shall maintain a museum for the benefit of members and students of the Society, and members of the public interested in the profession of pharmacy.

2. The museum will reflect the principles and practice of British pharmacy and the history of the Society.

3. The Council shall establish a constitution for the maintenance and management of the museum collection.

### Section XXVII: Regulations

1. The Council shall have power to make regulations for any of the following purposes:

(1)     For prescribing the qualifications of and fees to be paid by persons seeking to be registered as students.

(2)     For prescribing the times, places, forms, fees and dates of entry for, and methods of conducting, the examinations to be held in accordance with the Pharmacy Acts.

(3)     For prescribing the subjects and the standard of knowledge thereof to be required of candidates presenting themselves for examination.

(4)     For prescribing the scope and length of training to be undergone by candidates presenting themselves for examination and the evidence thereof to be submitted by the candidate.

(5)     For prescribing the character and length of curricula to be taken by candidates, the institutions at which such curricula may be taken, and the evidence thereof to be submitted by the candidate.

2. All such regulations and all altered or new regulations shall, before becoming operative, receive the approval of the Privy Council and copies shall immediately thereafter be obtainable by members and students free of charge upon application to the Registrar. The approval of the Privy Council to regulations shall be notified in The Pharmaceutical Journal immediately after its being received.

### Section XXVIII: Bye-laws

1. Any proposal to make, alter or revoke a bye-law shall be in writing and, being delivered at a Council meeting by a member of Council to the Chairman, or brought up on the report of a committee, shall thereupon be read, and, if seconded and approved, notice of the approval by the Council of the said proposal and of the intention of the Council to make, alter or revoke the said bye-law, as the case may be, at the expiry of not less than 60 days from the date of the said notice, shall be given to the members in The Pharmaceutical Journal.

2. Any member applying to the Secretary for a copy of any proposal to make, alter or revoke a bye-law shall be entitled to receive a copy free of charge.

3. At the meeting of the Council held next after the expiry of 60 days from the date of The Pharmaceutical Journal in which notice of a proposal to make, alter or revoke a bye-law

was given, the Secretary shall report any observations received by him upon the said proposal. If the Council shall thereupon confirm the said proposal and make, alter or revoke the said bye-law, as the case may be, but not otherwise, the Secretary shall forthwith submit the bye-law so made, altered or revoked, as the case may be, to the Privy Council for confirmation and approval.

4. If no observations are received by the Secretary upon the said proposal he shall notify the Council in writing, and shall forthwith submit the bye-law as prepared to the Privy Council for confirmation and approval and report this at the next meeting of the Council.

5. Notice of the confirmation and approval by the Privy Council of the making, alteration or revocation of any bye-law shall be given in The Pharmaceutical Journal.

6. Every person upon becoming a member and every person upon becoming a student shall be entitled to receive a copy of the bye-laws free of charge.

## First Schedule

## Form of voting paper

THE ROYAL PHARMACEUTICAL SOCIETY OF GREAT BRITAIN
VOTING PAPER
*For the election of seven members of Council*
OR
*For the election of five Auditors*

| Order of Preference | Candidates |
| --- | --- |
|  |  |
|  |  |
|  |  |
|  |  |
|  |  |
|  |  |

INSTRUCTIONS FOR VOTING

(1)    You have a single transferable vote.

(2)    Vote by placing the figure 1 (and no other mark or figure) against the name of the candidate who is your first choice; placing the figure 2 against the candidate of your second choice; and so on until you are indifferent as to the candidates whom you have not marked.

(3)    A later preference is considered only if an earlier preference has a surplus above the quota required for election, or if an earlier preference is excluded because of insufficient support. Under no circumstances can a later preference count against an earlier preference.

(4)    Enclose your completed voting paper in the addressed envelope provided, seal the envelope, sign it on the back and transmit it through the post or otherwise to the address shown so as to be received there not later than 12 o'clock noon on the second day after the annual general meeting, excluding for this purpose Saturday, Sunday and Bank Holidays.

**Second Schedule**

### Model Rules for Branches

1. The name of the Branch shall be*..................... Branch of the Royal Pharmaceutical Society of Great Britain.

2. The objects of the Branch shall be to further the interests of the Society and its members more particularly by:

(1)    serving as a medium of contact between the Council of the Society and members in the Branch area;

(2)    cooperating with the Council generally in the work of the Society;

(3)    promoting a corporate spirit amongst members and securing the observance of such standards of professional conduct as will uphold the dignity of the Society;

(4)    providing opportunity for members to raise and discuss matters of common interest and to express their collective opinion thereon;

(5)    arranging lectures and courses of instruction for members and students upon scientific and other subjects appertaining to pharmacy;

(6)    organising social functions and encouraging social intercourse between members;

(7)    promoting friendly relations and cooperation between members of the Society and members of the medical and allied professions;

(8)    urging upon members the claims of the Benevolent Fund to their support.

3. Membership of the Branch shall be limited to members of the Society and, except as hereinafter provided, all such persons residing in the Branch area shall be members of the Branch. A member of the Branch may, subject to the approval of the Council of the Society, transfer his membership to another Branch and a member of another Branch may, subject to the approval of the Council of the Society, transfer his membership to the Branch.

4. The Branch area shall be such as the Council of the Society may from time to time decide after consultation with the Branches concerned.

5. The Officers of the Branch shall be: a Chairman, a Vice-Chairman, a Secretary, a Treasurer and such others as may be decided in general meeting.

6. The affairs of the Branch shall be under the control and management of a Committee consisting of the Chairman, the Vice-Chairman, the Secretary, the Treasurer, and any other officers and not more than†..................... other members. The Committee may appoint from their number subcommittees for educational, Benevolent Fund, social and other purposes, and delegate to them the powers of the committee in such respects.

7. General meetings of the Branch shall be held annually in‡..................... at such other times as the Committee may think fit, and at any time on the written requisition to the Secretary of not fewer than†............ members.

8. The business of the annual general meeting shall include the presentation by the Committee of a report of the work of the Branch, and an audited statement of accounts for the past year, and the election of committee and†............ auditors. The Committee shall forward to the Secretary of the Society a copy of the audited statement of accounts as soon as possible after the meeting.

9. The Officers of the Branch shall be elected§ ..................... The representatives of the Branch to attend the British Pharmaceutical Conference or any Branch Representatives' Meeting shall be elected at a general meeting of the Branch.

10. The Officers and Committee shall retire at the annual general meeting, but shall be eligible for re-election. Any vacancy occurring during the year may be filled by the Committee.

11. The Committee shall, on request, furnish the Council of the Society with such information about the activities and finances of the Branch as the Council may require.

* Insert the name of the branch.
† Insert the desired number.
‡ Insert the name of a month not later in the year than May.
§ Insert here either '. . . . . . by the Annual General Meeting' or '. . . . . . by the committee at a meeting to be held as soon as convenient after the Annual General Meeting'.

## Third Schedule

### The Annual Register of Pharmaceutical Chemists

| Date of Registration | Number | Name | Address |
|---|---|---|---|
| F | | | |

F in left margin indicates Fellow of the Royal Pharmaceutical Society

## Fourth Schedule

### Form of Declaration Under Bye-law Section II, Clause 2 (ii)

In pursuance of Clause 2 of Section II of the Society's bye-laws I declare that during the year 20.... I shall not be gainfully employed in any occupation for more than 13 weeks or the equivalent thereof. And I further declare that if subsequent to making this declaration I am gainfully employed in the relevant year for more than 13 weeks I will remit forthwith to the Registrar without demand the balance of fee. I further confirm that during 20.... (i.e. the previous year) I was not gainfully employed in any occupation for more than 13 weeks or the equivalent thereof. (The last sentence should be deleted if not applicable.)

### Form of Declaration Under Bye-law Section II, Clause 2 (iii)

In pursuance of Clause 2 of Section II of the Society's bye-laws I declare that I have attained my 65th birthday and shall not during the year 19.... be gainfully employed in any occupation. And I further declare that if subsequent to making this declaration I am gainfully employed in the relevant year for 13 weeks or less I will remit forthwith to the Registrar without demand the balance of fee as required by Clause 2 (iii)(a). I further declare that if subsequent to making this declaration I am gainfully employed in the relevant year for more than 13 weeks I will remit forthwith to the Registrar without demand the balance of fee as required by Clause 2 (iii)(b). I further confirm that during 20.... (i.e. the previous year) I was not gainfully employed in any occupation/I was not gainfully employed in any occupation for more than 13 weeks or the equivalent thereof. (The appropriate part of the last sentence should be deleted if not applicable.)

## Branch Representatives' Meetings: Rules of Procedure

1. Except as the Council may otherwise decide from time to time, the meeting of Branch Representatives held annually in May shall be for the purpose of discussing and voting upon motions submitted by Branches and by the Council of the Society.

2. A motion with an explanatory paragraph to be submitted by a Branch must have been approved by a general meeting of the Branch and must reach the Secretary of the Society not later than the third Friday in January for the meeting to be held that year.

3. Between the third Friday in January and the meeting of the Council in March, there will be a meeting to which each Branch which has submitted a motion will be asked to send a representative to discuss and, if necessary, clarify, modify or withdraw the motions received.

4. At their meeting in March, the Council will review the list of motions received and may instruct the Secretary to delete from the list any motions that are in their opinion trivial, irrelevant or obscure. A copy of the list, with the addition of any motions to be submitted by the Council, will then be sent to each Branch.

5. If motions covering similar ground are submitted, the Council may at their discretion group or, in consultation with the Branches concerned, amalgamate the motions.

6. Branches may submit motions up to the time of the meeting on urgent matters of importance that have arisen since the third Friday in January. The Chairman will decide whether any motion is of such a character as to be eligible for submission under this rule.

7. Except with the prior consent of the Council, or with the permission of the Chairman of the meeting, motions may only be submitted in accordance with the above procedure.

8. The order in which motions are to be taken shall be decided by the Council in the light of the recommendations made at the meeting mentioned in Rule 3.

9. The President or, in his absence, the Vice-President, or in his absence some person elected by the meeting, shall be the Chairman of the meeting.

10. Subject to these rules, the procedure of the meeting shall be governed by the ordinary rules of debate, movers being allowed five minutes, seconders three minutes, other speakers three minutes. The mover shall be allowed three minutes to reply to the discussion.

11. After a motion from a Branch has been moved and seconded the Chairman, or other speaker nominated by the Council, may, at some stage in the discussion, state any views of the Council or give any information in the Council's possession which the Council may consider will assist the meeting in discussing the motion. The meeting will at an appropriate time be asked whether any Branch wishes to submit an amendment.

12. In the event of there being no representatives present from a Branch in the name of which a motion stands on the Agenda it shall be permissible for any representatives to move and second such proposition.

13. When the vote on a motion has been taken, any Branch representative may inform the Chairman that the Branch concerned wishes its abstention from that vote to be recorded.

14. A vote will be taken at the end of the Branch Representatives' Meeting on any motions which, due to the lack of time, cannot be debated and they shall stand referred to the Council.

15. A motion that has been defeated at a representatives' meeting or a motion to the same effect that has been defeated shall not be included in the Agenda of a representatives' meeting, without the consent of the Council, until after the next two representatives' meetings have been held.

16. A Branch may not submit more than two motions annually.

## Regional Organisation: Model Rules

At the inception of the regional organisation of the Branches of the Society the Council suggested the following model rules for the regions:

1. The name of the region shall be decided by the regional committee subject to the approval of the Council.

2. The object of the region will be to carry out those activities of the Society, which, in the opinion of Council, can be planned or coordinated at regional level. Before undertaking any activity in addition to those suggested by the Council, the regional committee must consult headquarters.

3. Membership of each region will be limited to members of those Branches, which, as determined by the Council, are within the region.

4. The Officers of the region shall be a Chairman, a Vice-Chairman, a Secretary, a Treasurer and such others as may be decided by the regional committee.

5. The affairs of the region shall be conducted by the regional committee which will be constituted as follows:

(a)    A representative from each constituent Branch who is a member of the Branch Committee, or a nominated deputy.

(b)    The Head of the School of Pharmacy plus the Regional Course Organiser.

(c)    Any member of Council who is also a member of the region; or, should there be no member of Council fulfilling this requirement, one member of Council by invitation and preferably residing near to the region.

(d)    One British Pharmaceutical Students' Association representative from the School of Pharmacy.

(e)    The Regional Pharmaceutical Officer.

(f)    The pharmacist Regional Representative of the PSNC and NPA.

(g)    A representative of any major section of the profession not already represented on the committee through other appointments.

The regional secretary shall not be a member of the regional committee.

6. The Officers shall be elected annually by the regional committee and, excluding the regional secretary, shall only be eligible to serve for a maximum of two years in any one office. The regional secretary will be eligible for reappointment each year.

7. The regional committee will normally meet three times each year or at such other times as the Officers think fit.

8. The regional committee may appoint subcommittees or working parties to deal with any matter which, in the opinion of the regional committee, requires specific attention over a long or short period, respectively. Such subcommittees or working parties may include coopted members.

9. The regional secretary shall submit to the Society, before a date specified by Council and prior to the annual meeting of regional secretaries, a report of the region's activities during the preceding financial year.

10. The regional treasurer shall submit to the Society, before a date specified by Council and prior to the annual meeting of regional secretaries, a statement of account for the preceding financial year.

11. The financial and administrative year for the region shall be April 1 to March 31.

# Statutory Committee Regulations

## The Regulations – The Pharmaceutical Society (Statutory Committee) Order of Council 1978 (SI 1978 No.20) Came into Effect on 1 February 1978

**Part I: General**

1. (a) In these Regulations:

*the Act of 1954* and *the Act of 1968* mean respectively the Pharmacy Act 1954, and the Medicines Act 1968;

*the Committee*, *the Chairman* and *the Secretary* mean respectively the Statutory Committee appointed under section 7 of the Act of 1954 and the Chairman and the Secretary of that Committee;

*the register* unless the context otherwise requires and *the Registrar* have respectively the same meanings as in the Act of 1954;

*registered pharmaceutical chemist* has the same meaning as in the Act of 1954;

*representative* has the same meaning as in section 72(4) of the Act of 1968;

*the person affected* means the registered pharmaceutical chemist, body corporate, representative or other person affected by any information received by the Committee; and

*retail pharmacy business* has the same meaning as in the Act of 1968; and

*the relevant Acts* has the same meaning as in section 80 of the Act of 1968.

(b) The Interpretation Act 1889, applies to the interpretation of these Regulations as it applies to the interpretation of an Act of Parliament.

2. These Regulations shall come into operation on the 1st day of February 1978, and the Regulations approved by the Royal Pharmaceutical Society (Statutory Committee) Order of Council 1957 are hereby revoked save in relation to the procedure to be followed by the Statutory Committee in the exercise of the jurisdiction conferred on them by the Pharmacy and Poisons Act 1933:

Provided that:

(a) such revocation shall not affect anything duly done or suffered under those Regulations; and

(b) any notice, direction, inquiry, application, proceeding or thing given, made, instituted or done under the Regulations confirmed on the 4th day of May 1957, shall, if in force immediately before these Regulations come into operation, continue in force and be deemed to be given, made, instituted or done under the corresponding provisions of these Regulations on the actual dates when the same were respectively given, made, instituted or done;

(c) without prejudice to the generality of the foregoing, such revocation shall not affect any inquiry or proceeding which has been stayed, postponed or adjourned or where decision has been postponed and such inquiry and proceeding shall be resumed and the decision therein given under the provisions of these Regulations.

## Part II: Cases Arising out of Convictions or Misconduct

3. When the Secretary receives information from which it appears that:

(a) a registered pharmaceutical chemist, or a person employed by him in the carrying on of his business, has been convicted of a criminal offence, or been guilty of misconduct; or

(b) a body corporate carrying on a retail pharmacy business has been convicted of an offence under the relevant Acts; or

(c) a member of the board or any officer of or person employed by a body corporate carrying on a retail pharmacy business has been convicted of an offence, or been guilty of misconduct; or

(d) a representative or person employed by a representative in the retail pharmacy business in respect of which he is the representative has been convicted of a criminal offence, or been guilty of misconduct; or

(e) a person applying to be registered as a pharmaceutical chemist has been convicted of a criminal offence, or been guilty of misconduct; or

(f) a person whose name has been removed from the register under section 12(1) of the Act of 1954 or a person employed by him in the carrying on of his business, has been convicted of a criminal offence, or been guilty of misconduct; the Secretary shall submit the information, or a summary thereof, to the Chairman.

4. Where the information in question is in the nature of a complaint charging misconduct, the Chairman may require that any allegation of fact contained therein shall be substantiated by a written statement signed by a responsible person, or, if he thinks fit, by a statutory declaration and any such statement or statutory declaration shall specify as

respects any fact not within the personal knowledge of the declarant, the source of his information and the grounds for his belief in its truth.

5. The Chairman may in any case direct the Secretary to invite the person affected to submit in writing any answer or explanation which he may wish to offer.

6. When he has considered the information, the evidence available in support thereof and any answer or explanation submitted by the person affected, the Chairman shall deal with the matter as follows:

    (i) if he is of the opinion that:

        (a)    the case is not within the jurisdiction of the Committee; or

        (b)    the complaint is of a frivolous character; or

        (c)    owing to the lapse of time or other circumstances the complaint may properly be disregarded;

    he shall decide that the case shall not proceed further;

    (ii) if he is of opinion that the conviction or misconduct alleged is not of a serious nature or is for any other reason of such a character that the matter can be disposed of without an inquiry, he may, after consultation orally or by letter with the other members of the Committee, decide that the case shall not proceed further but may direct the Secretary to send a reprimand to the person affected and caution him as to his future conduct;

    (iii) in any other case he shall direct the Secretary to take the necessary steps for the holding of an inquiry by the Committee:

Provided that, if it appears to the Chairman in a case arising under paragraph (b) or paragraph (c) of Regulation 3 that the person affected has no present intention of continuing or commencing to carry on a retail pharmacy business, or in a case arising under paragraph (f) of that Regulation that the person affected has no present intention of practising pharmacy, or seeking employment in a pharmaceutical capacity, he may postpone dealing with the matter until evidence of such an intention is submitted to him.

7. The Chairman shall report to the Committee any case in which he has not directed an inquiry to be held.

8. Where the Chairman has directed an inquiry to be held, the Secretary shall give such notices and take such other steps as are required by Part III of these Regulations, and shall instruct a solicitor to investigate the facts of the case and to present (or brief counsel) to present the case to the Committee at the inquiry:

Provided that, where a complainant undertakes to present his case to the Committee, it shall not be necessary for the Secretary to instruct a solicitor.

9. If the solicitor instructed as aforesaid reports that, as a result of his investigations, he is of the opinion that the evidence available is insufficient to prove the conviction or misconduct alleged the Committee shall consider his report and decide whether an inquiry shall be held, and give such directions as they think fit. In the interval all proceedings shall be stayed and the Secretary shall give any necessary notices to persons concerned, including the complainant.

10. If at any time after an inquiry has been directed and before it has been held information is received by the Secretary or by the solicitor instructed as aforementioned which might have justified the Chairman in not directing an inquiry in the first instance any such information shall be referred to him and he may direct that the inquiry shall not proceed further, and in that case, shall report such direction to the Committee.

## Part III: Inquiries

11. (a) Where directions have been given for an inquiry to be held, the Secretary shall, not less than twenty-eight days before the day appointed for holding the inquiry, send to the

person affected a notice specifying generally the matters into which the inquiry will be held, and stating the day, hour and place appointed for holding the inquiry:

Provided that where the person affected and the complainant (if any) so agree the period of notice required by this Regulation may be reduced to such period as may be agreed.

(b) The notice shall be in the form set out in the Schedule to these Regulations, (not reproduced) with such variations as circumstances may require, or in a form to the like effect, and shall be accompanied by a copy of these Regulations.

Where a complainant has undertaken to present his case to the Committee, the Secretary shall send to him copies of the notice and of these Regulations.

12. A notice required by the last preceding Regulation to be sent to any person shall be sent by registered letter or recorded delivery letter addressed to him, in the case of a registered pharmaceutical chemist at his address in the register, in the case of a body corporate at its registered office, or where the body corporate is a firm or partnership in Scotland, its usual place of business, in the case of a representative at his address last notified to the Registrar and in the case of any other person at his last known place of abode.

13. A notice sent to any person in accordance with Regulations 11 and 12 may be amended with the consent of the Committee or of the Chairman and written notice of the amendment shall be sent to such person in the manner provided by Regulation 12 or otherwise brought to his notice by the Secretary before the inquiry is held or in the course of the inquiry:

Provided that the person affected shall have the right to demand an adjournment of the inquiry if reasonable notice of any amendment materially affecting the particulars of the misconduct alleged in the notice of inquiry has not been given before the inquiry commenced.

14. The person affected shall, after giving reasonable notice to the Secretary, be entitled free of charge to inspect, and to be supplied with a copy of, any information or summary sent to the Chairman in pursuance of Regulation 3 or any written statement or statutory declaration sent to the Committee in pursuance of Regulation 4 and the notice of inquiry shall direct his attention to this Regulation. A complainant who has undertaken to present his case to the Committee shall, after giving reasonable notice to the Secretary, be entitled free of charge to inspect, and to be supplied with a copy of, any answer or explanation submitted in pursuance of Regulation 5 by the person affected.

15. The Chairman may at any time postpone the opening of the inquiry and direct the Secretary to give any necessary notices to persons concerned, including the complainant.

16. The inquiry shall be held in public except that the Committee may at any time direct that the public shall be excluded from an inquiry or any part thereof if it appears to the Committee that in the interests of justice or for some other compelling reason the public should be so excluded.

17. The person affected and a complainant presenting his case to the Committee may be represented by a solicitor, or counsel; alternatively, a body corporate may be represented by a director or officer thereof.

18. At the opening of the inquiry the Secretary shall read the notice of inquiry and, if the person affected be not present or represented, satisfy the Committee that the notice was duly sent to him. The person affected or the person representing him in accordance with Regulation 17 may waive the right for the notice of inquiry to be read.

19. If a complainant who has undertaken to present his case to the Committee does not appear, or fails in the opinion of the Committee to present his case properly, the Committee may nevertheless proceed with the inquiry or may adjourn the inquiry, in which case they may instruct a solicitor in accordance with Regulation 8, and Regulations 9 and 10 shall apply during the adjournment.

If the person affected does not appear and the Committee are satisfied that notice of the inquiry was duly sent to him, they may proceed with the inquiry in his absence, or may adjourn the inquiry.

20. Subject to the foregoing provisions with respect to non-appearance, the order of proceedings shall be as follows:

(a)    statement of the case against the person affected and production of evidence in support of it;

(b)    statement of the case of the person affected and production of evidence in support of it;

(c)    reply to the case of the person affected: provided that, except by leave of the Committee, a reply shall not be allowed where the person affected has produced no evidence other than his own.

21. Evidence may be received by the Committee by oral statement, written and signed statement, or statutory declaration. A witness shall first be examined by the person producing him, then cross-examined and then re-examined. The Committee shall disregard oral evidence given by any person who refuses to submit to cross-examination may, in their discretion, decline to admit the written statement or declaration of a person who is not present, and shall disregard it if, being present, he refuses to submit to cross-examination.

22. Members of the Committee may put through the Chairman, or on his invitation, such questions as they think desirable.

23. The Committee may at any stage of the proceedings adjourn the inquiry to a subsequent meeting of the Committee and, where the day, hour and place for such meetings are not appointed at the time of the adjournment, the Secretary shall, not less than twenty-one days before the day appointed, and in the manner specified in Regulation 12 give notice to the person affected and to the complainant, if any, of the day, hour and place appointed:

Provided that, where the person affected and the complainant (if any) so agree the notice may be waived or modified.

24. When the inquiry is resumed, no fresh evidence shall, except by leave of the Committee, be produced unless either:

(a)    the substance thereof has, not less than ten days before the resumed hearing, been communicated to the Secretary and to the person against whom it is to be produced; or

(b)    it is in the nature of a reply to any such evidence.

25. On the conclusion of the hearing the Committee shall deliberate in private and shall decide:

(a)    whether the conviction or misconduct alleged is proved;

(b)    if so, except in a case falling only under paragraph (b) of Regulation 3, whether such conviction or misconduct is such as to render the person with regard to whom it is proved, or is such as would if he were a registered pharmaceutical chemist render him, unfit to be on the register;

(c)    if so, whether one of the directions specified in section 8(1) of the Act of 1954, section 80(1) of the Act of 1968 or section 80(2) of the Act of 1968 or section 80(4) of the Act of 1968 should be made; and

(d)    whether any reprimand or admonition should be addressed to the person affected: Provided that the Committee may postpone their decision or any part of it, either generally or on such terms as they may approve.

26. The Chairman shall announce in public the decision of the Committee and if the decision or any part of it is postponed the Chairman shall announce such postponement and shall state the terms, if any, on which it is made.

27. If the Committee postpone their decision under paragraph (c) or (d) of Regulation 25 they may when the case is resumed take into account before reaching a decision thereon any information then or previously given to them concerning the conduct of the person affected

since the original hearing, provided that they shall not take into account any adverse report without giving the person affected a reasonable opportunity of answering it.

28. The Secretary shall communicate to the person affected and to the complainant, if any, the decision of the Committee and to the Registrar any direction to be acted upon by him.

29. Where under any of the foregoing provisions of these Regulations an inquiry is adjourned from one meeting to another, or a decision or any part of it is postponed to a future meeting, the validity of the proceedings at the later meeting shall not be called into question by reason only that members of the Committee who were present at the earlier meeting were not present at a later meeting, or that members of the Committee who were present at the later meeting were not present at the earlier meeting.

## Part IV: Applications for Relief from Consequences of Previous Decisions

30. An application to the Committee:

(a)    under section 8(2) of the Act of 1954 for the restoration of the name of the applicant to the register; or
(b)    under section 8(1) of the Act of 1954 for variation of a direction given by the Committee under that subsection; or
(c)    under section 83(1) of the Act of 1968 for the revocation of a direction given by the Committee under section 80 of the Act of 1968, shall be made in writing to the Secretary stating the grounds on which it is made and must be signed by the applicant, or, in the case of a body corporate, by a member of the board thereof.

31. No application for restoration of a name to the register shall be entertained by the Committee unless supported by a statutory declaration made by the applicant and accompanied by at least two certificates of the applicant's identity and good character. One of such certificates must be given by a registered pharmaceutical chemist and another must be given by a registered pharmaceutical chemist, a fully registered medical practitioner for the purpose of the Medical Acts 1956 to 1969, a justice of the peace or a legally qualified holder of a judicial office. The statutory declaration must identify the applicant with his application, the statements made therein and with the required certificates.

32. In a case where the name of an applicant for restoration was removed from the register under section 8(1) of the Act of 1954 on a complaint made by a person who himself appeared to present the facts of his complaint to the Committee, the Secretary shall, if he knows that person's address, give notice of the application to him and inform him that he may submit in writing to the Committee any objection to restoration. The Secretary shall communicate the substance of any such objection to the applicant and the applicant may reply thereto in writing.

33. In considering an application under this part of these Regulations the Committee may take into account any information in their possession concerning the conduct of the applicant during the period which has elapsed since the original direction was given. The Chairman may direct that the substance of any adverse report be sent to the applicant who shall be given an opportunity of submitting a reply thereto in writing. In these circumstances consideration of the application shall not take place until after such reply is received or a reasonable time for submitting a reply has, in the opinion of the Committee, elapsed. No adverse report shall be taken into account unless these steps have been taken.

34. Unless the Chairman directs that the application shall be considered in public, the Committee shall consider the application in private.

35. (a) Unless the Committee decide to grant the application without a hearing, the Committee shall afford to the applicant if he wishes an opportunity of appearing before them in person or by a solicitor or counsel and of adducing evidence.

(b) The Committee shall inform the applicant of his rights under the preceding paragraph of this Regulation but shall be entitled to proceed with the application if the applicant declines to appear or to adduce evidence before them or if the applicant fails to appear or adduce evidence on an occasion fixed for such purpose of which notice in writing shall have been sent by post to the applicant at the address to which a notice under Regulation 12 would have been sent to him.

(c) If the original direction was given following a complaint, the Committee may afford the complainant an opportunity of being heard or of submitting evidence as to any matter which appears to the Committee to be material.

36. Subject to the provisions of Regulation 35, the procedure of the Committee in connection with the application shall be such as they may determine.

37. The Committee may if they think fit adjourn consideration of the application from one meeting to another, and the provisions of Regulation 29 shall apply with the necessary modifications to the later meeting.

38. The Secretary shall communicate to the applicant and to the objector, if any, the decision of the Committee and to the Registrar any direction to be acted upon by him. Any such communication to the Registrar shall, in an appropriate case, direct his attention to section 11(2) of the Act of 1954.

# Proposals for New Disciplinary Procedures and the Introduction of Competence Based Practising Rights

## Proposals for a First Order Under the Health Act 1999

### Introduction

In 1998 the Royal Pharmaceutical Society began a wide consultation on its proposals for reforming the profession's 60 year-old disciplinary legislation. (*Pharm J* May 2 1998 p.622).

In an introduction to the consultation document, the Society's President said that reform of pharmacy's disciplinary legislation was long overdue and that a structure was needed to ensure that, as the profession plays an increasingly important role in the delivery of health care, pharmacists provide professional services of high quality.

In 1998, following consultation with the membership, the Society proposed fundamental changes to its present disciplinary legislation. The opportunity to implement changes based on those proposals arose in 2000. This opportunity will, in addition, allow the Society to introduce measures to ensure that members of the profession are required periodically to demonstrate that they have undertaken prescribed requirements in relation to Continuing Professional Development (CPD) in order to retain their practising rights.

In February 2001 the Society published a further consultation document on its amended proposals relating to disciplinary provisions and CPD built on those in the 1998 document (*Pharm J* February 16 2001, insert). They reflect the government's commitment to ensuring greater public involvement and accountability, and the goal of having consistency across the profession. The Society is confident it can meet the government's requirements for professional self-regulation while also upholding the best interests of the pharmacy profession.

The Key government requirements are similar to those issued in the government consultation documents: for the new Nursing and Midwifery Council to replace the United Kingdom Central Council for Nursing Midwifery and Health Visiting and the new Health Professions Council (see pages 286 and 291).

The consultation documents provide for the key functions for the new Councils to be:

- Establishing and keeping the Register ('registration');
- Establishing and reviewing standards of proficiency, and the training required, for admission to the Register ('education');
- Establishing and reviewing standards of conduct and ethics ('standards setting');
- Establishing and reviewing arrangements to protect the public from those who are unfit to practise ('discipline and health');
- Establishing and reviewing requirements for re-admission and renewal of registration ('competence based practising rights').

It is proposed that procedures will be implemented to require CPD to be undertaken by pharmacists:

- Applying for re-admission to practice following a period of absence
- As a condition for the periodic renewal of practising rights.

### Disciplinary Povisions

Below is the skeleton format of the new disciplinary procedures proposed by the Society.

### Committees

It is proposd that the Society's Council delegates its regulatory power in relation to discipline to two Committees; an *Investigating Committee*, replacing the Council's Infringements Committee, and a *Disciplinary Committee* replacing the Statutory Committee. In all cases, members of the Committees will have security of tenure, to ensure that they are independent of influence. Lay members will be appointed after public advertisement and in consultation with the Privy Council. Pharmacist members of the Appointments and Investigating Committees may be members of the Council of the Society.

There will be no common membership between the Disciplinary Committee, the Investigating Committee and the Appointments Committee.

An *Appointments Committee*, established by the Council, will appoint members of the Disciplinary Committee panel, with the exception of the Chairman and Deputy Chairman, who will be appointed by the Privy Council. The Council will appoint members of the Investigating Committee, in the case of the lay members, following consultation with the Privy Council.

The *Appointments Committee* will comprise five pharmacists and four lay members and will have a quorum of five members with a professional majority of no more than one. Members of the Committee will serve for a period of four years, with the possibility of renewal of membership, and with security of tenure.

The *Investigating Committee* will comprise eight pharmacists and seven lay members and will have:

(i) a quorum of five members with a professional (pharmacist) majority of no more than one;
(ii) pharmacists reflecting differing fields of pharmacy practice;
(iii) at least one pharmacist and one lay person from each of the home countries.

Members of the Committee will serve for a period of four years, with the possibility of renewal of membership and will have security of tenure.

A panel of pharmacists and lay people (the *Disciplinary Committee*) will be appointed by the Council to hear disciplinary cases. No member of the Society's Council will be eligible to serve on the panel. Panel members will serve for a period of four years, with the possibility of renewal of membership and will have security of tenure. For each case a *Disciplinary Committee* will be selected, which will comprise:

(i) a legally qualified Chairman or Deputy Chairman appointed by the Privy Council;
(ii) five members;
(iii) a professional/lay split of three to two;
(iv) no Council members;
(v) members sitting who are selected taking into account the field of practice of the pharmacist appearing before the Committee;
(vi) members sitting who are selected taking into account the home country of the pharmacist appearing before the Committee.

### Procedures

1. The Professional Standards Directorate will inform the Investigating Committee of all complaints, including those for which no further action is proposed. In this way, the Investigating Committee will have a screening function. The person who is the subject of a complaint will be notified promptly, and be given an opportunity to submit written observations within a prescribed period.

2. The role of the Investigating Committee will be to investigate an allegation and, if appropriate, to refer the matter for hearing by a Disciplinary Committee. Where the Professional Standards Directorate receives evidence to support an allegation that, if proved, would be of such a serious nature as to present an immediate and unacceptable risk to the public, an emergency meeting of the Investigating Committee will be convened to consider 'fast-tracking' the case through the disciplinary procedures.

The Investigating Committee will determine whether a case should proceed to a full Disciplinary Committee or Health Committee* hearing, and if not, will have the power to issue a written warning or advice to the person who is the subject of the allegation. The Investigating Committee may also decide that the case should proceed no further.

The remit of the Disciplinary Committee will be to hear and determine all complaints referred to it by the Investigating Committee. Following preliminary consideration of the evidence, the Disciplinary Committee may make an interim suspension order, or a conditional registration order where they consider that if they did not make such an order the public may be at risk. The person adversely affected by the interim directions will have the right to be heard and represented as to why such an order should not be given.

When a full hearing is convened, decisions of the Disciplinary Committee will be made by majority vote. In the case of equality of voting, the Chair will have the casting vote. The Disciplinary Committee will also be competent to give interim directions in adjourned cases and in cases pending an appeal.

* Note – The Society has power to establish a Health Committee under the Pharmacists (Fitness to Practise) Act 1997. Regulations to introduce the health procedures should be implemented in the course of 2001.

It is proposed that the Disciplinary Committee will be able to make the following directions in relation to a case:

  (i) no further action;
 (ii) a caution. This will be noted in the Register for a period not less than one year and not more than five years;
(iii) conditional registration. An individual's registration will be subject to certain conditions for a period not exceeding three years;
 (iv) suspension. An individual will be suspended for a specified period not exceeding one year. At the end of that specified period, the Disciplinary Committee will review its decision to suspend and shall be competent to either renew the suspension for an additional specified period, or give any other directions available within its powers;
  (v) strike-off. An individual's name will be removed from the Register. The Committee may order that the direction take effect immediately;
 (vi) referral to the Health Committee;*
(vii) restriction of right to act as a superintendent pharmacist of a limited company;
(viii) disqualification from running a retail pharmacy business;
 (ix) financial penalties. These may be directed against an individual or body corporate, involved in pharmacy business;
  (x) removal of premises from the Register;
 (xi) award costs. This direction may be given only in exceptional circumstances.

Disciplinary measures may be noted in the Register. Review of directions may take place whenever the Disciplinary Committee determines, or on application of the pharmacist affected. Reviews may also take place on receipt of new evidence.

### Appeals Procedure

Any appeal should be to the High Court, or the Court of Session in Scotland, within 28 days of receipt of the Disciplinary Committee's decision.

## Competence Based Practising Rights

The Society's education division is in the process of exploring ways to develop its CPD pilot scheme in order to satisfy the government's broad requirements. The result will be a practical CPD facilitation programme to be undertaken by all practising pharmacists.

It will be a continuous process, i.e. cyclical. The Society will provide a framework for pharmacists to devise their own Personal Development Plans, to be maintained throughout their careers as pharmacists. The cycle is underpinned by the idea that pharmacists will be required to identify their personal professional needs and improve their skills as practising pharmacists for the benefit of patients as well as for their own benefit.

## Competence Audit Committee

This Competence Audit Committee will set the framework for, determine the details of, and monitor the operation of, the CPD requirements for eligibility to practice.

It is proposed that the Council will delegate powers relating to post-qualification education to the Competence Audit Committee which will comprise eight pharmacists and seven lay members and will have:

  (i) a quorum of five members with a professional majority of no more than one;
 (ii) pharmacists from many different fields of pharmacy practice;
(iii) at least one pharmacist and one lay person from each of the home countries.

---

* See note on page 505.

Members of the Committee will serve for a period of four years, with the possibility of renewal of membership.

It is anticipated that each pharmacist will be required to submit CPD documentation to the Society every two to three years, thus to a large extent the individual pharmacist will determine the direction of his/her CPD. There are many different aspects of any effective CPD program; while the list below is by no means exhaustive, it attempts to identify some elements included in any cycle:

- Continuing education;
- Critical incident analysis;
- Audit;
- Writing;
- Experiential learning;
- Learning from colleagues;
- Teaching;
- Problem solving.

The Society has stated that a CPD program tailored to individual needs will be a key tool for ensuring sustained practitioner competence at a time when the health care professions are under close scrutiny from the public, media and government. CPD-related registration, it is hoped, will assist in increasing the confidence of the public in the pharmacy profession as well as the confidence of practitioners themselves in their professional activities. The key goal for the pharmacy profession through the implementation of such a large-scale project must be to provide high quality, dependable, and up-to-date services to the public.

*18*

# Proposed Code of Ethics and Professional Standards

## April 2001

### Preface

The Code of Ethics is in the process of undergoing substantial revision. Parts 1 and 2 below were adopted at the Society's Annual General Meeting in May 2000.

This has now been amended and the following text will be presented to the Annual General Meeting in May 2001. If endorsed by the membership, this text will be in force by the time this book is published.

### Part 1: Pharmacists' Ethics

The public places great trust in the knowledge, skills and professional judgment of pharmacists. This trust requires pharmacists to ensure and maintain, throughout their career, high standards of personal and professional conduct and performance, up-to-date knowledge and continuing competence relevant to their sphere of practice whether or not they work in direct contact with the public.

The Royal Pharmaceutical Society of Great Britain seeks to safeguard and promote the interests of the public and the profession by identifying the key responsibilities of a pharmacist.

'Ethics' has been described as the systematic study of moral choices; it concerns the values that lie behind them, the reasons people give for them and the language used to describe them. Ethical decision-making is the process whereby one recognises that a problem needs to be overcome or a difficult choice made, identifies the possible courses of actions, chooses one, takes it and then accepts responsibility.

The exercise of professional judgment requires identification and evaluation of the risks and benefits associated with possible courses of action; on occasions there may not be a right or wrong answer.

Different people may reach different decisions on a single set of circumstances and each may be justifiable. Many of the issues pharmacists are called upon to resolve are unambiguous and the decision will be obvious. However, when faced with ethical dilemmas, pharmacists are expected to use their professional judgment in deciding on the most appropriate course of action. They must be able to justify their decisions to their peers, any person or organisation which may be affected by their actions including individual patients, the public, the National Health Service, their employers and other health care professionals. Pharmacists may be accountable to any of these.

Disreputable behaviour, a breach of a professional responsibility or requirement identified in the Code could form the basis of a complaint of professional misconduct. The Society's disciplinary committees, in considering whether or not action should follow, take into consideration the circumstances of an individual case and do not regard themselves as being limited to those matters which are mentioned in this document.

## Key Responsibilities of a Pharmacist

Pharmacists understand the nature and effect of medicines and medicinal ingredients, and how they may be used to prevent and treat illness, relieve symptoms or assist in the diagnosis of disease. Pharmacists in professional practice use their knowledge for the well-being and safety of patients and the public.

- At all times pharmacists must act in the interests of patients and other members of the public, and seek to provide the best possible health care for the community in partnership with other health care professions. Pharmacists must treat all those who seek their professional services with courtesy, respect and confidentiality. Pharmacists must respect patients' rights to participate in decisions about their care and must provide information in a way in which it can be understood.
- Pharmacists must ensure that their knowledge, skills and performance are of a high quality, up-to-date, evidence-based and relevant to their field of practice.
- Pharmacists must ensure that they behave with integrity and probity, adhere to accepted standards of personal and professional conduct and do not engage in any behaviour or activity likely to bring the profession into disrepute or undermine public confidence in the profession.

## Part 2: Standards of Professional Performance

### A. Personal responsibilities

Pharmacists' prime concern, irrespective of their sphere of work, must be for the well-being and safety of patients and the public. Some roles that pharmacists undertake attract specific professional responsibilities. For example, pharmacists who own a pharmacy, super-intendent pharmacists, or pharmacist managers in hospitals and trusts must ensure that procedures designed to minimise risks are formulated and applied. Pharmacists providing professional services in any sphere of practice must ensure that their own work procedures are safe and effective.

The public and the profession are entitled to expect that pharmacists providing services will comply with the specific professional responsibilities associated with them and comply with any other accepted codes of practice and statutory requirements applicable to their sphere of practice.

### A.1 Pharmacists providing professional services

Pharmacists assuming responsibility for any pharmacy function, whether as an employee, locum, adviser or otherwise, are professionally accountable for all decisions to supply a medicine or offer advice, and must ensure that:

(a)     they only accept work where they have the requisite skills and fitness for the tasks to be performed. All pharmacists must establish sufficient information about the work to enable an assessment to be made;

(b)     they undertake continuing professional development relevant to their professional duties;

(c)     all activities they undertake are covered by professional indemnity arrangements;

(d)     they do not work in conditions that do not enable them to comply with the key responsibilities of a pharmacist;

(e)     the requisite facilities, equipment and materials are accessible to enable the provision of the service to professionally accepted standards;

(f)     if any tasks are to be delegated, they are delegated to persons competent to perform them; for example, any assistant who is given delegated authority to sell medicines under a protocol should have undertaken, or be undertaking, an accredited course relevant to their duties;

(g)     they and other staff work within standard operating procedures where these exist;

(h)     they agree terms and conditions and abide by them;

(i)     they honour commitments to provide professional services unless this is impossible. If they are not able to honour a commitment, the pharmacy owner or other responsible person must be informed at the earliest opportunity in order that alternative arrangements may be made;

(j)     they take action to report to the prescriber and relevant authorities suspected adverse drug reactions where this is likely to assist in the future treatment of the patient, or the future use of the medicine;

(k)     before accepting employment pharmacists must disclose any factors which may affect their ability to provide services. Where pharmacists' religious beliefs or personal convictions prevent them from providing a service they must not condemn or criticise the patient and they or a member of staff must advise the patient of alternative sources for the service requested;

(l)     if they become aware that a person has received pharmaceutical care of a standard less than the person had a right to expect they provide, if possible, an explanation of what happened, whether or not they are the person responsible;

(m)     they report to the Society concerns that a pharmacist's professional competence or ability to practise may be impaired and put the public at risk.


## A.2 Pharmacists who own a pharmacy, superintendent pharmacists and pharmacist managers in hospitals and trusts or other fields of practice

Before assuming the role of pharmacist owner, superintendent pharmacist or pharmacist manager in a hospital or trust, pharmacists must be satisfied that they are able to comply with the responsibilities set out below. Pharmacist owners, superintendent pharmacists and pharmacist managers in hospitals and trusts or other fields of practice have a personal professional responsibility:

(a)     to ensure the observance of all legal and professional requirements in relation to pharmaceutical aspects of the business. They are responsible for ensuring that a retrievable record of the pharmacist taking responsibility for the provision of each pharmacy service is maintained and that an identifiable pharmacist is accountable for all activities of non-pharmacists involved in the provision of pharmacy services;

(b)     to ensure that all professional activities undertaken by them or under their control are covered by adequate professional indemnity arrangements;

(c)     to satisfy themselves that the supplier, the source and the quality of any medicines or pharmaceutical ingredients are reputable. Medicines must normally be obtained from licensed wholesalers, the manufacturer or via a central purchasing or inter-branch transfer system. Records must be kept of the source of all medicines obtained by any other means and of measures taken to ensure the safety and efficacy of them. This standard is not intended to cover loans from professional colleagues;

(d) to ensure that all staff are informed of the professional activities they are expected to undertake. Clear instructions should be provided, designed to identify and minimise risks, and reviewed regularly. Where possible standard operating procedures should be drafted;

(e) not to seek to impose conditions on pharmacists which may adversely affect their ability to comply with their professional and legal duties;

(f) to ensure that adequate support staff and information about the pharmacy are provided to enable all pharmacists including temporary staff and locums to perform their duties effectively;

(g) to satisfy themselves that pharmacists employed or engaged by them are aware of the need to undertake continuing professional development relevant to their professional duties;

(h) to ensure that pharmacists and other staff employed by them or under their management have the requisite knowledge, skills and fitness to perform work delegated to them and comply with work instructions;

(i) to ensure that pharmacists and other staff employed by them are sufficiently competent in English. Competency in other languages common to the area is desirable;

(j) to ensure that working conditions, facilities, equipment and materials enable the provision of services to professionally accepted standards;

(k) to have procedures to deal with incidents where there is a threat to the health of a patient or the public, and review practices in the light of incidents;

(l) to ensure that effective measures are in place for protecting the confidentiality of person-identifiable data;

(m) to ensure that an effective complaint handling procedure exists, whereby all complaints are dealt with promptly, constructively and honestly;

(n) to report to the Society concerns that a pharmacist's professional competence or ability to practise may be impaired and put the public at risk;

(o) to notify the Society in writing of any changes in the ownership of registered pharmacy premises, or superintendent pharmacist of a body corporate.

### A.3 Preregistration tutors and pharmacists supervising preregistration trainees

Preregistration tutors and preregistration managers must ensure that section XX of the Society's Byelaws, relating to preregistration training, is complied with.

Tutors and preregistration managers must ensure that:

(a) preregistration trainees they assess understand and comply with the key responsibilities of a pharmacist and are competent. The public may be put at risk if a tutor or manager confirms the competence of a trainee who has not attained the required standard;

(b) preregistration trainees receive wide-ranging experience of professional practice;

(c) preregistration training meets the needs of the trainee;

(d) preregistration trainees are properly supervised, in particular in relation to their responsibilities for services to the public;

(e) the progress of preregistration trainees is reviewed regularly, with honest and constructive feedback;

(f) preregistration trainees are encouraged to self-appraise their performance;

(g) reports of trainees' performance provided to the Society are honest and objective;

(h) they reflect on work processes and outcomes, evaluate their own performance and take action to develop their expertise and knowledge.

## B. Professional competence

The profession, the public and the National Health Service expect pharmacists to develop their professional performance to provide a high level of care to patients.

(a)    Pharmacists must continually review the skills and knowledge required for their field of practice, identifying those skills or knowledge most in need of development or improvement and audit their performance as part of the review.

(b)    Pharmacists must, each year, undertake a minimum of 30 hours continuing education structured to meet their personal needs, and be able to provide evidence of such.

(c)    Pharmacists must be ready and able to provide information and advice about any medicine supplied by them or under their authority.

(d)    Pharmacists giving advice to prescribers, patients and others must be able to demonstrate competence and knowledge of medicines within the relevant therapeutic class.

(e)    Pharmacists must be alert to potential adverse drug reactions and drug interactions and respond accordingly.

## C. Confidentiality

The public expects pharmacists and their staff to respect and protect confidentiality. This duty extends to any information relating to an individual which pharmacists or their staff acquire in the course of their professional activities. Confidential information includes personal details and medication, both prescribed and non-prescribed.

Pharmacists must ensure that:

(a)    the confidentiality of information acquired in the course of their professional activities is respected and protected, and is disclosed only with the consent of the individual other than in the circumstances defined below in (b);

(b)    information is disclosed without the patient's consent only in the following circumstances:

  (i)  where the patient's parent, guardian or carer has consented to the disclosure and the patient's apparent age or health makes them incapable of consent. Pharmacists should be aware that information about services provided to adolescents should not normally be disclosed to their parents;

  (ii)  where disclosure of the information is to a person or body empowered by statute to require such a disclosure;

  (iii)  where disclosure is directed by a coroner, judge or other presiding officer of a court, Crown Prosecution Office in England and Wales or Procurator Fiscal in Scotland;

  (iv)  to a police officer or NHS fraud investigation officer who provides in writing confirmation that disclosure is necessary to assist in the prevention, detection of or prosecution of serious crime;

  (v)  where necessary to prevent serious injury or damage to the health of the patient, a third party or to public health;

(c)    they do not disclose information relating to the prescribing practices of identifiable prescribers or their practices, other than for the necessary purposes of the NHS, unless the prescriber has given his written informed consent to the disclosure;

(d)    access to confidential information within the pharmacy is restricted to those who require that information and who are themselves subject to an obligation of confidentiality;

(e)    the requirements of data protection legislation for data collection and use are complied with;

(f)    confidential information is effectively protected against improper disclosure when it is disposed of, stored, transmitted or received;

(g)    pharmacy computer and manual systems which include patient-specific information incorporate access control systems to minimise the risk of unauthorised or unnecessary access to the data. Pharmacy computer systems which include patient-specific information and which are linked to the Internet or other networks must incorporate measures such as data encryption to eliminate the risk of unauthorised access to confidential data.

## Part 3: Service Specifications

The application of the key professional responsibilities described in Part 1 to the following activities indicates that the provision of these services should incorporate the following professional requirements. Pharmacists should build upon these requirements when developing professional services to enable the public to receive services that reflect the best possible pharmaceutical practice. These service specifications must be read in conjunction with each other to ensure that in providing a service account is taken of all relevant professional requirements.

When providing any professional service pharmacists should ensure that the tenets of clinical governance are followed:

- that an identifiable pharmacist is accountable for all activities undertaken;
- that they and staff providing services are suitably trained and competent to perform the tasks required;
- that any necessary equipment and suitable facilities are available for the provision of the service and that these are maintained in good order;
- that risk assessment and management procedures have been identified and are followed;
- that adequate records are maintained to enable the service to be monitored.

The following service specifications cover a range of services; some are core services which will be provided by the majority of pharmacies, others are additional professional services which pharmacists may wish to be involved in.

## 1. Publicity, promotion and information

It is in the public interest for pharmacies to provide information about their opening hours and services available. Any information or publicity material regarding pharmacy services must be accurate and honest. The public and the profession would not expect any products or services advertised or otherwise promoted, to be injurious to health when properly and responsibly used.

(a)    All information and publicity for goods and services must be legal, decent and truthful; be presented and distributed in a manner so as not to bring the profession into disrepute; and not abuse the trust or exploit the lack of knowledge of the public.

(b)    Information and promotional material relating to professional services must be compatible with the role of pharmacists as skilled and informed advisers about medicines, common ailments, general health care and well-being. It should be presented so as to allow the recipient to decide independently whether or not to use a service and should not disparage the professional services of other pharmacies or pharmacists.

(c)    Pharmacists must not make any unsolicited approach, for promotional purposes, directly to a member of the public by way of a telephone call, e-mail, or visit made without prior appointment.

(d)    Pharmacists must ensure that promotions (materials and campaigns) for medicines aimed at the public:

  (i) emphasise the special nature of medicines;
  (ii) do not make any medicinal claim not capable of substantiation;
  (iii) are consistent with the summary of product characteristics approved by the Medicines Control Agency as part of the licensing procedures;
  (iv) do not promote a medicine by way of endorsement by a pharmacist, or comparison with other products. A pharmacist may recommend a product in response to a request for advice from an individual patient;
  (v) do not promote inappropriate or excessive consumption or use of medicines or their misuse, injudicious or unsafe use which may be injurious to health.

(e)    Pharmacists may advertise the prices at which they sell medicines and price discounts. Promotions for Pharmacy medicines which seek to persuade consumers to obtain medicines which are not wanted or quantities substantially in excess of those wanted are considered to be professionally unacceptable.

## 2. Stock

The public and the profession are entitled to expect all stock to be obtained from a reputable source and be of high quality and fit for the intended purpose.

(a)    Pharmacists must not purchase or supply any medicines, food supplement or health-care-related product where they have reason to doubt its quality or safety.
(b)    Pharmacists must report to the Royal Pharmaceutical Society, the Medicines Control Agency, Veterinary Medicines Directorate or the marketing authorisation holder any instance where they suspect that they have been offered or have been supplied with counterfeit or defective medicines. Such medicines must be isolated from other pharmacy stock and withheld from sale or supply.
(c)    Pharmacy stock must be stored under suitable conditions appropriate to the nature and stability of the product concerned. Particular attention must be paid to protection from contamination, sunlight, atmospheric moisture and adverse temperatures. During storage medicines must be retained in the manufacturer's original packaging. Pharmacists must exercise their knowledge of stability of materials to segregate for disposal any substances which are likely to have deteriorated, or which have been in stock for unduly long periods, or which have reached their expiry dates.
(d)    All stocks of medicines in the pharmacy must have batch and expiry details. Medicines may only be removed from blister or foil packs at the time of dispensing to assist an individual patient.
(e)    Medicines returned to a pharmacy from a patient's home, a nursing or residential home must not be supplied to any other patient.
(f)    Pharmacists must not purchase for sale on registered pharmacy premises, any product which may be injurious to public health or bring the profession into disrepute. This includes tobacco products other than nicotine replacement therapies, alcohol and products intended to mask signs of alcohol or drug consumption.

## 3. Pharmacy premises and facilities

The public and the profession expects all parts of pharmacy premises to be kept clean and orderly to reflect the professional health-care image of pharmacy, and to facilitate a safe system of work. The public is entitled to expect that any part of premises from which professional services are provided are readily identifiable and well maintained. The public and the profession expect a pharmacy offering professional services to have the resources to ensure competent provision of the service. These requirements apply to both registered retail pharmacy premises and hospital pharmacies.

(a) Premises must be safe for the public and people working there. All statutory requirements must be complied with, e.g. health and safety, occupier's liability, disability discrimination legislation etc., and high standards of hygiene must be ensured.

(b) A designated area reserved for pharmacy services should be easily identifiable, and arranged to enable services to be provided efficiently. Arrangements for the sale of Pharmacy medicines must ensure that the sale is made by a pharmacist or a person acting under the supervision of a pharmacist. Pharmacy medicines must not be accessible to the public by self-selection.

(c) The size and organisation of the dispensary must reflect the volume and work flow, and facilitate effective communication and supervision.

(d) Refrigerators used for pharmaceutical stock must be capable of storing products between 2°C and 8°C. They must be equipped with a maximum–minimum thermometer which is checked on each day the pharmacy is open and the maximum and minimum temperatures recorded. Appropriate action must be taken to rectify any identified deficiency.

(e) Arrangements must be made for the regular collection and safe disposal of pharmaceutical waste and other refuse.

## 4. Supply of prescribed medicines

### 4.1. Dispensing procedures in community pharmacies and for hospital out-patients

The public is entitled to expect the service to be accurate, accessible, and reasonably prompt, the medicines to be of appropriate quality, with a sufficiently long expiry date to cover the course of treatment, and to be suitably packaged and labelled for the intended recipient. The profession expects pharmacists to seek to maintain adequate stock holdings.

(a) Dispensing must be under the supervision of a pharmacist, who must be available to intervene and advise.

(b) Every prescription must be professionally assessed by a pharmacist to determine its suitability for the patient. Pharmacists must ensure that the patient receives sufficient information and advice to enable the safe and effective use of the medicine.

(c) Pharmacists must implement procedures to minimise the risks of dispensing errors or contamination of medicines, incorporating checks to reduce special risks associated with particular products.

(d) Where a product is ordered on a prescription a pharmacist must supply a product with a marketing authorisation, where such a product exists and is available, in preference to an unlicensed medicine or food supplement.

(e) Except in an emergency, pharmacists must not substitute any other product for a specifically named product without the approval of the patient or carer and the prescriber, or a hospital drug and therapeutics committee.

(f) All solid dose and all oral and external liquid preparations must be dispensed in reclosable child-resistant containers unless:

(i) the medicine is in an original pack or patient pack such as to make this inadvisable;
(ii) the patient has difficulty in opening a child-resistant container;

(iii) a specific request is made that the product shall not be dispensed in a child-resistant container; or

(iv) no suitable child-resistant container exists for a particular liquid preparation;

(v) the patient has been assessed as requiring a compliance aid.

(g) Labelling of dispensed products must be clear and legible and include the details required by the labelling regulations under the Medicines Act and where appropriate any cautionary and advisory labelling recommended by the current *British National Formulary*.

(h) Where it is not possible to dispense a prescription in its entirety, the patient, their carer or representative, should be informed at the outset and be given the opportunity to take the prescription to another pharmacy. A legible note detailing the name and quantity of the medication outstanding must be provided and a record kept in the pharmacy. Wherever possible the patient, their carer or representative, must be informed when the balance will be available for collection.

(i) Dispensed medicines should normally be supplied directly to the patient or their carer in the pharmacy, where there is an opportunity for face-to-face contact and the pharmacist has access to records and references which enable him to provide the best pharmaceutical service. Service specification 8 must be complied with whenever dispensed medicines are not to be handed over in the pharmacy direct to the patient, their carer or representative.

## 4.2. Medicines for hospital in-patients

Patients, hospital staff and management teams are entitled to expect pharmacists involved in the supply of medicines to ensure that the systems in place are adequate to assure the safe and accurate supply and usage of medicines.

This service specification applies to all supplies of medicines for hospital in-patients whether supplied as ward stocks or on an individual named patient basis.

(a) Pharmacists must adopt procedures to support appropriate use of medicines and minimise the risks of dispensing errors or contamination of medicines, incorporating checks to reduce special risks associated with particular products.

(b) Medication must be clearly and legibly labelled.

(c) Sufficient information must be provided to ensure that all medicines supplied to in-patients are likely to be used safely, effectively and appropriately. Patient information leaflets must be available to the ward.

(d) Medicines brought in to hospital by patients remain the property of the patient; they must not be supplied to anyone else.

(e) All medicines returned from a ward or hospital department must be examined under the direction of a pharmacist, to assess their suitability for being returned into stock. Date-expired medicines must be destroyed.

## 5. Patient medication records

The public is entitled to expect the best available pharmaceutical care from pharmacies. In order to provide that care, pharmacists and their staff need timely and accurate information to be held on pharmacy computer systems or in manual records.

Patients are entitled to expect that any information stored about them will be pertinent, accurate and up to date, stored securely and treated as confidential and used only for the purpose for which it is was obtained.

Pharmacists must be aware that individual patients have a right, under data protection legislation, to inspect records held about them provided that suitable notice is given.

The pharmacy patient medication record system must:

(a)   be notified to the Data Protection Commissioner;

(b)   incorporate access control mechanisms to minimise the risk of unauthorised or unnecessary access to patient-specific data;

(c)   have the facility to identify drug interactions and be able to highlight those which are potentially hazardous;

(d)   provide for the collection, storage and display of patient medication records containing the following as a minimum;

> (i)   sufficient information about the patient to allow accurate identification;
> (ii)   the identity of the patient's GP;
> (iii)   prescription details (quantity supplied, directions, date of dispensing, any balance owed).

## 6. Repeat medication services

A repeat medication service is operated in co-operation with local prescribers, in which pharmacists will provide professional support to assist in the rational, safe, effective and economic use of medicines.

(a)   The pharmacy must operate a patient medication record (PMR) system, notified to the Data Protection Commissioner, and ensure that an audit trail exists to identify each request and supply so as to enable the service to be monitored.

(b)   The request for the service must come from the patient or their carer and be recorded in writing. Pharmacists may not act as the carer for this purpose.

(c)   Unless this information is already available from the prescription form, pharmacists must establish with the prescriber the period for which repeat prescriptions will be issued. Pharmacists must be alert to the possibility of the patient needing earlier review. On dispensing the final repeat the pharmacist must remind the patient or their carer preferably in writing of the need to visit the prescriber.

(d)   Pharmacists may institute a patient reminder system but may not request a repeat prescription from a surgery before obtaining the patient or carer's consent.

(e)   At the time of each request the pharmacist must establish which items the patient or their carer considers are required and ensure that unnecessary supplies are not made. At this stage pharmacists must also use their professional judgement to decide whether concordance or other problems encountered by the patient may require early reference to the prescriber.

(f)   Records of all interventions should be kept in order to be able to deal with any queries that may arise and to advise the prescriber.

## 7. Prescription collection services

Prescription collection services encompass any scheme whereby a pharmacy receives prescriptions other than directly from the patient, their carer or representative.

(a)   Prescriptions must be collected by individuals acting in accordance with directions given by the pharmacist.

(b)   Pharmacists must ensure that the procedures for the collection of prescriptions safeguard patient confidentiality and the security of prescriptions.

(c)   The request for the ongoing service must come from the patient or carer, and the pharmacy must ensure that a procedure for recording the initial request, preferably consisting of written authorisation, exists.

(d)   All requests to the doctor for repeat prescriptions must be initiated by the patient or carer and be made directly to the surgery unless the pharmacy is offering a repeat medication service in compliance with Service Specification 6.

(e)   On receipt of prescriptions pharmacists must ensure that the pharmacy is authorised to receive and dispense them. Any prescriptions received for which the pharmacy does not have the patient's or their carer's consent must be returned to the surgery for collection by the patient or carer or be directed to the pharmacy authorised to receive the prescription.

## 8. Delivery services

A delivery service is one where medicines are handed over to a patient or their carer other than on the registered pharmacy premises. The provisions detailed in this service specification also apply to rural collection points. On each occasion that a service is requested, pharmacists must use their professional judgement to assess whether direct face-to-face contact with the patient or their carer is necessary.

In addition to complying with all other professional requirements relating to the sale or supply of medicines pharmacists are responsible for ensuring that the delivery mechanisms used:

(a)   are safe and that the medicines will be delivered promptly to the intended recipient with instructions for use. Unless alternative delivery arrangements have been made, medicines must only be handed over to the patient or their carer and before doing so the delivery person must confirm with the patient or their carer that the name and address of the patient is correct;

(b)   cater for any special storage requirements of the product;

(c)   enable a verifiable audit trail to be kept identifying the initial request for the service and each delivery and attempted delivery so that the service can be monitored. Wherever possible a signature should be obtained indicating safe delivery of the medicines.

## 9. On-line pharmacy services

The public is entitled to expect the same high-quality pharmaceutical care irrespective of whether the service is provided on-line or face-to-face on pharmacy premises. At all times pharmacists must act in the best interests of the patient and seek to provide the best possible health care.

Pharmacy web sites must clearly display the name of the owner of the business and the address of the pharmacy at which the business is conducted.

In addition to complying with all other professional requirements relating to the sale or supply of medicines pharmacists must ensure compliance with the following:

(a)   Security and confidentiality

    (i) Pharmacists must ensure that the confidentiality and integrity of all patient information is protected. All patient data transmissions must be encrypted to prevent the possibility of access by the Internet service provider or any other unauthorised party;

    (ii) NHS patient data must comply with security standards and other requirements of the relevant Health Department;

(b)   Request for supply of medicines

    (i) In all cases where a pharmacy medicine is requested or recommended, pharmacists must ensure that sufficient information is available to enable a professional assessment of the request and that they have an opportunity to provide appropriate counselling or advice. Advice must be available to all prospective purchasers of GSL medicines and vitamin and mineral supplements;

    (ii) Pharmacists providing on-line pharmacy services must advise patients to consult a convenient pharmacy whenever a request for a medicine or the symptoms described indicate that the patient's interests would be better served by a face-to-face consultation;

(c)    Information and advice

    (i) All information related to specific products must comply with the marketing authorisation, the patient information leaflet and the Medicines (Advertising) Regulations;

    (ii) Information relating to medicines must include all relevant details of contra-indications and side-effects;

    (iii) Non-patient-specific health-care advice, such as that relating to the treatment of symptoms or specific conditions, first aid, travel precautions etc., provided on pharmacy web sites must be of a high professional standard, and the pharmacist assuming professional responsibility for the provision of that advice must be identified;

    (iv) Product recommendations may only be given in respect of individual patients and a record must be kept of the pharmacist assuming professional responsibility for the recommendation;

    (v) Before a patient receives a Pharmacy or Prescription Only Medicine, pharmacists must ensure that the patient receives sufficient information to enable the safe and effective use of the medicine. Procedures for dealing with requests for supplies of medicines and/or delivery arrangements must ensure that this occurs;

(d)    Record keeping

    (i) The pharmacy must maintain information about supplies of medicines sufficient to guard against risks of abuse or misuse;

    (ii) Records must be kept to identify the pharmacist authorising every supply of a Pharmacy or Prescription Only Medicine following an e-mail request to purchase.

## 10. Sales of pharmacy medicines

The public is entitled to expect that medicines purchased over the counter will be safe, effective and appropriate for the condition to be treated and the intended recipient. The following requirements apply to Pharmacy Medicines intended for human use and Pharmacy Only veterinary medicines.

All staff whose work regularly includes the sale of Pharmacy Medicines must be competent and instructed to refer customers to the pharmacist where appropriate. Pharmacists responsible for the provision of professional services in a pharmacy must ensure that the following standards are observed in the sale of Pharmacy Medicines.

(a)    Pharmacists or assistants asked for advice on treatment must obtain sufficient information to allow an assessment to be made that self-medication is appropriate, and to enable a suitable product or products to be recommended. Advice on the use of products must be provided.

(b)    Pharmacists must ensure that when a product is requested by name the procedures for sales of medicines provide for professional advice and intervention whenever this can assist in the safe and effective use of Pharmacy Medicines. Pharmacists or assistants must provide any advice, relevant to the product and the intended consumer.

(c)    Pharmacists must be personally involved whenever this is necessary to provide an acceptable standard of pharmaceutical care. Assistants must be trained to know when the pharmacist should be consulted.

(d)    Procedures must ensure that the particular care needed is provided when supplying products for children, the elderly, and other special groups or individuals or where the product is for animal use.

(e)    Pharmacists must ensure that they are involved in the decision to supply any medicine, which requires their intervention. Such medicines may include those that have recently become available without prescription, that may be subject to abuse or misuse, or where the marketing authorisation for non-prescription use is restricted to only selected conditions. Pharmacists and their staff must be aware of the abuse potential of certain OTC products and should not supply where there are reasonable grounds for suspecting misuse.

## 11. Supply of emergency hormonal contraception as a pharmacy medicine

Pharmacists in personal control of a pharmacy must ensure that the following standards are observed in the supply of emergency hormonal contraception as a Pharmacy medicine. As with all medicines, pharmacists must have sufficient knowledge of the product to enable them to make an informed decision when requests are made.

(a)     Pharmacists must deal with the request personally and decide whether to supply the product or make a referral to an appropriate health care professional.

(b)     Pharmacists must ensure that all necessary advice and information is provided to enable the patient to assess whether to use the product.

(c)     Requests for emergency hormonal contraception must be handled sensitively with due regard being given to the patient's right to privacy.

(d)     Only in exceptional circumstances should pharmacists supply the product to a person other than the patient.

(e)     Pharmacists should, whenever possible, take reasonable measures to inform patients of regular methods of contraception, disease prevention and sources of help.

## 12. Complementary therapies and medicines

The public trusts pharmacists to offer informed advice on treatments and medicines, and the profession expects pharmacists to ensure that they are competent in any area in which such advice is given.

Pharmacists providing homoeopathic or herbal medicines or other complementary therapies have a professional responsibility:

(a)     to ensure that stocks of homoeopathic or herbal medicines or other complementary therapies are obtained from a reputable source of supply;

(b)     not to recommend any remedy where they have any reason to doubt its safety or quality;

(c)     only to offer advice on homoeopathic or herbal medicines or other complementary therapies or medicines if they have undertaken suitable training or have specialised knowledge.

## 13. Health care information and advice

Pharmacists are encouraged to contribute to the promotion of healthy lifestyles. By increasing public awareness of health promotion issues and participating in disease prevention strategies, pharmacists can work actively towards improving the nation's health.

The public and other health care professions are entitled to expect pharmacists and their staff to be able to provide up-to-date, accurate and reliable advice and information on a wide range of health care issues.

Pharmacists and staff providing information and advice on health-related issues must:

(a)     have an adequate level of current knowledge and information about relevant subjects;

(b)     ensure that all advice is independent and not compromised by commercial considerations;

(c)     seek appropriate and sufficient information from the enquirer to enable them to provide informed advice;

(d)    continually review their knowledge and keep up to date regarding new products and new policies for health promotion;

(e)    be aware of local and major national and topical health promotion initiatives;

(f)    work in partnership with patients and other health care professionals in seeking to promote healthy lifestyles and respect patients' rights to be involved in decisions about their health.

## 14. Diagnostic testing and health screening

Pharmacists working in primary care are well placed to provide diagnostic testing and health screening services to the public, who would expect any such service to be safe and accurate.

Pharmacists providing diagnostic testing or health screening services must:

(a)    ensure that before providing a service all staff have completed any training required to ensure competency with the equipment and procedures to be used and in the interpretation of results. They must be aware of the limits of the tests provided. The pharmacy must have a designated area, not in the dispensary, with suitable facilities to perform the tests and provide counselling;

(b)    institute and operate an appropriate quality assurance programme in order to ensure the reliability of the results produced;

(c)    ensure that equipment is maintained in good order to ensure that performance is unimpaired;

(d)    keep up to date with developments in the field and ensure that they are aware of current advice or local guidance on when to refer patients to their general medical practitioner;

(e)    before undertaking a test provide an explanation to the patient of the procedure to be adopted and obtain the patient's consent;

(f)    communicate test results to the patient in a manner in which they can be understood. Patients should be fully informed about the significance of the results and must be provided with any necessary counselling and available information;

(g)    ensure that adequate documentation is maintained to enable the service to be audited.

## 15. Emergencies

Increasingly the public looks to pharmacists in community practice for help and assistance, sometimes in emergencies.

(a)    Pharmacists must consider using their rights to make emergency supplies of medicines whenever a patient has an urgent need for a medicine. They must consider the medical consequences, if any, of not supplying.

(b)    Where pharmacists are not able to make an emergency supply of a medicine they should do everything possible to advise the patient how to obtain essential medical care.

(c)    Pharmacists must assist persons in need of emergency first aid or medical treatment, whether by administering first aid within their competence or by summoning assistance and/or the emergency services. The Society's booklet, *Emergency First Aid – Guidance for Pharmacists*, provides guidance on action in life-threatening situations.

## 16. Collection and disposal of pharmaceutical waste

These services include the collection and disposal of unwanted medicines returned to the pharmacy by patients and other members of the public, or from wards, clinics or other departments in a hospital, and the disposal of obsolete pharmacy stock.

(a)     Within the hospital sector, pharmacists must ensure that a standard operating procedure dealing with waste management, including pharmaceutical waste, is in place.

(b)     Pharmacists must ensure that a contract has been made with an authorised carrier for the collection and disposal of pharmaceutical waste at regular intervals or on demand.

(c)     All pharmaceutical waste must be segregated from pharmacy stock and promptly transferred to disposal containers.

(d)     Pharmacists must ensure that consignment notes and any other requisite documentation are completed and copies kept to comply with legal requirements.

## 17. Advisory services to nursing and residential homes

This service specification applies to any service intended to facilitate the safe, effective, and appropriate usage of medicines, dressings and appliances, their storage, stock control or disposal, and the associated record keeping in nursing and residential homes and hospices.

Pharmacists providing advisory services must ensure that:

(a)     they have undertaken adequate training relevant to the services being provided;

(b)     they visit the home regularly by appointment. All staff visiting the home should carry identification;

(c)     they have contact, regularly and as frequently as needed, with medical and nursing personnel responsible for the care and medical treatment of residents;

(d)     they undertake professional assessments to ensure appropriate usage of medicines in the home;

(e)     they assess and advise on procedures to ensure safe and accurate administration of medicines;

(f)     all necessary supplementary information, e.g. patient information leaflets, is available at the home;

(g)     they advise on the safe disposal of unwanted medicines supplied by the pharmacy and of other pharmaceutical and clinical waste, in compliance with legal requirements;

(h)     adequate records are maintained to enable them to deal with any queries that may arise and to enable audit of the service;

(i)     where they do not supply the medicines to the home they liaise with the pharmacy that does.

## 18. Domiciliary oxygen services

Domiciliary oxygen services comprise the supply of oxygen and associated equipment to a patient's home and the provision of advice on the use of oxygen in the home.

(a)     The pharmacy must operate a patient medication record system, notified to the Data Protection Commissioner.

(b)     The pharmacy must have the facilities, as laid down in statute, for the safe storage of oxygen cylinders and oxygen concentrators and display the required statutory warning signs.

(c)     Personnel involved in the provision of domiciliary oxygen services must be suitably trained to undertake the tasks required of them and should carry identification.

(d)     All patients receiving domiciliary oxygen for the first time must be visited by the pharmacist or a suitably trained and competent member of staff to instruct the patient or their carer on the use of oxygen in the home.

(e)     Pharmacists must ensure that all necessary safety information is provided to the patient or their carer.

(f)     Sets must be serviced regularly in accordance with the manufacturer's recommendations.

(g)    Pharmacists must maintain adequate records of supplies and advice given to enable the regular audit of the service.

## 19. Services to drug misusers

Services to drug misusers include the dispensing and/or supervision of patient self-administration of methadone and other products dispensed on instalment prescriptions.

(a)    The pharmacy must operate a patient medication record system, notified to the Data Protection Commissioner.

(b)    Pharmacists must liaise with health care professionals and others involved in the care of the patient having due regard for the patient's confidentiality.

(c)    If pharmacists anticipate or experience problems of unacceptable behaviour by a patient, they should enter into an agreement with the patient for the future provision of the service. This should detail the services that the pharmacist will provide and also outline the pharmacist's expectations of the patient, the reasons why and any action to be taken if the patient's conduct becomes unacceptable. Pharmacists may decline to provide a service to a patient whose conduct is unacceptable.

(d)    The pharmacy must not deviate from the instructions given on the prescription. Sugar- and/or colour-free products have a greater potential for abuse than syrup-based and coloured products, and must not be dispensed unless specifically pre-scribed.

(e)    Patients must be treated with respect and courtesy, and where self-administration occurs due regard must be given to the provision of a quiet area in order to provide some privacy for both the patient and other members of the public.

(f)    Only in exceptional circumstances should pharmacists supply clean injecting equipment for drug misusers if the pharmacy has no arrangements for taking back contaminated equipment. Purchasers of injecting equipment should be advised of the availability of disposal facilities at the pharmacy and should always be encouraged to dispose of used syringes and needles safely.

## 20. Needle and syringe exchange schemes

Needle and syringe exchange schemes involve the provision of clean syringes and needles and the collection of contaminated equipment used by substance and drug misusers.

(a)    Pharmacists must be aware of local facilities for drug misusers and have established contacts with other health care professionals involved in the care of drug misusers.

(b)    All staff who may be involved in the service must be instructed on procedures to be followed to minimise risks.

(c)    Supplies of syringes and needles must be made by pharmacists or trained staff.

(d)    Individuals must be encouraged to return used contaminated equipment in approved disposal containers, but a supply of clean equipment must not be refused if they omit to do so.

(e)    Used equipment must be disposed of, preferably by the individual, into a properly designed sharps container available in the pharmacy.

(f)    Suitable arrangements must be made for the disposal of full sharps containers.

## 21. Extemporaneous preparation/compounding

This service specification is not intended to cover the reconstitution of dry powders with water or other diluents.

The public is entitled to expect that products extemporaneously prepared in a pharmacy will be prepared accurately, suitable for use and meet the accepted standards for quality assurance.

Pharmacists wishing to be involved in extemporaneous preparation must ensure that they, and any other staff involved, are competent to undertake the tasks to be performed and that the requisite facilities and equipment are available.

(a)   A product should only be extemporaneously prepared when there is no product with a marketing authorisation available and where the pharmacist is able to prepare the product in compliance with accepted standards.

(b)   Equipment must be maintained in good order to ensure that performance is unimpaired.

(c)   Pharmacists must be satisfied as to the safety and appropriateness of the formula for the product.

(d)   Ingredients must be of sourced from recognised pharmaceutical manufacturers and be of a quality accepted for use in the preparation and manufacture of pharmaceutical products. All calculations and, where possible, measurements should be checked. Pharmacists must pay particular attention to substances which may be hazardous and require special handling techniques.

(e)   The product must be labelled with the necessary particulars, including any special requirements for the safe handling or storage of the product, and an expiry date.

(f)   Records must be kept for a minimum of two years but if possible for five years. The records must include the formula, the ingredients and the quantities used, their source, batch number and expiry date. Where the preparation is dispensed in response to a prescription the records must also include the patient's and prescription details and the date of dispensing. A record must be kept of personnel involved, including the identity of the pharmacist taking overall responsibility.

## 22. Aseptic dispensing services from non-licensed units

Aseptic dispensing includes manipulations such as reconstitution, dilution and transfer of a sterile preparation avoiding microbiological contamination and maintaining a physicochemical stability, under the supervision of a pharmacist.

(a)   The preparation of products intended for administration to humans must be in accordance with the principles of Good Manufacturing Practice throughout the process. This is encompassed in the documents *Quality Assurance of Aseptic Preparation Services* and *Aseptic Dispensing for NHS Patients* and any subsequent revisions.

(b)   The decision to prepare a product aseptically should be made in the context of the clinical needs of the patient. The pharmacist must ensure that the product complies with the standards to be expected for that product.

(c)   Personnel involved in aseptic dispensing must be suitably trained to enable them to work safely and competently.

(d)   The facilities and the service as a whole must be regularly audited and faults and deficiencies once identified must be promptly rectified.

## 23. Patient group directions

Pharmacists involved in writing and/or approving patient group directions are accountable for their content and must therefore ensure:

(a)   they only approve directions which comply with legal requirements;

(b)   that the staff training specified will enable safe operation of the patient group direction;

(c)   that the appropriate people have been involved in the drafting and approval of the patient group direction;

(d)     they have up-to-date knowledge relating to the clinical situation covered by the patient group direction, the medicine and its use for the indications specified in the patient group direction;

(e)     they are familiar with their role and responsibilities and the government advice set out in relevant guidance.*

Pharmacists involved in the supply and/or administration of a Prescription Only Medicine under a patient group direction must:

(f)     ensure that they have up-to-date knowledge relating to the clinical situation covered by the patient group direction, the medicine and its use for the indications specified;

(g)     ensure that they have undertaken any training required for operation of the patient group direction;

(h)     be satisfied that the patient group direction is legally valid and that it has been approved by the relevant health authority or other NHS body;

(i)     ensure that when supplies are made the agreed protocol is followed and that the information specified in the patient group direction is recorded. These records must include the identity of the pharmacist assuming responsibility for each supply.

---

* HSC 2000/026 (England only), WHC: (2000) 116 (Wales only) or HDL (2001) 7 (Scotland only).

# National Health Service: England and Wales Terms of Service for Chemists

The following terms of service are as set out in Schedule 2 to the National Health Service (Pharmaceutical Services) Regulations 1992 (SI 1992 No.662, as amended).

## General

### Interpretation (reg.1)

*HA* means Health Authority.

1. In this Schedule, unless the context otherwise requires, any reference in a paragraph to a numbered sub-paragraph is a reference to the sub-paragraph bearing that number in that paragraph.

### Incorporation of provisions (reg.2)

2. Any provisions of the following affecting the rights and obligations of chemists and doctors who provide pharmaceutical services shall be deemed to form part of the terms of service for chemists or, as the case may be, of the terms of service of doctors who provide pharmaceutical services:

(a)    these regulations;
(b)    the *Drug Tariff* in so far as it lists drugs and appliances for the purpose of section 41 of the Act;
(c)    so much of Part II of the National Health Service (Service Committees and Tribunal) Regulations 1992 (SI 1992 No.664) as relates to:

(i) the investigation of questions arising between chemists and persons receiving pharmaceutical services and other investigations to be made by the pharmaceutical discipline committee and the joint discipline committee and the action which may be taken by the HA as a result of such investigations; and

(ii) appeals to the Secretary of State from decisions of the HA.

## Part II: Terms of Service for Chemists

### Directed Services (reg.2A)

A chemist with whom an HA makes an arrangement for the provision of any directed service shall comply with the terms and conditions of the arrangement.

Directed services means *additional pharmaceutical services* (s.41A of the 1977 Act).

### Provision of pharmaceutical services (reg.3)

3. (1) Where any person presents on a prescription form:

(a) an order for drugs, not being scheduled drugs, or appliances, signed by a doctor; or

(b) an order for drugs specified in Schedule 11 to the medical regulations, signed by, and endorsed on its face with the reference 'SLS' by a doctor; or

(c) an order for listed drugs or medicines, signed by a dentist or his deputy or assistant; or

(d) an order for listed drugs or medicines, or listed appliances, signed by a nurse prescriber,

a chemist shall, with reasonable promptness, provide the drugs or medicines so ordered, and such of the appliances so ordered as he supplies in the normal course of his business.

(1A) If the person presenting the prescription form asks the chemist to do so;

(a) he shall give an estimate of the time when the drugs, medicines or appliances will be ready;

(b) and if they are not ready by then, he shall give a revised estimate of time when they will be ready (and so on).

(1B) Where a chemist reasonably believes that a form presented to him as a prescription form in accordance with paragraph 3(1) is not a genuine order for the person named on the form (for example because he reasonably believes the form has been stolen or forged), he may refuse to provide the drugs or medicines or listed appliances specified on the form.

(1C) Before providing the drugs or medicines or listed appliances ordered on a prescription form as specified in paragraph 3(1):

(a) the chemist shall ask any person who makes a declaration on the prescription form, that the person named on the prescription form does not have to pay charges by virtue of either:

(i) entitlement to exemption to charges under the Charges Regulations (SI 1989 No. 419, as amended); or

(ii) entitlement to remission of charges, under the Remission of Charges Regulations (SI 1988 No. 551, as amended)

to produce satisfactory evidence of such entitlement unless the declaration is in respect of entitlement to exemption and at the time of the declaration the chemist already has such evidence available to him; and,

(b) if no satisfactory evidence is produced to the chemists the chemists shall endorse the prescription form to that effect.

(2) Any drug which is provided as part of pharmaceutical services and included in the *Drug Tariff*, the *British National Formulary* including any Appendix published as part of

that Formulary, the *Dental Practitioners' Formulary*, the *European Pharmacopoeia*, or the *British Pharmaceutical Codex*, shall comply with the standard or formula specified therein.

(3) Subject to any regulations in force under the Weights and Measures Act 1985 and subject to sub-paragraphs (4) to (12) a chemist shall provide pharmaceutical services only in response to and in accordance with an order on a prescription form, signed as specified in sub-paragraph (1)

(4) Where an order, not being an order to which the Poisons Rules 1982 or the Misuse of Drugs Regulations 1985 apply, which is issued by a doctor, a dentist or a nurse prescriber on a prescription form for drugs does not prescribe their quantity, strength or dosage, a chemist may provide the drugs in such strength and dosage as in the exercise of his professional skill, knowledge and care he shall consider to be appropriate, and, subject to sub-paragraph (5), in such quantity as he so considers to be appropriate for a course of treatment, for the patient to whom the order relates, for a period not exceeding five days.

(5) Where an order to which sub-paragraph (4) applies is for:

(a)  an oral contraceptive substance; or
(b)  a drug which is available for supply as part of pharmaceutical services only together with one or more drugs; or
(c)  an antibiotic in a liquid form for oral administration in respect of which pharmaceutical considerations require its provision in an unopened package;

which is not available for provision as part of pharmaceutical services except in such packages that the minimum available package contains a quantity appropriate to a course of treatment for a patient for a period of more than five days, the chemist may provide that minimum available package.

(6) Where any drug, not being one to which the Misuse of Drugs Regulations 1985 apply, ordered by a doctor, dentist or nurse prescriber on a prescription form, is available for provision by a chemist in a pack in a quantity which is different to the quantity which has been so ordered, and that drug is:

(a)  sterile;
(b)  effervescent or hygroscopic;
(c)  a liquid preparation for addition to bath water;
(d)  a coal tar preparation;
(e)  a viscous preparation; or
(f)  packed at the time of its manufacture in a calendar pack or special container;

the chemist shall, subject to sub-paragraph (7), provide the drug in the pack whose quantity is nearest to the quantity which has been so ordered.

(7) A chemist shall not provide, pursuant to sub-paragraph (6), a drug in a calendar pack where, in his opinion, it was the intention of the doctor, dentist or nurse prescriber who ordered that drug that it should be provided only in the exact quantity ordered.

(8) In this paragraph:

(a)  *calendar pack* means a blister or strip pack showing the days of the week or month against each of the several units in the pack.
(b)  *special container(s)* means any container with an integral means of application or from which it is not practicable to dispense an exact quantity.

(9) Where, in the case of emergency, a doctor or nurse prescriber personally known to the chemist requests him to provide a drug, the chemist may provide that drug before receiving a prescription form, provided that:

(a)  that drug is not a scheduled drug;
(b)  that drug is not a Controlled Drug within the meaning of the Misuse of Drugs Act 1971 other than a drug which is for the time being specified in Schedule 4 or 5 to the Misuse of Drugs Regulations 1985; and

(c)   the doctor or nurse prescriber undertakes to give the chemist such a prescription form within 72 hours.

(10) Except as provided in sub-paragraph (11) a chemist shall not provide a scheduled drug, by way of pharmaceutical services or otherwise, in response to an order by name, formula or other description on a prescription form.

(11) Where a drug has an appropriate non-proprietary name and it is ordered on a prescription form either by that name or by its formula, a chemist may provide a drug which has the same specification notwithstanding that it is a scheduled drug, provided that where a scheduled drug is a pack which consists of a drug in more than one strength, such provision does not involve the supply of part only of the pack.

(12) Where a drug which is ordered as specified in sub-paragraph (11) combines more than one drug, that sub-paragraph shall apply only if the combination has an appropriate non-proprietary name, whether the individual drugs which it combines do so or not.

(13) A chemist shall provide any drug which he is required to supply under this paragraph in a suitable container.

(14) A chemist shall not give, promise or offer to any person any gift or reward (whether by way of a share of or dividend on the profits of the business or by way of discount or rebate or otherwise) as an inducement to or in consideration of his presenting an order for drugs or appliances on a prescription form.

## Premises and hours (reg.4)

4. (1) Pharmaceutical services shall be provided at each of the premises from which the chemist has undertaken to provide pharmaceutical services at such times as, following an application in writing by the chemist, shall have been approved in his case by an HA or, on appeal, the Secretary of State, in accordance with the following provisions of this paragraph.

(2) An HA shall not approve any application submitted by a chemist in relation to the times at which he is to provide pharmaceutical services unless it is satisfied that:

(a)   the times proposed are such that a pharmacist will normally be available:

   (i)   subject to sub-paragraph (4) for no less than 30 hours in any week; and
   (ii)  on five days in any such week; and

(b)   the hours when a pharmacist will normally be available in any week are to be allocated between the days on which he will normally be available in that week in such a manner as is likely to meet the needs of persons in the neighbourhood for pharmaceutical services on working days between the hours of 09.00 and 17.30 (or 13.00 on an early closing day).

(3) In this paragraph *available* means, in relation to a pharmacist, available to provide pharmaceutical services of the kind he has undertaken to provide and *availability* shall be construed accordingly. *Working day* means Monday to Saturday excluding a Good Friday, Christmas Day, 28th December if 26th December is a Saturday or a bank holiday which falls on any such day; and *an early closing day* means any working day when most shops in the neighbourhood are habitually closed after the hour of 13.00.

(4) The HA may approve an application to provide pharmaceutical services for less than 30 hours in any week provided that it is satisfied that the provision of pharmaceutical services in the neighbourhood is likely to be adequate to meet the need for such services on working days between the hours of 09.00 and 17.30 (or 13.00 on an early closing day) at times when the pharmacist is not available.

(5) An application for approval pursuant to sub-paragraph (2) shall be made in writing to an HA.

(6) The HA shall determine an application within 30 days of receiving it.

(7) Subject to sub-paragraph (8), in determining any application, the HA shall either:

(a)    grant approval;

(b)    grant approval subject to any requirement that it considers appropriate for the purpose of ensuring that a pharmacist is available for the provision of pharmaceutical services at such times as are necessary to meet the need for such services on working days between the hours of 09.00 and 17.30 (or 13.00 on an early closing day); or

(c)    refuse approval.

(8) Where the HA is considering whether to grant approval subject to any requirements, as mentioned in sub-paragraph (7)(b), it shall consult the Local Pharmaceutical Committee before determining the application.

(9) An HA shall notify the chemist in writing of its determination, and, where it refuses an application or grants an application subject to any requirements under sub-paragraph (7)(b), it shall send the chemist a statement in writing of the reasons for its determination or, as the case may be, for the imposition of the requirements and of the chemist's right of appeal under sub-paragraph (10).

(10) A chemist may, within 30 days of receiving a notification pursuant to sub-paragraph (9), appeal in writing to the Secretary of State against any refusal of approval or against any condition imposed pursuant to sub-paragraph (7)(b).

(11) The Secretary of State may, when determining an appeal, either confirm the determination of the HA or substitute his own determination for that of the HA.

(12) The Secretary of State shall notify the chemist in writing of his determination and shall in every case include with the notification a written statement of the reasons for the determination.

(13) At each of the premises at which a chemist provides pharmaceutical services he shall exhibit:

(a)    a notice provided by the HA specifying the times at which the premises are open for the provision of drugs and appliances; and

(b)    at times when the premises are not open, a notice, where practicable legible from outside the premises, specifying the addresses of other chemists in the pharmaceutical list and the times at which drugs and appliances may be obtained from those addresses.

(14) An HA shall notify the chemist in writing of the names and addresses of other chemists included in the pharmaceutical list whose premises are in the neighbourhood and of the times at which they are required to provide pharmaceutical services.

(15) Where a chemist is prevented by illness or other reasonable cause from complying with his obligations under this paragraph he shall, where practicable, make arrangements with one or more chemists whose premises are situated in the neighbourhood for the provision of pharmaceutical services during that time.

(16) A chemist may apply to an HA for a variation of the times at which, in accordance with a determination under this paragraph (*the earlier determination*), a pharmacist is required to be normally available, and sub-paragraphs (3) to (13) shall apply to the making and determination (*the subsequent determination*) of an application under this sub-paragraph as if it were the first application by that chemist for the purpose of this paragraph.

(17) Where an application made under sub-paragraph (16) is approved, the earlier determination mentioned in sub-paragraph (16) shall cease to have effect and the subsequent determination mentioned in that sub-paragraph shall have effect instead:

(a)    where the subsequent determination is made by an HA and no appeal is made, from the day falling eight weeks after the date on which the chemist receives notification of that HA's determination; or

(b)    where the subsequent determination is made on appeal, from the day falling eight weeks after the date on which the chemist receives notification of the Secretary of State's determination.

(18) Where it appears to the HA, after consultation with or at the request of the Local Pharmaceutical Committee, that the times at which a pharmacist is available no longer meet the needs of persons in the neighbourhood for pharmaceutical services on working days between the hours of 09.00 and 17.00 (or 13.00 on an early closing day) it may review the terms of:

(a)    any approval granted by the HA under sub-paragraph (7)(a) or (b) or by the Secretary of State under sub-paragraph (12); or

(b)    any direction given under sub-paragraph (20)(a) by the HA or, on appeal, by the Secretary of State.

(19) On any review under sub-paragraph (18) the HA shall:

(a)    give notice to the chemist of its proposed changes in the times at which the pharmacist is to be available; and

(b)    allow him 30 days within which to make representations to the HA about its proposals.

(20) After considering any representations made in accordance with sub-paragraph (19)(b), the HA shall either:

(a)    direct the chemist to revise the times at which the pharmacist is to be available in the manner specified in the direction; or

(b)    confirm that the existing times of availability continue to meet the need for pharmaceutical services on working days between the hours of 09.00 and 17.00 (or 13.00 on an early closing day).

(21) The HA shall notify the chemist in writing of its determination under sub-paragraph (20), and where it gives a direction under head (a) of that sub-paragraph it shall include with the notification a statement in writing of the reasons for its determination and of the chemist's right of appeal under sub-paragraph (22).

(22) A chemist may, within 30 days of receiving a notification under sub-paragraph (21), appeal in writing to the Secretary of State against a direction under sub-paragraph (20)(a).

(23) Sub-paragraphs (11) and (12) shall apply to any appeal made under sub-paragraph (22) but as though in sub-paragraph (12) any reference to a determination were a reference to a direction.

(24) A chemist in respect of whom a direction is given under sub-paragraph (20) shall revise the times of availability of the pharmacist so as to give effect to the direction:

(a)    where the direction is given by the HA and no appeal is made, not later than eight weeks after the date on which he receives notification under sub-paragraph (21); or

(b)    where the direction is given or confirmed on appeal, not later than eight weeks after the date on which he receives notification of the Secretary of State's decision.

(25) Where it appears to the HA, after consultation with the Local Pharmaceutical Committee that the times at which a pharmacist is available:

(a)    on working days before the hour of 09.00 or after the hour of 17.30 (13.00 on an early closing day); or

(b)    on any Sunday, Good Friday, Christmas Day or bank holiday;

are not adequate to meet the needs of persons in the neighbourhood for pharmaceutical services at those times or on those days, the HA may, subject to sub-paragraphs (26) to (28) direct the chemist to revise the times at which the pharmacist is to be available in the manner specified in the direction.

(26) If the HA has been directed under section 41A(1)(a) or (b) of the Act that it must or may make arrangements for a pharmacist to be available to any person in the HA's area for consultation outside the hours referred to in sub-paragraph (25) no direction shall be given unless sub-paragraph (26A) have been complied with.

(26A) The requirements referred to in sub-paragraph (26) are that:

(a)    the HA must have offered to make such arrangements with the chemist; and
(b)    the arrangements offered must have been such that under them a pharmacist would have been available at the revised times which the HA proposes to require in its direction under sub-paragraph (25)

but it is immaterial whether or not the chemist accepted the offer of such arrangements.

(26B) If the HA has not been directed in the manner referred to in sub-paragraph (26) no direction shall be given under sub-paragraph (25) unless a fee, allowance, or other remuneration to be paid to any chemist so directed is included in the *Drug Tariff* or has been determined by the HA by virtue of regulation 18(1A) (as the case may be).

(27) Before giving any direction under sub-paragraph (25) the HA shall:

(a)    give notice to the chemist of the revised times at which it proposes the pharmacist is to be available; and
(b)    allow the chemist 30 days within which to make representations to the HA about its proposals and shall take any such representations into account.

(28) The HA shall notify the chemist in writing of a direction under sub-paragraph (25), and shall include with the notification a statement in writing of the reason for its direction and of the chemist's right of appeal under sub-paragraph (29).

(29) A chemist may within 30 days of receiving notification under sub-paragraph (28), appeal in writing to the Secretary of State against a direction under sub-paragraph (25).

(30) Sub-paragraphs (11) and (12) shall apply to any appeal made under sub-paragraph (29) but as though any reference to a determination:

(a)    in sub-paragraph (11) were to a direction; and
(b)    in sub-paragraph (12) were to a decision.

(31) A chemist in respect of whom a direction is given under sub-paragraph (25) shall revise the times of availability of the pharmacist so as to give effect to the direction:

(a)    where the direction is given by the HA and no appeal is made, not later than eight weeks after the date on which he receives notification under sub-paragraph (28); or
(b)    where the direction is given or confirmed on appeal, not later than eight weeks after the date on which he receives notification of the Secretary of State's decision.

### Provision of drugs and fitting of appliances (reg.5)

5. (1) Drugs shall be provided either by or under the direct supervision of a pharmacist.

(1A) Where the pharmacist referred to in sub-paragraph (1) is employed by a chemist, the pharmacist must not be one:

(a)    who having been disqualified under section 46(2)(b) of the Act (or under any corresponding provision in force in Scotland or Northern Ireland) from inclusion in the pharmaceutical list of a HA (or in Scotland of a Health Board, or in Northern Ireland of a Health and Social Services Board), is also the subject of a declaration under section 46(2)(c) of the Act (or any corresponding provision in force in Scotland or Northern Ireland) that he is not fit to be engaged in any capacity in the provision of pharmaceutical services; or
(b)    who is suspended by direction of the Tribunal, other than in a case falling within section 49B(3) of the Act.

(2) Subject to paragraph 3(1) a chemist shall make all necessary arrangements:

(a)    for measuring a person who presents a prescription for a truss or other appliance of a type requiring measurement and fitting by the chemist; and
(b)    for fitting the appliance.

## Particulars of chemists (reg.6)

6. A chemist shall give the HA, if it so required, the name of any pharmacist employed by him for the provision of drugs for persons from whom he has accepted an order for the provision of pharmaceutical services under paragraph 3.

## Charges for drugs (reg.7)

7. (1) Subject to regulations made under section 77 of the Act, all drugs, containers and appliances supplied under these terms of service shall be supplied free of charge.

(2) Where a chemist supplies a container in response to an order for drugs signed by a doctor under paragraph 43 of Schedule 2 to the medical regulations or by a nurse prescriber or supplies an oxygen container or oxygen equipment, other than equipment specified in the *Drug Tariff* as not returnable to the chemist, the container and equipment shall remain the property of the chemist.

## Remuneration of chemists (reg.8)

8. (1) A chemist who has undertaken to provide supplemental services within the meaning of regulation 16 shall, on request, make available to the HA all records made in accordance with regulation 16(2)(b).

(1A) A chemist who has undertaken to provide additional professional services within the meaning of regulation 16A shall, on request, permit the HA or another person on its behalf at any reasonable time to inspect the premises from which those services are provided for the purpose of satisfying itself that those services are being provided in accordance with the undertaking.

(2) The HA shall make payments, calculated in the manner provided by the *Drug Tariff* or in accordance with any determination made by virtue of regulation 18(1A) subject to any deduction required to be made by regulations made under section 77 of the Act) to chemists in respect of drugs and appliances, containers, medicine measures and dispensing fees.

(2A) The HA shall make such payments, if any, as are provided for by the *Drug Tariff* or in accordance with any determination made by virtue of regulation 18(1A) to chemists who provide additional professional services within the meaning of regulation 16A.

(3) Where a chemist so requires, the HA shall afford him reasonable facilities for examining all or any of the forms on which the drugs or appliances provided by him were ordered, together with particulars of the amounts calculated to be payable in respect of such drugs and appliances and the HA shall take into consideration any objections made by the chemist in relation to those amounts.

(4) Where so required by the Local Pharmaceutical Committee or any organisation which is, in the opinion of the Secretary of State, representative of the general body of chemists, the HA shall give the Local Pharmaceutical Committee or the organisation in question similar facilities for examining such forms and particulars relating to all or any of the chemists which it represents.

## Professional standards (reg.8A)

8A. (1) A pharmacist whose name is on the pharmaceutical list shall provide pharmaceutical services and exercise any professional judgment in connection with the provision of such services in conformity with the standards accepted in the pharmaceutical profession.

(2) A chemist who employs a pharmacist in connection with the provision of such services shall secure that the pharmacist complies with the requirements set out in sub-paragraph (1).

## Incorporation of provisions (reg.9)

Deleted by SI 1995 No.644.

### Withdrawal from pharmaceutical list (reg.10)

10. (1) Subject to sub-paragraph (2), a chemist may at any time give notice in writing to the HA that he wishes to withdraw his name from the pharmaceutical list and his name shall be removed accordingly at the expiry of three months from the date of such notice or of such shorter period as the HA may agree.

(2) Where representations are made to the Tribunal under the provisions of section 46 of the Act (disqualification of a practitioner) that the continued inclusion of a chemist in the pharmaceutical list would be prejudicial to the efficiency of pharmaceutical services, he shall not, except with the consent of the Secretary of State, be entitled to have his name removed from such list pending the determination of the proceedings on those representations.

### Complaints (regs.10A and 10B)

10.A (1) Subject to sub-paragraph (2) a chemist shall establish, and operate in accordance with this paragraph, a procedure (in this paragraph and in paragraph 10.B referred to as a *complaints procedure*) to deal with any complaints made by or on behalf of any person to whom he has provided pharmaceutical services.

### *Rider A*

(2) The complaints procedure to be established by a chemist may be such that it also deals with complaints made in relation to one or more other chemists.

(3) The complaints procedure to be established by a chemist who provides pharmaceutical services from more than one set of premises may be such that it relates to all those premises together.

(4) A complaints procedure shall apply to complaints made in relation to any matter reasonable connected with the chemist's provision of pharmaceutical services and within the reasonable control of:

(a)    the chemist;
(b)    where the chemist is a body corporate, any of its directors or former directors;
(c)    a former partner of a chemist;
(d)    any pharmacist employed by the chemist;
(e)    any employee of the chemist other than one falling within sub-paragraph (d);

and in this paragraph and paragraph 10B references to complaints falling within this sub-paragraph.

(5) A complaint may be made on behalf of any person with his consent, or:

(a)    where he is under 16 years of age:

> (i) by either parent, or in the absence of both parents, the guardian or other adult person who has care of the child; or
> (ii) where he is in the care of an authority to whose care he has been committed under the provisions of the Children's Act 1989 or in the care of a voluntary organisation, by that authority or voluntary organisation; or

(b)    where he is incapable of making a complaint, by a relative or other adult person who has an interest in his welfare.

(6) A complaint may be made as respects a person who has died by a relative or other adult person who has an interest in his welfare, or where he was as described in paragraph (a)(ii) of sub-paragraph (5), by the authority or voluntary organisation.

(7) A complaints procedure shall comply with the following requirements:

(a)    the chemist must specify a person (who need not be connected with the chemist and who, in the case of an individual, may be specified by his job title) to be responsible for receiving and investigating all complaints;

(b) all complaints must be:

  (i) recorded in writing;

  (ii) acknowledged, either orally or in writing, within the period of three days (excluding Saturdays, Sundays, Christmas Day, Good Friday and bank holidays) beginning with the day on which the complaint was received by the person specified under paragraph (a) or where that is not possible as soon as is reasonably practicable;

  (iii) properly investigated;

(c) within the period of 10 days (excluding Saturdays, Sundays, Christmas Day, Good Friday and bank holidays) beginning with the day on which the complaint was received by the person specified under paragraph (a) or where that is not possible as soon as is reasonably practicable, the complainant must be given a written summary of the investigations and its conclusions;

(d) where the investigation of the complaint requires consideration of any records relating to the person as respects whom the complaint is made, the person specified under paragraph (a) must inform him or the person acting on his behalf, if the investigation will involve disclosure of information contained in those records to a person other than the chemist, or a director, partner, or employee of the chemist; and

(e) the chemist must keep a record of all complaints and copies of all correspondence relating to complaints, but such records must be kept separate from any records relating to the person by whom the complaint is made.

(8) At each of the premises at which the chemist provides pharmaceutical services he must provide information about the complaints procedure and give the name (or title) and address of the person specified under sub-paragraph (7)(a).

10.B (1) A chemist must co-operate with any investigation of a complaint by the HA in accordance with the procedures which it operates in accordance with directions given under section 17 of the 1995 Act, whether the investigation follows one under the chemist's complaints procedure or not.

(2) The co-operation required by sub-paragraph (1) includes:

(a) answering questions reasonably put to the chemist by the HA;

(b) providing information relating to the complaint reasonably required by the HA;

(c) attending any meeting to consider the complaint (if held at a reasonably accessible place and at a reasonable hour and due notice has been given), if the chemist's presence at the meeting is reasonably required by the HA.

N.B. The various forms for application to the pharmaceutical list are listed in the Schedules but are not included in this appendix.

**APPENDIX TWENTY**

# National Health Service: Scotland Terms of Service for Chemists

The following terms of service are as set out in Schedule 2 to the National Health Service (Pharmaceutical Services) (Scotland) Regulations 1995 (SI 1995 No.414 (S.28), as amended).

### Schedule I: Terms of Service for Pharmacists

#### Interpretation (reg.1)

*HB* means the Health Board.

1. In these terms of service unless the context otherwise requires:

(a)    *prescription form* means a form provided by the Agency for issue by a doctor or dentist or nurse prescriber to enable a person to obtain pharmaceutical services,

(b)    except in relation to a pharmacist who has notified the Board or Primary Care NHS Trust under regulation 3(7) that he wishes to be excluded from the arrangements for the supply of contraceptive substances and appliances referred to in regulation 3, *drugs* includes contraceptive substances and *appliances* includes contraceptive appliances;

(c)    any reference to a numbered paragraph is a reference to the paragraph bearing that number in these terms of service and any reference to a numbered sub-paragraph is a reference to the sub-paragraph bearing that number in that paragraph.

#### Incorporation of provisions (reg.2)

2. Any provisions of the following affecting the rights and obligations of pharmacists shall be deemed to form part of the terms of service:

(a)     these regulations;

(b)     the *Drug Tariff*;

(c)     any scheme made under regulation 8;

(d)     so much of Part II of the National Health Service (Service Committees and Tribunals) (Scotland) Regulations 1992 as relates to:

> (i)    the investigation of complaints made by or on behalf of persons against pharmacists and other investigations to be made by the pharmaceutical service committee and the joint services committee and the action which may be taken by the Board or Primary Care NHS Trust as a result of such investigations, including the withholding of remuneration from pharmacists where there has been a breach of the terms of service;
>
> (ii)   appeals to the Secretary of State from decisions of the Board.

### Provisions of pharmaceutical services (reg.3)

3. (1) Subject to sub-paragraphs (2) and (3) a pharmacist shall supply, with reasonable promptness, to any person who presents on a prescription form:

(a)     an order for drugs, not being scheduled drugs, or for appliances signed by a doctor;

(b)     an order for a drug specified in Schedule 11 to the National Health Service (General Medical Services) (Scotland) Regulations 1995, signed by, and endorsed on the face with the reference 'SLS' by a doctor;

(c)     an order for listed drugs, or for drugs, not being scheduled drugs signed by a dentist or nurse prescriber;

(d)     an order for listed drugs or listed appliances signed by a nurse prescriber;

such drugs and appliances as may be so ordered, and any drugs so supplied shall be in a suitable container.

(2) A pharmacist shall not accept for dispensing any prescription form transmitted from or received at a registered pharmacy which is not included in the pharmaceutical list.

(3) A pharmacist shall not supply any drugs or listed appliances ordered on a prescription form other than at a registered pharmacy which is included in the pharmaceutical list.

(3A) (a) Subject to sub-paragraph (b) a pharmacist shall, before supplying a prescribed item to any person presenting a prescription form with a declaration claiming either charge exemption under regulation 7 of the National Health Service (Charges for Drugs and Appliances) (Scotland) Regulations 1989 or charge remission under the National Health Service (Travelling Expenses or Remission Charges) (Scotland) Regulations 1988 request the evidence of the patient's entitlement to such exemption or remission.

(b) Sub-paragraph (a) shall not apply in respect of claims for exemption under regulation 7(1)(a) to (f) of the 1989 regulations where the pharmacists has information in his possession at the time of supplying the item which confirms that the patient is entitled to the exemption claimed.

(c) Where the person presenting the prescription form does not show valid evidence of entitlement and the pharmacist, in respect of a claim for exemption does not have evidence in his possession to confirm that the patient is entitled to make that claim, the pharmacist shall mark that patient's prescription form accordingly before supplying the prescribed item.

(4) Where an order, not being an order to which the Poisons Rules 1982 or the Misuse of Drugs Regulations 1985 apply, issued by a doctor or a dentist or a nurse prescriber on a prescription form for drugs or listed drugs does not prescribe the quantity, strength or dosage thereof, a pharmacist may supply such strength and dosage of drugs or listed drugs so ordered as he shall consider to be appropriate, and, subject to the provisions of sub-paragraph (5), in such quantity as he considers to be appropriate for a course of treatment of the patient to whom the order relates, for a period not exceeding five days.

(5) Where an order to which sub-paragraph (4) applies is for:

(a)     an oral contraceptive; or
(b)     a drug or listed drug which is available for supply as part of pharmaceutical services only together with one or more drugs or listed drugs; or
(c)     an antibiotic in a liquid form for oral administration in respect of which pharmaceutical considerations require supply in an unopened package

which is not available for supply as part of pharmaceutical services except in such packages that the minimum available package contains a quantity appropriate to a course of treatment for a patient for a period of more than five days, the pharmacist may supply for the patient to whom the order relates, such minimum available package.

(6) Where any drug, not being one to which the Misuse of Drugs Regulations 1985 apply, ordered by a doctor or dentist or nurse prescriber on a prescription form, is available for provision by a pharmacist in a pack in a quantity which is different to the quantity which has been so ordered, and that drug is:

(a)     sterile;
(b)     effervescent or hygroscopic;
(c)     a liquid preparation for addition to bath water;
(d)     a coal tar preparation;
(e)     a viscous preparation;
(f)     packed at the time of its manufacture in a calendar pack or special container;

the pharmacist shall subject to sub-paragraph (7) provide the drug in the pack whose quantity is nearest to the quantity which has been so ordered.

(7) A pharmacist shall not provide, pursuant to sub-paragraph (6) a drug in a calendar pack where in his opinion, it was the intention of the doctor or dentist or nurse prescriber who ordered the drug that it should be provided only in the exact quantity ordered.

(8) In this paragraph:

(a)     *calendar pack* means a blister or strip pack showing the days of the week or month against each of the several units in the pack;
(b)     *special container* means any container with an integral means of application or from which it is not practicable to dispense an exact quantity.

(9) All drugs and preparations supplied by pharmacists shall, where a standard or formula is specified in the *British Pharmacopoeia*, the *British Pharmaceutical Codex*, the *British National Formulary* (including any appendix published as part of that Formulary), or the *Drug Tariff*, conform to the standard or formula so specified, and in any other cases shall be of a grade or quality not lower than the grade ordinarily used for medicinal purposes.

(10) All appliances supplied by pharmacists shall conform to the specifications included in the *Drug Tariff*.

(11) Subject to any regulations in force under the Weights and Measures Act 1985, a pharmacist shall provide pharmaceutical services only in response to and, subject to sub-paragraphs (4), (5) and (6) in accordance with an order on a prescription form, signed as specified in sub-paragraph (1), except that in a case of urgency where a doctor or nurse prescriber personally known to a pharmacist requests him to dispense a drug or appliance the pharmacist may supply that drug or appliance before receiving such a prescription form, only if:

(a)     that drug is not a scheduled drug;
(b)     that drug is not a Controlled Drug within the meaning of the Misuse of Drugs Act 1971 other than a drug which is for the time being specified in Schedule 5 to the Misuse of Drugs Regulations 1985; and
(c)     in any case, the doctor or nurse prescriber undertakes to furnish the pharmacist, within 72 hours, with such a prescription form.

(12) Except as provided in sub-paragraph (13) a pharmacist shall not supply by way of pharmaceutical services under the Act or otherwise, any scheduled drug which is ordered by name, formula, or other description on a prescription form.

(13) Where a drug has an appropriate non-proprietary name and it is ordered on a prescription form either by that name or by its formula, a pharmacist may supply a drug which has the same specification notwithstanding that it is a scheduled drug.

(14) Where a drug which is ordered as specified in sub-paragraph (12) combines more than one drug, that sub-paragraph shall apply only if the combination has an appropriate non-proprietary name, whether the individual drugs which it combines do so or not.

(15) A pharmacist shall not give, promise or offer to any person any gift or reward (whether by way of a share of or dividend on the profits of the business or by way of discount or rebate or otherwise) as an inducement to or in consideration of his presenting an order for drugs or appliances on a prescription form.

(16) A pharmacist shall not, except with the consent of the Secretary of State, provide at a health centre services other than pharmaceutical services in accordance with section 27 of the Act.

## Premises and hours of business (reg.4)

4. (1) Pharmaceutical services shall be provided at the premises specified in the application made by the pharmacist for inclusion in the Board's or Primary Care NHS Trust's list, and the premises shall be open for the supply of pharmaceutical services during the hours specified in the scheme to be made by the Board or Primary Care NHS Trust for that purpose under the regulations.

(2) At every premises from which pharmaceutical services are provided there shall be exhibited a notice to be provided by the Board or Primary Care NHS Trust in the form prescribed in Schedule 2. There shall also be exhibited at such premises, at times when those premises are not open, and in such a manner as to be visible at all times, a notice in a form approved by the Board or Primary Care NHS Trust indicating the facilities available for securing the dispensing of medicines urgently required.

(3) Pharmaceutical services shall not, except with the consent of the Board or Primary Care NHS Trust or, on appeal, of the Secretary of State, be provided by a pharmacist in premises occupied by a doctor other than at a health centre.

(4) No pharmacist shall provide pharmaceutical services from any pharmacy or other premises which are not included in the pharmaceutical list in respect of that pharmacist.

## Dispensing of medicines (reg.5)

5. (1) The dispensing of medicines shall be performed either by or under the direct supervision of a pharmacist.

(2) Where the pharmacist referred to in sub-paragraph (1) is employed by a chemist, the pharmacist must not be one:

(a) who having been disqualified under section 29(3)(b) of the Act (or under any corresponding provision in force in England or Wales or Northern Ireland) from inclusion in the pharmaceutical list of any Board or Primary Care NHS Trust (or in England and Wales of a Health Authority, or in Northern Ireland of a Health and Social Services Board), is also the subject of a declaration under section 29(3)(c) of the Act (or any corresponding provision in force in England and Wales or Northern Ireland) that he is not fit to be engaged in any capacity in the provision of pharmaceutical services; or

(b) who is suspended by direction of the Tribunal, other than in a case falling within section 32B(3) of the Act.

### Names of registered pharmacists (reg.6)

6. A pharmacist contractor shall, if so required by the Board or Primary Care NHS Trust, furnish to the Board or Primary Care NHS Trust the name or names of pharmacists employed by him in dispensing medicines.

### Drugs, etc. to be supplied without charge (reg.7)

7. (1) Subject to the provisions of any regulations made under section 69 of the Act all drugs, containers and appliances supplied under these terms of service shall be supplied free of charge.

(2) Where a pharmacist supplies an oxygen container or oxygen equipment, other than equipment specified in the *Drug Tariff* as not returnable to the pharmacist, the container and equipment shall remain the property of the pharmacist who shall have no claim against the Board or Primary Care NHS Trust in the event of the loss of, or damage to, such container or equipment except as may be provided in the *Drug Tariff*.

### Method of payment (reg.8)

8. (1) A pharmacist is required to furnish to the Board or Primary Care NHS Trust or to such other person or body as they may direct, on dates to be appointed by the Secretary of State after consultation with an organisation which is in his opinion representative of the general body of pharmacists, the prescription forms and other forms upon which the orders for drugs and appliances supplied by him were given, arranged in such manner as the Board or Primary Care NHS Trust may direct, together with a statement of accounts containing such particulars relating to the provision by him of pharmaceutical services as the Board or Primary Care NHS Trust, with the approval of the Secretary of State, may from time to time require.

(2) A pharmacist whose name is included in the pharmaceutical list shall supply, in response to a request from the Secretary of State and within one month of the notification of the request any information which the Secretary of State may require for the purpose of conducting any inquiry into the prices, payments, fees, allowances and remuneration specified in these regulations.

(3) The Board or Primary Care NHS Trust shall, if any pharmacist so requires, afford him reasonable facilities for examining all or any of the forms on which the drugs or appliances supplied by him were ordered, together with particulars of the amounts calculated to be payable in respect of such drugs and appliances and if he takes objection thereto, the Board or Primary Care NHS Trust shall take such objection into consideration.

(4) The Board or Primary Care NHS Trust shall, if so required by any organisation which is, in the opinion of the Secretary of State, representative of the general body of chemists, afford the said organisation similar facilities for examining such forms and particulars relating to all or any of the pharmacists and shall take into consideration any objection made thereto by the said organisation.

(5) Payment will be made for drugs and appliances in the *Drug Tariff* at the prices specified therein and for drugs or appliances not in the tariff in the manner set forth therein. The payment to be made for containers and in respect of dispensing fees shall be calculated in the manner set forth in the tariff: provided however in either case that the amount payable shall be reduced by an amount equal to any charge made or recoverable under regulations made under section 69 of the Act.

(6) If the Secretary of State, after consultation with such organisation as is mentioned in sub-paragraph (1) of this paragraph, is satisfied at any time that the method of payment herein before provided for in this paragraph is such that undue delay in payment may be caused thereby, he may direct that the amounts to be payable to a chemist shall be calculated by such other method, whether by averaging the amounts payable to a pharmacist or otherwise, as appears to him designed to secure that:

(a)    payment may be made within a reasonable time; and

(b)    payments to a pharmacist shall, as nearly as may be, remain the same as if the payments had been calculated in accordance with the first mentioned method of payment;

and payments calculated by any such other method shall be deemed for all purposes to be payments made in accordance with these regulations.

(7) No pharmacist shall be paid in respect of the supply of drugs or listed appliances indicated on a prescription form unless that supply takes place at a registered pharmacy included in the pharmaceutical list in respect of that pharmacist.

## Professional standards (reg.8A)

8A. Without prejudice to any rule or implication of law to that effect, a pharmacist who provides pharmaceutical services in accordance with arrangements made in the regulations shall do so in conformity to standards generally accepted in the pharmaceutical profession.

## Complaints (reg.9A and 9B)

9A. (1) Subject to sub-paragraph (2) a pharmacist or pharmacist contractor shall establish, and operate in accordance with this paragraph, a procedure (in this paragraph and in paragraph 9B) referred to as a *complaints procedure* to deal with any complaints made by or on behalf of any person to whom he has provided pharmaceutical services.

(2) The complaints procedure to be established by a pharmacist may be such that it also deals with complaints made in relation to one or more other pharmacists.

(3) The complaints procedure to be established by a pharmacist or a pharmacist contractor who provides pharmaceutical services from more than one set of premises may be such that it relates to all those premises together.

(4) A complaints procedure shall apply to complaints made in relation to any matter reasonable connected with the pharmacist's or pharmacist contractor's provision of pharmaceutical services and within the reasonable control of:

(a)    the pharmacist;

(b)    where the pharmacist is a body corporate, any of its directors or former directors;

(c)    a former partner of a pharmacist;

(d)    any pharmacist employed by the pharmacist contractor;

(e)    any employee of the pharmacist or pharmacist contractor other that one falling within sub-paragraph (d);

and in this paragraph and paragraph 9B references to complaints falling within this sub-paragraph.

(5) A complaint may be made on behalf of any person with his consent, or:

(a)    where he is under 16 years of age:

    (i) by either parent, or in the absence of both parents, the guardian or other adult person who has care of the child; or

    (ii) in the care of an authority under Part II of the Social Work (Scotland) Act or in the care of a voluntary organisation, by that authority or voluntary organisation; or

(b)    where he is incapable of making a complaint, by a relative or other adult person who has an interest in his welfare.

(6) A complaint may be made as respects a person who has died by a relative or other adult person who has an interest in his welfare, or where he was as described in (a)(ii) of sub-paragraph (5), by the authority or voluntary organisation.

(7) A complaints procedure shall comply with the following requirements:

(a)    the pharmacist or pharmacist contractor must specify a person (who need not be connected with the pharmacist or the pharmacist contractor and who, in the case of an individual, may be specified by his job title) to be responsible for receiving and investigating all complaints;

(b)    all complaints must be:

> (i)  recorded in writing;
> (ii) acknowledged, either orally or in writing, within the period of three days (excluding Saturdays, Sundays, Christmas Day, Good Friday and bank holidays) beginning with the day on which the complaint was received by the person specified in (a) of this sub-paragraph or where that is not possible as soon as is reasonably practicable; and
> (iii) properly investigated;

(c)    within the period of 10 days (excluding Saturdays, Sundays, Christmas Day, Good Friday and bank holidays) beginning with the day on which the complaint was received by the person specified under paragraph (a) or where that is not possible as soon as is reasonably practicable, the complainant must be given a written summary of the investigations and its conclusions;

(d)    where the investigation of the complaint requires consideration of any records relating to the person as respects whom the complaint is made, the person specified in paragraph (a) must inform him or the person acting on his behalf, if the investigation will involve disclosure of information contained in those records to a person other than the chemist, or a director, partner, or employee of the pharmacist; and

(e)    the pharmacist or pharmacist contractor shall keep a record of all complaints and copies of all correspondence relating to complaints, but such records must be kept separate from any records relating to the person by whom the complaint is made.

(8) At each of the premises at which the pharmacist provides pharmaceutical services he must provide information about the complaints procedure and give the name (or title) and address of the person specified under paragraph (7)(a); and where he supplied supplemental services he must provide the same information to the person referred to in regulation 3(3)(a).

9B. (1) A pharmacist must co-operate with any investigation of a complaint by the Board or Primary Care NHS Trust in accordance with the procedures which it operates in accordance with directions given under section 17 of the 1995 Act, whether the investigation follows one under the chemist's complaints procedure or not.

(2) The co-operation required by sub-paragraph (1) includes:

(a)    answering questions reasonably put to the pharmacist by the Board or Primary Care NHS Trust;

(b)    providing information relating to the complaint reasonably required by the Board or Primary Care NHS Trust;

(c)    attending any meeting to consider the complaint (if held at a reasonably accessible place and at a reasonable hour and due notice has been given), if the pharmacist's presence at the meeting is reasonably required by the Board or Primary Care NHS Trust.

## Withdrawal from pharmaceutical list (reg.10)

10. (1) Subject to sub-paragraph (2) a pharmacist may at any time give notice in writing to the Board or Primary Care NHS Trust that he desires to withdraw his name from the pharmaceutical list and his name shall be removed therefrom at the expiration of three months from the date of such notice or of such shorter period as the Board may agree.

(2) Where representations are made to the Tribunal under the provisions of section 29 of the Act that the continued inclusion of a pharmacist in the pharmaceutical list would be prejudicial to the efficiency of the service, he shall not, except with the consent of the Secretary of State and subject to such conditions as the Secretary of State may impose, be entitled to withdraw his name from the list pending the termination of the proceedings on such representations.

(3) The name of any pharmacist whose business is carried on by representatives in accordance with the provisions of the Medicines Act 1968, shall not be removed from the list so long as the business is carried on by them in accordance with the provisions of that Act, and the representatives agree to be bound by the terms of service of the pharmacist.

### Records to be made available (reg.11)

11. A pharmacist who has undertaken to provide supplemental services within the meaning of paragraph (3) of regulation 3 shall on request make available to the Board or Primary Care NHS Trust all records kept in accordance with sub-paragraphs (b) and (c) of that paragraph.

## APPENDIX TWENTY-ONE

# Proposed New Regulations for the Health Committee

The Council of the Pharmaceutical Society of Great Britain, in exercise of their powers under sections 13B(6), I3G(1) and (2) and 13K(4) and (5) of the Pharmacy Act 1954 and of all other powers enabling them in that behalf, hereby make the following regulations:

### Part I: Preliminary

#### Citation and commencement

1. These regulations may be cited as the Pharmacists (Fitness to Practise) (Procedure) Regulations 2000 and shall come into force in 2001.

#### Interpretation

2. In these regulations, unless the context otherwise requires:
   *the Act* means the Pharmacy Act 1954;
   *allegation* means an allegation such as is referred to in section 13B of the Act to the effect that the ability of a pharmacist to practise is seriously impaired because of his physical or mental condition;
   *appeal notice* means the notice referred to in regulation 31(1);
   *chairman* and *deputy chairman* mean the persons appointed by the Privy Council in accordance with Schedule 1B to the Act to be the chairman and deputy chairman respectively of the Health Committee; and references to the chairman in the context of a hearing include the deputy chairman sitting as chairman;
   *Committee member* means a person appointed by the Council in accordance with Schedule 1B to the Act to be a member of the Health Committee;

*the Council's representative* means a solicitor or Counsel instructed to represent the Council in presenting the case for the allegation before the Health Committee or an Appeal Tribunal, as the case may be;

*determination* means a determination by the Health Committee whether an allegation is well founded;

*the Health Committee* means the Health Committee of the Society constituted under section 13A of the Act;

*legal assessor* means a person appointed by the Council to be a legal assessor in accordance with paragraph 6 of Schedule 1B to the Act;

*medical examiner* means a registered medical practitioner chosen by the President under regulation 6(2);

*notice of hearing* means the notice referred to in regulation 10;

*notice of review hearing* means the notice referred to in regulation 27;

*pharmacist* means a registered pharmaceutical chemist as defined in the Act;

*the President* means the President of the Society;

*the relevant documents* means the documents described in regulation 8(1);

*review hearing* means a hearing for the purpose of reviewing a conditions of practice, order or a suspension order under section 13D of the Act;

*Statutory Committee* means the Statutory Committee of the Society constituted under section 7 of the Act.

## Part II: Arrangements for the Initial Consideration of Cases

### Statement provided by complainant

3. (1) Where an allegation is made or referred to the Council they shall, unless the allegation is received in the form of a written and signed statement specifying the allegation made in respect of the pharmacist, write within 28 days to the person making the allegation requesting him to provide such a statement.

(2) Nothing in this regulation shall affect the duty of the Council to investigate any allegation which is not supported by such a statement.

### Action following allegation

4. (1) Where an allegation is made or referred to the Council, the Council shall write to the pharmacist:

(a) notifying him that information has been received which appears to raise a question whether his fitness to practise is seriously impaired by reason of his physical or mental condition, and indicating the nature of the alleged condition

(b) either:

(i) inviting him to agree within the permitted period to submit to examination by one or more medical examiners to be chosen by the President under regulation 6(2) and to agree that such examiners should furnish to the Council reports on his fitness to practise; or

(ii) if the information received by the Council includes reports on the pharmacist by medical practitioners who have recently examined him, and it appears to the Council that such reports afford sufficient medical evidence that the pharmacist's fitness to practise may be seriously impaired by reason of a physical or mental condition, so informing him;

(c) informing him that it is also open to him to nominate one or more other medical practitioners to examine him and report to the Council on his fitness to practise;

(d) inviting him within the permitted period to submit any observations or other evidence which he may wish to offer as to his own fitness to practise; and

(e) informing him that if he refuses to be examined or if, having agreed, he subsequently fails to submit to medical examination, or if he does not reply within the permitted period, the matter will be referred to the Health Committee forthwith.

(2) The Council shall, with every notification given by them under sub-paragraph (1)(a), if it is then available, send to the pharmacist a copy of any such statement as is referred to in regulation 3, and if it is not then available send a copy of such a statement upon it becoming available.

(3) The Council may enclose with any notification sent under sub-paragraph (1) a summary of the information received by the Council and copies of any reports on the pharmacist mentioned in sub-paragraph (1)(b)(ii).

(4) In this regulation, except in cases to which regulation 5 applies, *the permitted period* means the period of 28 days beginning with the day on which notice of the allegation is sent to the pharmacist.

### Urgent cases

5. (1) This regulation has effect in any case where:

(a) an allegation is made or referred to the Council; and
(b) the Council consider that, were the allegation to be well founded, it would be necessary for members of the public to be protected without delay.

(2) Where this regulation has effect:

(a) the permitted period for the purposes of regulation 4 and section 13B(3)(b) of the Act (within which the pharmacist may give the Council his observations on the allegation) shall be five days, beginning with the day on which notice of the allegation is sent to the pharmacist; and
(b) the Council shall state their reasons for specifying a permitted period of five days in the notification of the allegation.

### Medical Examination

6. (1) If the pharmacist agrees to submit to a medical examination in response to an invitation sent under regulation 4(1) the Council shall make arrangements for such an examination.

(2) Every such examination shall be carried out by a registered medical practitioner chosen by the President from among those appointed by the Council to examine pharmacists in respect of whom allegations to which section 13B of the Act applies have been received.

(3) The Council shall send to any medical examiner chosen by the President under sub-paragraph (2) and any other medical practitioner nominated by the pharmacist under regulation 5(1)(c) the information received by the Council and shall ask them to report to the Council:

(a) as to whether the ability of the pharmacist to practise, is seriously impaired because of his physical or mental condition and, if so, whether he should be allowed to practise on a limited basis only;
(b) on their recommendations, if any, as to the management of his case.

### Enquiries by Council

7. On receipt of an allegation the Council shall make such other enquiries as seem to them to be required in order to investigate the allegation, having regard to the urgency of the matter in a case where regulation 5 applies.

## Consideration of allegation by Council

8. (1) The Council shall consider the relevant documents, that is:

(a)    any written and signed statement such as is referred to in regulation 3, other than any part of such statement which, pursuant to regulation 4(2), has not been disclosed to the pharmacist;

(b)    any further information received from the person who made the allegation, other than so much of such information as, pursuant to regulation 4(4), has not been disclosed to the pharmacist;

(c)    any observations in writing and evidence provided by the pharmacist under regulation 4(1)(d);

(d)    the report of any medical examiner, and of any other medical practitioner, who carried out any examination under regulation 6; and

(e)    the results of any enquiries made under regulation 7;

and shall decide whether in their opinion the information which those documents contain discloses a case to answer.

(2) If the Council conclude that there is a case to answer, they shall, when referring an allegation to the Health Committee:

(a)    inform the Health Committee of their conclusion and of the reasons for it;

(b)    send copies of the relevant documents to the Health Committee; and

(c)    inform the Health Committee whether the Council consider the case to be an urgent case.

## Notification to pharmacist of decision of Council

9. (1) Where the Council give a pharmacist notice under section 13B(4) of the Act that there is a case to answer, they shall send to the pharmacist copies of the relevant documents other than those submitted by the pharmacist or previously given to him.

(2) The Council shall give notification of their conclusion under section 13B(4) of the Act that there is a case to answer, or, as the case may be, under section 13B(5) of the Act that there is no case to answer, within seven days of their conclusion, and they shall send a copy of the notification to the person who made the allegation concerned.

## Part III: The Hearing

### Notice of hearing and documents to be sent to pharmacist

10. (1) The Health Committee shall make arrangements for the consideration of a case referred to them and shall send to the pharmacist a notice stating the date, time and place of the hearing.

(2) The notice of hearing shall be sent before the beginning of the period of 14 days or, where regulation 5 has effect, of seven days ending with the day of the hearing.

[or (2) The notice of hearing shall be sent before the beginning of the period of 14 days ending with the day of the hearing, or where regulation 5 has effect, in time to allow such notice of the hearing as is reasonable in all the circumstances of the case.]

(3) The notice of hearing shall:

(a)    indicate the grounds for the belief that the pharmacist's fitness to practise may be seriously impaired; and

(b)    state the day, time and place at which the Health Committee will meet to consider the matter.

(4) Where the pharmacist has not submitted to a medical examination in response to an invitation issued under regulation 4 the notice of hearing shall contain further invitation to submit to such an examination prior to the hearing.

(5) When sending a notice of hearing the Health Committee shall:

(a) inform the pharmacist that it is open to him to be represented at the hearing and also to be accompanied by his medical adviser; and
(b) invite the pharmacist to state whether he wishes to attend the hearing.

(6) The Health Committee shall send with any notice of hearing:

(a) a copy of these regulations and copies of any reports and any other of the relevant documents except where the same have been submitted by the pharmacist or previously given to him; and
(b) a request for the pharmacist to state, within the period of eight days or, where regulation 5 has effect, four days, beginning with the day on which the notice was received, whether the pharmacist will require evidence of any part of the information or the findings and opinions contained in the reports supplied under sub-paragraph (a) (or previously given to him) to be given orally before the Health Committee.

(7) If the pharmacist requires the presentation of oral evidence the Health Committee may fix a new date for the hearing and, if so, shall issue an amended notice of hearing.

### Defective notices

11. (1) Where before a hearing begins or at any stage during the hearing it appears to the legal assessor that a notice of hearing is defective, the chairman shall inform the pharmacist of the defect.

(2) If the legal assessor is satisfied that it would not prejudice the interests of the pharmacist if the notice were corrected, the chairman may ask the pharmacist if he consents to the notice being corrected so as to enable the hearing to proceed.

(3) If the pharmacist consents to the amendment the hearing shall proceed on the basis of the amended notice.

(4) If the pharmacist does not give his consent, or if the legal assessor is not satisfied that the notice can be amended without prejudice to the interests of the pharmacist, the Health Committee shall issue a fresh notice which if necessary shall specify a new day, time and place for the hearing.

(5) Regulation 10 shall apply to a fresh notice issued under sub-paragraph (4) and for the purposes of regulation 10(6) any documents or information sent with the defective notice shall be treated as having previously been given to him.

### Preliminary circulation of evidence

12. Before the hearing, the chairman shall secure that there is sent to each Committee member selected to hear the case copies of:

(a) the notice of hearing;
(b) the relevant documents; and
(c) any other documents or evidence submitted on behalf of the pharmacist or the Council.

### Oral evidence by authors of reports, etc.

13. The Health Committee shall consider whether it requires the author of any report or written evidence to attend the hearing to give oral evidence at the hearing.

## Conduct of hearing

14. (1) The Health Committee shall sit in private unless the pharmacist requests the hearing or any part of it to be held in public or the Health Committee decides that it is appropriate for the hearing or any part of it to be held in public, in which case the Health Committee shall direct that the whole or part of the case shall be held in public; and the person making the allegation in question may attend any part of a hearing held in private unless the Committee direct otherwise.

(2) Where the pharmacist has indicated a wish to attend the hearing but does not for whatever reason, the Health Committee shall decide whether to adjourn or to continue in the absence of the pharmacist.

(3) Where the pharmacist is neither present nor represented:

(a)    the chairman of the Health Committee shall consider whether the notice of hearing has been received by the pharmacist; and
(b)    if the notice does not appear to have been so received, the Health Committee may nevertheless proceed with the hearing if it is satisfied that all reasonable efforts in accordance with these regulations have been made to serve the notice of hearing on the pharmacist.

## Further provisions as to hearing

15. (1) At the opening of the proceedings the notice of hearing shall be read out.

(2) Where in any case:

(a)    the pharmacist has, in accordance with regulation 10(7), required that all or part of the information or reports be supported by oral evidence; or
(b)    the Health Committee has, in accordance with regulation 13 or at any time subsequently, decided that oral evidence should be given the persons on whose testimony or opinions such information or reports depend shall be called as witnesses; and such witnesses may be examined by the Council's representative, and may be cross-examined by or on behalf of the pharmacist and may then be re-examined.

(3) Where in any case the pharmacist has declined medical examination the Council may adduce evidence of the facts alleged and the pharmacist or his representative may cross-examine any person giving evidence and the Council's representative may then re-examine that person.

## Calling of witnesses where no previous notice has been given

16. (1) If, in any case where no prior notice has been given on behalf of the pharmacist that all or part of the evidence shall be given orally, the pharmacist requests such evidence to be given orally, the Health Committee having consulted the legal assessor shall decide whether, in the interests of justice, it should adjourn the hearing in order to secure the attendance of any witnesses or whether to proceed with the hearing without taking such oral evidence.

(2) If any such witness is called he may be examined by the Health Committee or the Council's representative and may be cross-examined by or on behalf of the pharmacist and may be re-examined.

## Presentation of the pharmacist's case

17. At the conclusion of the Council's case the chairman shall invite the pharmacist to answer the allegation and give evidence (whether by himself, or by any witnesses who attend in accordance with these regulations, or both) as to the pharmacist's fitness to practise.

## Interim suspension orders

18. (1) This regulation has effect when the Health Committee is minded to make an interim suspension order in accordance with section 13F of the Act.
    (2) Where this regulation has effect the Health Committee:

(a)    shall inform the pharmacist that it is minded to make an interim suspension order, stating the reasons for which the order may be made, and
(b)    shall allow the pharmacist to make representations as to whether such an order should be made.

(3) Where the pharmacist is not present or legally represented at the hearing, the Health Committee shall give him the information referred to in sub-paragraph (2)(a) in writing and shall adjourn for such time as may be reasonable in the circumstances to allow the pharmacist or his representative to make representations under sub-paragraph (2)(b).

## Questions to witnesses and pharmacist

19. (1) At any time during the hearing questions may be put to any witness by any member of the Health Committee and, with the leave of the chairman, by the legal assessor.
    (2) Whether or not witnesses are called members of the Health Committee may put questions to the pharmacist.

## Adjournment of hearing

20. (1) The Health Committee may at any time adjourn a hearing:

(a)    in order to obtain further medical reports or evidence as to the physical or mental condition of the pharmacist or to hear evidence pursuant to regulation 15(2)(b);
(b)    where provision is made for an adjournment by any of these regulations, other than this regulation; or
(c)    for such other purposes as may be appropriate in the circumstances.

(2) If the Health Committee adjourns an inquiry it shall determine the month and year in which the hearing will resume and shall indicate any evidence, or further evidence, of the pharmacist's fitness to practise which it will require at the resumed hearing.

## Determination that fitness is not impaired

21. If the Health Committee makes a determination that the fitness to practise of the pharmacist is not seriously impaired by reason of a physical or mental condition it shall either:

(a)    refer a complaint about the pharmacist to the Statutory Committee; or
(b)    conclude the case.

## Determination that fitness is impaired

22. (1) If the Health Committee makes a suspension order directing the registrar to suspend the registration of the pharmacist it may decide when it will review the order, and may also advise the pharmacist of any steps which it considers should be taken prior to any review of his case by the Health Committee.
    (2) If the Health Committee makes a conditions of practice order imposing conditions with which the pharmacist must comply while practising as a registered pharmaceutical chemist it shall specify those conditions, and it may also advise the pharmacist of any steps

which it considers he should take prior to any review of his case by the Health Committee.

## Announcement of determination of Health Committee

23. The Chairman shall at the conclusion of the hearing announce the determination of the Health Committee under the foregoing regulations and the reasons for the decision in such terms [and with such recommendations] as the Health Committee shall have approved.

## Communication of decision of Health Committee

24. As soon as possible after the determination by the Health Committee, the Committee shall notify the pharmacist in writing of:

(a)  the decision of the Health Committee, [and] the reasons for the decision [and any recommendations approved by the Health Committee]; and
(b)  the pharmacist's rights to seek a review of the decision or to appeal against the decision.

## Part V: Review of Order

### Review of order on application by pharmacist

25. (1) Where:

(a)  a conditions of practice order or a suspension order is in effect in respect of a pharmacist; and
(b)  the pharmacist has made a written application under section 13D(2) of the Act for the review of the order; and
(c)  the application is not one which the Health Committee is precluded from considering by reason of section 13D(3) of the Act

the Health Committee shall make arrangements for a review hearing.

### Review of order on initiative of Health Committee

26. Where:

(a)  a conditions of practice order or a suspension order is in effect in respect of a pharmacist; and
(b)  the Health Committee has decided otherwise than on written application by the pharmacist under section 13(D)(2) of the Act that the order should be reviewed under section 13D(1) of the Act;

the Health Committee shall make arrangements for a review hearing.

### Medical reports: medical examination

27. (1) Before the date is fixed for a review hearing as regards any pharmacist the Health Committee shall obtain from one or more medical examiners such report or reports as it thinks fit.

(2) If a medical examiner reporting under this regulation wishes to examine the pharmacist, the Health Committee:

(a)  shall invite the pharmacist to submit to a medical examination within the period of 28 days beginning on the day on which the invitation to submit to such examination is sent; and

(b)   if the pharmacist agrees to be examined shall make arrangements for such examination.

(3) The date of the review hearing shall not be fixed until every such examination has been arranged.

(4) Regulation 6(2) and (3) (appointment of and documents sent to medical examiners) shall apply to any medical examiner who is requested to report under this regulation as if references to the Council were references to the Health Committee, and every such medical examiner shall also be sent a copy of every report obtained by the Council under regulation 6.

(5) Every updated medical report obtained in connection with the pharmacist shall be included among the documents to be circulated, prior to the review hearing, pursuant to regulation 12 (as applied to review hearings by regulation 29).

## Notice of review hearing

28. (1) The Health Committee shall give the pharmacist notice of the date, time and place of the review hearing to which regulation 25 or regulation 26 applies before the beginning of the period of 14 days ending with the day of the hearing.

(2) The notice of the review hearing sent to the pharmacist shall include a copy of the determination or determinations of the Health Committee in respect of the pharmacist and such other information as the chairman may decide should be included.

(3) The pharmacist shall be invited to attend the hearing and shall be requested to notify the Health Committee, before the beginning of the period of seven days ending with the day of the hearing, whether the pharmacist intends to attend the hearing and what, if any, witnesses the pharmacist proposes to call.

(4) A copy of the notice of the review hearing shall be sent to the Council and the Council shall be invited to submit for consideration at the hearing evidence relevant to the physical or mental condition of the pharmacist.

## Application of certain regulations to review

29. (1) The regulations referred to in sub-paragraph (2) apply to reviews with all necessary modifications and as if for any reference to the notice of hearing there were substituted a reference to the notice of review hearing.

(2) Sub-paragraph (1) applies to the following regulations:

Regulation 11 (Defective notices)
Regulation 12 (Preliminary circulation of evidence)
Regulation 13 (Oral evidence by authors of reports, etc.)
Regulation 14 (Conduct of hearing)
Regulation 15 (Further provisions as to hearing)
Regulation 16 (Calling of witnesses where no previous notice has been given)
Regulation 17 (Presentation of the pharmacist's case)
Regulation 19 (Questions to witnesses and pharmacist)
Regulation 20 (Adjournment of hearing)
Regulation 23 (Announcement of determination of Health Committee)
Regulation 24 (Communication of decision of Health Committee)

## Notification of result of review

30. The Health Committee shall notify the pharmacist in writing of the decision of the Committee and the reasons for its decision, and of the pharmacist's right to seek a further review or to appeal against the decision made by the Committee.

## Part V: Appeals

### Notice of Appeal

31. (1) A pharmacist who wishes to appeal to the Appeal Tribunal under section 13J(1) of the Act shall do so by notice in writing addressed to the clerk to the Appeal Tribunal sent within the period of 28 days referred to in section 13J(3) of the Act.

(2) The appeal notice shall state the grounds on which the appeal is made.

### Withdrawal of appeal

32. A pharmacist who has made an appeal under section 13J of the Act may withdraw the appeal at any time by notice in writing to the clerk to the Appeal Tribunal.

### Appointment of Appeal Tribunal

33. On receipt of an appeal notice the chairman of the Appeal Tribunal shall select three members of the Appeal Tribunal Panel constituted under paragraph 3 of Schedule 1C to the Act to act as the Appeal Tribunal for the purposes of the appeal.

### Arrangements for appeal hearings

34. (1) The Health Committee shall provide the Appeal Tribunal with copies of any papers in its possession relating to the hearing and any review hearing, so far as requested by the Tribunal; and copies of any papers so provided shall also be sent to the Council and to the pharmacist.

(2) The clerk to the Appeal Tribunal shall make arrangements for the appeal hearing and shall:

(a)    send to the pharmacist before the beginning of the period of 14 days ending with the day of the appeal hearing:

(i) a notice of appeal hearing giving notice of the date, time and place of the appeal hearing; and
(ii) a copy of these regulations;

(b)    send to the Council a copy of the notice of appeal hearing,
(c)    send to the members of the Appeal Tribunal panel selected to hear the case copies of the appeal notice.

### Proceedings on appeal

35. (1) The appeal hearing shall be held in private unless the pharmacist or the Council require it to be held in public.

(2) At the opening of the appeal hearing the appeal notice shall be read out.

(3) The chairman of the Appeal Tribunal shall invite the pharmacist to make his case against the order which is the subject of the appeal, following which the Council's representative shall be entitled to reply.

### Application of certain regulations to appeal hearings

36. (1) The regulations referred to in sub-paragraph (2) apply to appeals with all necessary modifications and as if for any reference to the Health Committee there were substituted a reference to the Appeal Tribunal, and as if for any reference to the notice of hearing there were substituted a reference to a notice of appeal hearing.

(2) Sub-paragraph (1) applies to the following regulations:

Regulation 20 (Adjournment of hearing)
Regulation 23 (Announcement of determination)
Regulation 24 (Communication of decision)

### Orders overturned on appeal

37. A suspension order or a conditions of practice order made in respect of a pharmacist shall cease to have effect on the determination of an appeal by the Appeal Tribunal.

## Part VI: General

### The legal assessor

38. (1) The legal assessor shall be present at all proceedings before the Health Committee.

(2) Subject to sub-paragraph (3), in proceedings before the Health Committee, the advice of the legal assessor shall be tendered to the Health Committee in the presence of every party, or person representing a party, attending the proceedings before the Health Committee.

(3) In any case where advice is tendered by the legal adviser after the Health Committee has begun to deliberate as to its findings and the Health Committee considers that it would be prejudicial to the discharge of its duties for the advice to be tendered in the presence of the parties or their representatives, such advice may be tendered in their absence, but the legal assessor shall, as soon as reasonably practicable, personally inform them of the question which has been put to him by the Health Committee and of his advice, and the information so given by him shall be recorded and a copy of the record shall be given to every such party or representative.

(4) If on any occasion the Health Committee does not accept the advice of the legal assessor, a record shall be made of the question referred to him, of the advice given and of the refusal to accept it (together with the reasons for such refusal) and a copy of the record shall be given to every party, or person representing a party, to the proceedings before the Health Committee.

(5) Copies of written advice, made for the purposes of either of sub-paragraphs (3) and (4) above shall be available on application to the clerk to the Health Committee to every party to the proceedings who does not appear before the Health Committee.

### Service of documents

39. (1) Any notice or other document required by any provision of these regulations to be given or sent to any person may be given or sent:

(a)    except in cases to which sub-paragraph (b) below applies, by leaving it at, or by sending it by post (by a postal service in which delivery or receipt is recorded) to, his usual or last known address, which in the case of a pharmacist shall be his address in the Register or, if his last known address differs from the address in the Register, his last known address;

(b)    in the case of a notice of an allegation to be given where regulation 5 applies, by leaving it at the address referred to in sub-paragraph (a) above.

(2) In any other circumstances, documents sent for the purposes of these regulations may be sent by ordinary first class pre-paid post.

### Legal representation

40. A pharmacist may be represented at any hearing under these regulations by a solicitor or counsel or by any other person acceptable to the Health Committee or the Appeal Tribunal, as the case may be.

### Evidence on oath

41. The Health Committee and the Appeal Tribunal may require that any person giving evidence at a hearing under these regulations shall do so under oath, and may at any stage in the course of the evidence of a person not under oath, require that person to swear an oath.

### Admission, etc. of evidence

42. Subject to sections 13G(3) and 13K(6) of the Act the Health Committee and the Appeal Tribunal shall not be bound by rules of evidence in any hearing under these regulations but shall refuse to admit any evidence, or shall disregard any evidence adduced which in the opinion of the legal assessor is of a character which makes it unsafe for any reliance to be placed upon it.

### Power to require attendance at hearings

43. The Health Committee and the Appeal Tribunal may require the attendance of any person to give evidence at any hearing under these regulations and the production of any document or other material as evidence and may issue subpoenas to secure the attendance of any witness and the production of any document or other material.

### Giving of notices, etc. by Health Committee

44. Where under these regulations the Health Committee is to give notice or send any notification or other matter to a person, it may do so acting by such officer or clerk of the Council as the Committee may designate for the purpose.

# Index